The African Religions of Brazil

The African Religions of Brazil

Toward a Sociology of the Interpenetration of Civilizations

ROGER BASTIDE

Translated by HELEN SEBBA

THE JOHNS HOPKINS UNIVERSITY PRESS
BALTIMORE AND LONDON

This book has been brought to publication with the generous assistance of The Tinker Foundation Incorporated.

Originally published in Paris in 1960 as *Les Religions Afro-Brésiliennes: Contribution à une Sociologie des Interpénétrations de Civilisations*
Copyright © 1960 by Presses Universitaires de France

English translation copyright © 1978 by The Johns Hopkins University Press

Manufactured in the United States of America

The Johns Hopkins University Press, Baltimore, Maryland 21218
The Johns Hopkins Press Ltd., London

Library of Congress Catalog Card Number 78-5421
ISBN 0-8018-2056-1 (hardcover)
ISBN 0-8018-2130-4 (paperback)

Library of Congress Cataloging in Publication data will be found on the last printed page of this book.

Contents

Foreword

At the time of his recent death, Roger Bastide left an unusually rich scholarly legacy—some 28 books (not counting their many translations), 337 journal articles, 80 chapters in edited volumes, 70 conference papers, 37 forewords or introductions, and 250 book reviews.[1] Of these, *The African Religions of Brazil*, first published in 1960, is the masterwork. In introducing this translation, I will try to sketch in with some very quick strokes something of the place of this book in the total *oeuvre*.

Bastide, already the author of two books on the sociology of religion,[2] left France for Brazil in 1938 at the age of forty, intending to study dreams and mental illness among the poor urban black population. Arriving at the still-young University of São Paulo (which during those exciting years played host as well to many other foreign scholars, such as Claude Lévi-Strauss, Georges Gurvitch, Fernand Braudel, and Melville Herskovits), Bastide carved out a special niche for himself in the turbulent intellectual life of this rapidly expanding metropolis. While engaged in the personal adventure of discovering what he soon realized was, for him, a whole new world, Bastide wrote about it, prolifically, producing a stream of critical essays and reviews for the daily newspapers and intellectual journals, on Brazilian poetry and novels, on painting, architecture, and sculpture.[3] Within the university, Bastide patiently effected what M. I. Pereira de Queiroz has called "a genuine revolution" in the methods and concepts of Brazilian sociology, a reorientation that has been carried forward with vigor by his students and colleagues; later in his stay, he was responsible for introducing the discipline of social psychiatry into the Brazilian medical schools.[4] But all the while, Bastide was patiently conducting his pioneering fieldwork on the spiritual life of Afro-Brazilians, focusing particularly on the *candomblé* of Bahia, and devoting a span of time to empirical investigation that set him quite apart from most of his French ethnological contemporaries.

Shortly before his death, Bastide wrote that his arrival in Brazil had provoked in him a *crise de conscience*, an intellectual and spiritual crisis. Approaching the world of *candomblé* "with a way of thinking [*une mentalité*] shaped by three centuries of Cartesianism . . . an ethnocentric mode of thought, . . . I [realized that I] would have to 'convert' myself to a new way of thinking if I ever hoped to understand it."[5] Elsewhere he wrote that "the sociologist who studies Brazil no longer knows what set of concepts to use. The ideas he has learned in Europe or North America are no longer valid"; Cartesian distinctions between past and present, sacred and profane, the living and the dead, no longer hold.[6] Bastide argued forcefully for the "Brazilianization" of the social scientist's perspective. After praising Herskovits's work in demonstrating the nonpathological, institutionalized nature of Afro-Brazilian trance, he noted:

> On the other hand, Herskovits risked locking Afro-Brazilian data into an international system of explanation [functionalism] which, like all international systems, will one day be rejected as a distortion of reality. . . . Few years will pass in Brazil before blacks become aware of their need to create an Afro-Brazilian science themselves, based on their own experience.[7]

For Bastide, one entrée into this new world of Brazil was through the study of poetry; the other was through the *candomblé*.

Near the end of his life, thinking back on his own rites of initiation into *candomblé*, Bastide gave thanks to the members of the cult group, who had somehow understood his intense need for new "cultural nourishment." In a personally revealing passage whose gustatory metaphors defy my translation skills, he wrote:

> Je serai jusqu'à ma mort reconnaissant á toutes les *Mai de Santo* qui m'ont considéré comme leur petit enfant blanc, les Joana de Ogum ou bien les Joana de Yemanja, qui ont compris mon désir de nourritures culturelles nouvelles, et qui ont . . . senti que ma pensée cartésienne ne pourrait supporter ces nourritures nouvelles en tant que vraies nourritures, non en tant que relations purement scientifiques, qui restent à la superficie des choses sans se métamorphoser en expériences vitales, seules sources de compréhension, sans qu'elles les répétrissent d'abord pour me les rendre assimilables, exactement comme les mamans noires roulent entre leurs mains fatiguées les aliments de leurs bébés pour en faire une petite boule qu'elles mettent amoureusement dans la bouche de leurs enfants.[8]

Bastide believed that this "conversion," as he called it, permitted him "to rethink *candomblé* . . . from the inside rather than the outside, and to effect a fundamental shift in my logical categories."[9] Emerging from this "crisis," Bastide moved on to the second subjective station of what he calls "the spiritual itinerary" leading to *The African Religions of Brazil*: his "enchantment . . . which has never disappeared," stemming from his realization that *candomblé*, far from being a mixture of folkloric traits ("uprooted survivals, deprived of their vigor"), expressed a rich and subtle metaphysics, and revealed itself as a system of knowledge that, "while different from our own, was as valid intellectually as that of Plato or Spinoza."[10]

Reacting against what he saw as the sterility of much of contemporary British social anthropology, against the limitations of North American functionalism, against the "folkloric" or "antiquarian" approach, and against ethnocentrism and racism of any stripe, Bastide attempted to enter and grasp *candomblé* as a living system of symbols. Drawn always to what Françoise Morin has cleverly characterized as the "anthropology of abysses," the mystic search for the Other's existential experience of the sacred, Bastide saw religion as a central part of mankind's ongoing cultural activity;[11] the anthropology of religion was, for him, a matter of going beyond "the chaos of religious facts" in order "to understand man as manipulator of the sacred, and constructor of symbolic worlds."[12] For Bastide, trance and dreams, myths and madness, could be viewed as special languages, and he argued early that the discovery of their semantic and syntactic structures must be a major goal.[13] Yet this never became for him the formal exercise that it did in the hands of some of his contemporaries. In his approach to religion, Bastide insisted that he was closer to the tradition of Halbwachs, Lévy-Bruhl, Leenhardt, and Griaule than to that of Durkheim, Mauss, and Lévi-Strauss.[14] Anthropology, he wrote, must always "*déchosifier* social facts in order to humanize them. . . . It ought to cease treating cultures like dried herbs placed between the pages of a thick tome, cease classifying cultural manifestations like objects in a museum. A myth is not a dead thing, a dried flower; it lives and moves like the dreams of a sleeper."[15] Speaking to this theme soon after Bastide's death, his close friend Jean Duvignaud noted that

> Bastide never transformed the people whom he knew and loved into a catalogue of scientific file cards. The blacks and Brazilians were not for him an instrument of professional advancement. They were living people, his own contemporaries. He willingly let them speak for themselves; it was their words he projected. . . . He was . . . one of a small number of analysts who do not reduce living people or societies to symbols. He had thought deeply enough about Marx and Freud to know that social life is not reducible.[16]

After sixteen years in Brazil, Bastide returned to Paris, where from 1958 to 1968 he held the Chair of Ethnologie Sociale et Religieuse at the Sorbonne. From 1962 to 1974 he also directed the Centre de Psychiatrie Sociale at the École Pratique des Hautes Études. There he began to mold his data on Afro-Brazilian religion for publication, all the while continuing his writing and research in sociology, applied anthropology, social psychology and psychiatry, and literature.[17] Bastide wrote, in retrospect, that his return to France had been necessary "in order to allow my thoughts to sift themselves out through a twofold 'distancing,' geographical and temporal, which I had to effect between the world of the *candomblés* and myself."[18] *The African Religions of Brazil*, which appeared close on the heels of his rich monograph on *candomblé*,[19] was an attempt to synthesize the results of some two decades of work.

Nevertheless, it is important not to see this book as an end point. For the decade and a half following its publication, Bastide continued to criticize, modify, and develop the views expressed here. Among the many issues to which he repeatedly returned was the phenomenon of "acculturation." Dissatisfied with the perspective of scholars from Nina Rodrigues to Herskovits, who tended to review "syncretism" as "the mechanical juxtaposition of cultural traits borrowed from two different civilizations,"[20] Bastide chose rather to focus on "the interpenetration of civilizations," stressing always the ongoing, processual aspect of these phenomena. In syncretisms, he sought to uncover "coherent systems," not simply "mixtures";[21] he wished to delineate "models of structural coherence . . . at the level of ecology, of beliefs, of ceremonies, or magical rites," and he was certain that they "would never be simple."[22] Drawing more explicitly on Marx and Freud than most of his North American contemporaries, he also actively engaged and reacted to the work of Lévi-Strauss and the French structuralists; a late essay on syncretism and *bricolage* is one of the finest examples of how far his ideas had progressed since *The African Religions of Brazil*.[23] But Bastide's point of departure in studying "acculturation" never wavered:

> There are never . . . cultures in contact but rather individuals, carriers of different cultures. However, these individuals are not independent creatures but are interrelated by complex webs of communication, of domination-subordination, or of egalitarian exchange. They are a part of institutions, which have rules for action, norms, and organization.[24]

His achievement, in *The African Religions of Brazil*, is to analyze, within a single conceptual framework, individuals, culture, and social and economic infrastructures, and to clarify the dialectic relationship between the historical transformation of these infrastructures and the religious phenomena in question.

The Brazil of the forties and fifties was, as Bastide well knew, in rapid flux, and after his departure from that country both infrastructures and Afro-Brazilian cults continued to develop apace. From Paris, Bastide followed with interest this ongoing transformation of Brazilian society and culture, as well as the development of new historical and sociological concepts with which to analyze it. In 1972 he set forth some thoughts on the changes that had occurred since the time of his initial research on *candomblé*. He noted the effects of tourism and the entry of mulattoes and whites into some groups, leading to a kind of "Americanization"; yet at the same time there had been an increase in the intensity of communication between Brazil and Nigeria, a two-way movement of people, goods, and ideas that was contributing to a "re-Africanization." He noted also the efforts of the Catholic church, since Vatican II, to "recuperate" Afro-Brazilians by means of a conscious, new "syncretism." And he discussed the consequences of the massive shifts in population from northeastern Brazil to the shantytowns of Rio and São Paulo. Summing up, he pointed to "a metamorphosis of religious, ideological, and political superstructures, closely tried to the upheavals that have occurred in the social and economic infrastructures, under the dual pressures of urbanism and industrialization," and to comprehend it he suggested research on such diverse phenomena as "marginalization as a consequence of . . . rapid economic development, . . . the degree of cultural 'resistance' among the migrants, [and] the semeiology of the new religious values."[25] In this same vein, Renato Ortiz, one of Bastide's students, recently pointed out that

if . . . [in *The African Religions of Brazil*] Bastide viewed Umbanda as an Afro-Brazilian religion, it is because he studied it in its infancy, at the moment when this new movement was gaining momentum and detaching itself from *macumba*. . . . [But today,] if *candomblé* and *macumba* can still be considered African religions, Umbanda might better be viewed as . . . the "national religion" of Brazil.[26]

The study of these ongoing religious developments had by this time become recognized as a rich field for research. (Bastide's own comments on the more recent results of this work, much of it by Brazilians, may be found in a 1974 review article in English.)[27] Indeed, in 1973 Bastide himself undertook a research trip to Brazil to analyze the situation first-hand. His summary notes on his findings reveal a characteristically broad field of investigation, ranging all the way from a microstudy of the symbolism of postures and gestures in *candomblé* to the development of a sociological model to account for the relative popularity of the various "brands" of religious experience then being offered in Brazil's pluralistic society. And these findings were to serve as the basis for a new book; shortly before his death Bastide signed the contract for *Les Religions Africaines au Brésil Vingt Ans Après*.[28] The task, perforce, now passes to those young Brazilians to whom he dedicated his 1973 volume of collected essays. In the introduction to that book he restated the focus of his own life-long interest in Afro-Brazil,[29] and it may stand as a fitting point of departure for those who would carry the work ahead. This focus, he wrote, was on

the study of black Brazilians as creators of culture. In contrast to those who would see in Afro-Americans simply consumers, imitators, or assimilators of white Western culture, and to those who view *candomblé* or *vaudoun* or *santería* . . . as African survivals, without any living significance and therefore "condemned," I have had the deep feeling, living

among Afro-Brazilians, that they were, like all peoples, not simply imitators or carriers of an ancestral heritage but the creators of original cultures
that they offer to the world. For they, too, have a moving message to
offer, and for the whole of mankind.[30]

RICHARD PRICE
Wassenaar, The Netherlands
December 1977

Acknowledgments

Many people have cooperated to make this publication possible, including a number of senior scholars who lent encouragement in its very early stages. A generous grant from The Tinker Foundation supported the long and difficult translation, which was expertly carried out by Helen Sebba. The Brazilian sociologist Duglas Teixeira Monteiro, a former student of Bastide's, kindly provided a rich introduction to the volume. Eugene K. Galbraith worked diligently to improve Bastide's many incomplete references and inconsistent spellings in the notes, and Scott V. Parris read the translation with care, suggesting a number of very useful clarifications. Beginning even before the establishment of the series in which this book appears, and continuing right through the writing of the present foreword and introduction, Sidney W. Mintz has provided encouragement and sound counsel. The publication of this book has been a complicated project; we hope it does credit to the memory of its author.

R.P.

Introduction
to the Translation

This book is the result of unusually extensive research. Over the course of many years, while working in Brazil and after his return to France, Roger Bastide patiently built up his understanding of Afro-Brazilian religious realities through the careful collection of data and the ongoing elaboration of partial interpretations. It would therefore not be an overstatement to say that this book represents the culmination of a whole life dedicated to research in the fields of sociology and anthropology.

When Roger Bastide initiated his Brazilianist studies in 1938 the data available on the black population and, in particular, on African religions in Brazil were fragmentary, scattered, and lacking in scientific rigor. Moreover these data were shaped by the particular "psychological" framework common to the theorists who collected them, and as a result often reflected a "white" bias.

Bastide, entering the scene in the role of the patient ethnographer (which indeed he was never to abandon) and rejecting the temptations of hasty sociological analysis, tried to fill the gaps in the existing data. This he did in a very special manner. In the first place, his "Brazilianist" stand resulted from a complete identification with Brazilian culture and society. Being by temperament interested in literature and art, he produced vivid critical essays in these fields, which he recognized as rich in promise for his investigations as a sociologist.

In the second place, Bastide did not turn to the study of Brazilian reality simply from the perspective of a detached scholar. His lucid and extremely erudite approach reflected a genuine passion for the object of study, and his enthusiasm usually led him to a deep understanding of the phenomena being investigated. In his case, this impassioned approach was not due to what is sometimes called a "personal equation," but resulted rather from a clear methodological choice. "Pour faire de la sociologie il faut aimer les hommes," as he once said. But he does not merely love them in general. On the contrary, he turns his interest to the poorest layers of the Brazilian population, and among these, particularly to those who are doubly disfavored—the blacks.

These are among the considerations that allow Bastide the remarkable statement made in the final lines of the Introduction: "Africanus sum."[1] Having been accepted as a member of one of the religious communities he studied, Bastide put into practice his chosen methodological approach, indicated in the comparison he drew between Gilberto Freyre's stand in *The Masters and the Slaves* and his own: they look through opposite ends of the tube.[2]

It should not be forgotten that although Bastide has become known as a specialist in the sociology and anthropology of religions, his research on Afro-Brazilian religions is part of a wider concern: the study of the "social condition" of the people of color within the multiracial Brazilian environment. This is why his sociology of African religions in Brazil is also a sociology of the "interpenetration of civilizations," and in a certain sense also a sociology of interethnic relations. This book, along with the essay that resulted from the joint investigations of Bastide and Florestan Fernandes on racial prejudice in São Paulo, serve to define the major lines of this more general field of interest.[3]

A final introductory observation should be of some relevance. *The African Religions of Brazil* is a sociological, not an ethnographic, study, as the author himself points out.[4] It is neither a detailed account of rites and beliefs nor an analysis focused on particular expressions of Afro-Brazilian religiosity. Rather, it is a vast and ambitious attempt to bring into a comprehensive sociohistorical perspective all religious behavior of African origin as it manifested itself in the country as a whole, from the time of the slave trade to the present. Although the book includes abundant ethnographic data and anthropological analysis of beliefs and rituals, these are presented only as the foundation for the essentially sociological project that the book is intended to be.

■ ■ ■

From a theoretical and methodological viewpoint, Bastide grapples throughout the book with a number of classic problems in sociology and anthropology. Indeed, the author seems almost to be trying to "settle accounts" with certain crucial questions in the academic tradition of these subjects. Certainly Marx plays the central role in the discussion. Marxist concepts can be found from the first lines of the Introduction to the final passages of the Conclusions, but they are presented and discussed in the course of a very personal interpretation, forming a sort of theoretical alternative that Bastide contrasts with his own ideas while elaborating the positions he endorses.

The discussion of the problems posed by the Marxist interpretation of religious phenomena leads Bastide to the selection of two main questions: the question of ideology, or rather of ideology/religion, and the question of the relations between superstructures and infrastructures. I shall consider Bastide's treatment of these two issues in turn, referring frequently to the text itself.

With respect to the first question, Bastide's point of view reveals itself throughout the book: he believed that there is a correspondence between the transformation of religion into ideology and the emergence of a distortion of the sacred. For example, in referring to a study on Haitian voodoo, which asserts that after first having been the expression of the resistance of slaves against slaveowners it became an instrument of political domination used by the mulatto bourgeoisie, an "epiphenomenon," he notes that it is in a class society that this sort of distortion can be expected to occur.[5] Further on in the book, within a different context, Bastide observes that slavery had broken the bond between the world of African values and the social structures they reflected. There followed the risk that values would be left "temporarily floating in a vacuum" which would lead them to be transformed into ideology, or at least to lose their sacred meaning, while being penetrated by "racial animosity and anger and with economic grievances."[6] This might have taken place, for example, when Catholic saints (e.g. St. Anthony) and *orixás* (e.g. Ogun) were thrust against each other as a manifestation of the antagonism between slaves and slaveowners. For Bastide this is one example, among others, of the "degradation of the sacred."[7]

However, says Bastide, the sacred is not always degraded in this manner. For instance, by spreading the belief in post-mortem compensation, the slaveowners tried to make the black (Catholic) church an instrument of domination. Manifestly or not, then, the caste of slaveowners considered religion an "opiate," but such tactical use of religion did not always result in alienation, as was desired by the dominant group. The black man who adhered to Catholic brotherhoods reinterpreted the Christian saints and saw in them, as in the *orixás*, not the mediators for the attainment of divine grace, but the guardians of life in this world. Reinterpreted in African terms, such Catholicism could scarcely be said to provide "opium for the people."[8]

The author's point of view becomes clearer in his Conclusions to Part II. Whereas in the Marxist conception, religion is seen as a response to the contradictions within the mode of production, for Bastide this interpretation is infinitely more adequate if applied to magic.[9] Magic helps people to face uncertainty, while religion strengthens the bonds between individuals. An example of this, as shown by the author, would be the predominantly magic-oriented mystical behavior of the slave masses. I would go on to suggest that the tensions and hostilities within the slave system were intensified by the almost complete suppression of freedom of activity imposed in the name of security. On the other hand, both the free Negroes before Abolition and, obviously, the liberated masses after it felt the need for some sort of ethnic or racial communion, and the religion of the *orixás* served as a basis for this.[10]

Bastide's position in relation to the question of ideologies becomes clearest of all in the final pages of the book.[11] He takes off from a reference to the two concepts of "ideology" that appear in Marx's writings, the first including every form of superstructural manifestation, the second, although still a conceptual tool, expressing a situation of class struggle. In this second formulation, ideology becomes the weapon of a fragmented world, and is related to the concepts of unhappy consciousness, alienation, and mystification.[12] While expressing, at a conscious level, a given stage of the development of productive forces, and when centered on a sacred that could be considered "pure" and "authentic" insofar as it is rooted in a given social situation[13] that serves as the basis for "axiological communion," religion is ideology, but only in the sense of the first formulation. This is how the author should be understood when he says that the sacred is always "a level of the global reality," never "a problem to resolve," never an "ideology."[14]

My observations so far lead me to one of the principal frames of reference used by Bastide.[15] It appears that the author operated on the basis of an implicit "measuring stick": the concept of "authentic" religion. It is from this point of view that he analyzes the two opposite directions taken in the process of gradation (or degradation) of religion: that which leads to magic (which we could qualify as "disnomic," as opposed to the magic we could label "eunomic"[16]) and that which leads to religious ideology.

It should be noted that the author's main point of reference—"authentic" religion—is not constructed on the basis of a deliberate methodological procedure. The concept is never plainly expounded, although it is latent throughout the text. Bastide, in fact, deals with Afro-Brazilian sects that are quite close to this concept of religion. In empirical terms his points of reference are the northeast Dahoman and Yoruba centers. These nuclei "act as a kind of brake"[17] in relation to the process of disintegration undergone by the Afro-Brazilian cults, a process that is more intense the farther we go from these particular groups.

However, even in these empirical paradigms of "authentic" religion, "religious values, the basis of axiological communion, were subjected to external pressures resulting in a compromise moving between the sacred and the ideological."[18] This is why Bastide, in referring to the economy of *candomblé*, which is based internally on cooperation and externally on potlatch, mentions the infiltration of new values bringing about a disintegration created by the capitalist spirit. Being in contradiction with the values of *candomblé*, these new orientations tend both to engender compromise with the outside and to heighten internal stress, which may in turn lead to deep modifications of black religiosity, as is the case with Umbanda. And thus a "canker" penetrates *candomblé*.[19]

In its turn, Umbanda is presented as the empirical paradigm of religious ideology.[20] The presence, however much degraded, of the sacred in its values, together with the tendency inherent in every sect toward the constitution of axiological communities, keeps Umbanda a religion.[21] This suggests, although Bastide does not attempt it, that it would be possible to identify a sort of vector directed from the extreme of religious ideology to the extreme of "authentic" religion.

In the final pages of this book Bastide refers to "threats" to Umbanda and actually, to every religious ideology. These threats result from the break-up of what I would call the organic bonds between the superstructure of religious values and the infrastructures. The mystic values fluctuate —as Bastide puts it metaphorically. They are no longer the significant expression of the infrastructure, but become merely its reflection. The organic bonds between the two levels that still subsist in the *candomblé* paradigm (where religious representations are directly connected to economic, aesthetic, and political ones) are, in the case of Umbanda, destroyed. Bastide nicely characterizes the continuity between the two sets of values in the first case in noting that here "the values were structured, while the structures were given value."[22] However, once this continuity is interrupted, as in the case of Umbanda, the defense mechanisms against the tensions and conflicts characteristic of a class society are destroyed. The Umbandist communities would thus no longer constitute "niches," and their corrupted sacred values would but reflect the damages done by the wider society.[23] The precise nature of this "threat" remains something of a question. In the light of Bastide's arguments as to the disintegration of sacred meanings under the stressful conditions of the slave regime,[24] this menace could be understood as the tendency toward increasing magical content. At the level of mystical values, it should then be possible to detect, in the heart of Umbanda, a tendency toward "disnomic" magic— *macumba*—which according to the author is clearly beyond the dividing line between religion and magic.[25] This assertion is at least partially confirmed by actual data on Umbanda, which seem to indicate that besides the process of reorganization leading from the extreme of "anomic magic" to the extreme of religious ideology there exists a trend pressing in the opposite direction.[26]

Finally, by focusing on the extremes of "disnomic" magic and "authentic" religion, one can complete Bastide's frame of reference. In this case, too, there are two opposing tendencies. The first, analogous to the vector pointing from religious ideology to "authentic" religion, is in this case, though pointing in the same direction, a vector originating at the extreme of "disnomic" magic: "there is a tendency to structure magical collective

representations, like religious ones, within the frameworks of institutionalized organizations."[27] The second tendency constitutes a process parallel to the "degradation" of the sacred into ideology. It leads from the
extreme of "authentic" religion, or "eunomic" magic, to that of "disnomic" magic: "the social structures of the slave era affected even religious representations, orienting them toward magic."[28]

■ ■ ■

Roger Bastide refuses repeatedly to consider the origin of religion, or to
discuss the place occupied by religious values within the totality of social
values.[29] He does not wish, he says, to invade the field of philosophy by
entering into a discussion of a theory of values. All values, including
religious ones, are considered levels of social reality.[30] However, this
supposed barrier existing between science and a philosophy of values is,
either implicitly (as is more often the case) or explicitly transgressed by
the author himself. He writes, for instance, that "the utilization of 'the
sacred,' transcendence in respect to the social, the participation of the
human in something that goes beyond it,"[31] distinguishes religious values
from all others.

Such a stand by Bastide would be of no significance had he placed it "in
brackets," thus keeping his analysis of values in scientific perspective.
However, it acquires a different meaning if the recognition of a supra-
empirical basis for religious values is implied, as if the latter expressed
something above the human. If, to this transcendence—different in kind
from the transcendence postulated by Durkheim for collective representations—one adds the rooting of these values and of the "axiological
community" of which they are the nuclei in social situations, one establishes the basis of Bastide's "authentic" religion.[32]

For Bastide, these social situations *may* act upon the axiological community, thus distorting the sacred by "introducing foreign elements such as
class interests and other impurities."[33] In characterizing religion, as opposed to religious ideology, the author clearly suggests a model in which
an "authentic" sacred would correspond to a perfect link between religious
values (associated with some sort of Transcendent) and the social situations they embody.

I wish to make clear the undoubted relevance, in some cases, of such
notions as that of the "authentic" sacred—at the level of both aspiration
and values and as an uncomfortable presence within the religious ideologies that are accommodating toward the *world*. Moreover, it is worth
stressing that in other cases (in millenarian and messianic ideologies, for
instance) aspirations and values point in the direction of a radical quelling
of the category of the sacred itself (and therefore also of the profane).
Finally, it is essential that the dynamic role of these aspirations in religious
and social structures in general be taken into account. Yet it is a very

different thing, in my view, to incorporate such values into a sociological model.

From the point of view of a value analysis (in which values are seen as elements of certain levels of the social reality, i.e. as "objective facts"), the "unauthentic" sacred is all one could expect to observe. In short, I am suggesting that the "corroding worm" (which for Bastide is chiefly of exogenous origin) that threatens the religious communities and the sacred things that constitute their nucleus is not present only in special social situations—i.e. the action of social situations on these communities does not represent simply one empirical possibility. These communities in fact present themselves to observation *only* under the influence of social contexts. Such considerations tend to suggest the presence of an inborn inner tension operating within every such religious community and as an intrinsic quality of the sacred values.

In Bastide's theoretical frame of reference, the category of the sacred lacks a contradictory and tensional character.[34] The consequences of this are of reduced significance, however, insofar as his practical starting point is the empirical paradigm provided by *candomblé* (though this is itself implicitly associated with the underlying concept of "authentic" religion). Nevertheless, the selection of this framework leads to obviously biased analyses of religious forms as Bastide ranges farther and farther from the *candomblé* pattern. Thus, the classification of this cult as religion at one end, and of Umbanda as religious ideology at the other end, is to my mind unacceptable.

There are strong indications that in elaborating these two concepts Bastide made use of the notions of communion, community, and mass, which are the "forms of sociability" in Gurvitch's depth sociology.[35] Thus, in reference to *candomblé*, Bastide says: "As long as the *candomblé* restores African civilization, the sacred remains dominant; individual consciousnesses are merged in a single system of beliefs; everyone shares the same values, irrespective of the social position of the *candomblé* members, free or enslaved, rich or poor."[36]

My own reflections, combined with this passage from Bastide's work, lead to the following arguments: (a) This "sacred," in the case of *candomblé*, conceals the external social contradictions that are manifested inside it. (b) The analysis of the ways this "sacred" is manifested could perhaps lead to the identification, within its own inner nature, of the reflections of the outer cleavages, whether in direct or inverted form. (c) Resting on the foundations of the "fusion of consciences into the same belief system," communion may figure as aspiration, but its obviously ideological character, revealed in its concealment of the suggested tensional nature inherent in the sacred, should not be overlooked. (d) The methodological operation (even if only implicit) by which this communion and the "sacred" to which it aspires define the ordering principle of a theoretical model cannot be accepted, since it introduces an ideological element into the scientific analysis.

However, the difference in character of the interconnections between infrastructure and superstructure in the cases of *candomblé* and Umbanda is undeniable, as Bastide demonstrates. Formed as a "niche" and warranted by the "principe de coupure,"[37] *candomblé* may, to some extent, embody an axiological orientation different in character and opposed to the one dominant in the wider society. Considering these conditions, the *candomblé*'s religious values, while expressing relevant facets of the profane lives of its members, pervaded them deeply.

Bastide points out the precariousness of this insulated state of the religion. For such isolation is only relative and always threatened by a magic or ideological degeneration. Nevertheless, these religious brotherhoods, which "grew up on the margins of the Luso-Catholic civilization,"[38] established a form of articulation between superstructure and infrastructure, during their struggle to defend their own boundaries, which is no doubt different from that existing in Umbanda.

While bearing in mind the reservations already expressed, one may say that in *candomblé*, values and symbols are living models of the infrastructures.[39] In line with Piaget's assertion, cited at the beginning of this book,[40] a material context can be extended into collective representations. However, this does not in any way alter the ideological character of the religion.

In the case of Umbanda, a kind of spiritualization of the religion can be said to have occurred. In the case of *candomblé*, religious values and symbols express social situations, while in Umbanda they reflect the lacerations of the human groups involved; they hover over the structural subversions that "depend . . . on other causalities or dialectics."[41] On one side, expression and symbol; on the other, image, reflection, and product. These formulations suit the realities they describe very well, but only insofar as they are seen as indications of dominant tendencies, and as long as the author's interpretation does not deny the existence of opposing tendencies in each case.

■ ■ ■

Bastide's approach to the problem of the relations between superstructures and infrastructures is the subject of the following pages. The questions I shall discuss are closely related to the ones treated above and are also, in a way, complementary to them.

Gurvitch's depth sociology[42] serves as a starting point for Bastide, who makes a brilliant demonstration of its application, while adding to it an original contribution on the problem of the interpenetration of civilizations. By bringing this theory to the level of empirical analysis, Bastide submits it to a decisive test.

In this case Bastide's orientation is quite clear, in contrast to the ideology question, for which his frame of reference and assumptions were never made explicit. However, it may be useful to underline some points of his analysis that have contributed to the solution of important sociological problems.

First, let us look at the discussion of what, in contrast to depth sociology, he names "plane sociology."[43] This singular term is used by Bastide to designate the analysis characteristic of a sociology that operates on a horizontal plane, seeking correlations between economic, political, religious, and other variables, while neglecting their vertical projections. Bastide argues that such variables must be examined at different levels of the social reality and within particular historical contexts, lest they run the risk of becoming mere abstractions. In short, for Bastide, the identification of the interrelations between phenomena cannot be accomplished if these are isolated from the dialectics between the superposed levels of the social situation or from the concrete conditions under which they take place. From a sociological point of view, "political," "economic," or "religious" variables are meaningful only if viewed from both these perspectives. Bastide's conceptions are thus equally far from "plane" sociological explanations, which ignore the different levels, and depth sociologies, which distinguish a single "determining" factor. In the first pages of the Introduction Bastide refers to those anthropological and sociological trends developed in the United States that employ the concept of "patterns of culture," as well as to Marxist and Durkheimian conceptions that distinguish different levels in the social reality. Derived from both these sources, his own depth sociology incorporates and transcends them by making space for the notions of totality and integration. He thus recognizes, in the dialectics of the superposed levels, the existence of "breaks, tensions, and polarities"[44] that are directly related to historical causality. In this way, the apparent irreducibility of the opposition between situational and causal explanations is broken.[45]

Second, the way in which historical causality is treated by Bastide should be noted. Among the different approaches to the problem of the interpenetration of civilizations, Bastide stresses three: that of those ethnologists and anthropologists who emphasize the gestalt of the cultures in contact; that of his Brazilianist precursors who valued the descriptive documentation of the history of acculturation, though their explanations suffered from the limitations of their psychological orientation; and the sociologically rich Marxist approach, which opens the gates to a social history or to a sociology not disdainful of history.[46] Reflecting upon these different trends he arrives at his own point of view: the meetings of civilizations is a process that cannot be studied outside the context of historically generated situations, such as that characteristic of modern slavery in America or the "colonial situation." Bastide confronts social structures and religion at different stages of Brazilian history and analyzes the variety of successive cultural patterns that appeared.

In Gurvitch's theory, the "esprit de système" is taken to an extreme, which sometimes leads to a sterile formalism, as is the case, for instance, with his characterization of social classes. By establishing a link between "situational" and "causal" analyses, and as a consequence of his historical approach, Bastide corrects this distortion and makes a major contribution to depth sociology.

Third, while trying to avoid both purely Marxist and purely culturalistic interpretations of the acculturation process,[47] yet at the same time deriving from them what is useful for his own sociology, Bastide calls attention to the significance of what he calls interest groups or ethnic associations.[48] He does not believe in an analysis of the interpenetration of civilizations that examines contact situations simply from either a purely cultural perspective or a perspective of the dualism of economic classes. He thus condemns both the culturalistic "flattening" that restricts itself to a single level of reality, and the depth sociology attached to a dualism that is a "sociologist's abstraction."[49] Hence, the groups that compose the dominant class (sugar-mill owners, merchants, church, state) and those belonging to the slave masses and freedmen (brotherhoods, "nations," religious groups) are seen by Bastide as participants in the concrete meeting of the horizontal plane of cultural contacts and the vertical plane of class opposition.[50] In other words, class opposition and the category of social class itself, rather than pertaining to a social vacuum, are embedded, so to speak, in "impure" structures, in which they mix with ethnic, racial, or religious oppositions.

Finally, Bastide's analysis of slave rebellions is a notable practical application of his theoretical conception. Those events present aspects of cultural resistance and of counteracculturation, but in a context in which they are directly related to racial opposition and to the antagonisms generated by a servile regime. This explains why the author accepts, in principle, the Marxist analysis of these confrontations as conflicts between social classes. However, in adopting this interpretation, he imposes the condition that *class* be defined "in its full complexity—its characteristic culture as well as its production system."[51] The examples offered in the book justify entirely the author's conclusion that "religion does not merely lend color to the social revolt; it is its very heart."[52]

Related to this discussion and informed by his views on "ideology" is Bastide's consideration of the Marxist interpretation of the religious elements in slave revolts as mere epiphenomena.[53] Similarly, we find later in the book a discussion of the interpretations of religion as the only channel left, since all others, particularly the political one, were closed.[54] Bastide reasons that to accept this interpretation would imply recognition of the power of the Marxist explanation, and, based partly on Balandier's analysis of African colonial messianism, he tries to avoid this, by distinguishing between two different situations. The first case embraces those instances in which religious resistance by the dominated civilization precedes deeper action by the dominant civilization. The second one includes those cases in which religious resistance arises after the emergence of the disintegrating effects of contact. Examples of the first situation would be the resistance of blacks against whites during the establishment of the first missions in Africa, and the *quilombos* and the upheavals of urban blacks in Bahia. The religious backlands' revolts in Brazil (Canudos and Contestado) and the African messianism of this century would belong to the second category, and the mystical direction taken by such movements is seen as an indication of the impossibility of giving a "secular" form to economic and political antagonisms.

Bastide seems to accept the epiphenomenal and therefore ideological character of the religious values and symbols of the movements of the second type. They can be viewed as an attempt to recover, at the level of more or less messianic and millenarian utopias, the irreparably lost equilibrium. However, he rejects these qualifications in the case of rebellions that occur prior to the integrating influence of social and cultural contacts.

Within the context of a dominant society and culture, the degree of compromise or accommodation on the part of the blacks engaged in the Bahia revolts and the *quilombos* seems to me to be a matter for continued discussion. Another controversial issue is the alleged ambivalence of black religiosity before as well as after Abolition (a question touched on by Bastide later in the book). Although I cannot take up these issues in the present format, I would add that it is not possible for me to accept Bastide's distinction without further qualifications, for reasons spelled out, in part, in the earlier consideration of the "ideology" problem. The basic question is whether or not we can apply to religious social movements (such as the backlands' uprisings mentioned by Bastide) and, in a certain way, though in different degrees, to "secular" rebellions as well, the statement made by Lukács about sixteenth-century peasant upheavals: "The ideological moments not only 'conceal' the economic interests, they are not only barriers and slogans in the struggle, but part and parcel of the actual struggle itself."[55]

■ ■ ■

Bastide's clear perception of the processes of change in interracial relations and religion is revealed in this book. His views on race relations were outlined even earlier, in 1955, in the study done in collaboration with F. Fernandes, in which he says: "Color prejudice becomes an instrument of economic struggle in order to make domination of one group over another more efficient."[56] Industrial and urban development, the clearer distinction between classes, the vanishing of traditional criteria for interethnic relationships, and the emergence of what Bastide calls "the multiracial masses"[57] produced a new type of prejudice and new modes of discrimination. I think we may add to these conditions those created by migration from rural to urban areas, proceeding from areas where black, white, and Indian interracial crossing had been occurring frequently and for a long time (e.g. from the northeastern backlands). Under such circumstances, in the big industrial cities the contingents of blacks formed of descendants of slaves who worked in the plantations of southeastern Brazil could scarcely avoid being absorbed by the racially "mixed" masses and had to struggle to establish their group identity.

Eleven years after the first edition of *Les Religions Afro-Brésiliennes* and sixteen years following his research on race relations in São Paulo, Bastide returned to the Brazilian racial problem and tried to compare it with the North American and South African situations.[58] He emphasized the significance of the American Negroes' reaction, marked by the search for an identity in their assertion of "blackness," when faced with a liberal and assimilation-oriented policy. An analogous, although still incipient, reaction is now taking place in Brazil, where a minority that asserts itself as *black* searches for that symbolic expression which could be specific to its group. It seems to be composed of a fraction of the Negro middle class which, while rejecting the traditional expressions of "blackness" sanctioned by the whites, tries at times to express it through the consumption of imported "soul music" at gatherings and meetings. Bastide seemed to be aware of this possibility, as well as of the extreme complexity of the situation. Be that as it may, he knew that simplistic interpretations that put excessive weight on homogenizing socioeconomic pressures while treating actual cultural factors on a secondary level were unable to explain what was happening.

Similarly, to the extent that Afro-Brazilian religious expressions are associated with ethnic groups (though open to whites who opt to "become Negroes") the trends of their evolution are not simple. The predominant tendency is no doubt toward the implantation of religious beliefs and practices that, in their syncretism, more or less derive from an already remote African tradition. Umbanda is, roughly speaking, an example of this process. However, the impetus with which this religion has expanded is uneven in the different regions of the country. The regions where the lines of cultural and racial identity were not attenuated by social factors existing in southeastern Brazil, and those where the traditional cults are deeply rooted, as in Bahia for example, have become foci of resistance.[59] On the other hand, because the Afro-Brazilian religion is so persistent, it is possible that it will become one of the constituents in the shaping of Brazil's "blackness." The likelihood of an "Afro" revival—whether or not within the framework of Umbanda—should not be underestimated.

In any case, Bastide's optimism in relation to the possible entry of

Brazil into an "organic period"—an optimism present in this book and referred to in connection with the emergence of Umbanda—is slightly altered in the author's more recent work. Brazil's economic development in the last years has been marked by the intensification of industrial concentration in large private, state, and mixed enterprises, by the impressive amount of external investment of multinational origin, and consequently by a "modernizing" impulse.[60] As a result, the disparities in the stage of development of the different regions has persisted, and the unevenness in the distribution of the national income and the deterioration of the real salaries of the working class have been aggravated. Add to this the tendency toward the disordered growth of the big centers and the almost complete suppression of freedom of political expression and we have created favorable conditions for the proliferation of certain types of religious behavior.

In these circumstances, it can be said that some of the tendencies pointed out by Bastide were greatly enhanced by the emergence of a new social picture as the stage for developing the religious beliefs and practices of the low-income population. Taking into account these new trends, I would like to conclude by considering a few aspects of the recent evolution of popular religion.

Firstly, a remarkable growth of Umbanda has been observed.[61] The number of Umbandists in the "mediumistic continuum,"[62] which includes Kardecist spiritualists (followers of Allan Kardec's doctrine) and Umbandists alike, has grown from 93,395 in 1964 to 256,603 in 1968 (from 11.5 percent to 28.4 percent of the population).[63] To appreciate fully the significance of these figures, it should be added that many Umbandists are registered in the census as spiritualists, while many others are registered as Catholics. The continuum's total number in 1968—a contingent of 900,925 people—should be viewed as an underestimate. Relevant, too, is the fact that the criteria of affiliation to these religious groups frequently lack precision. It is a well-known fact that residual spiritualist beliefs are widespread among the masses, even in groups that formally belong to nonmediumistic religions.

Secondly, a growth in the participation of Pentecostal groups in the evangelical population (in one way or another associated with the Protestant tradition) has been observed in the last decade. In 1970 the Pentecostal subgroup (which for purposes of ennumeration was limited to participants in communion) represented 62 percent of this religious contingent. The absolute figure is 2,992,335 among 4,814,728 evangelicals.[64]

The two religious groups referred to above—the Umbandists and the Pentecostals—and the old popular Catholic devotional practices are linked to the emergence of a seemingly very important tendency, i.e. the new clientele-based and instrumental orientation adopted in relation to religious "goods" and "services." This tendency has seemingly been accompanied by a persistence of communalistic forms of religious participation. The process under way is an increase in demands almost devoid of exclusiveness and characterized by a nonsectarian nature, which takes the form of a kind of "popular ecumenism." This does not imply that the specific differences between the various branches have been abolished. Actually, the preservation of the specific religious practices might be considered an important condition for the intense competition within the religious "goods" and "services" market.

Real agencies of production and distribution of religious "goods" and "services" spring up, particularly in the large urban centers, side by side with religious organizations that resemble the church or the sect type—this is what we observe at the concrete level. For the most part these "goods" and "services" take the form of blessings (given to the clients directly or transmitted through the radio) that are aimed at curing their diseases or solving their everyday problems. In many cases, the practice of blessing is accompanied by the emergence of special paraphernalia, such as religious pamphlets and records.[65]

A very important aspect of these phenomena is the fact that, while different in content and opposed from the point of view of the doctrines that inspire them, these various religious practices favor the emergence of agencies with similar patterns of activity. The latter can be found not only in Pentecostal and popular Catholic contexts, but also, with some differences, among Umbandists and even in sects of Japanese origin. On the other hand, the practices of exorcism that characterize certain Pentecostal agencies are in a way complementary to the animistic universe of Umbanda.

Such a state of affairs raises important sociological questions. What social conditions should be thought responsible for the exacerbation of those functions relating to uncertainty and magicoreligious control, at the expense of those functions related to the construction of meaningful worlds? Would the "market model"[66] be a more adequate frame of reference for the study of this religious field? Would any latent legitimations of a metareligious character guarantee the functioning of this "market"?

In any case, it should be evident, in conclusion, that whatever the orientation adopted by future research on Brazilian popular religion, Bastide's book, devoted to one of its main streams, constitutes the inevitable starting point.

Douglas T. Monteiro
Department of Social Sciences
University of São Paulo
São Paulo, Brazil

The African Religions of Brazil

Introduction

"Religious misery," wrote Marx, "is both an expression of true misery and a protest against true misery. Religion is the sigh of the afflicted creature."[1] This is how sociology in its beginnings linked religious values to social structures or, more precisely, to man's condition in society. But that link, the basic subject of the present investigation, was conceived in terms that were still far too narrow. Social life is seen as essentially a practical activity; it becomes identical with the forces of production. It is true that in his earliest writings the young Marx takes production in its widest sense, as the production of ideas as well as goods. Nonetheless he already perceives religion in the form of an ideology. This ideological character will be ever more sharply stressed as he progressively reduces his notion of production to the production of material goods alone. It is equally true that the Marxists have insisted above all that religion is the opiate of the masses and that the churches serve the purpose of lulling the workers' revolt to sleep and tying the exploited classes to the oppression of the ruling ones. But this is not the aspect of Marxism that concerns us here. Within the context of Marxist theory it is impossible to make religion a simple ideology invented by the masters to strengthen their hold over the slaves. Religion is not false because it is a one-sided vision of reality, an expression of the economic interests of the ruling class. This is merely a secondary aspect, a reaction of ideology to the social substructure, to the perpetuation of the class society. This aspect is of course important—so much so that in his political writings Marx insists less on the causal role of the modes of production than on the other side of the dialectical relationship. In these writings it is precisely the "false" ideas, those which no longer express the economic realities of the moment, that most effectively influence the course of historical events, since they enable the ruling class to maintain a power condemned by the facts.

Yet this aspect too is still secondary. For even if a class uses religion to strengthen its rule, this is not the origin of religion. Religion is born of "the

misery of man." How? This, for us, is the heart of the matter. Clearly we
find among the Marxists more or less fruitful attempts to link religion to
the techniques of production or, in a more general way, to the economic
factor, particularly in the case of early Christianity or totemism. But Christianity, like totemism, is no more than a solution designed to allay a more
powerful feeling—the feeling of fear. As one analyzes the main Marxist
texts on religion, one discovers beneath the new economic trappings the
old idea of the ancients: *primus in orbe deos fecit timor.* For what religion
expresses is not the economic relationships between human beings per se,
but the fact that these relationships are contradictory and yet not recognized as such. Engels more than anyone else insisted upon this aspect,
showing that primitive religion expresses man's anxiety in the face of the
mysterious powers of a nature beyond his taming, forces which therefore
assume the shape of superterrestrial powers, while contemporary religion
expresses the anxiety of contemporary man in the face of social forces
such as the law of supply and demand, economic crises, bankruptcies, or
unemployment, which the proletarian cannot foresee and which assault
him unexpectedly and brutally with such apparent strangeness and yet
inevitability that they too become supernatural and supersocial forces.
God is then no more than the image of blind capitalism. Consequently the
Marxist explanation of religion is in the end as much psychological as
sociological. It is sociological in the sense that it focuses on the failure of
the effort of human labor in the confrontation with nature or with the
contradictions of a social order, but it is psychological in the sense that
this failure or these contradictions operate only by arousing an eternal fear
and panic in the face of the irrational, the uncontrolled, the untamed.

Piaget praises Marx for having moved forward, in his discovery of the
relativity of the superstructures in relation to the substructures, from
ideological explanations to recognize action as the explanatory factor—
"things done communally to strengthen social group life as the expression
of a given material environment which extends into collective representations."[2]

In the pages to come we must not neglect this communal action. But in
moving from the sociological to the psychological, in reverting to the
explanation of religion by fear, Marxism is merely refining an outdated
solution. This explanation says in effect that there is no such thing as
religious feeling; there are only normal, easily identifiable feelings arising
from ordinary consciousness, and religion is merely an effect or an object
of such feelings.[3] Now religion, even where it takes a terrifying form,
where it expresses itself as anxiety, still seems to stem from a particular
domain, one which comes to light not only when human effort is defeated
but wherever "life touches its limits: in birth, death, coitus, wherever one
leans over the rim of existence and is seized by giddiness."[4]

The presence of religious forces, however, is not always a presence of fright; it may also be a presence of strength, peace, or joy. In saying this I am referring not just to contemporary Christianity but to the earliest forms of religiosity. Durkheim was to stress this aspect of the problem. We on the other hand cannot inquire into the origins of religion in the present work, because this would lead us from sociology into philosophy. (Even a sociological philosophy is still a philosophy.) Instead we shall study one particular case in an attempt to discover the various types of relations that can arise between the social structures (including economic conditions) and the world of religious values. We shall see that in certain instances these relations can indeed assume ideological character or be penetrated or colored by ideologies, taking this term not in the wider sense of intellectual production, of "works" of the collective consciousness, but in the more traditional sense of "unconscious deformation" or of the phantasmagorical play that goes on above the economic substructures.[5] What we do need to study, though, is how, why, and in which cases this distortion of the "sacred" occurs, always taking the "sacred" as a level of global reality, never as a problem to resolve, never as an "ideology."

Durkheim takes up the problem as Marx had posed it but gives it a much wider basis, making it easier for us to accept his position. To begin with, he twice refuses to identify religious feeling with fear: first in his definition of religion and again in his critique of naturalism. Primitive man, far from feeling crushed by forces against which he is powerless, "attributes to himself a mastery over things which he does not really possess but which, illusory as it is, prevents him from feeling dominated by them."[6]

Secondly, Durkheim refuses to treat religion as a simple epiphenomenon, as pure phantasmagoria. "It is inadmissible that systems of ideas such as the religions, which have held so considerable a place in history and to which, in all times, men have turned as a source of the energy they need to live, should be no more than a tissue of illusions."[7]

Finally and above all, in *Les Formes Élémentaires de la Vie Religieuse* religion is linked not to an economic substructure but to the totality of the social structure and its morphological articulation. Yet the causal problem preoccupying Durkheim is the same as in Marx, even though it appears here in a much richer and more complex form. "Religious conceptions are the products of the social environment, rather than its producers, and if they react, once formed, upon their own original causes, the reaction cannot be very profound."[8]

This last quotation, it must be noted, is taken from Durkheim's *Suicide* (1897), and we may ask whether, in the move from this book to *Les Formes Élémentaires* (1912), his thinking was not more-or-less profoundly modified. In distinguishing religious symbols from images, his thought turns away not only from religion defined as an ideology but also from religion defined as a simple representation, which was the idea developed in *Suicide*. Religion then becomes rather the expression of society, its structures and its rhythms, of the agglomeration or dispersion of human beings on earth.[9] The ambiguity is certainly not entirely overcome. Durkheim always seems to hesitate between religion as "product" and religion as "expression." The two themes are always closely intertwined in his work and it is difficult to separate them.

The difficulty lies in the fact that every human being is a social animal and that religion reduces to the consciousness of collective life. Religion is thus both the product of communion and the particular expression this feeling of communion assumes, namely that of a distinction between two worlds, the "profane" world of individual consciousness and the "sacred" world of collective consciousness, which is outside and above individual consciousnesses. There is no need to repeat here the critique of Durkheim's thesis, a critique which has been put forward often and well.[10] What strikes me is the discontinuity between the facts cited by Durkheim and the conclusions he draws from them. What emerges from the facts is the control of the group over the manifestations of the mystical realm,[11] the link between the rules of kinship and those of ceremonial life,[12] in short the impossibility of detaching religion from the global social phenomenon. It does not follow, however, that religion is produced by human agglomeration and the development of collective consciousness within this mass. Durkheim's conclusion goes beyond the multitude of examples he compiles in support of his thesis, inasmuch as they all merely show that religion is always incarnate in the social structure but not that social structure creates religion. *Les Formes Élémentaires* had the merit of eliminating certain shortcomings of Marxism by detaching symbol from image, but to explain these symbols in the final analysis through the state of society as an assemblage does not get us beyond that search for causes that we have already rejected as being philosophical.[13]

German sociology of religion, like its French counterpart, can be considered an attempt to go beyond the excessive narrowness of Marxism in its classical form. Cassirer even felt free to turn it around, opposing to historical dialectics what might be called the psychological eternity of the human mind. For Cassirer the starting point is not society but religious categories taken in the sense of a Kantian a priori. These categories can then be examined to determine how they serve to unify society and the world as well. To be sure, we can no longer speak of temporal causality. Religion is the cause of society not inasmuch as it chronologically precedes it but in the sense of being its logical condition. Society cannot constitute itself except in the categories of mystic thinking (*pensée mystique*), just as for Kant nature constitutes itself in the forms of sense perception or the categories of reason.[14] In Max Weber too we recognize above all an opponent of Marx who refutes him in his celebrated study of the origins of industrial capitalism by demonstrating the influence of ideological upon economic factors.

Weber's sociology of religion is of course not limited to this one essay, and it would be a caricature to turn him into an idealist pure and simple. To begin with, even in this essay Protestantism figures not as the total cause of total capitalism but merely as one cause among others, affecting only certain aspects of it. What Weber seeks is a common element, especially in the religious and economic factors, that would make the effective action of this causality intelligible. This element he finds in the social ethics of Calvinism. While religion does not act directly upon the economy, it always gives orientation to the moral behavior of individuals toward one another. These moral behavior patterns, and they alone, can modify economic relations.[15] Finally, while in his *Gesammelte Aufsätze zur Religionssoziologie* Weber insists on the causal action of religion, the opposite action seems to predominate in his *Wirtschaft und Gesellschaft* or, if not the causal action of the economy as a whole, at any rate that of classes or vested interests. Every class or social group—peasants, aristocracy, business bourgeoisie, craftsmen, or proletariat—has in fact its own religion, which gives expression to the group's position within society, to its dominance or subordination, and, even more frequently, to any change in this position, whether upward or downward.[16]

What sets Max Weber in opposition to Marxism is not that he reversed the materialistic chain of causes and effects. He is too much concerned with differences, with the complexities of reality, with variation in the causal sequences, to ignore the existence of an economic factor in the sociology of religion, just as Marx is interested in the reaction of the superstructures to the substructures. The true opposition, as we see it, lies in Weber's substitution of a sociology of understanding (*verstehende Soziologie*) for Marx's positive sociology. Marx, like Durkheim, studies social fact from outside, or, to put it another way, as "things" or at any rate as objectively explainable "actions." Weber does not stop at establishing variable correlations between the economic and the mystic facts; he wants to understand the deep significance of these correlations. He wants to grasp the meaning of types of human behavior. But this involves a danger that he has not been able to escape—the danger of subjectivism. For the understanding he seeks is attained by reference to the observer, i.e. the sociologist who interprets the correlations. This is to ignore the fact that the sociologist himself is part of a society, that he has been shaped by a given culture, and consequently that his own psychology has also been conditioned by social factors. In exactly the same way, the "meanings" of the modes of behavior he analyzes are dependent upon the total social phenomena within which these modes of behavior arise. We shall encounter this problem of understanding again as we move from sociology to ethnology. To conclude this critique, let me merely say that we cannot allow Weberian subjectivity to enter into the heart of our work.

While Weber is closer to the Marxist position—relations between religion and economic facts—Max Scheler seems closer to the position of Durkheim—relations between religion and the social structure, and not the economic one alone. Scheler distinguishes in effect between cultural sociology and the sociology of reality (*Kultursoziologie* and *Realsoziologie*). The sociology of religion belongs to the former, that of groups and institutions to the latter. Economic factors find their place in the sociology of real factors, but they rank only third, after the racial and political factors, which, from the viewpoint of social preponderance, precede them in time. As a result the question posed by Marxism becomes more meaningful for modern than for primitive religions. What, then, are the causal relationships between the two sociologies? There are, first of all, two independent causal chains. The spirit determines the content or, as Scheler puts it, "the thusness (*die* Soseins*beschaffenheit*) of the cultural content."[17] Similarly, human needs determine the formation and organization of groups or institutions. Side by side with this dual causality, numerous links exist between the world of culture and the world of social reality, but these links are complex in quite a different way. The content of culture plainly influences the very forms of organization, as, for example, the content of faith, Protestant or Catholic, and exerts its influence on the organization adopted by the respective churches. Spirit, however, whether individual or collective, is no "efficient cause" nor does it dynamically act upon reality. The actual relationships among men in society are not deducible from religious content or values. Conversely religions are indeed sociologically conditioned by the forms of actual relationships among men and by those of their groups, but these sociological conditions act only by way of selection. The dominant social interests—biological, then political, and finally economic ones—can do no more than either rule out certain possible realizations of the logic of the spirit or else promote or select them, but the real history, that of the social institutions or situations, is "indifferent" with regard to the history of spiritual life. The determinism of consanguinity, for example, will favor familial or tribal religion, which political determinism will later rule out, but the content of religion itself, whether tribal or political, depends on the pure causal logic of the individual or collective spirit.[18]

Scheler, it is true, establishes still another type of link between cultural sociology and the sociology of reality. Human needs, the vital impulses that are at the origin of groups or institutions, may well transcend the barrier separating the two worlds and penetrate to the level of ideas and values. But if they do, they are immediately transformed and "sublimated" by the spirit. In short, the author of *Die Wissensformen und die Gesellschaft* has grasped well the difficulty of the problem of the relations between what Marx calls the substructures and the superstructures when the problem is posed in terms of causal sequences. But, wanting to maintain these sequences at any cost, he can only resort to the most inflexible dualism and divorce the logic of the spirit from that of the real. Then, when he searches vainly for links, for reciprocal conditions, he encounters the very difficulty that Descartes encountered when he so radically separated mind from body that afterward he could never explain their union.

I do not believe that everything in the sociology of religion summarized here is to be dismissed. But does it not become useful only when it tries to escape, however clumsily, from purely causal explanation? Do not the difficulties it encounters always stem from the predominance it grants to causality over and above the other types of explanation? This leads me to examine another and radically different sociology of religion.

■ ■ ■

It would seem that contemporary sociology tends to substitute for the old isolated chains of sequences, detached from global reality, explanations based on situations, configurations, or integrations. And so the ancient traditional problem of the relation between economic and religious fact from which we started is replaced by the problem of the relations between the different aspects of one and the same civilization. The causal element then disappears in the face of the situational one.

Up to a point this movement corresponds to the transformations of classical logic as it abandons the Aristotelian notion of classes or substances and replaces them with a relational logic or set mathematics. One can indeed see the same process at work first in physics, then in psychology with Kurt Lewin's field theory, and finally in sociology. But though the new logic, which explains the parts by means of the whole instead of explaining the appearance of one phenomenon as the effect of another, has created a favorable climate for a social field theory, the determining factor in the rise of new sociological conceptions must, I think, be sought in the evolution of ethnology at the beginning of the twentieth century.

The massive difficulty in ethnology is the understanding of "the other self." Although the theory of evolution managed to conceal this difficulty for a while, it surfaced again when Lévy-Bruhl recognized the wealth and relativity of civilizations. Relations between human beings are not like relations between things. They have a meaning; they pose the problem of understanding. But can we interpret them within the framework of our own type of thinking, shaped, as it is, by our own society or our own value system, without falling into ethnocentrism? Can we communicate with the "other self" beyond the barriers of cultural differences? Lévy-Bruhl was well aware of the tragic implications of this question. Throughout his life he sought a method of entering into the mental attitudes of so-called primitives instead of projecting our own mental attitudes onto them.[19] But the result of this long quest was to proclaim the "opacity" of "primitive" thought to the thinking of the ethnographer who tries to grasp it. Toward the end of his life, Lévy-Bruhl's method was reduced to warning the researcher not to fall victim to the illusion that he has clarified what is by nature obscure to us[20]—surely an admission of the impotence of a sociology of understanding when it is applied to the world of human beings who belong to non-Western civilizations. This, at any rate, is how modern ethnology in general has understood Lévy-Bruhl's approach. As a result it abandoned any comprehensive interpretation and returned to an essentially positivistic method.

The study of structures thus wins out over that of collective ideas, and religion is perceived as part of that social structure rather than as a set of "mystic" ideas. The behavior of individuals and groups is no longer interpreted from within, through the ethnologist's own effort to "uproot" himself culturally, but from without, as "things" or, better still, "actions" that are interconnected, complementary, reciprocal, susceptible of objective scientific treatment. In this way ethnology tries to escape the difficulty by fleeing from life as it is lived into the mineral-like immobility of structures, sanctions, or organizations—at the risk of falling into ethnocentrism and value judgments—in an attempt to recover the neutrality of observation. There are, moreover, differences of degree in this immobilization, depending on whether one takes the term "social structure" as concrete and visible, taking account of the dynamism of societies[21] or of the phenomena of "deviant" and "alternative" behavior that permit the most rigid models to adapt themselves to the eventualities of life,[22] or whether one goes in the opposite direction and uses the term "social structure" in the sense of abstract rules or normative models, which of course vary according to the civilizations studied but reduce to a given number of formal types linked to the structure of the unconscious, which can then be grasped by a sort of psychoanalysis of institutions.[23]

Yet this does not fully exorcise the problem of understanding, for the ties between individuals or groups, sexes or ages, are defined by a system of symbols, including specifically religious ones, which gives them meaning. As Radcliffe-Brown has pointed out, social order ultimately depends on the existence in the minds of its members of feelings that control the behavior of individuals or groups toward others. A structure functions in accordance with the models, values, ideas, or ideals that have significance for its constituent elements. Thus the problem of understanding is not eliminated, it seems, but merely pushed aside. It can be solved in various ways. The first solution, proposed by Kardiner, leads us back once again to the psychological element. What gives significance to social institutions is the "basic personality." In this perspective the problem of the relationship between economy and religion, or between social structures and collective ideas, is no longer posed on the sociological level, in the actions and interactions of institutions. Instead it is transferred to the consciousness of the individuals who unify and integrate the institutions, in harmony or under internal and external tensions.[24] Yet the difficulty that Lévy-Bruhl exposed so plainly remains to be faced: how can the ethnologist be certain that he has grasped this significance? To go beyond mere interpretation or to verify his hypotheses, he may well use tests like the Rorschach,[25] but one must ask what good that will do, considering that the meaning of the responses has no universal validity, since there are as many responses as there are civilizations. The second solution consists in seeing in myths, collective ideas, or religious beliefs nothing but justifications or rationalizations (in the Marxist or Freudian sense) of the hidden, most essential realities. Lévi-Strauss provides a good example of this second solution when he criticizes Marcel Mauss for wanting to found the rules of exchange, of gifts and return gifts, of prestations and counterprestations, on the explicative notion of *hau*; when he argues against Mauss that the *hau* is merely the theory invented by the natives to explain their own cultural models and has no more value than any theory we might invent for ourselves; and when he thus reduces this *hau* theory to a simple epiphenomenon that conceals the unconscious structures of the mind that need to be discovered.[26] The approach of Lévi-Strauss seems to me the only truly positive one in ethnology, but can we stop there? Granet's work on China shows that on the contrary, religious beliefs go beyond the laws of exchange and solidarity, the fundamental rules of complementarity, the logic of relations, in explaining the complexity of the functioning of social models. The function of religion lies not so much in explaining these rules of exchange, these relations between groups, sexes, or ages, as in mitigating the formidable effects of their linking up. Religion is not so much an ideology of equilibrium as a remedy for ruptures.[27] Moreover, the social structure studied by Granet includes the dead, the deified ancestors, the totems, and the gods, as well as the living, all of whom have their own statuses and roles. Individuals not only have reciprocal relations with them but "participate" in them and identify with them, as Leenhardt has shown in his study of the Kanaka—so much so that the ethnologist cannot treat religion and the category of the sacred in terms of economics if he wants to understand the society he is studying. A civilization does not reveal its true meaning unless it is grasped through its mythical vision of the world, which is more than its expression or justification, being indeed its very mainstay.[28]

Has ethnology, then, no way to reach understanding, to grasp what is "different"? Evidently not, since this difference is cultural and does not stand in the way of the mental unity of mankind. If it is true that symbols reveal by veiling and veil in revealing,[29] then a definition can turn into a rule of method. The very mixture of veiling and revelation offers access to the veiled meaning by way of whatever is nevertheless revealed. This explains the evolution of ethnology, with the Griaule school, toward the depth study of the various levels of symbolic thinking.[30] The social structures are by no means forgotten, but now they are directly correlated with the world of mythical or ritual values. This school has been charged with exaggeration. But does not this charge arise precisely because its all too positive method clings only to the visible or links normative social structures to the unconscious mental ones at one stroke, with the result that it sees the symbol merely as an expression of that link rather than as an expression of meaning?

Be this as it may, ethnography enabled sociology to develop from a causal into an integrative discipline. Ethnology made it possible to eliminate theories that made capital out of certain supposedly privileged facts, such as the facts of production for the Marxists or the facts of religious social ethics for Max Weber. Ethnology demonstrated to sociology that in a society everything holds together, everything acts and reacts upon everything else, so that the cause of social phenomena must be sought in their interrelations with the structure of the whole. This development took place in two steps: first, the application of the descriptive methods of "cultural anthropology" to so-called civilized modern society (community studies); and second, the acceptance of structuralism and functionalism by American sociology.

American sociology was originally strongly influenced by German formalism, in whose wake it limited itself to reducing the social factor to a dusty cloud of interindividual or intergroup relations. What had so closely unified French sociology—the study of social institutions and organizations, of collective ideas and values, of the action of society on the psychic state of the individual—was split up into three different disciplines: sociology proper, cultural anthropology, and social psychology. Nevertheless a need was felt to overcome nominalism and reunite what had been divorced. Ethnography showed that interindividual relationships occurred within a certain global structure that gave them direction, thus enabling sociology to get rid of its nominalism. It also showed that this orientation took place according to norms or ideals, and this enabled the new sociology to link up with cultural anthropology. It is true that the Americans were bound by an academic tradition quite different from the French one. They did not go so far as to confuse society with civilization, especially since civilization can migrate and pass from one society to another. But in the work of Sorokin or Parsons, for example, the divorced pieces—society, civilization, personality—tried to join up again.

However, while American sociology has the merit of drawing attention to the importance of the total configurations, it also tended to flatten out, if I may put it that way, the various levels of reality that sociologists, whether they followed Marx or Durkheim, had so happily distinguished. Gurvitch has shown that "depth sociology," as he named it, had its origin in both, and there is no need to return to that point here.[31] The stratification of the depth levels of social reality made a much richer dialectic possible, one that did not even hesitate to have recourse to singular causal relations where it saw a need for it. It accounted simultaneously for the mutual relationships the new American sociology stressed and for the breaks, tensions, and polarities. In this way it made possible the transition from statics to change, from situation to cause; in brief it allowed explanation to be more effectively modeled on concrete fact in its perpetual transformation. Certainly we cannot derive cultural norms from anything other than human behavior, and this behavior is always grasped within an organized whole that is structured or is restructuring itself. Equally certainly, symbols are grasped within institutions, often are inseparable from them. And yet one cannot put norms, symbols, groupings, etc., on one and the same plane under the pretext that they function simultaneously.

The sociology of religion, as well as general sociology, must simultaneously take into account these two needed elements—configuration on the one hand, tiered depth levels on the other. Gurvitch has the merit of having proposed just that: a depth sociology with respect to both the total social phenomenon and the different forms it assumes.

The work of Gurvitch, which closes a long history of controversies, school struggles, and theoretical wavering, must, then, be the starting point for the present investigation. But it seems useful to begin with several comments about this work.

First of all, let us not forget that what Gurvitch proposed were operational notions, which means that the number of levels to be considered, or their order of importance, would vary from case to case. This is evident if we compare his *Vocation Actuelle de la Sociologie* with *Déterminismes Sociaux*, where the simple transition from description to explanation entails a revision of the number of strata and even a shift of the eighth level.

Secondly, depth sociology does not make the ancient problems disappear; on the contrary, it complicates them in order to be better able to resolve them in keeping with the wealth and complexity of reality. Thus the relations between the religious and the nonreligious appear simultaneously on the vertical and the horizontal plane. On one hand they enter into the study of the dialectic relations between the various depth levels of reality, from morphology to collective consciousness; on the other they appear on every one of these planes, for example between economic groups or social classes and religious organization, or again on the cultural plane between mystic symbols and political values. It must also be said that these two directions, vertical and horizontal, cannot be separated; they constantly intersect and cannot be dealt with separately. On the contrary, each social phenomenon must be placed on each of the two axes of the coordinate system.

Thirdly, Gurvitch has left aside the problem of interpenetrations between different types of global societies. Yet his unmistakable interest in them is obvious in passages like this: "One might perhaps assume that the equilibrium of the forms of sociability has a tendency to predominate over the specific hierarchy of the levels in the structuration and destructuration of the groups, while the tendency would be reversed in the case of the global society."[32] This seems to allude to certain American studies that show how contact between two civilizations can result in the disappearance of a global society that can dissolve in the form of sociabilities. But in a world where races, ethnic groups, and civilizations mix, the question arises how a more complete theorization of such phenomena can be achieved. We cannot know a priori whether they need to be related to a single total social phenomenon (as in the case of a native culture affected by foreign elements) or to two total phenomena (as Durkheim suggests when he defines colonization as the engendering of entirely new "social types").[33]

This brings us to a point where we may put aside the first problem that occupied us, that of the connections between structures and the works of religion, and look at the conclusions reached by the study of the interpenetration of civilizations to see whether they can satisfy us.

■ ■ ■

The interpenetration of civilizations is not a new problem arising from nineteenth-century European expansion. On the contrary, it might be said that the whole history of humanity has been one of cultural struggles, migrations, and fusions. The historians especially have applied themselves to this phenomenon, particularly to the encounter of the Greek and Asiatic worlds, the assimilation of the Mediterranean peoples into the Roman Empire, the religious syncretism that marked the end of that empire, the barbarian invasions, the Crusades, and the increasing diffusion of Western values throughout the rest of the world. But they studied this phenomenon as historians. That is to say, they concentrated chiefly on the special nature of each case; they did not try to use the comparative method to define a typology or at least a conceptual framework that might lead from description to explanation.

Sociology inherited this first formulation of the problem from historiography, but with Marx it searched for a theoretical model that could account for it. This model, obviously, was historical materialism. Religious syncretism results from the development of trade and the rise of cities where seafarers and travelers gather. It simply transposes to the level of superstructures the economic ties that link country to country, making them interdependent. But each "syncretism" has its own character and each one struggles against the others. Christianity triumphs as a consequence of the disappearance—or at any rate the decline—of the trading towns and of ruralization in the period of the barbarian invasions.[34] Unfortunately, by breaking the links between sociology and historiography in their attempt to find biological models to replace the older Marxist ones, the organic theories of society brought to the fore the very opposite phenomenon—the fixity of social types analogous to that of animal and plant species—thus preventing sociology from incorporating the study of the interpenetration of civilizations into its own field. Durkheim, who went beyond the organicism that he and Espinas took as their starting point, was to run into this problem again in his *Rules of the Sociological Method*, where he studied the relationships between social types. He distinguishes two cases. In the first and more general one, external causality touches society only peripherally. This leads him to discover not only the primacy of internal causality in the explanation of social phenomena but with it—and long before Herskovits—the phenomenon of reinterpretation.[35] The second case is the one where entirely new species come into being. Colonization may serve as an example of this. Durkheim himself studied only one instance of this phenomenon: the interpenetration of the paternal family of the Franks and the Roman patriarchal family. But the creation of a true sociology of civilizational interpenetration was blocked at the time by the so-called superstition of primitivity, the search for "origins"— the origin of religion, political power, etc. This made the facts of "acculturation" look like so many impurities, which, being unworthy of the scientists' attention, should be ignored and passed over.

The failure of certain forms of colonization in Oceania or Africa, the abortive attempt to assimilate the Amerindian masses into Western civilization, and the double crisis of European and North American capitalism, which forced it to push beyond its own restricted markets and concentrate on the underdeveloped countries, have now given top priority to this problem of interpenetration, which sociology tended to neglect around the turn of the century. But now the ethnologists and anthropologists, not the historians and sociologists, are in the lead. Hence the transition from the historical to the naturalistic approach.

Let us try to distinguish the one from the other. To begin with, the naturalistic approach has its roots—at any rate in the United States—in the traditional opposition between sociology and cultural anthropology, where the former studies intergroup relations, the latter intercultural ones. We thus have two unrelated notional systems: sociology, with its concepts of competition, conflict, and accommodation; and cultural anthropology, with its notions of selective acceptance, adaptation and syncretism, resistance and counteracculturation.[36] Secondly, acculturation studies follow the progress of ethnology, not of sociology. At the beginning, when culture was analytically defined by a set of traits, the encounter between civilizations was mechanically conceived and syncretist cultures were examined for traits belonging to the native civilization and traits borrowed from the alien one. Once ethnology brought to light the "gestalt" character of culture, the contact between peoples could be studied in terms of total cultures—undeniably a step forward. But this created a massive methodological difficulty for research, since such contact is selective inasmuch as it isolates from the cultural whole particular traits that it accepts while rejecting the others. This difficulty led cultural anthropology, in its third developmental stage, to the concept of the "cultural focus."[37]

As we shall see, we need to go beyond this naturalistic conception, though not without incorporating its results into the present work. What conclusions has it reached? First, it has made possible a typology that helps to transcend the historical individualization from which we had to start. Bateson, for example, distinguishes three cases: complete fusion of the original groups, elimination of one or both of the groups in contact, persistence of the two groups in dynamic equilibrium within a larger community.[38] Above all, this approach has brought into focus, with direct reference to the heterogeneity of interrelated civilizations, the two great processes of destruction and reinterpretation. In the first case, the cultural models that were structuring the society disappear. The society is reduced to the dust of interindividual relationships. External causality governs internal causality. In the second case, the alien elements are modified, metamorphosed into a function of the predominant models, and reinterpreted in terms of the receiving civilization. Internal causality then dominates external causality. In the first case pathology is at work, in the other, genetics.[39]

Nonetheless such naturalism is quite aware of its own shortcomings and tries to overcome them by successively introducing history and psychology into its description of the acculturation phenomena.

In the final analysis, naturalism interprets and explains the phenomena of civilizational interpenetrations in "quantitative" terms. The results of contact depend on the relative size of groups in contact (limited or large), on the chronological duration of the contact, on its territorial extent, etc., while acculturation always occurs under specific historical conditions, which are continuously evolving. Thus, despite Malinowski's indictment of "antiquarian research" in the name of his own functionalist doctrine, it becomes necessary to return to the historical continuum that explains why and how syncretism operates between different civilizations.[40] Herskovits requires the ethnologist to analyze the historical documentation in the archives and aptly reminds the Americanist that what ought to concern him is not the contact of Indo-European civilization with the African civilization of today but its contact with the African civilizations of the seventeenth and eighteenth centuries as we may know them through travelers of that period. Unfortunately this history one dreams of is either buried in the documents, where it is more than a simple chronological description of facts, or else it is conceived as a "cultural dynamics"—i.e. as a partial history, the history of cultural phenomena alone, divorced from the total social phenomena.[41] And precisely because this history is only partial, it must in the end fail to account for the acculturation phenomena, so that the ethnologist who is unwilling to limit himself to a mere description is finally forced to turn to psychology.

It is not civilizations that are in contact but human beings. Consequently, when two civilizations meet, it is psychic mechanisms that account for what happens. In the final analysis, then, the causal factor must be sought in the desires of individuals—the desire to differ from others, the desire for prestige, for a better lot, the desire to be imitated, reassertion of the claims of the self, affirmation of the defense of the self—and reinterpretation is linked not so much to the existence of cultural norms, of structural models (as with Boas), as to the recognition that the innovations or borrowings are mental and therefore cannot manifest themselves outside the limits set by the experience of the individuals themselves.[42] But this psychology cannot, in my opinion, be separated from the sociological conditioning within which it operates. This is a psychology not of isolated individuals but of individuals who belong to social groups, castes, or clans, where status differs with sex, age, or rank.[43] Whether we like it or not, the psychological factor thus sends us back to the sociological one. Let us agree in any event that the macroscopic process definitely resolves itself into a multiplicity of psychological microprocesses, just as the attempt has been made to reduce the visible phenomena of evolution (the appearance of new species) to an infinity of biochemical phenomena occurring at the level of genes. Obviously our explanation will never end, for it would have to encompass a complete examination of all the individuals in contact with one another, which is impossible even in the case of small groups. Fortunately, in every case where microscopic analysis proves impossible there is another level of explanation, the macroscopic plane, where the chaos of individual phenomena is neutralized, permitting new forms of regularity to emerge that are no less objective and visible than the earlier ones, as Durkheim and Halbwachs have confirmed in their studies of suicide—divergent as they are.[44]

By introducing novel methods of production, Soviet Russia has raised the standard of living in regions called "peripheral" (in relation to central Russia), many of which still belonged to "archaic" civilizations. Consequently contemporary Russian sociology too has a strong interest in the phenomena of acculturation, though it studies them on the basis of historical materialism, i.e. of the dialectic relation between substructures and superstructures. It thus goes beyond a psychologism that presupposes a psyche eternally identical with itself, tied to its own internal conflicts, independent of history, indeed capable of autonomously exerting causal influence upon the course of historical events. The consciousness of individuals is always determined by the conditions of the moment; it is in direct dialectic contact with socioeconomic transformations.[45] To take an

example, Guérin applied this new viewpoint to Haiti in an attempt to
understand the survival of voodoo, which, in a society where production
was based on slavery, once served a useful purpose in expressing the
people's resistance to their masters but which is today no more than a
doomed epiphenomenon used by the mulatto bourgeoisie to reinforce its
political dominance.[46] And indeed in a class society we cannot neglect the
influence of this type of group upon what is called acculturation. But we
must restore these groups to the context in which they belong: the global
society. Here we cannot rely on either economic or cultural history alone.
As Seppilli has said, the interpenetration of civilizations must be reintegrated into a unified, organic conception of the dialectic process of the
emerging total society.

This history is already far removed from historicizing history. If it is to
become social and sociological history, must it not go farther still? After
all, these historical processes unfold within given "situations," such as
slavery or colonization or aid to underdeveloped countries.[47] As Balandier has shown, contacts between civilizations can no more be studied by
divorcing them from these "situations" than can the phenomena or processes of evolution.[48] Of course what is true of colonization also holds for
all other types of "situation." The study of civilizational interpenetrations
reaches beyond "colonial sociology," one of its most important chapters,
but if it wants to be explanatory, it can never be anything but sociological.

So the conclusions I have reached in examining the successive interpretations of the acculturation phenomena tally with those that emerged from
the examination of our first problem. It is essential to view the encounters
between civilizations within the framework of a depth sociology and to
relate the play of the dialectic of social levels to the total social phenomenon, i.e. to the occurrence of various types of situations or configurations.

■ ■ ■

In our investigation of Afro-Brazilian religions the two themes whose
history I have briefly traced will mingle, interfere with, pursue, and at
times oppose each other—though without ever being mutually contradictory. Rather they will complement and enrich each other, since, as we have
seen, they derive from one and the same sociological interpretation.

Our thematic starting point is the relations between infrastructures and
superstructures or, to put it another way, the social conditioning of religion. We must be able to assess the role of the different depth levels of
social reality, the action and reaction of each level with respect to those
preceding or following it, and the action and reaction of the total phenomenon with respect to its parts. Is not the comparative method the one best
suited to this task? Yet this method has its pitfalls if the comparison
concerns different religions in different societies, or even if it deals with
civilizations of the same type where the elements of differentiation would

be minimal, so that the use of Durkheim's principle of concomitant variation would be preferable. This principle enables us to show how variations in symbols or values correspond to structural variations but it does not help us to grasp the dialectic of the emergent phenomenon *in statu nascendi*. It makes possible the formulation of working hypotheses but provides no way of verifying them. Similarly used in the case of different societies, the comparative method takes us from one global society to another, but it is quite difficult to find two such societies that resemble each other in more than one respect, since everything bears on everything else. Our best procedure would therefore seem to consist in staying with one and the same society as it destructures and restructures itself, developing its modes of production now slowly, now more abruptly, over the years, and creating new cultural works, so that we can then compare these diverse factors in the evolution of the chosen society. In short, we must substitute historical for geographical comparison. Nevertheless it is still comparison and not history, for what we want to do is examine structures and religions in this society at its different "ages." Unfortunately the material is never rich enough to allow us to follow the sequence of actions and reactions step by step. Still, this is a comparison that historical dialectics can complete, at least on some points, and its effectiveness will increase as we move toward the modern period, with its growing mass of documentation, which helps us to follow more closely the temporal changes on the various levels of reality.

As an example of the use of the comparative method, I have chosen the Afro-Brazilian religions, which established themselves and persisted amid radical changes in the social structure while undergoing modifications in their relation to it.

The blacks imported to Brazil belonged to different civilizations and came from the most diverse regions of Africa. But their religions, whatever they may have been, were linked to certain types of family or clan organization, to specific biogeographic environments (tropical forest or savanna), to village and community structures. The slave trade shattered all that. The slave was forced, willy-nilly, to become part of a new type of society based on the patriarchal family, the latifundium, the rule of ethnic castes. What happened then? This is the first question we shall have to answer. But the period of slavery lasted three centuries, and during those three centuries Brazilian society did not remain static. The eighteenth century, for example, saw the ascendance of mining over the great plantations. In the nineteenth century urbanization developed. Finally, as the empire drew to its end, miscegenation and the rise of the mulattoes gradually modified the ancient stratification of castes. How did the African religions react to all these upheavals? This is the second question we shall have to examine.

The decline of the slave trade (at first under British pressure), then the abolition of slavery, led to a crisis in Brazil that undoubtedly had economic and political repercussions (transition from empire to republic), but that affected the ancient structures even more seriously. The whole system of production changed. Forced labor was replaced by free labor. In addition, the demographic structure was altered by the influx of the colored peasants to the towns and by the arrival in the South of masses of European—and later Japanese—immigrants to replace the blacks on the plantations, which altered the territorial distribution of the races. The family system changed too. The *casa grande* group lost its Negro field hands and domestic servants. Finally, when capital formerly used for buying slave labor was freed for investment, the process of industrialization transformed Brazilian society from a caste society into a class society. All this had its repercussions on the Afro-Brazilian religions.

But all this occurred at different rates of speed in the different regions of Brazil. It has been said that Brazil is composed of historical layers rather than social strata and that to travel from the coast to the interior is to pass back successively from contemporary civilization to that of the empire, then to colonial times, and finally to the neolithic Indian period of the bush or the great Amazon forest.[49] Without going quite that far, the French sociologists who have worked in this field sharply distinguish archaic from modern Brazil.[50] Redfield's attempt in Mexico to trace the folk-urban continuum *in situ* is equally feasible for Brazil, and today we find more and more community studies in that country distinguishing between "folk communities" and "communities in transition." The rural and urban structures and civilizations are not identical. The structures of the northeastern cities, where industrialization is less advanced, differ from those of the South, where capitalism can still be observed at various stages of development in various regions. Consequently the religion of the black will take on a different complexion or express variations in status, living conditions, and unidentifiable social frameworks, depending on whether he is a countryman, a craftsman, a proletarian, or a member of some type of subproletariat.

What complicates the problem is the fact that this religion was influenced not only by those variations in social structure but also by the cultural pressure exerted by the white Catholic Europeans and by the dual policy of the Portuguese state, as represented by its governors, and of the Roman church, as represented by the members of its religious orders even more than by its plantation chaplains and parish priests. As a result, the superstructures, the religious ideas as well as the mystic symbols and cultural values of the Africans or their descendants, were subject to a dual influence. On one level they were affected by collective Christian ideas, European cultural symbols, and Portuguese values, and on a different level by morphological modifications, by organized or unorganized structures. Moreover, the Lusitanian religious culture also was an import. Like the

African one, it felt the impact of ecological change and of the destructuring and restructuring of Brazilian society in its formative stages.

So far we have focused on only one aspect of the dialectical processes we have to pursue. The Catholic religion not only was influenced by modifications of the social structure; it also shaped the new society, incarnating itself in it like a soul that from within shapes the body it is called to inhabit. Rome was never too far away to fight deviations and erosive influences. It tried more-or-less successfully to unify around its church the dispersed nuclei, the living cells of the Brazilian organism in process of gestation. In the same way, the African religion tended to reestablish in its new habitat the village community to which it was tied, and when it failed in this it created other instruments for its purpose. Like a living creature, it secreted its own shell, so to speak. It created original social groups similar to, yet at the same time different from, the African ones. Spirit cannot live divorced from matter, and if the matter is lacking, it creates a new kind. Marxism was right in cautioning us against idealism with the reminder that no social life can exist without matter to condition it; it erred in holding that social life always stems from matter. We for our part must not forget the collective psyche's power to create profound currents. Thus the problem of the interpenetration of civilizations complicates the deeper problem of the relations between the ordered levels of depth sociology without enabling us to transcend it.

Our task is thus a sociological one: to gain a better understanding of these dialectic relations, using an example that we consider outstandingly suitable in more than one respect. In bringing this introduction to a close it therefore appears necessary to examine what separates our interpretation of the Afro-Brazilian religions from earlier ones and what each interpretation can contribute to our enterprise.

Not until the end of the nineteenth century did these religions attract scholarly attention. The suppression of slavery created a formidable problem in Brazil, that of assimilating the blacks as citizens and as paid production workers. The increase in criminality, vagabondage, and prostitution, the return of blacks freed from commercial agriculture to simple subsistence farming—all this led the whites to wonder whether such assimilation was even possible. Was not African mentality different from white Brazilian mentality? Was black Christianity anything more than a varnish barely covering the persistence of ancestral "superstitions"? Had the conversion of blacks ever been anything but "pure illusion"? To prove this thesis of mental heterogeneity, Nina Rodrigues went to Brazil in 1900 to study black religion—the first scholar to do so.[51]

We must stress the work of Nina Rodrigues because all subsequent research developed out of it. As his disciple Arthur Ramos has said, Rodrigues was "the leader of a school" inasmuch as he established the two points of reference for the study of Afro-Brazilian religions that would hold good for the entire first half of the twentieth century: psychologism and ethnography. We with our hindsight may correct him and reject his racial prejudices or his stereotypes concerning the Negro, but we shall always have to follow the directions he took, those of psychology and ethnography.

Rodrigues was a doctor of forensic medicine, and naturally what struck him most forcibly among the African sects he worked with was what appealed to the physician, namely episodes of possession by spirits. This explains his approach. In the first place, he centered the whole cult on ecstatic trance, leaving aside other less spectacular but perhaps equally important religious manifestations such as the ritual of divination, private ceremonies, mythology, etc. Secondly, he proposed an interpretation of these religions within the framework of clinical psychology. In this perspective the initiation of believers into the cult looked less like acceptance into a society and a culture than like a process of unhinging the nervous system, a training in ecstasy. The notions of sleepwalking and dual personality then being elaborated by Janet thus served Rodrigues in his explanation of the mystical trance among Negroes at a *candomblé*. But since somnambulism was at that time equated with hysteria and since certain psychiatrists denied the existence of hysteria among blacks, Rodrigues was forced to prove first that hysteria was as prevalent among blacks as among whites and that African religious celebrations all took the form of induced somnambulism. Secondly, he had to show, even if it looked like retraction, that dual personality can appear in other disorders besides hysteria—in neurasthenia or imbecility, for instance. This led him to the final conclusion that the weak intellectual development of the primitive Negro plus the nervous exhaustion produced by the initiation ceremonies provoked neurasthenic states in the Africans and that hysteria did in fact exist among the Creole Negroes and mulattoes. In both cases African religion would represent a pathological phenomenon.

But the intensive cultivation of these pathological phenomena presupposed the prior existence of African sects unassimilated to Brazilian culture. Ecstasy therefore had to be recentered in the theological-liturgical context in which it manifested itself, and this required a shift from psychology (or psychiatry) to ethnology. Rodrigues, as I have pointed out, was not a professional ethnologist, but he made a tremendous effort to give an objective description of the world of the *candomblés* and to search the works of specialists on Africa for the roots of the Bahian religions. It is true that he exaggerated or overstressed any exotic elements, foreign to our mentality, that these religions contained, finding in them nothing but a web of superstitions. As a result he confused magic with religion, in the proper sense of that word, while unhappily neglecting the ordinary, everyday aspects of religious life. Even so, there can be no doubt that he was so determined to be objective that after more than half a century his description is still valid. In fact, Afro-Brazilian priests familiar with the work of his disciples consider Rodrigues's assessment the truest of all.

In the field of ethnology his great discovery was that of religious syncretism between African gods and Catholic saints. It was he who first discovered and (as Arthur Ramos points out) directed scholarly attention to the modern forms of acculturation. In this respect he was in a privileged position because in his day pure Africans and Creole Negroes still existed side by side. He thus came to distinguish two types of *candomblé*—the African and the national—and two types of syncretism—that of the pure Africans, who merely "juxtapose" the Catholic cult and their own "fetishistic" beliefs and practices and conceive the *orixá* and the Catholic saints "as being in the same category though perfectly distinct from one another," in contrast to Creole syncretism, in which he notes "a manifest and unrestrainable tendency to identify the [two] teachings." Rodrigues thus saw acculturation as a progressive Europeanization of the blacks, slowed by "the incapacity to progress, or the sullenness, of the Negro."[52]

In 1902 another physician, Oscar Freire of Bahia, wrote his thesis on the etiology of the concrete forms of religiosity in northern Brazil. The work goes a step beyond Nina Rodrigues in attributing to social factors what Rodrigues had attributed to race. But the most famous disciple of Rodrigues was undoubtedly Arthur Ramos, also a doctor of forensic medicine, who was to devote most of his life to a careful study of the African civilizations in Brazil. Ramos's great merit is his antiracism, his antiethnocentrism, his substitution of the principle of "cultural relativity" for the ancient notion of superior and inferior cultures. Nobody has done more to give the nonwhite Brazilian pride in his ethnic origins. Aside from that, his research criteria are still those of Nina Rodrigues: psychologism and ethnology.

Seen from the psychological viewpoint, his books show a widening of the thought of his predecessor. It is true that his interest is always in the possession episode and that he always links it to "morbid states," but first and foremost he used psychoanalysis to account for the phenomena of African survival. Myths and rites persisted insofar as they were anchored in the collective or racial unconscious, where they expressed general complexes of the Oedipus or Narcissus type. Syncretism was possible only where the Catholic saint—the phallic Saint George or the Mother Virgin, for instance—corresponded to exactly the same fundamental complexes as the *orixá*. Syncretism is no longer simply the result of the encounter between black and white consciousness. The objection to this psychology is not the principle of applying the resources of psychoanalysis to the phenomenon of acculturation but the fact that it is a psychology without sociology.[53] The unconscious, just like the conscious, is molded by the social structures, conditioned by the total social phenomenon in which it is anchored—in this case the phenomenon of the economic and political domination of one class of the population by another.

In a similar way Arthur Ramos's ethnology considerably widens that of Nina Rodrigues. Ramos knows more about the research conducted on the African continent and can therefore bring to light hitherto overlooked survivals. Above all, he broadened Rodrigues's Bahian studies to include other cultural areas of Brazil, particularly the *macumba* of Rio de Janeiro. Before then the only study of the *macumba* had been the suggestive but still journalistic account by João do Rio (Paulo Barreto). But this ethnology is still confined to the methodological framework of American cultural anthropology as corrected by Lévy-Bruhl's studies of the primitive mind. Consequently acculturation phenomena are described but they are not explained by going back to economic and social conjunctures. Civilizations do not mix in a vacuum: there are material foundations that condition the process and its consequences.

Besides Ramos, who may be considered the leader, one would have to name a number of other researchers who widened the scope of the inquiry still further to include other areas of Brazil (Gonçalves Fernandes on the *xangôs* of Recife, Nunes Pereira on the *Casa das Minas* in Maranhão) or other cult forms (Edison Carneiro on the *caboclo candomblé*). This was the period when the topic of the Negro swept poetry, the novel, and journalism, shouldering aside the Indian and the *caboclo* in literature and in the minds of the intellectuals. The high points of this period were the three great Afro-Brazilian congresses that brought together ethnographers, psychiatrists, anthropologists, linguists, historians, folklorists, and even sociologists: the 1934 congress in Recife organized by Gilberto Freyre, the one of 1937 in Bahia organized by Aydano de Couto Ferraz and Edison Carneiro, and the one held in Belo Horizonte, just before the outbreak of the Second World War, organized by Ayres de Mata Machado and Joã Dornas, Jr.

During the war years, Herskovits went to Brazil in the course of the great investigation of Afro-American acculturation that had already taken him to Dahomey, Haiti, and Dutch Guiana. He brought young Brazilian research workers to the United States to be trained in cultural anthropology. The second period in the history of research on the black people of Brazil opened when Herskovits's influence began to supplant that of Arthur Ramos. The two representatives of the new trend are Octavio da Costa Eduardo, who has studied the *voduns* of Maranhão, and Rene Ribeiro, who is making an exhaustive study of the religious sects of Recife. But this school has only refined the procedures of the earlier one, using new techniques and a new conceptualization, without changing its perspective. Afro-Brazilian religion continues to be interpreted via psychologism and ethnology.

However—and this may be the greatest contribution of Herskovits—
mystic trance has now been taken out of the clinical context to be linked,
by way of the theory of conditioned reflexes, to a normal cultural complex.
The two perspectives, psychological and ethnographic, are no longer divorced but are integrated as the reverse and obverse of one and the same
civilizational phenomenon. By treating trance as a ritual element, this new
viewpoint not only frees us—let us hope for good—from interpretations of
ecstasy based on the data of mental pathology; even more important, it
initiates the unification of the psychological and the cultural aspects. Unfortunately it does no more than make a start, since the cultural element is
still grasped in isolation, divorced from the social factors that condition it.
Yet in this respect Herskovits and his disciples are undeniably on the right
track. They recommend that the *candomblé* be studied in its totality, not
just as a religion. They point out that the African sects of Brazil have an
economic aspect, a sociological structure, which imposes itself upon and
shapes the relationships between individuals, and that no description that
neglects these aspects can be valid. Viewed in this way, their enterprise is
of course no more than a beginning, but it does reveal a concern with the
total social phenomenon. The error lies in neglecting the even greater
global phenomenon, Brazilian society as a whole, or in taking account of
its influence only in regard to syncretistic transformation, i.e. only inasmuch as that influence manifests itself inside the sects. To a certain extent
this viewpoint is valid, since African civilization in Brazil is "encysted," but
the dialectic of this encystment is totally missed. In short, my objection to
Herskovits is that he stays entirely within cultural anthropology instead of
moving ahead to a sociology of religious interpenetrations.

Less radically stated, my objection is that the relation between cultural
and social factors is seen solely in terms of functionalism and ecology. To
begin with ecology, the method recommended by Herskovits is the study of
small communities through participant observation. Now, the community
religion appears closely linked to the rest of social life and, since our
ethnologist has a concern for history, he grasps religion in its time-space
continuum. This study of black communities has taken us beyond the
preoccupation with the picturesque and the exotic that all too often marred
early ethnographic studies. It has made it possible to discover the daily life
of the inhabitants, their everyday behavior—knowledge essential to a better understanding of the whole. But this link between the cultural and the
social is still made from the standpoint of cultural anthropology and this
leaves it open to two objections. In the first place, community studies can
be meaningful only when the communities are linked with a regional or
national entity, because local civilizations are never more than particular
reflections of a larger society. Secondly, functionalism tends to be the only
aspect under which the social factors become accessible.

Cultural norms and sanctions represent the traditional modes of individual adjustment. . . . In the case of Afro-Brazilian cult groups, they not
only established themselves in particular units of people living together
within a larger society but also in the form of vectors of a system of values
and patterns which often differ from those of the other groups within that
society. In this way they provide the participating individuals with a system of beliefs and a new type of interpersonal relations, which are extremely helpful in reducing tensions, without forcing them to reject the
other values and life styles of Luso-Brazilian culture. People who lack the
opportunity to achieve their goals through positions and roles within the
global society . . . find here a system of beliefs, interpersonal relationships,
and hierarchy much like a type of relationship with the supernatural, or
of apparent control over the accidental, a system which enables them to
satisfy the psychological needs indispensable to their adjustment to the
world they live in.[54]

Let us first note the significance of this text in the reorientation now
achieved in Afro-Brazilian research. We began with pathology and have
arrived at the diametrically opposed conclusion that African religion is the
operational factor in the adjustment of the individual to society. Trance,
far from being a cultivation of the morbid, is a technique for resolving
tensions. I am in full agreement with this and have often stressed the point
myself. But where I see an effect, others insist on seeing a function. Now,
functionalism has its merits; it reminds us that every organism functions,
which some people occasionally forget. Sheer survival serving no purpose
would not last long. Too many accounts of Afro-Brazilian cults turn them
into dried-up museum specimens smelling of mothballs and disinfectant,
into precious objects to be displayed behind glass, properly catalogued and
filed. Brazilian Negro religion is a living religion.

Two comments, however, must be made. First, as Durkheim says, functionalist research takes second place to causal and historical research
because, although it shows why a specific phenomenon persists, it does not
explain why the phenomenon exists at all. This is particularly evident in
the case of the *candomblés*, whose functions have changed in the course of
time. Second, when one investigates the ultimate cause of a phenomenon
from a functionalist point of view, one always arrives at the same conclusion: securing the satisfaction of human needs if one begins with Malinowski; securing the survival of the group if one begins with Radcliffe-Brown.
In both cases the explanation is far too general to be of much use, since
the most diverse institutions, whether political, religious, or familial, satisfy the same desires for prestige, security, or new experiences. In the same
way, groups of every kind promote solidarity among their members. What
matters is not the banality of what these institutions have in common but
the differentiations. Why does the individual seek satisfaction here and not
elsewhere? Why does integration take place within this group and not

another? Only a sociological analysis of Brazilian society as a whole will enable us to answer these questions.

Unlike earlier scholars, Gilberto Freyre studies the racial situation in Brazil as a sociologist rather than an ethnologist or anthropologist, although he is a disciple of Franz Boas. It is true that he has not made a special study of the religious domain, confining himself to occasional comments—on the Saint George cult, for instance, or on the pantheistic sect of Pernambuco. Nonetheless he has outlined, at least for the colonial and imperial periods, the sociological framework in which the acculturation phenomena operated. This approach goes beyond the two opposite but equally value-determining viewpoints of blacks and whites. Acculturation studies had in fact talked about blacks only, but with Herskovits and his Brazilian successors this was not an apology for "whiteness," as Guerreiro Ramos charged. On the contrary, acculturation talk always centers on the blacks in order to discover, through the study of reinterpretations, how the African civilizations survived. However much Africa tries to hide behind the trappings of Western civilization, its traditional family structure survives in concubinage (*amasia*), its forms of collective labor in the *mutirão*, the economic independence of women in the sexual division of labor and the trading of the female group. The two objections raised by Guerreiro Ramos against Brazilian anthropology, its apology for the process of "whitening" and its pursuit of the exotic (the Negro as a theme rather than a problem), may be valid in the case of the first school I have discussed but they certainly do not apply to the second, which insists on the study of daily life and the importance of cultural "nonwhitening." Neither does Guerreiro Ramos distinguish between the sociological work of Gilberto Freyre and the work of the ethnologists. Yet there is a capital difference between the two conceptions, quite apart from the fact that they are connected with different sciences. What the anthropologists bring to light is the persistence of African civilization under the illusion of syncretism, while Gilberto Freyre elucidates the formation of a Brazilian civilization through the fusion of the contributions of the Indian, the Portuguese, and the African, so that the characteristics of African civilization are often more apparent in whites than in blacks, and those of the Luso-Amerindian civilization more apparent in blacks than in whites.

One might have hoped that Donald Pierson, a sociologist of the Chicago school who has written an important book on Bahia[55] and is a student of the *candomblé*, would adopt this integration of Afro-Brazilian religion into the context of sociological conceptualization. He did indeed make the attempt—for instance in examining the relations or reactions of the various social classes of Bahia, or of the various generations, with regard to the *candomblé*. But his book juxtaposes two "systems of reference," the system of the sociologists (conflict, accommodation, etc.) and that of the anthropologists (assimilation, syncretism, acculturation, etc.), rather than integrating them in a coordinated whole. He is caught in the American tradition, which separates the disciplines concerned with society and inter- personal relations from those dealing with civilization and the relations between values, ideals and collective ideas. The Afro-Brazilian sects are not treated in terms of the total social phenomenon, which alone makes interpretation possible. This was fully recognized by Tullio Seppilli, who proposes a definition of Afro-Brazilian acculturation based on transforma- tions of the social system.

According to Seppilli, the earlier interpretations are one-sided. An- thropology neglects social relations between masters and slaves and confines itself to the dynamics of cultural phenomena. Gilberto Freyre, by contrast, does describe those relationships but gives only secondary status to the fact that slave civilization is not native to the frameworks of Bra- zilian society but was imported from Africa, where it was the very basis of life. Somebody still needs to attempt a unified interpretation of syncretism, taking into account the relativity of the various causal factors and estab- lishing a hierarchy of psychological and historical integrations. This is exactly what Seppilli is trying to do. The framework he adopts is provided by the social situation of slavery and the subsequent proletarization of the blacks in its connection with the system of production (the monoculture of the plantations and the mines, the industrialization of Brazil). This is certainly the right road to take, and Seppilli's short articles represent a big step forward on it.

But while he vehemently repudiates one-sidedness and refuses to accept the economic explanation as the only one, Seppilli is unfortunately still too tied to Marxism. In the first place, he still defines religion as an ideology, and this prevents him from recognizing that Afro-Brazilian reli- gion is not per se an ideology, although in specific instances it may turn into one. This confusion between cultural product and ideology blinds him to certain important religious variants that remain to be examined. Sec- ondly, his explanation ultimately rests on modes of production rather than on social structures, and this allows him to grasp certain important aspects of the questions—the role of slavery, for example. In my opinion, how- ever, Afro-Brazilian religion is linked not so much to slavery as to the artisanal labor of the "free" Negroes. If this is so, then slavery must be restored to the totality of the social frameworks of Brazilian society: its family structure, its political, corporative, and religious organization. We need to bear in mind all the factors that come into play—demographic, economic, and social—at all levels and in all their interrelationships. So- cial dialectics is richer than Marxist dialectics.

Finally, this sociology cannot replace ethnology; it can only integrate and orient it. What Seppilli lacks is precisely this ethnological base. One example will show how indispensable it is. Having made no field studies

himself, and assuming the paucity of African myths purely on the evidence
of the books he has consulted, he mistakes the nonexistence of information
about them (which is actually only a research gap) for nonexistence of the
myths themselves. He then finds an explanation for this in historical dialectics. Hindsight never has any trouble finding explanations—particularly
if one has a system. We for our part must be wary of our models of
interpretation, our conceptual schemes, because we can always make them
accommodate anything we want to put into them, the false along with the
true. The role of ethnology consists in providing a solid base on which we
can build. That is why, after outlining in an article the conceptual framework of my research,[56] I embarked on a first-hand investigation of the
Afro-Brazilian sects, with no preconceived ideas and without having any
kind of theory in mind. My intention was first to verify the validity of
earlier descriptions and second to fill in what they had overlooked (worship of the dead, mythology, divination, private ceremonies, etc.). Obviously this investigation is quite inadequate when one considers the richness
of these cults,[57] but at least I am conscious of its shortcomings and shall
not undertake to explain what still remains to be discovered. My thesis is a
sociological one, but it rests on years of ethnographic observation.

As I conclude this introduction, I have one misgiving. Can a white undertake this ethnographic research or propose such a sociological interpretation? Here I am confronted by the negative view of Guerreiro Ramos, who
writes in his analysis of the problem of the Brazilian Negro:

> The theories about the Brazilian blacks are the product of alienated
> vision, an outsider's vision. Even when their authors are Brazilians, they
> abide by the tradition of old-time reports written for the mother country.
> . . . The epigones of our socioanthropology of the Negro since Nina
> Rodrigues merely add glosses to . . . the categories established for the sub-
> ject by European and American scholars. . . . Yet any true understanding
> of the situation of the Negro in Brazil requires a creative methodological
> and conceptual effort. It has special historical and social features that can-
> not be captured by procedures strictly parallel (to those of "export"
> scholarship). . . . To get rid of the humbug surrounding this topic—the
> Negro in Brazil—it is necessary to throw out these conceptual clichés, to
> try to examine the problem by bracketing out the connotations of our
> official science, and to endeavor to understand it by taking as the starting
> point a vital situation. . . . What vital situation? In the author's opinion it
> is the situation of a man whose skin is dark and who authentically affirms
> himself as Negro. What I am saying is that one begins to get a better under-
> standing of the phenomenon if one starts from the affirmation: *niger sum.*
> In the Brazilian setting, where everybody wants to be white, this experience
> of *niger sum* provides a highly rewarding scientific starting point, thanks
> to its dialectic significance. . . . Starting from this vital situation, the
> factual problem of the Negro in Brazil is primarily psychological and
> secondarily economic. Once one defines the Negro as a normal component

of the country's population, it is an absurdity to speak of an "economic problem of the Negro" as distinct from the problem of nonprivileged classes or the problem of pauperism.[58]

In essence two themes intertwine in this critique: the necessity of making *niger sum* central, and the rejection of "consular" or "export" scholarship. This is not the place to discuss the question whether one must begin with the experience of negritude to be able to understand racial relationships, or whether this experience may not rather be a deforming one—and if it is, as the Americans believe, whether one would not do better to choose a "neutral" observer, as they chose Gunnar Myrdal, a stranger to their country. But when we pass from the level of groups and organizations to the level of symbols and values, then understanding does presuppose participation or, to use the term of Guerreiro Ramos, a "vital situation." In Brazil, however, for reasons to be examined later, there is a dissociation between culture and race. In the *candomblé* we find Spanish "daughters of the gods" as well as French and Swiss members of the priestly hierarchy with various titles. (I am not of course speaking of foreigners who have been awarded honorary titles without any initiation formalities.) All that is required is to accept African law wholeheartedly. From that moment on, however white one's skin, one is caught up in the shared mystic rites, in taboos, and in susceptibility to magical vengeance. In fact it is possible in Brazil to be a Negro without being African and, contrariwise, to be both white and African. I can therefore say at the threshold of this book: *Africanus sum*, inasmuch as I have been accepted by one of those religious sects, which regards me as a brother in the faith, having the same obligations and the same privileges as the other members of the same degree. The experience to be recounted here is lived experience.

As for the criticism of "consular" sociology, this is, in my opinion, a useful warning against attempts to apply methods or concepts of European or North American sociologies to Brazilian realities without first subjecting them to criticism. Guerreiro Ramos's objection, however, holds only for the substantive type of conceptualization; it does not apply to the operational type, the type that is subject to verification by facts, modeled on facts, and that changes as the facts change. Our task is to understand Brazilian reality in all its originality, not to fetter it in generalities, and only in the final stage to extract from it whatever it can innovatively contribute to a theoretical sociology of dialectic relationships between social structures and religions and between heterogeneous civilizations.

I
The Dual Heritage

1
The Importation of
Portugal and Africa to America

The colonization of America was not orginally colonization by settlement. Like the British and the French, the Portuguese set up warehouses along the coast in order to trade with the natives, particularly in dyewoods. Far from imposing or propagating their own civilizations, the first whites to arrive in the New World adapted themselves to the Indian civilizations they encountered. In any case, those warehouses, which also served as markets and small fortresses, were few and far between, because Lusitanian commerce still looked principally to the Orient, with its wealth of spices, precious stones, and sumptuous fabrics. Not until the Portuguese were driven out of the East Indies did they turn their attention to America, America, however, had little to offer them: a few medicinal plants, brazilwood, multicolored parrots, and amusing little monkeys. If the new continent was to be opened up to commerce, the first task was to introduce new crops such as sugar, for which there was a steadily rising demand in Europe. Commercial agriculture of this type could not be successfully introduced without settlement of the new territories discovered by the white man.[1] Moreover, the Spanish were discovering, along the routes taken by their conquistadors, mines yielding silver and precious stones. Was it not likely that the vast hinterland of Brazil held similar resources? In its lust for gold, the mother country would soon organize *entradas* or *bandeiras*, expeditions to prospect for precious metals, and these too presupposed at least some degree of settlement.[2] During the sixteenth century colonization was to change its nature. While it remained linked to the

commercial capitalism characteristic of the age, its dominant feature was
to be settlement.

At the time, however, Portugal was short of labor, even for its own
farms. Small as the country is, in the sixteenth century much of it lay
permanently fallow for want of manpower. Wars of conquest, plagues, and
epidemics had made terrible inroads upon the population. This explains
why American colonization took a special form, why it was based on the
principle of slavery. Now, Portugal was quite familiar with slavery. Descendants of the conquered Arabs and—later—prisoners of war taken in
North Africa had been put to work in the fields. After exploring the
African littoral, Portugal had even initiated the enslavement of blacks. We
know that toward 1550 almost ten percent of the population of Lisbon
consisted of Negro slaves. So all that was necessary was to extend this
custom from metropolitan Portugal to Brazil and set the enslaved Indian
population to work on plantations to be established under the control of a
white minority for its own profit.³ These whites, stimulated by a more
sensuous climate and by contact with beautiful naked girls, would be allowed to interbreed with the Indians, producing vast numbers of bastard
mestizos who would constitute an intermediate class between the white
colonists and the wild Indians, thus alleviating the culture clash, spreading
Portuguese values throughout the *sertão*, and promoting settlement of the
country by a population more adaptable than the native one to modern
work modes.⁴

But if white colonists were to be attracted to an alien, inhospitable
country covered with vast forests and inhabited by cannibalistic Indians,
they would obviously have to be offered considerable privileges in return.
The coastline of Brazil was divided into twelve latitudinal sectors, and the
hereditary title to a *capitânia*, a slice of the country extending from the
seashore to the unknown hinterland, was granted to its "captain," whose
outlay for transportation and installations was repaid by sovereign rights
over his allotted territory. These included the right to appoint administrative authorities, to enact justice, to distribute land, and to impose taxes
and duties on his future subjects for his own profit. The character of this
earliest colonization has been much discussed. Some historians see in it a
transplanting of feudalism to America at the very moment when it was
crumbling in Europe. Others stress its capitalist aspect.⁵ In my opinion,
the juridical organization of the system must be distinguished from its
ultimate purposes. Juridically it was unquestionably a feudal system, but
this neofeudalism was no more than a means of attracting whites to Brazil
at no cost to the Portuguese crown. The real goal of the enterprise
stemmed in the last analysis from sixteenth-century mercantilist mentality.
In any case, there is no need to linger on the subject because these hereditary captaincies were doomed to failure and the mother country was forced
to look for a new system of settlement and to replace feudal by govern-

ment rule. In 1548 the crown appointed a governor general as its representative in the colony, and from then until the end of the colonial period centralization and the reinforcement of royal power steadily increased.

However, this political change had no influence on the development of the economy, since the production of sugar cane proved unsuitable for small-scale farming and, to be profitable, required big plantations. "Just to clear and prepare the ground properly—backbreaking work in this tropical virgin country so hostile to man—required the joint effort of many workers; it could not be done by small, isolated landowners. Once this had been achieved, the planting, cutting, and transportation of the crop to the mills where the sugar was made was profitable only if carried out on a large scale. Given these conditions, the small producer could not succeed."[6]

Monoculture demanded the latifundium, and the latifundium in turn demanded slavery. Naturally the colonists turned first to local—i.e. Indian —labor. This solution survived, in more or less hypocritical forms, for quite a long time in the extreme north and south of Brazil but in the late sixteenth century, and more especially in the seventeenth, Africans gradually came to replace Indians on the great sugar plantations. Historians have sought the reasons for this change in the labor force. The first and most important was the civilizational level of the Indian, who was accustomed to a nomadic form of life and agriculture and who, lacking the necessary "courage and initiative, firmness of mind, and organizational capacity," as Gilberto Freyre puts it, "was found wanting when it came to sedentary labor." The second reason was the stand of the Catholic church against the enslavement of Indians, which prevented their Christianization. While not wishing to underestimate this second factor, I consider it less important than the first, remembering that in Maranhão and São Paulo, where the whites were not rich enough to import "pieces of ebony" from Africa, the planters rebelled against the religious orders, which refused to allow them to enslave the Indians, and even went so far as to expel the Jesuits. If the Indians had shown any aptitude for agricultural labor, a *modus vivendi* could certainly have been reached—as happened in Spanish America. It was the Indian's failure on the plantations rather than protection by the church that caused him to be replaced by the Negro.[7]

How many blacks were imported to Brazil? Obviously a firm answer to that question would be extremely useful, since the stability of an implanted civilization depends on the number of migrants accompanying it. Unfortunately the official documents concerning the Negro slave trade were burned after the suppression of slavery, in an effort to expunge a blot on the country's escutcheon—a sentimental gesture which did nothing to simplify the historian's task. It is true that documentation concerning the customs duties paid when the slaves arrived is still preserved in the municipal archives of port cities, but much of it is still unpublished and in any case it is insufficient. Historians are therefore forced to generalize on the basis of fragmentary data or to suggest hypotheses, and it is not surprising that different writers should come up with different figures. If the variations were slight, we might reach an approximate answer, but they range from Calogeras's twelve to fourteen million[8] to Pedro Calmon's low estimate of two and a half million. The latter figure is obviously too low because it works out to an average of 8,333 Negroes per year, which is disproved by documents already published. Calmon himself realized this and later revised his estimate to six million.[9] Calogeras's figure, on the other hand, is too high because the transportation of 54,500 Africans every year would have required 185 ships (each carrying 300 men) serving the slave trade alone. In the eighteenth century, however, there were a mere 50 ships plying between Africa and the ports of northeastern Brazil, and they made only one voyage every two years. The number of sailing ships going to Rio could not have been much higher.[10]

There are two possible methods for arriving at more exact figures, the first based on economics, the second on history. Roberto Simonsen begins with a slave's average life span—seven years of active life, according to contemporary evidence—and with national production:

> According to our graphs, sugar production in the seventeenth century totaled approximately 180 million arrobas.[11] Allowing an average production of 50 arrobas per slave, which is not excessive for virgin land, and allowing for the loss resulting from the slave's seven year life expectancy, we can assume that sugar production in the seventeenth century absorbed 520,000 slaves. Of these a maximum of 350,000 would have been imported from the continent of Africa. . . . Between 1700 and 1850 the amount of sugar exported totaled 450 million arrobas at most. According to our reckoning, this total would have required at the very least 1,300,000 slaves. It seems reasonable to assume that one fourth of the total amount might have been produced by native labor and by slaves born in Brazil. This would mean that one million slaves were imported during this period. The eighteenth century was the century of gold. . . . We have already determined that the production of gold amounted to 200 grams per man. Assuming a general production of 1,200,000 kilos and an average life span of seven years, this would give a total of 860,000 slaves, of whom 600,000, or two thirds, would have been imported. Coffee did not begin to figure as a commodity of national importance until 1820. . . . During the period of the African slave trade, coffee exports never amounted to even 150 million arrobas. Average production per slave must have been over a hundred arrobas per year. Coffee therefore required the importation of no more than 250,000 slaves, which, added to the 1,000,000 Negroes for other agricultural products and for domestic service, gives a total figure of 3,300,000.[12]

Taunay, using historical documentation, arrives at a similar figure of 3,600,000. Between 1540 and 1560 the slave trade was much reduced. After 1560 it rose steadily, but by the end of the century it could not have been more than three or four thousand head per year. During the seventeenth century, when shipping was severely hampered by French and British piracy and by the war with the Netherlands for the conquest of Brazil, the highest possible yearly average is 6,000 slaves. In the eighteenth century, mining increased the need for labor, causing an increase in the number of Africans arriving, but the second half of that century saw the decline of the sugar industry and of mining, leading Taunay to suggest a yearly average of 13,000 slaves. While these figures remain hypothetical, Taunay has assembled copious documentation on the slave trade in the nineteenth century which leads him to assume that 1,562,000 Africans entered the country between 1800 and 1856. These figures may be tabulated as follows:

Sixteenth century	100,000
Seventeenth century	600,000
Eighteenth century	1,300,000
Nineteenth century	1,600,000
	3,600,000[13]

Mauricio Goulart, the Brazilian historian who has most recently addressed himself to this question, rejects hypotheses like that of Simonsen, whose data he finds too arbitrary.[14] He prefers to analyze documents and statistics, provided they are subject to critical appraisal to rule out useless documents such as the accounts of certain travelers whose fondness for the exotic led them to see Brazil as "a Negro country."[15] Nonetheless he too arrives at figures not very different from Simonsen's: 2,200,000–2,250,000 for the colonial period and 1,350,000 for the nineteenth century, giving a grand total of 3,500,000–3,600,000 Africans imported into Brazil.[16] Of course, far more Africans than that were abducted from their own countries and shipped to Brazil. Chained and herded together in the slave ships, they were decimated by contagious diseases, by hunger and thirst, and their bodies were thrown into the ocean. Sometimes no more than half the cargo would reach its destination.[17]

The consensus at the present time thus seems to arrive at an approximate figure of three and a half million blacks taken to Brazil from the beginning of colonization to the end of the slave trade, both legal and clandestine.[18]

While the slaving ships were unloading ever bigger cargoes of Africans, Portuguese emigration to Brazil also was accelerating, especially after the discovery of the gold mines in the eighteenth century and the development of commerical enterprises in the nineteenth. Unfortunately no reliable statistics are available on the racial composition of the population from century to century. According to Padre Anchieta, in 1585 it consisted of 24,750 whites, 18,500 civilized Indians, and 14,000 Africans. Rocha Pombo estimates the population of Brazil in 1600 at 30,000 whites, 30,000 blacks, and 70,000 civilized Indians or mestizos. In 1660, at the

end of the war against the Dutch, there were 74,000 whites and free
Indians and 110,000 slaves—most of them Africans or Creoles. In 1798,
according to Perdigão Malheiro, there were 1,010,000 whites, 250 Indians, 406,000 mulattoes or free blacks, and 1,582,000 black or mulatto
slaves. The official statistics for 1817–1818 give a total population of
3,817,000 for Brazil as a whole; of these, 585,000 were mulattoes and
free Negroes and 1,930,000 were slaves.[19] Thus at the beginning of the
nineteenth century the blacks dominated the whites demographically,
which explains how they managed to retain part of their cultural heritage
and even—for reasons I shall go into later—to influence the Portuguese
civilization. Nevertheless we should not forget that it was the whites who
gave the orders and directed, while the slaves were relegated to the margins of the national community, and that this stratification by color impeded more or less significantly the operation of the demographic factor.

   In the nineteenth century the ratio began to reverse itself, not immediately in favor of the white group but in favor of those of mixed blood.
Here again, though, the figures are not completely reliable. Rugendas, for
instance, estimates the total population of Brazil in 1827 at 3,758,000,
while Malte-Brun puts it as high as 5,340,000 for 1830. Rugendas's figure
for whites is only 845,000, for mestizos 628,000; Malte-Brun's figures for
these two groups are 1,347,000 and 1,748,000 respectively. Only on the
total number of blacks do the two writers come close to agreement.
Rugendas gives it as 1,987,000, Malte-Brun as 2,017,000. Even the statistics concerning slaves, which might have been most useful to us here, show
great divergence. In 1819 Councillor Velloso de Oliveira estimated their
number at 1,107,000; in 1850 Senator Cândido Baptista de Oliveiro raised
the figure to 2,500,000, and in 1869 Senator Thomaz Pompeu de Sousa
Brazil reduced it to 1,690,000.[20] Although the census of 1872 is unreli-
able, since most of the nonwhite people were illiterate and information
concerning their race was supplied by their masters (in the case of slaves)
or by census clerks (in the case of free men), it still provides the most
reliable data available and offers a way of checking the reversal referred to
above. In that year there were 3,854,000 whites in Brazil, 4,862,000
mulattoes or mestizos (this figure includes a certain number of Indian
mestizos), and only 1,996,000 Negroes.[21] The "whitening" or, as it is
sometimes called, the "Aryanization" of Brazil had begun.

   By then, however, the African heritage had had plenty of time—three
centuries—to take root and survive alongside the Portuguese one.

■ ■ ■

   A capital distinction must nevertheless be made between these two
heritages. Portugal imported its society along with its civilization. Slavery,
by contrast, broke up the African society, and the blacks, herded into the
slave ships, could bring nothing with them except their cultural values. The

Portuguese had to adapt to a new environment, and the modifications that his social organization and civilization underwent were chiefly ecological in nature. The African, on the contrary, had to adapt to a society quite different from his own, a society imposed upon him by the white man. He had to incarnate his own civilization in another social structure.

At first the white colonists tried to re-create in their new homeland the country they had left behind, with its vegetable and flower gardens, its wheat fields and vineyards, its chicken and livestock yards, its baroque churches and somewhat dark and austere stone houses. The burning tropical sun did not dispel their homesickness for their native villages, mountains or seashores, and they wished to create, in the true meaning of the word, a "new Lusitania." The ships that brought the new feudatories also brought artisans, monks, seed for crops, horses, and later even granite building blocks for houses and marble ones for raising churches to God. The new society in the making wanted to perpetuate Portuguese society down to its most minute details. We have already noted that the hereditary captaincies were an attempt to transfer the feudal system to American colonial soil. The same might be said of the first towns. Like Portuguese towns, they were administered by municipal councils composed of elected representatives of the "good men," i.e. the big landowners. The first artisans formed "corporations"—with their own judges, regulations, and examinations for the grade of master craftsman—and trade guilds under the patronage of a Catholic saint. The family itself, at least among the nobility, was no different from the *fidalgos* at the court of Portugal—much more extensive than the plebeian family because of its *criados*, members of the household who were educated, married off, and provided with dowries by the master and who in Brazil came to be called *crias*.[22]

This society, however, was forced to accommodate itself to different living conditions, just as the stone house usually had to give way to pisé or clay and open itself up to the outdoors through a covered terrace, a veranda of the oriental type which allowed the Portuguese to take the air during the pleasant twilight. Wheat and vines did not thrive. The colonist had to accept the habits of the Indian, married to his natural environment, and substitute manioc for flour, the hammock for the stuffy bed, native hunting and fishing equipment for his own traditional forms. For paddling up rivers he adopted the bark canoe or the pirogue. He acquired a taste for the indigenous fruits and for tobacco, chewing it or swallowing its smoke as the Indians did. The Portuguese *horta* or *chacara*, the vegetable garden and orchard, gave way to huge sugar cane plantations and this again forced the colonists to modify their old methods of production, their traditional farming techniques, and accept those of the Indians: the clearing of the forests and the nomadic cultivation of burned-over land.[23] All this, to be sure, lies within the sphere of ergology. The borrowings are material rather than social in nature, imposed less by the Indian as Indian than by necessities of environment and climate to which the Indian had found more effective responses than techniques or objects imported from beyond the Atlantic.

But these new conditions of life were soon to shatter the inherited social organization, breaking it up into a multitude of families lacking all organic connection. Brazil acted like a charge of dynamite upon the colony that was to be grafted upon it, exploding it into fragments. And while all the "fragments"—that is to say, the families—remained "Portuguese" insofar as their way of life (kinship or marriage rules, traditions, and rituals) went, their isolation, their dispersion throughout a vast country, and their remoteness from the mother country gradually tended to reshape them, so that their evolution took a different course from that of families that remained in Portugal. The typical Portuguese village, with its rich folklore, its neighborhood groups, its communal property, its habits of mutual aid and local cooperation, its firm anchoring in the parish church, never existed in Brazil. The metropolitan government tried in vain to establish villages and market towns, heaping praise and honors on the founders and creators of "settlements"[24]—those artificial villages, exotic stage sets erected in the bush, whose buildings stood empty most of the year, coming to life only on religious holidays or the days set aside for processions, or when the municipal council was in session and the plantation owners left their country estates to discuss their affairs and pay homage to God. Commercial agriculture in the form of plantations demanded the latifundium, and the latifundium in turn, with its itinerant cultivation of the land, its forest reserves, and its exhausted land lying fallow, separated men rather than bringing them together. Inside its *casa grande* and its estate, each family lived its own life in a kind of economic autarchy, self-sufficient, miles from its nearest neighbors, often linked with them only by waterway or by inhospitable roads not to be risked except for occasional visits, weddings, or anniversaries.

From the morphological point of view, then, there was an essential difference between the Portuguese rural society of the communal type and the Brazilian rural society with maximum dispersion of habitat. And this difference inevitably affected other adjacent levels of the social organization. First of all, this society was not a structured one. The centrifugal forces were stronger than the forces of cohesion. The only bonds that could hold these autonomous cells together were those of kinship or marriage. And marriage itself was often endogamous, sometimes between uncles and nieces, most often between first cousins.[25] Thus in addition to what Oliveira Vianna calls the feudal clan, the clan constituted within the estate by the plantation owner, his family, slaves, free men, serfs or *administrados*, and the Indians armed with bows and arrows who defended the sugar mill against attack, there was also the family clan composed of families connected by kinship and marriage. But the two types of clans remained independent of each other; their solidarity did not extend beyond their fluctuating, vaguely defined frontiers.[26] Quite the contrary. Bloody fights over disputed land or over love affairs unacceptable to the patriarch, amounting almost to vendettas and sometimes growing into clashes between armed bands, set one family against another, the Montes against the Feitosas, the Pires against the Camargos.[27] As a result, the history of colonial Brazil looks more like a chaos of dissension than a history of unifying, organic metropolitan administration. Of course the government did what it could to bring together these usually antagonistic *membra disjecta* in political solidarity. It appointed an "external judge" to represent the royal power vis-à-vis the councils of "good men," which upheld the interests of the planters or the big landowners. In Bahia it even changed the elective system of nominating municipal councillors to an appointive system. From the seventeenth century on it increased the number of government servants. But all its efforts were fruitless. This political unity remained a kind of superstructure, undeniably useful to the royal government when it came to raising taxes or defending the colony but never really rooted in Brazilian realities. To quote Pedro Vieira, who as a good Portuguese and a good Catholic was perturbed by this: "In the end every family constitutes a republic."

Yet, as I have said, although the Portuguese society had been shattered, every piece still remained a transplanted fragment of Portuguese society. The structure of the noble family—the only type of family that concerns us here, since it was the one that became the new nucleus of solidarity in Brazil—preserved the structure of the Portuguese *fidalgo* family while adapting it to a setting in which first Indians and then the Negro slaves replaced the white rural masses. Around the owner of the sugar mill or the cattle herds clustered all those who lived within the shelter of his *casa grande*. First his own family, over which he exercised absolute power, marrying off his children as he pleased, openly and without scruple betraying his wife with colored mistresses. Then of course his slaves, whom he could punish or even kill with impunity. His free Negroes—drivers of his ox carts, carpenters, blacksmiths, *tropeiros* to herd the cattle from the *sertão* to the coast, overseers to supervise the cane cutters, sugar refiners, etc. But also the "poor whites," small landowners forced to bring their crop to the master's mill, peasants to whom, in return for a few days' work, the master would grant permission to build a house or plant a garden on his land but whom he could turn away again any time he chose and who interbred with the Indians, perpetuating themselves through mestizo sons. In brief, a whole troop of "retainers," Indian *administrados* or hired hands, and protégés—"which makes a crowd," according to Gabriel Soares.

Thus in Brazil the sugar mill or the big estate devoted to crops or cattle replaced the Portuguese village. But, as anyone can see, this solidarity was of quite a different type. It no longer rested on communal work and democratic cooperation but on slave labor, on the disguised slavery of the mestizos, on family hierarchy. And the solidarity reveals its weakness when we move from the center (the *casa grande* of the master and the *senzala* of the blacks) to the periphery, to the small landowners without slaves or the farmers without land, who in their mud houses actually constituted a class of dependents something like the clients of Roman patricians. To strengthen itself, this solidarity had to acquire organic forms. It borrowed them from the Catholic tradition of "godparenthood" (*compadrismo*). The spiritual or religious bond reinforced the bond of economic or social dependence, correcting it and lending it an emotional or sentimental complexion it originally lacked. The *compadre* relationship could take many different forms—baptismal godfather at a child's birth, godfather at a marriage, even godfather for the bonfires celebrating the Eve of Saint John. It created between godfather or godmother and god-child a whole series of mutual obligations and sexual taboos, making this form of relationship as strong as a blood tie and at the same time safeguarding the hierarchy of social strata. These obligations included the godchild's duty to protect his godfather, the godfather's duty to educate his godchildren and provide a dowry for his goddaughters, and the godmother's or godson's obligation of aid, respect, and obedience.[28]

We should not be taken in by the sensuousness of the Brazilian, which Paulo Prado stressed so strongly in his *Retrato do Brasil*. This family retained its Portuguese Catholic values. The chapel stood adjacent to the *casa grande*. But the implanted Catholicism was that of the Counter Reformation, which, unlike Protestantism, revived the old worship of the saints and, along with it, some of the superstitions of the Middle Ages. But whereas in Europe worship of the saints was controlled, supervised, assigned to its place in a much larger dogmatic and liturgical whole, in Brazil the family, even more isolated from Rome than from Lisbon, incorporated it. It is true that the big plantations had their chaplain, who could serve as the representative of the church, the upholder of the European religious heritage. Indeed he was just that: the officiant at the Sunday mass, the schoolmaster who taught the master's sons Portuguese. Yet, as Gilberto Freyre has shown, he too fell victim to the isolation, to the sensuous climate of the *senzala*, the heady scent of the cut sugar cane. Above all, he was more dependent upon the white patriarch, who paid, fed, and housed him, than upon his hierarchical superiors. The bishops were to call repeatedly and insistently for the suppression of these chaplains, who were responsible for the regression of Catholicism from a communal religion to a religion of family clans, but they never succeeded in getting rid of them.[29] Moreover, the Brazilian patriarchate tended gradually to invade even the Roman church, to infiltrate it with its own interests and concerns and its rural nativism, for the youngest son of every big family was destined for the priesthood, while any daughters who failed to marry would shut themselves up in convents (or shut themselves up in a manner of speaking, since they usually took along a couple of slaves to wait on them and were in the habit of performing love comedies in the convent). In short, the morphological transformation the society underwent when it was transplanted from Portugal to Brazil had repercussions that reached far into the domain of symbols, values, and religious ideals through the creation of what might be called a "household" Catholicism centered on the worship of the patriarch's guardian saints and of the family dead, who were buried in the same chapel and surrounded by the same reverence.[30]

Nevertheless all these factors of dissolution or of cultural transformation were compensated or negated by opposing factors tending to preserve or revive Lusitanian civilization. The first of these was what American sociologists sometimes call "the frontier spirit," the racial pride of the adventurer, of the colonist, toward other ethnic groups whom he considers inferior. The white regarded the Indian and later the Negro as a machine for work or pleasure. He incorporated both of them into his family society, much as one might incorporate a herd of cattle into one's capital assets. Confronted with the seductions of a sensuous, enervating climate, the master draws himself up, clings fast to his European values to keep himself from going under, and proudly holds aloof from "men of color." This attitude varied from region to region. It was less marked in São Paulo than in the sugar mills of the northeast. In São Paulo the Portuguese and Spanish lived in closer symbiosis with the Indians—so close that the Tupí language came to dominate the language of the mother country.[31] The reason for this is that the Paulistas were a more plebeian population, less rich and more mobile than the noble owners of the great latifundia of Bahia and Pernambuco. The São Paulo civilization, isolated from the sea by the Serra do Mar and therefore more independent of the metropolitan civilization, interbred more freely; the civilization of the northeast was to remain more proudly Lusitanian.

But in the long run a heritage that does not renew itself through direct contact with its sources of inspiration is in danger of impoverishment. The material values of Lusitanian culture were indeed impoverished. Costume lost its distinctive regional characteristics;[32] furniture was reduced to a minimum.[33] It was the religious orders, particularly the Jesuits, that constituted a channel of communication between Europe and America. While the men sometimes held back, trying to avoid the expense and obligations of the processions,[34] the Jesuits maintained a hold over the women, whenever they came to town, through the confessional, and over the children through their schools.[35] It might be said that in Brazil a child was born twice: first as a Brazilian, a child of the plantation, exposed to the influences of his physical surroundings, brought up by blacks, playing with the black children, cantering his horse across vast solitudes; and then as a

Portuguese, within the drab walls of the *colégio*, where he learned Latin, the Portuguese "of the Kingdom," Thomist philosophy, and the art of obedience. These religious orders, constantly revitalized by brothers sent out principally from Portugal but also no doubt from Italy and Spain, would send to Europe for the plans, ceramics, statues of saints, and liturgical objects they needed for their churches, turning them and their sacristies, schools, and libraries into strongholds of the Lusitanian spirit. As Fernando de Azevedo so rightly said:

> It was through the concerted—and later successive—efforts of the Jesuits and the chaplains sent out from the Kingdom and educated in the colony, largely by the fathers of the order, that the rising tide of African influences was stemmed. . . . The efforts of the Jesuits and of the chaplains, who had been imbued with the Jesuit spirit and cultural ideals so that they might transmit them to the youth of the colony, were certainly not confined to protecting the Portuguese language from the Negro or native influences that were simultaneously threatening the paternal language, the authority of the church, morals, and behavior. They also raised a bastion against the disintegration of the culture vested in them.

Azevedo adds that these schools served not only as pillars supporting Portuguese values but also as channels of circulation for the elite, reshaping young whites and mestizos into priests, public servants, and educated men, good Catholics and good Portuguese (which at the time amounted to more or less the same thing).[36]

Finally there was the effect of the towns, or rather the ports, open to the vast outside world, where not only slave ships lay at anchor but also Portuguese vessels bringing European ideas and values, the latest fashions, Freemasonry and the theories of the eighteenth-century philosophers, Arcadia and pastoral poetry. As has been said, the towns were organized on the Portuguese model, but here again new conditions called for adjustments. There were not enough artisans to maintain corporations; apprentices could acquire the master craftsman's title without passing examinations, simply by being granted a license by the municipal councillors. These "masters" would in turn relinquish their functions to mulattoes or free Negroes so that they themselves might move up to the category of "good men."[37] In the end, the trade sodalities tended to turn into racial brotherhoods, as skilled workmanship progressively fell into the hands of the blacks. There were "aristocratic" brotherhoods open only to whites, mestizo brotherhoods, and Negro brotherhoods.[38] Yet despite these changes, the towns remained more Portuguese than Brazilian because the development of maritime trade attracted Portuguese merchants, bookkeepers, managers, and directors—the core of an urban bourgeoisie that was to clash with the rural society of sugar planters and landowners. In the "war of the *mascates*" Brazilian Olinda opposed mercantile Recife. The "war of the *emboabas*" ended in the expulsion of the São Paulo *bandeiran-*

tes from the mines they had discovered and in their replacement by Portuguese lured by the prospect of riches for the taking.[39]

The discovery of these mines, incidentally, was to transform the social structure of Brazil during the eighteenth century by producing on the central plateau an urban civilization, densely settled, avid for luxury, closely controlled by metropolitan Portugal. As a result, the umbilical cord linking the colony with the mother country was never cut. Century after century, new arrivals reinforced the bonds, renewing the vitality of ancestral values. And since civilizations change with time, an equilibrium could be restored between the two different directions in which the mother country and the colony were evolving. It is true that the later immigrants seem to have been of different ethnic stock. The first colonists came chiefly from the strongly Mozarabic provinces of Portugal; in the seventeenth century they began to be recruited from the Azores and in the eighteenth from the northern provinces.[40] These regional differences did not, however, prevent the immigrants from participating in the same culture.

Besides attracting Portuguese, the discovery of the mines resulted in shifts of population from the north to the south of Brazil and in the raising of cattle. The subsequent transportation of the cattle from the grazing areas to the centers of consumption not only created a vast communications network between the scattered cells of the family clans—a first economic step toward political unity[41]—but, by bringing people closer together, it made them aware of the homogeneity of their beliefs, feelings, and habits.

■ ■ ■

But while the Portuguese was able to maintain his society and civilization in the American tropics by adapting them, the African was not. Unlike the white, the black was forcibly uprooted from his land, shipped to a new habitat, integrated into a society that was not his own, in which he found himself in a subordinate economic and social position. Slavery shattered his African tribal or village community and its political organization and destroyed the forms of family life, leaving nothing of the original social structures intact. He entered a new system of stratification in which the white man occupied the summit, the free mestizo or the *caboclo* the intermediate level, leaving to him the lowest position of all, that of the slave. He was held fast by the big families that owned the plantations or the mines, the living cells of the new Brazilian society. From now on, they would replace clan, lineage, and village for him. On this point there is unanimous agreement: the African society could never be reborn in Brazil.

But the blacks' civilization was linked to that society. It constituted its authentic expression, either as its reflection, as the Marxists hold, or as its living source. Suddenly this civilization had been uprooted from its morphological and institutional base and left drifting, as it were, in the void. Was it not in danger of disappearing, along with the society, in the equally radical overturning of the old established conditions of life? Might it not perish along with the social frameworks that had hitherto conditioned it? Yet this did not happen. Of course the civilization had to adapt to new economic and social frameworks, to monoculture, slavery, and the sugar planter's family, but it survived. Everything indicated that a breach was opening between the various levels of depth sociology on the symbolic level, widening, yet leaving largely intact the collective representations, the values, and even the stirrings of collective consciousness, while the structures and norms that supported them were crumbling.

We must therefore examine the conditions in which first the slave trade and then slavery itself operated if we are to understand how the African culture was able to resist a revolution of this kind.

The first slaves must have belonged to coastal tribes, but when the trade intensified, as the plantations or mines increased their demand for slave labor, it reached deeper and deeper into the African continent and became more systematic. Children and women were abducted on the open roads; men were plied with liquor and fettered when they fell into a drunken sleep. The *sobas* made war on one another so that they could take prisoners and sell them to the European slave merchants. (This was the only reason for the clash between the Fon and the Yoruba.) Arab traders set themselves up as the major purchasers of human flesh. In these conditions, even if the slave trade never penetrated as deeply into the interior of the continent as certain historians maintain,[42] it must have been possible to find, in the embarcation ports of São João de Ajudá, São Thomé, São Paulo de Loanda, etc., people from the most diverse tribes, even from different ethnic groups. For this reason the terms used in Brazil to designate the imported Africans cannot be used to reconstitute their ethnic origin, since these terms usually refer to the ports of embarcation rather than to African tribes. In any case, a preliminary mixing took place even before embarcation, and if anything survived of the original civilizations, it could only have been their common features, not those that distinguished Mina from western Bantu or from eastern Bantu from "the opposite coast."

The slave trader would make a preliminary selection from this herd of human cattle crouching in the wooden sheds, their legs in heavy chains, their shoulders branded with hot irons. He refused to buy them in lots but looked carefully at their teeth, eyes, arms and legs, and sexual organs for indications of the slaves' strength, health, and reproductive powers. As a result of this selective process, their ethnic heterogeneity had been intensified by the time they embarked, since the lots had been broken down into individuals. Already—at least for those who did not die during the voyage —common misery was creating a form of solidarity other than the ancient tribal or village one, a solidarity which, insofar as circumstances allowed, would survive in Brazil. The blacks used the word *malungo* to designate those who had traveled in the same infernal ship, the same filthy hold, full of excrement and stained with urine, or been forced to prance along the deck under the lashes of the guard's whip.[43] All this must have contributed to the disintegration of the African cultures.

Once they arrived in Brazil, the blacks were housed in barracks (the Vallongo warehouse in Rio was a notorious one) to await the pleasure of the buyers. The buyers of course were motivated solely by their own selfish interests. If there were any couples in the shipment, they would separate husband and wife, mother and children. They took the "pieces" they needed without heed for their ethnic solidarities, concerned only with their future slaves' state of health and physical vigor. Thus, if several ships had arrived more or less simultaneously from different points in Africa and their cargoes had been mixed together, they might buy and take back to their plantations Mina along with Congo and "Guinea blacks" along with Angola. And even if this did not happen, the planter or mine owner would take only the "pieces" he needed to replace slaves who had died or to increase production. Slaves of the same ethnic origin would then be thrown together, on his estate, with others of quite different stock. We have testaments, family papers, account books of *fazendeiros*, which show how slaves from widely separated territories and very different civilizations always existed side by side. It is easy enough to identify these civilizations, at least roughly, since every African bore as his family name the name of his country: João Congo, Joaquim Benguela, Francisco Ibo, Maria Nagô, and so on. The leveling of all these ethnic groups by slavery was another obstacle to the survival of African civilizations in their full originality and diversity.

To comprehend this obstacle more fully, we need to pause for a while and try to determine the extent of this immense mixing of peoples and cultures and whether or not it could allow traits common to all of them to survive.

Silvio Romero posed the question of the origin of slaves imported to Brazil and claimed that they were nearly all Bantu. Jean Ribeiro and several other historians followed his lead.[44] Braz do Amaral[45] and Calogeras then broadened Silvio Romero's excessively narrow view and distinguished four big centers of exportation: Cacheo and Cape Verde; São Thomé (Guinea and Cameroun); São Paulo de Loanda (Congo and Angola); and the east coast center (Mozambique). But although these two writers did useful work as historians, they both had an inadequate knowledge of ethnography. Their lists of tribes are full of errors and confusion. It was Nina Rodrigues who, by interrogating the last Africans to be imported to Bahia and by using the methodology of comparative linguistics as well as ethnography, put the problem on an entirely new footing,[46] while Arthur Ramos deserves credit for finding the definitive answer to it.[47] On the basis of research carried out in various regions of Brazil, Ramos arrived at the following list of civilizations having representatives in Portuguese America:

1. The Sudanese civilizations, represented especially by the Yoruba (Nagô, Ijeja, Egba, Ketu, etc.), by the Dahomans of the Gêgê group (Ewe, Fon), by the Fanti-Ashanti group, known during the colonial era as Mina, and lastly by the smaller groups of Krumano, Ani, Zema, and Timini.
2. The Islamized civilizations, represented chiefly by the Peul, Mandingo, and Hausa, and to a lesser extent by the Tape, Bornú, and Gurunsi.
3. The Bantu civilizations of the Angola-Congo group, represented by the Abunda of Angola (Caçanje, Bengala, Umbengala, Dembo), the Congo or Cabinda from the Zaire estuary, and the Benguela, many of whose tribesmen were enslaved in Brazil, according to C. F. P. von Martius.
4. The Bantu civilizations of the east coast of Africa, represented by the Mozambique (Macua and Angico).

As this simple enumeration shows, Africa sent to Brazil cattle raisers and farmers, forest people and savannah people, representatives of roundhouse and square-house civilizations, totemic civilizations, matrilineal and patrilineal civilizations, blacks familiar with vast kingships and others who knew only tribal organization, Islamized Negroes and "animists," Africans having polytheist religious systems and others who worshiped chiefly their lineal ancestors.[48] Why was it that these diverse civilizations, originating in such diverse areas, did not destroy one another by sheer contact? Why were they not abraded by mutual friction? The answer is that here again the negative factors were counterbalanced by positive ones, primarily of a historical order.[49]

Originally all slaves from Africa were called "Guinea Negroes," but this expression must not be taken in a narrow sense, because in the sixteenth century Guinea extended from Senegal to the Orange river. Many of the Guinea Negroes who reached Brazil must have been true Bantu. Denunciations of the Inquisition in Bahia refer to a "Guinea Negro . . . son of the Angola race."[50] Nonetheless it is likely that during the early years of colonization the majority of slaves came from countries north of the equator, where white dominance was of longer standing and where trading between whites and blacks was more firmly established. During the seventeenth century, on the other hand, Bantu Negroes certainly predominated, first because Brazil was closer to Angola than to the regions north of the Congo, and secondly because the Bantu had proved themselves to be excellent field workers at a time when the plantation was dominant. As Wätjen tells us, the Angola black, who "showed a greater willingness to work and could be easily taught by the old slaves," was quite unlike the "quarrelsome, obstinate, lazy" Guinea Negro, who had little aptitude for obedience or work.[51] In the eighteenth century, Mina or Sudanese increasingly replaced Bantu because the discovery of gold-bearing sand required reinforcements of labor just at a time when a smallpox epidemic was raging in Angola, ravaging the population and keeping the traders in human flesh at a distance. Also, while Bantu were preferred for agriculture, Mina were preferred for the hard labor in the mines, "being stronger and more vigorous," as contemporary whites liked to say. This was also the period of the wars between the Yoruba and the Fon, which furnished many prisoners, and around the turn of the century the Dahomans sent a series of embassies to Bahia and Lisbon asking that their country be granted a monopoly of the slave trade. However, the treaty of 1815 between England and Portugal marked the first step in the total abolition of the slave trade, prohibiting the export to Brazil of slaves from countries north of the equator. From then until 1830, at any rate theoretically, all imported Negroes came from Angola or Mozambique. (The shortage of labor for the new coffee plantations accounted for the Mozambique, although those "obtuse" and "barbarous" Africans were not very highly esteemed by buyers.)[52]

Obviously this is only a rough survey, and the whole of Africa was always engaged in the slave trade. Even after the signing of the treaty of 1815, vessels would elude the British warships and unload clandestine cargoes of slaves transported from Dahomey or Guinea. Nontheless each century had its own ethnic stamp, so that each major group—Bantu, then Mina, then Bantu again—was able to some degree to establish its own civilization in Brazil before the mixing of ethnic groups caused them all to disentegrate irreversibly.

Of course time, in the long run, would erode all traditions, however firmly anchored in the new habitat. But the slave trade continually renewed the sources of life by establishing continuous contact between old slaves, or their sons, and the new arrivals, who sometimes included priests and medicine men. In this way, throughout the whole period of slavery, religious values were continuously rejuvenated at the same time that they were being eroded. We know little about Afro-Brazilian religions in those distant times, but we should certainly give up the notion of cult centers surviving through the centuries down to the present day (something that slavery precluded) and think rather of a chaotic proliferation of cults or cult fragments arising only to die out and give way to others with every new wave of arrivals. The *candomblés, xangôs*,[53] and *batuques* of today are not survivals of ancient sects reaching back into the Brazilian past but relatively recent organizations dating back no further than the eighteenth or early nineteenth century. Pierre Verger has shown that the *Casa das Minas* in São Luiz do Maranhão was probably founded in 1796 by perse-

cuted members of the royal family of Dahomey.[54] Nunes Pereira learned
from Mother Andresa that her *casa* was founded by "stowaways," i.e.
contraband blacks shipped after 1815 and freed upon their arrival in
Brazil.[55] We also know that the Engenho Velho *candomblé* in Bahia was
founded by two priestesses of the Shangô family brought to that city as
slaves in the early nineteenth century.[56] We should therefore think of the
religious life of Africans in Brazil as a series of events lacking any organic
links—traditions that were broken and resumed but that nevertheless retained from one century to the next, probably in the most diverse forms,
the same fidelity to the African mystique or mystiques.

To understand religious survivals or disappearances, we must consider,
in addition to these historical factors, factors of a more sociological nature
having to do with the forms of slavery. In the southern United States, until
the expansion of cotton growing, land ownership was based on small or
medium-sized holdings where the master relied on the services of only
three or four slaves. Here the process of acculturation was rapid.[57] In
Brazil too there were many small estates, each worked by a few slaves,
growing, for example, tobacco. But the dominant system, at any rate
socially and politically, was the big plantation requiring a minimum of
sixty to eighty slaves to plant, cut, and crush the cane. Even when animal
traction or water power replaced human labor in operating the mill wheel,
the number of slaves in the sugar mills increased rather than diminished.[58]
It continued to grow, and in the nineteenth centutury planters who owned
a thousand slaves were by no means rare. Obviously in these conditions
the African ethnic entities could regroup and re-establish a more restricted
solidarity within the black caste and around their religious leaders. The
history of these small communities has never been recorded. The whites
were interested only in their Negroes' capacity for work. But we know
from the accounts of travelers that when, as sometimes happened, a
plantation had slaves of royal blood, these individuals were treated by
their compatriots and by the people of color in general with great defer-
ence. They were respected and obeyed.[59] So it is easy enough to understand how small groups could emerge, how bonds of friendship, as well as
rivalries, could spring up and leaders arise within a mass which to white
eyes appeared amorphous. These groups managed to retain part of their
cultural heritage while their leaders, thanks to the prestige they enjoyed,
were able to impose the cultural forms of their country on slaves from
different ethnic stocks. This would explain the preeminence of the
Dahoman civilization in certain regions, of the Yoruba or the Bantu in
others. Ethnic solidarity, however, sometimes defied the prestige of the
chiefs. We know that when slaves were plotting a revolt or an escape,
other slaves belonging to rival "nations" would often denounce them to the
master.

The big plantation, where the number of slaves was too great to allow any give-and-take relationship with the master, thus made it possible for African values to survive to some degree. But to survive at all they needed to be revitalized at regular intervals by exposure to the great tide of collective consciousness. Marcel Mauss has shown the importance to the Eskimo of the rhythmic alternation of human dispersion and concentration in religious life. Durkheim has pointed out the importance to the Australians of celebrations that unite men in one and the same mystical exaltation. On the plantations, the blacks too shared the communion of celebrations, renewing the vitality of their symbols, values, and ideals in regular assemblies, held on fixed dates, around bonfires, to the drumming of tom-toms. Their masters' principal motivation in allowing the slaves to amuse themselves "after the fashion of their nation," on Sunday evenings or on holidays "sanctified by the Holy Mother Church," was a purely economic one. They had observed that if slaves were given a chance to enjoy themselves freely from time to time, they worked better than if they were required to labor continuously, day in and day out, without a break. Antonil, author of what might be called the sugar planter's bible, recommends allowing slaves to sing and dance on certain days of the year as the only consolation their sad estate allows; otherwise they become "melancholy, lacking in vitality and health."[60] To be sure, Antonil, a religious man, stipulates that these celebrations are to be held on the feasts of the patron saints of the master's family or of those of the slave caste, Saint Benedito and Saint Iphigenia. But the masters had still another reason for being generous about holidays and merrymaking, a reason less easily camouflaged by the chaste veil of religion: the high price of slaves. They saw dancing as a means of sexual stimulation that encouraged procreation, and hence as a cheap way of renewing their herd of human cattle without capital outlay. The whites may be said to have singled out dances of Bantu origin like the *samba*, the *coco*, the *batuque*, the *jongo*, and the *lundu* and steered African folklore toward them. The names vary from region to region, but the dance is always the same erotic one, centered on the selection of a sexual partner and the symbolic confirmation of this choice in the *umbigada*, the rubbing together of bellies, navel to navel.[61] At the same time, before the modest Catholic altar erected against the wall of the *senzala*, in the flickering light of candles, the blacks could perform their religious tribal dances with impunity. The whites believed them to be dancing to the glory of the Blessed Virgin or the saints, but the Virgin and the saints were no more than masks. The steps of those ritual ballets, whose significance quite escaped the masters, were tracing out on the floor of beaten earth the myths of the *orixás* or the *voduns*. The music of the drums abolished distance, bridged oceans, momentarily bringing Africa to life and creating a communion of men in one and the same collective consciousness, in an exaltation that was at once frenetic and controlled.

Proof of this is to be found in the fact that the African religions survived chiefly in the sugar-growing regions of the northeast. Apart from a few exceptions, they did not survive in the mining areas, because there the conditions of slavery were quite different. Work in the mines was infinitely harder. Unlike agricultural work, it was not subject to the rhythm of the seasons but imposed its tyranny the whole year round. Sand or gravel had to be moved, streams dammed, channels dug to concentrate or divert the flow of water. In a constant struggle against the mountains, rock slides had to be produced under artificial waterfalls, galleries hewn out in search of lodes. Since it was easy enough to steal nuggets by hiding them in the hair or swallowing them, the slaves were constantly supervised, both during and after working hours. Finally, confronted by a civilization of the capitalist type, in which adventurers enriched themselves before his eyes and which was ostensibly ruled by money, the black changed his mentality and began to think like the white man. The change was promoted by a whole series of measures such as the freeing of any slave who found a big diamond, and gifts of clothing or other rewards to those whose productivity was highest.[62] Some blacks not only gained their freedom but even became mineowners, thanks to a cooperative system of mutual aid. To be sure, this aid was restricted to a single "nation" or tribe, or even to one family, which proves that the African civilization was not completely dead but still retained some of its frameworks.[63] Nonetheless this desire to get rich was an obstacle to the maintenance of religious values.

The same applies to the cattle-raising areas, both in the pampas of the south and the *sertão* of the northeast. There stock raising required big estates but not much labor. The ranchers usually owned only a few Negroes to take care of their immense herds and their small gardens. These blacks, lost in areas dominated by Indian mestizos, could not withstand the impact of their environment and were easily contaminated by the surrounding civilization.[64] Finally, by the time coffee growing took over the state of São Paulo, making its way across the valley of the Paraíba from Rio, the days of slavery were already numbered. The country was being stirred up by abolitionist propaganda, and in this atmosphere the nature of black resistance was bound to change, moving from the cultural to the political level, from fidelity to the African religion to collaboration with the white abolitionists who came to the *fazendas* to help plan the escape of slaves.[65] Luiz Gama symbolizes this change. His mother was a daughter of the gods, perhaps even a *ialorixá*. He himself was a lawyer, founder of a Masonic lodge, and the great black artisan of the abolition of slave labor.[66] In the course of this book we shall have to come back to the idea that a kind of antagonism exists between the two solutions to the problem of the Brazilian Negro, the cultural solution and the political one. Wherever the former prevailed, politics never took hold; where the latter won out, the earlier cultural resistance crumbled.

Yet our survey of slavery is still not complete, for we have left aside one type that is particularly important to our subject: urban slavery. As has often been said, the city offers a different kind of anonymity from the country. It weakens social control, in this case the white man's control over the black, and offers those who are not their own master a liberty they do not enjoy elsewhere. Again, the city permits a greater concentration of individuals within a more restricted space. Even if each family owned only a few slaves, the total number in the city would be considerable. Travelers who happened to go ashore at Brazilian ports of call spoke of a "new Guinea," and this was not exaggerated. This concentration of urban blacks finally made possible something that was severely impeded, though not entirely precluded, by rural slavery, namely solidarity by "nation," i.e. the re-creation of ethnic entities in more or less organized groupings. In the first place, the cities had what were known as *negros de ganho* or "hired-out" Negroes—slaves who worked outside the master's house, returning to it in the evening with the money they had earned. Sometimes they were rented out as domestic servants; sometimes they were given a tray of merchandise to hawk in the streets. In their daily coming and going, these Negroes would encounter compatriots and talk of the country they had left behind. Groups from the same country would form associations and spend their days off and popular holidays together.[67] Many of these "hired-out" Negroes were porters who unloaded ships and carried the merchandise to the stores or who delivered a customer's purchases to his home—packing cases of all kinds, pianos, casks of wine, etc. Even before their manumission but especially afterward, these blacks would form groups known as *cantos* led by a "captain." As they carried their heavy loads, which often required four men, these *cantos* would sing songs in African languages. This indicates that individuals formed groups on the basis of their ethnic origin. Manoel Querino provides a good description of some of their rituals:

> When a captain died, a successor was elected or acclaimed and took office immediately. In the *cantos* of the business district [of Bahia] these proceedings were accompanied by a certain amount of ceremony in the African fashion. The members would borrow an empty cask, . . . fill it with sea water, pass ropes around it, and tie it to a long, heavy rail. Eight to a dozen Ethiopians, usually the most muscular, would support the barrel, and the new captain would climb up on it, holding in one hand the branch of a shrub and in the other a bottle of brandy. The whole *canto* would file past, heading toward the Pedreiras quarter, intoning monotonous chants in African dialects or languages and returning in the same order to their point of departure. The newly elected captain would accept the congratulations of the other *cantos* and, as he did so, would perform a kind of exorcism with the brandy, spilling out a few drops.[68]

We know that this ritual act, which persists today in the context of the *candomblé*, has a very specific religious meaning: nothing is to be eaten or drunk before an offering has been made to the divinities. For example, members of Afro-Brazilian sects never fail to sprinkle a few drops of the contents of their glass on the ground before drinking. Thus Querino's account reveals another, deeper solidarity beyond the ethnic one: the solidarity of communion in the ancestral religion.

Every night the *negro de ganho* would bring back a certain sum of money to his master, but anything beyond that stipulated sum was his own, and in this way the luckiest or most resourceful of them could save up enough money to buy their freedom. It was these freed Negroes more than any others who became the upholders of the African religions, assembling the faithful of their respective "nations" in their humble homes and assuming responsibility both for recruiting and for leadership of the sect. Toward the second half of the nineteenth century, the number of freed Negroes was steadily increasing, and this facilitated the solidification of African beliefs in the new habitat.

1798: 406,000 free mulattoes and Negroes; 1,582,000 Negro and mulatto slaves (Perdigão Malheiro's figures).

1817: 585,000 free mulattoes and Negroes; 1,930,000 Negro and mulatto slaves (Perdigão Malheiro's figures).

1847: 1,280,000 free mulattoes and Negroes; 3,120,000 Negro and mulatto slaves (Ewbank's figures).

Such are the most important positive factors that allowed the blacks to maintain their religious values in their new habitat despite the disappearance of the African social structures, which had been destroyed by slavery.

■ ■ ■

Every mother country has a certain policy toward its colonies. This policy may encounter resistance of all kinds, which it must heed, trying to adapt to it if it cannot be suppressed, but the policy will always be an active factor in determining, at least partially, the orientation and structural processes of colonization. In Brazil there were two policies, not one. Sometimes they were united, sometimes divergent. Their effects might cancel or balance each other, but they might also cumulatively reinforce each other. These were the policies of the king and of the church. The church, which had so vehemently defended the Amerindians' cause against the colonists and even against the metropolitan government, nevertheless accepted the enslavement of the blacks. It even profited by it. In 1768 the estate of Santa Cruz, which belonged to the Jesuits, owned 1,205 slaves; the Desterro convent in Bahia had 400 slaves for seventy-four sisters. These examples could be multiplied many times over.[69] But while the church accepted the enslavement of the African, it did so on certain conditions. In taking his body, it gave him in return a soul. While the white master might profit by slave labor, this right was counterbalanced by corresponding duties, first and foremost the duty of Christianization. Any black who had not been baptized before leaving Africa had to be evangelized on arrival, had to learn Latin prayers, receive baptism, attend mass, and partake of the holy sacraments. If this policy had been followed, it would have tended to obliterate the African religions or at least to syncretize them profoundly with Catholicism.

Some foreign travelers admired the Brazilians' treatment of their slaves: "Slaves in Brazil are treated like sons of the family. Great care is taken to baptize them and instruct them in the elements at least of the Christian faith. We may ask whether the slaves do not gain—and gain infinitely—in exchanging their barbarous liberty for these advantages of education and assured protection."[70] Yet we cannot trust this idyllic picture of Brazilian slavery. It is belied by too many official documents protesting against the refusal of the last rites to the dying and against baptism by the masters, without preliminary catechization, simply to conform to the regulations. In fact the whites were interested only in the physical strength of the Negroes and the profit it brought them. They were indifferent to the salvation of their souls.

Still the church could not totally abandon the slave to his sad lot, and since the master was indifferent to his religious obligations, the constituted church had to step in. The Negro or mulatto brotherhoods, modeled on those of the whites (of which we shall have more to say when we come to study Catholicism among the blacks), reflect the church's policy of uniting the Africans, or their descendants, within its bosom and beneath the Cross in order to incorporate them as a distinct entity in the vast religious community of Brazil. It was within these organizations, the Brotherhood of São Benedito (Saint Benedict the Moor) or of Our Lady of the Rosary, that assimilation and religious syncretism would develop. But it would be a multilevel syncretism. The religious orders, especially the Jesuits, had perfected a system for evangelizing the Indians based on two principles. The first was the acceptance of certain Indians values that were in no way offensive to the church and could therefore be retained so long as they were reinterpreted in Christian terms. (One example is the dances of the *curumiri* in which Indian chants were replaced by hymns to the Virgin Mary and which served as a background for theatrical performances something like mystery plays intended to instill Catholic dogma into the souls of the Indians through their eyes and ears.) The second principle was a determined, tenacious struggle, using guile or force, against values too radically opposed to Western ones (e.g. against the *pagés*). A split was made in Tupí rituals and myth: Tupan became God and Juruparí the Devil.[71] This same policy would be applied, though in a less systematized fashion, within the Negro brotherhoods.

Everything in the African customs that could be adapted to Catholicism was accepted, though of course it was reinterpreted and given another meaning. The existence of national kingships or tribal chiefhoods is one example. Their acceptance was facilitated by the fact that the kings of these fraternal orders were no longer chosen in the traditional way by hereditary succession within one family but were elected by the fraternities themselves. They were obeyed by their subjects and could serve as intermediaries between the white masters and their slaves, thus constituting for the whites ready-made channels of control over the black masses. Along with the coronation of a king of the Congo or of Angola, many other African customs were transferred to the fraternities: the custom of embassies or of interethnic wars, which became struggles between pagans and Christians, ending of course in the victory of the latter. How productive this policy was is debatable. It certainly adulterated the African religions and began the process of Catholic-African syncretism, but equally certainly it helped to maintain purely African values. We should note in the first place that these fraternities consisted chiefly of Bantu and that the Yoruba and Dahomans were less affected by them. Secondly, the Africans continued to speak their original languages, and although the church would have liked to bring over missionaries familiar with those languages to evangelize the Brazilian slaves, only one such attempt was ever made in practice.[72] Insulated from the control of their priests by the latter's linguistic ignorance, the religious brotherhoods often served as a refuge for much less orthodox beliefs. We do not know the basis for the assertion of Diogo de Vasconcellos that one of the brotherhoods of Our Lady of the Rosary was composed of daughters of the goddess Yemanjá,[73] but we do know that wherever black brotherhoods existed, African religion survived —in Uruguay, Argentina, Peru, and Venezuela—and that these African religions disappeared in those countries where the church refused to allow the brotherhoods to meet for dancing outside the church after mass.[74] I have observed over and over again that in northeastern Brazil these black brotherhoods are composed of the same individuals who frequent the candomblés and even hold high hierarchical positions in them.

Thus, in transforming the African cults, the church, without meaning to, often helped them to survive. Of course the brotherhood was not the candomblé, but it did constitute a form of racial solidarity, a nucleus which, in the dark of the evening, might well develop into a candomblé.

Sometimes when the church came to the defense of slaves, the state would oppose the church and side with the slaveowners. "If the slave (even if he is a Christian) escapes from his master into a church, he will not be protected by the church but will be removed by force."[75] In the same way the state often fought the effects of miscegenation, which, it believed, made the lines separating the social classes dangerously unstable. Honorary or public offices were denied to those living in concubinage with Negro women.[76] Mulatto women were forbidden to wear silk, lace, or costly jewels.[77] To discourage the free mixing of the sexes, which was threatening to modify the social structure of the country, the metropolitan government or its represenattives took measures to preserve or increase the separation of castes. Thus Portuguese policy aimed essentially at maintaining the existing social order. Although it did, at a very late date, intervene against the arbitrary rule of certain slaveowners, much more often it acted to defend their privileges—sometimes even against their own wishes, as in the case of the sumptuary laws concerning the clothing of mulatto women, who might well be the mistresses of rich colonists or even of bishops.

But this defense of the social order, of the slaveowners' interests, this intensification of the social separation of the castes, not to mention the advice—or even orders—not to free too many slaves lest this produce a threatening increase in the number of free Negroes,[78] also presented a danger, the danger of creating a class consciousness—and a revolutionary one—in the colored masses. By reducing Negroes and mulattoes, enslaved or free, to the same level in a country in which the whites were a minority, the state risked precipitating uprisings that might end in the burning of plantations, the murder of the masters, or even the loss of the colony.

But the state's first duty was to guarantee the security of that colony by guaranteeing the security of the privileged minority. This accounts for another aspect of Portuguese policy, one which can be summed up in the celebrated phrase "divide and rule." This policy was admirably defined by the Count dos Arcos at the beginning of the nineteenth century:

> Seen through the government's eyes, [the institution of the Negro dances known as *batuques*] is one thing; seen through the eyes of individuals, it is something quite different. The latter believe that the *batuques* infringe their dominical rights, either because they want to employ their slaves in useful work even on Sundays, or because they want to station them before their doors on these days of rest as a way of showing off their wealth. The government, however, sees the institution of the *batuques* as something that obliges the blacks unconsciously and automatically to revive every week the feelings of mutual aversion instinctive in them since birth, which are nevertheless gradually extinguished in their common suffering. These feelings may be regarded as the best guarantee of the security of the great cities of Brazil. If the different "nations" of Africa were totally to forget the furious resentment which by nature has divided them, if the Agomé were to become the brothers of the Nagô, the Gêgê of the Hausa, the Tapa of the Ashanti, and so on, a tremendous and inescapable danger would descend upon and destroy Brazil. And who can doubt that suffering has the power to create fraternization among its victims? Thus for the government to stand in the way of the only possibility of dissension between blacks would amount to indirectly preaching their union. This could only have terrible consequences.[79]

The Count dos Arcos was not mistaken. Negro revolts did occur, as we shall see, but they were always revolts of certain "nations," not of the slaves in general. They failed because they were discovered in advance. thanks to the treachery of rival "nations."

Moving from politics to sociology, however, we find that this policy permitted the constitution and organization of blacks in "nations," thus making it possible for their religious and cultural traditions to survive. The disintegrative effect of the mixing of various ethnic groups on one plantation or in one slaveowner's town house and of the mutually abrasive action of the different civilizations was halted by the policy of incorporating blacks into autonomous "nations." Nevertheless the Count dos Arcos was too good a Christian to accept the idea of this regimentation being achieved under the banner of the African religions. Was he perhaps also afraid that "fetishist" priests might become the leaders of revolts against the Christian whites—as indeed actually happened? In any case he draws a distinction between the prohibited African religious dances and the acceptable profane *batuque*. Here, we may note, he is conforming to a tradition that persisted throughout the whole period of slavery: the refusal to allow the perpetuation of African cults in Brazil.[80]

At a time when "Guinea Negroes" were rare, the Inquisition already expressed uneasiness over this question during its visitation of Pernambuco and Bahia. Later the municipal councils were ordered to investigate whether the region harbored "any persons utilizing fetishism or who may be witches—healing animals by blessing them, making use of diabolical relics, or having made a pact with the Devil."[81] As archives everywhere yield up their riches, they confront us with regulations prohibiting Negro assemblies of a religious character and with proceedings taken against "houses of fortune," *calundus* and *jurema* groups, and the subsequent arrest of the congregation and their priests.[82] And all to no avail, as Count da Ponte recognized in 1807.

By permitting the blacks to unite in brotherhoods, the church promoted the syncretism of Catholicism with African religion rather than the Catholicization of the blacks. By encouraging the splitting up of slaves into independent "nations," the government in turn initiated the cultural diversities among Africans that we shall encounter in the course of our investigations.

Certain conclusions can, it seems, be drawn from our analysis of the historical conditions in which the implantation of Africa in Brazil took place. First, slavery effected a breach between the superstructures and the infrastructures (using these terms without any Marxist connotation). The African social structures were shattered, the values preserved. But these values could live on only by creating for themselves new social frameworks, new institutions to incarnate them and make them viable, institutions capable of perpetuating themselves and of being transmitted from one generation to the next. In brief, the superstructures had to secrete a society. The movement is not an upward one from the morphological base toward the world of symbols and collective representations but the opposite: a downward movement of those values and collective representations toward the institutions and groupings. Of course African models were able to influence this restructuring, as were European models imposed from outside, like the brotherhoods or the Negro dance groups organized according to "nations."

Second, the negative factors of slavery seem to have been most active in certain sectors of society, such as the rural areas and especially the stock-raising and mining regions, while the positive factors of a demographic or institutional order seem to have operated chiefly in urban areas. As a result—and we shall verify this over and over again—the African religions are closer to their origins, purer and richer, in the big cities than in the country. In contrast to the usual pattern of religious or folkloric persistence, in Brazil it is the big city that constitutes the museum of archaic traditions.[83]

2
New Social Frameworks
for Afro-Brazilian Religions

Despite the unfavorable conditions of slavery, which mixed ethnic groups, broke down African social structures, and imposed a new work rhythm and life style, the religions the blacks brought with them from beyond the Atlantic did not die. Padre Vieira aptly characterized this opposition between a society dominated and regulated by Portuguese norms and the civilizations imported from Africa when he said that Brazil had its European body in America and its soul in Africa. But beliefs that remain buried in the depths of the heart, that find no expression in rites and ceremonies and do not lend themselves to organized collective forms, are inescapably doomed. Religion—or rather the Afro-Brazilian religions —had to seek out, in the social structures imposed upon them, "niches" where they could establish themselves and develop. They had to adapt themselves to a new human environment. This called for radical transformations of religious life itself. The superstructures that had formerly connected family, village, and tribe had to be linked with the new substructures: the big plantation or the urban center, slavery, a hierarchical caste society dominated by the white masters. This meant finding as yet unrecognized links, new gateways, that would allow mystical values to survive by incarnating themselves in the social fabric and at the same time make it possible for the social domain to be penetrated by values quite different from—and sometimes even contradictory to—the values of European origin that had hitherto sustained society either as models or norms.

Theoretically there were as many African religions capable of taking root in Brazil as there were transplanted ethnic groups. Nonetheless we may make the generalization that, without exception, all these religions were tightly linked to families, lineages, or clans. The cult of the Mozambique Bantu is the cult of the family ancestors, and the father exercises the priestly function. Only the ancestors of the chief are worshiped by all members of the tribe and serve as intermediaries between men and the supreme deity—the sky god or rain god. Ancestor worship also dominates the richer, more complex religion of the Angola blacks, in which the women are possessed by their family dead during religious ceremonies. In the Congo, it is true, animism is more developed, and there is a whole mythology, with a celestial god and an earth goddess. This mythology, however, is "domestically" linked to the great royal families, the gods being regarded as the founders of the ruling dynasties. Among other families the predominant cult is ancestor worship.[1] As for the Yoruba and Dahomans, they have a dual religion, rural and urban, well defined by Frobenius in *Die Atlantische Götterlehre*:

> The fundamental idea of the Yoruba religious system is the concept that every man is descended from a divinity. . . . All the members of any one family share descent from the same divinity. . . . It is quite irrelevant that this divinity may also be a storm, forge, river, earth or sky god, or the divinity of some force or activity. Every god has his descendants and the power to perpetuate himself in them through children. But under another aspect . . . every god has a specific function that is his alone. For example, there is the storm god responsible for providing the land with life-bringing rains. There is the iron god, who keeps the forge supplied with metal. . . . If there is a drought somewhere, all the people concerned jointly invoke the storm god, no matter what *orixá* the individual families may be descended from. If war breaks out, the whole community invokes the iron god (who also determines the outcome of wars), no matter what god the individual fathers may be descended from. . . . Hence every community must have its altar to the family god, served by an intermediary or headman, a family priest. Secondly, every urban community needs a temple or sanctuary for every important god capable of helping or harming it, where the great feasts and ceremonies can be celebrated by a high priest dedicated to that god. The family celebrant is called the *aboxa*, the community priest the *adjé*.[2]

For the moment we are not interested in how these two religions, which both invoke the same divinities, are coordinated or how it was possible to shift from one to the other. We shall concentrate on one idea. Each of the Yoruba gods (and the same is true of the Dahoman *voduns*) presides over one aspect of nature, with special priests and fraternities of initiates to serve him, for the benefit of the whole community. At the same time, each god also presides over one family, whose ancestor he is and whose cult is transmitted within the family through the male line.

But slavery, as we have seen in the previous chapter, separated mother m child, husband from wife.[3] It scattered throughout the most remote regions of Brazil members of a single line or clan who were sold into slavery at the same time.[4] How could a religion so closely tied to domestic life, to the souls of dead ancestors, real or legendary, totemic or not—a religion in which priesthood was the prerogative of the patriarch—resist such disruption? In discussing the effects of this structural change we must distinguish between blacks from West Africa and the Bantu. The Bantu could cope only indirectly with the disappearance of a cult centered almost exclusively in the worship of the dead. These indirect solutions all seem to have developed simultaneously, judging by the testimony of travelers and chroniclers of slavery. One solution was to cling to the idea that the soul returned after death to the country of the ancestors, either to be reincarnated there in free beings or to swell the ranks of deified ancestors and thus receive the worship denied it in Brazil. This was the solution adopted by family members divorced from their groups, not by groups enslaved as a whole. It often induced slaves to kill themselves in order to regain the ancestral paradise more quickly.[5]

The second solution was to reinterpret the other religions of Brazil—Indian, Catholic, or even those of other African ethnic groups—in terms of the cult of the dead. In the case of the Amerindian religions this was relatively easy because the maraca-shaking *pagés* would make the dead speak, causing the Indian women to fall into trance.[6] This explains the immediate acceptance of the *pagelança* or the *catimbó* by the Bantu.[7] For the Yoruba or Dahoman religions, which invoked divinities rather than ancestors as such, it was not so easy. Those cults, however, saw their gods as kings or heroes who had once lived on earth and been deified after death. And again trance was a central feature of their rituals. These factors helped the Atlantic Bantu to redefine their religon in Yoruba terms. Indeed the Congo or Angola "nations" often copied the *candomblés* of the West African Negroes, merely changing the names of the divinities (replacing Oxalá with Zumbi, Exú with Bombongira, etc.). Catholicism on the other hand forbade ecstatic transports or at least looked askance at them. Nevertheless the religious brotherhoods of Our Lady of the Rosary or São Benedito offered the Bantu a notion of "intermediaries" compatible with their own. In the first place, they identified the notion of the saints as intercessors between man and god with their own belief that the ancestors presented their requests to Zumbi or Zambi, the sky god. Identification was the easier inasmuch as the Virgin and the saints had lived on earth before ascending to the glory of God. Secondly, the existence of black Virgins and saints suggested that these Catholic "Negroes" had really been ancestors of their own races—not, of course, family ancestors but at least national ones. The Bantu were therefore more readily disposed than the other African peoples to accept the religious fraternities.

Later, toward the end of the nineteenth century, spiritism, with its mediums and materialization of the dead, developed in Brazil, and this obviously offered the later Bantu arrivals, or their descendants, the best solution to the problem of reinterpreting the religion of their fathers in European terms.

The problem was different for the Yoruba and Dahomans since their religion was dualistic, being simultaneously a lineage religion and a community religion. The lineage aspect was bound to disappear. The ratio of women slaves to men was far too low to permit the formation of stable couples.[8] A woman would sleep now with one man, now with another, as the fancy took her. While the men might belong to the same ethnic group, Yoruba or Dahoman, when she had a child, she could not know who its father was. This would not have mattered if the *orixás* or *voduns* had been inherited through the female line, but since they were transmitted through the male line, not to know the child's paternity was an insuperable obstacle to the domestic religion. Under the influence of Catholicism, religious marriage, blessed by the chaplain and accepted or encouraged by the white slaveowner, was introduced in an attempt to overcome this vast primitive promiscuity.[9] But, according to Couty, the attempt failed. Although the slaveowners kept the young slave girls confined to protect them from the men's lechery, once they were married, the girls would often poison their husbands with sweets made of herbs obtained from the witch doctor so that they might be free to take different sexual partners. In fact the death rate among married male slaves rose so high that on most big plantations widows had to be forbidden to remarry. Finally, adds Couty, morality was simply ignored and "the two sexes were allowed to mingle for two or three hours every evening."[10] In the towns too the slaves would leave the houses while their masters were asleep and meet in the darkness of the street or on the deserted beaches.[11] Such conditions, even after the introduction of marriage contracts, irreparably broke the chain of transmission of the *orixá* through the male bloodline.

On the other hand the second aspect of the Yoruba-Dahoman religion —namely the worship of nature gods by urban priests assisted by a fraternity of initiates for the benefit of the community—was able to survive by accommodating itself to the framework of "nations" reestablished by the Portuguese and Brazilian governments for the purpose of fomenting interethnic rivalries and so preventing the development of class consciousness and a general revolt of the blacks against the whites. Thus the living conditions imposed upon the West African ethnic groups caused a split between the domestic and the national aspects of their religion. This pattern, incidentally, had already emerged in Africa. Only the national aspect was retained, because organizations such as the *cantos* and "nations," dance festivals and *bantuques*, provided appropriate "niches," as I have termed them, where it could hide and survive.[12]

But how were these Brazilian substructures, the fraternities and nations created by the white man for his own purposes, linked with the superstructures of African values and collective representations? Unfortunately the historical documents that might provide the answer are lacking. We shall have to discover it indirectly when we come to study the social organization of the *candomblés*. For the moment we shall confine ourselves to two fundamental observations.

In Africa every divinity, Shangô, Omolú, Ogun, etc., had his or her own priests, fraternities, monasteries, and sanctuaries. In Brazil, even in the "black" coastal towns, the individual "nations" were too weak numerically to revive this kind of specialization. The sects therefore became small-scale replicas of the lost homeland in its entirety. Every *candomblé*, directed by a single priest, had to pay homage to each and every deity. Instead of specialized fraternities serving Ogun, Shangô, or Omulú, there was a single fraternity comprising daughters of all these gods. Thus all Africa was concentrated in the sect. That is the first point.

On the other hand, when the African sects were created by free Negroes the family ancestors were able to take their place alongside the nature gods. This was the case with the *Casa das Minas*, for instance. Here three "families" of gods were worshiped: the family of Da or Danbira (smallpox), the family of Kevioso (thunder), and the family of Davisé or Dahomé, i.e. the ancestors of the royal family of Dahomey, to which the founders of the *casa* belonged. In this case the two religions, family and national, survived together. But when the two were combined within one "nation," beliefs necessarily changed. The ancestors were equated with the *voduns* and assumed their theological forms, responding to the same rituals and producing the same ecstatic trances.[13] In other words, the new substructures were reflected in the superstructures, while allowing themselves to be contaminated by them only if they could, in turn, shape them to fit their own frameworks.

Before we can understand these "nations," *batuques*, and fraternities, we must see how they fit into the overall picture of contemporary society, a society characterized by monoculture, slavery, and big estates.

It has been repeated over and over again that Brazilian slavery was much more humane than its Anglo-Saxon or French counterparts. British or American travelers, familiar with the tragic lot of the working man in their own countries in the early days of industrialism, never failed to point out that the slaves could count on day-to-day security, were taken care of when they were sick, old, or infirm, and were, in general, better off than European or North American working men.[14] Saint-Hilaire, comparing the life of rural slaves with that of French peasants, found the former more fortunate than the latter.[15] I do not question these assertions; all sources agree, except perhaps for German travelers, who liked to dwell on cases of whites torturing Negroes or being murdered by their slaves. One suspects that their accounts may reflect a deliberate policy of discouraging German emigration to Brazil.[16]

But while I do not question them, I must still express certain reservations. The slaves' lot varied from region to region. They were treated better in Rio or Bahia, for instance, than in Maranhão or Pará.[17] Conditions also varied according to the category of the slave. Cowhands were better off than *charquedas* in the dried meat industry,[18] house slaves better off than field hands.[19] We should not forget that all these accounts date from the early nineteenth century, when the slave trade had already been restricted and would soon be completely abolished, thus enormously increasing the price of slaves.[20] The masters realized that it was going to become increasingly difficult to replenish their human livestock and that every worker represented a valuable capital asset. They therefore began to take appropriate measures to keep their slaves alive and in good health. They fed them better, set up infirmaries on their *fazendas* and called in "surgeons," granted time off to women about to deliver babies and to nursing mothers, and organized agricultural work so that it would not overstrain their Negroes.[21] In my opinion, economic factors of this kind were much more important in alleviating the hardships of slavery than the influence of Catholicism[22] or racial factors such as the indolence of the Brazilians.[23]

The works of Gilberto Freyre reveal a striking contradiction between his insistence on the humane nature of Brazilian slavery and his theory that slavery created a taste for sadism in the whites.[24] Certainly this sadism would not have developed if the whites had not taken pleasure in watching slaves being whipped, in forcing them to wear iron masks, shutting them up in chests, or cutting off the ears of runaways. Arthur Ramos devoted a whole chapter in one of his books to a minute description of the instruments of torture used in Brazil.[25] When abolitionist ideas began to flourish among college graduates, the *bachareis* and *doutores*, the rich landowners naturally had to be careful not to provide their most dangerous adversaries with ammunition. Relinquishing some of their prerogatives, they even ceded to government agents—to the police or the military—the right to administer punishment.[26] The Catholic church, long indifferent to the hardships of the Africans, passed certain measures on their behalf, including manumission of slaves through the Brotherhood of the Rosary. Any white man in whose house a runaway black took refuge was also given the incontrovertible right to buy that slave from his former master.[27]

But while these measures certainly mitigated the hardships of slavery, we should not be decieved by them. As Comte said, modern slavery is not the slavery of classical antiquity.[28] It is not based on the integration of one man into one family but on the economic exploitation of one race by another and on the profit motive. The "iron law of wages" applies to slaves no less than to wage earners. Indeed slavery, by its very nature, demanded harshness on the part of the master. The same travelers who stress the comparatively humane character of slavery in Brazil remark upon this fact, noting that Negro suicides, murders, and racial trouble are more frequent on the estates of "good" masters than elsewhere.[29] And indeed no one could work several hundred slaves unless he possessed an iron will. As Fernando de Azevedo rightly says, supported by Max Weber and by the history of his country:

> If it were to develop and survive, the patriarchal economy of the *casa grande* . . . had to use iron discipline to maintain in a state of servile submission the Indians and Africans who constituted two thirds—and later half—of the population. It was a bitter struggle for survival and domination. In the chaos of colonial society, the *casa grande* would not have been the disciplinary instrument it was, the instrument of order and agglutination, the centripetal force that regroups and holds together, without that fierce effort, lapsing sometimes into cruelty, to reinforce the armature of the system to meet the constant threat of attack by the field hands and of mutiny in the *senzalas*.[30]

The suffering inflicted on black children by little white boys who made them the butt of their pranks, the jealousy of the white woman who gouged out the eyes of her husband's black mistress or knocked out her teeth with a hammer, are of no more than anecdotal interest in the present study.[31] The essential fact is that the slave was the victim of systematic, brutal, self-serving exploitation. Not without reason does a famous proverb call Brazil the black man's hell, the white man's purgatory, and the mulatto's paradise. While it may have been a paradise to the free mulatto man and especially to the voluptuous mulatto woman, to the black slave it was sheer hell. Antonil said at the end of the seventeenth century that the slave needed "three p's—*pão, pau*, and *pano*" (bread, the stick, and clothing) —but that the Brazilian began with the wrong one, the stick, and treated his horses better than his slaves.[32] The master, it is true, found a way of deflecting the blacks' resentment by splitting the father-master figure in two: into the good father (the plantation owner) and the wicked father (the *feitor* or overseer).[33] It was the overseers who were responsible for the worst atrocities. They were recruited from the class of mulattoes and free Negroes, which enabled the exploiting class to divorce in the minds of the exploited the economic struggle against slavery from the Africans' racial struggle against the Portuguese.

As this exploitation disminished, however, beginning with the decline of mining and continuing throughout the nineteenth century until the abolition of slavery, the social structure was changing as a result of urbanization. The new structure again intensified the split between the exploiting and the exploited class, negating the integrative effect of the more humane attitude.

At first the Brazilian town was no more than an extension of the plantation. The planter who came to live in the capital or in one of the port cities
brought his rural tastes with him. The urban *sobrado* was a copy of the
sugar planter's *casa grande*, isolated from the other houses by gardens,
turning its back to the street, and concentrating its life in interior rooms
overlooking the courtyard, protecting the white women from the eyes of
strangers with jalousies and Moorish grille work. The *senzala* was brought
along too, to occupy the dampest ground-floor rooms, while the plantation
chapel was transformed into a family altar in an alcove off the drawing
room, where its golden hangings and flickering candles could be glimpsed
between half-open doors. Nevertheless the street, which linked the houses
and served as a meeting place and center for fraternization and gatherings,
finally triumphed over the isolation of the individual houses. It brought the
white woman out of her confinement to listen to student serenades beneath
her window, to attend balls and fashionable receptions, or to take her
place in her box at the theater, bejeweled like the statue of a saint. It lured
the patriarch away from his purely monetary interests into political clubs,
Masonic lodges, the spacious sacristies of the colonial churches, where he
could talk land, horses, or affairs of state. By way of the street and the
drawing room, the ancient antagonism between plantation owner and
Portuguese merchant diminished until it was finally extinguished in the
marriage of the master's half-ruined daughter to the young Portuguese
clerking in, or even managing, his father's store.[34]

But while the street helped the whites to develop a sense of racial
solidarity, it does not seem to have had a similar effect in bringing together
the different races and cultures. Far from promoting the integration of
black and white into one society, urbanization seems to have done the
opposite. We should perhaps except the great popular holidays, when
people of all colors joined the throng of merrymakers, and the religious
processions in which black and white fraternities paraded together. Yet
even then the races remained separate. The Brotherhood of the Rosary or
the Brotherhood of Saint Benedict would lead the procession, while the
white brotherhoods flanked the bishop's or the priest's dais. The festivals
allowed the black dances to coexist with the white celebrations but did not
promote interaction between the two.

The street had the same effect in producing ethnic solidarity among the
slaves as among the whites—and I am speaking of *ethnic*, not *caste*,
solidarity. Wherever the different "nations" came into contact, when the
women met at the fountain or the men met in the city square, they would
stop and talk. Thus the constituent elements of the old plantation,
formerly integrated in a unified system of production and protected from
the forces of dissolution by the patriarch's absolute authority, fell apart.
The *casa grande* became the *sobrado*, the *senzala* the *mocambo*. The
balance that had formerly existed between the rural Luso-Brazilian civili-

zation and the popular African civilizations gave way to antagonism
between the white European culture, derived from the schools of law and
medicine and from the seminaries, and the African culture that was developing within the "nations" in the form of a revival of ancestral religious
traditons.[35] It is true, as I have said, that the slaves' lot had improved.
Instead of slouching, half-naked, through the cane fields, he now wore a
frock coat and white gloves. While the purpose of this was to enhance his
master's prestige and maintain status in his neighbors' eyes, it also gave the
black a sense of human dignity which the old system of rural slavery had
crushed. Plantation slavery de-Africanized the Negro; urban slavery re-
Africanized him by keeping him in perpetual contact with his own centers
of cultural resistance, the fraternities and "nations."

Clearly the survival of African religions must be seen in the light of the
dualism between the conflicting classes. The struggle between civilizations
is just one aspect of the struggle between races or economic classes within
a society based on slavery. Since the black could not defend himself on the
material level against a regime in which the whites had all the rights, he
took refuge in mystical values—the only ones they could not take away
from him.[36] He fought with the only weapons left to him: witchcraft and
the *mana* of his warrior gods. But this reorientation of collective representations brought over from Africa was bound to change their significance.
There the divinities had been worshiped on behalf of the whole community
—a community of cattle raisers or farmers. Prayers were offered that the
cattle, the women, and the fields might be fruitful. In Nigeria and
Dahomey the great festivals are still agrarian ones.[37] But what was the
good of asking the gods to make women fruitful when they could bear
nothing but infant slaves? Better to pray that their wombs might be sterile.
What was the good of asking the gods for a good crop when agriculture
was a matter not of subsistence but of commerce for the profit of the
whites, the exploiters? Better to pray for drought or for epidemics that
would destroy the plantations, because for the slave a bountiful harvest
simply meant more work, more weariness, more hardship.

So the gods were subjected to a process of selection. Those who protected agriculture were discarded—and by the twentieth century were
entirely forgotten. But Ogun (god of war), Shangô (god of justice), and
Exú (god of vengeance) assumed a steadily increasing importance in the
slaves' minds. And in doing so they changed. Ogun ceased to be the
protector of blacksmiths or of iron farming implements. Exú as a god of
cosmic order was almost eclipsed by Exú the guardian of social order,
charged with averting the disorder of a society based on racial exploitation. Now, when the tom-tom was heard in the stifling nights, it was not
invoking rain, prosperity for the village, or glory for the tribe; it called to
other mysteries. Perhaps the brewing of love philters by means of which a
beautiful black woman could revenge herself on her haughty white mistress

by stealing her husband's heart. (Legal documents tell of many a husband who got rid of his wife and turned over his household to a colored mistress with whom he was infatuated.)[38] Perhaps the concoction of esoteric poisons from the toxic plants known as "herbs for sweetening the master"[39] that would eat away his brain and bring senility and slow death, or of potions to cause wombs big with future slaves to abort.[40]

In short, the African culture ceased to be the communal culture of a global society and became the exclusive culture of a social class, of one distinct group in Brazilian society—a class that was economically exploited and socially subordinated.[41]

■ ■ ■

Slavery not only divides; it also unites what it divides. Slavery united the African civilizations, now detached from their substructures, mutilated in the process and transformed from communal civilizations into class subcultures, with the European ruling-class civilizations. This produced the new phenomena of religious syncretism and cultural crossbreeding, which we must now examine. Here again, if we are to understand how the civilizations interpenetrated each other, through what channels, and with what consequences, we must study the social situation that conditioned and explained the interaction.

The *casa grande* on its elevated site dominating the plantation may have been remote from the nostalgia, the music, and the gods of the *senzala*, which housed its herd of slaves. The fact remains that they were both elements in one and the same reality, the great slave-based family. This family, isolated in the back country, constituted an organic entity whose parts were interdependent, a substitute for the Portuguese village. Of course the relationships that linked the members of this domestic community were not of the same egalitarian type that link village neighbors. These family members were hierarchized, and in this respect the community had more in common with the feudal clan than with the village. Social intimacy or distance depended upon the hierarchical rank of the individuals. At the very top stood the family of the white patriarch, the landlord and owner of the slaves. Immediately below them came the free men in charge of the relatively "high-class" production operations—the manager of the sugar mill, the supervisor of the refinery, the bookkeeper, and the small army of overseers who commanded the troops of slaves to the accompaniment of raucous shouting and the cracking of whips. At the bottom were the slaves. They in turn did not constitute an amorphous mass but were divided into two groups. One group consisted of the house servants, who spent the whole day inside the *casa grande* in close contact with the master's family—the cook, the seamstress, the weaver of homespun cotton cloth, the maids, nurses for the white babies, menservants, *negros de recado* (go-betweens who linked the plantation with its neighbors); the other comprised the field hands, who labored under the burning sun from dawn to dusk and sometimes longer. The latter group was of course numerically the largest and the farthest removed from the hub of the system, the *casa grande*.

This hierarchization by rank or status was also an ethnic hierarchization. The master's family was endogamous; it wanted no black blood in its veins. A wife was chosen with an eye to her racial purity and her fitness to bear her husband's children and propagate his line—an eldest son to replace the patriarch after his death, a youngest son to become a *bacharel* or a priest. The intermediate class consisted of poor whites who could survive only be integrating themselves as dependents within the only stable units in the colony, the big landowning families, and of mulattoes or free Negroes almost totally assimilated into the Portuguese civilization. The house slaves were selected for their beauty, intelligence, health, and cleanliness from the Creole blacks or the Mina or Nagô Africans, i.e. almost exclusively from the West African group. The field hands were usually Bantu or semi-Bantu. In short, social status increased with proximity to European values as represented by the master and his wife. Hence the only hope of rising on the social ladder and attaining the coveted positions, the ones that offered the most liberty, security, and prestige, was through de-Africanization.[42]

In this perspective, acculturation appears in its true light as a struggle for social status. Merely because I have spoken of a dominant race and an exploited one, it should not be assumed that white civilization was imposed by force, giving the slave a painful feeling of alienation. White civilization was desirable as a means of social mobility and—since insurrection had failed—as the only way out of an intolerable situation. It was pursued deliberately and systematically. The pursuit took two forms, the purely cultural form of adopting Catholicism and acquiring white habits and modes of behavior, and a biological form characterized by the expression "*limpar o sangue*," the purging of the blood by sleeping with whites and producing children with lighter skin, whose white fathers would help them along and who might in this way be freed from the yoke of slavery and enjoy an advantage when it came to economic competition. The purging of the blood of the shameful taint of blackness; the purging of the African civilization of its taint of barbarism; the acceptance of the masters' esthetic principle (that white was better than black) and his moral principle (that white ethics were better than "pagan" mores) as the sole criteria—there was no other way to rise socially in a society shaped and controlled by the white man.

The importance of trance in the religions of black Africa caused the earliest ethnographers to misunderstand Negro psychology. Blacks are not mystics. As has sometimes been said, their philosophy is closer to the Anglo-Saxon's than to the Asiatic's. It is essentially utilitarian and pragmatic; the only thing that counts is success.[43] The African's ambition to be a bureaucrat, an intellectual, or a civil servant, to wear a pince-nez and carry a ministerial portfolio, did not reflect idealistic aspirations or hatred of the machine or of manual work. It was simply a recognition of the superior social status the white man accorded to certain professions at the expense of others.[44] This utilitarianism explains the Negro's adjustment to his new situation in colonial or imperial Brazil and his effort to make the best of it. As we shall see in later chapters, it was not unthinkable to resort to force or to run away, but the circumstances had to be exactly right. Usually the slave, like the spider, the turtle, the rabbit, or the lizard in his folk tales, relied on trickery, the weapon of the weak which often triumphs over the stronger.[45] There is a whole folklore about the Negro slave in Brazil, known as the "cycle of Father John." It is a product of white-Negro collaboration and is therefore extremely ambiguous, since its thrust takes two different directions. Its white aspect is an apology for the "good" as opposed to the "bad" Negro. While the good Negro occasionally gives vent to his sadness in singing and twanging his *urucongo*, he accepts his lot and is devoted to his masters, regarding himself as a member of the patriarchal family, if only a poor relation. The cycle's black aspect is an apology for the crafty Negro who sweet-talks white women, succeeds in sleeping in the master's hammock, and gains a key position in the household by creating the impression that he is "white-souled," while all the time cherishing in his heart of hearts the essence of his African civilization: a knowledge of medicinal plants, magical rites, and the African names—i.e. the real names—of the Catholic saints.[46] Clearly acculturation does not consist entirely in cultural assimilation and the total obliteration of the native civilizations by the vast, oppressive darkness of slavery.

This is borne out by the fact that while the African, and to an even greater degree the Creole, accepted white values—slightly tinged with black—the propinquity of the races within the regime of slavery also enabled African culture to leave its stamp on the Luso-Brazilian civilization. The little white boy spent the first few years of his life among the black children, playing with them, swimming in the millpond or playing hide and seek in the cane fields, learning to set snares for birds in the surrounding forest. Before that, he had been suckled by a black nurse, who sang African lullabies as she rocked him, giving him love as well as milk. He was still taken care of by his *mãe preta*, who, when she put him to bed, would tell him stories of Quibungo, the great beast that ate little children, or of the little girl in the singing pouch, or the sailor married to Calunga, queen of the sea.[47] At the age when the mind is most malleable, most susceptible to outside impressions and influences, he was impregnated with totally African values. When he was sick, his black mammy treated him with herbs gathered by the witch doctor. On the chain around his neck bearing the holy medals of saints which his white mother had given him, she hung more potent charms dipped in the blood of sacrifical animals to protect him from the evil eye or from childhood diseases. Later, when his sexual awakening began, he would watch the Negro women bathing naked in the river and wear himself out in enervating, more or less erotic games with the little black girls, finally "proving his manhood" with some black girl he happened to meet in the fields. He would have an endless series of black mistresses and father an infinite number of mulatto babies, going to the African witch doctor, if his plantation had one, for potions to revive his sensuality when age or abuse had enfeebled it. And the influence of Africa did not end when he passed from childhood to adolescence but maintained its insidious, subtle hold throughout his life, chiefly through this eroticism, this worship of the black Venus.

In a similar way, though for different reasons, the white mistress of the household, shut up among her slaves, making preserves, supervising the dressmaker or the laundresses, enjoying *cafunés* from her maid's deft fingers,[48] hardly ever going out and rarely receiving visitors, even taking refuge in her own kitchen if a stranger appeared at her front door, finally came to think and feel as her slaves did, to share their superstitious fears and tales of magic, and to believe in Exú almost as firmly as she believed in the Devil. Not until the white family left the plantation and moved to town, thus exposing themselves to the European ideas shipped from Lisbon or Manchester along with cargoes of merchandise, did the forces tending to separate the two cultures overcome the forces of fusion. In rural Brazil the de-Africanization of the blacks went hand in hand with the Africanization of the whites, producing both mulatto children and a mixed culture.[49]

Gilberto Freyre made an excellent study of these diverse phenomena in *The Masters and the Slaves*, though from the viewpoint of the Brazilian civilization rather than the African civilizations that concern us here. We must now look at the phenomena from the opposite angle.

In Brazil the great sugar or coffee plantation replaced the African village community. It had to fulfill the functions of the village or the lineage: to integrate, provide security, organize and direct interpersonal relationships —in brief, to constitute the stable hub within which all roles and social ranks could find their equilibrium, their center of coordination. Despite conflicts of interest between the exploiting and exploited classes and the tensions generated by these conflicts, the Negro was to a certain extent caught in the solidarity that bound him to his master. He fought on his master's side in clashes between family clans; later he assassinated his master's political enemies and served as his bodyguard in electoral fights. In this way he lived in two societies at the same time: a racial class society, with its fraternities, "nations," recreation groups, and *batuques*; and a family society, upon which he depended to save him from starvation and from feeling abandoned in a strange land. His loyalties were split, and this split led, if not to the subordination of the African civilization to the European one, then at least to their peaceful coexistence—a pledge of future marriage.

This becomes even truer as we pass from the generation of "wild Negroes," as they were called, newly brought over from Africa, to the generation of Creole Negroes, born or raised on the plantation. Civilization, even when it puts its stamp on nature, even when it meets natural instincts or needs (which is not always the case, because it creates more needs than it satisfies), is never innate but always acquired. And the major instrument in the socialization of the child remains the family. Even when initiation rites include a tribal apprenticeship, this is always a kind of schooling; it never counteracts family training but merely completes it. But the black or mulatto baby born on the plantation was cared for by his mother only as long as she was nursing him. After that, some old woman, too old to work in the fields, took care of him, along with all the other children. Before long he came under the master's influence or the chaplain's, or, if he showed signs of intelligence and especially if he happened to be an illegitimate son of the patriarch or the chaplain, the schoolmaster's. Thus the Creoles underwent a double socialization: that of the African group, through the mother and the old woman who supervised the children's play and through the *senzala*; and that of the white family, with all its authority and prestige. Through these channels two civilizations met and mingled in his mind.

Racial parental dualism is the most singular phenomenon of slavery. It affected the little white boy just as strongly as the black one. The patriarch's son had a white father and a black mother. Sometimes his black mother shaped his character together with his white mother, who could then try to counteract the African influences. But often the white mother had married at fifteen or sixteen and borne her first child soon afterward. Living on a poor diet, taking no exercise, she often died very young, in which case the authority of the black mammy became even stronger.[50] The slave's son, on the other hand, may have known his mother but often had no idea who his real father was. In the final analysis his real father, if not his biological one, was the white patriarch, the plantation owner. Joaquim Nabuco and Luiz Gama are good illustrations of this parental dualism. Nabuco, orphaned at birth, was so attached to his colored nurse that the bonds of affection remained just as strong when he was at the height of his glory as a great writer, politician, and ambassador of his country. Although he was unquestionably a product of the most refined European civilization—so much so that literary critics sometimes accused him of being more foreign than Brazilian—one could never appreciate his sensitivity or his cast of mind without studying him, psychoanalytically as it were, in the light of the gentle molding he underwent at the hand of his *mãe preta*. Luiz Gama, it is true, had a Portuguese father who could have brought him up, but that father not only left him in slavery but even sold him to some traders, who shipped him from Bahia to the province of São Paulo. He was taken away from his mother, whom he sought persistently all his life but never found, though he continued to worship her. His true father, however, was the son of his Paulista master, who educated and reared him and forced him to study, shaping his mind and sensibilities according to European norms. These two leaders of abolitionism, the one devoted to his black nurse, the other to his slave mother, are a splendid illustration—in inverted form—of the drama of dual parentage, a subject which still calls for analysis.

In my opinion, the psychic mechanisms of acculturation can be much better defined through the psychoanalytic concepts of the superego, identification, and narcissism than through the processes of imitation, apprenticeship, adaptation, and suggestion. The factor that tended to unify the heterogeneous elements in Brazilian society and disseminate the same values throughout all strata of society was that the white lived in a patriarchal family and the black in a maternal one, so that they could not help but interiorize the same father. In doing so, they interiorized his culture, his view of the world and of life, his frames of reference, and his norms. Thus the separation of the ego from the superego proposed by Freud was translated for the black, and also for the white brought up by a black mammy, into a stratification of the two civilizations: the maternal African society, which was forced down into the unconscious, where it asumed the "foreign" character of repressed reality, which, however, did not prevent it from acting upon the ego; and the paternal Lusitanian civilization, which directed and constrained, sometimes with a touch of sadism. This explains why the voice calling to the white from the heart of the whirlwind or the whirlpool or from the depths of the unconscious was always the song of a black siren, while the black, peering like a modern Narcissus into the river of life to perceive himself more clearly, saw himself as white.

Of course these phenomena became more profound and substantial as one moved from the periphery toward the center of the vast patriarchal family—from the field hands, only tenuously linked to the center, crowded in the rooms of the *senzala*, to the Creole Negroes living in the *casa grande* to the same rhythm as the whites. But before going to bed, all the slaves had to assemble to receive the master's blessing, to praise him with a "Blessed be Jesus Christ, our Lord" in order to perpetuate and maintain within them the image of the white father.[51] Thus identification might be more or less complete, depending upon the class of the slave. In some of them identification repressed the native civilization. In others, where repression failed, it merely gave them a certain foreignness. And in the group of pure Africans who had arrived in Brazil as adults the father was never interiorized. He remained a kind of extra, superimposed from outside, not changing the native civilization but merely subjecting it to a control that had to be craftily defied by disguising black ceremonies with a white mask.

Secondly we must note that this process of interiorization applied only to master-slave dualism. Yet between these two poles of society there was an intermediate class of laborers, *administrados*, protégés, and small, free landholders. As Antonio Candido has rightly pointed out, sociologists have neglected the study of this interstitial stratum.[52] The reason is that it was originally small and closely linked to the patriarchal family by bonds of dependence, *compadrismo*, protection, and subordination.[53] As a result of white miscegenation with Indian and African women it grew into a network—though a loose one with many gaps—of miserable, illiterate peasants, isolated and often mobile, which linked the ganglionic cells of which the country was composed, the great families of the latifundia. Economically autonomous, living by subsistence family farming,[54] politically subordinate, and constituting a sort of "clientele" of the patriarchal clans,[55] this class, which was of no importance until the late eighteenth century, was immune to the process of acculturation. Its culture, made up of the debris of all the civilizations, poses different problems, which we shall examine later when we come to study rural Afro-Brazilian religions.

■ ■ ■

As I have already said, urbanization shattered the integrity of the seventeenth and early eighteenth century patriarchal family. Triumphing over the *sobrado*, the street introduced a twofold solidarity: that of the masters, whose original archaic civilization was being refined through contact with fashions, ideas, and values imported from Europe; and that of the slaves, the *negros de ganho*, and the members of the "nations," whose cultural losses were continually being made good by transfusions from Africa. But here again a compensatory phenomenon occurred, counteracting the dualism, slowing the formation of mutually antagonistic cultures, and reestablishing a certain unity. Gilberto Freyre made a study of this phenomenon in his book *The Mansions and the Shanties*, the sequel to *The Masters and the Slaves*. In fact Brazilian society has always known these two antithetical movements, the centrifugal one of emerging separate cultures, and the centripetal one that tended to integrate them in a single mestizo civilization, more white than Indian or black, since it was the whites who manned the controls, enjoyed the highest status, and, so to speak, operated the machinery of syncretization.

Miscegenation played an increasingly important role during the nineteenth century. Statistics show a growing preponderance of mulattoes, if not over whites, at any rate over pure blacks, despite the growth of the slave trade, which reached its peak at this time, just before abolition.

	Whites	Mestizos	Blacks	Indians
1835	845,000 (24.4%)	648,000 (18.2%)	1,987,000 (51.4%)	?
1872	3,818,403 (38.1%)	3,833,015 (38.4%)	2,970,509 (16.5%)	(7%)
1890	6,302,198 (44.0%)	4,638,495 (32.0%)	2,097,426 (12.0%)	(12%)

But miscegenation was now occurring in a different climate, a more sentimental one, one more strongly colored by Christianity. The wish to develop a herd of human livestock did not eclipse the sense of paternal responsibility, the father's affection for his illegitimate children or his concern that they be educated and attain a place in society. The sons of priests enjoyed a particularly privileged position,[56] as we see from the example of José de Patrocinio, one of the most brilliant journalists of imperial Brazil. A law passed in 1774 gave mestizos access to all positions, "honors, and dignities," leaving only the Negroes excluded.[57] In the nineteenth century some of the fraternities were democratically opened to men of any color.[58] The artisan class in the big cities was composed of mulattoes and free Negroes—tailors, shoemakers, hairdressers, bricklayers, and peddlers. The army was always the great ladder by which those of mixed blood could rise in society. This intermediate class was distinguished from the slaves by certain symbols, by no means the least important of which was the kind of shoes a man wore. Extremely small shoes emphasized the difference between the mulatto foot and the coarse, heavy, broad foot of the man who worked in the fields.[59] The opening of schools and academies for the illegitimate sons of the patriarch who enjoyed his patronage permitted the growth of a small colored middle class of physicians, engineers, lawyers, journalists, novelists, and poets—all elegantly dressed, their hair smooth and shiny with coconut oil, great talkers, and charming ladies' men. Romanticism, which stressed women's right to love and the sanctity of passion as against the prejudice of marriages prearranged by the families, promoted cross-color sexual unions. Concubinage between white men and black women yielded to the possibility of legal marriage between white women and light mulattoes—at least within the class of intellectuals and college graduates. The royal family of Brazil did all it could to promote the integration of successful mulattoes and intelligent Negroes into society. Colored *bachareis* and *doutores*, some of whom became court functionaries or were elected to the legislature, were received in the royal drawing room, at court balls, and at the emperor's "kissing of hands." They were rewarded for services rendered, just as whites were, with titles of nobility, after which they were commonly referred to as "chocolate barons."[60]

It was obvious, however, that this rise on the social ladder could be achieved only by espousing European values and ideals, by rejecting the African civilizations and becoming totally assimilated into the white culture.[61] Thus the vertical mobility of the mulatto or free Negro dealt a blow to the survival of African religions and counterbalanced the other effect of urbanization: the separation of the *sobrado* civilization from that of the *mocambo*, of society balls from street *batuques*, of the middle class from the "nations."

What concerns us here, however, is not so much this upward mobility in itself as its effects on survival and change in the African religions. Two important points must be noted. The mobility was on the part of individuals, not a social group.[62] Brazilian paternalism certainly never reflected a deliberate, systematic policy; it was the spontaneous emotional response of the "warmhearted man" to a specific social situation. But while the system must be absolved of any charge of hypocrisy, it is still true that the criteria for the rise of the mulatto or of the Creole Negro were always those of the masters and that his advancement was always controlled by the whites. No doubt the intelligence of the protégé, his personal qualities and professional aptitudes and ability, played a decisive role, but so did moral qualities, respect for established values, gratitude to his father, godfather, or protector, and "knowing his place." Besides being an individual matter, upward mobility was determined by skin color or by the number of generations that separated a man from the African slave caste. Light-colored people had better chances than dark; straight hair was more favorable than kinky; an aquiline nose was better than a broad flat one.[63] Thus the mulatto's social mobility inevitably threw into relief the plight of the forgotten masses, the imported Negroes. In brief, paternalism, while it certainly aided assimilation and the triumph of the white civilization, also split society up into subcultures, into a whole series of hierarchized but separate segments. The rise of the mulatto was but the obverse of the indifference that greeted the endeavors of José Bonifacio[64] and later of Brazilian positivists to establish an educational policy for the black group as a whole designed to make it upwardly mobile instead of depriving it of its most valuable elements. Mulatto social mobility stood out in brilliant contrast to the neglect of the slave class once it had been split up into rival "nations" to preserve the masters' peace of mind and relegated to the *batuques* for distraction from its sad lot. The result was that when slavery was finally abolished in 1888, Brazilian society, despite its colored aristocracy, was not a homogeneous society but consisted of disparate segments, all of which were bearers of different civilizations.[65] This explains how the African religions were able to survive relatively intact within certain segments of society that were immune to capillary attraction.

The second point is that, contrary to what many people believe, paternalism did not stand for freedom from prejudice since advancement depended upon the color of one's skin. In fact it inevitably fostered prejudice, first within the group of poor whites, who began to feel insecure, distrustful, and dissatisfied when they saw men of another race overtaking them and winning out in the struggle for economic or social status. Psychologists have demonstrated the connection between aggressiveness and frustration and the etiology of the scapegoat complex so clearly that there is no need to go into the matter here.[66] Among the poor whites prejudice was a defense or retaliatory mechanism against the policy of the patriarchs. But it was bound to erupt within this second class too, as a technique for controlling upward mobility. While the masters deliberately promoted this mobility, they were not blind to its dangers. They could not allow it to become a tidal wave that would sweep away the privileges of the whites. The mulatto *bacharel* or the Negro *doutor* had to be reminded at the strategic moment that he owed everything to the good will of his patron and that he had better not forget it. The policy had to alternate between opening and closing the sluice gates. The result was discriminatory measures that did not conflict with paternalism but were its inescapable counterpart. The alert early nineteenth century traveler Saint-Hilaire recognized this, at least as it affected the free Negroes. He stressed the fact that the number of blacks or mulattoes who grew rich was very limited, adding that if they rose too high the whites were astute enough to see that they quickly fell again.[67]

Gilberto Freyre's book may paint the rise of the mulatto or the colored college graduate in somewhat rosy colors, but it also outlines the steps of the antithetical policy that constituted its corollary. In the eighteenth century the blacks were forbidden to crown kings of the Congo, to own slaves, or to choose godfathers of their own race. Hospital patients were segregated by color. Sneezing or catcalls greeted a black who attended the theater wearing a top hat and frock coat. Certain Masonic lodges and political clubs were not open to mulattoes. Of course many of these measures were directed more against free Negroes or dark-skinned mulattoes than against light-colored ones, but, by making the latter aware of the insecurity of their position, they aroused in them anti-Negro prejudices even stronger than those held by the whites. They also made mulattoes much more susceptible than pure blacks to feelings of inferiority and marginality. This explains why a mulatto whose sensitive feelings had been hurt or who had been unable to realize his ambitions fully might revert to the black class, where he could become a leader or regain the superior status denied him elsewhere.

When we look more closely, we see that it was not the mulatto per se who rose but the mulatto college graduate who enjoyed the master's protection. Below him there was still the constantly growing mass of mulattoes who had no chance of realizing their ambitions by penetrating the interstices of the white group. To them the African religions opened their doors, offering high priestly positions, especially in the Bantu sects or the *terreiros de caboclos*. To quote Gilberto Freyre:

> We should not forget the stamina of the plantation "bad men"—most of them mulattoes or Indian and Negro half-breeds—nor of the longshoremen in many of our cities, nearly all of them mulattoes. . . . Even the

great leaders of what our Negro has kept as most uniquely his—his religious traditions—are today mulattoes. Mulattoes, many of whom are now greatly de-Africanized in their ways of living, but who re-Africanize themselves by going to study in Africa. As in the case of Father Adão of Recife, who made himself into a native religious leader in Lagos, speaking African as fluently as Portuguese.[68]

But if we except Father Adão, who went to Africa to drink at the source of the African religions, it was these mulattoes, whose life style, as Freyre points out, was already to some extent de-Africanized, who most profoundly adulterated the cults by introducing their own esthetic conceptions, as did Joãozinho da Gomea, or their semi-European ethnic identity, as did the founders of *umbanda* spiritism.

3
Slave Protest and Religion

The conclusion to be drawn from the preceding chapter is that in Brazil the African civilization (of which religion was an integral part) became a group subculture. It was therefore necessarily involved in the class struggle, in the slaves' dramatic effort to escape from their position of economic and social subordination. We must now look at Negro resistance to slave labor and at black racial protest.

Protest could be either individual or collective; it ranged from the murder of the white master to armed insurrection, from the flight of a slave who feared punishment to the establishment of *quilombos*. Later we shall examine the collective forms and see how they often crystallized around a religious nucleus. In cases of individual resistance or flight, however, the mystical element is nearly always lacking. Let us take a few examples. At Vila Rica, the slaves of José Thomas de Mattos revenged themselves for a whipping by falling upon the *fazendeiro* as he was giving them his evening blessing and killing him and his son. They then raped the women and gouged out their eyes, dismembered the bodies, and tied them down on ant hills to be devoured.[1] In Rio Grande do Sul a slaveowner named Gomes ordered his slave Jesuino to kill his rival in love and, when Jesuino refused, struck him with his whip. Jesuino turned around and plunged his knife into Gomes's heart.[2] These are typical examples of killings of whites precipitated by pent-up rage or by a spontaneous reaction to an unexpected offense.[3] Only in the case of Moslem Negroes, who found it intolerable to be dominated by Christians, does religion seem to have been a factor.[4]

But the white man was afraid. His fear grew as the number of Negroes increased. He needed to deflect the slaves' violence onto another object, and to this end he developed what might be called a strategy of frustration. This can best be described in psychoanalytic categories, the purpose being to "displace" hatred for the white master and turn it against a substitute object where it would be less threatening to society. The first substitute was the black himself. Dollard has shown that clashes between Negroes are very common in the southern United States and that they represent displacement of inadmissible antiwhite aggression.[5] All travelers and historians mention the fights that were constantly breaking out between the various African nations in colonial Brazil.[6] Alternatively, the blacks' hatred could be deflected onto the Indians by setting one race against the other, although such hatred did not come naturally to them. In the *quilombos*, as we shall see, blacks and Indians mixed fraternally, and Saint-Hilaire makes several references to Indian women's predilection for Negro men.[7] The whites, however, used batallions of blacks to expel the Amerindians and also used Amerindians to capture runaway slaves.[8]

When war was declared on a foreign country, slave resentment was directed against the enemy. This explains the formation of the African and mulatto regiments (called the "Henriques Dias regiments" after the great black leader of the war against the Dutch), commanded by their own officers, which played an active part in the fighting against the Batavians, against Duguay-Trouin's French expedition, and in the war against the *farrapos*.[9] But a white enemy was not always available to serve as a displacement object for the slaves' racial hatred. In that case it was directed against domestic enemies, which explains why the Negro was involved in all civil insurrections, in the Paulistas' war against the *emboabas*,[10] the wars of national independence,[11] and even in struggles between the royalist and republican parties under the empire,[12] as well as in political rivalries between individuals.[13]

As I have already mentioned, another mechanism with a parallel in psychoanalysis was also utilized: the splitting of the figure of the white father. The paranoiac typically invents a fictional family in which the father is split into an imaginary good, noble or rich father figure and the real father, whom the patient sees as unnatural and spiteful. This enables him to resolve the ambivalence of his filial feelings, which are a mixture of hatred and respect.[14] In the same way the Negro found himself confronted by two figures: the master who gave him his blessing at nightfall and who sometimes allowed him to spend the evening dancing, and the *feitor*, the overseer, always armed with his whip, who could be especially brutal if he happened to be a mulatto anxious to prove that he belonged to another race or a former Negro slave excessively proud of his authority. In this way, the slave's ambivalent feelings were disentangled and his respect was directed toward the white master, his hatred toward the *feitor*. In many crimes committed by blacks, the *feitor* was the sole target.[15] Under the empire another institution existed that achieved the same result: *compadrismo*. The slave's godfather would defend him against his master's brutality or save him from punishment if he tried to run away, so that a similar dualism came into play between the beloved godfather and the hated master.[16] In monasteries and convents slavery was usually more humane, but not always. There were cases of slaves being killed by priests and of priests marrying light-skinned mulattoes to much darker men so that the children would be too dark to cross the color line. Here again the master figure was split, in this case into priest and saint. "The Negroes say that they are not the slaves of the monks but of Saint Benedict, and the monks are merely his representatives."[17]

As slavery neared its end, the smoldering hatred had to find a new displacement object. European emigrants were called upon to replace the slave labor that would soon be unavailable. The Brazilian army also included foreign mercenaries, chiefly from Germany. The Negroes were quick to refer to the new arrivals as "white slaves" and happy to see men of their master's color working alongside them and living in houses much like the *senzalas*. This seemed to them a kind of nemesis. And when some of these whites revolted and the blacks were called upon to put down the revolt, they did so with a savage brutality that can be explained only by the assumption that they were using the Germans as a substitute for their white masters.[18]

The sublimation of frustrated aggression functioned in a similar way. The *capoeira* represents the sublimation of violent aggression in a game. The *desafio* represents the sublimation of racial hatred in a literary genre. We shall return later to these phenomena, which sometimes served as vehicles for religious protest. For the moment we shall confine ourselves to the most curious form this sublimation took: the Testament of Judas.

This was an old Portuguese custom that had been transplanted to the colony.[19] On Holy Saturday a straw man representing Judas was paraded through the streets of the village or town and finally drowned, burned, or hanged. Judas came to represent the establishment and became a symbol through which the common people could get rid of their inferiority complexes. But in Brazil, where the stratification of ages, sexes, clans, and races was particularly pronounced, the custom itself became stratified. In Rio there was a court Judas, with fireworks donated by the emperor. There was the white middle-class celebration, dominated by shop clerks; this was also accompanied by fireworks and ended with Judas being hanged by the Devil. There was the street children's Judas, where the black children always seemed to outnumber the white children. Finally there was the Judas of the masses, the Negroes, and the dark mulattoes. This one was stuffed with firecrackers and taken out at night to be hung from a tree and finally blown up.[20] The whites found an outlet for pent-up protest in making their straw man an effigy of an eminent government figure (as they did in Rio in 1831[21]) or by distributing from house to house "testaments of Judas" that ridiculed the local dignitaries.[22] But the Negroes took even greater advantage of this opportunity to release their racial aggression. The proof is that they represented Judas as a man being tortured by a black devil.[23] This was a dual retaliation. They were saying that it was a white man, Judas, who had betrayed Christ, and they, the Negroes, commonly called devils on account of their color, who had been chosen as instruments of divine justice.

Yet all this subterranean release of feeling did not prevent sporadic outbreaks of general insurrection among the colored people. Obviously the transition from individual hatred to collective resistance required some kind of common catalyst. As we shall see, the catalyst was religion.

The Negro had another means of protest against slavery. He could run away. At first this was always an individual gesture, and later, even during the empire, it resumed its individual character. Here the religious element played no part. A slave who had committed some offense and wanted to escape punishment would go off into the forest at night and disappear.[24] But during the colonial period and even in the early nineteenth century, runaways would join forces to avoid being recaptured or having to confront alone the perils of a precarious existence in a forest harboring wild animals and, sometimes, unknown Indians. And so a little group would form, which would gradually grow into a real town. These Negro republics were known as *quilombos* or *mocambos*. Here the ancient tribal customs were revived, especially when the fugitive who established the *quilombo* was a new arrival from Africa. As in the case of aggression, the transition from individual to collective action occurred at least partly under the aegis of religion.

But before examining these two great phenomena of collective resistance, the *quilombos* and the insurrections, I must say a word about a third possible way of escaping slavery—suicide. The proclivity to suicide, like the tendency to aggression, varied from one ethnic group to another. Mina killed other people; Gabon Negroes or Mozambique killed themselves.[25] But it is an established fact that although egoistic suicide (to use Durkheim's expression) is rare or nonexistent among so-called uncivilized peoples,[26] suicide was very common among slaves.[27] It was a form of resistance to white culture, the form preferred by the weak—escape from the oppressive presence through death. The Brazilian Negro was perfectly aware that his suicide was an act of war, for slaves were expensive, and when a whole group vowed to let themselves die or to posion themselves, this meant certain ruin for their master. The slaves made good use of this form of revenge.[28]

Particularly interesting to me is the fact that suicide was also a religious protest. Tschudi was astonished to find that good *fazendeiros* had a much higher suicide rate among their slaves than bad ones, and he did some research to discover the reason. He was told that it was probably because of the influence of the priests, the *quiombos*, who encouraged racial hatred rather than hatred for specific individuals. Tschudi found the explanation plausible. He also noted that many slaves, being descended from princes or small African kings, could not tolerate slavery and killed themselves in order to be reunited with their ancestors in the other world.[29] In any case, whether under the influence of the priesthood or of mythical beliefs, suicide had its origin in the mystical sphere. This is confirmed in an account by d'Assier of a conversation he had with a Negro. Captured by slave traders and shipped to Brazil, this man and his companions had decided to hang themselves "in order to get back to our own country as quickly as possible." But at the last minute their courage failed, and only one of them killed himself. The *feitor* cut down the body, chopped off the head, and stuck it on a stake. "Now he can go back to his own country if he likes. It doesn't matter to me. His head stays here, and any bastard who tries the same trick will get the same treatment. He'll go back without a head." "And you know," concluded the poor man, "you can hardly find your way back to your own country if you have no head." So he had decided to flee into the forest, where he lived on roots, fruit, and an occasional chicken, stolen during the night. But he had been recaptured and, old and resigned, was awaiting his approaching end. "I'm old. It won't be long before I return to my country."[30]

Nevertheless we must not forget that the religious element emerged only in response to suffering and in cases where suicide represented a gesture of resistance to slavery. The importance of the social element that accompanied the religious one is evident from the fact that it was nearly always male slaves who committed suicide. Because of the sexual divison of labor in Africa, women were more accustomed to field work than men; their lives had always been a kind of domestic slavery. Women slaves rarely killed themselves.[31]

The nostalgia for the lost homeland known as *banzo* has much in common with suicide. Many Negroes could not bear their new habitat. They went into a decline and gradually wasted away, finally dying of homesickness.[32] Yet one cannot speak of Negro patriotism or of a feeling of love for any particular geographical place. *Banzo* is to be explained by something quite different from what we mean by the word "patriotism," and here again religion was a factor. A man's birthplace was not simply a fortuitous concatenation of mountains, lakes, or rivers, but a sociogeographic entity in which the local myths, the distribution of tribes over the territory, the established meeting places of the secret societies, etc., were but parts of a single whole. The African does not, as we do, divorce the material world from the universe of values, each of which occupies an ecological position in the whole. He does not see the hillside just as a hillside, but as the abode of a certain spirit or the traditional center of a certain ceremony. Marcel Mauss has shown that to "primitive" people space is essentially heterogeneous; every point within it has its own properties, its distinctive characteristics. We might say that *banzo* was not, strictly speaking, homesickness but nostalgia for a certain ecological pattern of culture, for the tribal—and religious—configuration against the native ground, and if the slave died it was because that pattern could not be recreated in Brazil.

Nevertheless attempts were made to re-create it, to build a new Africa. They were spontaneous attempts, generated by the massing of fugitive slaves in one place. The time has come to look more closely at the *quilombos*.

Palmares

We do not know exactly where in the state of Alagoas the Palmares *quilomobos* were situated nor when they were founded.[33] In any event they date back to the Dutch occupation of northern Brazil, and an expedition was sent out against them as early as 1645, as we know from the campaign journal of João Blaer. At that time Plamares was divided into two sections, a large one with 6,000 inhabitants and a smaller one with 5,000.[34] The expedition came first to an old *quilombo* that had been abandoned because it was too unhealthy. Then it arrived at Palmares Grandes, which is described in the journal as follows:

> There were 200 houses, and in the midst of them stood the church, four blacksmith's shops and the headman's hut. The inhabitants included all kinds of artisans, and the king governed them with strict justice, not permitting fetishism among his people. When several Negroes ran away, Creoles were sent after them and they were captured and killed, so that terror reigned among them, especially among the Angola. The king also had a country house two miles away, with plenty of land.[35]

When the Dutch expedition arrived at the site, the *quilombolas* had fled, and they found only a few old men, women, and children.

The *quilombo* was gradually built up again and renamed Macaco (monkey). An anonymous manuscript gives a description of it:

> The king lives in his royal city, which is called Macaco after the animal killed there. It is the capital of all the towns and settlements. It is fortified by a wall of dry earth. . . . The ministers of justice responsible for law enforcement live there, and all the institutions of a republic have their counterparts here. . . . They obey one of their own people called Gaga Zumba or "Great Lord," and, whether they live in Palmares or in the surrounding country, they regard him as their king and master. He has a palace and houses for his family and is attended by guards and officers, who customarily have royal huts. He is treated with all the respect due to

a king and all the ceremonial due to a master. Those who come into his presence kneel on the ground and press their palms together in recognition and affirmation of his power. They address him as "Your Majesty" and obey him with reverence.[36]

The town consisted of 1,500 houses, and there was a church in which were found statues of the Infant Jesus, Saint Braz, and the Virgin of the Conception.

But Macaco was not the only city. The *quilombolas* were dispersed throughout the Serra da Barriga in numerous villages and fortified towns linked by dynastic ties. More than eighteen expeditions were sent out to destroy this "Negro Troy," as it has been called, but it always rose again from the ashes. The most famous was the one led by Fernão Carrilho, who so terrified the African fugitives that he "acquired the reputation of a *feiticeiro*."[37] This expedition was followed by an attempt to make peace between the Portuguese and the *quilombolas*.[38]

The peace, however, was temporary and quite illusory. The king's nephew, Zumbi, took up arms again, and the old war leader Domingos Jorge the Elder had to be summoned. With the help of his Paulistas, Indians, and local troops—and even, it was said, with six pieces of artillery—he waged a long, hard struggle, which ended in the almost total destruction of all the *quilombos* and the death of Zumbi.[39] The lands were shared out among the victors; the blacks who had escaped massacre returned to slavery. But Palmares was not completely dead. In 1703 a Negro named Camuango, who had escaped slaughter, established another small *quilombo* there, but it too was destroyed.[40] The rest of the Palmares survivors joined up with other *quilombolas* at Cumbé in Paraíba,[41] and these settlements were not wiped out until 1735.[42]

Palmares poses a whole series of problems. First, was it ethnically mixed or racially homogeneous? Ayres do Casal states that it was founded by forty Guinea Negroes.[43] This may be true of the first Palmares, founded during the Dutch occupation, but even so it does not follow that the early *quilombolas* were all West African blacks, because, as I have pointed out, the name "Guinea" was applied to the whole Atlantic coast of Africa. In any case, how significant was this tiny nucleus in a population numbering 11,000? In fact, the brave defenders of the Negro Troy seem to have been predominantly Bantu. The old woman named Madeleine who was sent to Palmares on an official mission was an Angola. A prisoner named Casper was the leader of the Angola. The name of one of the king's brothers, Bengola, probably indicates his ethnic origin and should read Bengala. Zumbi, the name of the last king of the *quilomba*, is a Bunda name for the god of light. The titles of the king's brothers, Gana Iomba and Gana Zona, come from the same language and are certainly corruptions of the word *ngana*, meaning "lord," while the names Zona and Iomba are probably connected with the word *mona*, which in Bunda means "brother," in Ambunda "son." The name Ganga is also a corruption of *nganga*, or "high priest." Nina Rodrigues connects the name Zumba with the word *cosumba*, whose prefix shows its Bantu origin.[44] This argument is supported by the fact that the Guinea Africans had a well-established mythology which was much more resistant to Christianity than was the vague animism of the Bantu. The existence of a church with statues of the saints therefore tends to confirm that Palmares was a Bantu *quilombo*. And finally a document recently found in the Lisbon archives states that the *quilombolas* referred to their cities as "Angola Janga" (little Angola).[45] Be that as it may, these Bantu obviously came from a wide diversity of nations, as is shown by the fact that the inhabitants of Palmares addressed one another as "Malungo." In one of his sermons Padre Vieira says: "The sense of kinship is so innate and spontaneous in the Negroes that they call everybody of the same color a relative and anybody who came over in the same ship a *malungo*, or comrade."[46] As we know, the cargo of a slave ship usually included captives from a wide variety of tribes. The fact that the people of Palmares called one another "Malungo" shows that they were not a tribe but a mixed group, now huddled together on a motionless ship of mountains and rocks, tossed on the green waves of a new ocean— the forest.[47]

The second problem posed by Palmares is that of social organization and its implications. Physically it consisted of a series of fairly widely separated fortified villages. But we know that, between these palisade-encircled towns, scattered settlements of small huts surrounded by plantations existed in clearings in the forest. These rustic huts were built of branches and thatched with *capim* grass.[48] This is all we know. There are several possible explanations for this ecological system. One family may have had two different types of house: what might be called a town house, where it lived the year round; and a country house, where it stayed at harvest or planting time. The king is said to have had a palace and a country house. Barleus's statement that the *quilombolos* danced until midnight in rural huts, making a lot of noise, does not necessarily mean that these houses were inhabited continuously. The dances may have been agrarian festivals celebrating the beginning and end of the harvest. It is also possible that the function of the towns was primarily political and military and that the social stratification was reflected in their physical layout. There was the royal capital, with its priests and magistrates and its council chamber, which might simply have been the men's communal dwelling house. There was Sucupita, where the king's brother lived, which was the military headquarters where soldiers were trained to defend the confederation. There were the *quilombolas'* local government centers, the seats of their civic authorities. Finally there was the scattered rural population, which spent all its time working its little gardens and withdrew to the towns only when attacked by the whites.

We know something about the clothing of these fugitives as well as their habitat. When Palmares sent an embassy to the governor, the Portuguese were so astonished by the Negroes' appearance that they left a detailed description of it. These "barbarians" were naked except for the genital area. Some of them had braided beards; others wore false beards or mustaches; still others were clean-shaven. We do not know whether these distinctions represented tribal survivals, differences of rank or social position, or possibly ethnic survivals whose function had changed and which had become symbols of social stratification. One thing is certain: social status was reflected in dress. We know that the chiefs wore costumes made of cloth stolen or bought from the Portuguese. They were the only ones who wore clothes, and it seems that they were also the only ones who had guns; the other Negroes were armed with bows and arrows, daggers, or machetes.[49]

The *quilombo* economy was complex. The men hunted and fished. Laert's expedition found abandoned traps in the forest, and Rocha Pitta mentions a lake full of fish near one of the *quilombos*. They practiced agriculture on a semiindividualist, semicollective basis. Rural property was family owned, but the whole village seems to have shared the work of cultivation. Barleus tells us that the land was worked twice a year, at planting and cultivating time, then again when the corn was harvested. The collective nature of the system is indicated by the fact that these two periods of agricultural work were accompanied by ceremonies and followed by a two-week holiday during which the inhabitants devoted themselves to pleasure or—as seems more probable to me—to religious celebrations, perhaps even to agrarian sacrifices such as those that survive today among the African Bantu. Thus the economy of Palmares was radically different from the economy of the white colonists. On the one hand we have the small family property, the field worked by the household and its slaves (for, as we shall see, the slaves did not abolish slavery); and on the other the great latifundium. On the one hand an economy still very close to that of the native land, observing its religious rhythm; on the other an economy based on monoculture, geared to commerce and profit, and completely secular, despite the fact that the chaplain always inaugurated the crushing of the sugar cane by saying a solemn mass and blessing the workers. We may note that the people of Palmares had no domestic animals.[50]

The economy was not however, purely agricultural. There were many artisans in the towns, although we do not know how many or the kind of work they were engaged in. The whites of course were interested only in the type of work that was potentially most dangerous to them: the manufacture of arms.

The *quilombolas* also did some trading. The large number of punitive expeditions sent out against them and the charges of assault, rape, and abduction submitted to the governor by their white neighbors should not lead us to forget that there were also long intervals of peace, when the Negroes traded amicably with the colonists, bartering field or forest produce for arms, gunpowder, and bullets, European clothes or cloth for their chief, and even, according to Rocha Pitta, who knew some of the original survivors, for money. We do not know whether this last statement is true and, if so, what they did with the money, whether they used it to buy jewelry or regarded it as having a magical value, or whether it was subsequently used for other purchases. In any case, like all primitive economies, that of Palmares was primarily a barter system, and the whites seem usually to have sought out the black *quilombolas* rather than vice versa. Barleus tells us that one of the Dutch expeditions was planned by a certain Bartholomeu Lintz who had lived in the *quilombo* for several days and returned with useful information. Although Barleus does not say so, it is obvious that Lintz could have stayed in Palmares only as a trader. Rocha Pitta gives us more details. The *quilombolas* and *fazendeiros* were in some kind of secret communication, and the *fazendeiros* would be given safe-conducts in the form of special signs or drawings that would permit their slaves to go up to Palmares without being molested or taken prisoner.[51]

But what impressed the colonists most deeply was the political organization of the *quilombo*. As I have already mentioned, the separate settlements formed a kind of federation under the authority of a king who ruled the whole "country" with the aid of powerful officials, often his own relatives, each of whom was in charge of one of the villages. The king was elected.

> As their king or prince, whom they called Zumbi (a name which in their language means "devil"), they elected one of their bravest and most intelligent men. Although his authority was elective, it was his for life. Any Negro, mulatto, or mestizo of superior judgment, value or experience was eligible. We have not been told and we do not know whether they were divided into parties . . . nor whether, in the course of the sixty years during which they lived independently, governing themselves, they killed one [king] in order to enthrone another.[52] They obeyed them all with alacrity and paid homage to the new king immediately after his election, which was carried out in the following way. Those voting for one man would stand in one place, while those who supported others stood apart. The office finally fell to the one chosen by the greatest number, so that the election was never the occasion for the slightest dispute.

The king was attended by magistrates responsible for the administration of the community, and there was a council house in the capital where communal affairs were discussed. Much has been written on the significance of this political regime. Because its leader was elected and the highest offices were open to everyone, Palmares has been described as a Negro republic and compared to Haiti. The *quilombo* has been seen as the first gesture of Brazilian independence against the colonial regime. Others, including the Dutch, thought that the Negroes merely copied the Portuguese system, no doubt confusing the men's house, which they called the "Big Council," with the municipal councils responsible for local government in the colony. Neither of the two views is correct. Nina Rodrigues comes much closer to the truth when he compares this form of kingship to African forms, though he weakens his argument by confining it to the royal rulers of runaway slaves. The truth is that to understand Palmares we need to examine not only the monarchic rulers of the insurrectionaries but also the social condition of the African Negroes, who were familiar with dynastic and elective systems and with the discussion of tribal affairs by adults or elders. More than anything else Palmares represents a return to the African tradition.

Another thing that has deeply impressed white historians is that the *quilombo* was not just a band of runaways, an amorphous chaos of individuals united in common protest against slavery, but a properly policed state:

> Homicide, adultery, and rape were punished by death, because things that could be perpetrated against the whites, with whom they claimed to be at war, might not be done to their own people. Slaves who came voluntarily to join them were given their freedom, but those they took by force remained prisoners and could be sold. Again, all those who had joined them voluntarily but decided to return to the hands of the whites were punished by death. However, slaves who had been captured by force were not punished by death if they deserted. All these laws were not written down but were preserved in memory and tradition, transmitted from father to son, so that, if the people were attacked and conquered, they would be inscribed in the memory of the second- and third-generation descendants of the earliest fugitives.[53]

Here again, deep in the Brazilian *sertão*, Palmares was simply observing the tribal laws of far-off Africa. These penalties for homicide, rape, and adultery are characteristic features of the moral code or the mores of the ancient communities from which these blacks had been uprooted. The retention of slavery by Negroes who had escaped from that very system is extremely significant when viewed as a "return to Africa."

About their matrimonial laws we know less. Certainly the traditional tribal system must have been disrupted, not so much by the mixing of tribes as by the shortage of women, who were less likely to run away. They were in fact so scarce that the *quilombolas* were forced to steal neighboring women. They did this with no regard for skin color, taking mulattoes and even white women.[54] We know, however, that polygamy existed, at least among the chiefs. Gangamusa, chief of the Angola nation, was married to two of the king's daughters, and the king himself had three wives.[55]

We are now in a position to define Palmares. It was not an original, "rational" creation of runaway Negroes intent upon establishing a republican constitution or an elective monarchy, upon promulgating laws and setting up law enforcement authorities of a totally new kind, but rather a phenomenon of cultural resistance, of "tribal regression"—an effort by Africans to combat the disintegration of their ancient customs by reviving the old Bantu systems.[56] It was analogous to the re-creation of Africa in the heart of Dutch Guiana which still survives and which has been analyzed by M. J. and F. S. Herskovits, among others.[57] Yet by its very nature no reactionary movement can ever achieve a faithful re-creation of the past. One is always affected by what one is fighting against, especially when contact with the dominant foreign culture has been fairly protracted. When we take into account the influence of the external environment, so different from the original habitat yet still pervaded in some way by native values, it is understandable that Palmares should have incorporated some extrinsic elements and should show a certain measure of syncretism. Its agriculture may have been much like that of Africa, but what it produced was Indian corn and sugar cane. Most of the place-names may have been Bantu, apparently reflecting a desire to Africanize the country and transform its geography, but certain features of the landscape were called by their Indian names. The religion of Palmares must be studied as part of this phenomenon of cultural resistance and syncretism—to the extent that our limited knowledge of it allows.

According to the Dutch, this religion was a clumsy copy of Portuguese Catholicism. They speak of chapels, statues of the saints, and priests, all based on white models.[58] Francisco de Brito Freyre said that the Negroes retained the Catholicism of their former masters, "but in a ludicrous way, out of ignorance rather than bad will."[59] We have also noted that the king of Palmares prohibited fetishism in the *quilombo*. This involves some serious but excusable confusion. The Bantu, whose mythology was relatively poor, identified their spirits with the Catholic saints, and the statues found by their conquerors were simply images of the spirits they worshiped. If it is true that fetishism was prohibited, this might be explained as a reaction by the Bantu against the *orixás* of the earliest Guinea fugitives or by the priests' rivalry with the *feiticeiros*. Rocha Pitta is therefore closer to the truth when he says that all the *quilombolas* retained of Catholicism was the sign of the Cross and a few garbled prayers, which they mixed with words and ceremonies taken from their native religions or simply invented.[60] Pitta's book, written so long ago, contains observations that prefigure discoveries made recently by specialists in cultural contact: the existence of syncretism, the retention of elements of the primitive culture, and the fact that this syncretism is not just an accumulation and jumble of juxtaposed elements but a symbiosis that produced new institutions.[61] This is probably what happened at Palmares.

What were the African elements in this symbiosis? We do not know, and we can only make an indirect guess. Barleus tells us that the neighboring white colonists were kept awake at night by noise from the huts of the runaway slaves and that the sound of stamping feet could be heard great distances away. These dances would last until midnight, and the Negroes would then sleep until nine or ten o'clock in the morning.[62] While the Bantu certainly have profane dances as well as religious ones, it is likely that some of this dancing was part of liturgical ceremonies. And since Barleus records this detail among others pertaining to the quilombolos' type of agricultural economy, we suggest that these ceremonies may well have been agrarian ones.

The religious character of the monarchy is much more evident. The recorded names designating the king and his brother and the commander of the armies are not personal but generic names or titles. And the titles are religious ones. Kanga, the king, is the Kimbunda nganga, the high priest; Zumbi is the supreme deity.

Clearly, resistance to the white man was as much religious as social.

The Other *Quilombos*

While Palmares was the most famous and certainly the biggest of the quilombos, it was not unique, and the history of Brazil, as well as its geography, offers plenty of evidence of the prevalence of collective flight and resistance to slavery and assimilation into the white culture. Many places still bear the name Quilombo in memory of the runaway slaves who settled there.[63] Many of the quilombos were built near inhabited places, but others were remote, deep in the forest. This brings up another phenomenon, which we shall study later: contact between the African and the Indian cultures, which inevitably had repercussions on the religion of both.

The first quilombo, situated in Bahia, dates back almost to the beginning of the slave trade—to 1575; it was destroyed by Luis Brito de Almeida.[64] A letter of 1597 from Padre Rodrigues states that "the colonists' major enemies are the insurrectionary Guinea Negroes, who live in the mountains, coming down to carry out their raids."[65] In 1607 a letter from the governor, Count da Ponte, informs the king of an uprising by Hausa Negroes, again in Bahia. In 1601 a quilombo cut the Bahia-Alagôas road at Itapicum.[66] In 1650 Captain Mancel Jourdan da Silva destroyed some quilombos near Rio de Janeiro after hard fighting.[67] In 1671 another quilombo is mentioned in the state of Alagoas.[68] In 1704 Dias da Costa was commissioned to "destroy the mocambos of Bahia, take the Negroes prisoner, and relieve the Maraca and Cucuriu Indians and the caboclos they had subdued." In 1707 Domingos Netto Pinheiro was ordered to reduce all the mocambos to be found in the Jacobina and Carinhanha mountains up to Rio São Francisco.[69] On the "River of Treachery" near São Paulo a *quilombo* existed from 1737 until at least 1787.[70] But the center of this type of resistance was Minas. This is not hard to explain. The discovery of gold and precious stones caused a shift of population. Slaves were diverted from agricultural work to hard labor in the mines. With the discovery of every new lode, every new nugget-bearing river, more Africans were brought in and immediately set to work in the new territories. They were harshly supervised to prevent theft. Travelers visiting the ancient cities of Minas Gerais were surprised to find that the architectural center of every town was the prison, with its thick fortresslike walls—evidence of the brutal punishment accorded to runaway Negroes.[71]

Such repression aggravated hatred. The white population was beginning to live in continual fear of possible revolt by the blacks. They believed that these uprisings were organized from outside, by the runaway Negroes in the *quilombos*. In 1719 there was a rumor that the Negroes were plotting to massacre the whites while they were assembled at mass on Good Friday. It was said that the *quilombolas* of Rio das Mortes had already elected the king, princes, and chief officials of the new state. The governor was skeptical at first but finally took precautions. Lieutenant General João Ferreira Tavares had the kings of the Mina and Angola nations arrested in Rio das Mortes, together with all the alleged officers-elect of the black republic. In 1756 the whites became alarmed again, and rumors were rife of a mutiny that would follow the same scenario. The Negroes were supposed to be going to wait until the whites were at mass on Maundy Thursday and then fall upon them, massacring the white and mulatto men but sparing the women. An officer is said to have discovered the plot, and the Africans, realizing they were lost, escaped to the forest.[72] While we have no grounds for assuming that such conspiracies actually occurred,[73] the rumors certainly reflect the atmosphere of terror that pervaded the country.

The whole area around Campo Grande and São Francisco was infested with fugitive Negroes who could not be eradicated. In 1741 João Ferreira had organized an expedition against them, but they had managed to escape and join up again and were now murdering prospectors on their way to Goiás in search of gold. In 1746, in another, more successful expedition, 120 Negroes were captured and their land was given to white pioneers. But in 1752, in an attack on Padre Marcos's expedition, 42 men, 19 of whom were slaves, were massacred, showing that the danger had not passed.[74]

The Minas *quilombos* were well organized and were certainly the most important after Palmares. They are said to have had a total population of 20,000 Negroes, plus the mulattoes, criminals, and brigands who had joined them. This population came from all over Brazil, including São

Paulo and Bahia, and was distributed among numerous villages, four of which, Ambrosio, Zundu, Gareca, and Calaboca, all in the neighborhood of Sapucaia, were large and fortified. Each of them had its king, officers, and ministers, who, it appears, ruled their subjects with blood-thirsty despotism. Their attitude toward the whites was ambivalent. They distrusted them, maintained an espionage service, and stationed guards along the roads and even in the white villages. On the other hand they lived by trading, and their secret agents bartered gold, skins, and farm produce for arms or food. A major expedition had to be sent out against them, commanded by Captain Bartholomeu Bueno de Prado, who returned bearing 3,000 pairs of ears as trophies.[75]

The *quilombos* refused to die out. In 1769, again in Minas, more *quilombos* were destroyed at Sabambaia,[76] followed in 1770 by the one at Carlotta in Mato Grosso. In 1772 fugitive Negroes allied with Indians to attack the city of San José do Maranhão.[77] In 1778 two *quilombos* on the banks of the Tietê in the state of São Paulo, composed of pagan Negroes between the ages of thirty and sixty, were wiped out.[78] Another coalition of Negroes and Indians is reported at Piolho in Mato Grosso in 1795. A large number of slaves had taken refuge there twenty-five years earlier and had raided the local Cabixé Indians to steal their women. These Indian-Negro unions had produced mestizos known as *caborés*. Francisco Pedro de Mello's expedition found six descendants of the former slaves serving as the chiefs, priests, and medicine men of the settlement, which, apart from these old Negroes, consisted of *caborés* and Indians. They lived by fishing and hunting, grew corn, black and broad beans, manioc, sweet potatoes, pineapples, tobacco, cotton, and bananas. They kept chickens and manufactured cotton clothing. At São Vicente (the first *quilombo* to be captured), with its six Negroes, eight Indian men, nineteen Indian women, and ten male and eleven female *caborés*, it was observed that the Indians and *caborés* were familiar with Christian doctrine and with the Portuguese language, which they had learned from the former slaves. A large *quilombo* was discovered close by, divided into two parts, about fifty paces apart, one having ten, the other eleven houses. The *quilombolas* had abandoned it to build a new settlement deeper in the bush, and this one was again divided into two sections, this time three leagues apart. One, with fourteen Negroes and five slaves, was commanded by a Negro named Antonio Brandão; the other, with thirteen Negro men and seven Negro women, by the former slave Joaquim Felix. This division into two parts may represent adoption of the dualistic division of the exogamous Indian clans.[79]

Quilombos were still being founded in the nineteenth century. In 1810 one was discovered at Linhares in the state of São Paulo.[80] About 1820 J. E. Pohl came upon one in Minas established by fugitives from the state of São Paulo. "They also had among them a minister to celebrate religious services," he notes.[81] In 1828 a *quilombo* still existed just outside Recife, at Cahuca. It was governed by a chief named Malunguinho and was surrounded by ditches and palisades, from behind which raids were launched. Apparently these *quilombolas* lived under a communal system, and this seems again to suggest a return to African traditions.[82] In 1829 some Indians were commissioned to destroy another *quilombo* at Corcovado near Rio.[83] In 1855 the Maravilha *quilombo* in Amazonas was destroyed.[84] And as late as 1866 Pará Negroes were still taking refuge in the Indian villages of French Guiana.[85]

Obviously the sociological documentation available for a study of the *quilombos* is not very rich. At the time, people were naturally less interested in the customs and internal organization of these fugitive-Negro hideaways than in taking military measures to destroy them. But it seems that, as was the case with Palmares, most of the *quilombos* exemplified tribal regression and the wish to escape to Africa. The fact that religion played a role in this cultural resistance is proved by the fact that all the inhabitants of the Tietê River *quilombo* were "pagans." Early in the nineteenth century the English explorer Richard F. Burton discovered African survivals such as the use of certain charms and of the poison stramonium among the *quilomboleiros* in the Diamantina area.[86] But as white civilization pushed inland from the coast, the fugitive Negroes came increasingly into contact with the Indians who had been driven back. It has often been said that the Africans and Amerindians were enemies, and it is perfectly true that the two races were often set against each other. But a shared hatred of the white masters sometimes led them to make common cause. Every time this happened, we find that it was a Negro who became the leader of the new community, either by enslaving the Indians, as happened at Bahia in 1704, or by virtue of his military or religious authority, as was the case at Mato Grosso in 1795. "Many a mulatto fleeing slavery or deserting from military service was proclaimed captive by the Indian tribe with which he sought refuge," wrote d'Assier in 1867.[87]

An even more curious fact is that in two cases the chosen leader was a black woman. The only plausible reason for this is a religious one: women were supposed to have special magical qualities because they were more susceptible to mystical ecstasy than men.

In this way a religious syncretism must have emerged whose dominant element stemmed from the African civilization. This civilization provided liturgy and mythology for the Negro priest and techniques of magic healing for the Negro medicine man. But what is even more curious is that this syncretism expanded to include features of white culture and that the Negro came to serve as an agent for the diffusion of Catholicism among the Indians—though it was probably a somewhat modified and corrupt Catholicism. The Indian too contributed his quota to this curious civilization born in the depths of the Brazilian *sertão*. The black tribal organization had been totally destroyed by the regime of slavery, surviving only in men's minds as a memory of ancient African divine monarchies. The Amerindians, on the contrary, had retained their ancient social structure. In my opinion it can be inferred from the documents I have cited that the *quilombos* created a social system which combined the dualist organization of the Indian tribe (the two sections or camps in the Mato Grosso *quilombos*) with the African tribal federation under the authority of a monarch-priest.

It is true that all this lies far back in the past. But the past did not die away without leaving traces, some of which still survive. We cannot know how far the fugitive slaves penetrated nor how widely their cultures were diffused. Martius believes that there were very few Amerindian tribes that had no contact with the Africans.[88] Roquette Pinto traces the origin of Nambikuara agriculture to the *caboré quilombos*.[89] Survivals of these *mocambos* of Negro fugitives have been found as far away as Alcobaça, near the Trombetas River in Amazonas. Here there was a *quilombo* directed by a Negro woman named Filippa Paria Aranha, who was so powerful that the Portuguese had to make an alliance with her instead of fighting her, and whose descendants became guides for travelers wanting to shoot the rapids of the Tocantins River.[90] When the Portuguese arrived at Passanha in the state of Minas, the country was populated with Malali Indians, among whom fugitive Negroes were living. Here again the Indians had accepted a black woman as their leader.[91] When Saint-Hilaire visited the Malali in 1817, they seemed to him more mulatto than Indian in physique, and their captain told him that his grandmother was a Negro.[92]

Saint-Hilaire visited the Minas Caribocas in 1819, when they were already facing extinction, being reduced to eighteen villages, and found that mulattoes and Creole Negroes were joining them and marrying Indian women in order to share the privileged position enjoyed by the Brazilian Amerindians. He found there a curious syncretism of beliefs in which Catholicism was restricted to an indirect role, since no priest was willing to enter the village. Their language was Tupí; God was worshiped under the name of Nhandinhan.[93] In other places the Amerindian religion was apparently dominant—in the village of Haut-des-Bois in Minas, for instance, where the Mancuni women married Negroes. During violent windstorms Saint-Hilaire observed women smoking outside their houses to drive away the hurricane. All this was done, of course, behind the official façade of Christianity.[94]

Because of the nature of the country, where wild wooded mountains were to be found right outside the big cities, small *quilombos* of pure Negroes could exist without interfering with the Indians. This was the case with the Marcel Congo settlement in the forest near Petropolis in Santa Catarina which was destroyed by Caxias in 1839.[95] We know little about the role played here by religion, but we can guess at it from the ethnic mixture suggested by the names of some of its members: Manuel Congo, Justino Benguela, Antonio Nagô, Canuto Maçambique, Afonse Angola, Miguel Crioulo, and Maria Crioula. The common denominator of all these diverse races could only be a Catholicism more or less colored by African fetishism.

This *quilombo* was involved in a whole series of murders, assassinations, individual or collective escapes, and revolts in which religion was a constant factor, along with physical or moral suffering. Freemasonry may even have incited people of color to plan a general insurrection in 1847, some time after the destruction of the earlier *quilombo* by Caxias, since this revolt was planned by a secret society divided into cells consisting of five people unknown to each other, each cell being linked by its captain to the leader of the insurrection, Estevão Pimentel, a free mulatto blacksmith. But the blacks were still unfamiliar with Masonic traditions and placed more reliance on the supernatural intervention of their protectress, a Negro woman named Klbanda, than on political action. It was this confident, semipagan Catholicism that proved their undoing and was responsible for the failure of the conspiracy. Although this attempted revolt came after the destruction of the *quilombo*, it sheds light on it and justifies the hypothesis that the religious element that sustained the faith of these humble people was not so much their ancestral fetishism as popular Christianity.

But these are later phenomena from the age of the empire. So far as the colonial period goes, I feel confident in saying that the *quilombos* were not merely a protest against the regime of slavery. They also represent the resistance of a civilization unwilling to die, a struggle in which African religion therefore necessarily played a major role. This view is confirmed by the fact that the *quilombos* changed as Negro tradition modified them.

Just as Charlemagne's deeds and prowess were celebrated in the *chansons de geste*, Palmares became the subject of a popular drama, interspersed with songs and dances, which survived in the black folklore of Alagoas until the early twentieth century. These *quilombos* of common colored folk always bore the stamp of racial protest:

> Don't worry, Negro!
> The white man won't come here.
> The devil will make off with him
> If he ever should appear.[96]

Sociologists studying the contact of heterogeneous civilizations are obliged to classify phenomena in conceptual frameworks to facilitate interpretation and to permit the phenomena of "counteracculturation" to be distinguished from those of syncretism. The latter differ from the former in that they represent accommodation to the dominant civilization. In fact these concepts operate only at a certain level of abstraction.

Syncretism is always more or less counteracculturative and acculturation is more or less syncretic.

Marronage represented a nostalgia for Africa rather than an attempt to re-create it (which in Brazil meant specifically to re-create the great kingdoms of Bantu Africa). The geographic, demographic, and political conditions were quite different, and concessions had to be made to them. Above all, *marronage* cannot be separated from the total social context in which it occurred: the context of the struggle between an exploited group and the ruling class. The *quilombo* or the *mocambo* was always on the verge of war, and one can fight only by adapting to the adversary. War, just as much as peaceful transactions, is one of the processes by which civilizations interpenetrate. It is true that the *quilombos* were set up by pure Africans, who had not had time to forget the realities of their own country, and not by Creole Negroes. This does not mean, however, that the Africans had not been marked by slavery and by catechization, perfunctory as it may have been: The Palmares sanctuary was the abode of Catholic saints. The runaway Negro brought the rudiments of Catholicism to the Indians of Mato Grosso living in places still untouched by Christian missions.

All, or almost all, of the African religious phenomena of the colonial era must be viewed in the light of this climate of cultural resistance. But resistance is not a normal phenomenon. It produces distortions, creates pathological states, rigidifies minds as well as institutions. A proposed Marxist interpretation of *marronage* is, in my opinion, unacceptable. *Marronage* did not represent first and foremost economic resistance to a specific system of labor but generalized resistance by the African civilization as a whole. The hardships of slavery merely intensified nostalgia for that civilization. The proof is that here religion is not divorced from the rest of social life, as it is today, but is closely intertwined with it, just as it was in the ancestral country. However, the Marxist concept of class struggle does offer the best key to the nature of *marronage*, provided the definition of class takes into account its full complexity—its characteristic culture as well as its production system. Seen in this perspective, *marronage* represents the first phase of the struggle: the withdrawal to the Aventine Hill. A second phase followed: armed revolution. The *quilombos* most clearly defined the seventeenth- and eighteenth-century modes of resistance; armed revolt was the typical form of the nineteenth century.

4

The Religious Element in Racial Conflict

We have seen the part played by religion in insurrections by slaves against the regime of slavery. But all men of color were not slaves. Gradually, chiefly in the cities, there emerged a lower class of manumitted Negroes, mulatto artisans, members of the militia and of the Henriques regiments, etc., which, although it constituted the lowest stratum of the free population, was nonetheless a step above the slaves on the social ladder.

This urban population was a marginal one. Being engaged in free labor, it had certain things in common with the whites. On the other hand its color excluded it from society in any real sense of the word. Its racial position therefore caused it great suffering, and the smallest incident was apt to release all its repressed resentment over silently borne injustices, all its pent-up anger, in outbursts of chaotic revolt. One might think at first glance that in this new type of insurrection, which we are about to examine, religion would not play a major role. The transition from slavery to urban working class was, after all, a step up, and in a white-dominated society upward movement inevitably meant assimilation; it meant relinquishing, short of one's color, everything one's ancestors had been able to bring with them from "barbarian" Africa. But did religion really play no part at all in these insurrections?

The first of them—known sometimes as the "tailors' conspiracy," after the trade of some of the participants (notably its leader), and sometimes as the "*bousio* conspiracy" because its badge was an African *bousio* shell hung on a watch chain—broke out in 1798.[1] The conspirators were all

common people—tailors, carpenters, bricklayers, laborers—mulattoes, free
Negroes, or even slaves. Against this obscure background the figures
of a notary, a rural Latin teacher, a lieutenant of artillery, and possibly a
priest emerge indistinctly, though these individuals were all released for
lack of evidence. These colored conspirators were not uneducated. Of the
nine slaves arrested, only one was illiterate. The mulattoes and free Negroes all could read; they had been introduced to the ideas of the French
Revolution by imprisoned French officers with furlough privileges whom
they met at fraternal gatherings. A mestizo slave named Luiz Pires possessed a hand-copied book "for disillusioning people on the subject of
religion"—no doubt the translation of a work by some eighteenth-century
philosopher.

Despite the role of people of color in this insurrection, it was based on
class, not race. It was a social revolt by the disinherited against the existing order. The sequestration orders show that the participants owned nothing but old furniture, worn clothes, and the tools of their trade. The
highest sum realized from the liquidation of individual property was a
paltry thirty-six milreis. The only man with any cash possessed a total of
eight milreis. Some of the conspirators were even living on public charity.
What they wanted was a regime of liberty and equality for all. "Take
heart, people of Bahia," read the proclamation they posted in the squares
and the churches. "The day of our liberty is at hand, the time when we
shall all be brothers and all equal."

But since the class of poor artisans consisted preponderantly of colored
people, racial grievances were inseparable from social ones. So we may
well ask whether religion was not, after all, implicated in this protest.

When one reads the record of the trial that brought the conspiracy to an
end, one is struck by the extremely confused thinking of the conspirators
themselves. Some of them were atheists, or at least anticlericals who had
drunk at the source of Enlightenment philosophy and to some extent digested what they had drunk. Others, like Manuel Faustino dos Santos
Lyra, whose papers included a considerable collection of prayers, in addition to liberal publications, were deeply religious. Nevertheless they all
seem to have supported the idea of divorcing the church of Brazil from the
church of Rome and founding an independent national church to be called
"Amerina." Its distinctive feature was to be its openness to people of color
as well as whites. To be sure, the dark-skinned people had their Brotherhoods of the Rosary and of Saint Benedict, but this segregation by color
within Catholicism offended the egalitarian conscience of the conspirators.
A pamphlet found in Luiz Gonzaga das Virgens's house complained that
mulattoes and Negroes "are not admitted to the corporations of the public
church" but had to be content with the right "to form separate chapters
established with their own money and at great effort," and that these
chapters were not recognized as being "of the same essence" as the brother-

hoods of the Holy Sacrament or the secondary or tertiary orders of the Franciscans, Dominicans, Benedictines, and Carmelites.[2] Clearly the religious protest was not, strictly speaking, religious; it was one of the forms assumed by racial protest. This revolution rested on a social and economic base, not a mystical one. It did not even succeed in giving people of color an awareness of belonging to any particular category or any consciousness of race.

The tailors' conspiracy failed. But racial protest had passed from the level of the *quilombo* to that of political insurrection, where it would remain. Twenty years later it resurfaced in the unrest that began in Pernambuco in 1817 and lasted until 1824. This movement promulgated the "Confederation of the Equator," Brazil's first major assertion of independence from the absolutist imperial regime.

The revolution of 1817 was political, not social. (Indeed, it proclaimed the inviolability of private property, thus reassuring the slaveowners.) It was a revolution of Brazilian-born whites against "the Portuguese." Nevertheless a few colored men of liberal tendencies played leading roles in it.[3] They included the mestizo Pedro da Silva Pedroso, who was exiled to Portugal. He later returned, his ideas unchanged, to collaborate with some whites in organizing the party of "pure liberals" that instigated the revolt of 1823.[4] Being very popular with the common people and the colored militia, Pedroso attracted whole battalions of mulattoes and Negroes to the movement. A popular junta was set up, but it soon became apparent that the liberals were unwilling to turn the political struggle into a racial one. The color line between white and black still existed, even when they were united in the same insurrection. The white revolutionaries tried to get rid of Pedroso by relieving him of the command of all the armed troops, but his popularity was so great that he won out, and it was the junta that had to resign, not Pedroso. Racial protest then had free rein.

Pedroso, it is said, liked to surround himself at table with Negroes and mulattoes. Holding a Negro woman in a tight embrace, he would say: "I've always liked this color. This is my race."[5] The colored masses, drunk and seminaked, roamed the half-empty cities—for the whites had fled or taken refuge in their homes—singing:

> The sailors and the whitewashed
> Can all go to hell.
> Only blacks and mulattoes
> Are welcome here to dwell.[6]

However, this period of exaltation, known as the "government of the *matutos*," was shortlived. The regular army put down the rebellion. Toward the end, the battalions of Negroes and free mulattoes abandoned it, and Pedroso had to give himself up to captivity.

When the structure of these revolts is carefully examined, they prove, despite the participation of free Negroes, to be mulatto rather than Negro uprisings, attributable more to the marginal position of the mestizo, caught between two cultures and rejected by whites and slaves alike, than to any clearly defined racial sentiment. This is confirmed by the fact that the regular army was assisted in putting down the revolutionaries by the sugar plantation owners, with troops consisting of their own farmers, cattlemen, and also slaves.[7] It is confirmed again by the uprising that broke out a year later, in 1824, again in Recife. Feelings had risen too high for calm to be restored immediately. As soon as news of the Negro revolt in Haiti reached Brazil, the mulatto regiment (as usual, the mulattoes), commanded by Emiliane Mandurucci, revolted. Its battle hymn went:

> I want to emulate Christovão
> The immortal Haitian hero!
> O my sovereign people,
> You emulate his compatriots![8]

This time, however, the revolt did not spread. In fact it degenerated into banditry. Recife was sacked, and the Negroes of the Henriques regiment had to restore order in the city.

As the nineteenth century progressed, the revolts assumed a more specifically social character. The reason for this is that after the imperial regime legalized party struggles, everyone had a chance to be heard except the poor and the downtrodden. Since the masses consisted predominantly of people of color, racial protest inevitably became involved in social protest. This is already evident in the *Cabanada*, a revolt of the "landless people" of Ceará against the white landowners. While this revolt does not concern us here, since the insurrectionaries were chiefly Indian, the *Balaiada* of 1838, in which Africans predominated, deserves some attention.[9]

At that time there were two parties in Maranhão, conservative and liberal. The latter party was named after a Brazilian bird, the *bemtevi*. For help against its adversaries, this party called upon a troop of colored bandits which was ravaging the *sertão*. The troop had been organized by Raimundo Gomes, a Negro nicknamed Blackface, who, having run afoul of the law, had fled to the bush, where other fugitives of the same type had joined him. Through his racial demands and by calling upon slaves to throw off their yokes and rise against their masters, Gomes had succeeded in expanding his forces considerably and had gradually turned his band of looters into an army bent on social reform. Among the men who joined him was a Negro nicknamed O Balaio ("The Basket") because he wove baskets. He is said to have offered the hospitality of his shanty to the officer charged with capturing the bandits and to have been rewarded by having his two daughters raped. Through his cruelty and his exploits O

Balaio quickly became the true leader of this army, which, besides Negroes, comprised mulattoes such as Redhead, *caboclos* such as Coqui, and
even whites, and which finally numbered 6,000 men.

The *Bemtevis* summoned O Balaio to Caxias to get rid of their adversaries. But when O Balaio's army accepted, it was not for the sake of
participating in a white quarrel but rather to take advantage of two opportunities: the chance offered to them as bandits to sack a town and the
chance offered to them as colored men to revenge themselves on the white
man. The chief magistrate of Caxias defended his city, but it was finally
taken and pillaged. What interests us here, however, is not the element of
banditry (although it was an essential element) but the racial grievances
that found an outlet in this revolt. In every city he occupied, O Balaio
would take a white woman and, when he tired of her, would call in a priest
and marry her off to one of his Negroes. Scenes of savagery occurred
which are conceivable only as outbursts of racial anger long nursed in
secret. A man's belly was split open and a *"petit cochon de lait"* sewn up
inside it. (Handelmann gives the real reason for this outburst of racial
anger when he tells us that the *Balaiada* was precipitated when a law
modifying the prerogatives of certain legal authorities provoked rumors all
over the *sertão* that the whites intended to reenslave all the people of color
who had gained their freedom.) Banditry finally became more important
to this once ill-treated Negro than hatred. The whites escaped with their
lives by offering him a high ransom. If the racial element had been the
preponderant one, O Balaio would not have forgotten the existence, near
the coast, between the Tutuoi and Pria rivers, of a *quilombo* of 3,000
Negroes on the Tocangura *fazenda*, whose ruler, Cosme, called himself the
Emperor of Brazil. But O Balaio never once thought of joining forces with
Cosme. The majority of slaves in the province remained loyal to their
masters and quietly went about their work.[10]

Glancing backward, we see that in the course of these political and
economic struggles a great change had occurred. The revolutionaries were
being recruited from ever lower social levels. At first they were drawn from
the white ruling class, then from the mulattoes and free artisans, then from
the militia, and finally from the illiterate masses. The last uprisings in
which people of color participated were of this fourth type. One was the
Praiero revolt of 1848, the object of which was to drive out the Portuguese
and which actually did result in the massacre of a certain number of them.
Preparations for this revolt included a press campaign organized by a
mulatto named Figueiredo (a socialist follower of Fourier), who advo-
cated the breaking up of the latifundia and the redistribution of the
land.[11] Another was the revolt of the *Guabirus* (1848), which also was
directed against European immigrants. It was indeed true that wherever
the white immigrant appeared he finally supplanted the colored (mulatto

or free Negro) artisan, who had previously earned a comfortable living. The revolt of the *Guabirus* was a struggle of starving mestizos or Negroes against the white "rats" who were taking the food from their mouths.[12]

A less well known uprising in Minas in 1820 is unusual in that it was a legal insurrection. When Portugal gave itself a democratic constitution,

> the Negro gold-panners of Guaraçaba [Guaraciaba], Santa Rita, Canta Galo and Saragua [Sabara?], aided by a very rich *fazendeiro* (also black), assembled at Fanado and proclaimed the validity of this constitution up and down the banks of the Abaete at Tapuias and Araguaia, where they joined the wild hordes of warriors who live on those tributaries. However there was a fierce fight between the Negroes of the Santa Barbara settlement and the inhabitants of Paraibuna, where the blacks are civilized. The black *fazendeiro* Argoins assembled an army of 21,000 Negroes, who were joined by two cavalry regiments. They mercilessly killed blacks who would not join the movement, and they made themselves flags and badges. A proclamation was issued to the people: "A constitution has been promulgated in Portugal making us equal to the whites. We swear obedience to this same constitution here in Brazil. . . . Death to the oppressors! Downtrodden blacks, revolt against your slavery! You are already free. Shed your last drop of blood fighting gloriously for the constitution established by our brothers in Portugal!"

Here we see the same desire for equality that had been demonstrated in Recife and Bahia. But it was quickly suppressed. The slaveowners—and even friars and bishops—took up arms and annihilated the movement in a blood bath.[13]

The religious or cultural factor that played such an important role in the founding of the *quilombos* seems to be lacking in this new series of revolts, in which the economic element was more important than the mystical one and in which racial grievances were inseparable from social ones. There were, however, other revolts, instigated by slaves rather than mulattoes or free Negroes, in which fugitives and *quilombolas* were only incidentally involved. In this type of insurrection, which we shall now review, the religious factor again played a major role.

These uprisings were usually instigated by Moslem Negroes. The first, which was suppressed even before it broke out, was scheduled for May 28, 1807. The Hausa had appointed a captain to command each section of the city of Bahia and a go-between to maintain contact with the slaves. Some people believed that their goal was to massacre the entire white population; others thought they intended to set the Nazareth Chapel on fire and take advantage of the ensuing panic to seize some ships and set sail for Africa. But they were betrayed, probably by a Negro belonging to another nation. Ten of the top captains were arrested before they could put their plans into action. Arms were found in the house of one of them, as were—and this is the point that interests us—"certain magical compounds they make use of, which they call *mandingas* and which, they believe, make them invulnerable and immune to all pain or injury."

In 1809 there was a second slave uprising. This time the Hausa allied themselves with the Nagô. Urban and rural slaves escaped into the bush, coming out to steal, set fires, and kill. They had to yield to the military forces dispatched against them, but the subsequent inquiry revealed the existence of a secret society of slaves known as *Ogboni* or *Ohogbo*. Now the *Ogboni* and the *Oro*, whose chiefs are the *Ologbo* (Ohogbo being one of their deities), are African secret societies which, as this evidence shows, were reestablished in Brazil by the descendants of Africans. Africanists have, it is true, stressed the political character of these societies, claiming that their principal object was to pursue and punish criminals. However, as Bascom rightly points out, this political activity was secondary (as is proved by the fact that the *Ogboni* had no voice in civic affairs), for the societies, which were comparable in nature to the fraternities of the gods, actually continued the cult of the Earth Goddess, a cult much older than the cult of the *orixás*, which had been superimposed on it. Clearly this is another case where the revolt of black against white had its focus in religion.[14]

On February 28, 1813, Hausa on the *fazendas* of Manuel Ignacio de Cunha Menezes and J. Vaz de Carvalho and on some of the neighboring estates set fire to their *senzalas* and marched on the village of Itapoan, where they joined the local Negroes and massacred the whites who tried to resist. They too, however, were finally decimated by the military. Again a mystical factor was involved, if not in the revolt itself, at any rate in the psychological preparations for it. At that time the Negroes enjoyed the right to assemble for religious ceremonies. Every Sunday they would meet in the main square of Bahia under the presidency of an elected chief and burn the whites in effigy. No one paid any attention. But if anyone had, he would have recognized a common rite of imitative magic, a sort of pre- paratory spell, a ritual celebrated before going into battle, performed to destroy the power of the patriarchal enemy in advance.

In 1826 there were two more attempts. An uprising in April of that year aborted, but its underlying religious factor is quite obvious from the arrest of a Negro king (unable to flee because of his wounds) who was crowned with a ribbon-trimmed cap, wore a green cloak with gold braid, and car- ried a red flag. His queen was killed outright.

In December a group of men decided to search out some runaway slaves who had set up a *quilombo* between the Cabula road and lower Urubu. In the bloody encounter a Negro woman was taken prisoner. She stated that the slaves had planned a general uprising in Bahia for Christmas Eve and she appeared to be telling the truth. In any case the crucial point here again is that the center of the *quilombo* and the headquarters of the conspiracy was a *casa de candomblé*, i.e. a temple of the fetishist Afro-Brazilian religion.

Two small localized revolts occurred in 1827 and 1828. This brings us to the most serious—or at any rate the best known—of the insurrections, which broke out in 1835. Although the insurrectionaries numbered 1,500 at most (including the black fetishists who later joined the Moslems), the revolt had been well planned. It was scheduled for the night of January 24, when the whole population of Bahia would be at church in Bomfim, leaving the city practically empty. The city had been divided among five groups who were to attack successively, throwing the soldiers into disarray. Having taken the cavalry barracks, the Negroes would proceed to the Bomfim church, where they would massacre their masters and, it was said, elect a mysterious queen of some kind.

On the evening of January 24, however, the plot was betrayed by a manumitted Nagô. Precautions were taken. The headquarters of the conspiracy, a house on the slope leading to the main square, was surrounded, but the Africans who were hiding there suddenly broke out, killing several police officers. Rioting began. There is no need to recount here all the details of that bloody night. At daybreak it was all over. The insurgents had been either killed or taken prisoner or had fled to the forest. From the nations to which the Negro prisoners belonged, it is clear that Moslems preponderated in the movement, but it also included fetishists. The breakdown was as follows: 165 Nagô, 3 Gruma, 6 Gêgê, 21 Hausa, 5 Bornu, 6 Tapa, 3 Cabinda, 4 Congo, 1 Cameroun, 1 Barba, 3 Mina, 2 Calabar, 1 Jabu, 1 Benin, 1 Mundu, plus 1 mulatto woman and 1 *cabra*, giving a total of 220 men and 14 women.

The 1835 insurrection was the last. Evidence found in the homes of the conspirators, as well as the trial and the interrogation of the prisoners, furnishes more details than are available in the case of earlier uprisings and enables us to determine whether these black revolts were of an economic and social character, like the *Cabanada* and the *Sabinada*, or are to be regarded as real religious wars.[15]

It was so obvious from the outset that religion played a major role in this last insurrection that the fact is mentioned in the report submitted by the chief of police to the president of the province in 1835:

> I can inform Your Excellency that the insurrection had been secretly contemplated for a long time and that the planning was better than might have been expected, in view of their brutality and ignorance. Nearly all of them can read and write in unknown characters, which look like Arabic as used by the Ussa and which seem to be combined with the Nagô language. . . . There were masters who gave lessons and who were responsible for organizing the insurrection, in which many manumitted Negroes were involved, and even some wealthy ones. A number of books were found, including

works of religious instruction. This instruction, they say, is derived from their various sects and is based chiefly on the Koran. . . . There is no doubt that religion played a part in the uprising. The chiefs persuaded these unfortunate people that certain slips of paper would prevent them from being killed. For this reason many of these slips were found on dead bodies and in the sumptuous clothing (probably belonging to the chief) seized during our house searches.

A study of the records of the trial led first Nina Rodrigues, then Étienne Brasil and Arthur Ramos, to support the view that the 1835 uprising was essentially religious in nature. In the first place, the majority of the leaders were priests or school teachers, and we know that Moslem teaching was religious in character. Pedro Luna was an *aluma* or *alufa*, i.e. a marabout, as was Luis, "Sanim, of the Tapa nation." Pacifico (whose Nagô name was Licutan) was called "The Sultan" by the conspirators. His prison guards reported that he received many visits, day and night, from Negro men and women "who would kneel before him very respectfully to receive his blessing." The affection in which he was held by all the Mussulmans of Bahia can be seen from their abortive attempt to storm the prison and set him free and from their efforts to raise the sum necessary to secure his release. The jailer also reports that a Nagô, talking to "the Sultan" through the bars of his cell, told him not to worry, because "when the fast was over they would come and set him free once and for all." In his analysis of this document Nina Rodrigues says: "The allusion to the insurrection and its connection with the propitiatory measure of the Mohammedan or Malê fast seems self-evident."

The *alufa* Dandara kept a school in the lower town. "He said that he was a professor in his own country and taught young men—but not for evil." In his house were found a warrior's tunic, a black rosary without a cross, and some *tabuas* in the Arabic language. Another school was kept by Manoel Calafate, Aprigio, and Conrado. There the property confiscated by the police included six little leather bags that served as amulets.

The conspirators would meet in the homes of these leaders to plan the revolt under the pretext of attending celebrations or dances. Moslem propaganda was the keynote of these preparations, as witnesses interrogated by the police all agreed. Gaspar da Silva Cunha stated that the papers shown to him were prayers, "and that he was pestered to learn them and to stop going to mass, as was his custom." Tia Marcelina stated that "the papers found are Mussulman prayers, written and made by the masters who taught them. These masters belong to the Hausa nation, because the Nagô do not know them, being called together by these Hausa and also by certain Tapa to learn them." Tia Marcelina also alleged that they hated her, claiming that she went to mass to worship the block of wood on the altar and that the statues had no religious value.

The conspirators spoke only Yoruba or Nagô among themselves and never used the Christian name they had been given, referring to themselves only by their real name: Ojô, Ová, Namosin, Sanim, Sule, Dada, Aliará, Edoum, etc.

The records have been preserved. They include plans for the revolt, written in Arabic. The slave Albino who deciphered them for the court testified that:

> Paper No. 2 was written more than a year and a half ago to protect the body from weapons of any kind. On it are prayers which, after being inscribed on the tablet, are washed off in water which you can drink to protect yourself from the danger of weapons. . . .
> The fifth, which was found covered with earth, shows roads underlined and a circle. It stated that on all the roads they had to take and in all the encircled places no harm would befall them, and the earth symbolized the dirt of the road.
> The sixth is a kind of proclamation to assemble people, with the signs and signatures of several individuals. The last is the name of Mala-Abukar, stating that nothing will happen on the road and that they can pass freely. . . .
> The ninth is a kind of tablet from which the Malê can tell the date of fasts so that they can kill sheep.
> Having been shown two tablets, one with lettering and the other without, Albino said that "the blank one had already been washed, as he had already described, so that the water could be drunk as a *mandinga*, but after it had been written on twenty times, and the other, the one with writing, was the second lesson of pupils learning to write.[16]

Another significant fact is that the costume of the insurrectionaries was very similar to liturgical vestments: a white robe with a red belt, red shirt, blue cap and white turban, and white shoes, with magic charms, coral ornaments, white rings, and amulets around the neck. In short, a whole symbolism of colors, letters, and numbers was enlisted in the struggle, so that victory would be certain.

This considerable body of facts unmistakably shows that the revolt of the Nagô and Hausa in early nineteenth-century Bahia represented a real holy war waged by the Mussulmans against the Christians. Nevertheless this view has recently been criticized by Aderbal Jurema, a historian of slave insurrections in South America. My distinction between popular or nativist movements and Negro insurrections seems to him untenable; he sees both as manifestations of the class struggle in its colonial form. He does not deny the existence of a religious element, but, invoking the famous Marxist distinction, regards the mystical factor as no more than an ideological superstructure, the only causal factor being the economic substructure. In his view religion merely lent a special complexion to the social demands of an oppressed class and introduced accessory practices that had no bearing on the insurrectionary movement itself—e.g. the use of amulets. Even today, Jurema argues, the *cangaceiros*, the bandits of northeastern Brazil, have their bodies "closed" to make them impervious to the bullets of the gendarmerie; but I do not therefore conclude that their banditry has mystical roots. Religion can certainly be a means to an economic end or can be used as a revolutionary tactic, for mysticism has always carried a potentially explosive charge that can serve as an instrument of propaganda or revolt. But the ultimate aim was to expel the whites from their estates, which would then be taken over by the Nagô. When Sabina asked the Negro woman Edum if she might see her lover during a meeting of the conspirators, Edum replied: "He will not appear until the time comes to take possession of the land." Thus, according to Jurema, Moslem and Catholic superstructures merely reflected the underlying antagonism between the material interests of slaves and their masters.[17]

Obviously these insurrections gave vent to diverse and complex feelings. There was a racial factor. The Hausa and Nagô, who in Africa owned slaves and land, could not tolerate being reduced to the status of slaves. These courageous, battle-hardened people could not submit. But the ethnic element was also a religious one. The social heritage of power and militarism these people bore within them was a Mohammedan heritage acquired in secular wars against fetishist Negroes which amounted to religious crusades.[18] There was undoubtedly an economic element too. Yet what these insurgents wanted to abolish was not slavery per se but merely the enslavement of the sons of Allah by Christian dogs. If they wanted to take over the land, it was not to cultivate it themselves but to have it cultivated for them by Creole Negroes and mulattoes. It was Mussulman hatred that precipitated the revolt and not class consciousness among the disinherited. Jurema's mistake lay in breaking down the culture into its constituent elements and seeking the causal factor among the cultural or social fragments thus produced. And of course the system of slavery itself, by bringing into contact the various tribes that were forced to work together and by uprooting people from their original habitat, tended to break up their culture and destroy its primitive unity through syncretism. But the Mussulmans, as we have seen, still had their schools and places for prayer; their traditions were very much alive. Moreover, according to scholars who studied the last generation of these Mussulmans, they did not associate much with other slaves, with fetishist or Christian Negroes, but lived in proud isolation.[19] So we should not distinguish between substructure and superstructure but rather look at their life in Brazil in its entirety, as an entity in which economic protest and cultural demands were inseparable. When we recall that virtually every civilization has its center of interest and that the center of the Moslem civilization is generally agreed to be religious fanaticism, the revolt of 1835 emerges as a real war waged against the Christians on all fronts— economic as well as religious. But it was waged on the economic front only because the white economy was an economy of Christians. We should not forget that the conspirators included free Negroes and that some of these were wealthy. Many of them could have risen in society. But, as Alain says, it may be possible to compromise with interests, because interests are always to some extent rational, but it is impossible to compromise with passion. And in these indomitable hearts fanaticism burned incessantly. Religion does not merely lend color to the social revolt; it is its very heart.

5
Two Catholicisms

However staunchly African civilization and religion may have held out, the influence of the Catholic environment was irresistible; some degree of syncretization was inevitable if they were to survive at all. Slave Catholicism in the colonial era presents some interesting peculiarities that lead us back once again to our central topic: the relations between social structures and the world of mystical values. Here we must pause for a moment before turning back to the African religions.

In an earlier chapter I outlined the distinctive characteristics of Brazilian as opposed to Portuguese Catholicism: the substitution of the plantation chapel for the cathedral or the provincial church, and the shift from a village religion to a domestic one in which the patriarch's patron saint and other protectors watched over all the activities of family life. Saint Joseph rocked the baby's cradle; Saint Anne lulled it to sleep at its nurse's breast; Saint Benedict protected it from being stung by great poisonous ants.[1]

What was the slave's place in this patriarchal religion?

There is certainly a great difference between the slavery of classical antiquity, which integrated the individual slave into his master's family through a religious ceremony, and colonial slavery, in which the slave had a purely monetary value. But this radical contrast is modified by the patriarchal nature of the two families. Patriarchalism links the Brazilian slave to his Greek or Roman counterpart; through it he too was to a certain extent integrated into the household and hence into its religion. But domestic solidarity did not preclude racial and social differentiation. This accounts for the separation of white from Negro Catholicism.

Wherever different races meet, we find analogous phenomena. In the United States the Puritan Protestant, always eager to propagate his faith, catechized the Negro, but blacks and whites worshiped separately. There were two separate church services, usually with different sermons. Segregation went so far that colored preachers came forward to take charge of the edification of their racial brothers. Two separate Protestantisms emerged, reflecting ethnic temperamental differences: the more emotional Protestantism of the blacks and the more rational Protestantism of the whites.[2] In Mexico, churches assumed a characteristic form, with the royal chapel standing adjacent to the church or, even more frequently, with the main chapel open on the side so that it overlooked both the nave and the cloistered patio, where the Indians stood during the mass. In this way the catholicity of the church accommodated itself to the separation of the whites, for whom the nave was reserved, and the conquered Indians, relegated to the courtyard.[3] In Brazil too the chapel was often divided into two parts, the *alpendre* or portico, and the nave. The benches in the nave were reserved for the white patriarch's family, while the slaves stood outside, participating in the mass from the portico, through the open doors. Thus the African was both included and separated; he shared his master's religion, but as an inferior being. Architecture followed the model of the color hierarchy.[4] An alternative solution was similar to the one adopted in the United States. The chaplain would hold two services at different times —an early one for the blacks and a later one for the white master's family. In 1584 the visitor Christovão de Gouveia wrote to the Jesuit general:

> On the *fazendas* and *engenhos* there are many slaves who do not attend mass, although there are priests saying it, because of the small size of the chapel and because these slaves go barefooted and, on account of their bad smell, their Portuguese masters do not admit them [to the mass] either inside or outside the church. Moreover, on holy days they go out into the woods at daybreak to look for food because their masters do not give them any. For this reason it seems to us that it would be very useful if His Lordship the general could request the pope to extend our privilege of saying two masses on the same day in different places to permit saying them in the same place at two different times—an early one for the slaves and a regular one for the Portuguese. If this privilege could be extended to the secular clergy for the same purpose, it would be of great benefit, because there are fifteen or twenty thousand souls there who are Christian in nothing but name.[5]

In this respect Brazil, like the United States, tended to separate the two forms of the religion. But it did not succeed completely because, by giving white leaders control over black Catholicism, it prevented race consciousness from expressing itself through the mystical experience. It was the emergence of the black preacher that enabled the United States to develop its two quite distinct forms of worship. This is borne out by the fact that after the Civil War the blacks themselves demanded separation of the churches and the establishment of Negro sects, realizing that their racial demands could then be much more freely expressed. In Brazil, however, even free blacks could not be ordained. Any colored priests there may have been came from the Cape Verde Islands or from Angola.[6] Later, it is true, light-skinned mulattoes were ordained,[7] but we know that the mentality of the Brazilian mulatto is different from that of the mulatto of North America, where a single drop of black blood suffices to classify a man as a Negro. As we have seen, it was easier for the Brazilian mulatto to find a place in the very mixed society, and he felt that he belonged to the white rather than the African group. In the United States mulattoes often became leaders of the blacks,[8] which rarely happened in Brazil. In consequence, religious leadership in Brazil was the prerogative of the whites, and black Catholicism existed side by side with the Catholicism of the white gentry but on a lower hierarchical level, being disdainfully regarded as similar in nature but inferior.

This similarity in nature accompanied by inequality of status was very clearly reflected in the life of the plantation family. Catholic rites set the rhythm of the day, just as they themselves followed the rhythm of the seasons and the yearly round. The slave participated in this Christian rhythm along with the whites but always in a subordinate position. It was constantly brought home to him that he belonged to the domestic community inasmuch as it was a religious community, but as an inferior being and by virtue of belonging to his master. In short, the structure of the patriarchal slave-owning family was an obstacle to Christian egalitarianism and to one of the characteristic tendencies of the church.

As an Anglo-Saxon observer, James Wetherell spoke of the slaves' natural politeness, of their readiness to greet anyone they encountered.[9] Indeed, in Brazil, as in the United States, a whole etiquette of race relations, a whole series of standard salutations, evolved to indicate social gradations.[10] In North America etiquette was more or less secular, but in Brazil it developed within the climate of Catholicism. To quote Walsh: "The constant salutation of a baptized negro, in the interior, is, 'Jesu Christo'; and the answer is, 'por sempre—forever.' . . . Another answer is 'a Deos,' a contraction of the sentence, 'Louvado seja Deos que faz santos—Praised be God who sanctifies us.' When I first met groups of negroes on the road, who all thrust out their hands to me, I thought they were beggars."[11]

This exchange of courtesies expressed the slave's submissiveness and at the same time the paternal role of the master. It united them in one and the same faith while stressing their respective hierarchical positions in the world of religious life. It marked the course of the day, especially in the morning before work began and in the evening when the slaves returned from the fields—the times when the black was in direct contact with his master. After receiving their assignments in the morning and before going off to work, the blacks would salute the plantation owner, saying, "Praised be Jesus Christ." The master would reply, "Forever." In the evening every man would kiss the master's hand, saying, "Father, give me your blessing" or "Praised be the names of Jesus and Mary."[12] Some would kneel in salutation; others did not.[13] In very Catholic families this ritual took an even more elaborate form, as on the *fazenda* of Donna Gertrudes at Jaraguá, which Kidder visited.[14]

Besides marking the rhythm of the slave's day with domestic ceremonies of this sort, Catholicism also marked the yearly cycle of *fazenda* life, so that the slave was integrated into the plantation, and particularly into its religious life, though always in a subordinate position. The most important of the great holidays that interrupted the round of work were the feast days of the family's patron saints, when mass would be celebrated in their honor. The Negroes were not admitted to the chapel and had to remain outside, but they would celebrate the conclusion of the mass by singing a hymn, sometimes in their own language.[15] Then there were the agrarian holidays, harvest time on the coffee plantations and the starting up of the sugar mill on the *engenhos*. Mello Moraes gives a description of the latter occasion in the days of the empire.

In April the slaves would clean up and put everything in order—house, courtyard, and sugar mill. On the evening before the master was to arrive, they would decorate it all with flowers, greenery, palms, arches of leafy branches, and garlands interspersed with flags, while the colored cooks would prepare the banquet, for which a steer, several sheep, and innumerable chickens had been killed. The next day the plantation owner would arrive, accompanied by his relatives and friends and by the local band, followed by the priest. It was said that the crushing of the cane could not be started until the mill had been blessed; otherwise everything would go wrong—the machinery would break down, future crops would fail, the slaves would die, or catastrophe would strike the family of the *fazendeiro*. The priest would say mass in the crowded chapel and then bless the mill. When he sprinkled the holy water, the Negroes would rush forward to catch as much of it as possible, for they believed that this water had magical protective powers.[16] The first stalks of cane were ceremoniously placed under the mill wheel, and the first juice was drunk. The festivities ended with a great ball. It goes without saying that this "sugar ball" reflected local social stratification. The whites danced together, while the slaves made merry in their own quarters and in their own way.[17]

On religious holidays the slaves did not work. Here again they participated in the great cycle of festivals from Christmas to Holy Week. But although their holidays coincided with the master's in date, they remained parallel festivals, conducted according to other rites.[18] The gap that separated them was accentuated by the fact that although the blacks were forced to celebrate when the whites did, the whites held themselves aloof from the blacks' religious celebrations, making it quite clear that while the black might respectfully try to rise to his owner's religion, the master was under no obligation to stoop to the Catholicism of his slaves. To take just one example, the Convent of Olinda, which owned about a hundred Negroes, granted them permission to celebrate their patron saint, the Virgin of the Rosary. The Negroes formed a committee to furnish candles and prepare the bonfire. They appointed a treasurer to pay the expenses and assessed dues to raise the necessary money. If a white showed his face, it was only to supervise the festival and make sure that it did not end in fighting and rioting.[19] A *fazendeiro* would sometimes even contribute to such expenses and in the evening make a brief appearance at the boisterous revels of his servants.

This religious separation forced the Negro into an awareness of his race just as it forced him to seek his own protectors. But his model was always the domestic religion, which, as we have seen, was essentially a cult of saints.

Thus black Catholicism, like the African religions, was to a certain extent a class subculture. If we wish to understand it, we must study it exactly as we studied those religions, from two aspects. We must first take the sociological viewpoint and examine white-black relations in a society of dualist structure: on the one hand exploitation and domination, on the other resistance and struggle. Then we must adopt the cultural viewpoint, examining the relations between this class subculture and the white civilization. In other words, we must define the values, norms, and collective representations peculiar to Negro Catholicism. Let us begin with the sociological viewpoint.

We do not know exactly when Negro Catholicism emerged. As early as 1711 Antonil refers to celebrations of the feasts of São Benedito and of the Virgin of the Rosary in the *engenho* chapels.[20] São Benedito (known to us as Saint Benedict the Moor) died in 1589 and immediately acquired the reputation of a miracle worker. Because of his color he soon became the protector of the blacks, although his cult remained marginal in Orthodox Catholicism and he was not recognized by the church until much later (1743) and was canonized only in 1807.[21] The veneration of the Virgin of the Rosary, initiated by Saint Dominic, had fallen into disuse and was revived just at the time when the Dominicans were sending their first missions to Africa, which explains why it took root and spread among enslaved Negroes.[22] These facts suggest that the worship of black saints or Virgins was initially imposed upon the Africans from outside, as a step toward their Christianization, and that the white masters regarded it as a means of social control to promote subservience in their slaves. Writing in the first half of the nineteenth century, Ribeyrolles still stressed that discipline on the *fazenda* rested on two foundations: the overseer and the chaplain or priest. The former supervised work with his whip; the latter broke the spirit of revolt with his cross. Ribeyrolles adds that this explains why the evangelization of Africans remained so superficial. The priest did not fulfill his mission out of love, but as a task imposed upon him by the plantation owner for his own profit.[23] In such conditions it is not surprising that the black in Brazil should have reacted just like his counterpart in the United States and transformed religion, which was being used as a means of controlling him and integrating him into a society that persecuted him, into an instrument of ethnic solidarity and social justice.[24] The dualism of these two Catholicisms and the transformation of a religion of social control into a religion of racial protest were intensified with the move from the plantations to the city because, as we have seen, the city loosened the bonds that in rural Brazil united people of different colors and social rank within the solidarity of the patriarchal family.

It is true that in the cities, in the seventeenth and early eighteenth centuries, trade guilds existed that might have brought working-class whites and free Negroes together. But in Brazil these corporations did not unite workers from the same trade in as tight a solidarity as they did in Europe. Certainly they played a part in festivals. The trades all participated as individual groups, each playing a different role. In the eighteenth century, for instance, in the São Paulo celebrations of the birth of a princess, the carpenters danced a quadrille, the cobblers performed the "dance of souls," the joiners constructed a great wooden ship and acted as its crew, the tailors also built a float, and the blacksmiths and saddlers dressed up in fancy costumes. But even in these celebrations race and trade apparently separated. The mestizos followed their white employers, but as a separate group. The tavern keepers, for example, also built a float, which was followed by Caiapó and Creoles dancing the *congo*.[25] Obviously a common trade did not unite people of different colors in a true religious communion.

Even more important than the trade guilds were the urban fraternities. In Minas particularly these played a major role in religion. While the religion of the seventeenth-century sugar plantations of northeastern Brazil was a domestic one, the religion of the eighteenth-century mining regions was one of fraternities. These brotherhoods were very numerous, and they competed jealously in decorating their chapels and accumulating power and wealth. People of color were caught up in this movement and organized fraternities modeled on those of the whites. In this way racial conflict was camouflaged by a mantle of religion, and ethnic resistance presented itself as rivalry between religious societies.

The white fraternities adopted statutes excluding from membership Negroes, mulattoes, and even anyone married to a nonwhite spouse. In a society in which women were always in short supply there were always many white men living in concubinage with mulatto women. This was commonly known and was tolerated by public opinion; it was not the illegal union that was forbidden but the misalliance.[26] The people of color were therefore forced to establish their own fraternities. The separation was so radical that the two groups finally became known as the "white church" and the "black church." They were in constant conflict, incessantly arguing over precedence in parades and funerals and over procession routes, and appealing to ecclesiastical or civil tribunals and even to Rome.[27] By insisting on rules and investigations, the white church could block as effectively as a wall topped with broken glass any application for membership by "new Christians" or individuals with "tainted blood." The black church in turn tried to penetrate the most forbidden sanctuaries— the most aristocratic and exclusive brotherhoods, like the Franciscans— through craftiness and humor. Let me cite one example: the famous quarrel between the Brotherhood of the Girdle of Saint Francis and the Third Order of Franciscans. In 1585 the pope sanctioned the establishment of brotherhoods of the famous Girdle of Saint Francis, white with three knots. The mulattoes of São João del Rei, Sabará, Mariana, and Villa Rica seized the chance to organize chapters of this brotherhood in Minas, since the Third Order was closed to them. The Tertiaries protested, not wishing to see people of color sneak into their white churches through the back door to hold celebrations "with guitars and drums" (as the complaint they addressed to Lisbon put it) or participate in processions "with their mestizo prostitutes, just as though they were no different from honest white people."[28]

The two churches were internally divided too. The white church involved itself in conflict between families or feudal clans. In São Paulo, for example, the Camargos belonged to the Franciscan brotherhood and the Taques to the Carmelite one.[29] Later, when society began to be hierarchized and a middle class emerged in Minas alongside the class of "good men,"[30] there were fraternities for the rich and others for the poor. The black church was also divided within itself, because the mulattoes did not wish to be classed with the blacks. In Diamantina rivalry between the black Brotherhood of the Rosary and the mulatto Brotherhood of Mercy provoked clashes.[31] In 1877, at Tijuco in the diamond-mining region, where every second chapel and all seven churches were built and maintained by the brotherhoods, the Africans, the Creole Negroes, and the mulattoes all had their own temples.[32]

In spite of their poverty, these fraternities served as a focal point for racial demands. They focused on a colored saint to whom the faithful felt not only a mystical attachment but a kind of ethnic kinship. The feeling is admirably expressed in a remark made by a Negro to Kidder as he watched a procession. *"Lá vem o meu parente* [There comes my kindred]," he said.[33] This feeling of kinship eclipsed the religious aspect of the saint, despiritualizing and humanizing him, making him just like his earthly brothers in all respects:

Saint Benedict's a saint
Whom every black adores.
He drinks brandy,
And when he sleeps, he snores.[34]

When Padre Correal visited Bahia in 1689, he was astonished to see in a procession a float depicting the Holy Virgin arguing with Saint Benedict, who was behaving in a most indecent fashion.[35]

In the end the ultimate purpose of these fraternities became an earthly rather than a heavenly one. They became a means through which slaves could gain their freedom. We have already told the story of Chico Rei, who freed his whole tribe under the aegis of Saint Iphigenia. The fraternities followed his example in all the towns of Minas, indeed all over Brazil. At first the brotherhoods were founded by blacks to demonstrate their gratitude to God for their liberation. The church of O Senhor do Bomfim in Copacabana was founded by a Negro *feiticeiro* whose magic had earned him a million cruzeiros.[36] In later years any Negro who gained his freedom would make a donation to the brotherhood for the benefit of the less fortunate, and in this way the fraternities were able to free a certain number of slaves every year.[37] In the end the whites even helped them. In several places it became the custom to grant freedom to the king of the annual *congada* with which the patron saint's feast day was celebrated.

Some travelers, however, give conflicting reports. Sometimes a slave who had been laboriously saving up money to buy his freedom preferred to give most of it to his brotherhood in the hope of being awarded a prestigious position and so becoming an important, respected figure. Thus the fraternities came to play a new role and serve a different purpose. For the colored masses they functioned as a selection mechanism and as training grounds for a certain type of leadership.[38] And indeed there were many offices these people could aspire to—first and foremost those of king and queen. The secretary of the fraternity, however, was often white, and the treasurer invariably so.[39]

The fraternity's final purpose—and by no means its least important for Africans accustomed to the cult of the dead—was to guarantee to every member a fitting burial place and funeral. A rule introduced in 1750 by the black Brotherhood of the Virgin of the Rosary in Villa Rica even extended burial privileges to the members' wives and children, who did not themselves belong to the brotherhood, paid no dues, and had no voting rights.[40] In this way a strong propensity of the black ethnic group was realized through Christianization.

Although churches were being built everywhere to the Virgin of the Rosary, Saint Benedict, Saint Iphigenia, Saint Elesbão, and other colored saints, it sometimes happened that a fraternity had no home of its own, either for lack of resources or because its temple was still under construction. In that case a chapel in a parish church would be set aside for it. But even here a process of selection came into play; the separation of the chapels symbolized the separation of the two Catholicisms. In Rio de Janeiro the same house of worship was shared by the canons of the chapter and the Negroes,[41] but it was not long before this produced conflict between the two races rather than the hoped-for cooperation. Sometimes, as happened in Bahia, the Africans rejected the whites and even the Creole Negroes in order to remain on their own.[42] Sometimes, as was the case in Pôrto Alegre, the whites expelled the blacks, alleging that the dancing and drumming that went on at their festivals was too noisy and unworthy of the house of God.[43]

It seems that Catholicism should have imposed limits on this segregationist tendency, since all men are brothers in the same god and all are called to the same communion table. There were several side chapels to choose from, but there was one, and only one, main chapel where the priest officiated. There were brotherhood churches in various quarters of the city, but in the center stood the parish church, or even the cathedral, representing the total urban community and abolishing social or racial differences. Here again, however, separation prevailed over union. Saint-Hilaire was astonished to see so many Negro women in the churches, but they did not mix with the white women. Differences of dress made it easy to distinguish the two, since the blacks wrapped their head and body in black cloth, while the whites covered their head with a black cashmere mantilla.[44]

In processions, when the whole city paraded through the streets, the faithful lined up in hierarchical order, guaranteeing segregation by skin color. Immediately behind the Holy Sacrament in the São Paulo Corpus Christi procession came Saint George mounted on his prancing horse. After him came the black fraternities, then the mestizos of the Carmelite brotherhoods and the Brotherhoods of Mercy and of Saint Elesbão. These were followed by trade guilds in predetermined order, beginning and ending with slaves—the bakery women and the vegetable peddlers.[45] In the procession of Saint Francis in Minas, the penitents, chiefly Negroes and free mulattoes, led the way, followed by the clergy, with the crowd bringing up the rear.[46] The Ash Wednesday procession was led by three mulattoes in gray dominoes; one of them bore a cross and the other two carried lanterns on heavy sticks. Behind them came a mummer disguised as a skeleton, who struck as the spectators with a cardboard scythe. He was followed by a group of whites representing Adam and Eve and Cain and Abel, then by the members of the Brotherhood of Saint Francis, bearing on their shoulders the litters of the saints. Only then came the band and the Holy Sacrament.[47] In 1753 the procession celebrating the "triumph of the Eucharist" was led by two groups of dancers, the Moors and the Christians, followed by musicians and allegorical floats. Then came the fraternities, which paraded in the following order: musicians and mounted

Negroes, the Brotherhood of the Holy Sacrament, the mestizo Brotherhood of the Chapel of Saint Joseph, the Negro Brotherhood of the Rosary,
the Brotherhood of Saint Anthony, a group of aristocrats or "good men,"
the white Brotherhood of the Rosary, and the Brotherhoods of Nossa
Senhora da Conceição, Nossa Senhora do Pilar, and the Holy Sacrament.
They were followed by the clergy, the angels, the Holy Sacrament, the
dragon being slain by Saint George, and finally by the military.[48] The
procession of Saint George followed a different order. First came the
military, then the Brotherhood of Saint George, and finally a troop of
slaves, with their own musicians, and the "Iron Man," a curious figure
riding a black horse. Behind them was borne the statue of Saint George.[49]

Obviously the hierarchy of color did not follow any fixed order. Everything depended on what was being celebrated. If it was a military saint, the
white soldiers led the parade; otherwise they brought up the rear. But in
general the mulattoes and Negroes seem to have come first and the whites
last. The order was one of increasing prestige, with the clergy in the middle
as though to guarantee the coherence and stability of such a mixed society.
In any case, for us the crucial point is that there was no mixing of color.
The church accepted the social stratification.

A more serious matter was that when people of color adopted a feature
of white Catholicism, that feature immediately declined in prestige. When
the sugar planter or *fazendeiro* moved to town, he brought along his family
altar and family worship. In his town house there was always a niche for
the saints and a candle burning before them.[50] But the family religion no
longer played the role it had played in the country. The street linked
the houses and served as a channel of communication between families; the
engenho chapel was replaced by the parish or fraternity church. At the
same time the street acquired its own sanctity. Here and there, at crossings
and in the heart of each neighborhood, there would be a shrine, where
every passer-by was supposed to perform an act of devotion. Foreign
travelers were struck by this.[51] But in general the street was the domain of
the common people; whites merely passed through. The slaves used the
street as a meeting place where they could linger and chat. For them it was
an instrument of solidarity. Through it, as we have seen, they escaped
from the domination of the paterfamilias and from integration into the
patriarchal family and renewed bonds and ties of social class.[52] For this
reason they, more than the whites, tended to make the street the center of
their Catholicism, preferring to worship the neighborhood saints rather
than those of the household. About 1850 Ewbank noted that it was the
blacks who were more enthusiastic in the performance of street devotions,
adding that, as a result, this urban religion lost caste in the eyes of the
whites.[53]

We must now determine whether this separation of the black and white
churches was accompanied by a corresponding difference in their Catholi-

cism. Obviously the unity of dogma promoted assimilation, and genuine colored saints did emerge, especially among the Creoles. Tollemare speaks of an unusually beautiful mulatto girl of eighteen named Gertrude who wanted to become a nun and who had had a miraculous premonition of the death of her mother, thus acquiring an aura of sanctity among all who knew her.[54] The Jesuits would reward the most devout Negroes with conspicuous favors such as admitting them posthumously to the Company. "João Francisco, mulatto, who has served for thirty years for the love of God, always with piety and in a satisfactory manner, who goes to confession and takes communion every week and lives an exemplary life, who has no taint of the Moorish or Jewish race, may be admitted to the Company in the hour of his death. He is worthy of it and deserves this consolation." Others were rewarded by being granted civil liberty.[55]

The segregation of people of color was an obstacle to this assimilation and tended to produce a parallel segregation of collective representations. The various "nations" still survived as organizing groups for festivals, and any of them could establish an ethnic religious fraternity of its own. In Bahia, for instance, the Brotherhood of Our Lord of the Redemption consisted entirely of Dahomans. The Third Order of the Rosary was composed of Angola Negroes, the Brotherhood of Our Lord of the Cross of mulattoes.[56] This church policy reflects a government policy and recalls the letter written by Count dos Arcos cited earlier. But in the end the policy created a differentiated Catholicism. This leads us from our first, sociological approach to the second, cultural one—to an examination of the values, norms, and collective representations peculiar to this "black church."

Jesuit catechization took as its starting point the idea that dogma must be adapted to mentality and that the Negroes had the mentality of grown-up children. They must be attracted by music, which they loved; by dancing, which was their great diversion; by vanity; and by their liking for titles and grandiose positions.[57] They should not be forced to break completely with their traditional customs, but these should be evaluated and the acceptable ones used as a springboard to help them attain the true faith. In this way a Negro Catholicism emerged which persisted within the fraternities and which, despite the unity of dogma and faith, presents special characteristics.

The procession of Saint Benedict included only blacks and mulattoes: the standard-bearer, the little colored angels holding their mothers' hands, the Brotherhood of Saint Benedict, the African queens (three in number, with Perpetua in the center, surrounded by two bands of Negroes fighting over her crown), the Brotherhood of the Rosary, and the *taieras*, whose silk clothing, it was said, was designed to reveal hints of lascivious bosoms. They all marched along singing:

> Virgin of the Rosary,
> Mistress of the world,
> Give me a fresh coconut
> Or I'll have to go to the well,
>
> Virgin of the Rosary,
> Mistress of the world,
> Give me a fresh coconut
> Or I'll have to go to the water pitcher.[58]

These naïve litanies beseeching the Virgin for fruit to assuage thirst have
their counterpart in the invocations of Saint Benedict:

> My Saint Benedict,
> I humbly pray,
> For the love of God the Father
> Let's have a *cucumbi* play.[59]

The characteristic feature of this celebration is not so much the familiar
tone in which the saints are addressed—contemporary whites used a similar tone[60]—as the fight over the crown of Queen Perpetua, which was an
integral part of the procession. When we add that the queen was protected
by a troop of Congo, the full significance of the ceremony emerges. It
represents a survival in the country of exile of ethnic struggles and African
monarchies. Christianity accepted it because in this way the struggle could
be given a symbolic meaning. The earthly crown became a symbol of the
celestial crown with which, according to the apostle, Jesus will reward the
faithful.

But the still vivid memories of African kingship emerge even more
plainly in the *congadas*. These festivals accepted the continuance of a
monarchic regime for Brazilian Negroes—in an adulterated form, of
course, and incorporated into the worship of Our Lady of the Rosary. The
earliest mention of a *congada* is in the town of Iguarassu in Pernambuco in
1700,[61] but it already existed, at least in fragmentary form, in the middle
of the seventeenth century,[62] and its origin can be traced back to Portugal.[63] Pereira da Costa tells us that each parish had its king, queen,
secretary of state, marshal, herald of arms, ladies-in-waiting, etc., who
were addressed as "Your Majesty," "Your Excellency" or "Madam." The
election was held on the feast day of Our Lady of the Rosary and was the
occasion for dancing, which varied in type according to the ethnic origin of
the king.

The custom gained ground and gradually spread all over Brazil. Like
the fraternities in which it originated, it gave rise to ethnic struggles and
rivalry between nations. At first the *congada* was a Bantu festival, and the
Nagô and Dahomans usually held aloof from it. Later it set the Congo
against the Angola and the Angola against the Mozambique. At Osorio in

Rio Grande do Sul the Mozambique followed the Angola *cucumbis*, neither singing nor dancing but simply playing their musical instruments. In Minas too the Mozambique were regarded as "the Congo's rank and file."[64] The Mozambique of São Paulo, however, believed that their dance had been invented and presented to their nation by Saint Benedict himself. In many places in that province the Mozambique finally triumphed over their rivals, the Congo, and in Monsanto they led the procession because, they claimed, they had been the first to encounter Our Lady of the Rosary.[65] Of course the slave class, through its solidarity, was able to surmount these tribal animosities. The Brotherhood of Balthazar, which dates back to 1742, was composed of Africans and Creoles, most of whom were slaves. Its archives contain lists of dignitaries with typically African names. Its king was called "Newangue," the queen "Nembanda," the princes "Manafundos," the *feiticeiro* (who often carried a snake coiled around his neck) "Endoque," the royal slaves "Uantuafunos." This shows that the kings were freely chosen, without regard for ethnic origin. The first, elected in 1742, was a Rebôlo, and the last, elected in 1811, a Cabinda.[66]

The festival was prepared well in advance. On Sundays and holidays members of the brotherhood would ask both blacks and whites for contributions to the expenses of the ceremony. This was in fact a very widespread custom, and every fraternity, black or white, did the same.[67] The king and queen and their secretaries of state and court attendants were escorted to the chapel by a long procession, with singing, music, and dancing. Then the priest consecrated the man whom the brotherhood had chosen by placing a cardboard crown on his head.[68]

The length of the king's reign was not fixed. Originally the elected sovereigns were probably former Negro kings who had been enslaved and to whom their subjects still owed fealty. To some extent the whites were able to turn the Negroes' allegiance to a king to advantage as a means of imposing their own laws upon the people of color. "Our king—and he alone—commands us all to work." According to Mario de Andrade, the ultimate purpose of these coronations was to induce the Negroes to submit to hard labor.[69] But the custom was not without its dangers, for the king exercised great authority over his subjects and could turn them against their white masters. A king named Miguel headed a Negro insurrection in Natal which, however, was a failure from the outset. Miguel was captured, deposed, and replaced by another slave named Luis.[70] On the other hand the Catholic church preferred to have the election and coronation of these kings coincide with Christian feasts, which are annual ones, and therefore tried to set the duration of a reign at one year, and this custom finally prevailed. But in this way the church diluted the concept of kingship and deprived it of its solemn, serious character, transforming it into mere entertainment. Spix and Martius compare these black kings to the kings of Twelfth Night in Europe and report that when the new monarch went to pay his respects to the governor of the diamond-mining region, the latter received him wearing his dressing gown.[71] Koster, however, recognized these kings' authority over their colored subjects, but said that the newly crowned king was the butt of endless joking.[72] It is therefore hardly surprising that the kings should gradually have lost their authority and been reduced to carnival kings.

The dances that accompanied the coronation were known as *congadas*, *cucumbys*, *congos*, *ticumbi*, or *turundu*, depending on the region.[73] They amounted to a theatrical performance consisting of several parts.

> The performance opens with the entrance of the dancers and the arrival of the king, singing. He asks the assembly for leave to celebrate the *congada*. Then the royal procession parades through the streets, dancing outside the church and the houses of the dignitaries. This is the most impromptu part of the festival and varies from place to place. There are semi-African songs, such as that of the queen:

> > *Quenguerê ôiá congo* of the sea
> > Turn, Calunga,
> > Here comes Manu.

There were quadrilles in the Portuguese manner, haunting folkloric songs, work songs from the plantation or the kitchen. There were animal dances in which the blacks mimed the movements of the animals mentioned in the song. Mello Moraes speaks of a snake dance performed by the king's son and a dance of the jaguar. Barroso mentions a crustacean dance.

> The second act of the festival is the embassy. Queen Ginga (or in Paranaíba Queen Ginga Ngambi) sends an ambassador to the king, sometimes on a mission of war, sometimes of peace. Even if their intent is peaceful, the clumsiness of the king's ministers and the hot-headedness of Prince Suena precipitate war between the Congo and the army of Queen Ginga. The prince is taken prisoner and sentenced to death.
> The third act recounts the death and resurrection of the prince. The queen, grieving over her son's death, summons the *feiticeiro*, who goes in search of his body:

> > *Feiticeiro*:   *E . . . Mamão! E . . . Mamão*
> > > *Ganga rumbâ, siniderê lacô*
> > > *E . . . Mamão! E . . . Mamão!*
> > *All*:   *Zumbi, matêquerê;*
> > > *Congo, cucumby-ôyá.*

> > *Feiticeiro*:   *Zumbi, Zumbi, ôiá Zumbi!*
> > > *Oiá Manêto muchicongo*
> > > *Oiá papêto.*

> Throughout these invocations the *feiticeiro* walks around the child's body, palpating and auscultating it, making magic passes, chanting mysteri-

ous spells, giving it plants and juices to inhale, placing little snakes beside
it and talismans with supernatural properties. Gradually the prince's body
comes to life again as the crowd rejoices:

> *Feiticeiro*: Who can do more than this?
> *Chorus*: The sun and the moon.
> *Feiticeiro*: An even more powerful god?
> *Chorus*: Saint Benedict!

In the final act the fighting begins again. If the play deals with a *caboclo*
who has killed a black, the *feiticeiro* fells him with a glance, and he falls
to the ground. If the subject is Queen Ginga, her army is finally defeated.
The king offers his daughter to the witch doctor in reward for his services.
The festival ends with more dancing, in which the Immaculate Virgin
of the Rosary is of course not forgotten.[74]

Obviously this play is strictly African in inspiration; one of the principal
roles is that of the pagan *feiticeiro*. Mario de Andrade, who has made a
more careful analysis of the *congada* than any other Brazilian scholar, has
discovered many traces of black Africa in the Portuguese verses. These
may be no more than tiny details, minor poetic themes, like these words
sung by the king:

> I don't need any more canaries
> In my kingdom,
> Eating up my grain. . . .

This is a common theme in African tales and recurs again and again in the
stories collected by Chatelain, Equilbecq, and Jacottet. Sometimes, however, essential features of the play are of African derivation, and that is
what interests us here. Firstly, the animal dances of the first act may well
be of totemic origin, because the Bantu, who created the *congada*, are
often totemic peoples. Secondly, the importance attached to the embassy
is very African. The Congo and Guinea kings liked to exchange ambassa-
dors and even sent missions to Brazil—first in 1750, again in 1795, when
two embassies were sent from Dahomey, and once again in 1824, when
the king of Benin sent one. Thirdly, the names of the characters are
historic names. Queen Ginga or Ginga Ngambi is none other than Queen
Ginga Bandi, who was reigning in 1621 and whose embassy to the Portuguese governor João Correia de Souza resulted in her being converted to
Christianity.[75] In some versions the king of the Congo is called Dom
Henrique, and this also commemorates actual events in Africa, where the
Christianized dynasty of the Portuguese Congo included many Henriques.[76] The prince's name, Suana, is not a personal name but a title,
which, according to Dias de Carvalho, was used in the eighteenth century
among the Lunda and which means "next in succession."[77] Mario de
Andrade compares the coronation ceremony, in which the new king assumes the crown of his predecessor, to a version of the *congada* in which

the father, before going into battle, hands on the crown to his son, while he himself assumes the attributes of the prince. Frazier came across this same exchange in Africa when he was studying the death of the king of vegetation. Mello Moraes's description even reveals a vestige of a circumcision rite occurring between the dances of the first act and the death of the king's son.[78]

Without doubt elements of white culture are intimately mixed here with African elements. But these elements of Western civilization should not blind us to the typically African character of the *congada*. One wonders how the church could so lightly have allowed an apology for the witch doctor's resuscitation of the dead to be incorporated into the life of the colored fraternities. The explanation is that Brazilian Catholicism was a continuation of Portuguese Catholicism, and in Portugal the custom of including masked dances and profane singing in religious festivals already existed. Certain high ecclesiastical dignitaries (including, in 1534, the bishop of Evora) opposed this tradition, but the king allowed it to continue, and it still persisted as late as 1855.[79] The colony inherited the custom. Foreign travelers give many descriptions of profane festivals celebrated in the shadow of churches and convents, where they were astonished to witness nuns performing love comedies and crowds following the procession playing ball with statues of the saints.[80]

It is therefore not surprising that the church should have incorporated the *congada* into the structure of the colored fraternities. In doing so, however—and this is the interesting point—it gave black Catholicism a different complexion from white Catholicism by infusing African elements.

Nonetheless the *congada* itself constituted an autonomous reality. While it might be associated with religious rites, it was also capable of existing independently. This led the groups that tried out and rehearsed the show between festivals to extend their activities beyond the actual coronation ceremony and the procession of the Virgin of the Rosary. The secular authorities turned to the *congada* to enliven big popular celebrations marking an important event such as the marriage of a princess or the birth of an heir to the throne of Portugal.

The church, on the other hand, was beginning to look askance at these African ceremonies incorporated into Catholic ones. It accepted the coronation, in a diluted form, but it was not so tolerant of the *congada* that followed it. In Rio it even forbade the coronation as part of the feast of the Rosary.[81] Thus the *congada* shifted from the domain of religion to that of folklore.

There is no doubt that we are dealing with two distinct forms of Catholicism. They stemmed from segregation by color, and they prevented the Negro from being totally assimilated into the religion of the whites. This explains critical comments by foreign travelers, especially Anglo-Saxons and Protestants, to the effect that the colored Brazilians were denaturing Christianity and turning it into a mixture of burlesque and immorality.[82] It would be more accurate to say that features of the African civilizations—especially Bantu civilizations—infiltrated the cult of the black saints and the *congadas* without the priests being aware of it. As I studied Catholicism, I seemed to be far removed from the African religions. I was not so far away as I thought, however, because the *congadas* were precisely one of those "niches" that I referred to earlier, where the blacks could cherish and conceal their gods or spirits, the better to worship them. To quote Arthur Ramos:

> In a description by Pereira da Costa, the eminent folklorist of Pernambuco, the African play performed by the Congo of Brazil, the name *Zambiapungo* (the name of the supreme Bantu deity) occurs in the blessing which the king gives to his secretary of state: "May God and Zambiapungo bless you, *qui tirindude* . . ." and in the subsequent lines:
>
> > Gladly comes our king,
> > Gladly comes our king,
> > To celebrate today
> > Glorious Saint Lawrence.
> > To this we owe the presence
> > Of our King Dom Carlo
> > Of Zâmbiapungo, Zâmbiapungo,
> > *Tirindoundê, o lê lê.*
>
> In the same Congo play, as more recently collected by Gustavo Barroso, I find the form *Zamuripunga* in the quatrain:
>
> > *Benedictim de Zamuripunga,*
> > May he destine you now to Heaven.
> > *Amulâ, amulequê*
> > *Amulequê, Amulâ.*
>
> In southern Bahia the blacks have a dance known as the *zabiapungo*. (In fact the words *zamuripunga* and *zabiapunga* are corruptions of *Zambiampungu*.) In D. Pereira da Silva's account of the Congo prayer we also find the name Calunga (the Bantu sea goddess), but its significance is not clear:
>
> > *Calunga ê meia ê*
> > *Zambuê*
> > *Calunga ê meia ê*
> > *Zambuê.*[83]

Black Catholicism was the precious reliquary, unwittingly presented to the Negroes by the church, in which they might preserve some of the highest values of their native religions, not as relics but as living realities.

6
Survivals of African Religion

To what extent did black Catholicism adulterate the African religions? Apparently the slaves did not openly resist being Christianized by the whites or regimented into the Brotherhoods of the Rosary and Saint Benedict. D'Assier describes the indifference with which they would submit to baptism upon reaching Brazil, contrasting them in this respect with the Indians, who liked to be coaxed with little presents, a bottle of *tafia* or a length of cloth, and who would sometimes even have a child baptized several times by different priests just to get more presents.[1] The new society in which the slave found himself disposed him to accept baptism— sometimes quite eagerly—as a way of improving his status, since the Creole Negroes ridiculed or even execrated "pagan" Africans, while the whites treated them as soulless animals. So he would hastily learn a few prayers by rote—although their meaning was beyond him.[2] Catechization, as I mentioned in an earlier chapter, was always perfunctory, if we except the Jesuits' attempts to bring over priests with a knowledge of the Angola language, and the slaves in monasteries and convents who regularly attended catechism classes and went to confession twice a year, at Christmas and Easter.[3] During the colonial period, Catholicism superimposed itself on the African religion rather than replacing it. In the shadow of the Cross, whether it stood in the *engenho* chapel or the city church, ancestor worship continued within what Nina Rodrigues called, even toward the end of the era of slavery, "the illusion of catechesis."[4]

The slaveowners were interested in their slaves' bodies, not their minds. They regarded them as machines for performing labor, not souls to be saved. Even in the eighteenth century Archbishop Sebastien Monteiro de

Vide bitterly complained that "the buyers are only concerned with setting their slaves to work and have so little interest in teaching them Christian doctrine that those who are offered the chance to be baptized within a year are few indeed."[5]

The chaplains—such as had not been seduced by the sensuous tropical climate—fulfilled their duties toward their flock as a purely professional obligation to which they brought no Christian charity. Even in the nineteenth century, when the moral climate had changed quite radically and the whites took more interest in the moral welfare of their work force, Ribeyrolles notes that the chaplains "do not evangelize; they simply perform a job. They baptize and marry the Negroes, but they do not instruct them."[6] Couty makes a similar comment at about the same time.[7] In fact the whites often regarded the attainment of Christianity by the black as a real danger—as a preliminary step toward equality between master and slave which might well lead to other steps, and hence as a first assault on their privileges. Thomas Lindley spoke for them when he said that participation in the religion of the country and the unreasonable familiarity that some people permitted to slaves made them presumptuous.[8]

But the indifference of the slaveowners was not the only factor involved. Some plantations had no resident chaplain, and the distances between *fazendas* was enormous, so that the priest's visits were rare and precious occasions. Frazier attributed the poverty of religious life in the province of Santa Catarina in 1713—among whites as well as blacks—to this isolation.[9] In Pernambuco a priest might have to cover twenty or thirty leagues on horseback to get from one estate or town to another, which made it impossible to visit them all every year.[10] Tollenare thought that religious instruction was possible only in the cities.[11] But the city presented its own problems. The street was the slave's avenue of escape from his master's strict supervision. At nocturnal *batuques* he met other members of his "nation" and sustained himself with memories of his native civilization. Then again, the white townsman devoted more time to political affairs than the country dweller; the white townswoman no longer bothered to teach her servants to make the sign of the cross or recite the Pater Noster.[12] The priests, who could and should have assumed the master's obligations in this respect, had no sense of mission (except of course for the regular clergy). Saint-Hilaire notes that in Minas priests were required only to say a low mass every Sunday and confess the faithful at Easter; they could devote the rest of their time to business or the practice of law. Priests owned mines and sugar mills; they even dealt in contraband gold and precious stones. Benefices were sold to the highest bidder. The priesthood became a profession rather than a vocation, with the result that vice triumphed and priests appeared publicly in church with their concubines and illegitimate children.[13]

Given these conditions, it is not difficult to understand why black

Catholicism should have superimposed itself on African religion rather than penetrating it or why the brotherhoods should often have developed into *candomblés*. Vilhena asserts that it is impossible to eradicate from the African's heart customs and ceremonies that "he imbibed with his mother's milk" and that his parents taught him. Among a thousand Negroes, he says, there may be one who voluntarily adopts Christianity. In all the others it will remain something imposed from outside, a superficial varnish.[14] Luis Vianna Filho found in the archives a document dated 1738 in which a Benedictine prior complains that although the Angola and Negroes of São Thomé and other localities have been baptized and are living among whites, they do not for this reason "abandon the superstititions they learned in their own countries, but organize societies (though secret ones) to set up their *calundus*."[15] In the early nineteenth century John Luccock noted that the Catholicism of the blacks and mulattoes in Minas was purely nominal, reduced to mere gestures devoid of spiritual significance.[16] Again in 1838 Kidder and Fletcher wrote that the Mohammedan slaves did not abjure their faith even when they were baptized and that the fetishist Negroes continued to practice their own religion although they considered themselves Christians.[17]

Unfortunately documentation concerning the survival of animism in the colonial and even the imperial periods is very sketchy. In those days no one had any feeling for ethnographic research. Such information as we possess is scattered throughout books of all kinds, from historical chronicles to travelers' accounts. The white was interested in his slaves' religion only insofar as it affected him personally, either when the raucous singing and the deafening drumming of tom-toms kept him awake[18] or when the black priest became the instigator or leader of a revolt or of a mass escape or mass suicides.[19] So long as their religion did not impinge upon his immediate interests, he closed his eyes to it. All we know about it has been filtered through his limited, self-centered, prejudiced awareness, which neglects the elements essential to a scientific study of African religions in Brazil and records only their superficial aspect and their repercussions on the regime of slavery. Even so, it is useful to assemble all the historical documentation we possess. We may be able to draw from it some not entirely negligible conclusions.

■ ■ ■

We have seen that by destroying the family system, slavery precluded the survival of ancestor worship in Brazil. But this religion was so deeply rooted in the moral code and the civilization of all the peoples of black Africa that it could not fail to leave in the slaves and Creole Negroes certain mental attitudes at least, certain modes of behavior and emotional patterns concerning such things as the importance of burial, separation rituals between the living and the dead, or the idea that the souls of the dead rejoin the great spiritual family of ancestors beyond the ocean. This obligation to render due respect to the dead, lest they avenge themselves by returning to disrupt the lives of their children with illnesses or nightmares, explains why burial rituals remained so important to all Afro-Americans,[20] even those who, like the Negroes of the United States, were most thoroughly assimilated into Western civilization.[21]

In Brazil, at least during the first two centuries of slavery, the whites' belief that the blacks were nothing but soulless animals made it easier for these rites to survive. The religious orders protested in vain against the way the blacks were abandoned by their masters at the moment of death.[22] The reverend fathers' teachings were never completely or universally obeyed, because they conflicted with the collective representations that viewed the black as a thing, not a person. Although this attitude was never analyzed in books or set down in writing, it went so deep that it still pervades popular folklore, expressing itself in verses like these:

> The white man: God made him.
> The mulatto: God painted him.
> The *caboclo* is a pig's fart,
> And the Negro's the Devil's shit.[23]

> The Negro isn't born, he appears.
> He doesn't die, he disappears.
> The white gives up his soul to God;
> The black gives up his to the Devil.[24]

> If the priest who says mass is white,
> It's because if a black said it, it would just be lies.
> The Negro is born to be a dog;
> When he dies, he dies barking.[25]

A whole series of proverbs stresses how impossible it is for a Negro to become a Christian. "The Negro goes to confession, but he doesn't take communion." "The Negro doesn't enter the church; he eavesdrops outside." "The Negro doesn't take part in the procession; he runs after it." One proverb goes to the very heart of our subject: "The Negro doesn't die; he comes to an end."[26]

We begin to understand why the whites did not go out of their way to give comfort to a slave at the moment of death.[27] Writing in the early nineteenth century, d'Assier stressed that in a slave's last hour only his fellow-slaves would stay with him and arrange for his burial.[28] This isolation permitted the traditional rituals and archaic ceremonies to survive, and everything indicates that after the blacks had accepted the Catholic fraternities so that they might bury their dead more ceremoniously in graveyards, Christian rites were merely superimposed on the "pagan" ones so deeply rooted in Afro-Brazilian mores.

The earliest documentation we possess on this subject dates back to the seventeenth century. During the visit of the Inquisition to Bahia in 1618, Sebastian Berreto informed the Jesuits of the blacks' funeral custom of slaughtering animals and washing in their blood in the belief that this caused the soul to leave the body and ascend to heaven.[29] During the Dutch occupation Pastor Soler wrote to a friend that when a Negro died, men, women, and children would surround the body to the beating of durms and question it, chanting: "Ai-ai-ai, why did you die? Ai-ai-ai, didn't you have any bread? Ai-ai-ai, didn't you have any fish?" and so on through a whole repertoire of food and drink.[30]

Debret's early nineteenth century descriptions of Negro funerals suggest a stronger admixture of Christianity, although he notes that the Christian element varied from one nation to another, being most marked among the Mozambique. Funerals of Negro women were attended only by women, except for two pallbearers, the master of ceremonies, and the drummer. During the procession the mourners would groan and shriek. When they arrived at the black church, the body was carried in, in a hammock, accompanied by eight female relatives or close friends, each resting her hand on the body.[31] The ceremony for a Negro king was even more impressive. A coin was placed in the dead man's mouth and a band tied around his head to keep his jaws closed. He was laid on a mat, wrapped in his ceremonial robes (if this was impossible, a drawing of him in this costume was made on a wall), and the dignitaries of the various Negro nations would come to pay their respects—the ambassador, the standard-bearer, the captain of the guard. All night his subjects would keep watch, making the air throb with the dull clapping of their hands or the beat of their musical instruments. The funeral procession was accompanied by a crowd throwing firecrackers, weeping, and singing; some would even turn somersaults.[32]

Kidder, hearing a noise, once went to his window, where he saw a Negro "bearing on his head a wooden tray, on which was the corpse of a child, covered with a white cloth, decorated with flowers, a bunch of them being fastened to its hand. Behind him . . . were about twenty negresses, and a number of children, adorned most of them with flaunting stripes of red, white, and yellow. They were all chanting some Ethiopian dirge, to which they kept time by a slow trot; the bearer of the deceased child pausing and whirling around on his toes like a dancer."[33]

Mello Moraes Filho wrote an account of a Mozambique funeral in 1830 which recalls Debret's. Women would accompany a woman's body, men a man's; both sexes followed the cortege of a king or a child, to the sound of much hand clapping, drumming, singing, and funeral lamentations.[34]

Superficial as they are, these descriptions prove that the African cult of the dead was very much alive. The accounts of Spencer Vampré are more interesting in that they describe how, in São Paulo toward the end of slavery, the Negro Brothers of the Rosary would address the dead man exactly as the Negroes of Dutch Pernambuco had done in the seventeenth century, intoning in their Creole dialect: "You, who loved life so much. . . . You, mouth, who talked so much. You, mouth, who ate and drank so much. You, body, who worked so much. You, legs, who walked so much."[35] The survival of this custom shows how resistant the African burial ceremonies were.

Rocha Pombo also notes that funeral rites are the richest source of survivals. The body was washed before being buried, as in Cameroun; sometimes the face was shaved. Before the burial, friends would hold a wake; this ceremony was known as the *velorio*, and the friends were called *carpideiras*. There was drinking and eating and hymn singing, and if the dead man's relatives could not pay the expenses of the wake, a collection was taken up, just as in Africa. Then the body was carried to the grave-yard, with the procession dancing *jongos* and *congadas* around it.[36] Obviously Rocha Pombo used the terms *jongos* and *congadas* loosely to denote Negro dances. Actually the funeral dancing carried on around the coffin had nothing in common with erotic dances like the *jongo* or entertainments like the *congada*; it was a specialized funeral rite.

The second area in which fairly circumstantial historical data is available is African magic. This magic made a deep impression on the whites for several reasons, chiefly because the Portuguese colonist was just as superstitious as his slaves, Indian or black. The scarcity of "surgeons," physicians, and apothecaries throughout the colonial period, even in the larger cities and the commercial ports along the coast,[37] forced those whose illnesses would not yield to plasters or infusions of herbs to consult "bonesetters" and *curandeiros* or "healers." Since the Africans were expert in the art of curative magic, they achieved a hold over their white masters and in this way were able to continue some of their native practices, which they combined with techniques of white witchcraft. A seventeenth-century poem by Gregorio de Mattos describes the workings of this medicinal magic.[38]

Obviously the Portuguese, living in a far-off foreign land full of pitfalls and unexpected dangers, in an often enervating climate, did not feel very secure. We know that magic is often linked to anxiety in the face of the strange and the unknown; it is an irrational technique for finding reassurance. All these factors—the superstitious nature of the early settlers, the lack of scientific medicine, the hazards that confronted the temperate European transplanted from the Mediterranean to the tropics—combined to keep alive the Brazilians' interest in magic.

This was doubly true of the Negro. Both as a foreigner—as *alien*—and as a black—for black was the color of the Devil—he had all the makings of a magician. But the white man's attitude toward him was ambivalent. On the one hand he accepted his medicinal magic, the love philters that could restore lost vigor to a sexually exhausted *fazendeiro*;[39] On the other he feared the slave witch doctor, who was familiar with toxic plants and could brew poisons to rid himself of a hated master. Antonil speaks of his mystical warfare and of "fetishes" manufactured by the blacks to do harm to planters or mineowners,[40] and I have already referred to it.

This explains two things. First, the frequency, throughout the colonial period, of judgments like the one of 1744 sentencing Louiza Pinto, free Negress of Sabara, native of Angola, to four years in prison "for the crime of witchcraft and for having, on presumptive evidence, made a pact with the Devil,"[41] or the one of 1888 against a Negro from São Antonio de Cachoeira who had "provoked revolution" in his neighborhood.[42] Second, the metropolitan government's official recognition of *curandeirismo*, as borne out by King Dom João VI's award of a pension of forty milreis to a soldier named Antonio Rodrigues who healed by the use of certain potent words.[43] During the imperial period travelers were struck by the white man's acceptance of African practices of curative magic.[44]

Sometimes this dualism in the white attitude toward magic allied itself with the dualism of the social structure, the town-country opposition. In rural Brazil, especially in more remote areas, the black enjoyed considerable prestige because he filled the role of the nonexistent doctor. Saint-Hilaire and Koster observed this during their travels in rural Brazil.[45] In the towns, however, African magic not only encountered opposition from the more enlightened (or more "Roman") clergy[46] but was also degraded by the whites, with their demands for aphrodisiacs and prescriptions to help them get rid of rivals in love or political enemies. In the cities this magic certainly retained more of its specifically African (particularly Bantu) character. It utilized bones stolen from graveyards, which were endowed with especially powerful "virtues". In 1881, when the body of Maria Moreira, an African, was exhumed in the lepers' cemetery three years after her death, the skeleton had no skull.[47]

The recognized need for magic, both good and evil, and the white man's fear of his slaves' witchcraft explain why documents dealing with African magic in Brazil are relatively plentiful. The subject aroused a practical interest that funeral ceremonies or religious dances lacked. The most explicit and detailed of these documents are the ones dealing with snakes— as is quite understandable at a time when antivenins did not exist and field hands were often bitten by those reptiles as they went about their daily work.

Tollenare tells us that Negro healers surrounded themselves with snakes, which would obey their orders after certain preliminaries. The *curandeiro* would hand on his secrets to his successor, and his teaching took the form of a religious initiation, about which Tollenare unfortunately gives no details. A woman friend of his was once so severely bitten by a snake that she was bleeding from all the orifices of her head. She called one of these healers, but he was not able to come himself and merely sent his hat.[48] It was placed on the head of the dying woman, who immediately began to feel better. That evening the witch doctor came himself and summoned the guilty snake. It duly appeared and slithered around the room, terrifying all those present, after which it coiled itself around the Negro, who killed it. In a city square in Recife, Tollenare watched a *feiticeiro* make two snakes dance.[49] A few years later Saint-Hilaire came across similar practices in Minas and São Paulo. The father of the priest of São João d'El Rey in Minas had a slave who handled poison-ous snakes with impunity. One day the priest threatened to strangle this man in order to learn his secret, and the slave revealed that he had become immune to snakebite by rubbing his body with "*urubu* herb." But, asks Saint-Hilaire, what is this herb?[50]

In those days many superstitions were attached to snakes. It was com-monly believed in some regions that the bite of a rattlesnake cured leprosy.[51] Koster refers to these Negro magicians not as "healers" but as *mandingueiros* and says that they could handle the most venomous snakes without danger, summon them with chanting or cries, and cure their bites. In the case of snakebite the patient had to let his head, face, and shoulders be covered by a tame snake, while the *mandingueiro* pronounced magic words. If someone who had been bitten by a snake could not call in one of these witch doctors, he had to go into hiding, because the bite would prove fatal if he were to cast his eye, even unwittingly, on a female creature, especially a woman.[52] D'Assier takes a different view from that of these two travelers. Speaking of the trigocephalous jararaca, a particularly poisonous snake, which, however, "does not seem to harm blacks," he says: "The Negroes have such an instinctive aversion to this reptile that many of them would rather be flogged than touch—never mind profane—a dead snake."[53] The contradiction, however, is only apparent; it may be attributable to a totemic survival or to some ambivalence in the notion of the sacred. In any case, what d'Assier says is certainly true because the Herskovitses encountered the same thing among the descendants of run-away slaves in Dutch Guiana.[54]

What is the origin of this snake complex in Brazil? Some writers believe that it originated in Dahomey, and there is no doubt that the *vodun* cult did exist during the colonial era; in fact the *Codex Felepino* mentions it, attributing it to "Guinea Negroes" in general.[55] Charles Expilly reports that he encountered the cult of the serpent Panga in Brazil but that it originated in the Congo. Expilly is even supposed to have devoted a whole book, entitled "Les Negres Charmeurs," to this subject,[56] but it was never published and I have had no success in tracing the manuscript. The de-scriptions cited here seem to indicate that there is no justification for speaking of a real cult, still less of a survival of ancient African totemism in Brazil. What we are actually dealing with is two associated types of "magic," which we may separate for the sake of clarity. On the one hand we have the Negro snake charmer, possibly of Moslem or Arabian origin (the term *mandingueiro* used by Koster to designate these snake charmers suggests a Mohammedan influence), and on the other the Negro healer of snakebite. The phenomenon is then seen to be merely one particular aspect of a larger whole—curative magic in general—which has already been discussed.

The third and last series of documents at our disposal deals with true religious cults. Unfortunately this is the scantiest category—understandably enough—since magic interested the white man as much as the slave and since funerals were public and attracted the attention of foreign travelers, avid for anything exotic and picturesque, while religion, by contrast, was secret. The oldest known iconographical document is engraving no. 105 in the *Zoobiblion* of Zacharias Wagner, who lived in Dutch Brazil from 1634 to 1641. The accompanying text reads: "When the slaves have worked hard for a whole week, they are given Sunday off. They usually assemble in specially designated places and spend the day in wild dancing to the sound of flutes and drums—men and women, children and old people alike. This is accompanied by frequent libations . . . often until they are too deafened and drunk to recognize one another."[57] But, as René Ribeiro rightly comments, "anyone familiar with the Afro-Brazilian cults of Recife will recognize at a glance that this is a *xangô*: the typical ring of dancers moving to the left in choreographic attitudes; the typical position of the *ogan-ilu* beating two drums of a type commonly found all over West Africa and an *agogo*; the jar of *garapa* beside the musicians; the typical position and pose of the priest. They failed to recognize one another not so much because they were 'deafened and drunk' but because they were possessed by their gods [*ficarem no santo*]—a psychological state of which the artist of course knew nothing."[58]

As I have already pointed out, we must not be deceived by the persistence of certain ritual movements throughout the centuries. The *xangôs* of today are not the successors of seventeenth-century *xangôs*. Evolution has not followed a straight line but a broken one in which sects are born, disappear, and reappear.

The first literary document, a satire by Gregorio de Mattos, also dates from the seventeenth century:

> All these *quilombos*,*
> With peerless masters,
> Teaching by night
> *Calundus* and fetishism.
>
> Thousands of women
> Attend them faithfully.

---

* [Here the word *quilombo* denotes a gathering of blacks, not a settlement of runaway Negroes.]

> So does many a bearded man [a Portuguese]
> Who thinks himself a new Narcissus.
>
> This much I know: in these dances
> Satan's an active partner.
> Only that jovial master
> Can teach such ecstasy.[59]

This text is interesting because it shows that "tourist *candomblés*," originated far back in history. The white element was not excluded from African religion; it participated in it, motivated no doubt by grosser impulses than an interest in ethnology or religious curiosity. This contact tended to break down traditional religion, change its function, and cause it to decline into magic or eroticism. But it must be observed that the cult the poet is describing is not Yoruba or Dahoman but Bantu. The term *calundu* he applies to it recalls certain Angola spirits of that name which take possession of women in labor.[60] The expressions "master" and *cachimbo* (pipe) suggest that these ceremonies attended by whites are analogous to those of the *catimbo*, the *caboclo candomblé*, and the *macumba*—i.e. that they are strongly syncretized with Indian and Catholic elements. The genuine African sects, by contrast, retained all their mysterious secrecy. They did not admit whites. In any event, black religion from the outset held a strange attraction for nonblacks, and this has continued. The satire of Gregorio de Mattos finds a parallel in the second half of the nineteenth century in a poem by Mello Moraes:

> What do I see? Snakes hanging everywhere.
> Hens on the floor and screech owls on the walls.
> Goats without heads are being grilled on coals.
> Enormous fetishes with outspread wings.
> Out of another room a joyful band
> Of dirty blacks bursts forth exultantly,
> Twisting and turning to the sound of bells.
> A flaming wick in earthen-colored oil
> Illumines these strange idol-worshippers.
> Women with skins of different colors dance,
> Their bodies sinuously intertwined,
> Naked, but for a cloth about their loins.[61]

Besides these iconographical and lyrical documents, only two other sources yield any information about African religion: police and administrative records and travelers' accounts of their journeys. During the colonial era, black religion was held to be witchcraft pure and simple, and since witchcraft was prohibited in Portugal, the royal decree prohibiting it came to be applied in Brazil to assemblies of blacks, which, in Christian eyes, had a demonic quality because of the frenetic dancing and especially the episodes of possession that occurred there.[62] In 1780 Count de

Pevolide denounced the dances that the blacks from the Costa das Minas performed "in the secrecy of their homes or in clearings, with a black mistress of ceremonies, an altar of idols, adoring live buck goats and other fetishes of clay, anointing their bodies with oils and cock's blood, eating cakes of cornmeal after pronouncing heathen blessings on them, making the countryfolk believe that those cakes so blessed bring good luck, working love spells on men and women." The Count added this comment: "So great is the credulity of some people—even people one would not expect to be so gullible, like the friars and priests brought before me after being arrested in the house searches I had ordered—that to purge their imagination I had to force the black occupants of those houses to admit to their deception in their presence. Later I was obliged to turn them over to their prelates for the correction they deserved."[63]

Under the empire, this problem presented itself in a slightly different form. Libertarian ideas had infiltrated Brazil from France and North America. The projected constitution of 1823 proclaimed freedom of religion for all Christian communities, "others being merely tolerated." This constitution was not ratified, however, since the constituent assembly was dissolved. The less favorable text that was actually promulgated read: "The Catholic, apostolic, Roman religion will continue to be the religion of the Empire. All other religions will be permitted, with domestic or private worship in special buildings not having the outward appearance of temples." Obviously this paragraph did not refer to slave religion; it applied only to the religion of foreigners, such as Jewish or Protestant merchants who came to settle in Brazil.

The criminal code of 1831 was more deeply rooted in Brazilian social reality and apparently tolerated fetishism on condition that it was confined to the *senzala* and was not practiced in public temples. Nonetheless this code contained one article, Paragraph 179, which gave carte blanche to police intervention: "No one may be prosecuted for religious reasons provided he respects the State and does not offend public morality."[64] In a society regularly disrupted by slave revolts it was easy enough to see black assemblies as a threat to the state, and animal sacrifices and dancing accompanied by mystical trance as offensive to public decency. Paragraph 179, which left the definition of public morality to the judgment of administrators or the regular police, provided legitimation for the campaign waged against the *calundus* and the *candomblés* under the empire, despite the constitution's fine façade of religious tolerance. In 1870, in southern Brazil, the "houses of fortune" (as the fetishist temples were called when the Portuguese expression replaced the old Bantu word *calundu*) were raided by the police and destroyed and their congregations were imprisoned.[65]

In 1876 new persecutions began. The municipal council of Campinas in São Paulo decreed: "The houses commonly known as *zangus* or *batuques* are forbidden. Penalty thirty milreis."[66] In northern Brazil, early in the nineteenth century, an African named Domingos was arrested at a *candomblé* in Bahia but released because he was able to prove that he was a lieutenant in the "Henriques militia."[67] In the same city in 1872 the police surrounded a *candomblé* of the Cross of Souls at midnight and arrested eight people, one of whom was a "madman," Raimundo Nonato, from whose body the *feiticeiros* conjured animals, spirits, and thirty red devils, as a result of which the unfortunate man's body was covered with burns and wounds. (The *feiticeiros* claimed that these were holes for expelling the spirits that were tormenting him.)[68] There is no need to quote further examples; unfortunately they tell us nothing about the organization of these sects, their rituals, or their numerical strength. The purpose of citing this documentary source is merely to show the vitality of a constantly persecuted religion that refused to die but has held out against all assault down to the present day.

Travelers' accounts, however, are more productive. The earliest one (dated 1728) is probably that of the "American pilgrim" Nuno Marques Pereira, who was unable to get any sleep at night because of the sound of drums and the "infernal din." His host explained that a *calundu* was being celebrated: "These are festivals or divinations that the Negroes say they were accustomed to perform in their own lands. When they get together, they perform them here too in order to learn all manner of things, such as what is causing illnesses, or to find lost objects, also to ensure success in hunting or in their gardens, and for many other purposes."[69]

Under the empire such descriptions become more plentiful. In 1821 Maria Graham saw Negroes dancing and singing to the moon and commented: "A superstitious veneration for that beautiful planet is said to be pretty general in savage Africa . . . and probably the slaves, though baptized, dance to the moon in memory of their homes."[70] At first sight this is a surprising comment because moon worship is not particularly common in Africa. It does exist among the Krumano, who furnished some slaves for Brazil, though not very many.[71] In fact the Portuguese connected far more superstitions with the moon than did the blacks. They used to present newborn babies to the waxing moon so that the child would grow with it:

> O, my moon,
> Moonlight, my godmother,
> Take your son
> And help him to grow![72]

Even if Maria Graham's interpretation was correct and the blacks were really dancing to the moon, we should not forget that in Brazil culture and race were two separate things and that many Creole slaves had inherited traits of the Portuguese civilization, while the whites had acquired many

African ones. It is therefore impossible to deduce the geographical origin of a custom from the color of the people practicing it. The moon plays a big role in Mediterranean culture; it is linked with water and women, with cycles of madness, and with the growth of plants. There is nothing African about this lore, even though Africans may have adopted it in their new habitat. It seems to me more likely that Maria Graham misunderstood the Brazilians' answers to her questions and that her statement should be rephrased to read "singing and dancing by moonlight."* This would refer to night dancing, which is an ancestral custom, not to dancing dedicated to the worship of the moon.

A little later, in 1839, Kidder and Fletcher mention "fetisches [*sic*]," which they associate with black secret societies for the celebration of native customs.[73] At Olinda in 1816 Koster notes that when the slaves in the *senzala* believed their masters to be asleep, they would sometimes invite other Negroes "to a nocturnal festival celebrated in deepest mystery like the festivals of the Good Goddess."[74]

This secrecy prevented travelers from observing African sects more closely. In any case they were more interested in eroticism than in religion. Tollenare, for instance, tells us in 1817 that the Negroes danced in couples surrounded by a ring of sepectators. "They would act out the lewdness of the monkey, the bear, or some other animal. With a coarse gesture the male would place a paw upon the woman. She would make as if to defend herself, run away, but finally yield, at which the two dancers would fall upon one another." Sometimes the couple would be joined by a third dancer armed with a stick, symbolizing the hunter. Often he would strike a young Negro, who seemed happy at being singled out in this way.[75] Tollenare, the gallant Frenchman, saw only sexuality in these animal dances, but they actually represent something quite different, although in a total civilization in which everything hangs together the sexual cannot be divorced from the mystical! Probably what Tollenare is describing is a dance that still exists in Africa and that some ethnologists believe to be the origin of black African theater. The dance is called the *nanzeke*. A group of men dressed as hunters confronts a group of masked men disguised as animals. Nanzeke kills a taboo antelope, which weeps at having been killed. The hunter's wife, known as the "guardian of the fetishes," intervenes.[76] This dance also occurs, in a form much closer to the Brazilian one, among the black Caribs of Honduras. Here there is only one hunter, and the dead animal is brought back to life by the *feiticeiro*.[77] Today these two fragments of the African dance coexist in Brazil: the groups of animals and hunters in the *ranchos* of Bahia,[78] the death of the sacred or taboo animal and its resurrection by the witch doctor in the *bumba-meu-*

---

* [Bastide has misread the text or read a bad translation. Maria Graham actually did write exactly what he says she should have written: that she "found parties playing, singing and dancing to the moonlight."]

boi. The African dance, along with European and Indian ones, is certainly one of the sources of the *bumba-meu-boi*,[79] although to my knowledge, this has never been pointed out. In this way more or less totemic survivals revealed themselves in the substructure of public dances—the only ones that foreign visitors could describe in any detail because they were the only ones they witnessed.

■ ■ ■

By separating people of different colors into stratified classes, each possessing its own civilization, the Brazilian social structure in the era of slavery naturally falsified the individual values of each class. Unable to comprehend a religion so different from his own, the white man wrote off black religion as "demonic" just because it was not Christian. Social dualism was extended—as well as justified—by the polarization of the forces of good, which descended from God to the plantation owner, and the forces of evil, which descended from Satan to his cohorts in the *senzalas* and the *mocambos*. In this way the white man stifled his qualms of conscience. In his eyes, the blacks' religious dances around stones bathed in the blood of sacrificial animals justified the social gap that separated him from them. Writing off the African civilizations as diabolical was a rationalization of the brutality and inhumanity of slavery.

Folklore, which keeps alive the beliefs of bygone centuries, still preserves traces of this more or less conscious falsification of the black religions and of the link between the slaves' paganism and the dualism of the social structure. Negro beliefs and religious rites are seen as the demonic aspect, the dark side, of this deep-rooted dualism:

> The Negro does not worship God;
> He worships Calunga.

> Every white man wants to get rich;
> Every mulatto is a braggart.
> Every gypsy is a thief;
> And every Negro is a *feiticeiro*.

> The mulatto is never without his knife
> Or the white man without his wisdom.
> The *cabra* is never without his brandy
> Or the Negro without his fetishism.[80]

> When an old Negro dies,
> He stinks so bad
> That Our Lady won't allow
> A black to enter Heaven.[81]

"The black has the foot of an animal, nails like wild game, a cleft heel, and his little finger is like Saint Paul's cucumber,"[82] says one description, which comes fairly close to the medieval Christian's traditional image of the Devil.

The white man might indeed have been mysteriously attracted by the dark paths of black religion, just as he was sexually attracted by women of color. As I have said, he might even have frequented *calundus* or organized African cults of his own. (Saint-Hilaire mentions a white ceremony in the village of Lage held in the "*mandinga* house," i.e. the house of African witchcraft. It consisted of a combination of Catholic prayers and *batuques* danced first by men alone, then by men and women together.)[83] But the fact remains that he always saw Africa in a Christian perspective, from the viewpoint of a Christianity more or less tinged with Manicheism. To participate in African religion was to descend into the abyss.

Until the beginning of the twentieth century the white man never made any effort to transcend his own concepts and culture in order to understand his slaves' religion. On the contrary, his distortion of African values justified his attitude. It was not until Brazil abolished slavery and proclaimed the equality of all citizens, regardless of skin color or ethnic origin, that the scholars could finally look at Afro-Brazilian culture with a minimum of ethnocentrism. The advance from a completely negative approach to a scientific one has something to do with the social situation that abolished, legally at least, the master-slave, white-black dualism of society. It resulted from a structural change that called for the integration of people of color into a unified, harmonious community, on a footing of equality.

Up until then, throughout the whole period of slavery, there had been a double falsification of values. We have seen how the whites degraded African values. Now we must see how the blacks degraded Portuguese values.

The black church, with its brotherhoods and carnivals, was superimposed on the *calundus* and the *cachimbos*. When the police raided a "house of fortune," they would sometimes arrest a king or official of one of these Catholic fraternities in the act of dancing or sacrificing.[84] In other words, the blacks inevitably conceived of Christianity in terms of their own conceptions of the sacred, just as their masters conceived of the African religions in terms of the Manichean dualism between God and the Devil. Unquestionably the masters wanted to turn the black church into an instrument of social control and racial dominance—perhaps an even more effective instrument than their bush captains and plantation overseers. (Here I refer the reader to some of the texts cited in Chapter 5 above.) All the time they were asserting that Saint Peter refused to open the gates of Heaven to Negroes or that the Blessed Virgin denied them entry because they stank, they saw nothing wrong with displacing the slaves' animosity onto thoughts of posthumous revenge. Earthly suffering, hard labor, and punishment endured would be requited in the beyond. The "valley of tears" of their earthly life would bring them glory in heaven after death. The ruling class—although it dared not admit it—did indeed regard religion as opium (to use Marx's expression) capable of breaking earthly resistance, castrating the spirit of rebellion in the oppressed, and dispersing opposition in vague messianic dreams.

But—and this comment might well serve as the basis for a critique of Marxism—this is to forget that the black reinterpreted Christianity in terms of his own utilitarian, collective religion. To call religion the opium of the people is not so much to define religion in general as to define a specific tactic of utilizing religion, with its emphasis on the immortality of the soul, at a strategic moment in the class struggle. The method was tried out in colonial and imperial Brazil. It proved successful—more successful among the mulattoes and mestizos than among the pure blacks, and more successful among pure blacks who had lost their native civilizations and were totally alienated than among the others. The little black angels one sometimes sees in Baroque churches in Minas or northeastern Brazil, hovering amid plaster clouds beside blond, blue-eyed cherubs, are proof of this. In other words, Marx's definition is applicable only in social situations where other Marxist categories appear, especially alienation. The black member of a brotherhood and a "nation," the *batuque* dancer, visualized the saints and the Blessed Virgin of his black church exactly as he visualized his gods or his ancestors, not as bestowers of celestial grace but as protectors of his earthly life. He asked them, as he would have asked his *orixá* or his *voduns*, for a good spouse, the return of a lover, the death of his enemies, deliverance from his earthly lot. Among the common people the cult of the saints undoubtedly took this same form. The Portuguese prayed to Saint Anthony to send rain; young girls prayed to Saint John the Baptist to send them a husband; old maids prayed to Saint Gonçalves. But they also asked their saints to cut short their time in Purgatory and to intercede for their admission to the heaven of the Lord God and the Virgin Mary. It was the latter aspect that escaped the black. As Ortiz puts it: "His theoanthropic economy is not one of long-term credit or enrichment, nor of capitalizing his interest by investing it in heaven, which, on the day of his death, will return eternal profits. It is a religion of immediate consumption, of barter rites, without credit or accumulated interest."[85]

In return for sacrifices, the ancestors protected their lineages. In return for festivals in their honor, the Yoruba or Dahoman divinities protected the village crops, hunting or martial expeditions, fishing trips at sea or in the lagoons. In the same way the miraculous saints were expected to help members of their fraternities in their daily lives—the only lives that interested them—in return for immediate payment or "promises." A lighted candle or an *ex voto* like those of the whites simply replaced the sacrifice of a cock or a goat. The principle remained the same—*do ut des*—but the reward was expected immediately, not in some problematic beyond.

Although Catholicism, in imposing itself on African religion, did adulterate it, it is only fair to say that, in the beginning at any rate, it was African religion that adulterated Catholicism. It did so by adopting the cult of the saints while robbing it of part of its significance and accepting only what could be adapted to a barter economy of gifts and countergifts, of exchange without celestial investment. To the slaves, Christianity did not offer compensation for their lot or sublimation of suffering. That sort of thing was comprehensible only to the white mentality and could appeal only to alienated blacks. The Negro church did not provide "opium for the people"—or at any rate did not provide it very effectively. It did not become the instrument of social control, the means of displacing animosity, that the whites had hoped it might be. Hence it did not serve as a link between the social strata. The dualism of the civilizations combined with class dualism to adulterate the specific values of both sides, reinterpreting the Africans' collective representations in Christian terms and the collective representations of the Portuguese in African terms, and underlining the paradoxical character that this "Catholic-fetishist syncretism" had shown from the very beginning. We shall return later to its paradoxical character, which has to do with the same words being used by the two parties in a different sense.

7
Black Islam in Brazil

In discussing survivals of African religion in colonial and imperial Brazil I have left aside the cults of the Mohammedan "nations." In listing the various ethnic groups that furnished slaves to Brazil I did, however, note that black Islam contributed its quota to the Brazilian population. In the new homeland this group jealously guarded its religious beliefs. Toward the end of the empire and during the early years of the republic, when documentation becomes more objective and accounts of Negro religions more detailed, writers begin to draw a careful distinction between the two major religions, which they refer to as the Mussulman and fetishist cults.[1] Yet the former has almost completely died out; in the words of Arthur Ramos, it is now no more than "a page in history."[2] For this reason it is included in the first section of this work, the section dealing with the historical evolution of the transplanted civilizations in their relations with the new social structures.

The Mussulman religion in Brazil was the religion of certain colored slaves known as Musulmi or Malê. The name "Musulmi" is self-explanatory; the name "Malê" has been much discussed.[3] Obviously it is a corruption of Mali, the name of one of the Mohammedan kingdoms of the Niger valley, inhabited in the thirteenth century by the Malinka. The Malinka are also known as Mandinga, and, as we shall see, in Brazil the word *mandinga* came to designate black magic. Strictly speaking, however, it was the Hausa, not the Malê, who introduced Mohammedanism to Brazil. While the Hausa certainly constituted the majority of Islamized Negroes, slavery threw them together with other tribes of the same religion, including some of the Nagô, the Bornú or Adamana, the Gurushi, Guruncu or

Grúnce, the Mandinga, and the Fuláh or Peul.⁴ Early travelers and historians also speak of Minas as Mussulmans, but the name "Mina," which originally designated not an ethnic group but a place—the big Portuguese slave market on the coast of West Africa—was, as we have seen, applied to anyone who did not belong to the Bantu groups. Hence some Mina were Mussulmans; some were not.

With very few exceptions, all these tribes were either pure Negro or of mixed Negro and Hamite blood. They were therefore Islamized animists, not Mohammedans by origin. Their old beliefs had not entirely died out.⁵ It was this Mohammedan-fetishist syncretism, not the pure Islam of Mohammed, that was introduced into Brazil.

These tribes were unusually successful in resisting Christianization and clung to their proud, intractable faith with jealous steadfastness. All travelers agree on this point. The best account of their intransigence is perhaps the one written by Count de Gobineau while he was ambassador at Rio:

> Most of these Mina, if not all, are outwardly Christians but actually Mussulmans. Since this religion would not be tolerated in Brazil, they practice it in secret, and most of them are baptized, with names borrowed from the calendar. Notwithstanding outward appearances, I have been able to ascertain that they faithfully cherish the beliefs they bring with them from Africa and zealously hand them on, since they study Arabic thoroughly enough to understand the Koran, at least roughly. This book is sold in Rio at 15 to 25 cruzeiros or 36 to 40 francs by the French booksellers Fauchon and Dupont, who import copies from Europe. Slaves who appear to be quite poor are willing to make the greatest sacrifices to acquire this volume, going into debt to do so and sometimes taking a year to pay off the bookseller. About a hundred copies of the Koran are sold every year. . . . So far as I know, the existence of a Mussulman colony in America has not previously been noted. . . . It explains the particularly vigorous attitude of the Mina Negroes.⁶

These statements are, it is true, contradicted by other data from Rio from the same period. It has been stated that a mosque founded by Mohammedan Negroes existed in 1840 in the Rua Baron Saint Felix, but the only evidence I have been able to discover is the existence of a black named João Alabah who occasionally requested police permission to hold celebrations in his house. Although he regarded the Mussulmans as "brothers," his religion did not go beyond fetishism. The only Mohammedan whose address Alabah was able to furnish stated that there was no mosque in Rio, and he could name only six Negro Mussulmans, who practiced their cult in their own homes. Perhaps these contradictory statements can be reconciled by the hypothesis that the Moslem "Mina" in Rio, although numerous, were all to some degree fetishists and stayed out of sight to avoid persecution, celebrating their rites in their own homes.

The Moslems were distributed practically all over Brazil. We know specifically that they existed in São Paulo, where, according to the testimony of a slave, there was a mosque for the practice of their cult,[7] and in the states of Alagoas, Pernambuco, and Paraíba.[8] But the greatest concentration was in Bahia, where they were the life and soul of the slave revolts and where, according to Nina Rodrigues, at the end of the nineteenth century they still constituted one-third of the population of African origin and maintained a highly organized cult.

> They have a central authority, the *iman* or *almany*, and many subordinate priests. Here the *iman* is called the *limano*, which is evidently a corruption or variation of the pronunciation of *almány* or *El imány*. The priests, who are actually marabouts, are known in Bahia as *alufás*. I myself am acquainted with several.[9] . . . The present *limano* is a Nagô named Luis, and the seat of the Mohammedan church is his house in Barris, at number 3, Rua Alegria. The *limano* is a big man, robust but very stooped with age. . . . His present wife is a Creole Negress who is over thirty and who spent some time in Rio de Janeiro, where she converted to Islam. She is a very honest, intelligent Negress who can read and write a little, and she is well versed in the Koran. Since she does not know Arabic, and the *limano* can neither read nor write Portuguese, they have in their home an Arabic Koran for the *limano* and a Portuguese translation for his wife.[10]

The second major center of the Moslem population after Bahia was Rio. Within a few years of Nina Rodrigues's description of the last Mohammedan survivors in Bahia, João de Rio wrote an account of the religions of the Brazilian capital. He distinguished two types of African religious survivals: the *orixá* and the *alufa* cults, i.e. the cults of the Yoruba and the Moslem sects.[11] He also noted that the Moslems observed the religious holidays of the other blacks, but this does not necessarily imply the emergence of a racial consciousness in resistance to slavery; it merely shows the depth of religious syncretism and the persistence of primitive paganism among the Islamized Negroes.[12] The Pernambucan cult illustrates this syncretism. There the *alufa* or Moslem priest would foretell the future by pouring palm oil and blood over three purple stones. One of these was known as the "Saint Barbara stone," and the others were meteorites.[13] Now Saint Barbara is the Catholic equivalent of Xangô, the thunder god, whose emblem is the thunderbolt or meteorite. Obviously the Islamic and Yoruba religions had intermixed.

The same was true in Alagoas, where the "Malê" sect of Tia Marcelina still existed in 1912. It was said that new initiates had to prostitute themselves to Ali-Babâ, the god of the sect, who assumed the form of "a child draped in red cloth, wearing necklaces of *ofás* and *oôs*." An *alufa* was in charge of the *orixá-alum* house, where the walls were painted with arabesques and the hymns that were sung showed some more or less remote Moslem influence: "*Edurê, edurê, alilala. . . .*" The ceremonies, however, invoked Yoruba divinities such as Oxalá, Ogun, Xangô, etc.[14]

Everywhere the Islamic cults disintegrated and merged with those of the other "nations," adopting their divinities and rituals and forgetting Allah and his prophet Mohammed.

But if the Mohammedan faith was so proud and so resistant to Catholic proselytizing, is it not paradoxical that it should have so suddenly died out or undergone such profound adulteration? There are several explanations. First, the number of Hausa diminished considerably after the revolution of 1813, when the troublemakers were either massacred or deported to Africa.[15] Those who remained made few converts, largely because of their racial or religious snobbery, which caused them to hold aloof from the other Africans, keeping to themselves and not mixing with their brothers in misfortune,[16] going to bed early while the other Negroes preferred to stay up late to celebrate their pagan rituals.[17] By establishing Catholicism as the religion of the masters and Mohammedanism as the religion of the insurrectionary leaders, slavery tended in early times to promote Islam, especially within groups that retained their African languages. But abolition and the theoretical equality of all Brazilians before the law destroyed one of the major incentives to conversion. The *iman* Luis told Nina Rodrigues how painful it was to him to see sons of Malê embracing fetishist sects or Christianity rather than holding fast to the faith of their ancestors.[18] Just as an animal species becomes extinct when its last representatives die out, Mohammedanism in Brazil, having lost all potential for renewal or propagation, died out along with its old adherents. But before it became totally extinct, just as its death agony was beginning, such men as Mello Moraes, Manoel Querino, Étienne Brasil, Nina Rodrigues, and João de Rio were able to observe and study it. From their descriptions we shall try to reconstitute the life of the black Islamic community in colonial Brazil.

It was essentially a Puritan community. Its outward morality, sobriety, and temperance contrasted strongly with the other Africans' noisy exuberance and their liking for alcohol and for singing and shouting. The Moslems' appearance, their quiet conversational tone, restrained gestures, and pointed beards symbolized their ethnic and religious separateness.[19] Above all, the Moslem's faith set the rhythm of his life, marking its every phase from birth to death, accenting the passage of the day from sunrise to sunset.[20]

It appears that a Mussulman baby was baptized at birth.[21] By the time he was ten he had been circumcised.[22] Then his instruction would begin, for the Mohammedans attached great importance to education.[23] Since his faith required the reading of the Koran, he had to be able to read and write Arabic script. Schools were therefore established in conjunction with the Moslem places of worship, in the homes of free Africans. House searches conducted after Hausa or Mina revolts produced alphabets, reading primers, and wall posters of lessons to be learned.[24] In Rio, Arabic grammars written in French were used.[25] Free members of the community even went to Africa to study so that they might later devote themselves to teaching the slave population of Brazil.

Marriage was a sacrament marking the end of childhood and the Mussulman's entry into adult society. The *iman* presided over the ceremony. He would begin by calling upon the couple to think carefully so that they would never regret the action they were about to take. After giving them a few minutes to reflect, he would ask if they were sincerely marrying each other by free consent. If the reply was affirmative, the bride, "dressed in white, her face covered with a tulle veil," placed a silver ring on the finger of her future husband, and he, "dressed in wide Turkish-style trousers," gave his future wife a silver chain as they repeated the words "*Sadaca do Alamabi* (I give this to you in the name of God)."

> They would then kneel, and the *iman* began the ceremony. He reminded them both of their duties and exhorted them to behave fittingly and not to violate their ritual obligations. In conclusion the young couple stood and kissed the priest's hand. The ceremony over, everyone adjourned to the house where the banquet was to be held. While everyone else remained seated, the bride walked to the center of the room, clapped her hands, sang a song, and returned to her place. Then came the wedding banquet of chicken, fish, fruit, etc., which included no alcoholic beverages.[26]

Now married life began. Polygamy was permitted and practiced among the Mussulmans in Brazil.[27] The women were subject to an extremely strict code of honor. "Any woman who failed in her conjugal duties was a general outcast; no one would show her any favor. Nevertheless the husband could not beat her. An unfaithful wife was allowed to leave her house only in the evening, chaperoned by someone whom her husband trusted."[28]

Married women retained some of the customs of their native country, especially the use of cosmetics. They painted their eyelids as a sign of beauty.[29] They did not, however, veil the face as they did in Africa.[30] It appears that these Malê led a quiet life, getting up and going to bed early, observing scrupulous rules of hygiene and keeping to themselves.[31]

When a Mussulman died, his body was washed, then dressed in a white shirt known as an *abada*. A cap with a white tassel called a *fila* was placed on his head; this was in fact the ritual headdress. The funeral was conducted in the Brazilian manner.[32] It was rumored that the bones of the corpse were broken and dislocated before it was placed in the coffin, but this seems not to be true; "they simply laid it on its side, not supine," in the coffin.[33] Although society prevented the Malê from conducting their funerals exactly according to their own tradition, they made up for this by hold their own festival of the dead twice a year. A description of one of these allegedly Mohammedan festivals was written in 1888.[34] The ceremonies consisted of three parts and were preceded by a preparatory period marked by abstinence from strong liquor, alcohol, meat, and cereals, which would have destroyed the effectiveness of the rites. During this time meals were restricted to a few vegetables and a little milk and water.

First Phase: The Prayers

The Africans assembled in a humble but roomy hut deep in the forest to meditate on death and the beyond.

> This group of penitents expiating the souls' wrongdoing included chiefs, deputy chiefs, and lower dignitaries of the hierarchy. All were dressed in a kind of alb and wore white caps; the chief was distinguished only by his striped robe and special headdress. . . . One feature of the cult was that these Africans spent the first night of the wake in monotonous chanting, accompanied by their primitive instruments. These prayers and lugubrious incantations ended before the second day of the funeral celebration. The women and families attended this opening ceremony and later devoted themselves to preparing the banquet and performing macabre imitative dances.

Second Phase: The Sacrifice

> At the stroke of midnight initiating the day of the banquet, the sacrificial attendants led ewes to the edge of trenches dug in the ground. With raised hatchets, they awaited the first glimmer of light before slaughtering them. The blood was not allowed to stain their hands but flowed into the trenches to nourish the spirits of the dead. The animals were then dismembered, and portions were reserved for those who were not present. This part of the ceremony was secret; no stranger was allowed to witness it.

Third Phase: The Banquet and Dances

The whole neighborhood was invited; even townspeople could participate.

> Wearing their turbans and *panos da costa*, embroidered skirts and light sandals, the Negroes plied the guests attending this strange feast with food prepared in their own special way. Dressed in white clothes similar to the costume of the Sahara desert and the sands of Oman, the high priest and his aides presided over the principal meals of these last two days. . . . Afterward, African matrons with tattooed faces would inconspicuously withdraw, moving superbly and carrying food concealed in the folds of their Angola robes. Walking circumspectly, with furtive looks and gestures, they scattered on the ground and under rocks food for the funeral banquet of the souls, who were supposed to come to share the commemorative offerings during the secret hours of the night.

Then, in the courtyard outside the hut, the dancing began, accompanied by African instruments. From the extremely literary description we learn that it was the high priest who indicated when the dancing was to begin, and also that various kinds of dances were performed, profane as well as religious, Portuguese as well as African, each "nation" following its own customs. The purpose of these concluding dances, which went on for three nights, seems to have been utilitarian—indeed financial—rather than religious. Their function was to raise funds for the festival, or so we can assume from the fact that this part of the ceremony was public. This assumption is confirmed by the following passage in Mello Moraes's text;

> One of the Negro dancing girls broke away from the circle and danced toward the secular spectators surrounding the performers. She was becomingly and richly dressed. Over her hand fell a shower of multicolored ribbons attached to a silver wand sixty centimeters long surmounted by [an ornament] the size of the palm of a hand, made of gold coins interspersed with pearls and *bouzios*. Singling out one spectator, she stopped in front of him and handed him the wand, inviting him to dance. If he accepted, there was general satisfaction and unrestrained joy. If he refused, he made up for it by contributing one or two *reis* for the festival. If he gave more, cheers and applause rewarded his generosity, and the death dancers would give him sprays of flowers interlaced with ribbons, to the accompaniment or prolonged, noisy acclamations. Then she approached another spectator, and another. . . .

An article by Ricard questions the Moslem character of this festival on the grounds that Mohammedanism is known to oppose the cult of the dead.[35] The point is well taken, but there is a possible explanation. We have seen how deeply the Malê cults in Alagoas were syncretized with Yoruba cults, so a contamination is entirely possible. We cannot judge black Islam in Brazil by the same criteria as black Islam in Africa or categorically deny the possibility that this cult of the dead in Alagoas, unorthodox as it was, may have been organized by incompletely Islamized blacks.

Be that as it may, religious observance set the rhythm of life for the faithful and determined the fate of the souls of the dead. The principles of the Koran dominated not only the essential frameworks of existence but daily life too. The devout Mussulman's day began at four o'clock in the morning. Dressed in a tight shirt, trousers, and a tasseled skullcap, all made of the whitest cotton, and holding his *teceba*, a rosary fifty centimeters long consisting of ninety-nine big wooden beads and ending in an ball, he stood on a sheepskin and recited his prayers.[36] This was called "performing *sala*." The Portuguese word *sala* is probably a corruption of *sara*, which, as we shall see, designated the most important religious ceremonies of the Moslems. No doubt the corruption stems from an awareness of the distinction between private and public worship and represents an attempt to express this distinction linguistically. Everyone who could do so recited his prayers four more times in the course of the day. The Bahian names for these five exercises were: *açubá* (morning), *al-lá* (noon), *ay-à-sari* (afternoon), *alimangariba* (sunset), and *adisha* (night); they were preceded and concluded by sacramental phrases such as *"Bi-si-mi-lai* (In the name of God, forgiving and merciful)."[37] Every prayer was preceded by an ablution, for which the Negro removed his ordinary clothes and donned a white shirt with long sleeves called an *abada*.[38]

On Fridays and holidays the *sara*, corresponding to Catholic mass, was celebrated. Manoel Querino has described this ceremony.

> In the morning a table covered with a white cotton cloth was set, presided over by the head *lemano*. After a light meal, the congregation, all holding rosaries, listened as the high priest pronounced the words: *"Lá-i-lá-la-lau, mama-dù dù araçù-lu-lai. Sa-la-lai-a-lei-i-sàlama* (O God, the one true God, it is Thy prophet who guides us). *Acheádo-ano-lá-i-lá, i-la-leu* (Thou art the only true god). *Acheádo-ano-mama dù ara-sululai* (And thy prophet is our master). *Ai-à-la-li-sa lá* (I bring my prayers). *Ai-à-la-li-sa lá* (I bring my prayers). *Ai-à-la-li-falá* (I bring my heart). *Cadecama-i-salá* (On Mount Sinai)." During the religious service the women would from time to time repeat the phrase *"Bi-si-mi-lai."* Then the priest would rise, turn his back to the congregation, raise his hands, then lower them to his chest, kneel, bow in reverence and repeat the words with which he had begun: *"Lá-i-lá, i-la-lau, mamadu-araçù-lu-lai. Sa-la-lai-a-lei-i-salama."* Then he shook hands with his cocelebrants, who in turn shook hands with the other people present, and the ceremony was over. While it was going on, the mistress of the house would approach the members of the congregation and with a movement resembling a genuflection, her arms crossed, would greet them with the words *"Barica de subá môtumba* (My respects)."[39]

Obviously slaves could not undertake the pilgrimage to Mecca because of their status, and free Negroes could not because of the distance,[40] but they always observed the fast of Ramadan.[41] The Mussulmans also abstained from certain foods, notably salt pork. They justified this taboo with a legend of Moslem missionaries dying of thirst in the desert who encountered a herd of pigs rooting around in the sand with their snouts. Suddenly they were astonished to see water spurt from the holes the pigs had made. They chased the pigs away, and a miraculous torrent gushed around their feet.[42]

For the Mussulmans the dog was a sacred animal provided it had never had sexual intercourse; "the moisture of its nostrils, if rubbed on the hands and face, inspired soothsayers to marvelous revelations." Otherwise dogs were not allowed to enter Moslem homes.[43] The Mussulmans were notorious among the other Negroes for their powerful magic. They had all kinds of amulets, talismans, and charms, most commonly in the form of Solomon's seals, and papers on which verses from the Koran were inscribed and which they carried in little bags hung around the neck.[44] A favorite procedure for gaining immunity to bullets—one which Nina

Rodrigues saw in use during Hausa revolts—was to write certain Arabic signs on a black tablet, then rinse the tablet and drink the water.[45] The same procedure was used to cast a spell, but in that case the water, instead of being swallowed, was sprinkled on a path that the victim would use. The signs inscribed and then washed off would then, of course, be curses.[46] How deeply this magic impressed other Africans can be seen from the survival of the names *mandinga* for an object used in black magic and *mandingueiro* for the practitioner.

We know little about the beliefs of these Mussulmans. Étienne Brasil's minute description of their theology is so general as to be applicable to Moslems anywhere in the world. What interests us is not Islamic beliefs and dogmas per se but those held by the Brazilian Mussulmans. Here we must be content with Querino's brief account: "They recognized only two higher entities, Olorum-u-luá (God the creator) and Mariana (the mother of Jesus Christ.) They held Satan in contempt; according to them he has no power in this world."[47] One of their prayers mentions "a refuge from evil spirits,"[48] which suggests that they had brought the djin cult with them to their new habitat.

One description of the Mussulman sect in Rio confirms the data from Bahia and, sketchy as it is, even provides some new details:

> The *alufás* practice a different rite [from the Yoruba]. They are Mohammedans with an underlying mysticism. . . . After the *suma* (baptism) and *kola* (circumcision), the *alufás* begin to read the Alcoran. Their obligation consists of the *kissium* (prayer). They pray after bathing and washing the feet and nose with their fingertips. They pray in the morning and they pray at sunset. I have seen them—black, their shining faces standing out among the white beards—performing the *aluma gariba* as the crescent moon rose in the sky. For these prayers they wear the *abada*, a white tunic with wide sleeves, and wrap the head in a red turban with a white tassel. They resume the *kissium* at night, seated on sheepskins or snow leopard skins. . . . At night they say the rosary or *tessuba*. They do not eat pork. They inscribe their prayers on tablets called *atô* with ink made of burned rice. Like the Jews, they fast for forty days at a time. . . . They have vicars-general or *ladamas* who owe obedience to the *lemano* or bishop. Their legal affairs are administered by *alikali* (judges) whose immediate subordinates are the *sagabamo* and by *assivajiu* (masters of ceremonies). Much study is required to become an *alufá*, and nothing keeps these blacks, who make a show of being serious-minded and marry with solemnity, from contracting an *amuré* with three or four women. When the young *alufá* completes his examinations, the other Mussulmans dance the *opa-suma* and lead him through the streets on horseback to symbolize his success. . . . These ceremonies are always performed on the outskirts of the town, in remote places.[49]

In Rio, as in Bahia, the Malê were regarded as masters of black magic, and many of them earned their living—and a good living—by selling spells and charms. João de Rio notes that, despite their monotheism, in preparing these spells they had recourse to *aligenum* (devils), a term which is obviously a corruption of *djinn*,[50] and that some of them had acquired great reputations in this art. *Alikali*, for instance, made *idams* to induce rain.[51]

How much of this rich tradition survives today? In 1937 the Bahia Union of Afro-Brazilian Sects still included a *candomblé* of the "Mussurumin" nation situated on the Rua da Liberdade and directed by Pedro Manuel de Espirito Santo.[52] We know little about it, but the corruption of the name "Mussulman" is in itself enough to suggest that its Mohammedanism—if any—must have been considerably modified. Some of the hymns sung at Bantu or Nagô *candomblés* include the name of Allah. Edison Carneiro noted two of these, one at Itaporan in 1936,

> Allah!
> Allah of God!
> Allah!

the other at a *candomblé* in Gantois,

> Allah!
> Oîô Allah!
> Babá quara dà.[53]

In Rio the spirits that incarnate themselves during the *macumba* establish "lines." One of these lines still exists and is called "the line of Mussurumin, Massuruman, Massurumin, or Massuruhy." Since Malê magic was considered particularly effective and dangerous, this line consists entirely of evil spirits who come down to earth to wreak vengeance. They are invoked by tracing on the ground circles of gunpowder surrounding cigarettes, drinks, pins, tobacco, chickens, etc. The gunpowder is lighted, and the spirits descend during the din of the explosion. The heads of these lines are called "Alufa," "Father Alufa," or "Uncle Alufa."[54] In 1934, in Alagoas, Arthur Ramos collected a Malê hymn to Ogun:

> Little Ogun is of the Malê race.
> Nu-ê, nu-ê!
> Little Ogun is of the Malê race.
> Nu-ê, ê-rê-rê-rê![55]

Olorun, the chief Nagô god, was finally merged with Allah, producing the new divinity Olorun-ulua (*uluà* being a corruption of *Allah*).[56]

In Bahia the name *ala* is applied to the white cloth used to make a kind of canopy beneath which the *filhas de santos* pass and also to cover the sacred stones in the *pegi*. In Pôrto Alegre it designates the cloth in which one of the cult drums is wrapped.[57] The term, however, is undoubtedly the Yoruba word for this white cloth rather than a specifically Moslem survival.[58]

Many features of Brazilian life that might at first sight seem to be of Arabic origin were introduced not by the Mussulmans but by the Nagô. This is true of geomancy, which is dying out.[59] It is interesting to note that in Bahia geomancy was often practiced by the Malê. The *babalaô* (soothsayer), Felisberto Salge, now dead, was addressed as "Mussurumi."[60] Informants of Protasius Frikel connected the cult of the *egun* (the dead) with Islam. "The Nagô and Gêgê do not work with the spirits of the dead. It is the Mussurumi and the Malê who evoke their spirits. Only the Mussurumi have a house of the dead . . . but the Malê are all dead. . . . Gunocô has gone back to Africa. . . . He speaks into the wind, but no one understands him any more."[61] With all due respect to this informant, the *egun* cult still survives, but, as Ricard has pointed out, it has nothing to do with Islam. Even though the leader of the cult may be named Aliba (recalling Ali-Babâ in Alagoas and the *alagba* or black African priest[62]), we must remember Verger's warning not to confuse terms that are similar in spelling but differently accentuated.[63] Nevertheless the fact remains that in Dahomey the *egun* secret society is often in the hands of Islamized blacks, while the *voduns* belong to non-Moslem blacks.[64] And Fernando Ortiz cites the Cuban masked dance of the *Kulona* (the Malê adjective *kulona* or *lonna* means "knowledgeable" or "erudite") as being connected with burial rites for the "little devils."[65] We may therefore assume that what these Mussulman blacks brought to Brazil was not so much Islam as the many elements of earlier cults that had been merged with Islam after it reached Africa. When Mohammedanism died out, only these early elements survived. Paganism, temporarily hidden beneath a Moslem veneer, broke through again in Brazil.

What happened in Brazil was the opposite of what happened on the black continent. In West Africa Islam triumphed over fetishism, steadily driving it back and gaining a firmer grip on the black continent. It even opposed the Christian missions—often victoriously. In Brazil, however, Islam died out, leaving the Gêgê-Nagô religion and Christianity in the lead. How can this sociological contrast be explained?

In the first place the Mussulmans never amounted to more than a minority of the colored population. They were also what might be called "passive" Moslems, i.e. Islamized blacks, converts, not pure Semites. Lacking all proselytizing spirit, the best they could do was to hold out as long as possible. In addition to this demographic explanation, there is also a psychological one: the Moslem's pride, his unwillingness to mix with other slaves, his desire to live in a world apart. Hence a change in his social situation produced a change in collective behavior; a proselytizing faith turned into a religion of mystical isolation.

So far as the fetishist Negroes were concerned, Islam and Christianity exchanged positions in moving from Africa to Brazil. In Africa Islam demanded less individual sacrifice than Catholicism or Protestantism. It discarded mythology in favor of dogma. It imposed certain taboos and prayers but required no strenuous moral effort. It accommodated itself to the sensuality of the Negro. In Brazil, on the other hand, Catholicism was the most appealing and the most tolerant religion. Confident that the influence of the environment would gradually change the African's heart and soul, all it asked of him was to learn by rote a few gestures and words, not to remake his personality. Hence in Brazil Islam came to represent Puritanism—especially because of its prohibition of excessive drinking, which was particularly hard on wretched slaves seeking an escape from reality in the sugar cane brandy known as *cachaça*.[66]

To the Negro the Mohammedan was not a comrade in slavery. Only in an insurrectionary situation—i.e., in exceptional circumstances—could he become a leader. The white man represented the world of liberty to which manumission gave access. But the *sine qua non* of such access was to imitate the whites. Hence the attraction of Catholicism.

All these factors combined to persuade the African to remain fetishist or to recognize only Christian leadership. This explains both Islam's lack of success in Brazil and the return of the last generation of Malê to the beliefs of their animist ancestors. Indeed, as the Malê came into contact with fetishists in Brazil, as their revolts failed and their numbers dwindled, the veneer of Mohammedanism began to disintegrate. All that remained was the old vital core, the ancient propensity for worshiping the forces of nature. The Mussulmans were absorbed by the Gêgê-Nagô cult. This produced another curious reversal. In black Islam Mohammedanism was the official religion, and the old cults were regarded as nothing more than magic rites. In Brazil, however, Mohammedanism became, and remained, sorcery. In differing demographic and social conditions, the collision of races and cultures can produce the most surprising happenings and the most contradictory religious metamorphoses.

8
Conclusions:
Religions, Ethnic Groups,
and Social Classes

Slavery split African global societies along a fluctuating line which, broadly speaking, separated the world of symbols, collective representations, and values from the world of social structures and their morphological bases. As his lineages, clans, village communities, or kingdoms were destroyed, the African clung more and more tenaciously to what remained to him of his native country, to the one treasure he had been able to bring with him—his myths and his gods. They lived on in his mind as mnemonic images subject to the vagaries of memory, but they were also inscribed in his body in the form of motor responses, dance steps or ritual movements, instantly aroused by the dull throbbing of drums.

Cultural anthropology is therefore to some extent justified in distinguishing between civilizations and social structures on the grounds that civilizations can pass from one structure to another, can change over to another society. Nevertheless it has studied the phenomena of "acculturation" too exclusively as simple consequences of civilizational contact and mixing, while neglecting the new social nexus in which such encounters take place. The laws governing the play of such interpenetration—if such laws exist—operate not in a vacuum but in global situations that determine its form and content. African values were transplanted to a new world, to a two-class society consisting of masters and slaves, a ruling and an exploited class. Thus the ethnic civilizations were transformed into class civiliza-

tions, and this inevitably reshaped and transformed them. That is why I
have devoted two chapters to the role played by religion in the resistance
of the blacks to the regime imposed upon them. I did so not just because
whites were, for good reason, more interested in the revolts of their slaves
than in describing their customs and mores, but because the topic was at
the very heart of our subject.

Marxism has quite rightly stressed the importance of the economic system and the role of the class struggle in the sphere of religious life. But
curiously enough, although its viewpoint is diametrically opposed to that
of cultural anthropology, both of them reach analogous conclusions. The
sacred becomes mere ideology, adrift above the social structures rather
than deeply anchored in them, and affected from without by their variations. In both cases, though for different reasons, all the rich dialectics that
play between the various levels of society are ignored. Both concepts tend
to divorce civilization from society or, more precisely, to link them solely
by a purely cause-and-effect mechanism, complicated only by having to
allow for the possible reaction of the causes to the effects—a reaction that
is itself mechanically conceived. I see the slave's resistance to subordination and exploitation in a different light and prefer to define it as cultural
resistance, as an endeavor not to let vital values inherited from his ancestors perish but to reestablish them, either in the secrecy of the *calundus* or
in the armed isolation of the *quilombos*. It was no accident that the whites
referred to these *calundus* as *mocambos* or *quilombos*. They sensed that in
both cases they were confronted by the same phenomenon: the resurrection on Brazilian soil of Africa, with its priests and rituals, even its
matrimonial customs and its kingships. To bring the global and not just the
economic character of this slave resistance into sharper focus I have
compared it with the revolutions of mulattoes and liberated blacks. In the
latter case religion does appear as an ideology, if it appears at all; in fact it
barely conceals the resentment of a social class eager to obtain equality
and seeking more economic or social opportunities.

One might no doubt object that resistance becomes religious only when
it cannot be political, that religion is the only way that remains open when
all others are blocked, and that the Marxist analysis therefore holds good
even if my definition of slave revolts as cultural movements is valid.
Balandier has demonstrated this brilliantly in the case of black messianism.[1] We find analogous phenomena in Brazil too. The fanatical
"Contestado" movement broke out only after political efforts in the
extreme south of Brazil had failed.[2] The muddy waters of the prophetic
"Conselheiro" movement obscure the *sertão*'s economic and political resistance to domination by the coast; lacking political leaders, it was
incapable of taking any form other than a religious one. We must, however, note that the revolts of the colonial period that we have studied are
not situated in the same time frame as those of present-day Africa or

twentieth-century Brazil. They have more in common with African resistance in the early missionary period, when blacks destroyed chapels and schools and assassinated priests and pastors. A good case could be made for differentiating two kinds of religious resistance: the type that precedes the more or less far-reaching impact of alien civilizations on native ones, and the type that follows this impact. To use the terminology dear to American sociologists, the former might be called an instance of cultural resistance and the latter an instance of counteracculturation. The former reflects the tragic collision of heterogeneous civilizations, the latter the disintegrative effects of the collision over the years and, as Balandier's analysis brings out, the desire to restore an *already destroyed* equilibrium by escaping into a past anterior to the tensions that have become unbearable. Yet although messianism arises in colonial societies when political nationalism is blocked, the explanation that every avenue except the mystic one was closed still does not hold for the Brazilian *quilombos*, or even for the Malê and Nagô revolts in Bahia.

It is also true that the fissure that slavery created between the sphere of values and the sphere of African social structures threatened, by leaving these representations temporarily floating in a vacuum, to transform them into ideologies or at least to divert them from their sacred significations and imbue them with racial animosity and anger and with economic grievances. As we shall see, this did indeed occur, and we find evidence of it today in the way the blacks visualize their gods. The Catholic saints and the *orixás* were certainly involved in the dualist structure of Brazilian society and were used in the class struggle. Saint Anthony, the most popular of the Brazilian saints in the colonial era, the protector of the country against foreign invaders, French or Dutch—he was even made a lieutenant colonel of the armies, with pay appropriate to his rank—was charged with recapturing runaway slaves. As Câmara Cascudo put it, the whites saw him as a kind of "bush captain with supernatural jurisdiction."[3] His statue would be thrown into some dark corner or turned upside down and left in this uncomfortable and humiliating position until the slave was recaptured.[4] Similarly, blacks who found their lot unbearable would seek retribution under the patronage of Ogun, the Yoruba war god. Despite the Catholic syncretism that identified Ogun with Saint George—a saint as blond as the sun itself, whose white horse trampled under foot a demon as black as a Negro—the blacks cherished the Ogun of their ancestors, armed only with an assassin's knife. Rio police archives mention a secret society whose badge was an iron bracelet (emblem of the sons of Ogun), typically yellow, with a fetish in the form of "a decorated drum symbolizing war."[5] In this analysis we must not lose sight of the many instances of such degradation of the sacred. The black was a member of two circles, his own social group and the Brazilian one, of which he was an integral part, although on the lowest rung of the social ladder. It was only natural—

especially if he happened to be a Creole—that he should carry over into his religion the effects of the tension between these two types of solidarity. But these effects were checked by other sociological phenomena.

After all, the slaves and, to an even greater extent, the Creoles were Christianized. Inasmuch as this resulted in the establishment of a black church different from, subordinate to, and controlled by the white church, Catholicism might have produced phenomena analogous to the ones so clearly exemplified by black Protestantism in the United States. It is true that color conflict sometimes took the form of conflict between religious fraternities; I have cited several examples of this. They were, however, struggles for prestige rather than an expression of racial hatred, and they indicate an acceptance of the dualism of society rather than a revolt against it—a desire to become part of the ruling community and to penetrate the white power structure under the guise of religion. In fact, the phenomenon dates back to the eighteenth century, when the discovery of gold began to modify the social hierarchy, when wealth was becoming a criterion for human classification, when, despite the objections of many people and despite the sumptuary laws aimed at keeping the black "in his place," events were proving the truth of the old Brazilian saying that "the rich Negro is white; the poor white is Negro." This mentality changed the direction of the racial struggle, steering it away from the class revolt of the rich mulattoes and their gradual metamorphosis into whites, and thus moderated any potentially excessive militancy in the Catholicism of the black church. But this did not mean that religion necessarily became merely an opiate for the people or the starting point of messianic movements. The man of color was not seeking escape from reality or compensation for his unhappiness in this world. He simply made religion a channel for upward mobility, a means for improving his status in everyday life. He conceived of Catholicism as a social activity rather than as a mystique, as an organization yielding benefits on earth rather than as a celestial savings bank, as an institution rather than as a faith. The exceptions, by no means rare, in which Christianity was lived out heart and soul should not blind us to this general rule, which was rendered more effective by the fact that the Portuguese Catholicism transplanted to Brazil was, to use Gilberto Freyre's words, more social than religious[6] and hence radically different from the Protestantism of revivals, camp meetings, and emotional impact to which North American blacks had to accommodate themselves.

The social structure of the colonial and early imperial periods was strongly dualist. We can ignore the intermediate class of rural *caboclos* or urban artisans because it did not represent a real middle class. As Couty so strikingly put it: "Brazil has no common people."[7] Tollenare actually worked out a plan for turning this illiterate, nonproductive intermediate class, caught in the conflicts between the big families, into a middle class of the European type.[8] Not until the time of the republic did such measures begin to take effect. But we must not be misled by this dualism of an aristocratic or bourgeois class and a slave class. Each of these classes was subdivided into interest groups so unaware of their shared beliefs and close ties that they engaged in constant rivalry. In white society the plantation owner opposed the Portuguese merchant; the *fazendeiro* opposed the Catholic church, which in turn opposed the metropolitan governors. What they all wanted, of course, was control over the black slaves, but they all conceived of such control in a different way. Some were interested only in putting the Negroes to work seven days a week or forcing them to perform erotic dances and thus replenish the herd of human cattle. Others thought only of their Christianization. Still others wanted to split them into mutually antagonistic "nations." The correspondence of the governors and the religious orders is full of endlessly reiterated disputes about forms of control.

The slave class was similarly divided into rival religious fraternities—African, Creole and mulatto—or into organized "nations," each with its own governor. Every group had its own autonomous life. Hence the social gap between a Malê and a Yoruba, a Yoruba and a Dahoman, a Dahoman and an Angola, an Angola and a Congo, or a Congo and a Mozambique was as wide as the gap between a mulatto and a white. To understand phenomena of intercivilizational relations in Brazil we need to study them in this chaotic context of interest groups or ethnic associations rather than within the rigid dualism of economic classes. Dualism is, after all, a sociologist's abstraction. The people involved were not so much the victims of dualism as of daily life and the immediacies of white or Negro rivalry. They were much less aware of the fundamental dualism than of the antagonisms between microgroups, which were more concrete and pressing and therefore seemed to them more real. This is why our explanation must steer clear of the purely Marxist interpretation as well as the purely culturalist one.

Let us return to our starting point: the split between the world of symbols or values and the African social structures. Religion survived as belief and feeling, but it was detached from the system of global society of which it had hitherto been a part and was confronted with the necessity of fitting itself into another such system. Collective representations had to create new organizational forms in which to incarnate themselves and through which to propagate themselves in time. There was certainly a movement from the dualist structure of society toward the realm of the sacred; I have devoted three chapters of this work to that subject. But we must not on that account neglect the opposite movement of the sacred to provide itself with or, so to speak, secrete its own structures, institutions, and morphological base. This second process could not operate freely, because the slave was deprived of liberty, and even the free Negro in the big cities remained under the control of the ruling class. At first, therefore, this process of re-creation had to adopt a posture of acceptance of, or accommodation to, permitted social realities. The African had to find, within the Brazilian social structure, what I have termed "niches" into which he could insinuate his native civilization. As we have seen, these niches were the *batuques*, the colored fraternities, the organizations of the *negros de ganho,* the urban "nations" established under the authority of kings or governors, and, to some extent, in the rural areas, Sunday dances. It is true that these were all groups through which one class controlled another, but they were modified at their depth levels of reality by the will of the blacks, or, more precisely, by the pressures of collective religious representations upon the individual members of the groups. Their transformation was facilitated by the social gap between the world of the whites and the world of the blacks, a gap that prevented the white from taking any interest in what those nocturnal creatures, his dark-skinned fellow-men, may have been up to in the dark of night. Sociologically the survival of archaic forms of civilizations like rural folklore in Europe or the folklore of workers' organizations in the early years of capitalism is to be explained by social distance rather than geographical isolation. Their disappearance results less from highways as such than from the democratization of mores, the leveling of classes, and the triumph of standardization over barriers.[9] In a slave system, social distances are at a maximum, and it is easy to see how the African civilization could insinuate itself into the niches provided by the Brazilian social structure.

But the initial adaptive phase was followed by a second creative one. The niche became a hiding place. Beginning with sacred values, the entire African society worked its way in, to reconstitute itself from the highest to the lowest levels of depth sociology, at least to the extent that demographic conditions and the rupture of the lineages permitted. Among the mass of slaves there was always a "bride of the gods," a priest, or a soothsayer to be found. We may cite one or two examples. The Ketu predominated in the Bahia *candomblés* because their city had been captured and destroyed by the kings of Abomey and their priests and princes sold as slaves in Whydah to Felix de Sousa, also known as Cháchá, a great trader in human flesh, who was himself of Bahian origin and who resold most of them to Brazil.[10] The water cult, which is extinct in parts of present-day Africa, still exists in America because its whole priesthood was reduced to slavery through the jealousy of the kings.[11] The Brazilian blacks were able to turn their *batuques* into *calundus* by organizing them on the model of the African religious fraternities. However, since the new habitat still had too few *filhos* or *filhas de santo* to establish separate brotherhoods, the blacks combined them in one organization. Around this solid core, which constituted the "nation's" center of gravity, other blacks of the same ethnic origin grouped themselves in a system of interrelationships, gradually establishing an organization with its own social statutes, status hierarchy, and specific individual roles within the group determined by relative closeness to the world of the sacred.

Thus the new emerging society was modeled on religious categories. The *calundu* replaced both the lineages, broken by enslavement and by the dispersion of their members among plantations far distant from one another, and the villages, now fewer in number, where life had once been lived according to the rhythm of the seasons. Marriage laws were preserved, except that the rule of exogamy was no longer applied to the clans but to what had replaced them: persons who had the same divinity "fixed" in their body. The great festivals also were continued but were detached from their agrarian basis. There is no need to dwell on these points because we shall look at them more closely later, when we compare the new system with African society. For the moment it is necessary only to indicate its origin and sources and to stress that such reconstitution of African society as was possible was accomplished in a downward process, starting from the African civilization, and that this new system retained a sacred character. Its internal structure was modeled on the mythic, of which it was no more than a symbolic realization.

The Afro-Brazilian religions can be understood only by examining them, as we have tried to do, in this dual perspective. On the one hand they clearly reflected certain effects of the master-slave structural dualism. They were modified by color conflict, and they reflected the structure of the global society. On the other hand, as a result of the breakdown of the major classes into interest groups or groups holding different beliefs, they formed the nucleus of a new Negro class structure. They were themselves creators of social forms.

But this African organization that was infiltrating the global society and growing inside it like a cyst, insulated by color discrimination, still found itself plunged into a new world, a world dominated by the values, cultural models, and collective representations of the whites. This explains the occurrence—and this is the contribution we may accept from culturalism —of pure exchanges of civilizations on the same level of sociological reality, independent of the effects, pressures, or reactions of the social structures. The slaves baptized by the chaplain were the same ones who performed ceremonial drumming in the courtyard of the *senzala*; the city Negroes who belonged to the Brotherhood of the Rosary were also members of the *calundu*. Hence it was possible for one religion to influence another, particularly as such interpenetration was facilitated by schematic similarities. What the blacks saw in Catholicism was a supreme god "who is in heaven" but so transcendent that to reach him it was advisable to go through a whole series of intermediaries: Jesus Christ his son; the Virgin Mary, beloved mother of Jesus; followed by the countless host of saints, each of them the patron of a trade or responsible for a well-defined social function—finding lost objects, curing eye disease or erysipelas, providing a husband for an unattractive girl, etc. Did not they too believe in a supreme god, generally a celestial deity, known by one "nation" as Olorun, by another as Zambi, who held himself aloof from worldly affairs or heard human prayers only through the intercession of his indispensable inter-mediaries, the *orixás, voduns,* or deified ancestors? This similarity gave rise to a religious syncretism that led the Bantu to equate all the Virgins and saints collectively with African gods and the Yoruba and Dahomans to identify each individual African deity with a certain Virgin or saint. For the moment we shall not study this syncretism in all its rich complexity but merely seek its historical origins. We shall discuss its complexity later.

Some believe its causes to be psychological in nature. However attached the black might have been to his ethnic divinities, he still borrowed and worshiped those of neighboring ethnic groups if they seemed more effective than his own in some particular field. The Yoruba and Dahomans there-fore exchanged gods and religious practices quite freely. The Catholic saints were the gods of the most powerful social class, the class responsible for the slave trade and the vast organization of slavery. Neither the *orixás* nor the *voduns* nor the ancestors, totemic or not, were strong enough to protect their unfortunate children from foreign exile and enslavement. Pragmatism therefore compelled the Africans to add the Christian gods to their pantheon and to incorporate into their sorcery the omnipotent "magic" of Catholic rites.[12] Clearly this conversion to Christianity en-tailed the same "Africanization" of Catholicism that we have already observed in another context.

Others prefer a psychoanalytical explanation: the mechanism of projec-tion. According to this view, slavery produced an inferiority complex in blacks, who saw Catholicism as the religion of the ruling class. By trans-ferring (or projecting) their beliefs and prayers from a barbarian *orixá* to a civilized saint, from a slave god to the god of their white masters, they raised their religious life to a higher level. This school of thought interprets syncretism as symbolizing the blacks' more or less unspoken desire for the upward mobility that was denied to them in social life—as a drama played out in the unconscious.[13] These two interpretations operate on the mental or psychic level and may well explain certain cases in certain social cate-gories. They are more valid for mulattoes than for Creoles and more valid for Creoles than for Africans. They should not, however, lead us to over-look the fact that at first the saints were no more than white masks cover-ing the black faces of the ancestral divinities. Even today members of *candomblés* are quite willing to admit this to anyone they trust. Secrecy alone could not guarantee the survival of the *calundus.* At any minute a raid by the militia or the police might interrupt the ceremonies. So the African character of the cult had to be concealed from white eyes as far as possible by superimposing on the *pegi,* where the stone fetishes ate the bloody offerings, a Catholic altar decorated with paper flowers, white cloths, statues, and chromos of the saints. Naturally they chose the saints who were closest to the divinities actually worshiped by their sect. But the songs of praise rising toward the candles burning on the altar actually invoked Ogun behind Saint George or Omolú behind Saint Lazarus. This is where our attempt to understand religious syncretism should begin, even though that syncretism was transformed when the last of the Africans died out and when maritime contact between Brazil and the west coast of Africa declined or was completely broken off.

The conclusion to be drawn from our last observation is that, while culturalism may rightly confine itself to one single level of social reality, the civilizational level, and attempt to determine how civilizations interpenetrate or clash, the phenomena of syncretism vary in the course of time. But the variation is not the effect of time per se; in other words, the causative factor is not duration itself. The variation results from the social situations having been modified, and this brings us back once again to sociology. The thesis that I believe is finally beginning to emerge from the lengthy first part of this study is that if features of the African civilization were transmitted to the Portuguese class, it was because the slaves were hierarchized as field hands, artisan slaves, and house servants, and because the last of these were in intimate contact with their masters. In other words, the process of transmission must be examined within the structure of the patriarchal Brazilian family. Conversely, if features of the Portuguese civilization were increasingly transmitted to the Negro class, it was because those two classes were never rigid, impenetrable, double-barred castes and because Brazilian society always contained built-in channels for upward social movement (assimilation of the black into the white value structure always being the condition for such upward mobility).

Abolition of the slave trade, then of slave labor, caused the African religions to break with the social structure that had enabled them to survive in Brazil and to coagulate with Catholicism. (The word *coagulate* is used here in preference to *syncretize*.) Would not such a structural upheaval be a mortal blow to these survivals or early forms of religious interpenetration?

■ ■ ■

As René Ribeiro said: "It is no longer the African natives who perpetuate African traditions but the third or fourth generation of their descendants. Yet the fact remains that throughout the generations, in a new habitat and new living conditions, fathers have continued, consciously or unconsciously, to hand on their life style to their sons."[14] How did the old colonial *calundus* manage to survive all the revolutions in the social structures? How was the African civilization able to maintain itself in an antidualist—or at any rate legally antidualist—society in which slaves were now citizens enjoying the same rights and dignity as their former masters? Some writers have adduced psychological reasons to explain this. To quote Herskovits: "The tenaciousness of African cultural elements, even in the face of the most severe attack—in social organization, in language, in religion, and in the arts—are [sic] but cultural correlates of the tenaciousness with which certain personality characteristics of Africans have held over in their New World descendants, even where acculturation to Euroamerican patterns has been extensive."[15]

But unless we assume that each race has a characteristic mentality and its own special psychology (which is contrary to the findings of contemporary science) this explanation does not resolve the problem; it merely defers the solution. If the Afro-Brazilian has managed to retain traits of his African personality, it is because that personality was shaped by an African cultural milieu. Emotional attitudes, modes of mentality, categories of thought, are the product of education. On the other hand, if we admit (though only with strong reservations on the present writer's part) that in Brazil this training in emotional response and African modes of thought originates not in the black family but in the candomblé (as Frazier believes),[16] then we come full circle without having found the answer to the question: how is it that candomblés still exist?

Evidently we must seek the answer in sociology, not psychology. But before embarking on the search, let us note that the resistance of the African sects is so deeply rooted that persecution by the police or ecclesiastical authorities has never been able to break it. Since many of their members considered themselves good Catholics, attended mass, and belonged to the Brotherhood of the Rosary, one might have expected the bishop of Bahia's pastorals, his threats to excommunicate the filhas de santo for "apostasy," and his orders to the priests to deny them communion to bring many children of the candomblés over into the Roman fold.[17] This did not happen. We shall not dwell on this form of persecution, for in Brazil there was always a wide margin of tolerance between dogma and practice. Police persecution was more violent, especially when it was connected with political movements, as was the case in Alagoas, for instance, in 1912, when a popular revolt against a pro-Negro governor who was a protector of the xangôs ended in the brutal destruction of the African sanctuaries in Maceió.[18] The only thing such persecutions accomplished was to turn public ceremonies into secret ones, a festive religion into a catacomb religion, its noisy drums silenced, its hymns chanted sotto voce behind closed windows and doors.[19] Drawing an analogy with certain Catholic rituals, Gonçalves Fernandes aptly described the phenomenon as the substitution of a low mass (xangô reisado baixo) for the sung mass.[20] The attempt to terrorize the congregation of the faithful through persecution did not even stop its normal recruiting activities. During a visit to Recife at the height of the campaign against the sects, this writer saw three girls undergoing initiation tests in one of the most traditional of the city's *xangôs*. What social factors were responsible for this resistance and survival?

In the first place, although abolition of the slave trade put an end to the renewal of the African community, it did not entirely sever relations between Brazil and Africa. According to Carneiro, the Engenho Velho *candomblé* was founded by Iyá Nassô,[21] but Carneiro makes no mention of a point of great interest to us, namely that even though Iyá Nassô was connected with Bahia through her mother (who was a slave there before she returned to Africa to enter the priesthood), she was born in Nigeria and went to Bahia of her own accord, as a free woman, accompanied by a *wassa* (a member of the priesthood), to found a *candomblé*—the one at Engenho Velho. Her spiritual daughter Marcelina, who also left Africa of her own free will, later returned there, no doubt to perfect her knowledge of the cult and initiate herself more deeply into its secrets. After seven years—seven is the sacred number of the Yoruba—she returned, to replace Iyá Nassô, then on her deathbed, as supreme priestess of Engenho Velho. The abolition of slavery did not end the coming and going between the two continents. A very active trade in *ôbi* nuts, cowries, ritual black soap, and other cult objects is still carried on today, although it has declined since the end of the First World War.[22] Martiniano de Bomfim went to Lagos to learn the art of divination and later became the most prestigious *babalaô* in Bahia. He used his considerable authority to prevent the degeneration of the African cults and to reform the Opô Afonja *candomblé* by introducing certain institutions that did not exist in Brazil but that he had seen, or thought he had seen, in Africa.[23] In an earlier chapter I referred to Padre Adão of Recife, who also went to Africa to undergo initiation rites. Present-day blacks cannot of course afford to make the journey, but they still treasure a Bible in the Yoruba language or perhaps a newspaper from Nigeria as a spiritual link at least with the far-away country of their ancestors.[24]

But this intercommunication between Brazil and Africa explains only the purity of the myths and rites of the *candomblés*. It does not account for their continued existence. This existence is by no means a mere instance of popular conservatism or of folkloric survival. The African religion, as we shall see in the second part of this work, is a *living* religion. If it did not collapse in the seismic tremors that engulfed society after abolition, that was because it fulfilled a useful function and because modifications in the social structure, particularly the elimination of master-slave dualism, left a place for it in the new organization of the country.

Besides separating the races, slavery also linked them, as we have seen, allowing the black to participate to some extent in the life of the whites. In the social chaos of Brazil, the patriarchal family was the only unifying organization. Zimmermann in fact preferred the term "tutelary" to "patriarchal" because the family exercised a protective function toward the common people and slaves.[25] By bankrupting the big estates, abolition destroyed one of the few forms of solidarity that existed in Brazil, leaving in its place only the disorder of interpersonal relations, a scattering of atoms incapable of forming new social molecules. Thus abolition continued and aggravated the process of social distantiation, which began with the early forms of urbanization and which, by separating the races far more effectively than the *engenho* had done, made possible the establishment of the *candomblés*. The first words of the emancipated Negro were: "Now we'll have houses with windows and back doors!"[26]—a symbolic expression of his desire to escape from white control. (Through a back door one can leave the house without being seen. The *senzala* had only a front door facing the master's mansion or the overseer's cabin.) These words also expressed his even deeper desire to be in touch with the wider world, to open his windows upon European values. Indeed, when slave labor was abolished, the first thing the ex-slave did was to leave the plantation, which recalled painful memories of his servitude, and seek the anonymity of the city.[27] Unfortunately what he found there was not the house he had dreamed of but a *mocambo* of dried mud, roofed with palm fronds or grass, lost in a marshy waste far from the white settlement,[28] a *favela* built of boards on a slippery hillside,[29] or a filthy *cortiço* in some abandoned house or damp cellar.[30] The ecological segregation of blacks in Brazil was quite different from the racial segregation of New York's Harlem. It was not imposed by the whites to protect themselves from unwanted contact; it was the automatic result of the competition of different economic classes for a place in the sun.[31] But the result was the same: the loss of white protection, of the tutelary family, of affective paternalism, and the intensification of racial separation.

No doubt the black could have found a way out of this situation if a personal effort to rise in society had been an adequate substitute for paternalism and if he had been able to integrate himself easily into the new capitalist industrial society that, under the republic, had replaced the old society in which wealth and social prestige derived from ownership of land. But the ex-slave, untrained for the role of free citizen, could not become a "proletarian" overnight and thus replace the old family solidarity of the *engenho* or the *fazenda* by class solidarity.[32] After the decline and termination of the slave trade, when the number of free Negroes in Brazil steadily increased as the number of slaves decreased, emancipation brought only a rise in prostitution and vagabondage. Statistics show a continuously growing army of "idlers."[33]

Abolition hastened the disintegration of the black community. The ex-slaves formed not a proletariat—the proletarization of the black was a later phenomenon and represented a step forward—but a *lumpenproletariat*. This partly explains the contemporary stereotype of the Negro as a lazy drunkard or thief or an unsavory character living on a woman's immoral earnings. (Young black girls found it easier to adapt to the new urban society as domestic servants, maids, cooks, or laundresses.) In the economic competition fostered by emerging industrial capitalism, the dark-skinned black was thrust aside by the mulatto, and the mulatto in turn by the European immigrant or his descendants. But this atomization of the colored class was by no means a purely urban phenomenon. Pierre Denis's reliable account of rural blacks in Minas just before the First World War describes them as passively resistant to regular, sustained work, even when they were organized in teams commanded by an overseer whose job, "apart from the lack of a whip, is that of the guards in the days of slavery." They would work for the white farmer two or three days a week at most, when they needed money, and were essentially mobile, never settling in one place, moving from one *fazenda* to another as fancy or indolence dictated.[34] There the social atomization was just as acute as in the city. In the northeast, the region of the sugar plantations, the old bond that linked the plantation owner with the land, the *caboclos*, and the slaves had been replaced by the dehumanized relationship between the factory owner and his workers, who were no more to him than interchangeable registration numbers and extensions of his machinery. Abandoned children grew up all alone in the cane fields. The disorganized family was reduced to concubinage. The individual felt completely isolated, with no one to turn to, ready to throw himself into the abyss toward which sexuality and *cachaça* beckoned, impelled by the desire to destroy a personality that society no longer recognized.[35]

In this atomizing and dehumanizing of personal relations, the *candomblé* remained the only possible center of integration. To the extent that it had been a reconstituted African village, with the same laws of religious fraternity and models of mutual assistance linking its members in warm, mutual affection, it became the refuge and support of a population suddenly thrown upon its own resources. Costa Pinto's observations on the contemporary *macumba* in Rio might be applied even more aptly to the African sects immediately after the abolition of slave labor. "The prestige of its spiritual leader and his position in the cult keep him in constant friendly contact with the local police. His economic position permits him to help proselytes in distress. His personal relations with members of a higher class and his mental and verbal quickness make him a potential leader, and often an active one, in the small world of his town."[36]

Moreover the constitution of the republic proclaimed universal suffrage, so that candidates running for office became interested in winning over the *candomblé* leaders, who could deliver the votes of the whole sect. But some quid pro quo had to be offered for this support, and the bargaining process enabled the politician to replace, for the sect as a whole, the vanished plantation owner, to become the tutelary patron, supported by the patriarchal *babalorixá*. This, it seems to us, is the essential factor that enabled the African religious sects to hold out successfully and even to achieve sociological consolidation in the great crisis that marked the beginning of the republican era.

Nevertheless, in order to survive they had to adapt to new social conditions. The first of these was the disappearance of the Africans. The *calundus* were linked to the "nations"; their rites, like their divinities, varied from "nation" to "nation." The Bantu *cabula* was different from the Yoruba *candomblé*, which in turn was different from the Dahoman *tambor das Minas*. Ethnic recruitment had come to an end. Moreover, marriages now occurred between widely differing ethnic groups,[37] and the children of these unions were Creoles lacking ties to any specific tradition. Obviously such marriages promoted syncretism between the customs of African "nations" that had formerly been rivals. The cult center of a Ketu *candomblé* had a Grunce *mãe d'agua*.[38] Congo songs were sung in Angola *terreiros*. But by and large each sect preserved the ethnic tradition of its founders, and this created a breach between tribal origin and civilization, between ethnic group and culture, which enabled the old *calundu* to survive in spite of miscegenation. Its new members, however, were not recruited exclusively from one people, since peoples no longer existed. Recruitment was governed by other laws—neighborhood factors or the prestige of the cult leaders or personal friendships.[39]

While abolition destroyed the community spirit of the black class, it increased its contacts with the white world, although these contacts remained informal and cultural rather than social in nature. The black found himself caught up in party politics, in the economic competition of the labor market. When the church, following the tendency to integrate all Brazilians into one society, reversed itself and took a stand against the dualism of separate black and white churches, the Negroes also became part of its great festivals and processions, the Catholic functions that brought the broad masses together without regard for origin or color. Closer contact with the Luso-Brazilian world just at the time when contact with Africa was declining might have resulted in an erosion of values, norms, and ancestral beliefs. The black responded with what we may term "the principle of compartmentalization."[40] He escaped the law of marginalism by erecting an almost impassable barrier between his two conflicting inner worlds, which allowed him to maintain a dual loyalty to often contradictory values. Stonequist's well-known psychology of the marginal man[41] may apply to the alienated blacks of southern Brazil, but it certainly does not apply to the black who has remained faithful to the Africa of his fathers. The latter calmly lives in two cultures at once without their clashing, interfering, or mixing with each other within him in any way. To paraphrase Pasteur, one might say that when he attends a meeting of his union or professional group or goes shopping, he closes the door on his *pegi*, and when he enters his *pegi*, he leaves behind his Brazilian clothing and the side of his mentality that is touched by capitalism, a money-based economy, and a society based on Western models. This compartmentalization (which has equivalents among "developed" African peoples[42]) is not in any way painful; it does not represent a self-laceration or mutilation. On the contrary it is the most economical solution to the problem of the pacific coexistence of two worlds within a single personality. Thanks to this solution the *candomblé* was able successfully to resist any attack that society might make on it.

Compartmentalization was not, of course, total. The African sects were not entirely immune to infiltration by subtle influences from the white world. When we come to examine the phenomena of syncretism, we shall have to study these influences and their limits. In any case the sects were and are well aware of the danger. In order to resist it, they are today more tenacious and determined than ever in their loyalty to the values they inherited from their founders. This "return to Africa," to use the expression of Couto Ferraz,[43] has been translated into action by uniting all the traditional sects into one federation, which then excommunicates "syncretized" sects.[44] Today a movement is under way to purify the *candomblés* in reaction against the debasement of the *macumba* and to deepen the religious faith of their members.

In contrast to the dualism of the colonial and imperial periods, the policy of the republic has been one of national integration. In the nineteenth century some integration of the best elements of the colored class was certainly achieved; we have discussed the rise of the mulatto. But this integration was confined to selected individuals; the broad Negro masses were excluded. Republican policy, by contrast, aimed at the integration of all Brazilians without discrimination—*caboclos* and other Indian mestizos, Negroes, European or Japanese immigrants—and at the creation of a community united by common interests and especially by common beliefs and feelings. This homogenization of attitude and ways of thinking was to prove the greatest obstacle to the survival of the African sects. The state had replaced the tutelary family, and, while it did not offer the emotional type of support provided by the old patriarchal system, its support was still helpful in shaping the disorganized masses into an aware proletariat and in giving the black a foothold in the new capitalist production system or even in the colored lower middle class that was beginning to emerge. But all observers agree that the black's social rise was achieved at the expense of his African values. Writing of rural blacks, H. W. Hutchinson said: "Traditionally, the *preto* is linked with ignorance and superstition, and a most common example of his 'ignorance' . . . is his belief in *candomblé* [and] . . . his participation in the cult of Janaina. . . . Anyone who intends to climb the social ladder first disassociates himself from these rites."[45]

Pierson makes similar observations about the urban black. Examining the development of mass education, he notes that it takes place not in segregated schools but in classrooms where black children sit on the same benches as white children and play in the same playground or the same street.[46] Unlike older generations, the present generation despises or makes fun of the *candomblés*.[47] These remarks are perfectly justified. The great majority of *filhas de santo* are still recruited from the economically underprivileged, more or less illiterate masses.[48] The *candomblé* today is facing a trial of strength, and it is impossible to predict whether it will succeed in adapting to the new situation or perish. In conclusion we may note that present-day *candomblé* members include more and more lawyers, rich businessmen, and prosperous artisans, and that its priests and priestesses are capable of highly intelligent discussions with visiting ethnologists and respond to their arguments with sensitive understanding. We may also note that while the policy of integration was prejudicial to the traditional sects, it was not necessarily prejudicial to the more or less syncretic ones, which, far from diminishing, steadily increase in number every day, as we shall see.

In any case this concerns the future rather than the present. Here it suffices to say that the *candomblé* and other types of African religion have resisted all structural upheavals and so far have always found a way of adapting to new living conditions or new social frameworks. The time has now come to study them in their contemporary context.

II
A Sociological Study
of the Afro-Brazilian Religions

9
Geography and the Afro-Brazilian Religions

Pagelança and Catimbó

Except for the Maranhão region, where Dahomans predominated, all northern Brazil from Amazonas to the borders of Pernambuco is Indian country. Here popular religion—*pagelança* in Pará and Amazonas, the cult of the *encantados* in Piauí, *catimbó* or *cachimbó* everywhere else— bears a strong Indian stamp. The transplanted blacks integrated themselves into that religion, and we must therefore begin by determining how a popular religion of Indian origin differs from one of African origin and how, despite this structural difference, the Negro was able to accept the dogma and rituals of the Indian religion—though not, of course, without introducing some African elements of his own.

Catimbó in its earliest form appeared at the very beginning of colonization, when it was known as *santidade*.[1] It is mentioned in the confessions and denunciations of residents of Bahia and Pernambuco before the Inquisition tribunal of 1591–1592. The cult centered on a stone idol named Mary and was directed by a "pope" and a "Mother of God." Admission was by a kind of initiation corresponding to Catholic baptism. Its rites were deeply syncretized with Christian elements—the building of a church where the idol could be worshiped, the carrying of rosaries and small crosses, processions of the faithful led by the men, with the women and children in the rear—and with Indian elements—polygamy, singing and dancing, and the use of the "sacred herb" tobacco as it was used by Indian medicine men, the smoke being swallowed to produce the mystic trance known as the "spirit of *santidade*."

Sociologically the cult belongs to the category of messianism; it is heavily charged with resentment—the slave's resentment of his master, the native Indian's resentment of his conqueror—and it prophetically proclaims the victim's ultimate revenge against the Europeans. That, at any rate, is what a woman named Luisa Barbosa, who had belonged to the sect since the age of twelve, affirmed when she was questioned by the Inquisition. She said that the stone god would deliver the faithful from captivity and make them masters of the white race. In a fair turnabout their former masters would be working for them tomorrow, unless they should refuse to worship the god, in which case they would be changed into stones or trees.[2] Thus at the very dawn of colonization the cult of the *encantados* was already beginning to emerge. It was later to overcome the religion of the *negros da costa* to become the predominant religion in the whole region. These two names still distinguish the cult of the Indian-white mestizos from that of the Africans. *Santidade*, as the Inquisition fought and prosecuted it, has of course disappeared. But its essential features survive: the combination of Catholicism and Indian culture and the use of smoke.[3]

The connecting link between *santidade* and *catimbó* is the indigenous cult of the more or less vaguely Christianized *caboclos* of the *sertão*. Carlos Estevão de Oliveira provides a good account of it as practiced by the "caboclized" Indians of the old missionary village Brejo dos Padres, in whose festivals the ancient exogamous division of the tribe into the clan belonging to the son of the sun and the clan belonging to the son of the moon is still preserved. This is the *jurema* or *ajua* ceremony, which gets its name from one of the intoxicating liquors the Indians are so fond of. Luis da Câmara Cascudo has traced this cult back to the eighteenth century and Gonçalves Fernandes has specified 1740.[4]

> On account of its religious character it is secret; not all the inhabitants of the village may participate. *Ajua* is a miraculous drink made of the root of the *jurema* tree. I watched the whole process of its preparation. The root was grated, then rinsed to get rid of any dirt that might be present, then laid on a stone. After it had macerated, the pulp was placed in a jar with water and worked with the hands. Gradually the water became a foamy red mash. When the liquor was thought to be ready, the foam was skimmed off. Then old Seraphim lighted a tutelary pipe made of *jurema* root and, using it back to front—i.e. putting the bowl in his mouth—he blew the smoke toward the liquid in the jar in the form of a cross, making a dot at each of its angles. As soon as he had finished, a *caboclo*, the son of the chief, placed the jar on the ground, resting on two *uricuri* leaves forming a shelf. Then everyone present, including two old "singing women," sat down on the ground in a ring around the jar. The ceremony was about to begin.
>
> The chief and two assistants lighted their pipes. No one spoke. A re-

ligious atmosphere began to build up beneath the thatched roof that sheltered us. . . . The pipes passed from hand to hand around the circle. When they had returned to their owners, one of the singers tapped her maraca and began to sing. She sang an invocation to the Blessed Virgin, asking good fortune for the village. This was followed by pagan couplets addressed to the *encantados*. From time to time one could distinguish the names of Jesus Christ, God, the Virgin, the Eternal Father, and occasionally also the name of Father Cicero. . . . All this time the *caboclo* who had placed the jar on the leaves was respectfully and solemnly distributing the magic drink, which transported people into other worlds and enabled them to make contact with the souls of the dead, the protective spirits. . . . After this he knelt on the *uricuri* leaves and drank a little of the liquor; what remained was placed in a hole prepared for this purpose. All this was accompanied by singing and the shaking of the maracas. When one singer tired, the other replaced her. The pipes passed from hand to hand, from mouth to mouth. Finally the men and women rose. The singers began to bless the congregation, one by one, singing all the time. . . . Then they withdrew, after having affirmed their loyalty to the chief. But before leaving, one of them stood and murmured a prayer to one of the guardian spirits of the village.[5]

This ceremony is still Indian. It has a social function; it concerns the village as a whole. It is a tribal festival but is already infiltrated by Catholic elements. Nevertheless we are very close to *catimbó*. *Catimbó* did not come into existence until this primitive collectivity had disintegrated, until nothing remained of the old tribal solidarity, until the mixed-bloods had been dispersed or urbanized, caught up in the network of the new social structure of stratified classes, in which they occupied the lowest level. *Catimbó* is an individualistic cult, not a social one; people turn to it to have their physical ailments cured or their spiritual hurts assuaged. Half a century ago the old *pagé* Tarcuuá observed sadly to Count Stradelli: "There are no *pagés* any more. Today we're all healers."[6] Yet, as we shall see, the principal elements of the *ajua* ceremony still persist in the new proletarian religion.[7]

The first thing that strikes the observer is the poverty of the cult center, which is also the home of the *catimbozeiro* and of the ritual objects. It is a little adobe house, thatched with straw, with a small living room in which a table has been transformed into an altar. This altar is the connecting link between Indian and Catholic America. On it are cigars, bottles of brandy, small bows, statues of saints or a crucifix, an Indian maraca, and the "princess," which does not stand directly on the table but on a roll of tobacco wrapped in a brand-new piece of cloth. The "princess" is the large pan or bowl in which the *jurema* is grated and by way of which the invoked spirits descend. This is the receptacle of the *santidade*. Magic too has invaded the altar. Besides these ritual objects, it holds toads with their mouths stitched up, dolls to be stuck with pins, and small creatures encased in wax. The ceremonies are held at night, usually on Saturdays. They are "petition" ceremonies in which the *caboclos* come up one by one to ask the spirits for healing, for love, or for good fortune. Ceremonies may, however, be held on any day of the week—Monday, Wednesday, or Friday for white magic (smoke on the right) and Tuesday, Thursday, and Saturday for black magic (smoke on the left). There is also another festival, the Day of the Kings, about which we know little, but which seems, at least in Paraíba, to be similar in structure to the "petition" ceremony.

The ceremony begins with an entrance ritual that includes the preparation of the table and an opening song:

> Open, table!
> Open, *ajuca*!
> Open, portals
> And royal balconies!
> Open, royal portals and curtains!

Then comes a song asking the masters, or spirits, to consent to work. After another special song, candles are lighted to Saint Joseph to light the way, to Saint Cecilia to clear the paths, to Saint Anthony for protection, and to Saint Lucia to bestow clairvoyance. The spirits are about to descend; the house must be opened to them. With a big key the master goes through the actions of opening a door on the right for the good spirits and closing one on the left against the evil ones (unless it is a "ceremony of the left"—i.e. for malevolent purposes—in which case the movements are reversed). The session begins.

No one speaks, but there is smoking and drinking. The room is in semidarkness, lighted only by the flickering candles. The consecration of objects and of the congregation commences. It is performed by the master, using a perfume made of incense, rosemary, and other aromatic herbs contained in a half coconut shell. Then the master takes his pipe, lights it, puts it in his mouth back to front, and blows out the smoke through the stem over the various objects on the table and into the four corners of the room. Holding the crucifix in one hand and the pipe stem in the other, he invokes the spirits with songs and Catholic or spiritist prayers. From time to time he sounds a high-pitched call on a little whistle; this is the summons to the divinities.

From this point on, the session, which continues for hours, consists in the descent of various spirits or supernatural masters who reveal their identities by songs or "lines" and incarnate themselves in the body of the master or his assistant, or sometimes a member of the congregation, asking them for a drink of brandy or a cigar. The master and his assistant are in a state of concentration like that of the medium in a spiritist seance; when a spirit descends, their whole appearance and manner of speaking changes. The master is no longer himself but an old *caboclo*, hunched and tremulous, speaking in quavering tones, a shrill-voiced woman, a proud wild Indian with blazing eyes, or a jolly, garrulous Negro who cannot stop talking. One watches a spectacular procession of individuals, a constant shift of personalities. The supernatural world becomes a vast wardrobe of temperaments and characters from which the master borrows all kinds of disguises to conceal his real self. Each of the invoked spirits has its special function: one cures erysipelas, another rheumatism; one makes marriages, another unmakes them. Each assistant in turn approaches the master, who relays to him from the beyond instructions for obtaining what he wants. The most common curative procedures are blowing smoke on the afflicted part, massage, and suction—all Indian remedies. Sometimes, however, the spirit recommends a medicine; they have a copious pharmacopoeia based on plants, juices of herbs, and resins, inherited from the original inhabitants of the country, which we know about thanks to the research of Câmara Cascudo and Gonçalves Fernandes. In addition to these remedies, Catholic "obligations" are imposed: the repetition of certain prayers, making the sign of the cross, or lighting candles to a certain saint or spirit.

During this ceremony the *jurema* is prepared by the master's assistant, and toward the end of the session the sacred drink is distributed to all participants according to their capacity; they are given neither too much nor too little. *Jurema* causes one to die in one's present existence and enter a hallucinatory world that unrolls "like a movie," allowing the believer to penetrate the mysterious kingdom of the *encantados*.

The "table" is then closed with the same song that opened it, the word "close" being substituted for "open," and by making the sign of the cross. The candles are not extinguished; they must burn down. The cigars used to summon the spirits have not been fully smoked, since a new one is used for each spirit, but the master is allowed to unroll them and smoke them in his pipe on ordinary days. The dishes and glasses on the table, however, may be used only for religious purposes and are carefully put away.

In addition to these public ceremonies, there are private ones—for the critically ill, for example, for anyone who wishes to have his body "closed" to police bullets or to misfortune, or for anyone who needs the help of black magic to summon evil spirits against an enemy. In other words, the essential element of the cult is personal "petitions" of people too poor to afford a doctor and sufficiently superstitious to resort to supernatural methods. The public ceremony is basically no more than a rosary of individual "petitions." It bears no resemblance to the African ceremonies of Bahia or Recife, which have an organic social character.

The priesthood is as meager as the liturgy. At the top is the intercessor-priest; then his deputy, who presides over the ceremony in the high priest's absence; then several assistants or disciple-masters who answer the master when he is in trance and prepare the *jurema* and from whose ranks future masters will be chosen; then the disciples, the fraternity of devotees; and finally the servant who goes out into the *sertão* to search for *jurema* roots, transmits messages, etc. There is no initiation in the strict sense; the disciples learn the songs and secrets from the masters by talking with them in their free time. The future master, however, is distinguished by his ability to fall into trance, by emotional paroxysms, which are an indication of his future power, and by a kind of wart known as "the seed."

The mythology that sustains the cult is equally meager. It centers on *jurema* and the kingdom of the *encantados*. Originally the *jurema* was a tree like any other, but when the Virgin fled to Egypt to escape Herod, she hid the infant Jesus under a root of that tree, giving it a divine quality. The world of the *encantados* is divided into kingdoms. Some say there are seven of these: Vajucá, Tigre, Canindé, Urubá, Juremal, Josaphat, and the bottom of the sea. Others say there are five: Vajucá, Juremal, Tanema or the kingdom of Iracema, Urubá, and Josaphat. The kingdoms all comprise a certain number of states, and each state has twelve villages. Each village has three masters, so that each state has thirty-six masters. Each master has his own "line," the song that announces his visit to the earth. The principal masters are Indians: Master Itapuan (the ancient Tupí sun god), Master Tupan (the ancient thunder god), Master Xaramundy (the great healer), Master Mussurana (the Prince of Jurema), Master Iracema, and Master Turuatâ. Then there are the souls of the dead, especially of famous old *catimbozeiros* such as Master Carlos, Master Roldão de Oliveira, Master Pequeno, Mistress Angelica, and Master Germano, who was alive until quite recently but whose spirit "had the power." To this constellation must be added such Catholic spirits as King Heron (probably a corruption of Herod) and Saint Anthony, some mysterious water divinities (little girls dressed in green), and a number of Negro spirits.[8]

Such was the Indian religion within which the African slave in northern Brazil or his descendants made a place for themselves. To quote Adhémar Vidal: "Today Negro and *caboclo* customs in the practice of fetishism are totally confused. They all communicate within one and the same mystery. . . . *Catimbó* is practiced by members of the African race."[9]

It is true that the term *macumba* occurs in the capital of Ceara and in some places in the *sertão*, undoubtedly indicating African influence. Sometimes we even find the names of *orixâs* such as Shangô and Ogun, but these divinities have become "masters" or *encantados*. In this "African line," as in the "*caboclo* line," "brandy and tobacco—cigars or cigarettes —are used and when a 'guide' descends, the 'instrument' (i.e. the medium) sings the appropriate verses."[10] In Paraíba, which borders our third geographic region, the region of the *xangôs*, a line in one of the prayers used in the local *catimbó*—"Goum can do more than God can do"—may perhaps preserve the name of the African god Ogun.[11]

How and why did the black (with very few exceptions) accommodate himself so readily to a foreign religion? The reason is that most of the blacks in this region came from Angola and were therefore Bantu, whose mythology is less developed than that of the Guinea Negroes. They believe in spirits, but the spirits are linked to the forests, rivers, or mountains of their country; they are tied to geographic features—marshes or grottoes— and cannot migrate as people can. They are local gods. Hence when the Bantu was taken to America, he left behind not only his land but also the spirits that inhabited it. All he retained was his animist mentality. When he came to a new land that also was inhabited by spirits, he was obliged to accept these supernatural counterparts along with his new habitat. I myself have been fully convinced that this was so by hearing so many black *catimbó* members say: "We're Brazilians now. We must worship the gods of our new country."[12]

Under the influence of spiritism, however, the ancient Tupí divinities were joined by the spirits of the dead and of famous *catimbozeiros*, and some of these were Negroes. Moreover, the shift from one religion to another always involves some nostalgia or remorse, which explains why these African masters integrated themselves with the *caboclo* masters in the kingdom of the *encantados*, thus creating an "African line" alongside the "Indian line."

The most famous of the black masters who haunt *catimbó* ceremonies is Pae Joaquim. He is notorious for his good humor and infectious high spirits and likes to make jokes and play tricks with the table. He is one of the most beloved masters.

It is interesting that from São Paulo to Natal the mythology of this religion constantly draws a contrast between the Negro and the Amerindian. The Negro spirits like jokes; the *caboclo* spirits are proud and arrogant or wild. The refrain of Pae Joaquim's line is *"asquibamba"*— obviously an African word. I believe it to be a corruption of *t'chinbanda*, the Ambundo word for *feiticeiro*, healer or *pagé*.

> Father Joaquim is black and jolly, *asquimbamba*.
> A funny old black, *asquimbamba*.
> I don't think there's another like him, *asquimbamba*.
> Black, and as old as I am, *asquimbamba*. . . .[13]

Then there are Master Ignacio de Oliveira, a former *catimbozeiro*, and his son Master Carlos:

> [Master Carlos] is the king of the masters, omnipotent and as full of faults as a Greek god. He is jealous, fond of brandy, and lends himself to good and evil with the same spontaneity. His story is a traditional one. As a young man given to drinking and gambling he was the despair of his father Ignacio de Oliveira. One day when he was drunk, he fell from the trunk of a *jurema* tree and died three days later. He is the most frequently invoked of all the masters. . . . When he "alights," the medium's face is

transformed. He becomes cross-eyed, makes exaggerated gestures, and his lips are stretched into the shape of a beak.[14]

Another well-known black master in Amazonas is Pae João, who speaks first in an incomprehensible language—no doubt meant to sound African —and later in Portuguese.[15]

The study of these African lines helps us to penetrate the mind of the Negro of these regions and translates the old social structure into terms of religion. The Jesuits defended the Indian against slavery. Believing him to be endowed with a soul no less than the white man, they Christianized him as far as possible and admitted him to society at a higher level than the black. The colonists, who brought no white women with them to this new land, did not hesitate to marry his daughters; their children were somewhat better off than the native Indians, being serfs rather than slaves. Miscegenation with Africans did occur later, but, except in the case of the plantation owner's son seeking sexual initiation, it was rarely with pure-blooded blacks but rather with light-skinned mulattoes. The black was always relegated to an inferior position because he was not defended by the Jesuits, because he was a slave, and because of the darkness of his skin. Romanticism later glorified the Indian who defended his land against the white man rather than submit and who thus came to symbolize Brazil's political liberty in defiance of Portugal.

The conflict between the free *caboclo* laborer "associated" with the plantation owner and the enslaved black at the bottom of the social ladder has left its traces in folklore and literature[16] just as clearly as in the clash of the two societies. When drought forced the cowhands of the *sertão* to leave their desolate country of prickly cactus and seek refuge in the humid agricultural regions, the two societies met; the individualists of the *sertão* confronted the proletariat of the cane fields. Common misery did not bring them together.

> The *caboclos* remain on the margins; they do not adjust to the new mores. They simply temporize. They do not accept the African influence of the sugar-producing regions. . . . The sensual religiosity of the humble people of the cane fields is linked to a social complex that has nothing in common with the historical evolution of the people of the *caatinga*, the cactus desert. It can never be imposed upon the sensibilities of a people with a tradition of independence, with no past history of oppression—a people whose social development is unquestionably more advanced. . . . The migrants move physically to the sugar cane region, but their minds cannot break free of their scorched land. In the *brejo*, the region of moist black earth, they are always uneasy, deprived, ready to head back home at the first sign of rain.[17]

Catimbó allowed the black to get even with the ancient social structure that relegated him to a place below the *caboclo*. It was he who became the *catimbozeiro*, who directed the ceremony and gave orders to the *caboclos*.

He had totally reversed the situation. Through religion he had become the leader; the *caboclos* were now beneath him. Taking advantage of a superstitious environment and making the most of his color, which set him apart from other men and made him look more menacing, and of his gifts of divination and his own initiative, he climbed the ladder to the top. He needed no initiation. He acquired the magic power through his own efforts or by chance.

> Master Carlos is a good master
> Who learned without being taught.
> He spent three days
> Stretched out on the *jurema* root.
> When he got up,
> He was ready to work,
> Triumphant master of all the tables.[18]

Nor was that all. Death, far from destroying him, would bring another advantage. He might turn into an *encantado* and become one of the kings of the supernatural kingdom:

> Fine are the works
> Of Master Ignacio de Oliveiro,
> Still a king, still a king.[19]

When we move from mythology to ritual, the African contribution seems to be more sporadic. This is because ritual is always a function of a mythology, and the mythology of *catimbó* is radically different from that of *candomblé*. The African gods form a family linked by ties of generation and marriage; they constitute a system. The Amerindian spirits on the other hand are distributed geographically by villages, states, and kingdoms. They come together in a celestial geography, but they are not linked in any way. They are merely localized, strung out in a decentralized organization. The African mythology is modeled on the tribe and the extended family, that of *catimbó* on the political organization of Brazil as seen through the eyes of a devotee of fairy tales. When this native Indian mythology was accepted, all the ritual linked to African beliefs was dispossessed.

What made it possible for the black to accept this religion was the fact that, like his own, it centered on the descent of the god into the human body, with a subsequent transformation of the personality. Of course there are great differences. The black can receive only one *orixá*, the one to which he is dedicated, while the *catimbó* master can receive them all. The *orixá* is invoked through songs and music; the spirit first descends into the *catimbozeiro* and then sings to announce its presence. A characteristic feature of the *candomblé* is dance and the donning of symbolic costume; the *catimbó* ceremony is performed with the participants sitting around a table, as though at a spiritist séance, without any choreography.[20] The orixá can "mount its horse" without the aid of intoxicating drinks or narcotics; the spirit descends via tobacco and jurema. Singing at the catimbó is always individual; at the candomblé it is accompanied by choruses. Catimbó ceremonies are held in closed rooms, those of the candomblé in open barracãos. Indian maracas set the rhythm of the catimbó; drums mark the rhythm of the candomblé.

But the black was familiar with narcotics in his own country. He therefore introduced them into catimbó, thus enriching its pharmacopoeia. Indeed the characteristic feature of the African line is not so much the spirits that descend but the use, along with jurema, of diamba instead of tobacco and of maconha, a plant similar to hemp, brought to Brazil by slaves and formerly used to force suspects to divulge their secrets or to produce magic hallucinations.[21] It is also possible, though debatable, that the use of "fragrant baths" may have been copied from the initiation baths of neighboring candomblés or xangôs. And lastly the practice of some catimbozeiras in the south of combining the table with the Catholic altar is certainly an imitation of the xangôs. But the most crucial innovation may well be the very existence of catimbozeiras—women who perform the pagelança. The Indian pagé was always a man. In candomblé, however, the cult center is often headed by a woman (usually one who has passed through menopause.) So it is thanks to the example of the candomblé that women of today are able to perform the function of the old masculine pagé—and we may note in passing that many of these catimbozeiras are black or mulatto women.

The black, then, made his contribution to catimbó. But it was still the Indian element that came out on top. The factors forcing the African to break with his own traditions were too numerous and too strong. In these provinces, these conquered capitânias so unlike Bahia with its stable population, where foreign invaders were constantly having to be driven out, where herds of cattle were being dismembered and an effort was being made to achieve a precarious equilibrium between agriculture and cattle raising on hard, ungrateful land ravaged by drought, famines, and a high mortality rate, the first concern of the black, like the Indian, was to stay alive.

Catimbó is a religion appropriate to minimal social organization, to a population consisting of individuals or isolated families, to solitary souls. As Mario de Andrade has pointed out, its music reflects this isolation. It uses popular tunes, even city songs, and does not share the traditional ethnic character of the music of the condomblé.[22] There is no rivalry among catimbó cult centers; they ignore one another, going about their own business without regard for what their neighbors may be doing. As we have seen, the mythology and the circumscribed administrative units of the kingdom of the encantados justify the coexistence of independent sects. The authority and standing of a catimbozeiro is determined not by the relative purity of tradition or the ostentation of his cult center, or by its number of *filhos* and *filhas de santo*, as it is in Bahia, but by the number of villages in the celestial world that are under his master's jurisdiction, by the size of the territory belonging to the spirits that respond to his summons. So far as I can judge, *catimbó* devotees do not constitute solidly united organic entities. They drift from one cult center to another, as variations in the ceremonies or neighborhood faclilities may dictate. Here religious mobility is pushed to the extreme.[23] The determining factors are individual preference or need, daily life and its illnesses, love affairs, crops, unhappiness, and dreams of a better future. The spirits have no history— or very little. They are reduced to a function: King Heron for curing leprosy, Mistress Angelica for finding wives for bachelors, Master Manicoré for curing ulcers, the little green-skirted girls for protecting sailors. Yet this functionalism is not totally organized. There are healing spirits whose powers are effective in any illness. There is a constant shift from one spirit to another because—and we come back to this point again and again—the dominant factor is subjective feeling. The black who joins a *catimbó* does not do so as a member of a certain race, still less as a member of a "nation." He does so as an individual seeking a solution to his own problems. The only trace of the social structure that we can discern is the ancient conflict between the *caboclo* and the black and the black's use of his intuitive gifts and facility for trance to get even by becoming the "master," by appropriating the Indians' spirits and even commanding them. In this way religion became a channel of upward social mobility for a self-assertive minority.

The Religious Area of Maranhão

In the middle of this zone of Indian influence there exists a little enclave of African or, more specifically, Dahoman influence, namely the city of São Luiz and the surrounding transitional zone where *catimbó* and *tambor de mina* entered into quite extraordinary marriages. Although Froès Abreu pointed out that anyone wishing to study African survivals in Brazil should concentrate on Maranhão, where the blacks were most isolated from European civilizations,[24] and although Raymundo Lopes carried out some preliminary research, which remains unpublished and unaccessible,[25] this region of Maranhão was long neglected by the Africanists. The neglect is particularly curious in view of the Brazilian Africanists' eagerness to discover traces of the Dahoman civilizations in their country —a leitmotiv that persists from Nina Rodrigues to Arthur Ramos and from Ramos to Couto Ferraz, Gonçalves Fernandes, Abelardo Duarte, Edison Carneiro, and Waldemar Valente.[26] Unfortunately all these writers, taking Haitian or New Orleans voodoo as their starting point, have

confused voodooism with the serpent cult, ignoring the fact that this cult
does not play a major role in Dahoman religion (certain regions ex-
cepted), that there is a radical difference between the totemism of the
royal family of Whydah, which does in fact keep a sacred snake served by
a brotherhood of initiates, and the serpentine divinity of the rainbow,[27]
and finally that the snake is also the religious symbol of certain Yoruba
divinities and Congo spirits.[28] This has led some of those writers into
gross errors, such as discovering major Dahoman survivals in the Bantu
terreiros![29] This kind of research was on the wrong track; what was
needed was a first-hand study of the authentic Dahoman sects or "nations." The first, very belated study of Maranhão was made by E. Correia
Lopes;[30] it was followed by the folkloric mission of Mario de Andrade,
whose findings (to be used with caution) were published by Oneyda
Alvarenga.[31] Then came the important studies of Nunes Pereira, whose
mother was a tambor de mina initiate, and of Octavio da Costa Eduardo, a
disciple of Herskovits.[32] Pierre Verger[33] and myself—the last scholars to
visit Mãe Andresa—complete the list of those who have done research in
this area to date.

As I have just noted, there exists between the capital city of Maranhão
and the sertão a transitional zone where the African religions intermixed
with the Indian catimbó. The influence of catimbó can even be found in six
centers of the encantado cult in the capital city. The studies of Octavio da
Costa Eduardo help us to recognize this religious fusion and to understand
to some extent the nature of its morphological base. In the rural areas, the
white masters would not allow their slaves to perform their ritual dances,
thus making priesthood impossible. All the blacks could do was to cherish
and secretly hand down the names of a few especially powerful or revered
gods and a nostalgia for their proscribed religion. Any of them who succeeded in escaping or revolting quickly merged with the Indians and found,
in the pagelança, ceremonies that were in some ways similar to their
ancestral ones, notably in the passionate pursuit of ecstasy. But into
pagelança's aristocratic notion of priesthood they introduced their own
democratic attitude toward mystic trance. It could no longer remain the
privileged prerogative of the pagé, an individual charisma, but came to be
shared by everyone, broadening down from the priest to the whole congregation of believers. On the other hand initiation of the African type
disappeared, not only because slavery caused a breach with tradition, but
because this was an extremely poor population unable to meet the expenses of a costly ritual. Although catimbó does not include dance and its
ritual consists of a procession of unfortunate caboclos filing up to the
entranced master in search of advice and supernatural aid, the black tillers
of the infertile land of Maranhão continued to meet in a shelter consecrated to the gods to perform dances climaxing in the descent of the
spirits.

But in these out-of-the-way places where something of Africa managed to survive, everything has become as impoverished as the soil itself, as the little family plots yielding a bare subsistence. The cult center is impoverished—the little mud house with a Catholic altar on which a statue of Saint Barbara is enthroned, sometimes with a pole in the middle of the room, a lingering memory of the Tree of the World. The mythology has been reduced to a legion of Catholic saints and a few African gods known as *budus* (*voduns*), most of whom have assumed Brazilian names like Pedro Angaco, Maria Barbara, and so on, and who are still commanded by the mysterious Kakamado and his Indian spirits. Finally the magic itself has been impoverished, losing its spectacular character and its haunting liturgy. It now apparently confines itself to a series of prophylactic measures for the benefit of children in a land of horrifying infant mortality.

The shift of this peasant population from the African religion to one closer to the religion of the Amerindians is very clearly illustrated by the existence of vaguely remembered Dahoman *voduns*, such as Avrekete or Sobô, who do not descend—who in other words do not incarnate themselves during the ceremonies. Here the influence of slavery is obvious. The names of the divinities have not been completely forgotten, but because the ecstatic cult is no longer handed down through initiation, a god may have no sons or daughters in whose heads he can "arrive." These gods are now no more than figures in the collective memory. Only Legba, the most formidable of them, known in Maranhão as Legba Bogui, still has the power to possess believers, but he does so only to punish them for not keeping their promises to him. He likes to make people climb into a treetop and to leave them there, unable to get down. But interestingly enough—and this shows how the mixing of ethnic groups within the old rural slave population was reflected in the mixing of civilizations—when the people sing for Legba, they do not always call him by that name but often call him by the more typically Yoruba form "Barabara" (Bara).

No special priest presides over the ceremony. This tradition is one of those that live on in the memory of a people through their own strength, much as folklore does, without any specific organization to provide a sustaining base. The "society" that meets every month or two to dance or summon the spirits comprises the entire village. The personnel consists of two servants of the *encantados*, who set the dates of ceremonies, sweep the floor, make arrangements with the musicians, and solicit contributions to provide petroleum for the lamps. They are respected but have no religious authority, being merely administrators or sacristans of the cult center. So it is not surprising that here mystical ecstasy is not controlled by social pressure as it is in other African religions. It is simply an unbridled release from day-to-day life and the miseries of existence—the barbaric joy of possessing gods, of escaping from the profane sphere to share in the supernatural rapture. This explains the violence of some of the ecstatic seizures, which can be calmed only by sprinkling the possessed person with holy water dashed on the head, hands, and feet with a sprig of the sacred *esturaque* plant. Control has not been entirely abandoned, but it is less strong than in other cults; communal censure is less rigorous. According to a law that we shall verify again and again in the course of these pages, trance varies within the range between what social pressure requires and hysterical violence, depending upon the relative strictness or weakness of a traditional organization. But there is always some control, weak as it may be, because any religious life is obliged to create for itself a minimum of order if it is to survive at all, and in this case the order consists in such African tradition as was able to outlast the long night of slavery.

Initiation, for instance, has disappeared, replaced by free choice on the part of the spirits, who take possession of those they wish to hold in their power. Yet it is precisely here that a rudimentary form of control still exists. When a woman experiences her first mystic seizure in the room where the dancing is going on, her spirit is considered still unbaptized; it is like the first imported slaves—a savage. A year must go by before her *encantado* receives his name and reveals his personality, thus becoming reintegrated into the mythological frameworks. He then has a family and a civil status; he is "civilized." In other words, he will in the future possess the woman in a more regular and less frightening manner. To prevent possession from assuming exaggerated forms, certain precautions must be observed; for example, the subject must not engage in sexual relations during the preceding day.

The classic division of African ceremonies into two parts is seen again here. First comes the dance inviting possession and then the dance of the gods, with an interval between to allow for the change from profane to liturgical dress. After the trance, those who have been possessed don the religious costume, man's clothing if the *encantado* is male, woman's if it is female. (The sex of the possessed individual is of course irrelevant.) But the poverty of the rural areas naturally precludes beautiful liturgical costumes, so the most striking feature is transvestism (or at least partial transvestism). In any case the change of clothing interrupts the ecstasy and acts as an additional element of control and order. Thus within the unconscious of the believers, a network of regulations, flimsy as it may be, controls the outbursts of madness so that the dances and music, the songs and movements, can maintain their harmony, and the ceremony does not deteriorate into an excessively anarchic or disorderly spectacle. In this way a religion evolved in which the spirits were Indians or Catholic saints rather than African gods but whose ritual was obviously moving away from the tradition of pure *pagelança* and incorporating many elements of the African ceremonial.

On the outskirts of the capital city the African element gradually gained ground at the expense of the Indian element, although the latter remained preponderant. The gods formed a whole series of "lines" or families, depending upon their ethnic origin or geographic localization in nature. Although the African line is richer here than in the rural areas, it is still just one of many. There is a Nagô line in which the specifically Yoruba deities Labara, Ogun, Shangô, Yemanjâ, Shapana, Osain, and Abaluaie are mixed with the Fon *voduns* Lisa, Lôkô, Verekete, Sobô, Dosu, Nanamburucú, and Badê. There is a Taipa line that represents the Tapa or Nupe peoples. There is a *caboclo* line, a line of forest spirits, a line of sea nymphs, the Surrupira line of the little forest sprite worshipped by the Indians, whose real name is Curupira, and a line of the souls of the dead. It is like being at a crossroads of religions or in a blind alley where all kinds of mystiques have come together.

Probably these sects originally crystallized around a nucleus of fellowship in misfortune rather than a nucleus of religious faith. People of totally different origins came together, all bringing their own hopes and mythic memories, and their pantheons of gods coexisted side by side just like the men and women in the sanctuary. Syncretism is symptomatic of one of the conditions of slave societies: the mixing of races and peoples, the cohabitation of the most diverse ethnic groups in one place, and the creation, at a level above the self-centered "nations," of a new form of solidarity in suffering, a solidarity of color. But the remarkable thing is that this solidarity does not destroy the ethnic one, no doubt because each nation has its own divine ancestors. Thus in an era when this black melting pot no longer exists, the religion of the São Luiz cult centers reflects and preserves a moment in history, an ancient structure of colored society—the transformation of antagonistic "nations" into cooperating "nations" more conscious of what unites them than of what separates them.

Mere coexistence, however, was impossible. Inevitably there was interreaction among the mythic concepts themselves and increasing standardization owing to the low educational level of the cult members.[34] This modification of old concepts as they were exposed to different religious ideas more closely related to the people's living conditions can be traced in some of their songs. Another modification is that the *voduns* do not descend, as they do in Dahomey, just to visit mortals, just for the pleasure of "mounting their horses" and being worshiped. Like the *caboclo* spirits, they come to help suffering humanity; they come "to work."[35] The ancient concept of worship has been replaced by a utilitarian, pragmatic concept that is of course potentially present in ecstasy of any kind (the intensification of *mana*) but that is now fragmented into various "services" and objectified in urgent individual requests. Then again the *vodun* no longer comes from distant Africa, from what the Bahian blacks call the *ilu aye*, the "land of life"; it inhabits the neighboring forest or the Brazilian desert, just as the Indian spirits do.[36] The god is no longer a temporary immigrant or a link with the lost homeland. He has taken out naturalization papers and settled down in his adopted country, just as the slaves' descendants have. His love for the poor Negroes makes him want to stay with them, defend and look after them.[37]

A notion that we shall encounter again later among the pure Dahomans of São Luiz also has a place in this synthesized religion—the notion of "go-between" gods who serve as intermediaries between man and the higher deities. Here, however, it is the African gods who serve as "guides" leading to the Catholic saints. The colored population recognized the colonial power hierarchy, which ranged from the humble *voduns* of the slaves through the wild *caboclo* spirits up to the saints of the white men, the masters, the rich people. Verekete, for example, became the channel for reaching Saint Barbara.[38] This religion was also open to outside influences, which it accepted and manipulated to fit its own use and beliefs. It integrated and at the same time distorted what Europeans had created. To take an example, in the syncretic sects, spiritism, which is very common in Brazil and which reminded the black of his own "mysteries" since the medium receives the souls of the dead during trance, became a new "astral" line and took its place beside those I have already mentioned.

Since slavery disrupted the sacred African time rhythm, the blacks had to borrow the whites' yearly rhythm, whether Christian or profane, which explains why their major ceremonies coincide with Catholic feast days such as those of Saint Barbara or Saint Sebastian. It also explains why every year on Saint Lazarus's Day they make a "promise" to the dogs and give them a splendid meal of several courses served on a cloth spread on the ground.[39] But the most important festival is New Year's, because this marks the new beginning of the year. On this day all ritual objects are carefully washed with lustral water, which in some way restores mystic properties that may be draining away, dissolving, or otherwise becoming lost.

As these changes deepen, however, the African elements lose more and more of their original value. The private aspect of the cult seems to disappear—and it is precisely in the private cult that the control of ancestral tradition exerts itself most strongly since it requires that one dedicate one's whole day-to-day existence to the service of the gods. In the sects we are discussing, this organized cult demanding constant offerings and the alignment of one's entire life with the axis of the *voduns* gives way to sporadic sacrifices offered to a divinity whenever one has worries, love troubles, or an illness of some kind. Now it is chance that prompts the act of devotion, not the African calendar of the religious community.[40]

The Yoruba mother house, the cult center in the Rua dos Creoles in São Luiz, however, has retained much more of its African heritage. In its cult, as well as its mythology, it is much closer to the other Yoruba houses in Brazil, which we shall study in more detail in the next section. We might therefore leave it aside here, except that it too shows a certain propensity for contamination by the other cults of the region. In the first place it is not purely Yoruba. It is situated in a region where Dahoman influence was strongest, and it combines certain Fon *voduns* with the Nigerian *orixás*. For example, the family of the orixá Shangô includes such Dahoman members as Lôkô, Verekete, Lisa, and Abé. This is an imitation of the Fon house of Mãe Andresa, an effort to achieve greater African orthodoxy by copying what goes on in the purest sect of São Luiz without realizing that this so-called purity is in fact, from the ethnic point of view, a betrayal. Catholicism also has its place in the cult, not only in the form of the Catholic altar that dominates the group of dancers in the *barracão* where the ceremonies are held, but also in the Catholic prayers added to the purely African ceremonies during May, the month of Mary. Yet here Catholicism does not merge with fetishism; it simply coexists with it like a foreign body. The altar to the saints is located in the public, not the secret, part of the house—i.e. the "fetish room," where the stones in which the gods reside are kept. This room is known by a name of African origin which is difficult to identify: *vardenko*; it corresponds to the *pegi* of Bahia.[41] And behind the Catholicism the Indian *pagelança* insinuates itself too. Every year three "*caboclo* nights" are celebrated when, instead of the African divinities, Indian spirits descend.

Finally there is the Dahoman house of Mãe Andresa, which surpasses all the other sects in faithfulness to Africa. This is a corner of Dahomey transplanted across the Atlantic. The very names *comé* for the sanctuary and *gumé* for the indoor garden are contractions of Dagomé and Dahomey. The *quêrêbatan*, as the building itself is called, is the Fon *keregbatâ*. It is true that in this *Casa das Minas* we do not find all the *voduns* of Africa but only those belonging to three families: Kevioso, Dan or Danbira, and the royal family. The first family includes Badê, Avrekete, Lôkô, Lisa, two women, Sobô and Abé, and about a dozen other divinities. It is in charge of celestial phenomena, controls thunder, and even has a small domain in the sea (Abé). The second, although it is known by the generic name of Dan—i.e. the famous snake Dânh-gbi—actually corresponds to the Dahoman pantheon of earth gods: Sagbata, who inflicts smallpox on those who fail to honor him, Polibogi (another name for Sagbata), Aloge, Bosuko, etc. The names of the members of the third family—Dadaho, Koisi, Akaba, Zomadonu, Agongonu (Agonglo), Dosu, etc.—are those of kings who reigned in the seventeenth, eighteenth, or early nineteenth century or of their sons, although the family also includes Nao or Naedona, who is certainly the Dahoman sea goddess Naété. The youngest god in each family is conceived of as a mischievous little trickster persecuted by his father but protected from his anger by the love of his mother or sister, just like the youngest god in the pantheon of the Dahoman *voduns*.

In addition to this classification by genealogical families, there is another one based on age. There are old *voduns* like Sagbata or Sobô and young ones known as *tokhueni* (i.e. half-brothers born of the same mother by different fathers). The *tokhueni* "open the way" for the older gods and serve as their "guides." They descend at the beginning of the mystic trance to find out whether the other *voduns* can incarnate themselves; if so, they clear the way for them. Finally, in addition to the real *voduns* and the *tokhueni*, there is a third class of divinities, nine in number, which, so far as I know, no ethnologist has found in Africa, although there is no doubt that they originally came from Dahomey. These are the *tobossas* or *meninas*.

Thus in the *Casa das Minas* we find the very opposite of what we found in the other houses: an extremely complex, coherent, and perfectly organized theology.[42] This coherence can be explained only by the coherence of the social organization that sustains it. There is indeed a complete hierarchy ranging from the *vodunsi-ahé*, girls who are recognized members of the cult but have not yet undergone initiation, through the *vodunsi-hunjai*, who have completed those rites, up to the supreme priestess or *hunbono*. It is she who is in charge of the cult members and is responsible for maintaining discipline in the group and for the proper conduct of the ceremonies. The chief musician or *hunto* (from *hun*, the biggest of the three traditional drums) takes charge of the bloody sacrifices that provide food for the *voduns*. Initiation lasts a year, thus ensuring the Africanization of the initiate and the maintenance of the theological purity mentioned earlier. It begins with three days of ceremonies during which the future *vodunsi* takes an *amasin* bath to open her body to divine possession, receives her god, offers a sacrifice to him, and has a lock of hair cut off to symbolize her future enslavement to the *vodun* who is "master of her head." Then she spends a week in seclusion receiving instruction about the sect and learning dances and songs—the language of the gods. She comes out of seclusion to receive her *tobossa*. Her time of seclusion is now over, but her apprenticeship continues for months, until a great public ceremony marks its conclusion and she is presented to the assembly of the faithful. When we add that the initiates spend their life in the *quêrêbatan* under the benevolent authority of the *hunbono* like nuns in a convent (though they are allowed to marry), it becomes easier to understand how the Dahoman "nation" in São Luiz do Maranhão was able to remain so faithful to the norms and values of the ancestral religion even in their most minute details. The Brazilian world ends at the walls of the *casa*; its waves gently lap against this secret island, this miniature Dahomey, facing inward upon the garden and the veranda where the great annual ceremonies are held.[43]

These ceremonies follow the regular norms of African ceremonies. They consist of two parts separated by an interlude. In the first part, the gods are summoned with music and drumming, singing and dancing. The second part begins when the girls have fallen into trance and been possessed and have changed into their priestly clothing. A curious feature is that the ceremony begins with the songs of the *tokhueni*, since it is they who "open the way," but the girls who belong to the *tokhueni* cannot be possessed until the old *voduns* have been received.[44] The observation of an order of rank and age in an ecstasy which some writers firmly believe to be emotional clearly reveals the true nature of the trance, which, far from being a state of hysterical excitement, is a sociological creation—control of the individual by the group.

The *tobossas* do not descend during ordinary ceremonies; they have their own special festivals at New Year's and the carnival on Saint John's Eve. Since these are the spirits of little girls, the ecstatic state of possession assumes a childish character. Nunes Pereira, who has witnessed these ceremonies, says that the *vodunsi* play all kinds of pranks, prattle in childish language (at least so far as he could tell, since in this house all the songs are in the Fon language), and play charmingly with dolls.[45]

Another ceremony is the paying of the drummers, which has been described by Octavio da Costa Eduardo. The *vodunsi* dance in honor of the musicians and offer them little presents.[46] When an initiate dies, the "drum lament" or, to give it its African name, the *sihun* (the *sirrum* of Bahia), is performed. This ceremony is of course more strongly influenced by the Brazilian environment because it has to observe the customs and laws of the country. It is therefore a mixture of African rites (washing, the use of *amasin* and of calabashes and jars transformed into musical instruments on account of their association with the world of the dead) and Catholic ones (burial and the mass). Of course the days of the year are linked together by a whole network of private ceremonies and personal obligations to the gods, of sacrifices and taboos, so that the lives of these servants of the *voduns* are indeed dedicated and Brazilian time is transformed into mystic African duration.

The Region of the *Xangô* and the *Candomblé*

Throughout the northeast, from Pernambuco to Bahia, Yoruba influence is stronger than Dahoman. This is the region where most is known about the African religions, one that has been most thoroughly studied and written about. Here the African religion is known by two names: *xangô* in Pernambuco, Alagoas, and Sergipe;[47] *candomblé* in Bahia. But we must not be deceived by this dualism. These are not the names the Negroes gave to their cult but are white men's terminology.[48] From the African point of view we can study this region as a single cultural unit. This does not of course mean that there are no differences between the *xangôs* of Recife and the *candomblés* of Bahia. On the whole, however, the differences are minor. They can be quickly enumerated.

1. In Recife the true *babalaôs*, who practiced divination with the necklace of Ifá and who were assisted in their duties by one or more of their wives, the *apetebi*, have disappeared from the priestly hierarchy and have been replaced by ordinary priests or priestesses.[49] The same process has begun in Bahia, but there *babalaôs* still exist along with *babalorixás*. Similarly in the *candomblé* an important role is assigned to the *ogans*, who are the protectors of the sects, undergo initiation of a kind, and, although they never fall into trance, exercise priestly duties as master of the *pegi*, *ashogun* (sacrificer), etc. In Recife this category of priest does not exist, or, to be more precise, its only representative is the *ashogun*, who assists the priest in his duties and who may even play a leading role if the *xangô* is directed by a woman rather than a man.[50] In Bahia the counterparts of the *ogans* are the *ekedi*, women who act as servants to the daughters of the gods, wiping the sweat from their faces during the dancing, taking off their shoes, loosening their hair as they fall into trance, and later leading them into the house to dress them in the apparel of their divinities. In Recife this is done by the *yaba*, who constitute a sort of recruiting pool for the *terreiros*.[51] Lastly, the drums used in the ceremonies are different, although in both cases there are three of them. In Bahia variations also occur from "nation" to "nation," particularly in the way the skin is fixed to the drum head.

2. Private worship seems to have remained closer to the African norms in Bahia than in Recife, although observation of the Western seven-day week instead of the four-day African one has naturally resulted in modifications. In Bahia each day is consecrated to one particular *orixá*, and its sons or daughters provide fresh food for it on that day, either in their own rooms or in the *pegi* of the *candomblé*. In Recife, although each *orixá* does have its own day, there is a tendency to consolidate all these acts of private devotion on one day of the week, usually Friday, when all the children of the *terreiro* assemble in the sanctuary to kill the consecrated animals, cook them, offer certain portions (the *aché*) to the stones of the *orixá*, and eat the rest in a communal meal.[52]

3. In Bahia the ceremonies are more spectacular. The *yawos* or brides of the gods first dance in their ordinary clothing. After the trance they are led into rooms where they are first calmed and then dressed in their sacerdotal costumes and symbolic ornaments. They then return and dance until the end of the ceremony. In Recife the girls arrive already dressed in *bahiana* costume in the appropriate color of their divinity (or sometimes all in white) and do not leave the dancing room except to enter the adjoining *pegi* to pay their respects to the sacred stones. Even then they do not change clothes. Their shoes are taken off so that their bare feet may touch mother earth, and their jewelry, except for the necklace of their *orixá*, is removed.[53]

4. The architecutural structure of the cult house is identical in the two

cities: the *pegi* houses the stones or iron of the gods; the *barracão* is used for dancing; and in the *camarinha* the candidates for initiation are secluded. Opposite this complex, the temple of the *orixás*, is the house of the dead, known in Bahia as the *ile-sahim* and in Recife as the *"balé* room."[54] Here the souls of the dead are "fixed" in jars and receive appropriate sacrifices, just as the gods do. In Bahia, however, the gods are divided into two categories: indoor gods like Oxalá and Shangô, who are worshiped in the *pegi* inside the house; and outdoor gods like Exú and Omolú, who have separate huts of their own in the grounds of the *candomblé*. In Recife there is only one *pegi*, and even Exú, the *orixá* of doors, paths, and openings, lives inside the house, not outside. In Bahia the cult of the souls of the dead is in the hands of a secret society, the *eguns*; in Recife no special priesthood exists for this function. When we recall that the society of *eguns* is one of the African secret societies and that the distinction between outdoor and *pegi* gods corresponds to the distinction observed in Yoruba countries between *orixás* that have their temples in towns and those that have them in the bush, we see that Bahia is more faithful to tradition than Pernambuco. The same applies to the pantheon of gods. In Bahia Mahi divinities such as Anamburucú and Omolú do creep in among the specifically Yoruba gods, but this Nagô-Dahoman syncretism already existed in black Africa. In Recife, however, a local syncretism superimposed on the ancient one has introduced the Fon god Afrékété whose function, like that of the "guides" of the *Casa das Minas* in Maranhão, is to "open the way" for the other *orixás*.

To sum up, it seems that the major difference between *xangô* and *candomblé* ultimately consists in a difference of economic level, because the modifications of African norms introduced in Recife all can be explained by the necessity of adapting those norms to poorer social conditions.[55] This is corroborated by the fact that in Bahia, in addition to the big, wealthy, traditional *candomblés*, there exist what might be called proletarian *candomblés*, such as the one in the Rua de Liberdade, which have solved their problems in much the same way as the Recife *terreiros*— e.g. by having only one indoor *pegi*.[56] As we shall see, similar solutions occur in the equally impoverished conditions of Rio Grande do Sul.

Xangôs and *candomblés* are divided according to "nation." In Recife there used to be at least six of these: Gêgê, Jesha, Egba, Malê, and Angola. Today the Angola "nations" have disappeared, having merged with *catimbó*, whose territory, as we have seen, extends to Pernambuco. The differences between the Gêgê, Jesha, and Egba "nations" have been obliterated and survive only in music; there are separate Jesha, Nagô, and Gêgê songs. Of the fourteen "houses" registered with the Service for the Protection of Psychopaths, which protects and supervises the cult, twelve are Nagô, one Chamba, and one Congo. The Chamba house is not indigenous but was established by a priest from Alagoas.[57] In Bahia, where there are innumerable houses,[58] not all registered with the police, the various "nations" have remained quite separate. According to my count sixteen of them were Ketu, eight or nine Jesha, probably three Gêgê (the principal one being called "Bogun"—a corruption of *vodu* or *vodun*), approximately ten Angola (although many of these were disintegrating or being penetrated by Indian influences), and two or three Congo. The rest were *caboclo candomblés*—the Bahian form of *catimbó*—or mixed cults.

Unfortunately no one has made an exhaustive comparative study of the "nations." The Africanists confine themselves to very general descriptions that might apply to all or any forms of the cult.[59] Actually the differences are very great—in musical instruments; in language, which varies between Yoruba, Fon, and Bantu; in songs, drum rhythms, and names of divinities; in the ritual; and in the way the beyond is visualized. For instance, among the Ketu the *filhas de santo* are "fixed" in the jars in the *ile-sahim* after death, while among the Angola they inhabit the branches of sacred trees. I have tried to show the significance of these differences in a study of variations in funeral ceremonies among the Jesha, Ketu, Gêgê, and Angola.[60]

Yet the Africanists had good reason to neglect these differences. We have seen how the Dahoman *voduns* penetrated the "Nagô" cult in Maranhão. Here the opposite occurred: the Yoruba imposed their divinities and the structure of their ceremonies on the other "nations." The result is that today everyone worships the same gods in his own language, with his own music, in structurally similar ceremonies. Of course we must not exaggerate. The Bantu songs are still addressed to Zambi or Bombongira rather than to Oxalá or Exú, but this applies only to songs "in language," and the Angola and Congo, who prefer to sing in Portuguese, call their divinities by the Yoruba names, or even by the names of their Catholic equivalents.[61] Thanks to the close parallelism of the correspondences, the members of the various "nations" (with the exception of the Ketu and the Jesha) can maintain that the gods being invoked under different names are always the same ones. These correspondences, which justify the generalized use of the Yoruba terms even by members of different "nations," can be tabulated.[62] The arrow in the accompanying table indicates the movement of a god, unchanged, from one "nation" to another.

Apart from variations that need not be emphasized here, this being a sociological, not an ethnographic study, all the "nations" follow the same structural pattern in their public ceremonies. At dawn animals are sacrificed to the god who is being worshiped that day; this is the *despacho de Exú*. Then comes the invocation of the divinities in fixed order, from Exú to Oxalá, accompanied by ecstatic seizures, followed by dancing to the gods. The ceremony ends with a communal meal after the gods have been sent away through special songs. I have not found any important differences in the initiation ritual, which varies from sect to sect only in length,

Nagô Orixás	Gêgê Voduns	Inkisses	
		Angola	Congo
1. Olorun		Zambi	Zambiapongo
2. Oxalá	Olissassá	Lombarengenga or	Lomba
		Cassunbenca	
3. Exú	Elegba or Legba	Aluvais	Bombongira
4. Ogun	Gun	Roche Mucumbé	Incôssi Mucumbé
5. Oxóssi	Odé (Recife)	Mutalombo	Mutacalombo
	Agué (Bahia)		Gongonbira
6. Omolú	Azoani or Sakpata	Cajanja	Quincongo (=
			smallpox in
			Congolese)
7. Shangô	Sobô (Sogbo) or	Zaze	Kambaranguanje
	Badê	Kibuco	
		Kiessubangango	
8. Yansan	Oiâ	Matamba	Nunvurucomabuva
9. Yemanjá		Dandalunda	Pandá
			Kaiala
10. Oxun-marê ←	Obéssem	Angoro	Angoroméa
11. Ossain			Agué or Catendê
12. Irôkô (the	Lôkô		Catendê or Time
sacred tree)			
13. Oxun	Aziri		

being longer among the Yoruba than among the Bantu. Even funeral ceremonies vary only in details, except for the calling back of the dead person's spirit by priests of the *eguns* among the Ketu—a rite called *achêchê* by the Yoruba, *sirrum* by the Gêgê, and funeral *candomblé* by the Bantu. Throughout this region the prestige of the Nagô was so high that rivalry compelled the other "nations" to borrow the organizational system of their cult, along with their *orixás*, which they identified with their own *voduns* or spirits.[63] They borrowed not only the essential features of the Nagô rites but even their priestly hierarchy. First they adopted the distinction between the *babalaô*, the diviner, and the *babalorixá*, the spiritual leader of the *candomblé*. After the supreme priest or priestess come the following female functionaries:

the *iya kêkêrê*, the "little mother" or *pequena mãe*, who assists the priest or priestess in his or her various functions;

the *filhas de santo*, who spend seven years as *yawos* or brides of the gods, then are promoted to *vodunsi* in Gêgê *terreiros* or *ebomin* in Ketu or Jassa sects. The functionaries of the house, such as the *iya bassê* (the cook), the *iya têbêxê* (the woman who leads the singing), and the *dagan* and *sidagan*, who devote themselves to the cult of Exú, are chosen from among the senior *vodunsi* (seniority being reckoned not necessarily by age but by date of initiation);

the *ekedi*, who, as we have seen, act as assistants or servants to these brides of the gods;

the *abians*, who have "given food to the head" but not completed their initiation and who constitute the reserve of the *candomblé*.[64]

The male functionaries include the *filhos de santo* and the *ogans*, some of whom are merely honorary patrons of the cult while others fulfill important functions: the *pegi-gan*, who is responsible for the altar; the *ashogun*, who is in charge of sacrifices; and the musicians, particularly the chief drummer, the *alalbé-huntor*.

There is, however, one radical difference between the Yoruba-Dahoman and the Bantu "nations" (allowing for a few very rare exceptions). In Bahia (though not in Recife) the traditional Nagô sects are always under the authority of a priestess, the *yalorixá*, and the sodality of initiates consists exclusively of women. The Angola and Congo sects, on the other hand, are usually under the authority of a priest, the *babalorixá*, and the fraternity includes men as well as women, although women predominate. All indications are that the former "nations" tend toward a "matriarchy" (Ruth Landes even used this very term)[65] and the latter toward a "patriarchy" on the Luso-Brazilian model.

An even more charateristic indication of the influence of the Yoruba "nations" is the fact that in Bahia the Indian religion was forced to adopt their frameworks as models in order to survive. While in Pernambuco the Angola "nations" were invaded by *catimbó*, in Bahia the cult of the Indian spirits had to adapt itself to the norms of the African *candomblé*, thus giving birth to the *caboclo candomblés*.

These were noted rather than studied by Manoel Querino and Arthur Ramos. Edison Carneiro was much interested in them.[66] They are of fairly recent origin and are still vacillating between the Bantu *candomblé* and the spiritist seance. In the spiritist seance, as in *catimbó*, the *caboclos* "descend out of charity" to offer remedies for the troubles of their unfortunate devotees, especially in illnesses, and the "clairvoyant" recognizes in a glass of water set on the table the figure of the spirit about to incarnate itself. In Bantu *candomblé*, on the other hand, there is a genuine Africanization of the Indian spirits, which are identified with the *orixás*. Thus the Sultan of the Forests is identified with Oxóssi, the Yoruba god of the hunt, and Ogun de Cariri with Ogun. The siren known by the lovely names of Dona Janaina, Dona Maria, the Princess of the Sea, and Aiuka is identified with Yemanjá, the Yoruba goddess of the sea. Some *caboclos* even have Dahoman names—Malemba is Lemba, and Bôrôcô is Nanamburucú. Most of the spirits, however, are Indian—Tupan, Tupinamba, Jacy, and Caipora (a familiar demon in popular legend, a little one-legged boy who accosts lost travelers to ask for tobacco), the Saint of the Snake, Green Lake, Black Stone, etc. This difference in the mythology naturally results

in differences between the *caboclo* and the African *candomblés*. In th
place, the *terreiro* is known as the "village"; secondly, the "horses" c
gods are called "instruments" and are adorned with feathers, bows and
arrows, and Indian necklaces.[67] Of course the music and dances have
their own characteristic form based on Indian models.

The mention of dancing leads into an investigation of the influence of
the Yoruba "nations" on the Indian religions, an influence which was
strong enough to turn them into real *candomblés*. In fact the choreographic element, lacking in *catimbó*, here becomes preponderant. Generally speaking, only the *catimbó* master can receive the *caboclo* spirits.
Throughout the session he is constantly changing personalities like a one-
man vaudeville act. In the *caboclo candomblé* the believers constitute an
organized fraternity, and each member receives "his" or "her" *caboclo*, as
in the African sects. The spirits descend in a fixed order, first Ogun, then
the "strongest" *caboclos* such as Maronga and Itapicu. The "strongest" of
course vary from one *candomblé* to another.

Thus the prestige of the "Nagô" finally won out everywhere. Their
prestige derived from their having upheld the ancestral religion most faithfully in the original form in which it had been brought to America by
Ketu priests captured by the Dahomans and sold into slavery in Bahia.
Thanks to the initiation of generation after generation of new *filhas de
santo*, vestals of the sacred fire, the tradition has been maintained without
any adulteration or falsification. This is not the place for a comparative
study of the religions of the Yoruba homeland and those of the Nagô sects
of Recife and of the Ketu and Jesha sects of Bahia. That would require a
voluminous book. But this fidelity cannot be demonstrated without outlining this area of research and the conclusions to be drawn from it.

The comparison is handicapped by the fact that, except for Herskovits
and, more recently, Verger, Africanists have not worked in these two fields
simultaneously. On some points we know many things about Africa that
have no bearing on America and we possess plentiful American data on
topics that have not been studied in Africa. In other words, the material at
our disposal is not always comparable. Even so, it is undeniable that the
survivals infinitely outnumber the variations.

The survivals are connected with the following subjects: (a) the
monotheism of Olorun, complicated by the polytheism of the *orixás*, who
are known by the same names on both sides of the Atlantic;[68] (b)
mythology, since the principal Yoruba myths reappear in Bahia and
Recife, as well as in Cuba—myths of Ifá, Shangô and his loves, and
legends concerning *odu* divination;[69] (c) this divination itself, its various
forms (by means of *obi* nuts, the necklace of Ifá, shells, entrails of sacrificial animals, and dream symbolism), as well as its technical procedures
and the meaning of each throw;[70] (d) the cult of the dead and the
duration of funeral ceremonies;[71] the "*balé* room" (the *igbalé* of the

Yoruba *ara aruns*), the *babalaô*'s presidency over these ceremonies,[72] the very name *achêchê* that designates these ceremonies here,[73] and (at least in Bahia) the evocation of the spirit of the deceased by an *agé* of the society of the *eguns*;[74] (e) the priestly hierarchy and the names of the various types of priests and their respective function;[75] (f) the initiation ritual, which follows the African ritual step by step, beginning with the inaugural change of clothing, ending with the final *panan* ceremony in which the *filha* is bought back by her relatives,[76] and including confirmation of the *orixá* who is "master of her head;"[77] (g) the existence of secret societies such as the society of the *eguns* and possibly even of the *oro*;[78](h) the symbolic colors of the various divinities and their liturgical ornaments such as the cow's tail or the double-headed axe of Shangô;[79] (i) the assignment of the days of the week to different gods;[80] (j) the distinction between the *filhas de santo* and their slaves, which corresponds to the Brazilian distinction between the *yawos* and the *ekedi*;[81] (k) the cult of the *irôkô*, the sacred tree;[82] and (1) the fate of the soul after death.[83]

These similarities can be pursued down to the most minute details. The twelve *obás* or ministers of Shangô found in Bahia have their counterparts in the twelve *magbas* or assistants of the African Orishangô.[84] In both regions certain circumstances of birth determine that the child belongs to a certain *orixá*.[85] The yam festival is celebrated on both sides of the Atlantic.[86] These correspondences are so strong that in some cases the analysis of African data would apply to Brazilian data just as it stands. For example, in discussing the differences between *orixá* cults and the *egun* secret societies, Bascom notes that they cannot be differentiated either by the wearing of masks or by secrecy, because the masks are also worn outside the societies (in worshiping Obaluayé, for instance) and some of the ceremonies of the *orixá* cults are secret too.[87] This statement would apply just as aptly to Bahia or Recife as to the Yoruba in Africa. It would not be necessary to change a single word in the description of Obaluaye's costume, with the hood that hides the face, or of the secret character of the *candomblé*.

All in all, the changes the African cults have undergone are no more than what was required to adapt them to the new conditions of life. In discussing the transplantation of Africa to Brazil in the earlier part of this book, I mentioned some of these changes. The move to another hemisphere, where the seasons were reversed, threw the old festival calendar out of phase with the rhythm of vegetation. At the same time, the slaves were forced to hide their black gods behind white masks. They therefore fell into the habit of honoring their *orixás* on the feast day of the corresponding Catholic saint. (This is more true of Recife than of Bahia.)[88] The blacks could not contravene the laws or conventions governing burial rites, so, to avoid trouble with the police, they were forced to bury the body within twenty-four hours instead of waiting the three days prescribed by African law, and then to leave the body undisturbed instead of returning later to the cemetery to take away the skeleton, clean it, and give it a second funeral. The imposition of the seven-day week necessitated a revision in the assignment of days to the *orixás* on the basis of a four-day week. Above all, the relative demographic weakness of the individual "nations" precluded a separate fraternity for each divinity. Instead, one fraternity was established comprising all the sons and daughters of the *orixás*.

The point to be stressed is that even within these variations the African norms continued to apply. The holding of the festival celebrating the new yams in September instead of July or August is a kind of compromise between the Brazilian tendency to shift the date to make it coincide with the agricultural calendar south of the equator and the African tendency to stick to the original date. Although burial does not take place on the third day after death and there is no second funeral, these two dates are still solemn occasions in the *achêchê*, one marking the conclusion of the first funeral ceremony, the other the so-called anniversary rites.[89] If the seven-day week caused complications, we must remember that colonial Africa experienced such complications too and found analogous solutions.[90] Finally, even though the specialized fraternities under the authority of a priest dedicated to the cult of a single *orixá* were superseded by one fraternity that included all the children of the gods under the authority of a *babalorixá* or a *yalorixá* responsible for the Afro-Brazilian cult as a whole, this does not make the *candomblé* ceremony any different from the African religious ceremonies. During the African ceremonies, which are held in honor of a single god, other *orixás* may still manifest themselves and are regarded as "visitors."[91] Any of the *orixás* may possess their sons or daughters during the dancing at a *candomblé*, but this does not alter the fact that each ceremony is dedicated to one individual god and that the others are just "visitors," exactly as they are in Africa. In Bahia the priest or priestess may even refuse to allow an *orixá* to manifest itself during a ceremony held for a different god, although this very rarely happens.

When we look carefully at the transformations that seem to have occurred in the movement of a cult from one continent to another, we see that they are not really transformations at all but mere geographic variations or what the anthropologists sometimes call "cultural alternatives."

Let us begin with the geographic variations. The African *orixás* number between one and four hundred, and obviously they do not all exist in Brazil. But they do not all exist in every Yoruba settlement in Africa either. Travelers' accounts or local monographs by ethnographers show that every city, every village, worships a strictly limited number of gods.[92] By and large the *orixás* known in Brazil are those brought over by the inhabitants of Ketu or of Ijessa; those of other towns are unknown. There has been much discussion of the nonexistence in Bahia of Odudua, the earth mother, although the cult of Obatalá, the sun god, is celebrated. There is nothing surprising about this when one recalls the dispute between the priests of Odudua and Obatalá over which of the two gods created the world. Obviously if the accidents of slavery brought worshipers of the sun god to Brazil but no worshipers of the earth mother, the hateful memory of Odudua would not be transplanted to the new habitat.[93] Moreover, the gods exist only insofar as they incarnate themselves in mortal bodies—i.e. only if on earth they find living temples in the form of their children. To all intents and purposes a god who does not descend does not exist; he is said to have returned to Africa. It is quite possible that a certain number of *orixás* have been lost in this way over the years, thus reducing the numbers of the Afro-Brazilian pantheon, but this reduction does not really represent a loss of African substance, because it results from an African process —the sudden lack of brides for a god.[94]

Anthropologists who have studied social structures in the past have insisted far too strongly on the rigidity of behavior patterns. Now a well-justified reaction is occurring, and more attention is being paid to the alternative behavior patterns that civilizations offer to enable people to adapt to the multiplicity of actual situations and random circumstances. In my opinion, any opposition we may discern between African and Afro-Brazilian patterns is resolved when we study these alternative forms of action left open to the Yoruba people in Africa by their cultural norms. Indeed we realize that even though the Africans may be more readily disposed to adopt certain options among these alternatives, they are familiar with the others too—the ones that have become standard in Brazil because they proved more adaptable to new circumstances.

It is true, for example, that in Africa the *orixás* are regularly transmitted through the masculine line and according to lineage. But it is equally true that after illness or misfortune the *babalaô* may order a person to take an *orixá* that is not the god of his paternal family. In the latter case the child is born of the *orixá*; in the other he is his son. Thus one person may have two gods at the same time or abandon the god of his lineage and keep only the one who summoned him through the intermediary of the *babalaô*. Moreover, certain individuals can adopt the maternal *orixá* as well. The circumstances of a baby's birth—with the cord around its neck or with the head still adhering to the placental follicle—may determine the child's *orixá*, which in this case is not necessarily his father's. A baby born in the *camarinha* while his mother is undergoing initiation belongs by right to the patron god of the fraternity.[95] Thus, even though slavery disrupted the lineages and hence made it impossible for the traditional African pattern to be followed in Brazil, all these other alternatives were feasible and were indeed adopted. One's *orixá* may be inherited from either father or mother. It may be acquired after a series of misfortunes or illnesses— which are in effect calls from the god—and a subsequent consultation with the *babalaô*. It may be acquired as a result of the manner of a child's birth. Even the law requiring a woman who gives birth during the period of her initiation to dedicate her son to her own *orixá* exists in the Brazilian *candomblés*—as if through some mystical contagion the fetus were affected by the ritual his mother is undergoing. We are not dealing with factual differences but simply with the predominance of certain options in one country and different options in the other.

The same applies to the duration of initiation and to the sexual composition of the fraternities. Initiation lasts longer in Africa—it used to take three years—but an exception is made for men, who spend only nine months in the *camarinha*.[96] This option has become standard in Brazil, for men and women alike, at least in the traditional *terreiros*. While it was essential to adapt to a more competitive economic system that did not allow women to stay in the cult center longer than men, the nine-month stay does not represent a radical departure from the model but is merely the extension of an alternative behavior pattern from a single group to both sexual groups. For the same economic reason the Brazilian fraternities of the Yoruba "nations" are essentially female (apart from the rare exceptions of boys born during their mother's initiation). The wife who keeps house is not as indispensable to the home as the man who works outside it to earn their living. (In any case, as I myself have observed, when a woman is called by her divinity, a *filha* who is already "made" is sent to the home to take care of the house and children.) Yet this predominance of females does not violate the African model; the same tendency also exists in Africa, but for a different reason: because an initiated woman enjoys greater prestige, she is allowed to resist her husband's authority. Thus what is merely an alternative in Africa becomes the rule in Brazil.[97]

Central Brazil

African religions did exist in Central Brazil too, but as a result of urbanization and intensified industrialization they are undergoing a transformation and evolving into the essentially syncretic *macumbas* and into "Umbanda spiritism." Like the Malê religions we have already studied, they may be said to constitute a chapter of history.

Although the term *calundu* is as common in Minas as elsewhere in Brazil, African religious ceremonies were commonly known in that province as *canjerê*.[98] Little remains of them today. Aires da Mata Machado Filho discovered what may well be the last moribund survivals of these old Bantu religions in the area of Minas where the *quilombos* were most numerous, and the vocabulary he recorded does indeed show that there were priests known as *ngangas* or *ugangas* as well as witch doctors called

caquis.[99] The gods worshiped included Zambiapungo (perhaps representing syncretism between Zambi, the great god of the Angola, and Opungo,
the great god of the Congo), Angana-Nzambi, Calunga (the goddess of the
sea and of evil spirits), and Cariacariapemba, who can be identified with
the Christian devil.[100] In this region there exists a whole population of
Negro gold prospectors who have faithfully preserved their songs (*vissungo*), some of which are hymns to Bantu divinities. Since Mata
Machado Filho says that some of these songs are secret and may be heard
only by "initiates,"[101] it appears that a religious fraternity may still exist.

What was this religion? It is difficult to reconstitute it from the vestiges
that remain. All we can say is that, unlike the religions we have studied so
far, which have all been dominated by Dahoman or Yoruban models, it is
a Bantu religion. The word *engira*, which occurs in the hymn "*O moânda
engira auê*," suggests that it is akin to the *cabula* of Espírito Santo. We
know something about *cabula* from a pastoral in which a bishop of that
maritime province attacked it. The document is worth quoting because this
Bantu sect presents religious forms entirely different from any others we
are familiar with. After speaking of the strength of the sect, which had
more than eight thousand initiates, Dom João Nery continues:

> It believes in the existence of a good spirit named Tatá, which incar-
> nates itself in individuals and thus closely controls them in their temporal
> and spiritual needs. . . . Under penalty of death by poison it requires abso-
> lute secrecy of its devotees, who are known as *camanás* (initiates) to dis-
> tinguish them from *caiálos* (noninitiates). It has initiation rites, sacred
> words, actions, and gestures; the brothers greet one another in public with
> special rituals. . . . The assembly of the *cabulistos* is called the "table"
> (*mesa*). There are two capitular tables, those of Saint Barbara and Saint
> Mary; these are subdivided into many others by the same name. I have
> been told that there used to be a third, more mysterious and more central
> table of Saints Cosmas and Damian that exercised some kind of supreme
> control over the other two and whose initiates attended their assemblies
> wearing long black tunics covering the whole body from head to foot, like
> the sackcloth of old-time penitents. However we cannot confirm this. . . .
> The head of each table is called the *enbanda* and is assisted in his duties by
> one whom they call the *cambone*. The congregation of *camanás* constitutes
> the *engira*. Everyone must obey the *enbanda* unquestioningly, under penalty
> of severe punishment.
> The meetings are secret, held either in a prearranged house or, more
> often, in the forest at night. At the appointed hour everyone converges on
> the *camucite* (the temple), barefooted, wearing white shirts and trousers.
> They advance in silence, some on horses, others on foot, the *enbanda*
> bringing up the rear. A *camaná* or a *cambone* leads the way, carrying the
> table (with cloth, candles, and little statues). When they reach a certain
> point, they turn off the road onto a path known only to the initiates. Next
> they light the candles. When they arrive at the *camucite*, which is always
> situated under a leafy tree in the depths of the forest, they clear a circular

space of about fifty meters. They light a fire and set up the table to the east, grouping lighted candles symmetrically around the little statues. The lighting of the candles is a ceremony in itself. First one is lighted in the east in honor of the sea (Calunga), then another in the west and two more in the north and, south. Many more are lighted around the *camucite*. The candles are called *estereiras*. Then the *enbanda* appears, barefooted, with a handkerchief around his head or wearing a *camolélé* (a kind of cap) and a girdle made of fine white lace. Assembled before their master, the *camanás* imitate him, tying handkerchiefs around their heads. Then comes a kind of opening prayer, repeated as they kneel around the table. The *enbanda* stands, raises his eyes to the sky, concentrates his spirit, and intones the first *ninbù* (song):

> Authorize me, Calunga,
> Authorize me, Tatá,
> Authorize me, *bacúlo*,
> That the *enbanda* wants *quendá* (?).

This hymn, like the others, is accompanied by hand clapping. The *enbanda's* body writhes, his eyes twitch violently, he beats his chest with his fist, utters deep snorting sounds, and finally emits a ghastly strident cry. The hand clapping is called *quatan* or *liquaqua*. . . .

With the cry of the *enbanda* the opening song ceases. The *cambone* brings a glass of wine and a root. The *enbanda* chews the root and drinks the wine. As fumes of incense begin to rise from a vessel in which it is being burned, he intones the second *ninbù*:

> Bacúlo of the air
> Take me on the table
> And whirl me around.

The *enbanda*, sometimes dancing to the rhythm of the hand clapping, sometimes falling into ecstasy, receives the *candarù* (the embers of the incense) from the *cambone*, places them between his teeth, and begins to emit sparks from his mouth. Then he sings the *ninbù*:

> Three *candarás* are calling me.
> Three *tatás* are calling me.
> I am the young [or old] *enbanda*.
> Today I am to become a *curimá*.

The time has come for the initiation of the new *camanás*. If one of the candidates has remained all this time with his *compadre* at some distance from the *camucite*, he must now approach. The *caiálo* presents himself in modest dress: white trousers, unstarched shirt of the same color, feet bare. As soon as he enters the circle, he passes three times under the leg of the *enbanda*. This triple journey symbolizes faith, humility, and obedience to his future "father," as he will henceforth call the *enbanda*. Meanwhile the *camanás* are singing a hymn of thanksgiving for the reception of the new brother. The initiate then stands before the *enbanda* as the latter is handed the *enba* and rubs the *caiálo's* wrists with it and the top and back of his head. He gives him the root to chew so that he may swallow the juice, gives him a glass of wine to drink, and leads him to the place he will occupy in the future in the *engira*.

After the *enba* has been distributed to the other *camanás*, together with the root and the wine, the "ceremony of faith" takes place. The *enbanda* intones his *ninbù* to the clapping of hands, etc. Then he takes a lighted candle, blesses it, and proceeds to pass it between each person's legs, over his arms, and across his back. If the flame goes out in front of one of the *camanás*, he immediately exclaims: "Why has *Camaná* So-and-So no *ka-*faith *k'*at all?" The *cambone* replies, and the punishment of the poor *camaná* begins—two, three, or four strokes on the hands with the *quim-bandon* (whip)—until the candle no longer goes out. . . .

When the faith of all the brothers has been tested, the *santé* ceremony begins—the climax of the assembly. Everyone folds a white handkerchief into a band and ties it around his head, knotting it at the back of his neck. The light of the fire is dimmed; incense or resin is burned to perfume the air. An appropriate hymn is intoned, and the *enbanda* dances to hand clapping, making forceful movements to induce the spirit to possess the congregation. There is always more than one *enbanda* to a table, and the chief *enbanda* must make every effort to transmit the *santé* to the others. From time to time *enba* is thrown into the air to drive away the evil spirits and to blind noninitiates, so that the secret of the sect may not become known. Suddenly one of the participants, usually an *enbanda*, doubles up, drops his head, and rolls on the ground in contortions. His face stiffens; his body is rigid; raucous sounds issue from his chest. The *santé* has taken possession of him. Sometimes a simple *camaná* is elected to receive it. During his seizure he talks and holds forth about *cabula* matters (although he has never been taught anything about them) like the most highly trained, learned *enbanda*. . . . Everyone makes diligent efforts to receive the *santé*, practicing all kinds of abstinence to this end and performing the most ridiculous penances.

Once a man has been possessed by the *santé*, he may try to get to know his familiar guardian spirit in the following way. He goes into the forest with an unlighted candle and returns with it burning, having taken along nothing to light it with. In this way he brings back the name of his pro-tector. There are many of these—for example, Tatá Warrior, Tatá Flower of Calunga, Tatá Break-Mountains, Tatá Break-Bridge, etc.[102]

A former student of mine who has searched for traces of *cabula* in Espírito Santo has so far found only memories of it among very old Negroes. It appears that Carioca-type *macumba*, which has retained many elements of *cabula*, notably the names of the priest (*enbanda* or *um-banda*) and his assistant (*cambone*), has completely supplanted it.[103]

In Rio de Janeiro the blacks were separated into "nations" right up to the end of the first decade of the nineteenth century, i.e. until urbanization of the Brazilian capital reached a peak. Each nation was distinguished by its own religious traditions. Unfortunately there have been no extensive studies of these diverse traditions; often our only available source is journalistic reporting. Nonetheless it is possible to make a rapid survey of those religious sects.

First we must distinguish between the Yoruba and the Bantu "nations." The Yoruba are themselves divided into Nagô, Tapa, and Ketu "nations."[104] Specialization may even have been carried farther here than in Bahia, for we know of at least one house that seems to have been dedicated solely to the cult of Oxun-marê, the rainbow.[105] The religion of these Yoruba people was called "jujuism" in rural areas,[106] *candomblé* in the capital. Descriptions by João de Rio and Magalhães Corrêa mention exactly the same cultural features that we noted in the preceding section: the monotheism of Olorun complicated by the polytheism of the *orixás*,[107] the same names for divinities,[108] the same priestly hierarchy (*babalaô, babas* or fathers, *yawos, abas, ogans* or *agibonans, ashoguns* responsible for sacrifices, *anuchans* representing the dead, etc.),[109] the same assignment of the days of the week to the *orixás*,[110] the same divination procedures and the same *odus*,[111] the same society of *eguns*,[112] the same annual festivals for the gods,[113] the same music, accompanied by the same ecstatic trance, and the same initiation rites.[114] Anything we might say about this religion would be no more than word-for-word repetition of what we have already said. Yet these blacks were not in close contact with either Bahia or Recife. The similarity of their cults can therefore be explained only by their common ethnic origin. Africa reproduced its own image in various parts of Brazil, and if these regions all look like carbon copies, this is because every black remained faithful to the norms and values of his ancestors, wherever the slave trade happened to set him down.

In addition to the Yoruba "nations," to which we must add the Djé-djé "nation" (the Gêgê—i.e. Dahoman "nation" of Bahia), although we know nothing about it,[115] there were Bantu "nations" whose ceremonies were known as *macumba*. The earliest extant descriptions of these show that they were essentially nothing other than *cabula*. They had *enbandas* or *cambones*, who directed the cult, and *cafiotos*, who were the initiates. Like *cabula*, this cult was celebrated outdoors, the assistants standing or sitting on benches in a circle around the *canzol* or sanctuary. Candles were burned; hymns were sung asking the spirits' permission to begin the ritual. There was the same "mad" dancing, with the same episodes of possession by the *tatás*, who here too were regarded as guardian spirits.[116]

But the Bantu of Rio were no more capable than the Bantu of Bahia of resisting the prestige of the Yoruba *candomblés*, and they adopted much of the Yoruba sacerdotal organization. First, the male initiates were renamed *ogans*, the female ones *gibonans*. Second, the *orixás* were given symbolic "fetishes": a sword for Ogun, the *orixá* of the white race; shells for Oxun, the *orixá* of the sea; a bow and arrows for Ode, the *orixá* of the forests. These imitations obviously entailed a certain number of mistakes: the *ogans* of genuine African *candomblés* do not receive the gods; Oxun is a goddess of fresh water, not of the sea; and it is difficult to see how Ogun could possibly become the divinity of the white race! Be that as it may, syncretism had already begun.[117] All that was needed to produce *macumba* as it exists today was the adoption, along with these two Yoruba elements, of the *caboclo* spirits, the Catholic saints, and the spiritists' dead. *Macumba*, which is still fluid and in a constant state of evolution, reflects a new social structure, a structure born of industrialization and the proliferation of great octopus-like cities in the wake of the First World War. We shall therefore pause here, deferring the study of this new religious phenomenon until later.

The *Batuques* of Rio Grande do Sul

The final region where the African religions survive is the extreme south of Brazil, from Viamão to the Uruguayan frontier, including the two big centers of Pelotas and Pôrto Alegre. Here the religions are known as *batuques*. Achylles Porto-Alegre gives an account, unfortunately very brief, of the old *batuques* in the days of the empire, defining them as part entertainment, part cult, part funeral ceremonies. He regrets their disappearance, which went hand in hand with the extinction of the African Negroes, and sadly notes that there are hardly any Mina left and that the young people make fun of the ancient dances, although when he was a young man they were all the rage in the suburbs of the city. Some of them even aroused white people's curiosity—the Bomfim dances, for instance.[118] Porto-Alegre's regrets were premature; far from being dead, the *batuque* still survives today.[119] It has been studied by Arthur Ramos,[120] M. J. Herskovits,[121] and Dante de Laytano.[122] Some personal observations of my own will round out their findings.[123]

The number of *batuques* registered with the police is relatively high and is in fact increasing every year. The oldest cult center dates back to 1894. Ten new houses were opened between 1920 and 1930, twenty more between 1930 and 1940, and eighteen more between 1940 and 1945. There were then fifty-seven African religious societies in Pôrto Alegre, thirty of which were named after Catholic saints, two after African gods, one after a *caboclo* spirit, and ten after historic dates.[124]

They are sometimes registered as mutual aid societies, but actually the element of mutual aid is restricted to meetings and expenses of the cult center. In one of the houses visited, for example, the members pay two cruzeiros a month, and the *filhos* one cruzeiro. In addition everyone pays a trifling contribution for each ceremony, whether profane or religious. The statistics for Rio Grande show the following totals:

1940, 37 houses with a total of 1,185 members + 121 new ones
1941, 42 houses with a total of 1,387 members + 110 new ones
1942, 52 houses with a total of 1,776.[125]

The cult centers are situated in the suburbs where the density of the Negro population is highest: nine in Sant'Ana, seven in Asenha, seven in Auxiliadera, nine in Passos, six in Menino Deus, four in Partenon, four in Petropolis, four in Floresta, two in Navegantes, two in Bomfim, one in Cidade Baixa, and one in João Pessoa.[126]

As in Bahia, the blacks of Pôrto Alegre are divided into various "nations," which here again are not, strictly speaking, ethnic categories but communities with common traditions. The same phenomenon has thus occurred in the south and in the north: the racial group has become a cultural group. Although the blacks of a certain "nation" may be descended, through their ancestors, from the most heterogeneous tribes and may themselves be mulatto or even white, they are linked by membership in a special cult and by ties to certain religious traits.

These cultural nations differ in some ways from those in the north, suggesting parallel evolution rather than possible influence. Gêgê (Dahomans) and Jesha (Yoruba) certainly exist, but Ketu (the major group in Bahia) are not found in Pôrto Alegre, while two new groups, the Oba and the Oyo (both Yoruba) are. Another important difference is the absence of Angola or Congo *batuques* despite the large number of people of Bantu descent.

The Dahomans have perhaps preserved more relics of their native religious culture here than in Bahia. To quote Herskovits: "The name of Mawu, the great god of the Dahomeans, rarely heard or recognized in the North, is well known in Porto Alegre, as is Aida Wedo, the rainbow serpent. Sogbo, encountered in the North, and *vodun*, the Dahomean term for deity, are also found in the South. Linguistic survivals of this group would seem to be quite extensive."[127]

But the differences that distinguish the Gêgê from the Yoruba "nations" have less to do with the mythology, which is Yoruba, than with more concrete cultural traits: the use of falsetto in their songs (noted by Herskovits), their use of smaller drums and of the *agôgô* instead of the little bells used by the Oyo, the use of sticks rather than the hands for beating the drum skin, and the greater importance attached to the sacred stones. Each *orixá* has its own stone: Bara's stone is erect; Shangô's lies flat; Omolú has a stone riddled with little holes as though pitted by smallpox; Oxun's stone is yellow and semitransparent when washed.

Disregarding these differences between the "nations," we find almost everywhere the same *orixás* as in Bahia, with the same day of the week assigned to them:

Monday: Bara, Odé, Ossanha, Otin
Tuesday: Shangô, Oiâ

Wednesday: Sapata (Saponam), Obá
Thursday: Ogun
Friday: Yemanjá, Odé, the son she clasps to her breast
Saturday: Oxun
Sunday: Oxalá

A remarkable fact to which, so far as I know, no one has called attention, is that years that begin on a Monday are dedicated in their entirety to
Bara, those that begin on a Tuesday to Shangô, etc. One Gêgê cult house
held ceremonies every two weeks honoring the *orixás* in this same order
and beginning again when they reached Oxalá. The assignment of the gods
to the days of the week thus has a cosmic significance; it constitutes a
division of time, and the calendar is primarily a sequence of festivals. Here
we see traces of the mentality, studied to such good effect by Mauss, that
divides time into qualitatively heterogeneous parts, into mystic and ceremonial periods. Another curious point is that this temporal order of the
orixás does not correspond to the order in which they are honored in the
shiré or worship ceremonies, where they are evoked in a different order:
Bara, Ogun, Oiâ, Shangô, Odé, Saponam, Obá, Oxun Pandá, Boji, Oxun
Doko, Yemanjá, Oxalá, and Orunmila. The order may, however, vary
from one "nation" to another.[128]
     The structure of the ceremonies is the same as in the north. Before
beginning, a sacrifice must be made to Bara, so that the ceremony may
proceed undisturbed. As one journalist has described this: "The whole
congregation left the room. Bara descended upon the woman who served
as his horse. . . . Then a little jar of water was given to the god for the
despacho of Exuto-lâ. This ceremony is intended to honor the god and
prevent Exú from disrupting the session. Bara dances wildly in the middle
of the room. Then he goes to the street door and empties out the water in
the jar. He returns and repeats the action at the rear door. Exú is now
despachado. The congregation returns to the room."[129]
     The songs and dances are then performed in the fixed order known as
the *shiré*. In the north and in Rio three songs are dedicated to each *orixá*,
but here only Exú, Ogun, Oiâ, Aganju, Ogodo, Shangô, Odé, Ossaim, and
Saponam are limited to three; the others all receive at least four.
     The songs are accompanied by drumming. Three drums are not always
used; some houses have two, others only one. In one house I visited there
were two: one in the colors of Shangô, red and white, called the *iniam*; the
other in the colors of Ossaim, yellow and green, called the *yabaniam*.
These are small drums held on the knees, the *iniam* partly covered with a
white cloth (*ala*), the *yabaniam* with a yellow one. As in the north, the
drum is a god: it eats—i.e. the drum skin is sprinkled with the blood of a
sacrificial animal. It is deeply revered by the believers, who make an
obeisance to it on entering the room, immediately after making one to the
African altar and before saluting the *mãe* or *pãe*. This gesture of rever-

ence consists in lowering the hand toward the ground, then immediately raising it to the mouth.

The climax of the ceremony is the descent of the *orixás*. It follows the same rules as in Bahia and Recife. But here possession is more violent and rapid because the police do not allow the ceremonies to continue after ten o'clock (to protect the neighbors from disturbance), and this certainly increases the violence of the trances. When someone is possessed, he prostrates himself violently before the *pegi* or the *mãe de santo*, then stands up in a slower, more ritualistic fashion. Then, as in the north, he salutes the visitors with a kiss on each cheek. But here he also turns them around between his arms and blows all over their body to enclose them in a field of magic force. Finally, after raising his arms to the sky several times with clenched fists, he bends the elbows of the person he is embracing and stretches out his arms, palms open. He then passes his hands over both arms and over the outstretched hands, which he closes over this mystic caress so that the transmitted power cannot escape. Some of these actions are more reminiscent of *catimbó* or *macumba* than of *candomblé*. Those who have been possessed also pass their hands over the heads and both cheeks of any children who may be present; this represents the blessing of the god.

In Bahia, when the ecstasy is too violent, someone rests a hand on the back of the "horse's" neck until the possession becomes gentler. Here someone blows into both ears. If the calming gesture is delayed too long, the desperate "horse" projects his or her head so that relief may be given quickly. Those who are possessed assume the expression of the *orixá* they represent, but they do not change clothes.

Herskovits makes a statement concerning the descent of the gods which does not agree with information given to me:

> Unlike orthodox practice in the Yoruba-Dahomean cults of the North, a person may actively worship and become possessed by several deities. In this respect, indeed, Porto Alegre is more like Haiti and Guiana than northern Brazil. In the latter area, while a number of deities may "descend on the head" of a devotee, all but one will be "seated"—that is, sent away so they will not trouble him by possessing him. In the South, while a cult member is initiated for his principal god, the "master of his head," he can be possessed by any of the other gods who come to him, and will dance for all who do possess him at any given ceremony.[130]

I was told by a *yalorixá* that no one could receive more than one *orixá*, but that since there are gods who do not descend, their initiates may receive another divinity instead. For example, a devotee of Shangô-dada may receive Ogun in his place. This contradiction can probably be explained by the fact that my information came from different informants and hence from different cult centers.

The ceremony ends with the meal of Oxalá. Those who have been possessed sit in a circle on the ground and eat the dishes prepared for the gods from their cupped hands while the *mãe de santo* takes a little of the sacred food and distributes it to the congregation. It should be noted that the children have already received their share. During the dances of the *Beji* they are brought into the circle and given cakes.

There are private ceremonies in addition to these public ones. Statistics, generalizing from other religions, mention baptisms and funerals.[131] It is even said that, in rural areas, when a baby is born it is tossed several times in a white cloth and this constitutes its baptism. I have never been able to confirm this. Actually there is no real baptism corresponding to the Catholic one, but rather an initiation, of both children and adults. The initiation ceremonies follow this order:

1. The summons from the *orixá*, although its identity is still unknown.

2. The discovery of its identity by the same methods of divination used in the north, including *dilogun* (divination by shells).

3. The preparation of the *filho* or *filha*. The initiates are taught songs and dances as well as the dogma of the religion. This initiation is short, and what I have learned about it confirms what Herskovits says:

> One priestess volunteered the information that she was planning to spend two weeks of the next month in a town in the interior of the state, to initiate a woman who had been possessed by a god and whose family had called her to perform the necessary rituals. The entire ceremony, which would be entirely carried out at the home of the novitiate, would not take more than a week. All expenses would be borne by the candidate's family, and it was made clear that all essentials of initiation would be included in the intensive, individual training compressed in this period. Specifically mentioned was the giving of the cult-name and the making of the sacred cuts at the top of the novitiate's head, two of the most important items in the longer cycle of ceremonies in the North. That initiations in Porto Alegre itself are short (the maximum period indicated by anyone was three weeks) is further shown by the fact that the heads of the candidates are not completely shaven, but the hair is merely cut at certain indicated points.[132]

4. Initiation ends with a mixture of African and Christian rites: the gift to Yemanjá on the river bank (which in my opinion represents, as it does in the north, the throwing away of the objects used by the candidate during initiation, which he or she must never touch again), the mass at Nossa Senhora de Rosario, and finally the public initiation ceremony in which the candidate receives his or her new name and is taken by the *orixá*.

5. The new *filho* or *filha* then makes the rounds of all those present at the ceremony to thank them for their courtesy. No money is given to the initiate, all the costs being borne by his family. During the ceremonies, though, the spectators drop a few coins on one of the trays in the *pegi*.

The initiation constitutes the biggest difference we have so far encountered. The shortening of the initiatory cycle, which consists of qualitatively different units of time, makes it impossible to retain all the rites; some of them must be dropped, thus weakening the tradition.

As in the north, the funeral ceremony is called the *achêchê*. Apparently it is performed only for *filhos* and *filhas* who are "made"—i.e. who have completed all the steps of their training for the priesthood. The *achêchê* lasts for seven days after death. On the morning of the seventh day there is a mass in the Catholic church, and at night a four-footed animal is sacrificed. On the eve of burial the devotees dance around the bier on which the body has been laid, but, as in the Bahia *achêchê*, the *orixás* do not descend. On the final night a table is set with food (probably the sacrificial animal) and coffee. A place is set for the deceased. But the *achêchê* does not completely separate the member from his religious group or from his family. On the first, third, fifth, and seventh anniversaries of his death, offerings are made to him, so that his spirit is not finally sent away (*despachado*) for seven years. Even then it may still return to earth. Pôrto Alegre blacks believe in reincarnation, just as their African ancestors did. They explain the continuance of traditions such as the return of the *orixás* by the reincarnation of their forebears in the bodies of new-born children.[133]

Here again, however, cultural elements have been lost. The cult of the dead seems narrower in scope than in Bahia. The sanctuaries in the south do not include houses or altars consecrated to the *eguns*. Their worship does not go beyond the *achêchê*.

The last differences—though by no means the least—are those connected with the organization of the "nations" and the hierarchy of priests. This hierarchy is much less extensive, and the number and variety of priests are considerably smaller. Each *batuque* is directed by a *pãe* or *mãe de santo*, and priestesses seem to outnumber priests. In Bahia we differentiated between the *babalorixá* and the *babalaô* or diviner. Divination is also practiced in Pôrto Alegre, but here, as in Recife, it is performed by the head of the cult center. The term *babalaô* is known, but the difference between him and the *babalorixá* is not very clear. Sometimes he seems to be the husband of the *mãe de santo*, when the house is directed by a woman; sometimes this title is assumed by an initiate who is not completely "made." In the north, at least in Bahia, power is divided; here it is concentrated in the hands of one person.

No special priest exists to perform the duties of sacrifice; even *mães de santo* may kill the animals, and any "made" *filho de santo* may perform the sacrifice. The *ogans* and *ekedi* who assist in the religious ceremonies in the north and who are subject to certain ritualistic rules and have undergone a minor initiation do not exist in the state of Rio Grande. Thus the cultural organization has been reduced to two components: the *filhos* and *filhas* and the priests and priestesses. This simplification has its counterpart in a slackening of the "nation's" organization as a religious community. Of course the priest and priestess still exercise great authority over their children, but the initiation is now too brief and has lost the buying and selling rituals, which symbolize the fact that the initiate has ceased to belong to his family and now belongs to the sect and that to be restored to his place in his blood family the child must be bought back. In the north, the authority of the *babalorixá* tends to extend beyond the religious framework. In the south it is confined to it; elsewhere the family is sovereign. Anyone who has lived for a time in the world of the *candomblés* and the *batuques* will recognize how the solidarity that unites the members of a *candomblé* into a genuine family has been eroded in the *batuques*. Of course the "children" visit their *pãe* or *mãe*, but, judging from my own experience, their relations are to be described sociologically as neighborly or friendly and lack the closeness of the tribe or the secret society. In this respect Bahia is closer in spirit to the lost homeland of Africa. Yet some vestiges of the old African social structure do remain. For example, the members of the cult usually belong to it by hereditary right, except for those who have been personally called. I have already spoken of reincarnations. The *orixás* remain in the same family, but they can be transmitted by both the male and female lines. A *mãe de santo* I knew had inherited her *orixá*, Oxun, from her paternal grandmother. There are no absolute marriage rules, but the marriage of two people who belong to the same *orixá* is considered "dangerous." In this respect the Pôrto Alegre norm is closer to that of Recife (which, according to René Ribeiro, permits such a marriage on condition that one of the partners has first had his god taken away and replaced by another)[134] than to that of Bahia, where *orixá* exogamy is customary.[135]

This leads me to the conclusion that while the mythology and even the structure of the public ceremonies have maintained a high degree of purity, the organization of the cult is weaker than its African models. How is this evolutionary difference to be explained? I believe that the causes lie in the economic and social situation of the blacks in Rio Grande.

While the cult certainly includes people of some social position, such as retired army men or Masons, the general social and economic level of the colored population is low. Hence anything in the ceremonial that costs money loses in richness and importance. Comparing cult centers in the south with those in the north, we are struck by the absence of the vast assembly rooms, the clusters of houses, and sacred buildings scattered throughout the grounds. Here the cult house is the private home of the priest or priestess. On the days when the ceremonies are held, the living room becomes the assembly room, with brightly colored paper streamers suspended from the ceiling.[136] These houses are small, usually built of wood (forty-three of the fifty-two registered in 1942 were frame houses), and differ in no way from the other working-class dwellings in the proletarian suburbs. Instead of the great open *barracãos* of Bahia, we find small rooms holding at most two hundred people (though rooms of this size are extremely rare) and sometimes no more than five. Their average capacity is about fifty people.[137] Because of their small size, the Catholic altar, which would take up too much space, tends to disappear, being replaced by religious prints on the walls—Saint George slaying the dragon, or the Virgin Mary holding the infant Jesus. The *pegi* is much more modest, consisting of a sort of closet made of boards, totally different from the shrines in the *candomblés* of the north. The altars are covered with an immaculate cloth. Stones are seen chiefly in Gêgê sanctuaries; in Oyo shrines there may be statuettes of the saints (especially Saints Cosmas and Damian). There are vessels of holy water and dishes for the sacrificial articles.

One result of this meagerness is a different disposition of the mystic space. As we have seen, some saints have to be worshiped indoors; others —above all Exú—must have their shrines outside. Since some houses have neither a courtyard nor a garden, Bara sometimes has to be assigned a place at the entrance to the *pegi* rather than the house. Sometimes, instead of having their own little hut, the two Baras have to make do with some old piece of furniture, perhaps a small sideboard standing on rotting planks and holding a few bottles and two strangely shaped pieces of iron. In Bahia, Omolú and Oxóssi dwell outside the *pegi*, but in Pôrto Alegre they are crowded into the same closet-shrine, along with the other *orixás*, following the norm that prevails in Recife. Nevertheless the blacks are quite aware that Omolú and Oxóssi ought to remain outside the house. To quote Herskovits: "One priest exhibited a special outdoor shrine for Shapana (Omolu) in the restricted space available behind his house, while at another center an attempt had been made to 'seat' Oshossi in a small tree, growing near the entrance-gate."[138] The priestess of this house frankly admitted that here economic conditions presented obstacles to religion. "City life is difficult for us," she said, "but we do the best we can."

The low economic level also accounts for the shortening of the initiation period and the weakening of tradition that this inevitably entails. As a priestess complained to me: "You have to pay a terrible price for a sheep nowadays. You can't get away under one or two *contos*."

Probably this also explains why the descent of the gods is not marked by a symbolic change of clothing. As we have seen, this is true in Recife too. It also accounts for the erosion of the religious obligations and private worship of the *filhos* and *filhas*. Of course they still have to observe ritual taboos, since this costs nothing. Here the penalty for infringing an *eho* (taboo) is very severe: the violator is afflicted with a skin disease. But the *filhos* or *filhas* are no longer obliged to offer the customary sacrifices to their *orixás* on the anniversary of their initiation. As one of them told me:

"That's too expensive today. We can't do it more often than every two or three years. The *orixás* are like children. If you let them get used to a yearly sacrifice, they can't do without it and punish anyone who doesn't perform it. Right from the start you have to get them accustomed to receiving only occasional sacrifices, just as you train a child to eat at certain times."

In short, throughout this region the people of color's low standard of living is a constant threat to the purity of religious tradition and accounts for all the disorganization and erosion we have observed. Religious needs conflict with economic needs. All one can do is try to strike a flexible balance that will do the least possible harm to tradition. The mythology has not been seriously weakened, although the brevity of the initiation inevitably deprives it of some elements. Organization and ritual are more seriously affected: mystic space is concentrated in the *pegi*; mystic time loses certain moments of its duration, keeping only the essential parts of the ritual; the hierarchy of priests is reduced; sacrifice loses ground. What remains is the essential: the ceremony surrounding the descent of the gods. Indeed, ecstasy has gained in importance to make up for what has been lost elsewhere; it has become wilder and more violent and uncontrolled. Clustered around its descending gods, the cult still manages to hold off outside influence, deviations, and syncretism. Devotees of the African sects are very Catholic and see no disloyalty to their ancient traditions in observing church feasts. A *mãe de santo* will finish up all her housework on Wednesday and Thursday; on Friday, the day of the death of Our Lord, she does none at all. Nevertheless Catholicism and the African religions simply coexist; there is no more mixing here than in Bahia.

Internal Migration and the Afro-Brazilian Religions

The conclusion to be drawn from the preceding paragraphs is that the African religions inevitably suffered repercussions from modifications in the economic or social structures. Wherever black communities found niches in which they could organize themselves—in Bahia, Recife, and the capital of Maranhão—they were able to imprint their own values and cultivate them. But when these communities were atomized into a random scattering of interpersonal relationships, as happened in the *sertão*, they became peculiarly susceptible to influences from the environment, especially the influence of *catimbó*, while at the same time the low standard of living in the south forced them to modify their organization and rituals. The link between religious values and social structures will emerge even more clearly as we study the effects of internal migration.

Brazil always had to compensate for its demographic weakness by shifting its population from one corner of its vast territory to another. When the gold mines were discovered in the eighteenth century, populations hitherto concentrated in the northeast or in the São Paulo region were immediately moved to the future province of Minas to exploit them. The decline of mining at the end of that century was reflected in a return of these gold miners to the "Minas triangle," where they took up cattle raising, and to the state of São Paulo, where they established the sugar industry. The nineteenth century in its turn brought new shifts to the coffee *fazendas* and the Amazon forests. Every time a new source of wealth was discovered, hordes of people were lured from the poorest zones, or from areas being proletarianized by a slump in a certain product, toward the regions that promised new riches and prosperity.[139] Yet this mobility could never be more than a temporary solution because it prevented people from putting down roots and developing that attachment to the land without which there can be no steady enrichment of the country as a whole. The empire, and later the republic, tried to substitute foreign immigration for these domestic migrations. The idea now was not to move populations from one part of the territory to another in response to the changing labor market but to populate the whole of Brazil by attracting people from abroad.

This new policy, however, was handicapped by a series of negative factors. In the first place, even though it was feasible for the south, where the more temperate climate reminded the newcomers of Europe, only a few immigrants (chiefly Japanese) were able to adjust to Amazonas. In the second place, even in the south, immigration posed problems: the encapsulation of foreign populations, especially the Germans and Japanese, and the adverse reaction of Brazilian "nationals," who often lost out in the competition between races or ethnic groups and sought protection against the influx of immigrants from the authorities. This resulted in the establishment of quotas (excepting the Portuguese), which progressively reduced the numbers of European and Japanese immigrants just when coffee production and the industrialization of the big cities were creating an insatiable demand for new labor. Mussolini's fascist policy prohibiting Italian emigration to South America (which he saw as a hemorrhage that would prove fatal to his country), and—even more important—the Second World War, which cut the ties between Brazil and Europe, brought immigration to a standstill. As a result domestic migration, which had never entirely ceased, picked up again.

The prosperous areas with their high salaries and living standards (in the northeast São Paulo is known as "the promised land") acted as suction pumps, the poverty zones, especially the waterless region of scorched earth and prickly cactus, as evacuation pumps. Inhabitants of Ceará and Bahia and of the Minas *sertão* set out on foot, or by boat, train, or truck, toward the new land of Canaan, which promised them, if not figs and grapes, at least less arduous work and an easier living.[140] Some of these migrants came from the regions of *catimbó* and *candomblé*. It was only to be expected that human mobility should be accompanied by a corresponding religious mobility.

I myself have encountered in the working-class districts of São Paulo members of *candomblés* or *xangôs* who had left their native region to try their luck elsewhere, usually as builders in a town where a new house was being erected every fifteen minutes. But we must not forget that the African religion is a "nonmobile" religion. Its sacrifices and rites are addressed to sacred stones in the *pegi*. They can be performed only by special priests who have undergone the appropriate initiation. Worship—even private devotions—is impossible outside the *terreiro*. The admission ceremony consists essentially in establishing a mystic participation between an individual and his god's "fetish." A member of the Gantois *candomblé*, for example, would be an outsider in the Engenho Velho *seito*; if he did attend a ceremony there, he would be unable to worship his *orixá* or be possessed by it.[141] The cult is geographically restricted to a specific sacred site and could move only if that site were to move along with it. A *candomblé* member who has left his native region is therefore obliged to return home for a few days every year if he wishes to perform the obligatory devotions to his god. The presence of members of African sects in São Paulo does not therefore necessarily mean that they have reestablished institutionalized organizations there.

The situation was different in Rio. Here *macumba* provided a substitute for the *candomblés* or *xangôs* of the immigrants. But the law I have just cited applied there too: the Rio *macumbas* had different stones, different priests, and a different ceremonial. Yet one intelligent, enterprising *babalorixá* with an instinct for the economic benefits he might derive from a stay in the Brazilian capital, where several of his former *filhas* as well as his *pequena mãe* were living, did not hesitate to transfer his *candomblé*, complete with stones, liturgical objects, and musical instruments, along with some of his former assistants—his *iya basse* and his *alebés*. Success rewarded this brave action, and the tourists guaranteed his new *terreiro* a glorious future.[142] Thus a trail was blazed for the migration of rites and gods. I know of at least three such attempts in São Paulo. The first was made by a *babalorixá* from the Bahia *sertão* who moved to the city on two separate occasions but could not find a job to support himself. The second case was a *babalorixá* from Alagoas who arrived with great trunkfuls of cult objects, having moved his *xangô* lock, stock, and barrel. Although he found compatriots, he did not succeed in establishing his sect and had to return home after a year. The *babalorixá* from Bahia who had done so well in Rio later decided to set up a kind of branch *candomblé* in São Paulo, where a dozen or so of his former *filhas* were living. Indeed he had several times been invited by Paulistas who were resisting Vargas to celebrate sessions of black magic there. Nevertheless the *terreiro* he founded is evolving in the direction of Umbanda spiritism instead of remaining faithful to purely African norms.

How are these failures or semifailures to be explained? One reason is probably that the blacks who leave Bahia for the south come from the arid areas, from cattle-raising or mining regions, or from the São Francisco basin—i.e. from sparsely populated, isolated regions where *candomblé* is virtually nonexistent. Another reason is that country dwellers are more attracted to pioneering country than to cities, so that such *candomblé* members as may exist in the state of São Paulo are scattered throughout the numerous coffee *fazendas* and are not in touch with one another. There are other reasons too, chiefly the dichotomy of two economic structures, two life styles, two worlds of conflicting values. It has often been said that there are two Brazils, not one: "archaic" Brazil, still colonial in character, oriented to the past rather than the future; and modern Brazil, with its skyscrapers, huge factories, and scientific agriculture, feverishly striving toward the future.[143] Domestic migration plunges people from the most archaic Brazil into the most modern. The encounter might of course have produced a civilizational clash that the African religious sects could turn to their advantage by becoming a refuge from social tensions. But this did not happen. In this melting pot of people and values, the northerner cleaves to his new environment. If he finds himself working in a city as a factory hand or a builder, he accepts the ideals of his rivals and workmates. The individual effort needed to shoulder his way into society supersedes *compadrismo* and cooperative give-and-take. The monetary economy takes precedence over the community economy of prestations and counterprestations. He becomes infected by a mentality to which material interests and their advancement by political parties and unions are more important than spiritual interests and which regards work as a surer source of reward than magical procedures. But the *candomblé* is based on community, not individualist spirit; on an economy of gifts and counter gifts, not a profit-seeking capitalist one; on material success as a consequence of the regular fulfillment of religious obligations, not as the reward for unremitting work and the will to succeed. The African sects cannot reestablish themselves in such a hostile environment, even in the interstitial zones of the abandoned suburban proletariat. Their only chance is to adopt the forms of Umbanda spiritism, the only ones through which the black community can adapt is religion to urbanization and industrialization—as we shall see in a later chapter.

That the hostility of the environment is indeed the decisive factor is proved by the fact that wherever a sanctuary of the gods has migrated successfully, it has been within the archaic, community minded, precapitalist Brazil rather than from one of the two Brazils to the other.

In addition to the route that took migrating populations from the barren *sertão* to the "promised land," there is another leading from Ceará and

Maranhão to Amazonas with its rubber and chestnut trees. Those who took this route merely exchanged one hardship for another: the merciless sun for the stifling humidity, the scorched earth for the mysterious forest teeming with mythical or real monsters, with hidden Indians and terrifying shadows. They left an apocalyptic land petrified in the rigor mortis of a planet for a world of unfinished Creation, where land and water merge, where life emerges from rotting vegetation, where the moans of death are mingled with those of childbirth. Here man sees little reward for his effort; his creative activity is frustrated by the malevolence of the forest, by landslides produced by the rising waters of the Amazon, by the countless prison bars with which the rain isolates him in his solitary drudgery. If anyone makes a profit, it is not the migrant but his employer. Already hampered by the hostile physical environment, he chafes at the contrast between what he was promised by the recruiting agents of the big Amazon companies before he left and the economic realities that confront him: the inadequate pay, spent before he even draws it, to cover what he owes to the company store, his only source of supplies. Obviously the mental climate in which he now lives cannot help but promote a mystic search for supernatural protectors, for friendly spirits to preserve him from the diseases oozing out of the swamps, from the arrows that fly by night, from the tangled greenery, and from the monsters prowling around his hut.

Mario de Andrade was probably the first scholar to call attention to the coexistence of Negro *pagelança* with Indian *pagelança* in Amazonas,[144] but he never discovered the secret of its origin. The juxtaposition of the word *vodun* and the name Yemanjá in a hymn he collected (*"Dêrêcê Vodun, dêrêcê Amanjá"*) led him to think that the cult originated in Haiti.[145] Today, however, we know the true sources of this African *pagelança*. It stems from a kind of missionary activity by the *tambores* of Maranhão among their compatriots in Pará. The most thoroughly studied of these sects, the one known as Babassué, is, like the older Cambinda one, merely an extension of the debased suburban sects of São Luiz do Maranhão. The Babassué *terreiro* is especially susceptible to this debasement or, to use another word, to syncretism, because its *pãe* belongs to the Dahoman tradition, its *mãe* to the Yoruba one. There has been a marriage of cults as well as bodies.

The name Babassué is a contraction of Barba Couera, "the African name of Saint Barbara," patron saint of the sect.[146] The sect uses the same term—*vodun*—used in Maranhão to designate the gods, but also uses the term *orixá* (no doubt to avoid jealousy within the family).[147] Here we find the same syncretism between the Dahoman deities (Agungono, Averekê, Odé, Doku, Zamadan) and the Yoruba ones (Yemanjá, Ogun, Yassam, Omolú, Shangô, Oxalá)[148] that we find in similar cult houses in Maranhão. The sanctuary is called by the same Fon name— *kêrêbê* (*quêrêbatan*).[149] The same "mourning drum" is played when a cult member dies.[150] And of course Indian *caboclos* appear in the sanctuary, and the dances are held on a veranda.

The other *pagelança* sects in Amazonas have not been studied as thoroughly as *Babassué*. (My informants could furnish only songs and some fragmentary data on certain aspects of the cult.)[151] But their success was undeniable and offers an interesting contrast to the failures in São Paulo. This does not mean that the creators of the African *pagelança* sects were better organizers than the *babalorixás* who headed south but merely that they found a social climate comparable to the one they had left behind.

My use of the term "missionary activity" corroborates this. Even though the constituent nucleus consisted of emigrants from Maranhão,[152] it soon attracted a new type: sons of Amazonas, who brought along masters of *catimbó* or Indian *pagelança*—Master Noé (who received a particularly warm welcome since his name was easily confused with that of the Dahoman sea goddess Naété, known in Maranhão as Naê), Master Carlos (whom we have already encountered in *catimbó*), Master King of Urubá, Master Marajó, etc.[153] One point should be noted, however. The imported African tradition and the local Indian tradition do not fuse; they merely coexist. The sanctuary is composed of two parts: the "state" (with the statues of the saints)—i.e. the complex of *caboclo* states and villages described earlier in the section on *catimbó*, and the *pegi*, where the private rituals are celebrated near the *otas*—the stones of the *voduns*.[154] The funeral ceremonies have not been contaminated by *pagelança*, and the dances conform to the norms of the African dances of Maranhão.

Thus the mystic shadow of Africa, following on the heels of the migrating descendants of the original Africans, tried to project itself over the rest of Brazil, to invade new areas, to reproduce itself either through the migration of sects or through fission of the old ones. Its success varied according to the type of society it encountered on its way.

10
How the African
Religious Sects Function

These African cells scattered throughout the living tissue of Brazilian society are not scar tissue; they too are living cells. What exactly do I mean by "living"? Life is primarily the ability to adapt to the environment or to change it, to find an answer to the problems that present themselves or are presented by ever changing circumstances—in short, life is a self-renewing capacity for regeneration. If we were to concentrate on that meaning of the word, this chapter would have to address itself to the evolution of the African religions, and we should realize that from one single starting point (or from several similar ones) evolution may take many different directions and the collective consciousness may assume many different forms. In Haiti, for instance, voodoo, by mythicizing the African homeland, tends increasingly to incarnate the pride of the youthful Negro republic.[1] Hence its evolution goes hand in hand with the development of national consciousness. In Brazil, however, where the African religions are urban rather than rural, their evolution is following in the footsteps of urbanization and industrialization in an attempt to adapt to a changing society. We shall examine this course in a later chapter.

But the word *life* can be taken in another sense: as pure functioning. An institution or a group can be said to be living when it works, when its various mechanisms are running and meshing properly, just as an organism is living when it digests, breathes, and reproduces. In the present chapter we shall confine ourselves to this second sense. The Africanists who have described Afro-Brazilian sects have all too often treated them as museum specimens; in fact I know of only two books that give an adequate idea of their dense, teeming vitality, Ruth Landes's *The City of Women* and Henri-Georges Clouzot's *Le Cheval des Dieux.* Unfortunately as soon as a writer tries to communicate the impression of life—a life that must inevitably strike the Westerner as exotic—literature rears its head and he must take a stance, since art is always the product of a choice and, even if his aim is only to reproduce nature, he will reproduce it in the light of his own temperament. Ruth Landes presents a feminine view of the *candomblés* which is in keeping with the aggressive self-affirmation of North American women that observers unanimously agree is a basic trait of U.S. mentality.[2] Clouzot gives them a sadistic cast. His account of Bahia, like his movies, is tragically permeated with contempt for the human being. This being so, it is easy enough to understand why scholars have ignored the living aspect of the sects they were describing. They were afraid that to introduce anecdotes or describe actual happenings would remove their studies from the objective to the subjective plane, from the realm of scientific knowledge to that of literary evocation.

But surely the problem of life can be approached scientifically. The verb *function* in the title of this chapter also exists as a noun. Does not functionalism offer us a basis for assessing the life of the African sects while steering clear of poetry or drama? Herskovits called the attention of the second generation of Brazilian Africanists to the need for using the guiding concepts and the viewpoint of functionalism in the study of the *candomblés*. In a lecture delivered in Bahia he even outlined what he took to be the principal functions of the *candomblé*: to promote the security of individual members through close solidarity in a mutual assistance group and through identification with the gods, to help satisfy personal desire for prestige and improved social status by linking the latter with religious status, and lastly to satisfy mass esthetic or recreational needs through music, singing, and dancing.[3] Ribeiro took a similar position:

> [These religions] offer their devotees a system of beliefs and a new type of interpersonal relations which strongly promote the relief of tensions without requiring them to repudiate other values and styles of the Luso-Brazilian civilization. People whose position and role in the global society rule out all chance of attaining their objectives or even reconciling the realities of daily life with their ideals or desires . . . find there a system of beliefs, of personal relationships, of hierarchy, as well as a type of relationship with the supernatural and of apparent control over chance that enables them to satisfy their indispensable psychological needs—the first step in adjusting themselves to the world they live in. Participation in these groups, which are organized differently from the other groups of our urban

society, and the fair chance of achieving a prestigious position that will
confer a new—and often superior—status offer these people a more satisfying experience than any other available to them in our society.[4]

Obviously this functionalist conception is closer to Malinowski than to
Radcliffe-Brown, closer to psychology than to sociology. And it would be
easy enough to link it with Thomas's theory of the four desires. I should be
the last to deny that the African sects survive because they meet individual
needs or necessities, having called attention to these psychic factors in the
historical first part of this book and having devoted several pages of
Sociologie et Psychanalyse to the way in which ecstatic trance and identification with the gods relieves tensions.[5] But the Marxist explanation does
not contradict the functionalist one; it uses it as a point of departure in the
study of new forms of social groups that are capable of answering or
satisfying the same fundamental needs of human nature while integrating
the individual in a godless society. Jorge Amado's novel *Bahia de Todos
os Santos* is no more than an account of the dialectic that leads Jubiabá
from the solidarity of the *candomblé* to that of the trade union, from the
prestige he enjoys as a son of the god to the prestige awarded him as a
leader of a social class, from the poetry of dance to the poetry of the
strike.[6] But that merely amounts to saying—and this is the significant
point for us—that the same needs can be satisfied by different types of
groups. The functionalist explanation of the African sects is therefore too
broad, since it applies to any kind of institution, any type of solidarity or
group, constituted or self-constituting. Ribeiro was well aware of this when
he said that no other group in urban society could help people of color to
realize their ideals or their deep strivings as effectively as the African sect.
But why is this so? If we want to understand this institutional choice, we
are forced back to the fact that Brazilian society is composed of social
classes in which skin color symbolizes one's position in a hierarchy of
privilege or lack of privilege and in which racial prejudice continues more
or less hypocritically to impede the collective rise of a colored group that
poses a threat to another group's key positions within the global society.
Our effort to understand the African sects may lead us to study the psychology of their members, but that in turn is understandable only through
an analysis of the social structure. The ultimate explanation is the sociological one.

There is another reason for not dwelling on the functionalist position,
and that is that the desires or needs of human nature are always shaped by
the cultural environment.[7] For example, if the desire for interpersonal
solidarity is more effectively satisfied in the world of the *candomblé* than
in the trade union, in a precapitalist type of mutual assistance more readily
than in organizations of the modern type, this is because members of
candomblés have been raised in a certain environment since early childhood and shaped by certain norms of life. If prestige is sought through

relations with the divine and close participation with the supernatural, this is because the African's whole life cycle, from birth to death, is governed by learned rituals imposed both by the family and by the neighborhood. Moreover, the same individuals often belong simultaneously to very different types of organization, some of African, others of non-African origin— trade union, mutual aid society, Brotherhood of the Rosary or of Saint Benedict—each of which can adequately meet the desire for security, prestige (the fraternities and societies offer a whole range of ranks), esthetic entertainment (Catholic feasts, processions, or even secular dance clubs). Popular Catholicism, with its demands and promises, its miracles and *ex votos*, its "potent" prayers and its holy medals, offers the black—and the white too—the same possibilities of controlling change and manipulating fate, the same familiarity with the supernatural, as his own religion does. And yet the *candomblé* is not abandoned. It is not abandoned because, although these individuals belong to different groups, they have been conditioned by the education they have received, by the pressure of their environment, to seek their satisfactions in predetermined ways. Their ideals and desires are certainly those common to all human beings, but they have been given direction. The basis of the African sects is faith. Faith in the omnipotence of the *orixás*, in the supernatural sanctions that punish those who violate taboos. A faith that rests on thousands of happenings: children of the gods punished for their disobedience, profane men healed by sacrifices or by "giving food to the head." A primal faith inherited from the ancestors and transmitted from one generation to the next. The esthetic or moral ideals of individuals may change; new needs may emerge in response to the transformations of society, but such is the power of the ancestral tradition that these ideals and new needs will seek satisfaction within the old framework—though not, of course, without modifying it more or less radically.

While I have never knowingly slighted human needs or desires in the study of social phenomena, neither do I ever forget that these psychic factors are the reverse side of sociological phenomena. The psyche we are dealing with is always a socialized one, not some nonspecific human nature that predates the culture. My discussion of the way the Afro-Brazilian sects work is not based on any functionalist theory but quite simply on how the cogwheels of an organism mesh so that it may survive and propagate. It is based on the history of the organism and on what the biologists would call the physiology of a system. We must discover the laws that connect individuals located at a certain point in space and time. We must find out how human passions and group interests are reconciled and what this reconciliation entails in the way of clashes, compromise, and capitulation. Instead of describing strictly labeled and classified norms, symbols, and rites, we must watch the battles of the gods, the rivalry over prestigious positions, the day-to-day acts of love—as well as the petty shortcomings—that are lived out within the frameworks of the sects. We must watch living people at work within a living cell.

■ ■ ■

When we compare rural and urban zones, we find that such African behavior patterns as have survived do not all integrate themselves in the lives of individuals in the same way. Although the study of predominantly Negro rural zones is only just beginning, it seems that here survivals remain isolated and do not form specific complexes. Sexual, economic, and religious behavior all remain discrete. For example, in the municipalities of Caxias and Codo, both in Maranhão, we find polygamy. The first form in which it occurs is the common one where a man has both a wife and a mistress. This may well be a reinterpretation of African polygamy in Western terms, but it may also be something else: a legacy of slavery, a common practice of the white man that was adopted by the blacks. In any event this case is too controversial to serve our present purpose.[8] But we also find polygamy in a clearly African form: a man may have two or more wives living in different houses, usually in different villages, and spend a few days with one and then a few days with the other.[9] We find the land divided into two plots, one of which is assigned to the woman, who works it and is entitled to whatever she harvests from it.[10] We find communal labor, in the form—probably more typically Brazilian—of "day-labor exchange" (*trocar dias*) between neighbors. Here, however, such exchanges conform to the sexual division of labor: men exchange with men, women with women.[11] Lastly, we find the cult of the *encantados*. But although these various behavior patterns are all specifically African, they are not combined in any integrated system; they merely coexist.

In the towns, however, religion became the center of attraction, assembling in its shade every vestige of Africa that had been able to survive. The *candomblé* is more than a mystic sect; it is a genuine bit of Africa transplanted. Among banana plants, bougainvilleas, breadfruit trees and, gigantic fig trees from whose branches trail the veils of the *orixás*, or beside golden sandy beaches edged with coconut palms, stands the *candomblé*, with the huts for the gods, the living quarters, the roofed shelter where at night the beating of drums summons the ancestral deities. Women, girls, and men bustle about their work—cooking, having their hair dressed by the deft hands of old women. Half-naked children frolic under the fond eyes of mothers adorned with liturgical necklaces. It is as if one had taken a cutting of Africa and rooted it in Brazilian soil, where it bloomed again. Here sexual, economic, and religious behavior fuse in a harmonious unity.

The *candomblé*, or the other African sects mentioned in the previous chapter, unites these men, women, and children in a coherent, functional whole, not only through their common beliefs or feelings, through like minds and hearts, but also by molding their passions and desires, their attractions and jealousies, according to a series of mythic models that enable them to coexist, join forces, or cooperate in a communal task. Anything that might separate individuals and thus disrupt the group—eroticism, ruthless ambition, avarice—is controlled, not in order to suppress it but to make it compatible with the impulses of the other members. If the *candomblé* is alive and pulsating with vitality, this is certainly not because it stifles passions or discourages personal incentives. The life of the African religious sects resides in this interweaving of existences, this mingling of individual life stories, this multiplicity of personal histories whose threads finally come together to produce a sociological novel depicting an efficiently functioning human milieu.

A Brazilian of African descent once remarked to René Ribeiro: "[Free city blacks] don't get married. It was the sugar planters who invented that marriage business so that the poor Negresses would have babies and provide them with plenty of slaves." This does not mean that the urban blacks who founded the African religious sects lived in concubinage, but merely that they did not marry according to Catholic rites. They continued the African type of polygamy. Antonio de Moraes Silva's Portuguese dictionary alludes to this state of affairs when it defines *combarca*, a word in common usage in the African sects, as "two rivals in concubinage." Only the term *concubinage* is inaccurate. In addition to a legitimate wife, *babalaôs* in Recife had their *apetebi*, who assisted them in divination rites. These *apetebi* were in fact second wives; their relationship to the first wife was analogous to that of the second to the first wife in Africa. They were required to accept her blessing, to serve her as a daughter, and to be cherished by her in return.[12] Most *candomblé* priests in Bahia still practice plural marriage.[13] Of course concubinage exists outside these circles; a man may have several common-law wives, though usually successively rather than simultaneously. But this should not be confused with the sanctioned polygamy of priests. It is easy enough to distinguish between a ritualized African survival and the breakdown of the proletarian family.[14]

This does not imply that the African system is one of sexual license. On the contrary, sexuality is imprisoned in a whole series of taboos and strict rules. A woman undergoing initiation must remain "pure in body" during her residence in the *camarinha*. Later, whenever she is to receive her god, she must abstain from relations with a man for twenty-four hours beforehand. In fact this rule of physical purity applies to any religious ceremony of any kind. Moreover, as I have said, one day of the week is consecrated to each god, and on that day all sexual activity is forbidden to the girls dedicated to that particular deity.

But besides bending individual needs to its system of norms, the *candomblé* also establishes guidelines for bringing men and women together or keeping them apart; there are preferential marriages. In Brazil the law of exogamy can no longer be applied to genuine lineages; instead, it is applied to the spiritual reconstitution of lineages that makes a man and a woman who belong to the same *orixá* brother and sister. A son of Shangô may not marry one of Shangô's daughters; a son of Yemanjá may not marry a daughter of Yemanjá. That would be incest. Neither may the *babalaô* take as his *apetebi* any girl who pleases him. He may choose only from among the daughters of Oxun because according to myth only they have the right to play with the divining shells.[15] Polygamy too must follow strict imperatives. But a marriage between a son of Shangô and a daughter of Yansan (or vice versa) would be a felicitous one, because Yansan was the first or principal wife of Shangô. A son of Shangô may also marry a daughter of Oxun, because Oxun was Shangô's favorite concubine, the most beloved of his three wives, although he does not share with her, as he does with Yansan, mastery of the storm and the terrifying lightning.[16] The more strictly the law of preferential marriage is observed, the more harmonious will be the relations between members of the *candomblé*. Observation of the law of exogamy (mandatory if supernatural punishment in the form of misfortune, illness, or death is to be avoided) brings into play a whole set of complementary forces that create a balance of ritual functions and a climate of cooperative, friendly participation in the life of the African sects. While the *candomblé* certainly directs the eroticism of its members, this direction ensures that individual couples are not just separate atoms in the community, since husband and wife occupy different positions in the cult. In this way the functioning of the *terreiro* is not subject to the disruptive pressure of passions that might fragment it into families. On the contrary, these passions, when controlled and directed, become forces that promote intergroup solidarity.[17]

The African norms, different from but not inconsistent with Luso-Brazilian customs, continue to govern the life of the married couple—whether they are married legally or by common law. Hence there is a general tendency to accord women the utmost economic autonomy, which is not the case in the patriarchal Brazilian family. Of course the husband works and contributes his share to the household, but if he has more than one wife, each of them must make a living. They do so just as they would in Africa, by petty trading. They prepare dishes of *couscous* or little rolls of bean flour browned in palm oil, or cakes, or they pick fruit and peddle these things in the streets. The money they earn in this way is their own property. One reason why women have maintained their economic independence is that the man may abandon the home from one day to the next, leaving his partner alone with the children born of their temporary union. This explains the high incidence of matriarchal families in the black population of Brazil, as in the United States.[18] This matriarchal family is not an African survival. Indeed a comparative study of patriarchal and matriarchal families among Afro-Brazilians based on past statistics seems to show that matriarchal families increased with the decline of slavery and were more common at first among mulattoes than among Negroes (mulattoes having been manumitted by their white fathers much earlier than the Negroes).[19] The decisive factor therefore seems to be social disorganization, not a reversion to Africa. But even so, as a result of the domination of the children by the mother or grandmother, African ideals and collective representations are perpetuated more effectively in matriarchal than in patriarchal families, since the women are more conservative and traditional than the men. Here again, in the matrimonial system or the family structure, a reciprocal process is at work just like the one that directs erotic options. On the one hand the survival of an African norm— maximum economic independence of the woman—makes the maternal type of family possible; on the other hand the matriarchal family promotes the perpetuation of African ideals and hence the preservation and vitality of the traditional religious sects.

In spite of this, sexuality always presents a danger because of its very irrationality, which can upset the subtle interplay of these controls, correspondences, and reciprocal actions and reactions, especially when, through contact with whites, the black is exposed to new forms of love— the romantic, for instance. Strife between a husband and wife who both belong to the same cult center, and more especially between spouses belonging to different *terreiros*, a man's capricious decision to leave his partner of long standing for another woman, or a girl's decision to change lovers may precipitate a crisis in recruiting or in the orderly functioning of the sect. Here, where reason reaches its limits, the only recourse is magic. The *babalorixá* or the *yalorixá* possesses effective expedients to prevent a man from leaving one woman for another or to bring him back to his former partner—herbs that arouse love, philters that allay quarrels. Menstrual blood in the morning cup of coffee. A toad imprisoned in a basket full of earth, its eyelids sewn together with thread, its feet tied with a ribbon. *Urucabaca* wine in which the shirt of the loved one has been soaked. In addition to these popular remedies one can of course make promises and sacrifices to the *orixás* and consult the necklace of Ifá or the shells of Exú.[20] Here again, a potential source of internal conflict and danger for the *candomblé* ultimately increases its integrative force, since all problems can be resolved through the authority of the priests and the discipline they impose upon the members. It is always possible to punish those whose uncontrolled eroticism threatens the life of the sect, either through magic's power of suggestion over anyone who knows that he is the object of it or through the "punishment songs" performed on the day of a public ceremony. The latter produce an ecstasy so brutal, painful, and exhausting that when the trance is over the individual is compelled to abide by the law he was tempted to violate.[21]

What I have said about erotic behavior is equally applicable to economic behavior. Here too whites labor under gross delusions. They believe that the priests live on mass superstition from which they can earn plenty of money without working with their hands. Admittedly the capitalist economic system and the profit motive have been introduced into the *macumbas* and into some *candomblés* and *xangôs*, thus commercializing them. But we must not judge the traditional sects by modern caricatures. In the first place, the priests in charge of these "tourist *macumbas*" are not "made"—i.e. they have not undergone the long process of initiation and have only an indirect, incomplete knowledge of the "secrets" of the African religions. Secondly, the privileged status of the *babalorixá* and the *yalorixá* has its reverse aspect: more extensive duties, more numerous taboos. The higher one rises in the hierarchy, the greater the onus. Every rung on the sacerdotal ladder brings increased prestige but no more money. And lastly, it is not the rich outsiders who meet the major expenses of the *candomblé* but more often than not the insiders, who are often its poorest members. Here giving is not a duty but a privilege, which is not granted to everybody. The higher one rises, the more one gives. If the whites find this hard to understand, it is because it represents an economy quite unlike our capitalist one—the type Mauss so nicely defined as an economy of gifts and countergifts. The fee paid for consulting Ifá or having a magic ritual performed, for being initiated or "giving food to the head," is not a purchase price but an obligatory return for the surplus of being, strength, or life received in exchange. Even the word "exchange" is not very appropriate here because what we are dealing with is a manipulation of the sacred, and this manipulation requires a balance between the two parties. This is confirmed by the fact that the transaction is usually not in money but by barter. The god who relinquishes a little of his being as a gift to the mortal receives in return the sacrifice of a cock or a goat or an offering of food to replenish the force he has lost. Or there may be no exchange at all. The individual may simply provide the wherewithal for the procedure he needs—the animal to furnish the blood, the perfume in which the herb will be soaked, the necklace to be washed. A third possibility is that a member may help the less fortunate members of the sect by standing as godfather to future *yawos*, for example, or furnishing their liturgical clothing. In return the *yawo* will nurse him if he falls ill, keep his house, or bring him food if he is alone. The countergift is always equal to the gift. There is no profit, no desire to gain an advantage, no wish to receive more than one gives. The balance is never disturbed. But even so, in order to disarm the criticism of their white opponents, most *babalorixás* and *yalorixás*, at least in Bahia, follow a trade. They earn their living by driving a taxi, selling vegetables, doing construction work, etc. The priests or priestesses in Recife who live on gifts, on services performed for clients, on divinatory consultations, do not all live in affluence by any means. In Pôrto Alegre each *batuque* is backed by a secular society that administers the *terreiro* with funds derived from small monthly contributions from all the *filhos* and from secular events like Sunday dances to which the young men pay admission.

To visitors the *candomblé* looks like a beehive, or perhaps like an African village where the behavior patterns of mutual aid and clan labor are still intact. The men build the dwelling houses and the sanctuaries of the gods; the women devote themselves to housework or cultivate gardens. But it cannot be said that either group is performing unpaid labor for the priest or priestess. They are working for the community. To be sure, the land may belong to the *babalorixá* or the *pegi-gan*, but we must not forget that priesthood is not hereditary and may not be transmitted within the family. (Parents are not even allowed to initiate their children in their own *terreiro*.) A *yalorixá* or *babalorixá* who dies is usually succeeded by the *mãe pequena*, so that the property of the *candomblé* must belong not to an individual, not to the priest in charge of it, but to the society. Even when the property is privately owned under the law, members of the group regard it as collective property. The *vodunsi* of Maranhão live and work communally in the *Casa das Minas*. Their husbands work outside it but return at night to their wives' home. In Bahia, if a daughter of the gods finds herself homeless, destitute, ill, or too old to care for herself, she may go and live in the *candomblé*. Thus religious solidarity is reinforced by socioeconomic solidarity, and this socioeconomic solidarity in turn rests on the spiritual communion that unites all members of the sect in one and the same faith.

We are constantly running across this give-and-take, which upholds the life of the African religious sects by interweaving personal relationships and making individual behavior patterns complementary. But the economy of the *terreiros* influences their functioning in yet another way. A study of the great Catholic orders that did not include an analysis of the economy of the monasteries, their resources and expenditures, would be inconceivable. Even the most religious societies cannot live without a material base to provide the faithful with their daily bread. Unfortunately we know little about the economy of the African sects, and no typical budget is available to us.[22] While we can of course estimate the value of the land and living quarters, such values, important as they are in a capitalist economy, have no meaning in a cooperative society where they merely represent inanimate objects, since the land and houses are not for sale but belong to the gods and, in practice if not by law, are common property, at least insofar as the traditional *candomblés* are concerned. Any budget of expenditure and income we might work out would be equally misleading because it would translate into monetary terms something that remains outside the monetary economy. Even if it were accurate, it would give an erroneous impression. It is of course possible to calculate the value of the work days contributed by builder members of the *candomblé* to repair a roof or expand a *pegi*, or of the hours the daughters of the gods spend cooking. We can even calculate the amount paid for room and board by the girls who live in the cult house. But this collective budget would be meaningful only if it were supplemented by budgets for all the members of the sect showing just what they contribute and receive, and this data would be practically impossible to obtain. Broadly speaking, we can say that, thanks to gifts and countergifts, financial stability is always more or less maintained. An *ogan* or an *obá* is obliged to present a yearly sacrifice to his god, accompanied by a private ceremony, the entire expense of which he bears. The initiation of a *filha* is expensive, costing several thousand cruzeiros, for it includes board for the time she spends in the *camarinha*, the four-footed animals to be sacrificed, and the liturgical clothing she wears on the day she receives her new name. If her parents cannot meet these expenses, however, godparents will be found to help out; her clothes will be made at home; after the ceremonies, visits will be made to friends who will bestow small gifts of money. In return every year the *babalorixá* or *yalorixá* will hold for the whole membership great public ceremonies including animal sacrifices, three to seven nights of dancing, and a great abundance of food graciously offered to everyone in attendance.

While socioeconomic cooperation is the rule in internal relationships, external relationships between *terreiros* are governed by the law of potlatch. The prestige of the *candomblé* depends upon the beauty of its ceremonies, the discipline with which they are conducted, the abundance of food, and the splendor of the rites. Of course, outlay for representation of this kind could be explained in capitalist economic terms as "propaganda" expenses that will be recouped through more numerous initiations and a rise in membership. But this is not the way the priest thinks. He is not concerned with what is still to come, with future credits. What matters to him is his own personal prestige and the collective prestige of the sect. He is engaged in sumptuary rivalry with other priests from which he will emerge either the winner or the loser, but never the same man as before.

Yet although the economy of the *candomblé* is different in kind from the Western economy, it too is subject to a phenomenon we have already observed in the sphere of sexual behavior: infiltration by new values and life styles. In the case of sexuality it was relatively easy to resolve the tensions between the old and the new, but the capitalist spirit, or to put it more simply a monetary economy, is disruptive in a different way. I am not speaking of the fake *candomblés* or *macumbas* opened up nowadays to exploit tourists, sanctuaries that live on the superstition of whites and concentrate on expensive magic rituals for sensation seekers and night club patrons. Although these centers may be directed by mulattoes and offer their sophisticated clientele a ballet performed by girls who are quite likely to be black, culminating in simulated African rites, they represent white rather than black religion. But quite apart from this commercialization of the mystic, even the most traditional *terreiros* are being invaded by a canker. Merely through contact with another world, the man of African descent has acquired new values, attitudes, and desires. Prestige derived from money is less expensive to acquire than prestige derived from status in the priestly hierarchy. As we have said, to rise in the world of the *candomblé* means accepting new obligations, taboos, and a curtailment of behavioral options. But to rise in society by means of money opens up new areas for spending and new sources of pleasure. The first course tends to diminish the pleasure of life; the second gives it wider scope.

Many of the changes taking place today are entirely attributable to this fact. For instance, in Recife and Bahia the *babalaô* is disappearing because to seek advice about the future by means of the necklace of Ifá is to increase the number of sexual and alimentary prohibitions imposed upon the man who in Africa headed the sacerdotal hierarchy. But the *candomblé* cannot function without consulting the gods before every ceremony and every sacrifice and at the beginning of each day. So the *babalaô* is replaced by the *babalorixá*. From the struggle that engaged these two types of priesthood as soon as the African sects were organized in Brazil, the priests of Ifá emerged the losers.[23] The first result of this was an impoverishment of the Afro-Brazilian priesthood as compared to its African counterpart. The second result was the disappearance of methods of divination that had been quite common in Recife and in Bahia, and hence an impoverishment of the ritual too. (All that survives now is divination with *obi* nuts or shells.) The third result was that no more sons of Ifá were initiated, no more of the little bags known as *kpolis* were made. The personal experience of Ifá died out. His songs, which are falling into disuse, will probably ultimately disappear from the collective memory.

Even if new attitudes toward life have not contaminated traditional African behavior, the monetary economy still exerts pressure in another way. Blood is the principal means of linking the world of men and the world of the gods. While the blood of two-footed creatures will do for small private rituals, the blood of four-footed animals is needed for the big annual rituals or for initiations. But these animals—goats, sheep, sometimes steers—become more and more expensive, while the earnings of potential candidates for initiation remain extremely low. In the old days, a semirural, semiurban population could raise, in the courtyard of the cult house, a goat or a ewe to be offered to the *orixá*. The smaller living quarters of today, the abandonment of the small suburban shanty for a standard apartment closer to the place of employment, require that these animals be purchased at the going market price—sometimes several thousand cruzeiros. The old patronage system cannot always provide a solution, with the result that godparenthood is fragmented and one person will contribute a quarter or a third of the cost of the initiation of the *yawo* he is sponsoring. Obviously this splitting of the cost among three or four individuals must inevitably weaken the bonds of affection that marked the old system. In the absence of interpersonal bonds of respect or affection, motivations come into play which may or may not be acknowledgeable: sexuality or sadism, misplaced curiosity. The donor may demand in return admission to secret rites that may be witnessed by only two or three of the top figures in the *candomblé*. He may seek the titillation of watching a tranced woman dripping with the blood of a goat slaughtered over her naked torso. He may demand satisfactions from the *yawo* beyond the prestige of being her godfather.

This process has only just begun; it goes back no farther than the end of the Second World War. There is no telling where it may lead, unless it is checked by the violent reaction now arising within the oldest and most traditional *candombles* against these new methods of meeting initiation expenses and the erosion of African moral standards they inevitably produce. Be that as it may, the economic factor tends to assume an increasingly important role in the life of the *candomblé*, thus modifying both its structure and its functioning.

The political aspect of *candomblé* life has been even less thoroughly studied than its economic aspect. But it would be wrong to neglect it. We have seen in Part I of this book how the *calundu* exercised leadership in the blacks' struggle against white exploitation. The *calundu* was the nucleus around which revolt crystallized, placing the power of the gods at the service of their enslaved children. The abolition of slavery eliminated this old established function of the African sects, but, as I have pointed out, this did not automatically improve the economic and social condition of the blacks. One might therefore presume that the sects would continue to be hotbeds of resistance for a subordinated, abandoned class of people of color in a competitive world where skin color was one of the criteria for upward mobility. Indeed two attempts were made to enlist some of the sects in political causes. The first, which occurred in the 1930s, was the infiltration of the *candomblés* by communism. This was the period in which Ruth Landes visited Bahia, and *The City of Women* contains a certain amount of information on collusion between religion and communism. But this first attempt failed. When communism was banned, it became dangerous for the *candomblé* to link its destiny to a proscribed party. It had suffered too much police persecution or harassment to stake its very existence on such a venture. Indeed in Recife the government closed down the *xangôs* on the pretext that the African sects were collaborating with a party not recognized by the law.

The second, much more recent attempt was Bishop Maura's propaganda campaign among devotees of *macumba* and Umbanda spiritism. To some extent this represents a religious protest against the Roman Catholic church rather than a purely political movement, but actually the two forms of protest are closely linked, since the disinherited masses may see the

Catholic church as a rampart of social conservatism. In fact Bishop Maura's Catholic Apostolic Church of Brazil is developing both a religious and a political program, and the latter has much in common with the program of the Communist party. Anti-Roman sentiment has always existed in Brazil, but never to the point of repudiating the Catholic heritage. The cult of the Blessed Virgin and the saints, with its attachment to the great liturgical festivals and spectacular processions, is so strong that anti-Roman sentiment always stops short of Protestantism. I have already mentioned this sentiment in an earlier chapter in connection with the Tailors' Revolt, which represented a kind of Brazilian Gallicanism. But it was not confined to the blacks and mulattoes; during the regency it expressed itself just as strongly among whites.[24] In any case, Maura demands that Brazilian Catholicism be freed from the "foreign" domination of Rome, rejects the authority of the Pope and of auricular confession, and seeks to establish a truly popular Catholicism responsive to the aspirations of the most wretched segments of the population. The movement's journal, *Luta*, provides ample evidence that since 1945 its priests have been attending Umbanda spiritism séances, blessing statues of the Virgin identified with Yemanjá, saying mass in *macumba* sanctuaries, and buying land where the Negroes can celebrate their "national Brazilian" festivals, regardless of the fact that these are proscribed by the Roman church. The movement has spread from Rio to Recife, where, according to Waldemar Valente, two or three *xangôs* are now more or less openly affiliated with the Catholic Apostolic Church of Brazil.[25] In my opinion it will not spread to the genuinely traditional *candomblés*, since it can gain a foothold only in centers that are disintegrating in the social chaos of octopus-like cities where industrialization and the proletarianization of the blacks pose new problems.

Why, then, are the African religious sects, which spearheaded the struggle against slavery, not equally active against those after-effects that still survive: color prejudice, racial discrimination, segregation of the mass of blacks in the lower strata of society? Why has the struggle passed from the hands of the religious groups to purely defensive political organizations such as the Black Front, the Federation of Associations of Brazilians of Color, etc.? The answer is not hard to find. In the first place, the democratic regime allows racial and class demands to be expressed through the legal channels provided by the constitution, and this form of expression is more effective than underground activity by religious groups. The Black Front was modeled on the protest movements of Italian immigrants in São Paulo and stemmed from the early strikes in which those immigrants organized their black fellow-workers as shock groups.[26] Again, these racial protest movements can arise only where prejudice and discrimination are rife; they cannot exist where racial democracy runs smoothly, as it does in Bahia. Repeated attempts have been made there to organize Negroes and dark mulattoes in racial political associations; all of them quickly collapsed.[27] Why indeed should blacks protest against whites when they see them kneeling humbly before their own *yalorixá* to ask her blessing and treating the few surviving *babalaôs* with the utmost respect; when they even see immigrants, especially Spanish women (Spaniards constituting the largest foreign group in Bahia), becoming daughters of the gods and submitting to the most exclusive, not to say tyrannical, authority of black priests? The African religion abolishes every hierarchy except the one based on relative closeness to the sacred. In the *candomblé* the racial situation is radically different from that of the secular world: here the dark-skinned dominate the light. As we have seen, mystic trance identifies the little waitress, the cook, or the bricklayer with the rulers of the sky, the storm, or the sea, dispelling feelings of inferiority and rancor over day-to-day humiliations—all the feelings that provoke or nourish racial protest.[28]

The elimination of politics from the life of the Afro-Brazilian sects confirms what the historical part of this book attempted to show: that black revolt as expressed in the *quilombos* or in slave insurrections was not a purely economic movement but essentially a cultural one—the pathetic outcry of a civilization unwilling to die. While there is no collusion today between political parties and religious sects, the *candomblés* certainly have a political policy. It continues the policy of the colonial *calundus* and is by necessity a cultural policy. Under the republic the blacks were wooed by candidates seeking their vote, but their decision as to which party to support was dictated solely by concern for the freedom of their cults and their potential growth. Some candidates sponsored ceremonies, paid for festivals, surrounded themselves with daughters of the gods, went to the polls with a "black guard" of male *candomblé* members in order to claim, along with Pedroso, O Balaio: "This race is my race." (This phenomenon, by the way, is not confined to Brazil. The Rosas dictatorship in Argentina also sought the support of the African religious sects.)[29] But the *candomblés* learned the danger of such excessively close alliances. If their chosen candidate and protector was not elected, the winner would immediately attack them. In Alagoas, for instance, popular rejection of a governor friendly to the local *xangôs* was expressed in the vandalization of the African sanctuaries. Perhaps the *candomblés* are vaguely aware that what happened in Argentina could happen in Brazil too, that the defeat of their protector might be followed by a tidal wave that could sweep away their religion forever. For this reason they follow the more prudent policy of supporting the party in power, whatever it may be, on condition that it leave the members of the *candomblés* alone. At first glance black espousal of the strongest party may look like fickleness. Actually the lack of political loyalty reflects a deeper loyalty—fidelity to the ancestral heritage.

Each factor we study in the functioning of the African religious sects leads to the same conclusion: any potentially disruptive element is always woven into a network of Africanizations in such a way as to transform it into a new element of social cohesion. We shall see this again as we look at the rivalries, jealousies, hatreds, and personal ambitions that in many groups might well dislocate interpersonal relationships. So far as I know, René Ribeiro is the only Brazilian Africanist to have called attention to this, and he did so precisely after completing an analysis of the sanctions and controls exercised by the sects over their members:

> While competition and rivalry do promote disintegration and conflict among cult members, they also act as integrative forces by stimulating the members to greater participation, by leading them to adopt behavior more in keeping with their goal of achieving a position in the hierarchy, and by forcing them to seek influence and prestige within the group through conforming more closely to its rules. On the other hand, competition and rivalry between the various cult groups and between individuals keep the priests and the members alert to possible infractions of the traditionally sanctioned and accepted norms and ever ready to censure the least ortho-dox cult centers and the most deviant members.[30]

These struggles and rivalries never flout African norms and are always contained within the framework of the *candomblé*. Thus they vitalize the group rather than destroy it, keep it flexible, help the machinery to run smoothly. The gods cease to be mere collective representations and become Homeric forces working alongside mortals—to the point where in studying the history of individual sects it is hard to tell whether one is dealing with a battle of men or a battle of gods.

A few examples chosen from different regions will illustrate this. We may begin with the battle between the *orixás* and the *eguns* in Pôrto Alegre. A particularly respected *yalorixá* had been trained as a young woman by an old *babalorixá* surrounded by African-born blacks. She was his senior initiate, and before his death her spiritual father gave her his necklace of Oxun, the sign and symbol of her right to succeed him. But during the night following the death of the *babalorixá* a younger *filha* appropriated the cult objects and secretly removed them to her own house. Her possession of the *pegi*, where the stones of the gods reside, automatically made her the chief priestess of the *batuque*. Her house, however, was located near the cemetery, and the spirits of the dead came in to take advantage of the ceremonies and enter the bodies of the initiates as they danced. One after another, *filhas* and *filhos* began to die of a mysterious ailment that struck them down with increasing rapidity, until one was dying every week. The Shangô of the *pegi* was consulted and revealed the reason for these deaths: he did not wish to remain in the company of the dead. And indeed a well-known Afro-Brazilian myth relates that Shangô is afraid of the *eguns* and flees at their approach.³¹ A mass was said for the souls of the dead. Shangô's stone was washed and purified, then solemnly carried to the door of the *filha* who was the rightful *yalorixá* of the sect. A Star of David was painted on her door, barring it for ever to the spirits of the departed. Thus the struggle of the two candidates for the supreme priesthood was interpreted on the level of reality in terms of the dramatic struggle between the *orixás* and the *eguns*.

One of the most prestigious *terreiros* in Bahia is under the protection of Shangô, to whom it is dedicated. When the old *yalorixá* who had directed it died, the *sidagan* of the sect was given temporary charge. The Ketu "nation" traditionally waits seven years before appointing a priest's successor. Then the secret society of the *eguns* on the island of Itaperica (the Isle of the Dead) evokes the spirit of the dead priest, who announces in the mystery of the night who is destined to succeed him. Now this *sidagan* was a daughter of Oxun. For seven years a battle raged between Shangô and Oxun to decide who was to prevail. There was of course no question of changing the patron god of the sanctuary, but Shangô's *obás* and the priests of Oxun enjoyed equal authority. The *obás*, who considered themselves the spiritual sons of the great Martiniano of Bomfim, wanted to maintain the ultimate authority over the *terreiro* and force the daughter of Oxun to submit to their will. She, however, acknowledged no authority above her own and was determined that the ministers of Shangô should do her bidding. In this clash of individuals motivated by purely human feelings both claims to the priesthood were supported by a god. Oxun was on the side of the *sidagan*, while Shangô supported his ministers—like Pallas and Aphrodite fighting above the walls of Troy.

The combatants are not always immune to remorse, but if remorse does break through, it always takes an African form. One of the most famous *yalorixás* in Recife who succeeded a *babalorixá* initiated in Africa made his son the *pegi-gan* of her *xangô* but took advantage of the rule prohibiting a father from initiating his child in his own *terreiro* to retain the supreme authority for herself. Nevertheless in some obscure recess of her being she was nagged by a consciousness of having done wrong—no doubt because Brazilian custom requires that succession be within the family. This guilt complex expressed itself symbolically as a conviction that the son of the *babalorixá* had cast a magic spell upon her to punish her for having assumed a position to which she was not entitled. The doctor who treated her until her death told me that there was nothing organically wrong with her, yet she slowly wasted away, deliberately destroying herself through her belief in the all-powerful black magic of the man whose spiritual heritage she had appropriated.

In ways like this, individual passions and interests, functioning within the framework of the African religious sects, lend the collective representations that hold the sects together and the machinery that keeps them functioning a characteristic dynamism.

■ ■ ■

So far we have started with interpersonal or intergroup relations and shown that they always develop in accordance with collective norms, values, and ideals. The forms of sexual, economic, political, or any other solidarity imply communal action in a shared faith, and it is because the whole membership of a *candomblé* shares the same collective representations, the same deep feelings, that potentially disruptive elements are ultimately transformed into elements that promote cohesion.

Now we shall follow the opposite course and begin with communal phenomena. We shall see that these communal acts are invariably accomplished through personal relationships. Forms of social solidarity and acts of collective communion are useful abstractions for introducing a little order into the complexity of concrete social phenomena, but we must never forget that they *are* abstractions, ideal poles, and that in reality these two poles are closely interdependent and maintain a reciprocal dialectic relationship.

Daily life in the religious sects consists of a series of private rituals, services performed by the daughters of the gods, individual contacts, visits, and consultations. The great public festivals, however, whether distributed throughout the year, as they are in Maranhão and Recife, or lasting for a whole week once a year, as in the big Ketu sanctuaries in Bahia, and the great ceremonies that initiate the new *yawos* into the African brotherhood are moments of collective communion. At these times the entire membership of the *candomblé* assembles to share in a common exaltation, in the ballet of the *orixás* who have returned from Africa to dance with their Brazilian sons. Some members come from a considerable distance, trudging several kilometers along a highway under the broiling sun, the mothers carrying their babies in their arms, the fathers holding little children by the hand.

Here we see the error of the Durkheimean school, which sees acts of communion ultimately as crowd phenomena. Durkheim built up his whole theory of the social origins of religion on an erroneous description of collective ecstasy. In fact there is no collective ecstasy, no mass madness, no trance produced by individuals coming together and being possessed by one and the same "collective soul." What there is, is an ordered set of individual trances, each of which has its own distinctive character and its own place in an overall network of personal relations. It is not the crowd, the enthusiasm, the concentration of individuals in a confined sacred space that generates the Dionysiac orgy. The gods do not descend haphazardly but in fixed order—the order of the musical leitmotiv. They respect all

kinds of restraints. Menstruating women and those recently bereaved cannot receive their *orixá*; neither can pregnant women as a general rule. If
trance were really produced by the emergence of a collective soul or by the
pressure of a crowd of individuals, visiting members of other *candomblés*
would be caught up in the general madness and would abandon their role
as spectators to join the ecstatic, convulsive dancing in the central ring.
Yet etiquette forbids nonmembers of the sect responsible for the ceremony
to allow themselves to be possessed by the gods. In other words, trance is
always controlled by the group. The most significant fact from our standpoint is that every trance is different because it is the trance of a different
god. The ecstasy of a son of Shangô cannot be compared with the trance of
a son of Omolú; the trance of Yansan is quite unlike that of Yemanjá.
Moreover the various deities are related by blood or marriage, rivalry or
friendship. Since the ecstatic ballet is essentially a rehearsal of the ancestral myths, each individual ecstasy must be related to the rest according to
models furnished by the pantheon, be it Yoruba or Dahoman, Bantu or
caboclo. The possessed girls dancing in the mystic ring in the center of the
room have not taken their places at random. Each has her assigned place,
which depends on her god's position in the pantheon and on bonds of
hierarchy or marriage. Oxun cannot precede Yansan, Shangô's first wife. If
Obá descends, she will quarrel with Oxun, for these two are rivals who
hate one another because of an ancient incident involving erotic magic.
Anyone who regularly attends *candomblé* sessions will easily distinguish
the adolescent ecstasies of the young gods (even if these gods are incarnated in old men) from the shuffling ecstasies of the old ones, female from
male ecstasies, the trance of the warrior *orixás* from that of the gods of
sensual pleasures. And these trances are not merely juxtaposed but are
interrelated, complementing one another to form a harmonious whole that
calls to life events played out long ago in the supernatural world. Certainly
there is communion, but it is realized only through a nexus of personal
relations and complementary individual roles, or by incarnating itself in
such a nexus. The outsider may get an impression of collective madness
provoked by the crowding together of people partaking of the same faith,
the same emotional exaltation. In fact he is witnessing a ballet—an
ecstatic one, to be sure, but a ballet staged by mythic tradition.

    Moments of communion also occur in other contexts of *candomblé* life
—in clashes between different *terreiros*, for instance. While bonds of
friendship link a mother house with its daughter houses when a split occurs,
each *candomblé* constitutes an autonomous community, the jealous rival
of other communities. At times these rivalries may become particularly
intense, and then the members become more strongly aware of their group
loyalty. As passions are fomented, a communal spirit develops in resistance to outsiders. How does this communal spirit manifest itself? By an
even more absolute respect for the ritual obligations that link the individ-

uals in a structured nexus of relationships. In other words, communion again reduces to a more effective functioning of interpersonal relationships, according to each person's status and roles within an ordered whole, only this time the process is conscious instead of being produced by controlled ecstatic actions.

The same applies to times of persecution or crisis. I myself was present on two occasions when collective feelings reached a peak: the prohibition of the sects by the police in Recife, and the publication of some photographs of secret rituals in Bahia. Because they could mean the end of the African sects or are a symptom of the erosion of ancestral customs, these persecutions and crises immediately provoke collective defensive reactions. I do not deny that these are the genuine collective reactions of a disturbed collective consciousness. To be convinced of this one need only experience the fervent excitement of the individuals involved; this is certainly the "soul of the *candomblé*" palpitating. But here again the communion is realized only through strict obedience to the norms that govern interpersonal relations. Communion is objectified in forms of solidarity which, as they function, intensify the communion.

Clearly, in studying the functioning of the African religious sects we must never separate the two poles of social organization—namely intermental relations and acts of communion. In his study of the development of moral sentiments Piaget carefully distinguished between the effects of family restraint and peer pressure. What is true of morality also applies to religion. Durkheim saw only the restraint of collective representations and defined religion as the creation of a common soul. In one sense he was right, for, as we have seen, relations between individuals invariably develop according to models provided by collective representations; their functioning requires the existence of communion in one and the same faith. But we must not forget the other aspect of religion: it represents a kind of peer group whose activities constitute a network of complementarities, a nexus of relationships between individuals playing different roles. In short, communion is always structured. We should not forget this, for in the next chapter it will provide the key to some of the problems of collective memory that Halbwachs left unresolved.

11
Problems of
the Collective Memory

All religion is a tradition—a dual tradition of stereotyped actions and rites and of mental images and myths. It has often been claimed that the two elements are inseparable, myths being a definition or justification of the ceremonial actions. And it is true that myth does seem to constitute a model to be reproduced, an account of a past event that took place at the dawning of the world and that must be continually repeated lest the world collapse into nothingness. Myth is not simply monologue or "precedent," as Lévy-Bruhl termed it. It is already an oral action intimately bound up with a manual one. Nevertheless those who perform the rite are not always completely cognizant of the underlying myth. There are various degrees of initiation, and only the top priests in the hierarchy are privy to the whole heritage of divine lore. Rite is encaged in the matrix of muscular capacity; its range is narrowly limited by the body. The scope of myth, on the other hand, is the almost infinite one of the creative imagination. It is capable of all kinds of proliferation—the unpredictable flowering of dreams. Bergson distinguished two types of memory: motor memory as a bodily function, and the memory of pure images capable of self-crystallization. This distinction is helpful in comprehending the difference between what is commonly accepted as rite and what is commonly accepted as myth, as well as the gap between the two.

This gap will help us to understand why the various elements of religious life in Brazil have shown varying degrees of resistance to change or oblivion. The rites have held out much more tenaciously than the myths. Of

240

course, just because we know little about a certain area, we cannot conclude that certain elements in a religious complex do not exist. At present
few Afro-Brazilian myths are known to us, but this does not necessarily
mean that there are none; it may simply reflect a lack of interest or
curiosity on the part of scholars. The scholars have been chiefly physicians
(Nina Rodrigues and Arthur Ramos for instance) who concentrated
almost exclusively on actions, particularly ecstatic ones. Our lack of
knowledge may also have something to do with the law of secrecy. All
ethnographers who have studied *candomblé* life have been struck by the
important function of "the secret" in protecting the cult against the whites.
The priests are reluctant to explain the profound meaning of rites, even
public ones, to people inspired only by curiosity. They are afraid that this
knowledge might be used against them or ridiculed as "superstition."
Nevertheless African myth is well preserved in the memory of the *babalaô*
or the *babalorixá*. The daughters of the gods are quite aware that their
dance steps speak a kind of motor language, that their movements and
hieratic actions recount past adventures of the *voduns* or the *orixás*. But
the researcher who shows a little love, reciprocal friendship, or simple
human respect will finally gain admission to the world of myth and thus
come to understand the symbolic meaning of the ceremonies he watches.[1]
Then he will immediately recognize the fragility of the oral compared with
the motor tradition.

Myth now survives only through its connection with ritual. In passing
from one generation to the next, from mouth to mouth, it has lost its
original richness of detail and been reduced to a mere explanation of
certain actions. The transplanting of African civilization across the ocean
was a process antithetical to the one Bergson studied in *The Two Sources
of Morality and Religion*: the process of decrystallization, nonprolifera-
tion, and loss of all poetic substance. It would be incorrect to say that the
myths have died out.[2] Ribeiro's research in Recife, Verger's in Bahia, and
my own show that many myths found in Africa have exact equivalents in
Brazil, among them myths about Exú, Shangô, Oxalá, and Oxóssi. The
legends that explain the diviner's *odu* were not lost in the move to a new
country; in fact today they are often carefully copied out in the cheap
notebooks of schoolchildren. But the fact is that myth now survives only
as a definition of rite. Only by allying itself with actions or with the rules
of divination did it save itself from extinction. Only to the extent that
Bergsonian pure memories are able to attach themselves to the more substantial motor mechanisms, which are less easily forgotten because they
operate within the living organism, have the stories of the gods been able
to survive—and even then not without losing some of their color, poetic
vigor, and richness.[3]

Perhaps we can now take a step forward and ask what has been lost to
myth and why. Although myth may shift events back into a mysterious

past, it still depicts a certain society. It reflects the structure of lineages, the emergence of chiefhoods, the laws of communal life. As we have seen, slavery destroyed the organization of Negro society. It is true that in Brazil this society was able to rebuild itself, and in doing so it certainly reinterpreted some of the more resistant archaic customs like polygamy or respect for old age. But it naturally rebuilt itself according to the norms and models of the surrounding Luso-Brazilian society. By applying to Brazil a test used by Clémence Ramnoux to study the transmission of legends[4] but using it on a sociological rather than psychological plane, I determined that what is lost when one moves from one social group to another is the collective representations characteristic of the archaic social structures, the parts of the legend connected with ancient forms of marriage or exchanges —in short, everything that is no longer meaningful to the Western world. I concluded that the vital elements in oral transmission are "the structures of contemporary society . . . as well as the changes in collective values, social representations, and ideals resulting from these morphological upheavals. This explains why we immediately try to rationalize and justify according to our own mentality anything that appears at all strange and why these strange elements are the first to be swept away into oblivion because we can no longer fit them into the social frameworks of memory."[5]

The allusion in the last sentence to Halbwachs's famous book is not a casual one. After all, it was he who established (with the help of other data) that "social thought is essentially memory, and . . . its content consists entirely of collective memories. But only those memories survive— and only that part of any one memory—that society, operating within its existing frameworks, is able to reconstruct at any given time."[6] The impoverishment of African myths is not the result of real forgetting of a psychological nature, induced by the destructive action of time, but of the lack of landmarks to which memories can attach themselves. Societal change, not erosion, is responsible for the loss of images.

This test may explain the impoverishment of myth, but having been designed to study change, not survival, it does not explain what preserves it. How are we to account for what survives? Arthur Ramos devoted half of his book *O Negro Brasileiro* to a psychoanalytical interpretation of African myths based on matriarchy, the murder of the father, the birth of the hero, and the twin nature of the human personality. But this interpretation (assuming that it is valid) applies only to myth at its origin—i.e. African myth, indeed the only type with which Ramos was familiar, thanks largely to the work of A. B. Ellis. According to Ramos, the images of the gods carried over by the Afro-Brazilians to their new habitat survived only because the racial archetypes of the Negroes remained unchanged. Shangô remained the phallic hero, Yemanjá the image of the maternal libido. In short, taking Ramos's hypothesis as a point of departure, the part of myth that survives is the part that best meets the inmost leanings of the black soul. To uphold this explanation one would have to accept that acquired characteristics can be inherited (which is controversial), that we are dealing with a black unconscious different from the racial unconscious of other peoples and possessing its own archetypes (which Jung would not admit), or that the social conditions in which Brazilian blacks live are a continuation of the original African ones. I have bent Ramos's theory to fit the last of these three premises.[7] If the lower-class black family is a matriarchal one in which the child is cared for by the woman, Yemanjá will continue to be conceived of in the image of the mother.[8] Nevertheless, if psychoanalysis is to elucidate certain aspects of the survivals, it ultimately has to call upon sociology. What survive are the complexes of the collective unconscious that are upheld by contemporary social conditions, and in the end these conditions are the essential factor. Moreover the psychoanalytical explanation of African survivals holds good only for some of them (the myths of Yemanjá, for example) but not all (divination through Ifá or Exú).

Octavio da Costa Eduardo, who made a study of animal stories in one region of Maranhão, remarks on the similarities between African and European stories. But these similarities do not adequately explain the tenacity of the African legends. The reason why these animal stories have survived, he says, is not that black memories are constantly reinforced by similar white stories. Even though the black and the white versions correspond structurally, the Afro-Brazilian stories respect the African models down to the most minute details; almost identical versions crop up in the memory of Haitian Negroes or of blacks in the southern United States. Thus da Costa Eduardo winds up with a sociological explanation for the survival of memories: "The process of memory is socially determined and is therefore to be explained in terms of attitudes, feelings, and collective conventions on the part of groups of individuals."

This sociology is a functionalist one. Legend preserves anything that fulfills a useful function within the community. The black, first a slave and later relegated to the lower levels of society, defends himself against his white master or against people of greater social prestige through the story of rabbits outwitting brute force by guile and intelligence. Among the Bantu, where these stories originated,[9] they are directed against the authority of a chief or an elder brother, but they have carried over to the Bantu's Brazilian descendants because these people were subjected to new constraints that called for similar stories as an outlet for desires for revenge and a means of projecting repressed feelings.[10] While I do not deny the importance of this function, our problem, the preservation of African elements, requires an investigation of other factors too. After all, the same function could have been served by the legends of Renard the Fox just as well as by stories of the African rabbit.

Their survival is explained not so much by the function of the stories as by the carry-over of the African social frameworks in the Maranhão communities (to which da Costa Eduardo also calls attention). European folklore is a folklore of the daytime and the evening; African folklore is of the night. In this region of Brazil it is forbidden, as it is in Angola, to tell stories until the sun has set. "These stories are normally told in São Antonio only during the evening, on the death of a child, and every year during the nights of Holy Week preceding Maundy Thursday and Good Friday, when men and women assemble in a house to perform their dances in honor of the spirits known as *encantados*. During those nights they customarily hold a funeral wake for the dying Jesus."[11]

Thus these stories are linked to funeral ceremonies, either real ones like the ceremonies for "little angels," as the Bantu call children who have died, or symbolic ones like those of Holy Week. They are not held just anywhere, but in the house of the *encantados*. They are a part of the ritual of communion by which the Negroes reconstitute their ethnic solidarity in the dark of the night. When the African village rises again in Brazil, these stories emerge from the depths of memory. This is the essential point. In the same way, the religious myths survive only in the organized setting of the *candomblés* or *xangôs*, being inseparably linked to ritual actions. Collective memory does not come into play unless the ancestral institutions have been preserved. Memories are so much a part of interpersonal relations, constituted groups, or human associations that they spring to life again only where these sociological phenomena are perpetually operative. Thus the functionalist thesis and the psychoanalytical one lead to the same conclusion: the primary importance of social frameworks in collective memory.

Halbwachs's strong insistence on this point, that the individual cannot remember without recourse to group thought and that forgetting is caused by the disappearance of the old social frameworks, makes further elaboration unnecessary. For one thing, Halbwachs was too firmly committed to the Durkheimian dilemma of the individual and the group—the group becoming aware of its identity in the course of time and the individual remembering only through his membership in a group. He was also too committed to the theory of collective consciousness, which led him to distinguish as many types of memory as there are groups in society. He forgot that every group is structured and is in the process of either destructuring or restructuring. To be more accurate, he did at one point (in a little article on the memory of musicians, each of whom plays a different role in the orchestra[12]) recognize the importance of the respective places of individuals in an organized whole, but he never revised his earlier theses in the light of this article. Yet to understand the reason for survivals or disappearances in African religious traditions we must concentrate on the structure of groups rather than on groups per se.

Religious rites are not performed by just anyone but by actors carefully chosen for each particular ceremony. The ceremonies themselves are distributed among the various social categories: the moieties or clans, sex or age groups, those qualified to handle what is sacred and the rank and file of the sect, family and community heads, farmers and the artisan castes. Each category has a special function quite distinct from all others, although all functions are complementary and seek the well-being of the community as a whole. The evocation of the dead is entrusted to the men, while possession by the gods is the prerogative of the female sodalities. Certain clans or *camarinhas* are responsible for producing rain; others nurture the sun. The various sectors of society are constantly exchanging services. The priests of Ogun bless the iron of the farming implements before they are used; the priests of Shangô protect the houses of righteous men from thunderbolts.

The assertion that religious ceremonies create great emotional exaltation through the massing of individuals has created an extraordinarily false impression. They have been interpreted as a re-creation of primeval chaos through the momentary abolition of all taboos and rules, through sexual license, and through an anarchic jumbling of classes and sexes, ranks and roles.[13] Nothing is further from the truth. Even in its apparent madness the festival is always controlled, and if sexual license or a certain reversal of values does creep in, these phenomena are obligatory; they occupy a preordained place in the sequence of the ritual and occur between predetermined partners. If exaltation occurs, it is a controlled exaltation, a frenzy which begins at a certain time, respects the hierarchic order, ranging from the director through his assistants down to the other people involved, and follows an invariable order, ending just as promptly at the time appointed for the conclusion of the rite. It has nothing in common with the madness of modern crowds. The ceremony is the image of the group and hence is structured like the group. While I do not wish to equate the social role with a theatrical one, we are nonetheless dealing with a kind of spectacle in which each actor has certain lines to speak and certain actions to perform. But these lines make sense only within the total dialogue; the actions acquire significance only when they connect with those of the other actors.[14] Social continuity thus depends on structural continuity, and if the latter were for some reason to be broken, the tradition would be in instant danger of crumbling. In short, collective memory can indeed be regarded as a group memory provided we add that it is a memory articulated among the members of the group.

It was precisely these articulations that slavery shattered. While it was quite possible for an entire priesthood that had offended a king to be reduced to slavery—and I have cited some examples of this—the slave trade usually did not strike at all segments of society uniformly. Hence certain key actors were missing, and, along with them, whole sections of the play.

Actions or roles were forgotten. In the case of Afro-Brazilian religions the forgetting was not so much the effect of a change of environment, of the necessity for the group to adapt to new living conditions, or of time, which obliterates everything, as the effect of the impossibility of getting together the whole team of actors in any one place in Brazil. Naturally they tried to reconstitute the complete ceremonial of their homeland. Like the actor who, in order to deliver his monologue on cue, needs to know his partners' parts too, the black slaves were able to restore whole portions of their traditions, especially when their fellow-exiles included priests, who, as directors of the spectacle, were more familiar with the ritual as a whole. As we saw in the section on the region of the *candomblés* and *xangôs*, fidelity to Africa is total, but it is a fidelity composed of separate pieces. As we shall see, mythology was caught up in the same process.

This explains why the cults of Orun, the sun god; Ogillon, one of the deities of the forge; Olokun, the sea god who plays such an important role in the town of Ifé and who reappears in Cuba; as well as of many other deities, do not exist in Brazil. In fact the *babalorixás* and *yalorixás* do not even know their names. Earlier in this book I explained the disappearance of Oko, the god of agriculture, as an effect of slavery: the slave had no need to perform rites to ensure the fertility of the fields, because the crop did not belong to him. But while this was certainly a factor, it was not the only reason, nor perhaps the most important one. As we have noted, the festival of the new yams (which, it is true, celebrates the consumption rather than the production of a crop, but which is nonetheless connected with agriculture) was continued in both Recife and Bahia. On the other hand the myth of Oko is incorporated in the myth of the birth of Shangô, son of Yemanjá,[15] who does exist in Brazil. The disappearance of Oko is therefore probably to be explained primarily by the fact that the priesthood that served him escaped enslavement. An interesting point is that the unknown rites and myths left gaps in the collective memory, and attempts were made to fill those gaps by using other myths or rites whose exponents or practitioners were available in Brazil. In Bahia, for instance, the fishing industry is in the hands of blacks, and they believe it necessary to make appropriate gifts and sacrifices to the ocean before embarking, so that the fury of the waves may be calmed. Since Olokun was unknown, he was replaced by Yemanjá, who had *filhas* among the slaves in Brazil, although this goddess, who lives on the Ogun River in Abeokuta, represents the liquid element in general and fresh rather than salt water.[16] In Abeokuta the daughters of Yemanjá used to offer gifts to the river. The black fishermen of Bahia have carried over this ritual, and every year, usually on February 2, although the date varies from one *candomblé* to another, they throw into the water bottles of perfume, flowers, little mirrors or combs, boxes of face powder or lipsticks—for Yemanjá is very vain.[17]

The religious tradition can be seen in two different aspects: as constraint and as structure. The former aspect has been stressed most frequently because the pressure of the older generations on the younger was regarded as the elementary process of social continuity. But this constraint operates within a certain division of social labor, and apprenticeship to the past changes with the make-up of the community. It is the structure of the group rather than the group itself that provides the frameworks of collective memory; otherwise it would be impossible to understand why individual memory needs the support of the community as a whole. If we need someone else in order to remember, it is because our memories are articulated together with the memories of others in the well-ordered interplay of reciprocal images. As I said in Part I of this book, this explains why African survivals maintained themselves infinitely more vigorously in the towns than in the country. If tradition were merely the force of the past, mere group constraint, it would simply have assumed the form of individual initiations, the handing on by the oldest members of the group to the youngest of a heritage of images, or the conversion of a few Bantu to the Yoruba religion. But when that did happen, only two or three roles were interiorized; the totality of the liturgical drama (and of the mythology, which is linked to it) disappeared. In the city, though, the old structure could more easily find many of its actors, if not the entire cast, so that the memories could be reconstituted almost in full.

But in Africa the different sectors of society, each of which retains memories that complement the memories of other sectors—the initiation and apprenticeship of a *babalaô* are different from those of a *babalorixá*; Ogun's ceremonies are quite unlike Omolú's—are also geographic sectors. The sanctuaries of the deities are scattered about a space that thus itself becomes structured. This brings us to another theme in Halbwachs's theory. Since memories are psychic by nature, if they are to survive they must survive in something durable; they must be attached to a permanent material base of some kind. Psychologists seek this material base in the brain; sociologists seek it in nature.[18] The localization of memories in material objects that endure in social time is the exact equivalent, it seems to me, of cerebral localizations in psychological theory. The transplantation of blacks from Africa to America and the consequent loss of certain sectors of society pose a problem analogous to the problem of the destruction of, or of lesions in, certain convolutions of the brain and the subsequent formation of new memory centers. When Halbwachs studies the topography of Palestine and shows the Crusades trying to localize the collective representations of the Christian church in a country profoundly modified since the death of Christ and the Arab invasion,[19] he comes close to the problem we are dealing with here: the problem of the memory of a religious group establishing new material centers to which to attach its mental images. The *candomblés*, with the temples, the *pegi*, the groves of sacred trees, the houses of the dead, the spring of Oxalá, represent a reconstruction of the sacred topography of the lost Africa. Moreover, the first sacred stones were actually brought over from Africa, still impregnated with the supernatural force of the *orixás*—a force that, through mystic participation, was transmitted to the whole of the surrounding space.

Nevertheless something analogous to what happened to Christianity when it left Palestine happened here too. The ecology was transformed into symbolism. In our cathedrals the Israel of the time of Christ is recreated. The church building traces on the ground the Cross of Golgotha; at its center stands the table where Jesus once shared with his disciples the bread and wine of communion. The sacristy or a lateral chapel shelters the manager of Bethlehem; the stations of the Passion are depicted on the walls. But these geographic localities now form a single mystic space. Henceforth the Jerusalem pilgrimage will take place in a compacted, telescoped ecology, which, while retaining its structure intact, will be reduced in format, in which history will become simply an invitation to prayer. In the same way, the spatial sectors of the Yoruba homeland that are concentrated in the restricted space of the *candomblé* or the sectors of Dahomey enclosed in the inner courtyard of the *Casa das Minas* vacillate between pure matter and spirituality. They belong to a reduced spatial structure that, to use Halbwachs's word, "preserves" memories and also to a symbolic structure. This explains why, when running water was introduced in São Luiz, the sacred spring of the *voduns* outside the *Casa das Minas* could be replaced by a spigot without losing any of its virtue.[20] This is not just ordinary tap water but water from a tap sanctified by its place in the cult house. Again, the Africans found new forms of vegetation in Brazil, and the *olosan* was obliged to reconstitute the sacred Yoruba botany on the basis of the likeness of certain leaves and their curative, stimulating, or soothing properties.[21] Similarity became identity when these plants were grown in the garden of the sanctuary and ritually gathered or when songs were sung to "draw the *aché*," songs that assimilated the new plants by imbuing them with the same spiritual atmosphere as in Africa. In the *candomblé* of today it is difficult to tell where the material recreation of the ancestral country leaves off and the symbolic image begins.

■   ■   ■

The foregoing arguments show that collective memory is a set of mental images linked on the one hand to the motor mechanisms of rites (although going beyond them) and on the other hand to morphological and social structures. Hence remembrance is precipitated whenever the assembled African community regains its structure and reactivates, in the linking of roles, the ancestral motor mechanisms. Place, society, actions, and memory now become one. Certain things, however, may hinder the process.

First, the Negro is more concerned with rite than with myth, with the practical value of ceremonies than with their intellectual meaning. Pure memories and motor habits are indeed inseparably linked, but it sometimes happens that the linkage breaks and only the memory of the actions remains. *Candomblé* religion is utilitarian even in its ecstasies, in the plunge into the vast, dark night of trance, for participation in the divine restores health, improves one's lot, and propitiates fortune. A certain kind of "salvation," material or social, individual or collective, is associated with the regular meticulous performance of one's assigned role in the total ritual. Hence, among the daughters of the gods, the mythic element, which presupposes a certain intellectual curiosity, is scanted, and this can have serious consequences because it makes the girls' conception of their deity more susceptible to new influences from white society. Let us look at those influences.

Unlike the *filhas*, the priests are not ignorant of mythic tradition. But this rich store of imagery is unequally distributed throughout the group. We have already mentioned the importance of the secret in the African religious sects as the black's defensive weapon against the white man. But some things are secret from the blacks themselves. Here one could speak of a structure and hierarchy of secrets. The cooperation of individuals in communal ceremonies does not preclude functional rivalry—*babalorixá* against *babalaô*, a jealous *mãe pequena* against the *yalorixá*, the *sidagan* against the *mãe pequena*—and this forces every actor in a leading role to surround himself with mystery to prevent his secrets from being revealed to possible rivals. Sometimes this rivalry is so intense that if a *babalorixá* dies without having had time to complete the "making" of his successor, the successor will constantly have to seek advice from the *mãe pequena*, who knows more than he does. I have personally observed this in more than one sect. This structuring and hierarchizing of the secret threatens to become a factor in the gradual disappearance of memories in the course of time. An informant of mine, who was always ready to explain the mythic significance of the ceremonies I was watching or of sexual and food taboos, sometimes had to admit his ignorance on certain points. The children of Shangô may not eat butter beans.[22] Why not? There is certainly some reason, said my informant. Shangô was once taken captive by his enemies. Perhaps this happened just when he was cooking butter beans. He didn't really know. Obviously there have been losses and they are irretrievable because contact with Africa has been broken.

It is important to recognize exactly what we mean by the secret. As a *babalaô* friend of mine (or rather an *olosan* who called himself a *babalaô*, because in Africa the gatherers of herbs are often the *babalaô's* assistants)[23] once said: "You can't reveal secrets all at once. It takes patience and time." He said this not to maintain his own magical aura but because the secret is part of the system of gifts and counter gifts that we have seen at work within the *candomblé* economy and because this system cannot be translated into terms of capitalist economy. The secret has a dangerous mystic force, like everything that one gives away and that has to be neutralized. The slowness with which secret *candomblé* knowledge is divulged makes the process a kind of inoculation, a graduated exposure to more and more potent things, to protect both giver and receiver from the danger inherent in the transmission of the secret. Countergifts serve the same purpose. These are not so much little presents—already a departure from capitalist economy—as small rituals to be performed, sacrifices to be made to the gods, religious activities to be carried out. But—and this brings us to the important point—such gradual initiation into the world of myth is not without its dangers. If the "transmitter" dies unexpectedly, whole portions of the tradition may be forgotten. So long as there are plenty of priests, the risk is not too high, but now that the *babalaôs* are dying out in Brazil, a whole segment of collective memory (that of the cult of Ifá) is threatened with extinction.

As I mentioned just now in connection with animal stories, the black belongs to two different social structures: his religious fraternity and the multiracial global community. The encounter of black and white in the latter structure produces attitudes, feelings, and values whose interaction within the collective memory may shed a new light on acquired images. The resentment of an exploited class, the frustration arising from class competition, the desire to "be whiter" may transform gods such as Exú or Ogun into national heroes, or goddesses such as Yemanjá and Oxun into consoling mothers. But in every case of memory metamorphosis the direction of the change is dictated by tradition. Of course attitudes or values acquired through participation in the second structural framework may act upon inherited African collective representations and alter their complexion. But since the individuals involved are also *candomblé* members, only the complexion of the memories can be changed, not their nature. An analogous phenomenon occurs in individual memory. Every memory partakes of both the past and the present and, inasmuch as it belongs to the present, is part of the total stream of consciousness. It is therefore modified in response to changing affectivity or central interests. Halbwachs's observation that not all traditional images are resurrected but only those that fit the present,[24] an observation by which he explains the evolution of the Catholic mystique, underlines the importance of the phenomenon I am alluding to: the penetration of the past by the present or, to rephrase it in terms of structure, dual participation in two different social worlds: the past-oriented African sects and the perpetually changing global Brazilian society.

The study of collective memory must therefore include, besides an explanation of retaining and forgetting, an explanation of the metamorphosis of collective memories. Among the most important of these are changes in the personae of the gods, for these are always carried along in the stream of group consciousness.

Leaving aside Olorun, who no longer intervenes in human affairs, the top god in the hierarchy is certainly Obatalá, usually known in Brazil as Orixálá or Oxalá (i.e. the great *orixá*). Most of his African characteristics —his white color, the requirement that his worshipers refrain from salty dishes and alcoholic beverages, his role in reproduction and in the development of the fetus—are well known to Brazilians, as are the African myths about the creation of the world and Obatalá's visit to Shangô, from which he returned in a pitiful state.[25] Some traits, however, have been lost. Actually Obatalá appears in the creation myth as a rival of Odudua, the earth mother, who is unknown in Recife and even in Bahia. Obatalá and Odudua merged in Africa, forming a hermaphroditic deity, or, as is more probable, they represent an originally hermaphroditic deity that later divided into two. A vestige of this hermaphrodism may survive in a song collected by Arthur Ramos in which the words *baba* (father) and *mother of god* are used in reference to Oxalá:

> Oxalá-king ô i, baba ô é
> Oxalá king.
> Odé mi orixalá ru
> Oxalá-king baba, orixalá
> Oxalá-king, O mother of god,
> Baba orixalá-king.[26]

Obviously the Afro-Brazilian mentality was profoundly shocked by this hermaphrodism, and before long Oxalá assumed an exclusively male form. Indeed the same thing happened in Africa, where the old link between Obatalá and Odudua finally disappeared, at least in some areas.[27] In Bahia, however, this god split into Oxalufan, the old Oxalá, "dragging his feet, his hunched body supported on a stick," and Oxaguihan, the young Oxalá, boyish and quick on his feet.[28] This distinction is difficult to account for in African terms; I see no other explanation than the influence of Catholicism. As we shall see in the next chapter, because of Oxalá's preeminence he was identified with Christ, and Christ is worshiped both as the newborn Jesus and as the good shepherd leaning on his crook.

The evolution of Exú seems to follow the opposite direction, and this is reflected in some regions of Brazil by his identification with the devil, the enemy of Jesus Christ. Early in the nineteenth century Nina Rodrigues already spoke of a "rudimentary dualism among primitive people" between the forces of good and evil.[29] Actually nothing is more foreign to African thought than Manicheism. All the gods are ambivalent; they can all do evil as well as good, and although Exú is a particularly mischievous character he does protect his worshipers and take care of those who make sacrifices to him. Nevertheless his sinister side tends to eclipse his persona as an African Mercury, an intermediary between mortals and the other *orixás*.[30]

The first point to note is that the Dahoman Legba cannot be definitively identified with the Yoruba Exú. The phallic aspect of Legba does reappear to some extent in the Nagô Exú, the figure holding a raised stick. But the *legbanos*, the priests who in public ceremonies simulated coitus with a great wooden phallus,[31] do not exist in Yoruba countries. Nevertheless something of Exú's phallicism survives in Brazil in the notion that he presides over the sexual act. All the same, in the special *pegi* where he is worshiped he is represented as asexual. Here images in the African collective memory conflicted with the collective representations of Luso-Brazilian morality and especially with the censure of the Jesuits, who in many churches even mutilated angels depicted with genital organs. In order to gain a foothold in the Brazilian environment Exú therefore had to renounce or conceal his priapic side. Even so the evolution of Exú in the Ketu houses or of Legba in the Gêgê ones has not gone as far as it appears to have gone in Haiti, where this deity, because of his great age, has become the symbol of sexual frigidity.[32]

What are the other characteristics of the African Exú? In the first place, he is a go-between, the intermediary between two worlds, the messenger who delivers human prayers. This is why all sacrifices are offered to him first. This intermediary role is reversed in his connection with divination by shells; here he transmits the orders of the other *orixás* to mortals. Secondly, he is a god of orientation, because he opens or closes gates. Offerings of cock's blood and entrails are made to him at the door of every house, in the main square of every village or at its approaches, and at crossroads. Thirdly, he is a mischievous god who loves pranks and likes to play tricks on people and make trouble between friends or create havoc in meetings. On the other hand he helps those who feed and respect him; he has a good heart in spite of all his nonsense. Lastly, because of his power he is regarded as one of the patrons of magicians.[33]

All these characteristics and many of the myths that illustrate them were carried over to Brazil, but some of them developed more fully than others. Because of slavery the blacks used Exú in his capacity as patron of witchcraft in their struggle against the whites,[34] so that his sinister side was emphasized at the expense of his function as a messenger. The mischievous god became the cruel god who kills, poisons, or drives men mad. But Exú's was a one-way cruelty; to his black worshipers he was a savior and compassionate friend. The abolition of slavery and the proclamation of the equality of all Brazilians before the law might have been expected to check this evolution toward the diabolical since it put an end to caste conflict, but police persecution of the African religious sects and party political struggles accentuated the tendency of the colonial period. For this reason the *ebó* sacrifice of today is still the magic *ebó* it became in the time of slavery. The black chicken that used to be sacrificed to Exú and thrown into the uninhabited bush is now stuffed with tobacco, roasted corn, and other ingredients and placed in the path of the intended victim.[35] I have mentioned that in Maranhão Mãe Andresa was unwilling to talk about Legba, and in Bahia Joana de Ogun trembled as she spoke of him. But this evolution (assuming that it is indeed occurring) is not proceeding at the same speed in every "nation." The Ketu have faithfully preserved the African image of Exú the intermediary who speaks through the shells in the name of the *orixás*, the god of orientation, a young boy, mischievous rather than spiteful, who takes good care of his "people."[36] On the other hand, in the Bantu "nations," where the mythology of Exú was (for good reason) unknown and where magic always played a bigger role than in the other "nations," this demoniac element is continually growing.[37] In the *carioca macumba* it will finally predominate.

Collective memories, we see, are attached to groups, and the degree of their resistance depends on the nature of those groups. But we also see that if the present affects the past, it is always along the line marked out by the past. Nothing is created; a selection is simply made among memories. For example, the *padé* of Exú (the preliminary offering made to him at the beginning of every ceremony), whose original function was to open a way between the natural and the supernatural worlds, is regarded in Brazil as a propitiatory sacrifice to prevent Exú from disrupting the proceedings. But this new interpretation of the *padé* already existed in some areas of the Yoruba homeland, where it is said that a preliminary sacrifice must be made to this god to prevent him from introducing "confusion."[38] So the present acts primarily as a kind of sluice gate that lets through only what can adapt itself to the new environment or at any rate what does not conflict with it, while holding back irreconcilable representations. Perhaps the present might also be compared to the Freudian censor, which represses in the unconscious anything that conflicts with the customs and ethics of the social environment. There is, however, one difference, a difference that stems from the twofold distinction between affective and intellectual memory and between the individual and the group—namely that the repressed libido goes on working while collective myths or representations that have fallen into desuetude are gradually forgotten.

Ogun's fate was very similar to Exú's, which is understandable since the two gods are linked by myth—Exú is Ogun's slave—and by liturgy— Ogun's songs and dances are performed immediately after Exú's. In Africa, Ogun is the god of iron and in this capacity presides over any activity that makes use of iron—agriculture, hunting, and war.[39] Blacksmiths hang the various emblems of Ogun from the roof of their forge and ask his help before embarking on the difficult task of smelting iron.[40] But this does not mean that Ogun is a caste god. Like all the other *orixás* he is a lineage or fraternity god. The smiths who worship him or the hunters who risk their lives in the bush are sons of other deities; they offer sacrifices to Ogun only as producers or users of iron. In Brazil, Ogun has retained his persona as the god of iron. He is represented by a set of small metal tools—hammer, hoe, spade, etc.—tied together, symbolizing agriculture, the forge, and skilled work.[41] But a whole set of functions over which this god presided in Africa has been dropped from his cult. The first of these is agriculture, and here the reason is probably the same one that caused Oko to be dropped from the Afro-Brazilian pantheon: the plantation slaves had no wish to invoke divine blessing on farming implements that would be used only for the profit of their white masters. The second is hunting, which no longer figures among the occupations of the urban Brazilian. Moreover there is a special *orixá* for hunting, Oxóssi, and people found it strange that two different deities should be responsible for the same function. Although the figure of Ogun the smith still survives in Afro-Brazilian myth, he is no longer the patron of ironworkers because the metallurgical industry is comparatively recent and exists chiefly in the south, where there are no longer any African religious sects.

Ogun's persona as a brutal and aggressive warrior and beheader was the one that won out.[42] His evolution took opposite courses in Brazil and Africa. The difference stemmed from social causes; it reflected in the realm of spiritual values the opposition between the colonial regime and the regime of slavery. The colonial regime, by preventing tribal warfare and maintaining peace—the Pax Britannica—throughout Nigeria, caused Ogun the warrior to die out and be replaced by Ogun the hunter. The rites that used to precede military expeditions have been transferred to collective elephant hunts (omitting the human sacrifices, of course),[43] and the Africanists explain Ogun's popularity by the importance of hunting in the economic complex of village life.[44] On the other hand, slavery set the exploited, subjected caste of blacks against the white ruling class. The slave system became a kind of endless struggle between the two races, and the two major weapons the black relied on to win were Exú and Ogun— magic and revolt.

We are now in a better position to understand why the myths about Exú, the slave of Ogun, and about Ogun clearing the way, like Exú, by cutting back the lianas along the paths with his sharp knife should have survived so successfully in the new habitat. These two gods' comradeship in the common struggle against the white man guaranteed their indissoluble partnership. There is no need to go into Ogun's role in black resistance in Brazil; an earlier chapter in this book has already dealt with it, and Gilberto Freyre has glorified it. This evolution was more marked among the Bantu than among the Yoruba. In their Portuguese songs the Bantu "nations" of Bahia refer to Ogun as "the minister of war," and, since there is more than one Ogun, they have even invented a "naval

Ogun" who is naturally referred to as "Admiral."[45] In the *macumbas* of Rio de Janeiro, Ogun is by far the most popular god, having triumphed over Shangô, still the best-known and best-loved deity in the northeast.[46] In my opinion this shift in popularity is probably due largely to the different social environment. The racial democracy of Bahia discourages resentment, while the proletarianization of the blacks in Rio has kept the racial struggle alive by projecting it into the class struggle. This is confirmed by the fact that, according to recent information, in Recife, where industrialization is more advanced than in Bahia, the cult of Ogun is now overtaking that of Shangô.[47] In any case in the course of this evolution Ogun, like Exú, is acquiring a sinister character and in Rio may even be invoked in black magic more frequently than he is worshiped in a religious sense.[48]

Le Herissé and Herskovits have shown that Xapanan was originally a chthonian deity, "the fetish of the earth,"[49] but this Dahoman god punished those who failed to worship him by infecting them with smallpox through flies and mosquitoes. In this way Xapanan became—and in Africa still is—predominantly the god of smallpox and other epidemic diseases.[50] The Yoruba accepted his cult because of their great fear of this type of malady, and a myth tells how he established himself in Nagô country by inflicting a terrifying outbreak of smallpox.[51] But his name has become taboo,[52] and today this deity is known as Omolú or Abaluayé. Absolutely everything the Africanists can tell us about Omolú indicates an extraordinarily terrifying deity who is greatly feared—his irascible character, the way he took his revenge on the other *orixás* who made fun of him because he took a fall while dancing,[53] the struggle for domination between his priests and the kings,[54] his priests' tyrannizing of the Africans and extortion of money from them. This sinister image was all the more easily carried over to Brazil since, in the days before vaccination, smallpox epidemics repeatedly decimated the population of the colony and their worst ravages were among the enslaved masses.[55] The name Xapanan still inspires fear and remains taboo. Under the name Omolú he became associated with Exú, a link that is marked by the fact that they are worshiped on the same day, Monday, and that in magic Omolú, who works with the souls in graveyards, is an ally of Exú.[56] Also the black is often too poor to afford a doctor and in any case has less faith in doctors than in healers of his own color, so Omolú gradually became the god of medicine.[57] This evolution, like the preceding ones, seems to be more rapid in the Bantu sects. When a black is possessed by this deity he sits down, and the congregation crowds around him seeking advice and remedies.[58] But Omolú is also found in the Yoruba sects of Recife, where he is held in great affection. There the mystic trance, in which the son of the god symbolically acts out the anguish caused by the disease, is regarded not as a punishment but as a purification.[59] It should, however, be noted that indications of this evolution are already to be found in Africa. As I have said, the present does not create; it simply releases such elements in the collective memory as are in accord with it. While the African may be afraid of Omolú, he also knows that by means of the appropriate sacrifices his priests can avert epidemics from their country[60] and that smallpox does not attack the friends of the god but only those who fail to worship him appropriately.

Shangô, by contrast, has tenaciously retained all his African characteristics in Brazil, perhaps because he is the master of lightning and because in tropical countries storms break with sinister fury. Ortiz suggests that this is true in Cuba, where Shangô is very popular.[61] Shangô's three wives— Yansan or Oiâ, Oxun, and Obá—have been included in this fabric of fidelity along with him. Nearly all the great myths concerning him or his wives that the Africanists have transcribed reappear in Brazil—his struggle with Mokwa and his deification,[62] his pursuit of Yansan,[63] Obatalá's gift of the magic power to spit fire and Yansan's theft of lightning,[64] Shangô's theft of Ogun's wife Oxun and the ensuing struggle,[65] the quarrel between Oxun and Obá and the story of the severed ear, etc.[66] The Brazilian Shangô has also retained his "masculine," not to say phallic, characteristics,[67] and the passion for justice that causes him to hurl thunderbolts only at thieves and dishonest people.[68] Even in its details the ritual of his cult presents astonishing analogies in the two countries. In Africa his children "work miracles" when they are possessed by this deity. In Ketu houses in Brazil at least one of these miracles can still be witnessed: the swallowing of glowing embers without suffering burns.[69] To this impressive list of common characteristics must be added Yansan's role as a queen who vanquishes death.[70] All I can say is that we may be witnessing a simplification of these divine images. Although a Recife myth shows Yansan paying court to Ogun and surreptitiously passing him a bunch of flowers while pretending to sell him little bean-flour cakes[71] (no doubt to demonstrate her independence of her husband), this goddess is usually represented as the ideal wife, faithful, and a good housekeeper to boot— the good woman of the Gospels.[72]

Even Oxun is caught up in this process of moralization. She is still the voluptuous, flirtatious woman, the image of the eternal feminine, but now her passage from Ogun's arms to Shangô's is reduced to an etiological myth explaining a taboo (why Shangô is a great okra eater).[73] Now she is regularly married to Shangô, thanks to his patience, which is finally rewarded when he succeeds in entering her father's house during his absence and becoming her lover.[74]

This attempt to make the African deities more moral, thereby modifying some of their mythical characteristics, is even more strongly marked in the case of Yemanjá, especially since she is often identified with the Immaculate Conception. This being so, how can one accept the idea that she married her brother and was later raped by her own son Aganju? The myth telling how the principal *orixás* sprang from the bursting belly of Yemanjá, first related by Father Baudin, then by Ellis,[75] shocks the more Puritan mentality of the Brazilian Negro of today. It is true that a myth collected in Recife by René Ribeiro tells of Yemanjá being seduced by Orumila, although she was the wife of Oxalá. "Yemanjá agreed to Orumila's request and one day went along to talk to him. We do not know what kind of conversation took place, but one thing is certain: she came back pregnant. By her husband Oxalá she had already had Shangô, Ogun, Odé, Oxóssi, Ewa, and Obá." Oxun was the child of Orumila.[76] Yet despite this myth, "most informants have so much respect for Yemanjá . . . that when one of them was questioned about this adventure, which can hardly be said to enhance the reputation of the goddess, she declared that it could never have happened, since Yemanjá was a virgin. When I asked her how, in that case, Yemanjá could be the mother of so many deities, her immediate response was to identify her with the Virgin Mother of the Catholics."[77]

African collective representations are affected not only by the Catholic environment but also by the glamor that surrounds the Indian—a legacy to the Brazilian imagination from romanticism that finds popular expression in the *catimbó* of Pernambuco, the *caboclo candomblé* of Bahia, and the *macumba* of Rio de Janeiro. We have already analyzed the undeniably religious character of these *caboclo* ceremonies, but in many *terreiros* they are also performed on the Brazilian holiday celebrating national independence. In Bahia I was always conscious of a certain patriotic note, a curious mixture of Bastille Day street dancing and mystic trance. In the time of Nina Rodrigues, Oxóssi, the Yoruba god of the hunt, was a secondary figure in the Afro-Brazilian pantheon. But since he is armed with a bow and arrow, symbolized by the *damatá*, and wears a parrot's feather on his head, he is not unlike an Amerindian in appearance and thus becomes a "national" rather than a strictly African figure. For this reason his importance in the cult continues to grow. This does not mean that he has lost his original characteristics. On the contrary, the Gantois *candomblé* remains remarkably faithful to collective representations in preserving the Yoruba mnemonic images. It even preserves, in the heart of Brazil, the society of African hunters presided over by this god; in fact today this society provides the core of the leadership of the sect.[78] But the Bantu, imitating the Ketu rather than inheriting the myths of the African ancestors, are nationalizing this god more and more.[79] In Recife the *caboclos* are considered subjects of the kingdom of Oxóssi.[80] Here once again we encounter that vitality in the African sects which, for all their fidelity to the rich ancestral heritage, keeps them actively involved in the conflicts of the gods. Some of the deities are on the rise—Ogun, Oxóssi, and Oxun-marê, the snake god, the rainbow, who was neglected twenty years ago but who, thanks to Máe Cotinha, the *yalorixá* of Mata Escura, is now a popular figure in black circles in Bahia.[81] Others are declining or dying out—certain forms of Shangô (Shangô Aira seldom appears any more) or of Omolú (Aruaru, well known in the time of Manoel Querino, no longer exists). Throughout the area extending from Recife to Pará, Yansan is becoming the principal goddess,[82] while from Bahia to Rio, Yemanjá is the most widely worshiped.[83] In this divine struggle for social prestige, collective memory still plays a part in the selection of images or myths.

Certain general conclusions concerning the sociological problems of memory can be drawn from this study of the gods.

1. There are two kinds of memory—motor and intellectual. The more closely collective representations and myths are interwoven in the web of actions, the more resistant to change they will be.

2. It is not the group itself that explains the phenomena of the preservation or forgetting of memories so much as the group's structure or organization. More generally, I have distinguished three operative structures: the sect, the sacred space, and the secret. Since memories are localized in specific separate yet complementary sectors, the presence or absence of these sectors in Brazil as related to Africa accounts for survivals and gaps in the collective memory.

3. Memories inherited from the ancestors survive only insofar as they can insinuate themselves into the existing frameworks of society. If the collective African memory persists in the new land, it is because the African sects "work." And because they work in symbiosis with the global Brazilian society, whatever is no longer in accord with the new environmental values is forgotten.

4. Although myth retains a certain richness of detail, it tends to decrystallize, to become schematized. Its principal function is now to justify or explain rites or the forms and types of sacrifices, taboos, and ceremonial sequences.

■ ■ ■

The Brazilian black is quite conscious of this loss of substance; he recognizes the steadily widening gaps that have appeared in myth and tries to fill them. But having changed worlds, all he has to fill them with is a set of new elements, extraneous to the African civilization, borrowed from the Western society in which he lives. In this way Catholic hagiography is paradoxically merged with the African mythology. While African ritual has been preserved in all its purity and while Catholicism can coexist with this ritual but, as we shall see, never infiltrate it, a number of legends inseparably link Africa with the Euro-American world of the West. The song sung in Recife in honor of Oiâ (Yansan) that begins *"E' minha quiquoe"* is explained as follows: "Oiâ used to raise hens—plenty of them, as pretty and plump as anyone could wish. After the Virgin had given birth to the Christ Child, she said she had a craving for some chicken. A woman who had once been a sinner but had become a saint overheard the conversation and without hesitation stole a hen and presented it to the Virgin. . . . When Oiâ noticed that one of her hens had disappeared, without knowing the explanation she began to sing "*E' minha quiquoe*, etc."[84] The unorthodox nature of this legend by contemporary moral standards and the unexpectedness of the "saint's" action, even though she may have been a former sinner, make it obvious, despite the fact that the original African version of this myth is not known to us, that here the Virgin and the saint stand for Afro-African deities lost to the collective memory of the Afro-Brazilian sect. Interpenetration of Christianity and African thought may even go so far that the myth preserved in the *batuque* or the *candomblé* may ultimately be the simple transposition of a legend of the saints or a story from the Gospels. A story told to Donald Pierson about the origin of smallpox and the life of Obaluayé is merely a transcription in African terms of the parable of the prodigal son.[85] The etiological myth told to me in Pôrto Alegre to explain why Shangô Dada does not descend is simply a retelling of the well-known legend of Saint John the Baptist spending his feast day, June 24, sleeping, because if he descended to join the crowd of his worshipers, all lighting bonfires and shooting off firecrackers, he would burn up the whole earth.[86]

Nevertheless the black is very conscious of the opposition between his religion and Catholicism. He sees his deities as closer to spirits or fairies than to the Blessed Virgin and the saints. The nursery tales he heard over and over again when he was little transported him to a supernatural world comparable to the world of his *orixás* and into a time that predates chronological time—the time of myth. This is why the African myths that had decrystallized and lost much of their Bergsonian lyric proliferation recrystallized in the mysterious atmosphere of Brazil, full of miracles and metamorphoses, of fairies and witches, of mermaids and ravening giants. The African hut yields to the medieval castle or to the palace at the bottom of the sea. God-kings move along the highways escorted by a troop of vassal-knights. Yemanjá, combing her long seaweed hair in the sparkling sea foam, grows the tail of a Greek mermaid. Shangô locks up his wife Oxun, like the martyr-princesses of our fairy tales, in a great tower with barred windows, where she weeps over her husband's infidelities until Exú, the new Prince Charming, sees her and, turning her into a dove, sets her free.[87]

The problems of forgetting and of filling the gaps in the collective memory lead on to the new problems of syncretism and the mutual interpenetration of civilizations.

12
Problems
of Religious Syncretism

As we have seen, throughout the period of slavery the black gods were forced to hide behind the statue of the Virgin or a Catholic saint. This was the beginning of a marriage between Christianity and the African religions in the course of which, as in all marriages, the two partners would change more or less radically as they adjusted to each other. Long before the scholars began to talk about the phenomena and processes of accultura- tion, Nina Rodrigues drew attention to this syncretism between the cross of Christ and the stone of the *orixás*. Distinguishing between the Africans, who in his day still existed, and the Creoles, who were beginning to estab- lish their own *candomblés*, he noted that the Africans simply juxtaposed the saints and their own deities, considering them to belong to the same category though completely separate. Among the Creoles, however, Catholicism was already infiltrating the African faith and transforming it into an idolatrous cult of statues conceived as images of the *orixás*. "In the mind of the African Negro the religious ideas instilled by Catholicism have always coexisted—and still coexist—with the fetishist ideas and beliefs brought over from Africa. The Creoles and mulattoes, however, show a manifest and unrestrainable tendency to identify the two teachings."[1]

Rodrigues quite rightly sensed that syncretism was an ongoing process and that its degrees should be distinguished, but he failed to recognize a phenomenon that was to counteract it. This was the African sects' resis- tance to assimilation—the "back to Africa" movement that I have already mentioned. Present-day observers are always struck by the priests' careful differentiation of their beliefs from those of Catholicism and spiritism—at any rate in cities like Bahia where there is no police persecution. (An immediate consequence of police persecution is that to avoid prison sentences devotees of African religious sects swear that they are "good Catholics.")[2]

One *candomblé* priest told me that Catholicism and the African religions are alike in believing that everyone has his guardian angel, but, while the Catholic is simply aware of this as a fact, the African knows the specific name of his angel: it is that of the *orixá* who "protects his head." Another similarity between the two religions is that both the *orixás* and the saints once lived on earth. Thus the two cults share a common point of departure in what might be described as euhemerism. But, added this priest, the Catholic canonizes his saints, while the African knows nothing of canonization. The *orixás* manifest themselves—i.e. they descend into the bodies of their votaries, causing them to fall into ecstatic trance—whereas the priests forbid the materialization of saints.[3] So far as spiritism is concerned, it is a cult of the dead, who enter into the medium in order to communicate with their devotees. In the African religion the *eguns* (the souls of the dead) do not manifest themselves in trance. "They do not descend, they appear," and they do so in the form of masked individuals who impersonate them. Or they may "speak from without," and then the voice of the dead on the island of Itaperica is heard. To put it briefly, in the sects we are concerned with, the *orixás* manifest themselves inwardly, the *eguns* outwardly. We are a long way from spiritism. Moreover, spiritism is a somber religion. The room is dimly lighted and lugubrious. The believers sit on benches, eyes closed, heads bowed in concentration. The only sound is an occasional sniff or gulp, a breath caught and held like the breathing of a woman in labor straining to deliver the spirit. The African religion is a joyous one, celebrated in an atmosphere of music, singing and dancing, festivity; faces reflect sheer gladness. These descriptions are accurate. But other priests, less afraid of offending their presumably Christian questioner, go much further in analyzing the differences. One even exclaimed: "I don't want anything to do with the saints. They're dead— *eguns*. But the *orixás* now, they're *encantados*!"—a remark that brings out the profound difference between a cult commemorating people who have died and been canonized and African polytheism, which worships the forces of nature—the sea, the storm, the sky.

Rodrigues's distinction between African and Creole *candomblés* must therefore be modified if it is to hold good today. As we shall see, it is now meaningful only if the distinction is drawn instead between the traditional Ketu or Gêgê *candomblés* and the Bantu, Angola, Congo, or *caboclo* sects.

Nevertheless both types closely equate the gods, *voduns*, or *orixás* with the Catholic saints. The colonial mask remains firmly affixed to the black god, even when the two are not identified in any way. This so-called syncretist phenomenon is not particularly Brazilian and actually predates the slave trade. The evangelization of blacks began in Africa a couple of centuries before the settlement of Brazil, and certain Dahoman gods and some of the Congo Negroes' spirits had already been identified with Catholic saints.[4] And in Cuba and Haiti, in Louisiana voodoo, and in the *xangôs* of Trinidad, we find correspondences between saints and African deities transplanted to America that are analogous to those found in Brazil.[5]

The prevalence of this phenomenon can be explained only by the structural, cultural, and sociological parallels (to the extent that we have seen them in action) that facilitated the infiltration of Catholicism into the African sects and its reinterpretation in African terms. Briefly summarized, they are:

1. The structural parallel between the Catholic theology of the saints' intercession with the Virgin Mary, the Virgin's intercession with Jesus, and the intercession of Jesus with God the Father and the African cosmology of the *orixás* as mediators between man and Olorun.

2. The cultural parallel between the functional conception of the saints, each of whom presides over a certain human activity or is responsible for healing a certain disease, and the equally functional conception of the *voduns* and *orixás*, each of whom is in charge of a certain sector of nature and who, like the saints, are the patrons of trades and occupations, protecting the hunter, the smith, the healer, etc.

3. The sociological parallel between the Brazilian "nations" or the Cuban *cabildos* and the Catholic fraternities.

But these parallels, which facilitated the approximate equation of saints and gods, were complemented by more specific parallels between individual saints and gods. Obviously Omolú, the god of smallpox, could be identified only with Saint Lazarus, whose body is covered with sores and who cures skin diseases, or with Saint Roch, whose dog licks wounds, or with Saint Sebastian, whom popular prints show bound to a tree, his flesh bleeding from arrow wounds. Oxóssi, god of hunting, could be linked only to warrior saints like Saint George and Saint Michael, whose statues show them impaling dragons with their lances or crushing some other monster under foot. Yansan is identified with Saint Barbara because she ate the "magic" of her husband Shangô and therefore spits lightning, while Saint Barbara is the patron of artillerymen and offers protection against thunder and fire. (According to legend, her father was struck by lightning when, enraged at her refusal to abjure Christianity, he tried to decapitate her.)[6] Ribeiro also suggests another reason. Chromolithographs often depict Saint Barbara "standing before a tower with three windows, holding a martyr's palm branch and often a chalice and the Eucharist," and Ribeiro believes that this symbolic reminder of her role as comforter of the dying may have helped to link her with Yansan, the only goddess who does not fear death, participates in the *achêchê*, and watches over the dead in the "*balé* room."[7] Saint Francis is linked with Irôkô because he is the saint of nature and pictures show him talking to the little birds under a leafy tree. The Beji, the divine twins, naturally seek out other twins like Saints Cosmas and Damian in the Catholic hagiography.

The importance of popular lithographs and statues is undeniable, and many writers have called attention to it.[8] Nor should we forget the stories of the Golden Legend or the superstitions of rural Catholicism, even though the latter were not recognized by the church. Shangô is identified with Saint Jerome because, according to unofficial tradition, Saint Jerome is the husband of Saint Barbara, while Shangô is the husband of Yansan (Saint Barbara). Nanamburucú is identified with Saint Anne because Saint Anne is the mother of Mary and the grandmother of Jesus, while Nanamburucú is the "oldest" deity of the Afro-Brazilians and the ancestor of all the *orixás*. As Ribeiro says: "This suggests that the mythological kinship between the various deities of the African pantheon and their position in the hierarchy must be taken into account in analyzing the identification of these deities with the Catholic saints," as must their specific functions and the way they are depicted in popular prints.[9]

But with a little good will correspondences are not hard to find, which is why a certain *orixá* may be identified with different saints at different times or in different places, as the table below clearly shows. Exú, for instance, may be the Devil because he is one of the masters of black magic; Saint Anthony because he leads people into temptation, is given to evil thoughts, and disturbs ceremonies (Saint Anthony was tormented by demons); Saint Peter because he opens or closes the ways and is the gatekeeper of the *candomblé*, having his *pegi* at the entrance to the houses, as Saint Peter keeps the gates of Heaven, opening and closing them with his great bunch of keys; or Saint Bartholomew because of the saying that on this saint's feast day, August 24, "all the devils are turned loose." Conversely, one saint may be identified with various *orixás*. Our Lady of Pleasures is sometimes identified with Obá because in Africa Obá is the patron of prostitutes,[10] sometimes with Oxun because she is the goddess of sensual love. Saint George, astride his white horse, his lance couched, may be either Ogun, god of war, or Oxóssi, god of the hunt.

All the same, the richness and complexity of our table of correspondences—this jumble in which several *orixás* represent the same saint and several saints represent the same *orixá*—is somewhat disquieting. We need a guideline to help introduce some order into this chaos of contradictions. To begin with, it should be noted that the table gives all identifications known for Brazil without any indication of the date of the research on

God	Bahia	Recife	Alagoas	Pôrto Alegre
Oxalá	St. Anne[a] N.S. of Bomfim[abcde] The Christ Child[e]	The Holy Spirit[o] N.S. of Bomfim[m] The Eternal Father[n] St. Anne[l] The Holy Trinity[n]	The Eternal Father[c] N.S. of Bomfim[r]	The Holy Spirit[stu] Sacred Heart of Jesus[u]
Exú-Legba	The Devil[abcde]	The Devil[lm] St. Bartholomew[hp] The Rebel Angel[o] St. Gabriel[i]	The Devil[r]	St. Anthony[tu] St. Peter[htu]
Shangó	St. Barbara[a] St. Jerome[bc] St. Peter[e] St. John as a Child[e]	St. John the Baptist (Ani-Shangó)[lmo] St. Anthony[l] St. Jerome[ho]	St. John[c] (Dada)[r] St. Barbara (Bonin)[r] St. Jerome[r] St. Anthony (Kilo)[r]	St. Jerome (Ogoda)[s] St. Michael the Archangel[t] St. Barbara[t] St. John (Dada)[h] St. Mark (Osseinha)[u]
Ogun	St. Anthony[a] St. Jerome	St. George[lmo] St. Paul[l] St. John[h]	St. Roch[c] St. George (Ogun Meji)[r]	St. George[stu]
Oxóssi-Odé	St. George[abcdgi] Archangel Michael[e]	St. George[ll] St. Michael[ilo] St. Expedit[lmo] St. Anthony[h]	St. George[r]	St. Michael and the Souls[t] St. Onophrius[t] St. Sebastian[su] O.L. of the Rosary[u] St. Roch[u] St. Iphigenia[u]
Omolu-Obaluayê	St. Benedict[bc] St. Roch[bcdef] St. Lazarus[cdef]	St. Sebastian[lo]	St. Sebastian[cr] St. Benedict[c]	N.S. of Bomfim[r] N.S. of the Passion[u] St. Jerome[u] St. Anthony[u]
Ifá-Orunmila	Holy Sacrament[dg] St. Francis[cd]			St. Joseph[s] St. Catherine[u] N.S. of Bomfim[u] St. Louisa (Orunmila)[u]
Oxun-marê	St. Bartholomew[d]			O.L. of the Immaculate Conception[tu] O.L. of the Rosary[u]
Irôkô-Lôkô Katende—Time	St. Francis[b] St. Sebastian[d] St. Lawrence[e] St. Gaetano (Time)[e] O.L. of Navigators (Time)[e] St. John (Katende)[d]			St. Lazarus[u] The Holy Spirit[u]
Nanamburucú	St. Anne[bc] O.L. of Candlemas[d]	St. Anne[hl] O.L. of Candlemas[h] O.L. of the Good Death[e] St. Barbara[l]		St. Peter and St. Catherine (Dahoman houses)[u] O.L. of Montserrat O.L. of the Rosary O.L. of Navigators St. Anne and St. Peter (Nagô houses)[u]

Rio de Janeiro	Pará	Maranhão	Cuba	Haiti
God[j] St. Anne[c] N.S. of Bomfim[c] St. Barbara[k]			Virgen de las Mercedes The Holy Sacra- ment Christ Crucified	
The Devil[c][j] St. Anthony[c]		"The Dog" (i.e. The Devil)[v]	The Souls in Pur- gatory *Anima Sola* St. Anthony The Devil	St. Anthony the Hermit St. Peter
St. Michael the Archangel[c] St. Jerome[b][c]		St. Peter (Nagô house)[v]	St. Barbara	St. John as a Child
St. George[j][c]		St. John (Nagô house)[v]	St. Peter	St. James St. Joseph
St. Sebastian[c]			St. Albert St. Humbert	
The Holy Sacra- ment[j] St. Lazarus[c]	St. Sebastian[l]	St. Sebastian (Nagô house)[v]	St. John the Baptist St. Lazarus	
St. Francis				
				St. Patrick
	St. Barbara[l]	St. Rita (Nagô house)[v]		

God	Bahia	Recife	Alagoas	Pôrto Alegre
Yemanjá	The Virgin Mary[a] O.L. of the Rosary[abc] O.L. of Compassion[dg] O.L. of the Immaculate Conception of the Beach[c] O.L. of Lourdes and O.L. of Candlemas[h] (Bantu houses) O.L. of Candlemas (Yemanjá-Saba)	O.L. of Sorrows[l] O.L. of the Immaculate Conception[lo] O.L. of the Rosary[l]	O.L. of the Rosary[r]	O.L. of Navigators[h] O.L. of the Good Journey[u]
Yansan-Oiâ	St. Barbara[bcf]	St. Barbara[lmo]	St. Barbara[r]	St. Barbara
Oxun	The Virgin Mary[a] O.L. of Candlemas[cdf] O.L. of the Immaculate Conception[bc] The Infant St. Mary in the arms of St. Anne[e] O.L. of Lourdes (Bantu houses)[d]	Mary Magdalene[hq] O.L. of Pleasures[l] O.L. of Carmel[hio] O.L. of the Immaculate Conception[o]	Mary Magdalene[c]	O.L. of the Rosary[tu] O.L. of the Immaculate Conception[s] O.L. of Sorrows (Nagô houses)[u]
Obá	St. Joan of Arc[d]	O.L. of Pleasures[ln] O.L. of Perpetual Help[o] St. Joan of Arc[o] St. Martha[io]	O.L. of Pleasures[r]	St. Catherine[st]
The Beji (the twins)	Sts. Cosmas and Damian[cd] St. Crispin and St. Crispinian[cd]	Sts. Cosmas and Damian[l]	Sts. Cosmas and Damian[c]	Sts. Cosmas and Damian[stu]
Ossain				St. Manuel[h] St. Onuphrius[s]
Aniflakete Verekete		St. Anthony		
Sakpatan				
Lisa				
Sobô				
Dosu				
Badé				

Sources: a = Nina Rodrigues; b = Manoel Querino; c = Arthur Ramos; d = Edison Carneiro; e = Thomas Kockmeyer; f = Pierre Verger; g = Donald Pierson; h = Roger Bastide; i = Oneyda Alvarenga; j = Jean de Rio; k = Magalhães Corrêa; l = Gonçalves Fernandes; m = Vicente Lima; n = René Ribeiro; o = Wal-

Rio de Janeiro	Pará	Maranhão	Cuba	Haiti
O.L. of the Immaculate Conception[b] O.L. of Sorrows[c]	O.L. of the Immaculate Conception[l]	O.L. of Good Childbirth (Nagô house)[v]	Virgen de la Regla	The Immaculate Conception O.L. of Grace
	St. Barbara[l]	St. Barbara[v]		
			Virgin of Charity	
			O.L. of Candlemas	
Sts. Cosmas and Damian[j]		Sts. Cosmas and Damian (Tosa and Tose)[v]	Sts. Cosmas and Damian	Sts. Cosmas and Damian (Marassa)
		St. Francis of Assisi (Nagô house)[v]		
St. Anthony[j]		St. Benedict the Moor[v]		
		St. Lazarus (Dahoman house)[v]		
		St. Paul (Nagô house)[v]		
		St. Barbara[v,w]		St. Peter[x]
		St. George[v]		
		St. Jerome[w]		St. Paul[x]

demar Valente; p = Pierre Cavalcanti; q = Jacques Raimundo; r = Abelardo Duarte; s = Leopold Bethiol; t = M. J. Herskovits; u = Dante de Laytano; v = Octavio da Costa Eduardo; w = Nunes Pereira; x = Milo Marcelin.

which they are based. Yet syncretism is fluid and dynamic, not rigid and crystallized. In Nina Rodrigues's day, for instance, Shangô was identified with Saint Barbara, patron of lightning.

> The identification of the protectors in the mind was strong enough to overcome sex discrepancies. Whenever I pressed fetishist believers to explain this physically absurd ambivalence, they would always come back with the question: "Isn't Saint Barbara the patron of lightning?" Among some blacks a still more curious inversion is found. Shangô's wife is Oxun; Saint Barbara's partner in protecting people from lightning is Saint Jerome. They simply turned this relationship around and made Oxun, Shangô's wife, the husband of Saint Barbara and hence Saint Jerome.[11]

Logic, however, proved stronger than functional analogies, and today the *orixás* are associated with saints of their own sex. Shangô has become Saint Jerome and Yansan Saint Barbara. Similarly, when Gonçalves Fernandes made his study of syncretism in the *terreiros* of Recife, he found certain equivalences that have now completely disappeared. Ogun, for example, was identified with Saint Paul, Oxun with Our Lady of Pleasures, but the latter has been replaced by Our Lady of Carmel, who, being the patron saint of the city, is very popular in Catholic circles. (For the same reason Oxun became the most popular female *orixá* in Recife). Yemanjá was identified with Our Lady of Sorrows or Our Lady of the Immaculate Conception, probably by analogy with Bahia.[12]

Correspondences are born and die with every age. But when we study them in space rather than time, we find even wider variations. Some of them are the same everywhere—Yansan and Saint Barbara, the Beji and Saints Cosmas and Damian. Generally, however, they change from Bahia to Alagoas, from Maranhão to Recife, from Rio to Pôrto Alegre. This is because Brazil grew out of independent settlements separated by veritable deserts, with no channel of communication except the sea. Thus every African center had to invent its own table of correspondences. Of course the same factors were at work everywhere, so that despite the chaos the correspondences are always comparable,[13] but local circumstances naturally affected their operation. In Bahia, for example, Yemanjá is still identified primarily with Our Lady of the Immaculate Conception of the Beach because she is the beloved protector of sailors and because every year the Virgin of the Immaculate Conception emerges from her church to bless the sea. In Pôrto Alegre, however, the procession of fishermen and sailors is dedicated to Our Lady of Navigators, so it is she, not Our Lady of the Immaculate Conception, who is identified with Yemanjá.[14] In Bahia, Ogun is identified with Saint Anthony because Bahia was the capital of Brazil during the colonial period, and Saint Anthony, who had victoriously defended the city against foreign invasion and been rewarded with the title of lieutenant, was an appropriate symbol of the warrior spirit. In Rio, however, where the blacks have always been more resentful of the whites and where Saint George used to take part in the Corpus Christi processions mounted on a real horse and acclaimed by the crowd, the Negroes wanted their own black Saint George, protector of murderers, *capoeiras*, and upholders of the black cause, so Ogun was linked with him rather than Saint Anthony.

Sometimes variability is so great that the correspondences change from one cult center to another. In Recife, for example, in the time of Gonçalves Fernandes and when I was there, Oxun was identified with Our Lady of Pleasures in Joana Batista's house, with Our Lady of Carmel in Master Apolinário's, and with Mary Magdalene in the African Center of Saint George. In Joana Batista's house Shangô was identified with Saint Jerome, in Master Apolinário's with Saint Anthony (probably because of the color prints showing demons tormenting Saint Anthony as he emerges from the *fires* of Hell), and in the Saint George center with Saint John the Baptist (because of Saint John's Eve bonfires). In Joana's house Ogun, who was usually equated with Saint George, was called "Saint Paul in the Portuguese language." In the Eloy *terreiro* Saint Anne, generally the Catholic equivalent of Nanamburucú, was the counterpart of Oxalá (apparently a vestigial survival of the androgynous character of that African deity).[15] It seems that originally every priest followed his own judgment in his intent to disarm the whites by masking his deities and labeling them with the names of Catholic saints.

The apparent confusion in the table of correspondences may also be due to the researchers' failure in some cases to indicate the ethnic origin of the sects they studied. It is possible that the Dahomans do not react to the Catholic hagiography in exactly the same way as the Yoruba. In fact two phenomena that ought to be clearly distinguished are often confused by the Africanists: regional syncretism and ethnic syncretism. My attention was called to this by the fact that in Pôrto Alegre, Herskovits found identifications different from those previously reported by Arthur Ramos for Exú and Shangô and for Saint Onophrius, whom Ramos linked with Osain, Herskovits with Odé (a form of Oxóssi). Herskovits states that the "nation" he visited was Oyo; Ramos does not cite the source of his information. When I visited Pôrto Alegre, however, I found that the Gêgê table of correspondences differed slightly from that of the Oyo "nation." Obviously geographic isolation is a factor in regional variations, but so is the isolation of the "nations," which are kept apart by rivalry. This isolation, to which I have already called attention, still persists in the form of competition and rivalry between *candomblés*. It has produced the same results as geographic isolation: variations in *orixá*-saint correspondences. As of now Dante de Laytano is the only scholar to have made a systematic study of these divergences between "nations." Unfortunately his findings have been published only in part, but they are sufficient to show the importance of the cultural affiliations of the *terreiros*.

Four Gêgê Houses		One Nagô House	
Oxalá	The Holy Spirit	The Sacred Heart of Jesus	
Yansan	Saint Barbara	The young Yansan The old Yansan	St. Catherine St. Barbara
Oxóssi	St. Sebastian	St. Roch	
The young Yemanjá	O.L. of Navigators	The young Yemanjá	O.L. of the Good Journey
The young Omolú	St. Jerome or St. Anthony	The young Omolú	N.S. of Bomfim
Oxun-marê	O.L. of the Rosary	O.L. of the Immaculate Conception[16]	

It would be useful to conduct a similar study in other regions of Brazil before drawing any final conclusions.

But it seems to me that the most important lead to follow in introducing a little logic into our table of mixed-up correspondences is the protean character of every deity. *Orixás* are not confined to a single form. There are at least twenty-one Exús, not just one. There are twelve different forms of Shangô, sixteen different forms of Oxun. It is therefore likely that each form (or at least the principal ones) will have its Catholic equivalent. Hence it comes as no surprise to find one *orixá* corresponding in our table to several saints or Virgins. What at first seemed capricious now appears as a more harmonious arrangement. Nina Rodrigues identified Yemanjá with Our Lady of the Rosary, whereas today she is identified with the Virgin of the Immaculate Conception. The explanation is that we are dealing with two different Yemanjás, since there is one Yemanjá who is always identified with Our Lady of the Rosary. Again, Oxalá is said to be the Eternal Father, although most scholars equate him with Nosso Senhor de Bomfim, but the difficulty disappears when one remembers that Oxalá is split into Oxaguiam and Oxalufan. Kockmeyer's table of correspondences for Bahia allows for this to some extent by carefully distinguishing an old and a young form of each god. Dante de Laytano does the same for Pôrto Alegre.[17] But we still need to go beyond this dualism and envisage the totality of the divine forms. Then we would see that Saint Jerome is not the counterpart of Shangô in general but of Shangô Ogodo, so that this correspondence does not prevent or contradict the identification of Shangô with Saint Anthony, Saint John, or even Saint Barbara, these saints being linked with other forms of the same god (Saint John the Baptist with Sangô Dada, Saint Mark with Osseinha, Saint Anthony with Shangô Nile, and Saint Barbara with Shangô Bonin). I believe that a study of this sort would simplify the problem of syncretism, especially in the case of Exú,

Shangô, and Ogun, although it would not completely eliminate the contradictions in our table of correspondences.

So far we have tried to define syncretism from the outside. We must now try to comprehend it from within—i.e. to discover the emotional or mental attitudes at work in the black psyche when it identifies its *vodun* or *orixá* with a Catholic saint. We must try to find out what inner feelings or images underlie this syncretism. I devoted almost the whole of one of my stays in Bahia and Recife to this problem, yet, as my studies progressed, I found that so far as the Negro was concerned it was nonexistent; it was a pseudoproblem. I had been reasoning according to the logic of Western thought, which is based on the principle of identity and noncontradiction. I had imagined that all outward syncretism must have its psychic counterpart, whereas the black did not see the contradictions that I saw, and psychic syncretism, if it exists, takes quite different forms from the outward syncretism with which I had assumed it to be linked. It is true that the endless questions I put to African cult members forced some of my informants to rationalize their faith, but on the whole I felt that their replies were largely dictated by the form in which I stated my questions and that I had forced my black friends to step outside their own mentality for a moment and assume mine. A spiritist who attended *candomblés* saw the *orixás* purely as effluents of the astral world—benign (guardian angels) or malevolent (Exú). Hence the names by which they are called, whether African or Catholic, are of no importance since these are purely spiritual forces. The *mãe pequena* of a former Gêgê house that had been taken over by an Angola sect told me that there are two hierarchized heavens. The first contains God, Christ, and the Virgin, and immediately below it is the heaven of the *orixás*. This was an admission of the superiority of Catholicism and of white to African civilization, but she hastened to add that it represented only her personal belief, not that of her colleagues. An *obá* of Shangô and a Recife *babalorixá* gave me the most logical replies, based on euhemerism. According to them, in the beginning there were only the *orixás*, and they accepted the bloody sacrifices. But *orixás*, like mortals, die and reincarnate themselves, and in the course of their posthumous evolution their souls were reincarnated in the bodies of white Europeans. Yet since they were still the same all-powerful *orixás*, the people recognized them as gods, despite their changed physical appearance, and canonized them, and these are the Catholic saints. This explains the belief that the spirit of the *orixá* and the saint are one and the same and that the saint's name is the Portuguese translation of the *orixá's*.[18] These rationalizations drawn from my own experience may be supplemented by one made to René Ribeiro by a Recife priest: "The saint we worship is a saint who never died. . . . There are the saints of Heaven (those of the Catholic church), but ours too have the power to speak with God. . . . When Jesus Christ ascended to Heaven, some of the apostles and some of His followers accompanied Him to the celestial court. . . . Others remained in the world where animals can speak. . . . Those other saints live in the *ayê*—in space."[19]

In general, however, the priests do not confuse saints and *orixás*, although they attend church and call themselves good Catholics. "We are no longer Africans," they like to say. "We are Brazilians, and as Brazilians we are obliged to worship the saints of the church too—especially as they are the same spirits under different names." This notion of a purely linguistic difference is the one that recurs most frequently in answers to questions. The saint is the *orixá* under a Portuguese name. For most daughters of the gods the problem I am posing is therefore no problem at all. If you ask a child what the wind is, he will reply with a simple tautology: the wind is the wind. The *filhas* give the same kind of answer. Why is Yansan Saint Barbara? Because she's the same. Tradition weighs so heavily on the beliefs of the faithful that they become oblivious of the contradiction between Catholicism and the African religion. As I said just now, the problem is a pseudoproblem. But this is true only of certain strata of the population or certain "nations." Thus our study has led us to take social structures into account and to open up the question of inward and outward syncretism—i.e. to reexamine it in the light of relationships between the levels of psychic life and the levels of society. In fact there are almost as many forms of syncretism as there are social strata. We need to reexamine the question as a whole.

■   ■   ■

First there is syncretism on the ecological level, which is quite understandable because the whites had to be given the impression that the members of the "nations" were good Catholics. It was therefore only natural that an altar with statues of the saints should occupy a conspicuous place in the *candomblé*, one immediately visible to any outsiders who might drop in. The defining characteristic of the ecological space is juxtaposition. Material objects, being rigid, cannot merge; they are located side by side within the same framework. Consequently the degree of syncretism is denoted here by the relative closeness or separation of what might be termed the Catholic and the African areas of the sacred space. Both in Bahia and in Pôrto Alegre every traditional *terreiro* has a Catholic altar and one or more *pegis* for the *orixás*. (In Recife, so far as I know, only the *terreiro* of Father Adão conforms to this norm.) The Catholic altar is located in the dancing room and often faces the entrance to make it more visible to visitors. The indoor *pegi* for Oxalá, Shangô, etc., is hidden away in the obscurity of a special room, where the stones of the gods repose in dishes and receive offerings of blood and food from their daughters. The outdoor *pegis* for the "open air" gods—Exú, Ogun, and Omolú—are scattered about the grounds in the form of small closed houses. Sometimes one finds both a cross and Exú's little hut at the entrance to the *candomblé*, but the cross stands neither on nor immediately beside the hut. Here again the two spaces, the Catholic and the African one, do not impinge on each other. Moreover the Catholic altar has no functional role in the ceremonies honoring the *orixás*. The daughters of the gods do not salute the statues of the saints as they do the *pegi*, by prostrating themselves, or as they salute the drums that evoke the gods and cause them to descend, by kneeling before them and touching the leather drumhead. Indeed, when they dance they turn their backs on the saints. One feels that this altar is just an extraneous decoration lacking any deeper meaning. It is true that the choice of statues to be displayed is dictated by the symbolism of the *orixá*-saint correspondences, but that is as far as it goes. Here both spatial and social distance between the objects are at their maximum.

In the Bantu *terreiros*, where as we have seen the collective memory is less well organized, the objects are closer together, though still separate. The esthetic needs of the blacks, which here are not counterbalanced by the desire to respect a mythology not entirely their own, compel the *babalorixás* to decorate their *pegis* to make them look more appealing and thus attract larger congregations. With this in mind, they adopt features they have admired in Catholic churches and chapels. For instance, they may cover the dishes in which the stones rest, immersed in blood or oil, with immaculate cloths or drape the ceiling with a canopy that falls in graceful folds. In what we have referred to as "proletarian" *candomblés* the very smallness of the house makes it necessary to bring the Catholic and African spatial areas closer together. Since it is difficult to find room for a Catholic altar, statues are replaced by colored prints hung on the walls, and since there is not room for all of them in the tiny dancing room, many are hung in the *pegi*. Thus the two theoretically separate spaces tend to impinge on each other. In the Recife *terreiros* such closeness is the general rule.[20]

In every case it is spatial rather than social distance that is abolished. That is to say, morphological syncretism cannot be taken as an identification of divinities with saints,[21] although it certainly promotes it. Finally, in *catimbó* (which, it is true, is more Indian than African, but which blacks have penetrated) the bowl of *jurema* lies next to the Christian rosary on the rustic table that serves as the altar, the *caboclo*'s cigar next to the Catholic candle. In Rio *macumba*, and still more in Umbanda spiritism, the Catholic and African areas are completely merged, and the *orixás* are totally identified with the statues of their Catholic counterparts.[22] The substitution of the statue or print for the stone in the *pegi* means that the two spaces have become one, so that the *orixá* and the saint can totally fuse in the affective awareness or the imagination of the votaries. The degree of psychic syncretism thus keeps pace with the degree of ecological syncretism so closely that it is impossible to tell cause from effect.

Moving along to the next level, that of rites and organized ceremonial structures, we distinguish two elements: the temporal framework within which the actions are performed, and their organization. The temporal framework presents the same problems and solutions as the spatial one. For members of traditional *candomblés* there are two religious time frames that do not intersect. During Holy Week the *terreiros* are closed, not in mourning but because the *orixás* have been sent away. During the month of May at the *Casa das Minas*, the Engenho Velho *candomblé*, and Father Adão's house in Recife, as well as in other cult centers, the litanies of the Blessed Virgin are recited in front of the altar in the dancing room. In Bahia at the conclusion of initiations everyone renders thanks to God by attending Catholic mass at the church of Bomfim. In Recife the daughters of Oxun go to mass at Our Lady of Carmel. Yet never is there any mixture of the Catholic and African rites. They are juxtaposed in chronological time exactly as we have just seen objects juxtaposed in space. Depending on the month or the moment, one shifts from one time frame to another without ever confusing the two.

Nonetheless the blacks' transplantation of African ceremonies from one hemisphere to another presented a difficulty: how to localize ceremonies linked to a certain rhythm of nature and society in a country having a different seasonal rhythm. The way this difficulty was resolved in Recife (though not in Bahia) represents the first instance of synchronization of the Christian and Yoruba time frames. The great festivals of the *orixás* were celebrated on the feast day of the corresponding Catholic saint. The Service for the Protection of Psychopaths (which supervises the activities of the *xangôs* in Recife) even tried to fix the dates of the major festivals of the African sects to coincide with the major feasts of the European calendar —Epiphany, the feasts of Saint John, Saint Anne, and the Immaculate Conception, and Christmas—but the *babalorixás* raised such violent objections that it had to yield. This shows that the African calendar did not entirely coincide with the Christian one.[23] Generally speaking, however, and excepting the festival of the new yams (which celebrates the beginning of the African year), Exú is celebrated on Saint Bartholomew's Day, Shangô on the Feast of Saint John, Ogun on April 23 (Saint George), Omolú on January 20 (Saint Sebastian), the Beji on September 27 (Saints Cosmas and Damian), Oxalá on New Year's Day, Yansan on Saint Barbara's Day, etc.

But combining the two calendars did not make the rituals any less heterogeneous nor did it standardize their organization. A mass may be interposed in the sequence of movements and actions, but it is not incorporated into the African ceremony. One goes to church in the morning and at night;

one dances to the throbbing music of the drums to the point of ecstasy. In the less traditional sects, however, extraneous elements are sometimes introduced to embellish a ceremony, and in this way the process of syncretism takes another step forward. This is most conspicuous in the Bantu sects and in *macumba* (which is essentially Bantu by origin). René Ribeiro cites an innovation (introduced by the only Chamba cult house in Recife) that in effect injects into the initiation ritual of a future *yalorixá* elements borrowed from *reisado* or *congado* folklore. Queen Ginga's embassay to the King of the Congo and the display of the gifts exchanged between the two kingdoms in testimony of friendship are transformed into an embassy from the entranced sons of Ogun to the enthroned daughter of Yansan and the display of the *yalorixá*'s diploma as a gift from Shangô.[24] What has happened here is exactly what we observed at the end of the preceding chapter in the case of myth. The *babalorixá* was no longer familiar with the ritual of enthronement for a *yalorixá* and had to search his memory for some appropriate procedure to fill the gap. In both cases the syncretism occured purely as a means of patching holes in the collective memory.

In the same study Ribeiro cites another instance of syncretism which is much more significant from our point of view. Fernando Ortiz stressed one difference between Christianity and the African religiôns that in his opinion precludes genuine conversion without a complete change of mentality. A black, he says, may accept the admission of miraculous saints to his pantheon but he can never accept a god who dies ignominiously on a cross.[25] Yet there is actually an African deity—Shangô—whom Frobenius characterized as "the dead and resurrected god."[26] Why, then, is this god never identified with Christ in our table of correspondences? The deity who corresponds to Christ is Oxalá, and even he is not conceived of as Christ crucified but as the good shepherd leaning on his crook. Ortiz's point is well taken, and we should not be misled by the terminology used by Frobenius, which smacks too strongly of Frazer's ideas. Shangô does die, but in exactly the same way as Ogun or Oxun, who sink into the ground. In each case what has to be explained is how a king or a living woman could mysteriously disappear and become a god. We are a long way from Christian dogma. But there exists in Recife a version of an African ceremony which in Bahia has remained pure. This is the invocation, prior to the ceremony, of all the *orixás*, even the "old ones" who no longer descend. It is performed kneeling, to the accompaniment of the *shiré*. In Recife this ceremony too has been contaminated by folkloric elements borrowed from the *reisado* and has assumed the new form of "praising God." In the *reisado* the songs of praise are addressed to the statue of Christ on the Cross and accompanied by maracas; here they are addressed to Oraminha as the father of all the Shangôs. Ribeiro explains the contamination and the important role Shangô plays in the ritual by the myth telling how Shangô, like Christ, died as a king and was reborn as a god.[27] If this interpretation is correct, it would indicate that the African mentality has been radically transformed and Christianized to allow Shangô to be identified with Christ on the Cross. The ritual syncretism would then be explained by an earlier assimilation of collective representations involving a shift from one social stratum to another.

This is possible. A study of other ceremonies will lead us to the same conclusion. As we have seen, the African (or his descendants) may participate in Catholic rites. When he does, he transforms and reinterprets them to fit the values of his own civilization. If he goes to mass after the initiation ceremony, the Latin words he hears are not, in his mind, addressed to God but to his personal *orixá*. If he walks behind the statue of Our Lady of the Immaculate Conception in a procession, he believes he is walking behind Yemanjá, not the Virgin. The washing of the church of Bomfim in Bahia, which takes place in January,[28] is a typically Portuguese festival. It was introduced by a soldier going off to war in Paraguay who promised Jesus that if he returned unhurt he would wash the atrium of His church. The blacks adopted the custom, but in doing so they changed its meaning. They say that they do this in honor of "the old one." But Jesus, who died at the age of thirty-three, can hardly be described as old. Obviously "the old one" must be His African counterpart, Oxalá. Moreover the blacks attend this festival not as individuals or as families but in groups; each *candomblé* sends its own truck. And lastly, the water they bring with them in flowered containers is not just ordinary water; it comes from the sacred spring of Oxalá. Now the Africans have a ceremony called "the water of Oxalá," which consists chiefly of purifying the stones of the gods once a year and renewing their *mana* by washing them with water from this sacred spring.[29] Two similar ceremonies have been merged. One might almost say: *bis repetita placent . . . deis*. The washing of the church has been reinterpreted in African terms as a doublet of the ritual for purifying the divine stones.[30]

Conversely one of the musical instruments used in the African ceremonies for summoning the divinities is a little bell known as the *adjá*. Since the *adjá* resembles the little bell rung during the mass at the moment of the consecration of the Host, in Recife it is sometimes used to call the attention of the congregation to the climax of the fetishist ceremony: the praising of Orixálá, the greatest of the *orixás*. Here the African rite is reinterpreted in Catholic terms.[31]

Thus the level of ceremonial organization leads us back to collective representations just as the ecological level did. Indeed there is in syncretism a constant shifting back and forth between the various levels of social reality that must reinforce one another in order to function. But this does not prevent each level from remaining relatively independent within the whole phenomenon. Each follows its own laws of development. One might say that there is a spatial logic that is not the logic of actions, just as the logic of actions is not the logic of ideas.

Now that we are entering the domain of collective representations, we must distinguish between religion and magic. Syncretism does not work in the same way in both. The law of religious thought is the law of symbolism and mystic analogies or correspondences. The law of magic thought is the law of accumulation, intensification, and addition. The slaves who were taken to Brazil were of widely different ethnic origins and they sought analogies between their respective deities. Of course there was no question of identifying them—of confusing Zambi and Oxalá, for instance—or of merging them; it was simply a matter of recognizing equivalences. Each "nation" retained its own gods, but they were linked by all kinds of mystic correspondences. One might say that they presented the same supernatural reality in different languages or different civilizations. What was needed was some kind of dictionary that would make it possible to pass from one religion to another, thus demonstrating the unity of the slave class in respect to ethnic origin. The task of compiling such a Yoruba-Dahoman dictionary had already begun in Africa. It was simply continued in Brazil and extended to include the Bantu. Obviously it was a dictionary of analogies, not synonyms. The Nagô Exú was not the Fon Elegba. Neither was the Bantu "man in the street" (Bombomgira) the same as Exú. But these three deities had common as well as divergent characteristics; they were alike. It was in classifications of this sort that Catholicism found its niche. Catholic-African syncretism presents nothing new or extraordinary compared to syncretism among the African religions themselves. The African gods are not identified with the Catholic saints. How often have I heard Bahia blacks protesting against Exú's being referred to as the Devil! They are well aware of the gulf that separates the two. "No, Exú is not the Devil. He's not bad." How can one find the perfect Catholic counterpart for Oxalá, originally an androgynous god? No adequate translation has been found, and Oxalá vacillates between the two sexes, between Nosso Senhor of Bomfim and Saint Anne,[32] as in Cuba he vacillates between Christ and the Virgen de las Mercedes.[33] In any case not all the *orixás* can find counterparts in the Catholic hagiography; the African pantheon is more extensive than the Christian one. As a black said to Kockmeyer: "Everything the church has we have too, but we have a lot more besides. The Catholic priests don't know everything."[34]

Devotees of the African cults are therefore quite aware of the differences between the religions, but they are also aware of their resemblances. Hence it is just as feasible to compile a table of correspondences between *orixás* and saints as between *orixás* and *voduns*.

Syncretism, however, assumes different forms depending upon the nature of the collective representations that come into contact. And when we move from religion to magic or to healing, which is merely another form of magic, we are moving from one group of collective representations to another group that does not follow the same structural laws. In fact religion constitutes a relatively closed traditional system linked to the total social and cultural life, confined within the boundaries of the tribe or "nation." Hence when two religions come into contact, the result will be either religious stratification, with one of them being considered the only true religion and the other relegated to the realm of mysterious cults or black magic, or an attempt to establish equivalences between the gods and place them on a common value level. But the two religions will always tend to persist as entities. The law of magic is the exact opposite and always has been, from classical antiquity to the present day, from the land of the Eskimos to the South Sea islands. Magic is associated with the omnipotence of desire and retains all the excited illogicality, all the unyielding passion, of desire, which never gives up hope. Specialized sorcerers certainly exist who practice only certain types of rites, who have their own formulas and procedures. But if these procedures fail, they have to take stronger measures and find more powerful techniques. Beliefs that originate in the emotions are not willing to recognize defeat. Failure does not arouse skepticism toward magical practices; it just forces them to become more complicated. In order to succeed, the sorcerer takes more precautions. He goes through every name of the god or spirit he is invoking because if he omitted one he would draw a blank. He invokes him in all languages, for if he did not use the most mysterious and archaic tongues, the spirit would not hear his call. He piles action upon action, words upon words. In this respect magic is rather like some experimental science based purely on "experiments to see what will happen." The sorcerer tries out everything he knows or can think up in the hope of achieving his goal. This law of accumulation, which is characteristic of magical (in contrast to religious) thinking precisely because it is bound up with individual or collective desires, actually sets in motion the process of syncretism.

Newly arrived in Brazil, the black found himself exposed to a popular Catholicism that was familiar with and treasured the "potent prayers" of medieval Europe against various diseases, sterility in women, and the accidents of life,[35] and that in the colonial or imperial chapels amassed *ex votos* testifying to miracles performed by the Virgin or the saints in response to desperate prayers or promises.[36] With such "experimental" proof before his eyes, he could not fail to recognize that the whites, like the Negroes, were the masters of benign or formidable powers. Some connection may even have formed in his unconscious mind between the stronger *mana* of the Catholic religion and the whites' higher place on the social ladder. This explains why he grafted the Catholic tradition onto his own—but not before he had rethought and reinterpeted it in terms of magic. He then fortified and enriched it with procedures drawn from his own tradition, mixing Christian and African rites to make them more efficacious. And it must be stressed that he did not borrow from Catholicism alone. Since the law of magical thought is the law of accumulation and ever-increasing complication, the black looked everywhere for ways to intensify magical dynamism. This explains why Mussulman magic survived although the Mussulman religion died out. The non-Moslem black unhesitatingly accepted it to enrich and fortify his own magic, adding the *mandingas* of the Malê to his own spells. This is why blacks were not afraid to use Indian techniques during the colonial period or to pore over the books of Cyprian of Antioch or Albert le Grand in the nineteenth century and even over Tibetan or Rosicrucian books of magic in the present day. Far from promoting skepticism, the spread of education and literacy widened the scope for potential syncretism.

Nevertheless these borrowed elements introduced into African magic changed in character and function. Magical syncretism is not the automatic result of contact between civilizations or of the pressure of the Luso-Brazilian civilization on the civilization of slaves or their descendants. Strictly speaking, magical elements were not combined with Catholic ones. African magic was supplemented, enriched, and intensified by the use of Catholic techniques that in this newly created complex immediately acquired a magical character. The black does not see the priest saying mass as a priest but as a formidable magician who would like to reserve all his secrets for whites and withhold them from blacks, so as to maintain white supremacy. Father Ildefonso was asked by a *babalorixá* named Chico: "Where do you hide the key for opening and closing the body?" Catholic rites are not seen as religious rites but as magic ones, efficacious in themselves. To quote another dialogue reported by Father Ildefonso:

"Father, I've been ill for six months and getting worse for the last two. But if I confess I could get well."
"My friend, confession does not benefit the health of the body but that of the soul."
"Father, you don't know. [Obviously he was afraid to say: "You don't want to."] If you confess me, I'll be cured. My neighbor had a spirit tormenting him. When Father Gaspar came to see him, he confessed and was cured. My mother has consulted the *feiticeiro*, but he couldn't do anything for me. . . . Now there's nothing for it but confession."[37]

We may note that Chico's *candomblé* shows the highest possible degree of syncretism in all the magical expedients I have mentioned: African deities in the form of saints, Oxun in the form of Our Lady of Lourdes (because of the spring), magic herbs, toads, snakes, lizards, dolls, molasses—the whole lot, even down to the fortuneteller's crystal ball. "The small change is for summoning the saint. The string helps. The crystal ball tells who cast the evil spell. The person appears in it. The ball changes color; it turns black or blue. Sometimes a knot forms in it. When the white ball turns black, there's nothing to be done. The person will die."[38]

Magic always tends to be quantitative. The *balangandan* worn by Bahian women is a silver frame hung with the *figa* of the ancient Romans, the Jewish Star of David, the symbolic fish and dove of Christianity, African horns to protect against the evil eye, *candomblé* drums, keys, the four-leafed clover of European sorcery—a touching conglomeration of world-wide magic.[39] This syncretism is facilitated by the relative homogeneity of magical symbols all over the world and throughout the ages—the phallus, the knot, the eye, and the hand—and by the monotony and poverty of the substances used—excrement, nail clippings, hair, strongly scented herbs, strangely shaped roots. Thus syncretism assumes different forms in religion and in magic according to the different laws that govern the structuring of the various types of collective representations.

But the divergence between religious syncretism (through correspondences) and magical syncretism (through the piling up of elements) should not make us forget that the differences between Africa and Catholicism diminish (a) as we move downward from the supreme priests to the sons and daughters of the gods, then to the *candomblé* members still tenuously attached to the sect though operating on its periphery rather than at its center, and (b) as we move from the traditional to the Bantu sects more or less complicated by *caboclos* and from there to the *macumba* of Rio.

This evolution is easy to understand. In the first case, moving downward from the priests or priestesses, we come first to highly Africanized individuals on a lower intellectual level who are less interested in myth than in rites, less concerned with collective representations than with practices, because of the favorable effect these may have on their lives in general. Next come people who belong to the Brazilian rather than the African society and who in their hyphenated allegiance to two different mental worlds derive reassurance from identification with the *orixás* and the saints. In brief, the intensity of the syncretism varies with the degree of participation in institutionalized groups.

In the second case several factors tend to bring the African religion and Catholicism closer together. First, the Bantu assign a more important place to magic in the activities of the *candomblé* than do the Yoruba. Anyone privileged to spend a few days in both types of *candomblé* and observe the type of callers received by the *babalorixás* or *yalorixás* and the advice given to them will recognize this essential difference. As for *macumba*, it openly crosses the line separating religion from magic, particularly black magic. The *macumbeiros* are constantly being asked to make *despachos* against football clubs, politicians, or rivals in love. Thus the law of magical syncretism, which brings Catholicism and Africanism together, tends to replace the law of religious syncretism, which confines itself to compiling a dictionary of correspondences or analogies. Another factor is that the Bantu songs, like those of *macumba*, are generally in Portuguese, and their composers indiscriminately use the god's African name and the other name by which he is known—that of the Catholic saint. By calling the *orixás* by their Portuguese names, they identify the two in the minds of the singers or listeners. A last point to remember is that the color of the participants grows lighter as one passes from the traditional *terreiros* to the Bantu ones and then to *macumba*, which has as many white as mulatto devotees—and far fewer pure black ones. Interracial marriage finds a parallel in the marriage between civilizations. "Mulattoism" is a cultural as well as a biological phenomenon. *Macumba* is a mulatto or rather a mixed-blood religion (since it combines Indian elements with African and white ones). But this cultural mulattoism can only be explained by, and always occurs together with, mulattoism in the form of the mixing of races or blood through marriage or concubinage.

While the ecological and ceremonial levels led us in a rising dialectic to the level of collective representations, our study of the latter has led us, in an inverse dialectic, to a lower level, that of social structures.

■ ■ ■

Civilizations may meet and live side by side without mutual penetration. Contrary to what one might expect, this does not happen because they shut one another out in mutual hostility. A state of war is not prejudicial to cultural fusion. It brings the civilizations together as much as it separates them, because to win a war it is necessary to learn from experience and borrow the victor's most effective weapons. We have seen how, in Brazilian *quilombos* such as Palmares, the saints made their way into the chapels of the runaway slaves fighting against the white planters. So-called counteracculturation movements begin to operate only after a more or less prolonged exploitation of one ethnic group by another, so that the civilization to which one returns is not the authentic one of former times but a mythical version of it, and the counteracculturation always bears in its wake some of the characteristics of the rejected civilization. Cultural exchange seems to be at its lowest in times of peace, not war, as the example of India shows. In peacetime, civilizations in contact are mutually complementary—cattle raisers or crop raisers, pure agriculturists or craftsmen.[40] This state of complementary though hierarchized activities was typical of Brazil in the days of slavery. Under this system of labor the blacks and whites could not get along without one another. The black was his master's "hands and feet"; he supplied the indispensable labor force without which the white would never have been able to establish himself and prosper in Brazil. On the other hand the white provided the minimal security his slaves needed, protecting them against raids by wild Indians and the hazards of disease, infirmity, or old age. As I have shown, before the "nations" came into being, the great plantations replaced the African village for the slave, providing him with a cooperative environment in which security made up for the loss of liberty. The two worlds, the world of the blacks laboring in the fields and that of the whites living in the *casa grande*, did not interpenetrate. Africa simply coexisted with Europe.

But in addition to these rural slaves there were the house servants, maids and black nurses, and the mistresses selected by the master for his sexual pleasure. Two courses were open to the black who could not bear his subjection: to revolt or to seek integration into the dominant group, even in a subordinate position, for the sake of the advantages this would bring him. This integration, however, entailed the de-Africanization of the black in his new environment and a parallel though less profound Africanization of the white. In any case, from the colonial era on, the two systems existed side by side—the encystment of the different races and the integration of individuals into one community. These two phenomena are constantly at work in the network of interpersonal or interracial relations in Brazil. The social class has of course replaced the closed caste. But class barriers, especially when their hierarchy coincides with a color hierarchy of some sort, still confront the black with the same dilemma as before: encystment or participation. The degree of syncretism or assimilation depends upon the degree of encystment or integration of individuals into the global society. To be more precise, both cases actually constitute integration (since individual isolation, far from promoting the preservation of some kind of culture, tends to turn men into animals interested only in survival), but in one case it is integration into a partial community, in the other into society as a whole. In the conclusion to Part I of this book we saw that the abolition of slave labor completely disorganized the black group, leaving it without any institutional frameworks—even deleterious ones—to support it. In this situation we found that the *candomblés* provided one of the rare community niches within which uprooted men deprived of all social ties could re-create communion.

Yet today *candomblé* members too are caught up in the movement of integration into Brazilian society as a whole and as a result of economic competition in the labor market (which arouses or revives color prejudice and racial discrimination) are forced back upon themselves and compelled to form encysted communities.[41] Today one should perhaps distinguish between cultural encystment, which would reach its highest point in the *candomblés*, though without leading to racial encystment, and racial encystment, which would be strongest in the southern part of the country, though without leading to cultural encystment. However well justified this distinction may be, it should not distract us from the first correlation we established: the correlation between the degree of participation and the degree of syncretism, especially since, as we have seen, the principle of compartmentalization enables the black to participate in the economic or political activity of the region he lives in while remaining loyal to his African norms and values. We must always view the facts of syncretism in the dualist context of Brazilian society. Even Pierson, who, in *Negroes in Brazil*, places so much stress on miscegenation and racial democracy, is forced to admit that when one moves from the lower to the upper class one finds oneself in a totally different world.[42] Hence encystment and integration or integration into a community and integration into the global society always operate in tandem, and we may safely follow this lead in seeking to understand the phenomena of syncretism.

In Bahia multiracial integration occurs within the framework of cultural encystment. Whites and mulattoes are linked with *candomblé* life primarily in the capacity of *ogans*, the patrons and protectors of the *terreiro*, or as its political friends. The godparent relationship, which links the various levels in the hierarchy of color, takes the form of godparenthood *de santo*—i.e. the godfather pays all or part of the expenses of an initiation. The most prestigious members of the Negro group belong both to the world of the *candomblé*, where they often hold important offices, and to the Luso-Brazilian world, where they may be businessmen, property owners, or members of Catholic fraternities. Consequently syncretism, which was originally merely a mask, a means of distracting the white man's attention and evading his watchful eye, is transformed into the system of equivalences, of correspondences between saints and *orixás*, that I have described in some detail. The saints and *orixás* are not confused; they are not identified—or at any rate not completely. In fact in Ketu, Jesha, or Nagô *terreiros* they are quite sharply distinguished. But they are linked, as the blacks are linked with the whites without completely merging with them. In Pôrto Alegre, as we have seen, the survival of the *batuques* varied even more clearly with the social distance between the black masses and the middle- and upper-class whites. Yet the blacks are Catholics too; they were integrated into Brazil primarily through Christianization. So here too correspondences were established, facilitated by the blacks' participation in the festivals of the Rosary, although never to the point where saints and *orixás* were merged. To put it briefly, the more closely integration adheres to the community type, or the greater the social or cultural encystment within which it occurs, the less profound the syncretism. What I have said about the Yoruba religion also applies exactly to the Dahoman religion of Maranhão. It may be noted that in the *Casa das Minas* most of the *voduns* have never found a Catholic counterpart.[43] Here the syncretism is primarily between the calendar of African festivals and the Brazilian calendar, civil as well as religious: Christmas, Carnival, the feasts of Saint John and Saint Sebastian.[44]

In the areas of *pagelança* and *catimbó*, however, the blacks are much more thoroughly integrated into the surrounding society, as is reflected in the acceptance of *caboclo* spirits. The same is true of Rio, where the surrounding society is white and preponderantly Catholic rather than of mixed blood. Syncretism occurs as the saints are accepted and gradually replace the *orixás*. But the black is never integrated directly into society as a whole; his integration always proceeds by way of the social class system and—as has been true from the outset—by way of the dualism of Brazilian society. It is certainly integration, but with what? With the lower-class masses of mixed-bloods or part-whites.[45] That is, with a Catholicism that is not the official one but the superstitious Catholicism of medieval European peasants. With a society in which miscegenation Africanizes the whites as much as it de-Africanizes the blacks. Hence integration with a class (the form that black integration into the global society assumes) does not do away with the African religions altogether but, by pushing syncretism to its limits, denatures and corrupts them. The corruption takes different forms in rural areas and in big cities—i.e. according to whether the black is integrated into the lower peasant class or into the urban proletariat. The next two chapters will go into this.

13
Two Types of Disintegration

The Rural *Candomblé*

In spite of the current trend toward industrialization, Brazil is still essentially a rural country. Not only is the major part of its labor force employed in agriculture but the ratio of agricultural workers to the total population is one of the highest in the world.[1] So even though the social structure of rural Brazil has changed since the abolition of slavery, the dualism of colonial times still persists. A series of economic crises including both the sugar and the coffee industries bankrupted the landed aristocracy. In some periods and some regions the great estates were broken up (not to say atomized) and subdivided into tracts that were finally allotted to immigrants or their children in small or medium-sized holdings. Other periods and other regions saw the reconsolidation of the vanished latifundia and the acquisition of vast expanses of land by a few individuals or by capitalist development companies. Thus, in the country as a whole, changes in ownership had little effect on the pyramid of rank and social status. Still at the top are the big landowners, who usually employ administrators to supervise the working of their *fazendas* or plantations and who account for almost half of the total wages paid out to agricultural workers. Below them—a long way below—come the *sitiantes*, small landowners employing a few hired hands but relying chiefly on family members to work their land. They range in type from the modern scientific farmers of the pioneering regions of São Paulo and Paraná to the backward, traditional ones of the *sertão*. Next come the classes of farmers who pay a fixed rent to the landowner for whom they work, sharecroppers who give them

285

half or two-thirds of their crop, and tenants whom the landlord allows to
live on his land, on somewhat precarious terms, in return for a few days'
work a week. At the bottom are the day laborers. The figures for 1940
break down as follows:

Big landowners	252,047	2.67%
Small landowners and sharecroppers	3,309,701	
Family members working for the above	2,665,509	63.20%
Hired farm hands	3,164,203	33.47%
Unknown	62,052	0.66%

But to comprehend the meaning of this table we must coordinate it with
the distribution of the land:

	Number	Acreage
Large properties		
Latifundia (over 1,000 hectares [2,471 acres])	1.46%	48.31%
Large properties (200–1,000 hectares [approximately 500–2,500 acres])	6.34%	24.79%
Medium and small properties		
Medium-sized properties (50–200 hectares [approximately 125–500 acres])	17.21%	15.90%
Small properties (5–49 hectares [approximately 12–125 acres])	53.07%	10.45%
Very small properties (less than 5 hectares [10 acres])	21.76%	0.55%

Clearly the pyramid showing who works the land is still the inverse of the
pyramid showing who owns it.[2]

The black who did not desert the country for the blandishments of the
city was integrated into this social structure. In the cattle-raising areas,
where he had never been badly off and where the horse acted as a kind of
leveler, he became a tenant farmer or sharecropper. His social status
changed but his condition remained the same. In the central region of
Brazil he constitutes the mass of farm labor, working by the day according
to his own needs, never settling in one place. His mobility varies from
region to region, ranging from seven or eight miles in isolated mountainous
country to six or seven hundred in the pioneering zones.[3] In the northeast
the black often became a *sitiante*, but usually he did not acquire his small
farm through his own labor. When a sugar planter freed a slave, it was the
custom to give him a parcel of land to live on.[4] As everywhere else, these
people today are largely sharecroppers, tenants, or day laborers.

These blacks, like the *caboclos* and the poor whites, are very widely
dispersed. The density of population in Brazil is estimated at five or six
inhabitants per square kilometer. They are not totally isolated of course.
People who live reasonably close together form *bairros*—what might be
called neighborhood groups. But distances are too great for this neighborhood relationship to be anything but a very loose one. From time to time
they spend an evening together in some kind of religious activity, and the
communal labor known as *mutirão* or *puchirão* also brings them together.
But such moments of communion are few and far between.[5] Obviously

this kind of isolation and the mobility of day laborers prevents the blacks from keeping up their beliefs and cults. Thus the modern social structure has perpetuated the disintegrative effect of the slave regime. As we have seen, by mixing Africans of different ethnic origins and by closely supervising black festivities, this regime prevented the formation of organized "nations." Practically all that remained to the black was his magic—black magic to be used against the whites, curative magic to heal his own sick. The isolation and mobility that succeeded slavery, and the mixing of blacks, *caboclos*, and whites in the same *bairros*, made it possible for the descendants of the first Africans to keep up their magic as a personal defensive weapon or as a substitute for medicine in regions too sparsely populated to support a doctor, but prevented the organization of institutionalized African cults. In the absence of structured groups the collective memory could not function; it dissolved into a multiplicity of individual memories that were themselves subject to the corrosive action of time. As we shall see, only rural Catholicism offered frameworks capable of bringing the mass of scattered peasants together, and rather than sink into even deeper solitude the black integrated himself into that religion. The question is whether in doing so he did not insinuate some of his African memories or reinterpret Catholicism in the light of African attitudes. We shall therefore return to the problem of black Catholicism in a later chapter.

For the moment, however, we are looking for authentic survivals from Africa. They did not exist—could not exist—in the type of rural structure I have briefly analyzed. The black adopted the ideals of his environment. D'Oliveira maintains that there is no African influence at all in rural Brazil, where the black allowed himself to be totally assimilated by the *caboclo* culture. This is perfectly true.[6] Outwardly there is no great difference between the poor whites, cut off from the church by distance; the mixed-blood descendants of Indians civilized by the Jesuits but cut off from ongoing Christianization by the Pombal government's expulsion of the Jesuit order; and the blacks, perfunctorily evangelized on the plantations but seeing Catholicism chiefly as a symbolic bond with their fellow-men and fellow-sufferers. When we remember that interracial sexual liaisons and marriages were continuously mixing blood, the profound disintegration of Africa in rural Brazil is easy enough to understand.

But between these rural areas where the African religions disintegrated and the state capitals where they survived there exists an intermediate social environment: the small towns in the interior of Brazil, more country than urban to be sure, which nevertheless bring the population together in one place, promote more permanent and more highly developed neighborhood relationships, and provide an opportunity for upward mobility through the school, skilled craftsmanship, and the frameworks of local government. The social stratification of these country towns corresponds exactly to the racial composition of the population. As a general rule the members of the local gentry—the big landowners, the lawyers, doctors, and politicians—are all white; the mulattoes or mestizos form the middle class; and the dark-skinned blacks are lumped together in the lower class, living on the outskirts of the town where it merges gently with the country-side. There is no doubt that, as one popular saying puts it, "money whitens"—to which another adds, "whiteness is worth money." That is to say, the racial element plays its part in the competition between all those who want to rise in society, and even here the lighter one's skin, the easier it is to climb the social ladder.[7]

These two conditions—a higher concentration of blacks within a con-fined area and their relative segregation in the lower class—favored the emergence of organized African sects. Unfortunately the ethnographers have neglected the study of these sects for the understandable reason that they presented only impure survivals, whereas the big coastal cities offered a chance of discovering genuine "Africanism." Sociologists were not much interested either. The result is that data on the subject is very scarce—or, to be more precise, quantitative data that would enable us to ascertain the extent of this organizational movement and of African survivals. However we do possess more or less complete information about certain sects, the ones sometimes known as "rural *candomblés*." The sample is sufficient to show how deeply beliefs and rites had been eroded.

Da Costa Eduardo has described what remains of the Dahoman reli-gions in the small town of Santo Antonio in Maranhão. The town has no Catholic church, and the inhabitants consist chiefly of illiterate black peas-ants. The ancestral deities are not dead; the names Verekete and Sobô are still known, and these two Dahoman gods have been joined by the Yoruba deity Eowa and the Angola Calunga, who is here considered a goddess of death although in Rio she has survived as queen of the sea. But these gods do not descend.[8] I believe that the reason for this is the lack of the initiation ceremony. We have seen that the *voduns* and *orixás* cannot descend unless they have been "fixed" in the heads of their children. The Santo Antonio blacks have not forgotten this, but since they no longer know the secrets of the initiation rites, the gods of their fathers can now survive only as mental images, not as living realities. They have been replaced by *encantados* because the cult of the latter is much simpler, requiring no significant outlay for sacrifices while still allowing the devotee to experience the same joy of possession in the mystic trance. The *encan-tados* are known as *budu* (i.e. *voduns*), and the highest one has an African name, Kakamado. One of the spirits they worship, Maria Barbara, may even retain, behind her Portuguese name, some of the characteristics of Nanamburucú. Curiously enough, in this moribund ancestral mythology the image of Legba (whom a praise song refers to by one of his Yoruba names, Exú-Bara) has been preserved much more faithfully than in the mother-house in the capital of Maranhão.[9]

Dances are held twice a month, on Sundays, in a house with a fine Catholic altar. No special sacrifices are made to the *encantados*, but once a year the liturgical objects are washed with a mixture of water and wine; this is all that survives of the festival known in Bahia as "the water of Oxalá." Some houses, however, still retain the specifically African, not to say Dahoman, feature of the pole in the center of the room around which the dancers circulate counterclockwise. There is no priest in the strict sense, and, as I have said, no initiation. This is replaced by baptism, according to the Catholic rite, of the spirit that descends upon a new "horse." In contrast to the practice in traditional sects, the *encantados* mount men as often as women. They speak through the mouths of their sons and daughters, offering advice and remedies and suggesting how best to solve the problems of daily life.[10] All in all, these ceremonies seem to fulfill a twofold need: providing entertainment in a small town with little else to offer and supplying material and spiritual leadership to an isolated population abandoned to its lot.

What we know of the rural *candomblés* in the state of Bahia generally bears out this description. Each has its own character, as though each individual sect had retained scraps of some distant, tattered collective memory. On the Salvador–Santo Armaro road I came across a *candomblé* where only three gods out of the entire great Afro-Brazilian pantheon were known. I believe that this attenuation of the mythology can be explained only by the fact that slavery brought very few initiates to this area, and, while they were able to continue the cult of their own individual *orixás*, they could not revive the others. Since the *orixás* are inherited by family, following either the paternal or the maternal line, they were limited to those of the original settlers. In Vila Reconcavo there are several *candomblés*, but "owing to the pressures of modern life almost no one has the time necessary to spend in the full preparation for a *filha de santo* (servant of the god) or a *mãe de santo* (caretaker of the gods) and much of the old ritual is being forgotten and discarded, and newer and simpler innovations are in evidence."[11]

Farther out in the *sertão*, at Monte Serrat, where the *candomblé* is in closer contact with *caboclos*, it has been more deeply penetrated by the *encantado* cult. Here the blacks worship and are possessed by *orixás* known by their Catholic names—Saint Barbara (Shangô), Saint Roch (Omolú), Saint Anthony (Ogun), or Our Lord of the Good Death (Oxalá)—and also by Indian spirits such as Tapuya and Tupinamba (neither of whom has a Catholic equivalent). But the element of worship is disappearing, just as it is in *catimbó*, and the primary function of the cult is to cure illness. As Câmara Cascudo says, *catimbó* is not a cult but a consultation.[12] The principal object of the rites of these new *candomblés* is to free people from the *encosta* (intruder) or *caboclo* who has made them sick.

Not content with prescribing remedies and medicinal herbs and offering advice while in trance, the sons and daughers of the gods also shake the patient violently, to the lugubrious throbbing of the drums, in order to drive the enemy out of his body. These sects become a kind of battleground where the Afro-Catholic deities, aided by Indian spirits, fight it out with the demonic *caboclo* spirits, where Africa clashes with the mestizo Brazil of the Amerindians. The racial clash is shifted to the supernatural world, and the ethnic conflicts of the rural society are resolved in myth. As is often the case in Africa, the members of these *terreiros* are former sufferers whose *encosta* was cast out through the power of the god who subsequently became their protector.[13] They then took regular instruction from a *pão* or *mãe de santo* (the *babalorixá* or *yalorixá*) to learn the songs, rituals, and techniques of healing. One of these *terreiros* is directed by a mother who is also a healer. She heals essentially through prayers to the saints and Catholic benedictions, but those whose health is restored are expected to acknowledge their obligation by sponsoring a ritual dance in the *candomblé*.[14]

Although one of the Vila Reconcavo *terreiros* is directed by a white lawyer (probably without clients), *candomblé* is associated in people's minds with the lower class. For this reason anyone who wants to rise socially through schooling, good connections, marriage with a lighter partner, or political help in obtaining some minor official position, rejects *candomblé* along with anything else that might remind the people whom he hopes to impress of his cultural ties with Africa.[15] Conversely, whenever a town grows through the influx of country people who settle at the base of the social pyramid, *candomblés* spring up and multiply. In Juazeiro, which has become a major pilgrimage center (a sort of Brazilian Lourdes), *pães de santo* looking for new opportunities have recently founded four or five *candomblés* in defiance of the church. Apparently the competition is keen, for each of them is sharply critical of his colleagues, accusing them of "knowing nothing." Two of them have no *terreiro* of their own and have to rent a room in town, where they hold consultations, give initiation instruction, etc. The others have their own houses, where, as in Bahia and Recife, there is always an *egun* room beside the *pegi* and Exú's hut. But sacrifices are not made for the souls of the dead; candles are simply lighted on Fridays, and the bones of all the sacrificial animals are deposited in this room. When a daughter reaches a high position in the priestly hierarchy, she takes all these bones into her possession; otherwise she would be possessed by the spirit of an *egun* instead of her own *orixá*. The same thing would happen if the *sirrum*, the funeral ceremony corresponding to the final African burial, were not held seven years after a death.

These *candomblés*, which appeal to a heterogeneous population in which Indian mestizos outnumber blacks, are now trying to adapt to the new racial and social situation, for example by using songs in Portuguese rather than the African languages and by supplementing the *orixá*-saint correspondences indicated earlier with new mystic equivalences between these same *orixás* and Indian spirits.[16] Thus each god has three names: an African one such as Oxóssi, a Catholic one such as Saint Sebastian, and an Amerindian one such as Urubatão. We shall find a similar solution in Umbanda spiritism.

Curiously enough, in Rio, urban disintegration came before rural disintegration. At the beginning of the twentieth century *candomblé* still existed. In the capital it was soon transformed into *macumba* through contamination with Bantu and Indian survivals and with spiritism, but in the Rio *sertão* it lived on under the name of "jujuism." Its existence, however, was only sporadic; Magalhães Corrêa speaks of its "rarity."[17] In the rural areas a mixture of folk medicine and magic predominated. As Silvestre observed in 1935, "the *macumbeiro* has become a *curandeiro*,"[18] the priest a mere healer. The same is true in the interior of the state of São Paulo.[19]

Superstitious peasant beliefs, whether Catholic or Indian, African or European, do not simply drift around in a void. We have seen that collective representations need to be attached to a group, to a flesh-and-blood institution, in order to live on. Here these superstitions crystallize around certain individuals who appear to have more *mana* than others, to be endowed with extraordinary powers—*macumbeiros*, healers, dispensers of blessings, mediums. In the big cities Africa is incarnated in the sects; here it can survive—if at all—only to the extent that it can incarnate itself in individuals. The black plays a major role in this crystallization of rural collective representations. Simmel's pages on the association of the "foreigner" with the "foreign," on the sinister character of the outsider, are famous. The Negro is doubly foreign, being both African and black. The group therefore relegates him to magic—preferably to curative magic, since doctors are in short supply and it might as well make use of him.

But the black is too cut off from the collective memory of his ancestors, too closely integrated with the Brazilian environment, to have retained anything more than vestiges of his mythology or ritual. The only figure from his former pantheon that remains to him is Exú, no longer an interceding god but a diabolical one, master of black magic. This Exú assumes different aspects depending on the kind of work he is supervising. Exú-Banana-Tree is invoked on banana plantations; Exú-Stump-Puller requires the sorcerer to wear a black suit; Exú-Guinea "works" with guinea fowl; Exú-of-the-Seven-Crossroads accepts offerings where roads intersect; Exú-Bambua whistles in the reeds; the magic ritual of Exú-Seven-Keys requires seven virgin keys; Exú-Stone-Puller works only with rocks; Exú-Tiriri is well known in the *candomblés* of Bahia.[20] Magical drawings are made for him in chalk of a particular color for each name, and he is offered sacrifices or libations of brandy. But this god cannot fill out a whole mythology by himself. The defunct African gods are therefore replaced either by Indian spirits or by Catholic saints. The house of every *macumbeiro* has its little chapel, beside which the magic rites are performed, interspersed with prayers, Paternosters, and Ave Marias.[21]

These *macumbeiros* are often former patients cured by another *macumbeiro* who subsequently dedicate themselves to the service of the healing spirit, or people who have found themselves to be mediums when attending a spiritist meeting in some city. Others suffered "attacks" in childhood or had "visions," and their families or neighbors, taking this as a sign of divine election, sent them to a *feiticeiro* to be "initiated." The initiation usually consists of a quite rudimentary apprenticeship imparting a knowledge of certain herbs, certain "potent" prayers, etc., complicated by tests designed to create an ineradicable affective association between this empirical knowledge and the supernatural. One such test might be to spend a night in a cemetery talking with the dead. Some of these blacks came originally from Rio, where they attended urban *macumbas*. Life histories that have been collected show that they all belong to the socially disrupted lower class (broken families, serial concubinage, high child mortality, alcoholic parents, geographic mobility, etc.). But it cannot be said that this social disorganization is reflected in a disorganization of beliefs. On the contrary, it is these beliefs, even if disorganized, that constitute their only integrative link with the rural environment in which they live, provide them with status and role, and guarantee them a certain amount of security and recognition from the local people.

Although this rural *macumba* is essentially individualist and amounts to little more than a series of consultations by the sick, victims of snakebite, or people seeking revenge on an enemy, and although it is not in any way an organized cult, it may become a nucleus for loose groupings of believers. In areas where the population is widely dispersed, where Catholicism and its festivals cannot overcome the fear of loneliness or meet the desire for revivifying collective communion, the evening gatherings held by a magician or famous woman healer provide relief. These are semireligious, semiprofane meetings. Catholic prayers are recited; candles are lighted for the souls in Purgatory; the sick are healed. In addition to all this, stories are told—tales of animals or legends of Pedro Malazarte. On the outskirts of big cities or in the small towns of the interior, these meetings tend to take the form of what is known as "low spiritism," which is characterized by the manipulation of three "streams," the *caboclo* or Indian, the African, and the white, whose names are derived from the spirits received by the mediums in séances—spirits of *caboclos*, old Negroes, or whites such as Pedro II or Joan of Arc.[22]

Because of the way rural *macumba* is organized and because it develops in nonorganic contexts, it can degenerate into criminality. In Itapeva, Vicencia da Sila Melo was ordered by God and the Blessed Virgin to kill her grandmother, who had been turned into a snake, and then walk about naked, carrying the banner of the Holy Ghost. To cure his sick father and drive out his demon, the black healer João Martins da Buri dragged him out of bed so violently that he killed him. He inflicted burns on a neighbor to exorcise him,[23] and finally organized a purification procession that ended with the drowning of many members of his family. Joaquim Pedro de Avaré, a black, celebrated marriages by order of the spirit, and when the spirit ordered him to leave his old wife and live with a pretty young *cabocla* from his neighborhood, he did so, "although reluctantly." He was arrested, in the company of a group of devotees, just as he was about to sacrifice his baby to the spirit. Obviously the commands of the spirits or the Catholic saints simply express the desires of the individual's own unconscious: to murder an old woman who must be fed, although she makes no financial contribution to the family, or a crippled child who is a heavy burden to the household, to change wives, etc. But these repressed desires, which surface in the state of trance (or ecstasy) and are tinged with mystic representations, find an outlet and a vindication in *macumba*.[24] Such is the final avatar of these religions, which once flourished so splendidly. As they disintegrate, becoming more and more individualized, merging with the country landscape, their last vestiges, which are no more African than Indian or Catholic—or are all of these at once—finally degenerate into the distorted figments of criminal madness.

Certain conclusions can be drawn from this analysis:

1. Disintegration becomes more pronounced as distance from the Dahoman or Yoruba centers of the northeast increases, since these centers act as a kind of brake.

2. Contributory factors to this disintegration are: (a) the disappearance of initiation rites, i.e. the lack of African socialization or culturalization; (b) the poverty of the peasant class, which precludes animal sacrifices; (c) the needs of the rural masses, lacking all medical care, which practically force the priest to become a healer and the cult to degenerate into the mere consultation of spirits.

3. In the erosion of religious institutions the first thing to be affected is the mythology. One of the rare figures to survive is Legba in the Dahoman area, Exú in the others. A step below him come the *eguns* or spirits of the dead. The gaps that remain are filled by new figures: the saints of Catholicism, the *encantados* of *catimbó*, the *caboclos* or "Africans" (depending on the region) of "low spiritism."

4. The line of erosion leads from the rural *candomblés*, which still celebrate ceremonial festivals, to the individualism of Carioca or Paulista *macumba*, while a parallel line leads from trance, which is still controlled

by the group and serves its interests, to individual trance, which is ultimately no more than a reflection of the *macumbeiro*'s personal libido.
The disorganization of the cult ends in the disorganization of the self.

Urban *Macumba*

As noted earlier, in Brazil the city was originally just an extension of the
fields. It is true that the discovery of the mines and the arrival of the
Portuguese court in Rio resulted in an initial wave of industrialization, but
real urbanization is a relatively recent phenomenon that certainly did not
begin to influence religious values until the twentieth century. But although
this movement is of course linked to population growth, it does not appear
everywhere with the same intensity. There are towns that are still basking
in their traditional rural atmosphere, and there are the great tentacular
cities, notably Rio de Janeiro and São Paulo, which in 1950 each had over
two million inhabitants.

What strikes the sociologist even more forcefully than this trend toward
concentration is the rapidity of the urbanization process, which did not
really get under way until after the First World War. The following
figures will give an idea of its pace:

Year	Population of Rio de Janeiro	Population of São Paulo
1872	274,972	31,385
1890	522,651	64,934
1900	691,565	239,820
1920	1,157,842	579,033
1940	1,764,441	1,326,261
1950	2,413,152	2,227,512[25]

This modification of Brazilian society is due to the industrialization of
the country, which is proceeding at an ever-increasing rate. Formerly a
producer of tropical agricultural products, sugar, and coffee, Brazil, especially in the south, has become a country of huge factories. In the
colonial era Portugal, anxious to protect its export trade, prohibited the
creation of local industry.[26] After independence, England's proclamation
of free trade confined the development of the country to agriculture. Not
until the slave trade was abolished could capital hitherto reserved for the
purchase of slaves be applied to the establishment of local industry. Only
after the great electrical power centers of São Paulo and Rio had been
built, when the crisis in the coffee industry was forcing the plantation
owners to look for new sources of profit, did industrialization really come
into its own in those cities, bringing with it accelerated urbanization of the

south. Until 1913 industry was almost entirely confined to foodstuffs and textiles, but the two world wars forced the Brazilians to build up industries to manufacture all the products they had formerly imported from Europe or the United States. After World War II, São Paulo alone accounted for 40 percent of the total factories and mills in Brazil,[27] but Rio was already catching up. In 1947 it had 101,302 industrial plants and 2,040 wholesale warehouses.[28] These factories and businesses attract more and more labor from the rural areas. The number of apartment houses in Rio grew from 30,918 in 1872 to 405,999 in 1950.

Industrialization might have brought the blacks an opportunity to earn a living and a channel of upward mobility. But they were slow to benefit from it, being held back at first by economic competition from poor whites and immigrants. They were therefore not immediately integrated into the social class system of the capitalist regime. They formed a kind of sub-proletariat, and the development of urbanization, which destroyed their traditional values without providing new ones in exchange, meant for them only a stepping up of the process of social disintegration. One might say that as the city developed, it had two successive effects on the Negro: first a disintegrative impact and then a reintegrative one, as he finally gained a foothold in the class system, particularly in the construction and mechanical fields. *Macumba* is an illustration of what happens to the African religions during a period when traditional values are being lost. Umbanda spiritism, on the other hand, reflects the reorganization, on new foundations and in accordance with the new attitudes of proletarianized blacks, of such elements of the African homeland as *macumba* had allowed to survive. We shall study this spiritism in the next chapter. For the moment we may confine ourselves to the phase of urban disintegration.

Arthur Ramos defined *macumba* as syncretism between the African, Amerindian, Catholic, and spiritist cults. We may add that the African elements were heterogeneous. In mapping the religious geography of Brazil, we saw that at the beginning of the twentieth century there were two "nations" in Rio: the Yoruba, who worshiped *orixás*; and the Bantu, whose cult is known as *cabula*. *Macumba* started out as *cabula* with an admixture of certain *orixás* and certain Yoruba rites. The superseding of the "nations" by organized sects was the first erosive effect of the big city. Within the colored masses ethnic and cultural bonds were dissolved. Another solidarity emerged—not yet the solidarity of class but the solidarity of misfortune, of comradeship in the struggle to adapt to the New World and in loneliness. But this first syncretism, which juxtaposed two systems of belief, could not form a very coherent system. Through the chinks in this new theology, hesitantly trying to find itself, other elements crept in, especially when it began to appeal to whites, who soon became almost as numerous as blacks in *macumba*. The first of these extraneous elements was popular

Catholicism (aided by the fact that the Catholic saints already had their *orixá* counterparts). Then came the spiritism preached by Allan Kardec.* *Macumba* was born of this encounter and fusion. To consolidate itself, the emerging proletarian class needed a minimum of intellectual and affective homogeneity, which it could attain only by pooling in the new frameworks of industrialization the mystic experiences peculiar to each of its constituent races. *Macumba* represents this minimum of cultural unity that is indispensable if men are to achieve solidarity in a world that offers them nothing but insecurity, disorder, and mobility.[29] To put it another way, it reflects the transitional city in which the old values have been swept away but not yet replaced by those of the modern world. As the city grows and is split up into neighborhoods, no overall class solidarity can develop; it is fragmented into neighborhood solidarity. The *macumba*, no longer anchored in a structured collective memory, is individualized, although it still remains a group. Almost every priest invents new ritual forms or new spirits, and the fierce competition between cult groups is reflected not in greater fidelity to the past, as it is in Bahia, but in the very opposite: aesthetic or dogmatic innovations. These are accepted by people who once again have nothing in common except their situation at the bottom of the social ladder and whose forms of sociability—their family and profession —are also disorganized. Hence the fluidity of this constantly changing religion, which defies accurate description. I shall not attempt to do more than outline its essential general characteristics.

The supreme priest is known by the Bantu name of *embanda* or *umbanda*—actually the Angola *kimbanda* transported to Brazil.[30] He is assisted in performing the ceremonies by one or more associates, the *cambones*, a word whose African etymology Ramos never succeeded in discovering, despite extensive research. The daughters of the gods, on the other hand, are known by the spiritist name mediums (media in the feminine). Those in the top category are the *sambas*; the principal *samba* performs functions analogous to those of the *mãe pequena* of the *candomblé*.[31] The term *ogan* is known, but is used here to designate the drummers. The mythology includes all the great gods of the Yoruba pantheon, though often they have different Catholic equivalents. The counterpart of Oxalá, also known as Zambi (through Bantu influence), is Jesus Christ; that of Ogun, who, as I have said, is especially popular, is Saint George. Shangô corresponds to Saint Jerome, Oxóssi to Saint Sebastian, Oxun to Our Lady of Aparecida, etc. But these *orixás* are no longer worshiped in the form of stones or pieces of iron, receptacles of supernatural forces, but as Catholic statues adorning the altar of the sect. There

---

* [Allan Kardec (pseudonym of Hippolyte Rivail [1809–1869]) was an influential French spiritist and author of *Le Livre des Esprits* and *Le Livre des Médiums*. Kardecism is discussed in Chapter 6.]

is no *pegi*, but, at most, a curtain below the Catholic altar hides dishes in which food offerings to the *orixás* are placed.

These gods may descend in one of their many forms. Even Exú has sons and daughters who receive him, and their trances have a particularly spectacular quality. In fact ecstatic possession in general takes a form different from that in Bahia, where it is relatively calm and controlled by the group. Here it tends toward hysteria. This is understandable since the mediums no longer have a mythology with which to regulate trance and provide a model of divine activity. Ecstasy therefore degenerates into passionate gesticulation by individuals whose inner beings are disorganized by the transition from a normal to an altered state. Although the *orixás* do descend, *macumba* differs from *candomblé* in its veneration of familiar spirits derived from the *tatas* of Bantu *cabula*. Due to the influence of spiritism, however, these protective spirits are long-dead Indians or Africans whose souls drift about the astral world—Father Joaquim, the Queen of Guinea, Old Lawrence, etc. They are divided into *caboclos* (representing the contribution of the native religions), fathers and mothers, "aunts" (the name by which blacks refer to old women), and grandfathers. Of course each god or spirit has his own distinctive color, necklace, favorite food, and special drinks. There is no need to go into detail about this unstable mythology. The number of familiar spirits varies from one *terreiro* to another, and here the mediums' imagination, conscious or unconscious, has free rein.[32]

Membership in the sect is conferred by initiation, which begins with a purification bath. Only a symbolic lock of hair is cut off, and seclusion in the *camarinha* is shorter to allow for the greater responsibilities of modern city life. Sometimes it lasts only a week, but the usual stay is three weeks, during which the candidate is taught precepts, songs, and dances. The reception of the new initiate into the sect is the occasion for a great ceremony known as "the crossing" because the priest takes an iron sword and traces a cross first on the back, then on other parts of the candidate's body.[33] The public ceremonies are a mixture of Africanisms, "low spiritism," and magic. They open with songs for Exú, and the singing continues until the *embanda* receives an *exú*, who gives orders to the *cambones* before withdrawing. As in Bahia, Ogun is honored after Exú, and he in turn incarnates himself in the priest. Only after these two manifestations can the Indian or old African spirits descend. They are easy enough to recognize because in trance the Indian's eyes are always open, the African's closed. These spirits advise the assistants, provide remedies for the sick, and solve problems of daily life, particularly matrimonial ones, for anyone who asks. Thus the ceremony winds up as a consultation session.

Certain elements of the *macumba* ritual deserve a little more attention. The animal sacrifice, which in the *candomblé* is performed in the morning in the presence of a very small group of believers, takes place in the *macumba*—if at all—during the public ceremony, constituting its climax. A cock is killed and its blood is allowed to trickle over a woman's body. One feels that the spectacular element is now the only one that counts and that commercialized *macumba* is the next step. Just as the Catholic priest or his acolytes swing the thurible or burn incense, the *embandas* begin their rituals by censing the cult house and the assistants. More and more importance is attached to this censing with aromatic herbs, which has given rise to a regular commerical business. The herbalists of Rio sell "censing herbs" for all kinds of ailments—spiritual as well as physical. The gods or spirits are invoked not only by drumming and by songs in the African language but also by designs drawn on the ground in special chalk; these are known as *pontos riscados*. These designs are not unknown in Africa and are also found in Haiti, where they are known as *vêvê*.[34] But they have been drastically changed and have lost the simplicity of the circular and other more or less geometric forms of their African models through imitation of European books on magic.[35]

Umbanda spiritism has driven *macumba* out of the Rio suburbs into the small towns that form a kind of proletarian ring around the city. Duque de Caxias has now become one of the major centers of this type of African sect.[36] While the *macumbas* still serve as centers for the healing of bodily or spiritual ailments, they have also become places of free entertainment.[37] The craze for the exotic, the blasé public's hankering for new sensations and shows, and the craving for mystery that haunts many people attract large numbers of whites to some of these *macumbas*. One quite often sees a number of Chevrolets parked outside a humble house waiting for their owners. This white invasion, which, on the evidence of the poem by Gregorio de Matos quoted in the historical section of this book, dates back a long way, has produced what has been called the "tourist *macumba*." Intelligent priests grow rich by putting on well-staged choreographic performances, spiced with a touch of sadism, to attract well-to-do clients who are all too ready to pay extra to see some "magic" performed or to watch rites of a more secret nature.[38] Mulattoes, white Brazilians, and even foreigners become *embandas* themselves in the hope of making an easy fortune. The *terreiro* of Oxun is directed by the young son of an Italian immigrant named Fernandes Copolillo, assisted by a black *mãe pequena* from Bahia. In a *terreiro* in the suburb of Ramos a Lebanese woman named Judith Kallile used to take orders from the *caboclo* Jurema.[39] The Rio *macumba* is becoming more and more debased, losing all its religious character and deteriorating into a stage show or mere black magic.[40]

It is not only in Rio that *macumba* flourishes. We also find it in the state of Espírito Santo, where it works chiefly through *exús* and *caboclos*, i.e. African gods and Amerindian spirits. The *exús* preside over magical activities and the *caboclos* over "works of charity," consultations with the sick

and the unfortunate who come seeking solutions to their personal problems. The Catholic saints play a role too—those who have been identified
with *orixás*: Saints Cosmas and Damian, Saint George, Saint Barbara,
Saint Anthony—but they remain discreetly on the altar and take no active
part in the ceremonies. In addition to the *exús*, other African elements are
found, e.g. the two Angola deities Kanjira and Calunga (the sea goddess).
As in Rio, however, the chief feature of the ceremonies is the descent of
familiar spirits, the souls of old *caboclos* or dead Negroes.[41]

   Macumba also exists, in an even more eroded form, in the city of São
Paulo.[42] It is practically certain that it once existed there in the form of
organized cult groups practicing censing, sacrifices to Exú, and magic
drawings, and venerating the same mixture of saints and African or Indian
spirits. My informants were especially struck by the importance of outdoor
ceremonies held "in the forest," certain details of which recall the Bantu
cabula of Espírito Santo.[43] These religious groups, however, were harassed
by the police and were soon replaced by "low spiritism," which is protected by law. Nevertheless *macumba* has not totally disappeared; it
has simply changed from a collective form to an individual one, degenerat-
ing from religion into magic in the process. The lone, sinister *macumbeiro*,
feared as a formidable sorcerer, has today replaced the organized *macumba*. My study of these sects and individuals, based on police records,
newspaper files, interviews, and life histories, shows that here even more
than in Rio the whites have infiltrated this mystico-magic movement and
by their presence have removed it even farther from its African orgins. (It
is true that the ratio of black *macumbeiros* to the percentage of blacks in
the population as a whole is very high, but numerically there are more
whites than blacks.)[44] Moreover these whites are often foreigners. I recorded thirty-three cases of healers, *macumbeiros*, or *feiticeiros* of Portuguese, Spanish, Japanese, or other non-Brazilian nationality. The
syncretism already in progress is accelerated by the introduction into *macumba* of the magic elements these immigrants bring with them from their
own countries.

   While the Carioca *macumbas* are located for the most part on the
outskirts of the city, in São Paulo they are scattered all over it, although
they are of course strongest in the inner city, where the density of blacks is
highest and living standards are lowest. A particularly interesting feature,
which I was able to study from a notebook confiscated by the police that
contained the addresses of all those who had sought consultation, is the
wide dispersion of the clientele. Almost every section of São Paulo had
contributed to the support of the *macumbeiro* who had been arrested, and
the highest number of consultants came from the most distant neighborhoods, not the closest. The magical character of the sessions is obvious
both from the services requested and from the ritual used. Urbano Mendes
Falcano cured the sick, arranged or prevented marriages according to the

client's wish, obtained jobs for the unemployed, and revealed winning lottery numbers. The white *feiticeiro* Paulino Antonio de Oliveira found lovers, reconciled estranged spouses, stitched up hernias, and supplied remedies, for stomach and heart trouble and for toothaches. Paulista *macumba* is the great source of hope for people out of work, out of love, and out of money. This is not a science of magic but folk magic suited to the extremely low intellectual and economic level of the big-city masses. The materials it uses are those used for magic purposes all over the world, but they are enriched by procedures the immigrants have added to Indian, African, and Luso-Brazilian methods. A Syrian will use talismans, books of astrology, and Arabic prayers, a Frenchman the Star of David and cabalistic signs. The rituals, however, are very meager and rely chiefly on roots, herbs, and daggers. Confining ourselves to the African elements that have managed to survive in this jumble of objects and rites, we find— chiefly among blacks of course—the mystic trance inspired by Exú, master of magic; the *despacho* of Exú performed with half a black chicken stuffed with shreds of tobacco and kernels of corn and deposited on the doorstep of the enemy whose death one seeks; and the *pontos riscados*, or designs used in Carioca *macumba*, around which candles are burned and in the center of which flash powder is exploded to chase away evil emanations. And of course, as in Rio, these African elements are accompanied by "potent prayers" to the saints of the Catholic church and by magnetic passes borrowed from spiritism.

In brief, we find in São Paulo the same syncretism we found in Rio, with one fundamental difference: here the mystic trance is not the trance of an entire social group, occurring as part of a ceremony that comprises both cult and consultation, but the trance of one individual, the *macumbeiro*, who alone receives the spirit of an African or *caboclo* in the course of a private ceremony or magic consultation session. This individualization, whether it occurs in the city or the country, cannot fail to arouse the erotic or criminal instincts of those who yield to it.[45] We have come from one extreme to the opposite one. *Candomblé* was and still is a means of social control, an instrument of solidarity and communion. *Macumba* leads to social parasitism, to the shameless exploitation of the credulity of the lower classes, or to the unleashing of immoral tendencies that may range from rape to murder.

■ ■ ■

The reader will have realized that I am using the word "degeneration" in two different senses, speaking sometimes of cultural, sometimes of social, disorganization. The two phenomena are too closely linked to be separated in an account aimed only at concrete description. Now, however, it will be useful to differentiate them.

The African religious sects might be called cuttings of Africa rooted in foreign soil. Out of these preserved and transplanted mystic values a whole society was able to reconstitute itself. The images of the collective memory secreted a shell to protect themselves against external enemies as well as a medium in which they could take root and live. Cultural disorganization attacks this civilization on every level of social reality—bringing a loss of values and of the mystic representations and ceremonies that acted out and rehearsed its myths, the fading away of the images of the gods, animal sacrifices, initiation, and the priestly hierarchy, and a diminution of the sacred space in all its rich complexity. It is difficult to say whether gaps in the collective memory were responsible for this diminution of the space, the ceremonial life, and the hierarchy, or whether the structural impoverishment of the sect destroyed the web of collective memories. Probably this depended upon circumstances. In any case a general and progressive impoverishment of the African heritage constituted the first form of disorganization.

Social disorganization is a more general phenomenon that in certain historical or geographical circumstances affected not just the descendants of the Africans but all other racial strata of the Brazilian population. It consists in a weakening of interpersonal solidarity and of bonds of communion or community, and in the isolation of certain segments of society and of individuals within these segments. In the country and in the city there are nonintegrated groups—or, as I would prefer to say, nonintegrated people—who are not part of any framework. In moving from, say, the rural *candomblé* to the healer-magicians or from the *macumba* of Rio to that of São Paulo, we follow the line of this second form of disorganization. As Arthur Ramos perceived, "the Negro is no longer much concerned with all that, and his responsibility decreases as a result of various factors of a cultural and social order, which, by restricting his natural practices, have alienated them from their meaning and transformed them into sorcery or something of that sort—i.e. into practices in which whites and mixed-bloods now play the leading parts."[46]

What are the relationships between these two forms of disorganization? The question is very important for a theory of acculturation. We need to determine to what extent the disintegration of a civilization is merely the counterpart of better social and cultural integration or, alternatively, the effect of a disorganization of the community, a pathological weakening of social solidarity. Those who study civilizational clashes and interpenetrations often tend to see syncretism as an intermediate form of adaptation between cultural encystment and definitive assimilation, and hence as a normal, beneficial process.

First we should note that cultural encystment in the *candomblé*, the *tambor das minas*, the *xangôs*, and the *batuques* actually went hand in hand (to varying degrees) with excellent social integration. The principle of compartmentalization that kept religion separate from economic, political, and professional life enabled members of those religious sects to be good Brazilians and good Africans at the same time. Except during periods of persecution, there is no tension between mystic attitudes and feelings and national ones. This is by no means surprising. Coexistence without interpenetration is a common phenomenon not restricted to Afro-Brazilians. We white Westerners, living in multiple social groups, are continually switching from one role to another without realizing that the groups' underlying attitudes may be contradictory. In the same way *candomblé* members switch from one world of values to another according to the activities they are engaged in without any signs of strain. We might even say that the stronger their attachment to the *candomblé*, the more successful their integration into Brazilian society is likely to be. All the problems of modern society, problems that grow more numerous and complex as urbanization increases, find a solution or compensation in the religious sect, which gives humble people a sense of their own worth by associating them with the divine and offsets economic insecurity, urban isolation, and family disintegration by providing a cooperative center of communion and a nucleus of mutual assistance.

Conversely cultural integration can exist in situations of social disintegration. Here we must consider two cases, both of which are pertinent to our topic. When two heterogeneous civilizations come into contact—the Anglo-Saxon and the Indian, for example—this may entail the destruction of the native tribal society and the destructuring of interpersonal bonds without the old religious values necessarily being affected by the impact.[47] But quite apart from these civilizational clashes, all societies are subject to the weakening of bonds of solidarity. When Comte founded sociology, he based it on the differentiation of organic periods and periods of crisis, the latter being defined by "individualism" as against "social consensus." Durkheim later showed individualism to be the basis of another form of solidarity, the organic form, but made a point, in *The Division of Labor in Society*, of analyzing the pathological forms of this new solidarity. It is clear that homogeneity of beliefs and feelings and the sharing of values and cultural norms do not prevent certain segments of the population from being cut off from the collectivity as a whole. All societies have their rejects, cast out from the home where their fellow-men cluster around the communal hearth.

The disintegration of African religions may therefore represent either (1) a backlash from better cultural integration into the rest of society achieved through the rejection of particular values and the acceptance of new ones in the form of syncretisms, or (2) an effect of the pathological disintegration of national solidarity and a consequence of the community's rejection of all social failures.

Because of the archaic-modern dualism of Brazil, cultural syncretism, in the case of the rural peasants of more or less mixed blood or the subproletariat in the big modern cities, really represents assimilation with the rest of the population. As we have seen, it creates an indispensable corpus of common belief for the multiracial masses. But it also represents a crisis in a society evolving at breath-taking speed from a communal to a societal form, rejecting from this new Brazil anyone who cannot keep up. The greater the gap between the two Brazils, the more numerous the rejects. The economic and social insecurity of these abandoned masses, the degeneration of normal family life into mere concubinage, the decline from professional mobility to unemployment or vagabondage, from African polygamy (reinterpreted and hence institutionalized) into unrestrained prostitution or sexual parasitism—all these factors promote the metamorphosis of religion into magic, of a communal cult into the individualism of the *macumbeiros*. We should therefore speak of a social rather than a cultural marginalism, which affects the whites as much as blacks, the unsuccessful immigrant or the new arrival as much as the citizen. In this marginal population *macumba* finds its "masters" as well as its preferred clientele. It is therefore necessary to distinguish between cultural "mulattoism" and this social marginalism. Mulattoism represents the marriage of civilizations, miscegenation between cultures in contact, while marginalism represents a shouldering aside, a collapse of social solidarity.

Yet this social marginalism may be no more than a transitional phase resulting from the exaggerated speed at which the country is being transformed. With the proletarianization of the blacks, the assimilation of the immigrants, and a general rise in the standard of living of the masses, other phenomena appeared, phenomena of cultural and social reintegration. In this restructuring process, what remained of the African religions in the gigantic metropolitan cities was itself restructured, giving birth to Umbanda spiritism.

14
The Birth of a Religion

The first effect of urbanization was to destroy the blacks' sense of community. Its second was to initiate a reorganization of social bonds in the form of class solidarity. Industrialism offered blacks new opportunities of making a living and merging with the proletariat. Brazilian workers are protected by a law requiring that two-thirds of the labor force of every industrial employer be native citizens (regardless of color), but, since native-born children of immigrants count as native Brazilians, in practice the black is always relegated to subordinate or unskilled jobs. S. H. Lowrie's studies of the ethnic origins of the population of São Paulo show that on every level the original population has been superseded by descendants of immigrants or of mixed couples:

Type of Sample	Number in Sample	Percentage with Brazilian Father	Percentage with Brazilian Grandfathers
University students	501	71	60
Children interviewed in city parks	1,624	54	21
Children born in free hospital wards	600	73	48

But Brazilians of long-standing citizenship belong in the main to either the top or the bottom class, while the middle class consists largely of the children of immigrants.[1] And those in the lower class are for the most part people of color. Negroes and mulattoes constitute 1 percent of the upper class, 3 percent of the middle class, and 27 percent of the lower class.[2]

Although there is undeniably some vertical mobility among people of color, particularly among light mulattoes, the fact remains that only five out of every thousand physicians or lawyers are black, two out of every thousand merchants, ten out of every thousand white-collar workers, thirty out of every thousand civil servants. On the other hand, out of every thousand stevedores 997 are Negro; out of every thousand domestic servants, 999.[3] And in major cities such as São Paulo and Rio even domestic servants have to face foreign competition. Until comparatively recently classified newspaper advertisements would often state: "No colored need apply";[4] aristocratic households preferred white maids or Japanese housemen.[5]

This pressure or competition from the whites made it difficult for the black to raise his low standard of living, despite the labor laws and the opportunities offered by industrialization. As we have already seen, high rents resulting from the high price of land together with equally high interest rates forced the blacks to congregate in the marginal zones of the big cities, in the *mocambos, favelas*, or *corticos*. Government programs for providing workers' housing and low-rent apartments have not yet succeeded in correcting this situation, because the spreading cities absorb ever-growing masses of rural Brazilians who can find no place in which to live except these slums. We have seen how the family disintegrates in these marginal zones. Concubinage exists everywhere, but in traditional cities like Bahia or in the interior it becomes a genuine common-law marriage in which the father feels just as responsible for his wife and children as he would if he were legally married. In the sprawling metropolitan cities, however, concubinage takes the form of serial short-lived marriages. The many temptations of the big city make each successive illicit union briefer and increase the likelihood of one of the partners deserting the home.[6] Then, as effect reacts on cause, a consequence of the black's poverty becomes an obstacle to his rise in society and chains him even more inescapably to his mediocre life. From this point of view concubinage represents passive submission to fate, while marriage—and religious marriage even more than civil—is already a revolt against it, the black's declaration of his wish to adopt white behavior.

Other statistics illustrate the miserable situation of the black race as compared to that of the white. In Rio infant mortality is 228 per thousand for mulattoes and Negroes, 123 for whites. In São Paulo the ratio is 257 per thousand as against 118. For the country as a whole the death rate for blacks is 28–29 per thousand as against only 23–24 for whites.[7] In this respect the big cities are particularly deadly:

Blacks and Mulattoes (São Paulo)

Year	Births	Deaths	Deficit
1934	14,017	17,189	3,176
1939	19,122	20,686	1,564[8]

Even the statistics for mental illness eloquently reflect this state of affairs. While there is more psychosis among whites, the blacks have a higher incidence of reactions to toxic and noxious substances and of alcoholism and syphilis—symptoms of escapism from harsh reality into the twofold artificial paradise of drunkenness and eroticism.[9] An analysis of family budgets offers further evidence of such escapism. The black's spending does not follow the same pattern as the white's and diverges noticeably from the pattern of the white immigrant. The latter allots most of his income to food and housing, while the black spends it on clothes and miscellaneous expenses. When, half-starved, he escapes briefly from his slum, clothes make him feel more equal to the richer whites on the city streets. And to him miscellaneous expenses mean not the education of his children, not insurance or health care, but tobacco, liquor, the big Negro dances, and carnival paraphernalia, on which he often spends everything he has saved in a year.

But things are changing. The black is no longer as resigned to his lot as he once was. And the more education he has had, the less willing he is to accept it. We might even say that the spread of education marks the dividing line between the old and the new generations. While illiteracy is still one of Brazil's problems, the difference between the "old" and the "new" Negro is obvious when we compare the literacy rate of 9.29% for elderly Negroes with the 28.5% for young ones.[10] These figures apply to the country as a whole, but school attendance is higher in the cities and black literacy increases as we move from the rural zones to the traditional towns and on to the great metropolitan cities (although here too it remains lower than that of whites). In Rio the literacy rate is 53.64 percent for blacks, 75.07 percent for mulattoes.[11] Of course people of color rarely go beyond primary school, but, even so, education has a double effect. On the one hand it arouses new attitudes and feelings and integrates them with the rest of the population. On the other hand, it brings home to them their pitiful situation at the bottom of the social ladder and makes them more aware of racial discrimination and of the discrepancy between their theoretical upward mobility and their low, semiproletarian status.

It is undeniable that the only reason the educated man of color can see for his low standard of living and his inferior position is the existence of an annihilating prejudice. Dreams that I have collected from various black servants reveal nothing but elemental desires, but the life stories I have collected from mulattoes show that every man of color has at one time or another come up against a preconception or been handicapped in relationships with whites by a pathological shyness. This has given rise to a psychology of resentment, which may lead to revolt either against others or against oneself. This resentment then expresses itself in political rationalizations and, in the cities, in religious manifestations.

The first place to look for evidence of Negro ideologies is in the press and in the establishment of racial interest groups.[12] Here three very different periods can be distinguished. During the first, the black journalist wrote for white newspapers, or if, like Patrocinio, he was himself managing editor of a newspaper, he opened it to whites. This was the period of communion. The struggle followed the line of political party, not color. But the Negroes finally realized that, after using their votes to get elected, the politicans were betraying them. This led to the second period, the period of encystment or the formation of groups for the defense of people of color. The process was gradual and almost reluctant. The first Negro newspapers were more literary than political, more interested in social events than in protest. They belonged to the small-town, provincial type of paper that concentrates on anniversaries, weddings, and obituaries and publishes the announcements of black dance groups and athletic clubs, draft notices, and an odd poem or two. But gradually these papers were transformed into militant organs. By 1920 it was obvious that by propagating ideas of liberty and fraternity the First World War had aroused aspirations in the colored class and that these people were no longer willing to remain at the bottom of the social ladder. The Black Front, with its symbols and paramilitary troops, was founded in São Paulo in imitation of Fascist or Nazi models and quickly established local units throughout the country. It acquired a polemical journal called *The Voice of the Race*. When Getulio Vargas came to power and suppressed the political parties, both the Black Front and its journal disappeared. The third and final period began with Brazil's return to democratic liberty at the end of World War II. The blacks reestablished their class organizations, convened regional or national congresses to discuss their own problems, and founded new newspapers. The democratic element of communion was clearly gaining the upper hand over the militant element.

The reason for this is that in a racial democracy the black is split. Split between rebellion against the white, who tends to reject him, and rebellion against himself, which intensifies his feeling of inferiority. Split between African militancy and the desire to be assimilated, through miscegenation, into the great white mass. In the United States the mulattoes belong with the Negroes. In Brazil the mulatto escapes from the colored caste and turns against the blacks. It is he, not the white, who holds the deepest prejudices against his darkest brothers.[13] This split expresses itself in an ambivalent ideology that I shall now try to define. It reflects the new urban conditions and in a contradictory way combines the promise of upward mobility for the black with his encystment in the most squalid neighborhoods. Just when democracy and industrialization open prospects of liberation, competition from the immigrant pushes the man of color down a little farther.

This ambivalence, the blacks' simultaneous desire to remain separate from and to identify with the whites, is reflected in the advertisements for

products for straightening kinky hair[14] that appear in black newspapers
next to articles attacking such products as a rejection of "the race."[15]
These papers reject traditional folklore as barbaric, preferring to organize
tennis clubs or aristocratic recreation of that kind,[16] yet they also advo-
cate giving children black dolls instead of blond, blue-eyed ones for
Christmas or New Year's.[17] On the one hand they attack the policy of
whitening the race on the grounds that it involves the abandonment of
people of color.[18] This line of protest leads to violent xenophobia,[19] and
even to the demand that Negroes marry only within their race. They warn
against the blandishments of the whites, who are interested only in ruining
colored girls, not in raising them to their own level.[20] On the other hand
they point out that Brazil's uniqueness stems from the amalgamation of
the three ethnic groups—the Indian, the African, and the European—and
this leads them into a defense of "mulattoism" based largely on the arguments of Gilberto Freyre. But it is interesting to note that a subtle trick of
the unconscious twists this "mulattoism" into a means of resisting the
Aryanization of the country. It is claimed that one can be a true Brazilian
only if one has Negro blood in one's veins. Here again patriotism leads to
hatred of the foreigner, and the ambivalence is perpetuated.[21]

But black newspapers and organizations have another function besides
protest, the function of what we may call "valorization," of heightening
the Negro's sense of his own value, thus helping him to get rid of the
inferiority complex that handicaps him in competitive life.[22] Innumerable
comic strips, highly colored, naïve, and standardized, depict the glorious
deeds of heroes or saints of color in newspaper after newspaper, year after
year. Thus an Afro-Brazilian time frame is created that is marked off by its
own commemorative landmarks—a Negro historical time incorporated
into Brazilian historical time but nevertheless possessing its own tem-
porality, something like a current flowing within a wider river yet never
merging with its waters. This is not merely a chronological time frame but
also an affective one, full of memories of past suffering, bright interludes
of hope, flashes of anger and of admiration—the exploits of a race. For
this reason these biographies or fragments of history are not much concerned with objective truth. They are nascent legends or myths, for only
legend has dynamic action value. The aim is always to bolster the Negro's
confidence by reminding him of a glorious past, to point up the lesson that
the black is capable of "evolving" to the level of the white. Nevertheless
the ambivalence persists because this valorization does not extend to
Africa. That barbaric continent of savages is best forgotten. These newspapers seem almost afraid to recall the origins of the black race. When
they do look beyond Brazil, it is not to Dahomey but to great North
American Negroes like Langston Hughes or to European ones like René
Maran. Instead of trying to bring out the uniqueness of a civilization, this

upgrading of the black image seeks to prove that the black can be totally assimilated into white civilization.

Moreover this past record of assimilation promises a better future. Valorization cannot rely entirely on reminders of the lives of great Negro figures; it is demonstrated in action. This leads the colored press into Puritanism. The Negro is relegated to the bottom of society by his image as a lazy, sensual drunkard or thief. He can rise only through education and respectability. Therefore the press condemns alcoholism and licentiousness,[23] and the Negro organizations promote literacy programs, educational conferences, and Negro theater. This Puritanism even prescribes the proper way to dress, blow one's nose, behave in society and at table, etc.,[24] because what counts in the racial struggle is not so much internal values as external ones—keeping up appearances.[25]

Yet here again the Negro is torn by conflicting feelings. If he relies on appearances alone, one factor will always be decisive: his blackness. So we must reverse our approach and start from the inside rather than the outside. If we take this course, we shall find ourselves, at the end of this ideology, which has so far been political or social rather than religious, back in the domain of the mystic. There is a tendency to assume blackness of soul from blackness of skin, but the soul has no color. The qualities of intelligence and the virtues of the heart are the same in all men. It is not the cowl that makes the monk; neither does the Nessus shirt of skin color make the man. Thus Puritanism leads to an affective idealism, an attempt to escape from epidermal distinctions into that which unifies, equalizes, and identifies: the luminosity of pure spirits.[26] And here again the blacks have the advantage over the whites because spiritualization is produced primarily by suffering, especially unjust suffering. The slave was tortured, beaten, and cursed, like Jesus Christ. His earthly existence was a second Passion, a second crucifixion. Yet he does not answer wrong with wrong. On the contrary it is he who, in the sweat of his brow, has created all the wealth of Brazil, the fortunes of his masters, the greatness of his new homeland. A new myth emerges—the messianic myth of world salvation through the blacks, the mysterious alchemy that creates goodness out of injustice. Other foreigners came to South America to make their fortune; the African came only to create happiness out of his own martyrdom. His miserable lot, which formerly called for revolt and escape, is now seen as a glorification of the oppressed, redeeming race.

Of course this is just one theme among many, but it is symptomatic of a new climate that will be most apparent in another setting—within religious groups. While changes in social structure bring changes in attitudes and the overthrow of values in all urbanized zones, these changes and upheavals may take different forms. In São Paulo they are chiefly political, in Recife and Rio more strictly mystical. But, as we shall see, the mystic forms

express exactly the same ambivalences and resentments. Before studying
these forms within the religious sects, we need to isolate them in their pure
state, as revealed in the colored press. Having done this, we are in a better
position to understand the pantheism of the Pernambuco blacks and Umbanda spiritism.

■ ■ ■

The pantheistic sect of Pernambuco did not have a very long life. It was
founded about 1935 and was officially registered as a cult in 1937. In
1938 it, along with all the other African sects, was prohibited by the very
Catholic governor of the state. Unlike the xangôs of Recife, which continued a clandestine existence, this pantheism totally disappeared. Nonetheless it is worth studying as an expression of the new religious tendencies
referred to above.

Gilberto Freyre was the first to mention this sect, which he took to be a
Mohammedan survival because of its worship of Venus, the morning star,
and because its adherents dressed entirely in white.[27] But those who have
studied it most extensively, including Pierre Cavalcanti and Gonçalves
Fernandes, have been physicians, and their interpretation is marred by an
excessively narrow psychiatric viewpoint.[28] I would not attempt to deny
the existence of pathological phenomena in this religion (glossolalia during
trance, for instance), and the linguistic poverty of the songs is an obvious
sign of a corresponding poverty of thought. But neither would I go so far
as to speak of a schizoid mentality on the grounds that the decoration and
architecture of the pantheist temple recalls the surrealism of André Breton.
On the contrary it represents an effort, however clumsy, to break away
from African "barbarity," a striving for a new kind of beauty. We should
not forget that the founder of this sect, José Amaro Feliciano, was a
schoolteacher and wanted to use all his learning for the benefit of the new
religion. All that can be held against him is the fervor of the neophyte
carried away by his newly acquired knowledge and expressing it before
having digested it.

We should also remember that the pantheistic cult of nature developed
in an area of xangôs and catimbós, of healers and practitioners of black
magic, where many spiritist sects also flourished. Around 1913 the town of
Beberibe was made famous by a white healer, Bento the Miracle-Worker,
who with the aid of a fluidic water restored the sick to health, cast out
demons, and found husbands for old maids.[29] Now, Feliciano's cult also
set great store by healing waters, whose miraculous virtue it attributed to
planetary irradiation. It is undeniable that the sect was influenced by the
religious milieu in which it was born and by the xangôs and local healers.
But influence does not necessarily mean mere continuation. In my opinion
Feliciano's movement represented a reaction rather than a tradition. He
was forced to break with everything around him because his aim was to

give the Africans a religion better adapted to their new needs. To parody the words of Jesus, he came not to abolish the *xangôs* but to fulfill them by spiritualizing them, by freeing them from the crude fetishism that makes them ridiculous in the eyes of educated people and by extracting their essential marrow, the worship of the forces of nature, purged, as far as possible, of all anthropomorphism and mythology.

Thus astrology—i.e. the theory of the irradiation of the miraculous water by the planets—provides a means of explaining medicinal magic if not rationally, at any rate in a way that reason can accept. Freemasonry, whose influence is apparent on the organizational level in the separation of the leaders of the sect from the devotees, tried to turn the new religion into a sect of universally recognized value. Spiritism became the language into which the phenomena of mystic trance were translated, and this language, accepted by scholars and studied by parapsychology, reassured the African that his experience was no longer that of a primitive barbarian but had a human and not merely racial value. On the eve of public ceremonies this sect used to build sphinxes out of sand that were supposed to be incarnations of "inhabitants" of the forest, the waters, or the planets. This practice reflected a desire to identify the African civilization with that of Egypt, reputedly the earliest and one of the most beautiful civilizations that ever existed.

This evolution of the mythology was accompanied by an evolution of morality in the direction of Puritanism to counter the image of the lubricous, lazy, drunken, or thieving Negro that, as we have seen, is one of the stereotypes through which the whites perceive the blacks. This explains the prohibition of alcohol, smoking, and coveting one's neighbor's wife, as well as the spirit of humanity and fraternity that constituted the ethical basis of the sect and was demonstrated in mutual aid and cooperation in work and in adversity. It also explains the strict discipline and the control maintained over the behavior of the members of the pantheistic sect through fixed bylaws.[30] This puritanical morality also led to the founding of a journal entitled *The Paladin of Good*, which was dedicated to promoting the triumph of "Harmony, Love, Justice, and Truth throughout the entire Universe." What the sect was trying to do was to create in the eyes of the whites a new, more authentic image of the black as a laborer in the service of the good. But it also wanted this new image to be associated not with the Christianization or Westernization of the Negro but with his greater faithfulness to the genuine Africa. The old symbols had to be transmuted. Fraternity is nothing but a reinterpretation of the collective work of primitive Negroes, virtue a spiritualization of their old taboos. The idea was to move forward from traditional customs but by sublimating them.

Basically *xangô* was a cult of the forces of nature. Its gods were hypostases of the sea, lightning, or tempestuous winds distorted by "fetishism." In theory pantheism was supposed to be a deification of nature identified with divine unity, but the sect went only halfway and remained bogged down in dynamic pluralism. One lost oneself in the forest, plunged naked into rivers, exposed oneself to the nocturnal influences emanating from the stars or the moon. The astrology of astral irradiation improved on African fetishism, perfecting it and making it "scientific." Feliciano derived complete pedagogical and medical systems from this astrology. Living a simple life close to nature, practicing vegetarianism and abstaining from alcohol, tobacco, and sexual excess, would produce a gradual improvement in racial health. Children were to be brought up in contact with the forces of nature, in harmony with the cosmic rhythm, beyond all the injurious influences of an artificial civilization. Thus the aims of the pantheistic movement represented a significant effort to find in the African heritage a counterbalance to the mechanistic civilization that capitalism was establishing in Recife and in the sugar factories, a civilization that brought in its wake the proletarianization of the people of color.

Admittedly this movement represented a departure rather than a series of doctrinal realizations. Polytheism crept in again by way of spiritism and mystic trance. Nature—its waters and rocks, its waterfalls and forests— was peopled by all kinds of "inhabitants"; even the heavenly bodies were inhabited. Like all the African sects, the cult consisted in producing a state of trance, of possession by one of these planetary "inhabitants." During the state of possession songs were dictated that were later interpreted by "definers" who were supposed to abstract a philosophy from them. The mythology of irradiation was merely superimposed on possession by spirits; it did not replace it. Magic also was involved, since the worshipers "incarnated" the spirits in little sand sphinxes made for every session. We are not far removed from the fetish in which a god resides. But the fetish was, so to speak, "civilized" when it relinquished the form of a thunderbolt or a stone polished by the sea and assumed a form that symbolizes one of the oldest and greatest of civilizations in the world. In any case this minor regression was of little importance. The essential thing was the feeling behind the not entirely successful effort, the revelation of a new mentality seeking an outlet, the glorification of a refashioned Africa. Maybe pantheism did not destroy polytheism; maybe it did not entirely transcend anthropomorphism. No one could expect Feliciano to be an African Louis Menard or another Renouvier. At least he tried to present the religion of his forefathers in a form more acceptable to civilized people by eliminating the excessively bloody sacrificial rituals and the mythology of gods prone to all-too-human adventures and by bringing in astrology and Egyptian mythology.

In my opinion this new religion was the first sign of the change that had overtaken the lower classes of society as a result of better schools, compulsory education, the mixing of races in factories, and the new needs inspired by transformations of the social structure. But the desire to remain true to Africa is more than just an underlying idea. It reflects something real, an awareness of difference derived from first-hand experience, a conflict in the world of values. There is one point in Feliciano's preaching that has been neglected by observers but that to me seems of capital importance, bearing in mind the profound influence of Catholicism in Brazil. This is his diatribe against Christ: "Optimism is the very crux of the life of our devotees. Christ, they say, came to this earth and at the end of His life He failed. If He was the son of God, why did He suffer so much? Suffering is wrong."[31]

Whereas the *xangô* sects equate the *orixás* with the saints and spiritism submits to the guidance of Jesus, in pantheism we see the black becoming aware of his fundamental antipathy—in a country saturated with Christianity—to the Catholic religion and its dogmas of original sin, grace, and redemption through suffering. The religion of the South American black is a religion of joy. Asceticism, if it exists, does not take the form of monastic asceticism but of a magic ritual that will open one to the divine. The link between nature and the supernatural has not been destroyed by man's misuse of liberty, which only suffering can expiate; it is automatically realized in rapturous ecstasy when the music and dancing call the gods down to earth. Suffering certainly exists, but it is an evil, not an instrument of good. By suffering, Christ showed that He was not a god and lacked the essential attribute of godhead: might, power, *mana*. Similarly, and for the same reason, Feliciano, while making use of spiritism, refused to accept its Christian tinge and Christian dogmatism. Spiritists regard this world as a vale of tears, a place of suffering and expiation. The dual law of karma and metempsychosis transforms living men into imperfect spirits of light who must suffer if they wish to regain the astral plane after death. Nothing is more foreign to the African mentality.[32] Feliciano's laughter is an echo of the Greek laughter that greeted Saint Paul's sermon on the dying god. If that comparison seems far-fetched, at least it reveals, beneath the attempt to upgrade the religion of nature by translating it into Western terms, a still-vital African mentality that, although eager to advance, insists on remaining authentically African.

■ ■ ■

Spiritism was introduced into Brazil about 1863 and was immediately successful.[33] At the present time [1960] the country has about 465,000 spiritists, and while the number may seem relatively small in relation to the total population of fifty-two million,[34] we must remember first that these are all practicing spiritists (whereas the Catholic group includes nonpracticing members) and second that spiritism is a purely urban phenomenon.[35]

In estimating the depth of the spiritist faith and its effective range, comparison with other religious denominations should therefore be restricted to urban frameworks.

This last sentence already shows the significant effect of structural factors on the world of religious values. Spiritism meets certain needs of the big-city proletariat and disinherited classes. Even the more traditional small towns in the interior of Brazil, which cling firmly to the past and have changed but little since the days of the empire, confront it with their Catholic, patriarchal conservatism. The regular attendance of spiritist séances is made up of misfits, uprooted people lost in the crowd— domestic servants, rural artisans who have forsaken the country for the great human agglomerations, low-grade white-collar workers, minor police officials, etc. Moreover, as it evolves, spiritism adapts itself to social categories and takes on different complexions.[36]

One type of spiritism is that of the intellectuals, doctors, engineers, civil servants, and even members of the teaching profession—the type that claims to be scientific. Yet behind their experimentation with parapsychology one senses a predilection for the mysterious, the restlessness of a soul in search of a religion. Saint Thomas wanting to reach out and touch the miracle. A second, more widespread type preaches the modern-day gospel of Allan Kardec. Although it is open to everyone, most of its adherents are lower-class whites. Unlike European spiritists, they are not looking for a way to communicate with their departed loved ones; this is not a reaction to death. These simple people have never examined the idea of immortality critically enough to require proof in the form of communication with the dead. For them spiritism is an answer to the desire for salvation, both physical and spiritual. To the struggle against illness and poverty. Against bodily infirmities, which can be cured with the help of fluidic waters, by prescriptions dictated by spirits acting through mediums (who are often paid by pharmaceutical companies for pushing their products), or even by surgery performed by spirits—though in spiritual operations involving no letting of blood. Against the troubles of the world: separated couples, abandoned children, permanent unemployment—all of which are caused by past wrongdoing that has to be expiated but that can also be dispelled by magic passes to drive away the evil spirits responsible for them. The spiritist knows, moreover, that this world of suffering is a transitory one and that his soul will find happiness again in the astral realm. In brief, spiritism has been transformed by the Brazilian environment, which still puts more faith in the healer than in the doctor and does not divorce the supernatural from nature.

Spiritism in turn affected this environment by preaching a morality of fraternity and love. (According to the law of karma, happiness on the astral plane depends on one's actions in this world.) Through its federation it has created schools, day care centers, dental clinics, and hospitals to relieve some of the deficiencies of proletarian life in the big city. Spiritism's triple sociological function—the fight against disease, the fight against spiritual poverty, and the inculcation of morality—is illustrated by its three different types of meetings, usually held on Mondays, Wednesdays, and Fridays. There are meetings for the consultation of spirits, special meetings for spirits in distress, and meetings for the training of mediums. All meetings include prayer, reading of the gospel according to Allan Kardec, and moral homilies during which the spirits of the dead are incarnated in the medium. Here city people without status, who have lost their place in Brazil's old patriarchal structure and not yet found, in a trade union or a political party, an organization to provide them with a measure of security, seek a new cosmic or mythic framework to sustain them. They find a place in a hierarchy of spirits that extends from the earth to the planets, where there is one law for all in a supernatural society hierarchized according to merit or virtue. They escape from human loneliness in a mystic association with this new supernatural society.

Spiritism is further modified as it passes from the white to the colored lower classes. Now the spirits that incarnate themselves are those of Indians or Negroes—as though racial segregation persisted in the beyond and as though communication between the natural and the supernatural worlds could be established only by following the color line. Of course spiritism retains its medical aspect here too, strengthened by the fact that the tradition of the healer and of curative magic and the attribution of illness to the mystic action of sorcerers or to the vengeance of the dead are still basic principles of the primitive mentality. One change, however, is already evident. The leader of the session, the one who speaks with the mediums, questions the spirits, drives them away or gives them orders, becomes a thaumaturge. In the new sect he occupies the place held by the *pagé* or medicine man in Amerindian society or on the continent of Africa. The disembodied spirits are no longer in control; the magician becomes the master of the spirits.

A second important change is the transition from spiritism in the strict sense to animism. The Bantu (the predominant ethnic group in southern Brazil) worshiped the dead; they believed in the reincarnation of their ancestors. The Indians in turn peopled nature with spirits. Spiritism gave this animism a kind of scientific justification. The fact that white people were spiritists clearly proved that animism was not a barbaric religion or an indication of a retarded mentality. Now the man of color felt justified in following the line of his old civilization. For him spiritism became an extension of the religion of primitive man, which is primarily a passionate quest for trance or ecstasy—a new way of establishing communication with the invisible and receiving information or advice from it. The whites recognized this, which explains their use of the pejorative term "low spiritism" to designate this third and last level of spiritism in Brazil. For

Indian mestizos or descendants of slaves, however, it was already a step upward, an attempt to catch up with the whites and to show that the line of civilizational evolution extended to animism. This is the ultimate sociological function of spiritism: to reassure the man of color of his own value by showing him that he is not a "primitive, semicivilized" being beyond the pale of Western culture but that he thinks and feels exactly as the other members of the Brazilian community do.[37]

As it evolved, this low spiritism obviously did not remain confined to the colored class. Whites infiltrated it and in many instances became its leaders. Nevertheless the vast majority of its adherents are blacks or mulattoes for the simple reason that by and large the class stratification corresponds almost exactly to the color stratification.

Low spiritism recognizes two different "lines" (as the streams emanating from the dead are called)—the Indian and the African. Sometimes separate séances are devoted to the descent of the Indian and the black spirits; sometimes they incarnate themselves during the same one, though never simultaneously. The ritual divides the mediumistic manifestations into two parts; the African spirits are usually summoned after the *caboclos* have departed.

The myth of the wild Indian was created by poets and romantic novelists after Brazil attained independence. It was a literary creation, stemming from Chateaubriand and Fenimore Cooper, and in Brazil it inspired the work of José Alencar and Gonçalves Dias. But during the romantic era the gulf that now separates the general public from literature did not yet exist. It was not the intellectuals alone who glorified the "native Brazilian"; their approbation was shared by the whole Brazilian community. Light mulattoes passed themselves off as descendants of native Indians; some of them even dropped their Christian names in favor of Indian ones. A drop of Amerindian blood in one's veins was something to be proud of, a drop of Negro blood something to be ashamed of, on the grounds that the African accepted slavery while the Indian preferred death to submission. Hence the myth of the free, brave warrior. Brazil's shaking off of the Portuguese yoke was interpreted as the native's revenge against the invader.[38] The schools perpetuated this myth, as did the wide dissemination of Alencar's novels in cheap popular editions, and it percolated from the literate to the illiterate population. Finally it surfaced in spiritism. The Indian spirits that descend to possess the mediums take their place in this system of collective representations. They are brash, violent, and bellicose. They shout and shake deadly arrows. They preach liberty. They are no longer cannibals on the lowest level of material civilization, as they were at the time of contact, but are defenders of Brazilian independence and bearers of a rich spiritual culture. Better still, they restore the self-esteem of descendants of slaves by not hesitating to descend into the bodies of blacks and mulattoes. Popular poetry generally pits the *caboclo* against the Negro. As Leonardo Motta says, "Any Indian mestizo singer competing against a Negro will always attack his Achilles heel: the Negro's feeling of inferiority."[39]

In these literary contests the black reacts with brutal insults, but his very brutality shows that he has been hurt. He knows that the public is not on his side. Spiritism allows him, by receiving a *caboclo* spirit, to rise mythically on the scale of values, to identify himself with a champion of liberty, to become the spokesman for bravery or Indian pride. Unconscious complexes are certainly at work, but they operate sociologically, within the struggle of the colored groups, through the acceptance of certain collective stereotypes. Unable to pass for Indian because of his color, the black succeeds in transforming himself into one through spiritist valorization.

To defend itself and to justify slavery, white society created two types of Negro, the "good Negro" (Pai João) and the "bad Negro." This was not a peculiarly Brazilian reaction but one common to all slave societies. Analogous images are found in the United States.[40] The North American Negro in his resentment accepts this image of the murderous "bad Negro" who rapes white women and is in a constant state of revolt against his class enemies, and he lives up to it.[41] The Brazilian Negro, on the other hand, having found a compensation in his ability to incarnate Indian spirits, accepts the image of the bad black together with all the stigmas the whites have attached to it and, as he is assimilated into the common mentality, turns against himself a myth that was originally directed against his color. Spiritism actually differentiates between two kinds of African spirits: bad blacks, who descend only to do evil, to bring to earth nothing but illness, misfortune, and discord, and whom the head medium is supposed to dismiss after a little homily to improve their attitude; and good Negroes, who descend only to lend a hand to suffering humanity.

This "bad Negro" is nothing other than the image of the runaway slave, the criminal, while the "good Negro," typified by Pai João, is the submissive, conformist slave who does not protest but, as they say in the United States, "knows his place," like a domestic animal. Pai João is the gray-haired old African who tells stories of "the times when the animals could talk," who entertains his master's children with plaintive old songs, who may take a beating but returns good for evil—devout, always ready to make the greatest sacrifices. He is the Uncle Remus of Brazil. His feminine counterpart is Mãe Maria, who shared her milk with the little white boy and is more attached to her foster son than to her own child. The two pillars of a resigned race. The more closely the black modeled himself on this preconceived image, the more surely he could count on his master's condescending affection. The myth served to make slavery less bitter and the African more submissive. It is curious to find the people of color today accepting this stereotype of their own accord instead of revolting against it. Let us see what Leal de Souza has to say about the old Negroes Pai Domingo, Pai Miguel, Mãe Congola, and Mãe Maria d'Aruanda, and how the image that spiritism gives them even mitigates the arrogance of the Indian.

The authentic *caboclo*, emerging from the forest after an apprenticeship in space and appearing in the tent,* shows the intolerant zeal of the newly converted Christian. He is as intransigent as a monk, scolds us for our faults, and even criticizes our attitudes. When he hears the laments of those suffering under the bitterness of life, he gets angry and tells them that spiritism is not meant to help people in their material life, and he attributes our suffering to mistakes and faults that have to be paid for. But after two or three years of contact with the terrible hardships of our existence, his intransigence is mitigated and finally he comes to the help of his incarnated brother. But the black, who has groaned under the overseer's whip on the plantation, cannot see other people's tears without crying himself and, even before being asked, removes the obstacles from our path. The African is a little different from the Bahian Negro. The former in his goodness helps anyone he can, though he sometimes becomes irritated with the vain and the ungrateful. But the Bahian Negro is full of compassion for them too.[42]

Nevertheless color prejudice did creep into Brazilian spiritism. As I indicated earlier, mediums working with the Indian or African lines are disparagingly called "low spiritists." We must look more closely into this. The color line, subtle as it may be, certainly exists in Brazil to the extent that the Negro is encysted in his color or his culture, at any rate so long as he has not been "whitened" or lost in the mass. The spiritism of Allan Kardec is willing to take mulattoes or Negroes to its bosom provided they receive spirits of whites. To quote Lourenço Braga, champion of the cause of colored spiritism: "The Umbandists are unjustly attacked by the Kardecites. The Kardecites believe that the Umbandists are mistaken in accepting the spirits of *caboclos*, Indians, etc., as guides and protectors, alleging that these spirits are inferior or backward and not worthy to be guides of centers or tents or protectors of mediums."[43]

Other stereotypes also are involved in this summary condemnation: the drunken Negro, the thieving Negress, the colored prostitute, the coarse, ignorant, lazy, or lying black man. How, then, can they accept the idea that after death such people can become spirits of light, capable of lighting on their way not only their ethnic brothers—which might perhaps be understandable—but even whites?

The barriers that cannot be erected in earthly society because democratic laws prohibit them are transposed to the society of the spirits. The question whether Negroes have souls used to be open to discussion. Spiritism uses the law of metempsychosis to represent the man of color as a being in whom bygone wrongs are expiated—a spiritual regression, a descent into animality. It is willing to accept blacks in subordinate positions but would not tolerate one as a general or an ambassador, much less

---

* [The spiritist cult center (and more specifically the sanctuary) is called a "tent."]

as general of the disembodied spirits or as ambassador of the beyond. Inevitably the Negro reacts to this. Umbanda spiritism is the expression of his reaction. According to Captain José Pessoa, the decision to found Umbanda was taken and implemented at Niterói in the state of Rio "over thirty years ago" in a *macumba* he was visiting for the first time. Up to that time Pessoa had been a Kardecite spiritist. The *pãe de santo* invested him with the office of president of the Tent of Saint Jerome, which was to function in the capital, and told him that Umbanda was to be organized as a religion.[44]

The success that greeted this new sect, first in Rio, then in the states of Minas and Rio Grande do Sul and in São Paulo and Recife, proves that it answered the needs of the new mentality of the more highly developed black, socially on the rise, who realized that *macumba* lowered him in the eyes of the whites but who was nevertheless reluctant to abandon his African tradition altogether. Umbanda represents an upgrading of *macumba* through spiritism.[45] When whites began to join it, bringing with them half-digested smatterings of the writings of philosophers, theosophists, and occultists, this naturally contributed to the upgrading. At least it contributed to it to some extent—up to the point where the upgrading became rejection and the African origin of Umbanda was forgotten. For there was a Negro upgrading and a white upgrading and as we shall see the two intersected because of the two separate groups of adherents: the colored and the ones of European stock. So here too the racial struggle was continued, though certainly in a more subtle, less obvious manner.

It is just as difficult to describe the early stages of Umbanda as it is to trace them historically because we are dealing with a religion that is still taking shape, that has not yet crystallized or become organized and is proliferating in an infinite number of subsects, each having its own ritual and mythology. Some of these are closer to *macumba* in assigning a more important role to African dancing and musical instruments, others are closer to spiritism, while still others veer toward magic or astrology. In an attempt to remedy this anarchy of forms and beliefs, which threatened to impede the spread of this new church, a congress was convened in Rio in 1941 to standardize its ritual and systematize its dogmas.[46] Even so, its heterogeneity still precludes a clear, precise summary of Umbanda. The individualism of the tent leaders is stronger than the spirit of the federation, and when one reads the early reports of Leal de Souza or João de Freitas one realizes that standardization still has a long way to go.[47] The very success of this new religion has led inadequately trained mediums or exploiters of mass credulity to found new tents by mixing elements of *macumba* and spiritist dogma, with no attempt to harmonize the two.[48] At the time of writing the Brazilian capital and the state of Rio alone have thirty thousand tents, and the head of each tent draws his inspiration from the revelations of his own mediums![49] The original federation was swamped. In 1950 an attempt was made to revive it, but this one too seems ineffectual. The leaders of the movement blame either communism or the police,[50] but the real reason for the failure is that this is a nascent religion that has not yet found its forms. The confusion is so great that when some "federated tents" tried to remedy it by "codifying" the rules, these federations (of which there are now four in Rio) fought one another. In order to establish a minimum of order and coherence, it was even proposed that an Umbanda pope be nominated![51] I shall therefore refrain from trying to introduce nonexistent order into this parturient chaos, even though my exposé may as a result seem somewhat confused. We shall have an Ariadne's thread to guide us through the labyrinth: the raising of the man of color's self-esteem in reaction against a society created by whites for whites.

To begin with, what does Umbanda mean to its own adherents? What mystic reality does this mysterious-sounding word designate? Its etymology is clear. *Umbanda* comes from the Bantu *Quimbanda* (root: *ymbanda*), the Angola name for the supreme head of the cult.[52] This being so, we might expect the man of color readily to accept the idea that the Umbanda religion had its origins in Africa—all the more so since the sect has overtones of nostalgia for the "lost continent." But this nostalgia runs up against linguistic ignorance. To quote Leal de Souza: "I don't know what *Umbanda* means. The *caboclo* of the Seven Crossroads calls acts of charity '*Umbanda*' and procedures for neutralizing or undoing the work of black magic '*Demande*.' "[53]

On the background of this linguistic ignorance the self-assertive imagination of the mulatto and later of the white Umbanda devotee would embroider the most remarkable variations. To counter the criticism of the Kardecites they wanted to establish the initiatory origin of the religion and link it with the oldest and highest civilizations. One way was to concentrate on the old Negroes and make Umbanda a continuation of the Lemurian religion, which predates that of India. "It should not be forgotten that African magic is the heritage bequeathed to the Negro race by the ancient Lemurian civilization, the highest that ever existed."[54]

It is true that between this early Lemuria and Umbanda there is a transition: the Africa of tom-toms and fetishes dripping with blood. The paradox that bronze-skinned slaves should have brought the highest of the initiatory mysteries to Brazil has to be explained. "Umbanda comes from Africa, there's no doubt about that, but from eastern Africa—i.e. from Egypt. . . . The African barbarity permeating the remaining vestiges of this great initiatory line of the past is attributable to the debasement that verbal traditions inevitably suffer, especially when they have to transcend space and time and traverse climates and ages poorly adapted to the grandeur and resplendency of their teachings."

Obviously valorization is turning into rejection, a condemnation of the barbarian peoples who misunderstood and destroyed the Egyptian religion and brought its distorted relics to Brazil—the dross of slavery, the scum of humanity.[55] It is true that a black reaction within Umbanda asserted that the Negro succeeded in preserving or reviving the initiatory secret within the secrecy of his priesthood. At the First Congress of Brazilian Spiritists the following thesis was approved in plenary session: "The initiatory religious ideal was launched on the African continent by the divine Kariru kings who had come from the lands of Lemuria, of which Africa was a part."[56]

The second way open to us, which also takes Lemuria as the starting point, leads to another rejection. Lemuria borders not only Egypt but also India, and Umbanda thus becomes an esoteric Hindu doctrine.

> Umbanda is not a combination of fetishes, sects, or beliefs originating among uncivilized peoples. It is—and this has been proved—one of the greatest streams of human thought, which existed on earth more than ten thousand years ago and whose roots are lost in the impenetrable depths of the most ancient philosophies.
>
> AUM—BANDHÂ (OM—BANDÁ)
> AUM (OM)
> BANDHÂ (BANDÁ)
> OMBANDA (UMBANDA)
>
> The word *Umbanda* is of Sanskrit origin, the oldest and most beautiful of all languages, the source-language, so to speak, of all others in the world. Its etymology goes back to *Aum-Bandhâ*, i.e. the limit within the limitless. The prefix *Aum* has a high metaphysical meaning. All masters of Orientalism consider it sacred because it is the emblem of the Trinity within Unity. *Bandhâ* signifies constant movement or the centripetal force emanating from the Creator that envelops the created being and leads him toward perfectibility.[57]
>
> But this is not the end of the confusion. Christianity also enters in, and some spiritists believe Umbanda to be the name of "an angel of the Eternal of the category of Saint Michael or Saint Raphael."[58]

The same aspiration lies behind all these contradictory explanations. Behind the nostalgic vision of the ancestral Africa is a determination to deny that Africa fathered Umbanda, a determination to reduce the slaves transported to Brazil to merely one link in an initiatory chain that leads back far beyond them—back to Egypt or India or to Jesus Christ. Yet at the same time the myth of Lemuria makes the primitive black the champion of the highest civilization, which, debased though it undoubtedly was by tropical heat, exterminatory wars waged by the whites, and cosmic catastrophes, never totally perished. In this play of mythological representations, amid all this etymological confusion, we can discern two ideologies merging or clashing: the ideology of the black who wants to upgrade his image as his position on the social scale improves, and that of the white who, even as a devotee of Umbanda, still harbors color prejudice in the depths of his unconscious. The sacred is always the meeting place of human interests and class attitudes; it always reflects urban structures.

But we are still in the domain of rationalization. In the domain of fact, as it appeared to the founders of Umbanda, the African religion looked like a crude mixture of elements, some of which—communication with spirits, for instance—could readily be accepted, while others such as animal sacrifices and orgiastic dancing were shocking to a civilized mind. Rio *macumba* therefore split into Umbanda spiritism, which retained only the civilized elements, and Quimbanda magic, which was associated with demonic powers. This split made it possible to upgrade the ancestral tradition by purging it of anything disgusting to modern-day man.

But the founders of Umbanda, who came from both Kardecism and *macumba*, had another task to perform: to unite the cult of nature gods with the descent of the spirits of the dead into the bodies of mediums. After the rupture with pure *macumba* came synthesis. And Allan Kardec himself provided part of the solution. One of his principles was that the spirits form in space groups or phalanxes of entities on a common moral or intellectual level that come together as a result of their affinities.[59] Was it not reasonable, then, to suppose that in addition to the professional groups posited by Kardec—the spirits of priests that descend chiefly into priestly mediums, the disembodied intellectuals who are particularly attraced to scholarly parapsychologists—there should also be ethnic phalanxes in which the dead are grouped according to their racial origin— phalanxes of *caboclos* or old Negroes? And was it not likely that these groups in interplanetary space should obey leaders who might well be the gods of the *candomblé*? These were the foundations on which both the dogma and the ritual of Umbanda were built.

Leal de Souza had already distinguished these seven lines in the earliest form of Umbanda spiritism:

1. Oxalá (Nosso Senhor do Bomfim)
2. Ogun (Saint George)
3. Euxoce[60] (Saint Sebastian)
4. Shangô (Saint Jerome)
5. Nhan-San[61] (Saint Barbara)
6. Yemanjá (Our Lady of Conception)
7. The Souls[62]

Today Umbanda is still divided into seven lines, but no longer exactly the same ones:

1. Oxalá	directed by	Jesus Christ
2. Yemanjá	directed by	The Virgin Mary
3. Orient	directed by	Saint John the Baptist
4. Oxóssi	directed by	Saint Sebastian

5. Shangô	directed by	Saint Jerome
6. Ogun	directed by	Saint George
7. African	directed by	Saint Cyprian

The first line consists of spirits of various nations, but principally of Negroes who were good Catholics during their earthly lives. The second protects sailors and women. The third comprises Asiatics and Europeans; the fourth and fifth *caboclos*. The spirit that presides over the sixth line is ambiguous, while the Africans are disembodied spirits from the peoples of Africa, still very close to the material world. Here again, in the very midst of the upgrading process, we find a survival of color prejudice.

Each of these lines is subdivided into phalanxes or legions:

Oxalá	Legion of Saint Anthony		Catholic saint
	Legion of Saints Cosmas and Damian		Catholic saint
	Legion of Saint Rita		Catholic saint
	Legion of Saint Catherine		Catholic saint
	Legion of Saint Expeditius		Catholic saint
	Legion of Saint Benedict		Catholic saint
	Legion of Saint Francis of Sales		Catholic saint
Yemanjá	Legion of the Sirens	Commander: Oxun	Yoruba god
	Legion of the Water Sprites	Nanamburucú	Yoruba god
	Legion of the Caboclos of the Sea	Indayá	Indian spirit
	Legion of the Caboclos of the Streams	Yára	Indian spirit
	Legion of the Sailors	Tarimá	Indian spirit
	Legion of the Calungas	Calunguinha	Bantu god
	Legion of the Guiding Star	Mary Magdalene	Catholic saint
Orient	Legion of the Hindus	Commander: Zartá	
	Legion of the Physicians	Joseph of Arimathea	
	Legion of the Arabs	Jymbaruê	
	Legion of the Japanese, Chinese, Mongols, Eskimos	Ory	
	Legion of the Egyptians, Aztecs, Incas	Inhoarairy	
	Legion of the Carib Indians	Itarayacy	
	Legion of the Gauls, Romans, and other Europeans	Marcus I	
Oxóssi	Legion of the Urubatão		All Indian spirits
	Legion of the Aragiboia		
	Legion of the Caboclo of the Seven Crossroads		
	Legion of the Redskins		
	Legion of the Tamôios		
	Legion of the Jurema Caboclos		
	Legion of the Guaranys		
Shangô	Legion of the Inhaca		
	Legion of the Caboclo of the Sun and the Moon		
	Legion of the Caboclo of the White Stone		
	Legion of the Caboclo of the Wind		
	Legion of the Caboclo of the Waterfalls		
	Legion of the Earthquake Caboclo		
	Legion of the Negroes		

Ogun	Ogun Seashore Ogun Yára Ogun Break-Forests Ogun Megê Ogun Naruê Ogun Malei (Mussulman) Ogun Nagô	
African Line	Legion of the People of the Coast Legion of the Congo Legion of Angola Legion of Benguela Legion of Mozambique Legion of Loanda Legion of Guinea	Commander: Father Cabinda King of the Congo Father Joseph Father Benguela Father Jerome Father Francis Zan-Guinea

Thus we wind up with an extraordinary syncretism of nations, African gods, Nagô like Ogun and Bantu like Calunga, Amerindian nature spirits such as the *yáras*, the mothers of the waters, and Catholic saints. Quimbanda, which is under the authority of Satan and represents the other, unaccepted side of *macumba*, also is divided into seven lines:

1. Line of the Souls	Umulum (Omolú)	People of the cemetery ghosts
2. Line of the Skeletons	John Skeleton	People of the cemetery ghosts
3. Nagô line	Gererê	People of the spirits that haunt crossroads
4. Mussulman line	Exú-King	People of the spirits that haunt crossroads
5. Mossoruby line	Kaminalôá	African savages (Zulu, Kaffir, etc.)
6. Line of *Quimbandeiro* Caboclos	Black Panther	American savages
7. Mixed line	Exú of the Countryside or Streams	Evil spirits of various races[63]

Here again collective representations reappear and creep into spiritism. We have seen how *macumba* establishes a reign of terror within the population—and by no means only within its illiterate segment. The *macumbeiro* has acquired the identity of a formidable, evil sorcerer. Umbanda, instead of pointing out that *macumba* is a religion, accepts this erroneous popular conception as a concrete fact. Thus Quimbanda, identified with *macumba*, becomes a kind of inverted spiritism, a black magic working through disembodied savages, ghosts, and skeletons under the direction of two of the most formidable Negro deities, Exú, god of the lost crossroads, and Omolú, god of smallpox.

Besides retaining essential elements of *macumba* and *candomblé*, Umbanda spiritism has kept another feature of the African religion: the system of mystic correspondences between colors, days, forces of nature, plants, and animals. But far from being regarded as survivals of a primitive mentality subject to the law of participation, these features too were upgraded and assessed with the occultist doctrines of Proclus and Paracelsus in mind. The works of modern apologists for Umbanda cite an extraordinary assortment of philosophers' names, ranging from Plato to Victor Cousin, who, as leader of the eclectic school, ranks as the patron of religious syncretism.[64]

Thus these correspondences lead away from a spiritism that believes in phalanxes of the dead commanded by African or Indian deities or by Catholic saints, leaders of the space legions, and bring us closer to occultism. Umbanda becomes the African form of white magic. "The African gods are merely personifications of the forces of nature." The existence of the *exús*, for example, is explained by the fact that man is the meeting ground and battlefield for two kinds of cosmic forces—negative ones leading to materiality (the *exú* side) and positive ones leading to spirituality (the *orixá* side). Similarly the bisexuality of Obatalá symbolizes the union of the active or masculine principle with the passive or feminine one.[65] To preserve spiritism in its strict sense amid this syncretism, the *caboclos* and old Negroes therefore had to become centers of irradiations, mediations between men and the astral forces. "What we call African magic is the effect of the work performed by the phalanxes of entities from the astral plane, which themselves belong to several different planes. These phalanxes combine forces to reduce and neutralize the negative discharges that are constantly bombarding the planet, projected or attracted by the wickedness or materiality of its inhabitants."[66]

Consequently the ritual, like the dogma, juxtaposes spiritism and occultism rather than merging them. First it invokes the descent of the astral fluids in response to songs addressed to the African gods, Exús, Oguns, Shangôs, and Oxóssis, and then it invokes the descent of the disembodied *caboclos* and old Negroes. Fortunately the merging of these *caboclos* and Africans with the forces of nature is much more pronounced in other sects. "The entities that descend are not spirits of the dead, have never been incarnated and never will be. They are spirits of nature, elemental beings (*orixás*). Such entities have always been immaterial on the physical plane; their greatest material density is confined to the astral plane."[67]

In the eyes of the Umbandists, Annie Besant upholds this new conception of the African religion since she affirmed that on the astral plane, besides spirits of the dead on their way toward the light, there exist spirits of nature, grouped in countless legions—salamanders, water sprites, gnomes, etc.—which are linked with the seven elements of matter and direct their force, constituting channels through which divine energy can be transmitted to earth to nourish its life. At the head of each of these divisions, says Annie Besant, is a higher being known as a *deva*, leader of a mighty army, a supreme intelligence who controls a province of nature administered by elementals of that specific class.[68] This definition makes it clear that Umbanda merely translates a Western idea into Brazilian terms of *caboclos* or Africans. The *devas* of India become *orixás* and, like the *orixás*, "precisely because they are spirits of nature, have more affinity or esteem for such humans (whether incarnate or disembodied) as have or have had most contact with virgin nature (forest, thicket, countryside, mountain, spring, stream, sea, air, rain, sun, moon)." It is therefore quite understandable that in order to communicate with the living they should make use of "disembodied Negroes or Indians (*caboclos*) who, during their earthly existence, took from the riches of the kingdoms of nature only that which was indispensable to them, in contrast to the civilized man, who ambitiously, greedily, and violently strips nature bare in his implacable destructiveness."[69]

This represents an attempt to introduce a little logic into the confusion between spiritism and *macumba*, a reaction of the modern mind to a concrete situation, to a syncretism born of the clash, in the great cities, of different religions that nevertheless were serving the same people and meeting the same needs and whose adherents showed a disconcerting religious mobility. The creation of Umbanda is a purely sociological process dictated by social causes alone and to be explained only by the contact of civilizations. But while the common man can accept the inner contradiction because he is not even aware of it, the thinking man wants to go further than the marginal man, divided against himself. Hence these rationalizations. Nonetheless they remain fragile or temporary rationalizations, for beneath the harmony of the system the myths are still in conflict. One of the two streams will come out on top, now spiritism, now African *macumba*, but *macumba* raised to the level of a sophisticated theogony. We may study some of the rationalizing philosophies that are fighting it out, but we cannot yet know which one will triumph and become the official dogma of unified Umbanda.

Let us look first at the philosophy that is farthest from Africa, that of the Morning Star sect.[70] Of course this sect too accepts the existence of *caboclos* and old Negroes; otherwise we should be beyond the range of Umbanda. The disembodied spirits are divided into (a) guides, who no longer come down to earth and are responsible only for the heavenly bodies, who are incarnations of the vital forces of nature, administrators of earthly or astral energies; (b) the spirits of light, who receive their orders from the guides and who act as guardian angels and medium-protectors; (c) *marumbos*, who disobey the guides because their affection for beings that are still living makes them unwilling to leave the earth; (d) the suffering spirits, who continue to cause illnesses, and the obsessive spirits, which incite to evil.

But in addition to the spirits there are also the forces of nature, emanations of divine energy, and these forces combine in lines with the spirits, which are then defined by their irradiations rather than their anthropomorphization. There are five of these lines:

1. The line of Exú, in which all the errors of man's negative side come together.
2. The line of the Souls, composed entirely of suffering spirits.
3. The Quimbanda line, which works with the terrestrial forces and with

the spirit of the moon and of Neptune. This is the domain of black magic, the spiritist name for *macumba*.

4. The Uruanda line, which represents the transition to Umbanda and which assembles the spirits that have left the Quimbanda line and sets them on their way toward the light.

5. The Umbanda line, which works only with the forces of nature—but of divine nature.

"The Umbandist works with all the forces of nature, wherever they are materialized. In the forest he confirms his faith; in the river he rids himself of his faults; in the sea he reaffirms his belief; on the mountain he invokes the Angelus; on the rock he asks for fortitude. . . . Umbanda reaches the heavenly bodies."

This shift from the African religion to astrology is the most original feature of the new sect. This is not the place to analyze a transition that takes us a long way from Africa, but we must bear in mind that the forces of the heavenly bodies, the forces of nature, the lines, and the groups of spirits are all linked, so that the ultimate function of spiritism is to make magical use of these astral forces, which may help or harm man in his spiritual rise.

In addition to this movement, which submerges Africa in European occultism, there is another, more interesting to us, which abides more closely by the African tradition. But this movement runs up against the difficulty we have already mentioned: that Umbanda mediums also receive the spirits of the dead, old Negroes and *caboclos*—a flagrant contradiction of the exclusive worship of the *orixás*. How is this to be explained? Some make a distinction between major *orixás* and the protective spirits of mediums. In this case the old Negroes and *caboclos* are transformed into minor *orixás*.[71] A second solution is to distinguish "lines" and identify them with the African "nations" of history. Umbanda would then have evolved out of the black sects that existed in Rio—Nagô, Gêgê, Cabinda, Congo, Malé, Angola, Mozambique, Rebôlo, Cassange, and Benguela— each of which became a line. Now, these lines include the line of the Souls, i.e. spirits of *babalaôs* who failed to complete their missions on earth and who return after death to do so. This would mean that the *exús* and *tatas* would still be worshiped chiefly in the *terreiros* of Guinea origin, while the line of the Souls would derive from the funeral ceremonies that I have termed *achêchê* but that are better known in Rio as *voumbi*.[72] Although this cult of souls would bring us close to spiritism, it would still conform to the true African tradition and represent just one more manifestation of it.

Just as there has been an attempt in this movement to resolve the difficulty of spiritism by linking souls with the *orixás*, an attempt has also been made to resolve the difficulty of syncretism with Catholicism by distinguishing two types of Christianity: a popular Catholicism that ignorant minds confuse with the African religion, and a magical Christianity, the Christianity that Joseph of Arimathea taught to Jesus. It is this latter type, and this type alone, that is found in—or rather identified with—true Umbanda.[73] In this way the new religion, while still proclaiming itself to be "African," manages not to offend the spiritists or the uneasy Catholics who are drawn to it. On the contrary it attracts them because it deifies the dead as *orixás* and sublimates Christianity in a higher magic.

Obviously if the African gods are to be retained in a spiritism of this kind, they will have to undergo a fairly radical transformation to enable them to adapt themselves to the governing lines of the system. Some of the general characteristics of these deities are respected. Shangô rules over rocks, Ogun over iron, Oxun over sweet water, Yansan over bamboo (because of her connection with death, symbolized by bamboo), Oxóssi over forests (where he hunts), Omolú over cemeteries, Exú over crossroads, Yemanjá over the sea.[74] But gradually these deities rise from the plane of natural forces to the plane of moral ones. Ogun ceases to be the warrior of the *candomblés* and becomes the champion of justice, not so much because he is identified with Saint George fighting monsters as because he holds an intermediate position between the material and the astral planes, between Horus and the souls, the former standing for terrestrial life and the latter for life after death. Because of this intermediate position he stands for man's moral conscience, which controls his body and rewards or punishes his earthly conduct after death.[75] Oxóssi is no longer the divine hunter. Undoubtedly because of his identification with Saint Sebastian, always shown pierced by arrows, he reminds us that "only when we have overcome the imperfections of our physical and astral bodies can our spirit enter the mental body and prepare itself for the higher life."[76] Shangô, who in Africa hurled his thunderbolts at the guilty alone, is represented holding a scales to weigh human actions and determine the fate of souls after death. As for Yemanjá, as mistress of the sea she becomes the great purifier of earthly passions. The Ibeji, the Yoruba twins, restore to our troubled hearts the purity of childhood, still uncontaminated by sin. "The old Negro personifies humility; the *caboclo*, energy; the children, innocence; and the sirens, hygiene."[77]

In some tents in Minas, the phalanxes of Yemanjá are invoked at the opening of the session in order to "discharge" all the impurities introduced into the building by man's "sinful body." Other Umbandists do not carry the moralization of the *orixás* quite so far and prefer to give them a more practical character. Yemanjá protects sailors and helps anyone who wishes to improve himself to follow the path of righteousness.[78] Oxóssi resists black magic, heals the sick by means of herbs or magnetic passes, and always has a moral homily for suffering brothers.[79] Shangô helps the unfortunate, raises the humiliated, lifts sorcerers' spells, and also restores

justice here on earth.[80] Ogun protects against evil spirits who have strayed
from the path of goodness and insinuate themselves into humans and cause
them suffering. He is also the defender of liberty[81] and for this reason has
sometimes been identified with Stalin (through a communist correspondence that conflicts with the Catholic one) and the leader of the revolt
against capitalist oppression.[82]

But it is with Exú and Omolú that the metamorphoses of the gods
assume their most curious aspect, although these metamorphoses still start
from the African originals. As we have seen, Omolú was much feared by
the Brazilian blacks, on whom he inflicted terrible smallpox epidemics but
whom he also protected, provided they observed his cult, so that he became, especially in the Bantu "nations," a kind of "poor people's doctor."
This ambivalence continues in Umbanda, but both aspects are exaggerated. Omolú is now the deity of cemeteries, leader of the phalanxes of
the dead and the legions of the skeletons. This makes him the commander
of innumerable evil Exús, although in African tradition there is no connection between these two *orixás*. These evil Exús include Exú-Death's-Head,
who carries off souls; Exú-Embers, who sets fires; Exú-Pemba, who causes
venereal diseases; and Exú-Pagan, who separates couples. As a result
Omolú becomes, with Exú, one of the two great masters of black magic.[83]
This explains why he appears more often in the works of Quimbanda,
which have an evil intent, than in those of Umbanda, which are beneficent.[84] Nevertheless Omolú is not confined to the line of the Souls but can
work in any of the lines, for he has a strong influence over all the entities
of space. The Umbandists explain this by the earthly friendship between
Lazarus (the Catholic counterpart of Omolú) and Jesus. After ascending
to Heaven, Jesus is believed to have charged his old friend with the mission of interceding with all the spiritual phalanxes on behalf of the
living.[85]

While possession by Exú is rare in *candomblé*, Umbanda spiritism, as
a continuation of *macumba*, sees the possession of mediums by the Exús
as an essential part of the ritual. In *macumba*, Exú is identified with the
Devil and is the master of magic, and Umbanda too has inherited this
demonic conception. While the *orixás* are the leaders of the phalanxes of
good spirits that descend into the bodies of mortals, the Exús and Omolús
are the leaders of the evil spirits that visit misfortune and illness upon men.
And that is not all. We are surrounded not only by spirits but also by
fluids, and these fluids may be good or harmful. The spirits, children of
light, emit good fluids whose beneficent effects the Umbanda ritual makes
accessible to us. They help us to rise morally and inspire in us love of our
fellow-men. The harmful fluids, however, cause us to sink into criminality
or sensuality and draw us downward toward the earth from which they
emanate. Hence the distinction between black magic (Quimbanda), which
uses *exús* to spread dissension among our enemies, and white magic

(Umbanda) which uses only good forces. To be more precise, Umbanda may have recourse to *exús* but only for the purpose of lifting spells or driving out these spirits prior to any ceremony in the tent.[86] In this dual rite of expulsion or spell-lifting Exú will work only for pay. He is therefore the only *orixá* who receives sacrifices—usually tobacco or brandy offered at a crossroads.[87]

The dualism of good and evil thus has the effect of making the educated nonwhite Brazilian, living in a progressive big city and steadily rising on the social ladder, unwilling to have anything to do with the cult of Exú. To practice this cult would only justify the whites' image of him as an inferior being with a propensity for evil. Eager to rise spiritually, he is of course obliged to give African tradition its due and allot a place for the Exús, but he de-Africanizes them and Aryanizes them by means of Judeo-Christian thought. Inventing another false etymology, he derives the name Exú from Exud, the rebel angel whom God struck down with lightning and hurled from the heights of Heaven to the depths of Hell. This makes it easier for him to identify Exú with Lucifer.[88] Yet this rejection of tradition arouses a kind of unconscious guilt. To identify Exú with Lucifer is to relegate a significant part of Africa to the realm of the diabolical, thus justifying European criticism of the black civilizations. We therefore find a second tendency in Umbanda: a desperate effort to save this god.

Exú now becomes the elemental force, the great cosmic fluid, "the subconscious of God." It was he who was created when God said: "Let there be light." So he is ultimately the perpetual vibration of the ether, the life of the universe, and hence the great magical agent who can be used for good as well as evil. "Without him no one can do anything."[89]

But, like *mana*, this universal energy can be individualized, giving rise to personal *exús*. These fall into two classes: *exús* such as Carangola, Ganga, Tiriri, etc., who are personifications of the fluids of nature, linked to the major *orixás* as their personal servants; and *exús* who are the protectors of individuals. (Just as every *orixá* has his *exú*, every human has his *caboclo* and his *exú*.) The former, anthropomorphized forces of nature, are generally represented as terrestrial forces or forces that bind us to the earth, and therefore people who desire happiness, fortune, and earthly pleasures make use of them. But those who wish to rise spiritually should try to avoid their influence and move from the plane of these material forces to the plane of the astral and, later, the mental forces.[90] As for the *exús* of the second class, "everyone has a higher and a lower self. Thus in Umbanda each medium has a familiar spirit who protects him, or a *caboclo*, but he also has a familiar *exú* who defends and looks after him."

This familiar *exú* is the vegetable or animal soul, the instinctive part of our being, indispensable to our survival—what the Umbandists call the "pagan soul." Here, as in the case of the terrestrial fluids, the function of

Umbanda is "to train and purify [this soul] by transforming it into a luminous body or, as Saint Paul put it, by changing animal man, the son of earth, into spiritual man, the adopted son of God."[91]

The African gods have been transformed, and these transformations reassure the black as to his moral value and the intellectual richness of his ancestral beliefs. There has certainly been an upgrading in the domain of dogma, following and reflecting the rise of Negroes and mulattoes in society. Every change in the structure is accompanied by a corresponding change in the world of ideal values. The gods "rise" along with their devotees. Unfortunately in rising they degenerate. Indeed our study of collective representations reveals a constant ambivalence of feeling between fidelity to Africa and rejection of it, because in order to "rise" the *orixás* are obliged to become white. We shall find the same vacillation as we move on now from representations to rites.

Aluizio Fontenelle recognizes that the cause of the transformations the African religions have undergone lies in the black's desire to model himself on the white. "Quimbanda perpetuates the determination to maintain the old African traditions, while Umbanda seeks to break away from the uncivilized side of those practices—thanks to the influence of the white man, who is too educated to countenance them."[92] Yet the desire to break with them, which marks the social rise of a colored group, is combined with a desire for continuity, which reflects the discrimination encountered in this difficult process. The black's proud reply to those who dismiss his civilization as barbarian is to save whatever can be saved, whatever does not conflict too conspicuously with the new ways of thinking he has acquired in school or in his contacts with other Brazilians.

This is why Umbanda, although it is certainly spiritism of a kind, differs so strongly from Kardecism. Ordinary spiritist sessions end with a moral homily; the ceremonial is meager or nonexistent. While its ritual is by no means as rich and complex as that of the *candomblé*, Umbanda still shares the latter's sense of and love for ceremonial.[93] In Kardecism the manifestations of the spirits require only that the medium be in a semiconscious state; there is no trance. In Umbanda, as in *candomblé* (and even more so since the mythology exerts no control), the spirits manifest themselves through extremely emotional and violent ecstasies.[94] In Kardecism there are no fraternities. In the course of meetings certain people may show themselves to be endowed with mediumistic talent and may then be sent to the "medium school" attached to the cult center, where this talent will be "developed" or "perfected." Membership in an Umbanda sect is conferred only by initiation (known as "crossing"). Although much briefer and far less spectacular,[95] this initiation still represents a bond between the new religion and the old. Thus in the domain of ritual as in the domain of collective representations, we are dealing with a process of sublimation rather than elimination.

Let us take a look inside an Umbanda tent. Regardless of its type, the ceremonial will follow more or less the same lines. As in *catimbó*, the ceremonies begin with the censing of the room and the congregation. Then the *cambones* and *sambas* enter. Before sitting down, they allow themselves to be enveloped in the acrid smoke of fragrant herbs that the leader wafts toward them from his swinging censer. A song accompanies their entry, and the monotonous litany continues until the last medium has taken his place. Besides purifying himself with smoke, the medium salutes the altar and the table by striking the surface of the latter three times with his head, loudly and forcefully. The second part of the ritual is the summoning of the entities and their incarnation in the mediums. This is performed to the sound of *pontos cantados* "pulled" for the various phalanxes in turn in a fixed order that varies from sect to sect.

The third part is devoted to the sick people in the congregation or to those who have a request to make of the spirits. Each client has a number, handed out to him at the entrance. The mediums are seated on low benches near the *cambone*, who assists them with a lighted candle and a box containing such objects as the spirit may need: tobacco for smoking, brandy for drinking. The medium is in paroxysm, but the initial violence has worn off. No more writhing on the floor; no more convulsively twitching muscles or agonized gasping. But tightly closed eyes. Episodes of glossolalia. His face assumes the mask of an old Negro or a *caboclo*, a mask of gentleness or of arrogance. The clients, also seated on low benches, recount their sad stories—unemployment, a missing husband, a rebellious child, a persistent illness. The *caboclo* or African smokes and drinks and gives advice or prescribes remedies—opening the golden door of hope. The séance ends with a moral homily or a prayer. Then the closing song is sung, automatically causing the disembodiment of the spirits and the medium's return to a normal state.

We immediately recognize what Umbanda has in common with the other forms of spiritism and what sets it apart. The sermon, the prayer, and the reading from Allan Kardec or the Gospels are partly or entirely replaced by songs. The mediums do not sit around a table in the dimness of a poorly lighted room; the congregation sits on benches as if in church, praying and concentrating amid the panting of laboring women, big with the spirit to which they are about to give birth. There is an atmosphere of rejoicing rather than sadness, and the trance regains its spectacular quality. Nonetheless the ultimate purpose of the Umbanda and the regular spiritist meeting is practical and utilitarian. Both seek to provide some relief to suffering humanity.

Variations are sometimes introduced into this ritual pattern. In some Rio tents the session opens with the singing of the *pontos* of Ogun, Exú, and Ganga, so that these evil spirits may not disturb the work under way. The *pontos* of the guide-leader and of Yemanjá, Ogun, Oxóssi, and

Shangô follow. The songs of Araribgoia or of the Indians are sung only after the practical, charitable part of the ceremony, to mark its conclusion.[96] If, during a meeting, a suffering spirit descends instead of the entities or the phalanxes of nature (this would represent a rebellion of the medium's unconscious against group control), the leader makes a little speech telling it that it is already dead and liberated from matter, that it has no need to seek a new body. This is done "gently and with kindness." if an evil spirit—one of the spirits that work in black magic—descends, it must be driven away by more material means. *Pontos riscados* may be drawn or gunpowder exploded. An offering of tobacco, alcohol, or even an animal may be made at a crossroads to the phalanxes of Exú, the people of the cemeteries.[97]

Some Minas sects, although recognizing the necessity of summoning Quimbanda spirits from time to time to give them a moral lecture and help them to rise spiritually, recommend that the ceremonies not be opened by hymns to the Exús, because if they get into the habit of descending into spiritist tents they will be unwilling to leave again and will do harm. Here the séance is opened by the old Negro Pai João. The phalanxes appear in the following order: first the *caboclos* going out to battle against the forces of evil, ready to drive them away with their arrows or spears; then the children, who come and play for a moment, creating an atmosphere of purity; then the sirens, the people of the sea, who symbolically lead the mediums to ocean beaches so that by plunging into the salty foam they may cast off the impurity of the sinful body.[98]

Our study of the ritual leads to the same conclusions as our study of the myths. The upgrading of Africa is accompanied by a more or less conscious rejection. Everything that disturbs modern man's conscience is abandoned or relegated to secrecy. This may be the work of the whites, who have joined Umbanda in large numbers, but the collective representations are constantly shifting back and forth between the preconceived ideas of the whites and the resentment of the people of color. The formation of a mixed racial group in which the mestizos finally take over creates a certain homogeneity of feelings and ideas, attitudes and behavior, produced by the synthesis of individual consciences. These affective complexes cannot be analyzed in order to separate the contributions of the various ethnic groups without destroying precisely this common reality. In sociology there is no genuine theorem of combination of forces. From our point of view the essential thing is that even where the whites are in the majority (the color breakdown varies from sect to sect),[99] Africa still casts its great black shadow over Umbanda.

Thus the racial struggle persists, moving from the social to the mystic plane without basically changing its character. Leal de Souza describes a spiritist meeting in which the leader reprimanded a Negro spirit who tried to incarnate himself in a medium for one fault alone—being a Negro.[100]

But, as I have said, in Brazil the racial struggle takes more subtle forms. The idea is to get rid of everything reminiscent of Africa as quickly as possible so that the three main color groups may be merged into one. The Kardecites may moderate their criticisms but they still exist. They may present Umbanda as a sort of kindergarten, Kardecism as a sort of university, and the spiritism of Christ the Redeemer as a transitional phase representing secondary education.[101] Or they may admit that Umbanda is a step up from the African religion inasmuch as it recognizes two separate lines of white and black magic and rejects the latter, and inasmuch as its ritual is slanted toward prayer and the reading of the Gospels. Indeed this represents a step forward on the road to true spiritism. But unfortunately, they say, the Umbandist stops along the way because Kardecism is difficult and demands much study as well as the virtue of patience, which the black does not possess. It is quicker to drive away evil spirits by shooting off gunpowder than by teaching goodness and steering them toward virtue. Above all, in his racial materialism the Umbandist clings to the spirits of *caboclos* or old Negroes and classifies the phalanxes of the beyond according to geographical criteria (people of the East) or ethnic ones (Indians and Africans), while in true spiritism the question of spirits is secondary and the essential thing is man's moral progress.[102]

Here, in the domain of religion, we have a process analogous to the one we have just seen in the social sphere: the mixing of bloods and the domination of the whites. But behind the soft words, the black is quite aware of the old prejudice, as vigorous as ever, scourging and humiliating him. "The old Negroes, those obscure heroes who knew the rigors of slavery, are dear to the Umbandists because they were a sacrificed race— though only after getting rid of their black outer covering, often so vermin-ridden that the worms found nothing to feast on. As incarnate beings— even after Abolition and even today—they are still despised in the land of the white man. When shall we succeed, through our messages and communications, in instilling true fraternity into the brothers of Planet Earth?"[103]

But the Umbandist's revision of *candomblé* was all for nothing. However much he has sugar-coated the religion of his fathers and denounced *macumba* as a place of sorcery, the Kardecites still reproach him for what little he has preserved of the religion of his ancestors—the censing, the herbal baths, the *pontos riscados*, the gunpowder, the casting of shells to divine the future, and, above all, the *caboclos* and Africans who, through the intermediacy of the medium's body, come asking for tobacco or brandy, who smoke and drink, more like poor, degraded lower-class human beings than spirits of light. Since his rejection was ineffectual and since one cannot, in full view of one's adversary, stop at half-measures and hold on with one hand while letting go with the other, the Umbandist was forced to meet attack with counterattack. An apology for the man of color begins to take shape, an apology that will end in messianism. "The work of Umbanda temples requires white or blue chalk, brandy, "Christ's blood" (port wine), beer (*marambaia*), a plug of tobacco, a pipe, candy for the children, lighted candles, statues of the saints, shells, and salt water. Although all this seems unnecessary to the Kardecites, each object has its value; they all serve to attract the phalanxes of spirits, with their respective fluidic bodies, which are commanded by higher spirits."[104]

And indeed the *pontos riscados* drawn on the ground are immediately recorded on the astral plane and act as appeals to the spirits to descend and help us.[105] At the same time, these drawings touch the eye, concentrate thought, and establish a magnetic fluidic current between our souls and the summoned phalanxes.[106] Moreover, if one studies the magic of Eliphas Levi, the cabala or theosophy, one comes upon the swastika, the Star of David, and a whole series of symbols that recur in Freemasonry, with its eye and compass, and in Christianity, with the Cross. Why, then, do the Kardecites limit their criticism to the Umbandists and even "feel it an honor to join the Masonic, Rosicrucian, or theosophist orders"? Does this not show, in spite of all they say, that their criticisms are ultimately nothing but camouflaged or rationalized racial prejudices?[107] The Kardecite finds the brandy shocking, yet the priest drinks wine during the mass. And the principle is the same. In one case it is done to embody the force of Christ, in the other to cause the entry into the medium of the forces that will give him the power or defend him against the evil spirits.[108] Tobacco smoke drives away deadly fluids and helps to heal the sick, just as censing creates an atmosphere propitious for receiving vibrations and for the irradiation of the guides. The science known to Mager, d'Arsonval, and Lesourd as *radiesthésie** offered a positive basis for the use of these aromatic or smoke-producing herbs. Here again the Kardecite, who confines his attack to Umbanda and never says a word against the use of incense in Catholicism or the Magi's gift of myrrh to the Christ Child, shows that sentiments other than love of truth inspire his criticism. Less acknowledgeable sentiments too.[109] The gunpowder and firecrackers relieve the atmosphere of excessively material fluids that prevent the spirits of light from descending into our midst. Although the Umbandists tend to use this process more and more rarely, as though admitting that their critics are right, they might well have found a justification for it in popular Catholicism, for in Brazil all the great church festivals, especially the feasts of Saint Peter and Saint John, are celebrated with explosions of gunpowder and firecrackers. Neither should the Kardecite be surprised by herbal baths, considering that Catholicism preaches the washing of

---

* [The English linguistic equivalent of *radiesthésie* is *rhabdomancy*, but the French term designates a much wider science, which might better be called psychometry. Besides water divining and the finding of lost objects, *radiesthésie* includes medical diagnosis and healing based on "radiations" and natural substances.]

feet,[110] Hindus purify themselves in the waters of the Ganges, Christians make the pilgrimage to Lourdes, and sick people take the waters at Vichy![111] Initiatory and cleansing baths (obligatory every Friday) have a twofold spiritual effect derived from the purifying water and the medicinal herb, the water being saturated with planetary fluids and the herb with magic virtues that any medical science worthy of the name should recognize.[112] As for the offerings, these are not to be confused with the *despachos* of black magic, but symbolize the adoration of a pure and loving heart.[113]

This Umbandist strategy reveals a good deal about the inmost feelings of its adherents. On the one hand we have the upgrading that we have so often seen in operation, the step forward from barbarianism to science— and to science on its highest level, not the still all too empirical science of the laboratories but the higher knowledge of the occultists or theosophists. And at the same time and as a result of this, we have the denunciation of color prejudice in its most hypocritical and insidious form because, once the value of the ritual has been proven, the only remaining explanation for Kardecite criticism is that the white spiritists still cling to their racial prejudice, hatred, and ethnocentric feelings.

Why should the souls of whites be the only ones capable of doing good on earth? How much pride or ethnocentrism lurks within Kardecism? No single nation is the cradle of the manifestation of spirits; they manifest themselves from everywhere, in many different ways and in response to all kinds of needs because they are not the work of man but a divine emanation and therefore scattered throughout the universe. "Africa is not a separate part of divine creation."[114]

> The Kardecites believe that the Umbandists are mistaken in accepting the spirits of *caboclos* and Africans as guides or protectors, alleging that these spirits are inferior or backward and not worthy to be guides of centers or tents or protectors of mediums. But what condition, I ask, must a spirit meet to qualify as a guide or protector? The unanimous reply will be: to be virtuous. I ask again: is being virtuous the privilege of a single race? The *caboclos*, the Africans, and others can be guides because they too, like people of the white race, have developed morally through suffering and thus become virtuous.[115]

Moreover, if it is true that suffering is the road to virtue, the Indians and *caboclos*, who had to endure the violence of the white colonists or the injustices of cruel masters, are more likely than the whites to become spirits of light in the beyond.

We are close to messianism. For the Negro, like the Indian, answers evil with good. "The despised Negroes, mistreated by the whites, are now invoked to come to the aid of those who often, in former incarnations, put them on the block or hunted them down in the shade of palm trees in Africa. Thus they fulfill the words of Jesus: 'He that shall humble himself shall be exalted.' "[116] Having learned in the forests the secret of herbs or the magic that drives away demons, they use their knowledge for the benefit of their former persecutors.[117] Did not God assume human form to save humanity? Did He not lead the most humble existence, that of a carpenter, and did He not surround Himself chiefly with poor, common people? Did He not give Mary Magdalene, the sinner, the privilege of witnessing His glorious resurrection? Why, then, should He not choose the humble *caboclos* and unfortunate Negroes to carry the light to the whites? We may go even further. It is possible that in the course of their successive rebirths on earth rich or educated whites should have preferred to incarnate themselves in *caboclos* or blacks so that they might suffer more and thus advance spiritually. "Who knows whether these spirits, when they foresake earth and their material frame forever in their victorious return to the beyond, may not review their whole past and prefer to continue in the humility of their last incarnation as a quicker way of achieving total dematerialization?"[118]

The man of color's sense of retribution goes even further. For Umbanda will triumph over its adversaries. Even now the *caboclos* and old Negroes do not descend into mulattoes or mixed-bloods alone. "They even make their way into palaces and embody themselves in ladies of high society and eminent men."[119] The black sees the entry of white civil servants, businessmen, and industrialists into Umbanda as a reversal of values: the *caboclo* is no longer a savage, the African no longer a slave subject to the white man's every whim. They have become gods of the new religion before whom their former masters humbly bow their heads.

But in religious life, as in social life altogether, black messianism cannot be separated from Brazilian nationalism. It is not confined to purely racial protest. It casts a harsh, cynical light on those Brazilians who would like to forget that their country was born of the encounter of three races and to see only its white, European aspect. Intransigent nationalism takes shape more quickly among the lower classes than in the more cosmopolitan, Westernized upper classes. This lower-class nationalism manifests itself in spiritualism exactly as it does on the political level. Umbanda is its expression. If we admit, say the Umbandists, that Brazilian civilization is a product of the merging of Indian totemism, African fetishism, and Iberian Catholicism, why should we want to break with our past? Instead of obstinately looking toward the Rome of the popes or the France of Allan Kardec, we should start out with Brazilian realities and create a religion for our mestizo people.[120] That is why Umbanda and Umbanda alone can unite in one harmonious whole all the colors and ethnic groups that have come together to merge on American soil.[121]

But this earthly nationalism remains ambivalent. On the one hand it is an expression of *"brasileirismo"* (a neologism dear to the younger generations). It stresses the country's "marginalism" or "mulattoism." It rebels against a patriotism that denies Negroes a front place. In this context the true significance of setting up Pai João, who descends in Umbanda, against the Saint Benedict of the Catholic chapels is revealed as a caste struggle. Saint Benedict is a white expedient for chaining the slave more closely to his servile condition by allowing him his own ambassador to God, much as the tribune used to defend the Roman plebians before the people. This expedient unites, but at the same time it divides. And lest the Negro become too proud of his tribune, the white explains the blackness of Saint Benedict either as a punishment—"because his mother thought ill of her godmother"—or as one of God's miracles through which "this brother was transformed from white to black to escape the persecution of the infidels." Saint Benedict's halo is a halo of color prejudice rather than the conventional halo of the white saints. As Jacy Rego Barros says, "Pai João was perfectly integrated into *brasileirismo*. We propose him as a substitute for Saint Benedict, whose legend is unexpressive and foreign."[122]

But how much longer will black messianism be content with the myth of Pai João? With the old Negro and the *caboclo*? Will the Brazilian of color ever be able to call a halt along this road, which has taken us from the upgrading of Africa to its most flagrant rejection? Even if Umbanda represents a step forward from *macumba*, it still sometimes constrains the black like a prison because it is still a segregation—segregation from his white Kardecite brothers.

Max Weber effectively showed that the theory of karma denies people of low caste all possibility of social rise except through posthumous reincarnation in a higher caste.[123] By the same principle, our spiritism represents a means of ascent to the man whose hopes and aspirations are blocked by the dual barrier of color and social class. It is the only means through which children of darkness, imprisoned in their skin, can dream of transforming themselves, in their future existence, into children of light. It goes even further; it numbers the years before deliverance. The Quimbanda spirits will disappear in two thousand years, passing from a lower to a higher plane.[124] In 1937 the phalanxes working with the sea in the Morning Star sect passed from the terrestrial to the astral plane.[125] But if Quimbanda is going to disappear, "Umbanda will no longer be necessary. There will remain only the Kardecite law—i.e. scientific and philosophic spiritism."[126]

According to this theory of spiritist evolution, the messianism of liberation from the nocturnal body, which will be replaced by a fluidic one, from a body that will grow less and less bituminous and carbonaceous and more and more luminous and spiritualized (white narcissism accepted by the black libido), will some day join up with the dream of the fraternization of races in a unified Kardecism in which all sects have been abolished, all prejudice eliminated.

What does this mean if not that the black is ready to reject all the remaining features linking him to his African traditions provided Kardecism will divest itself of its white ethnocentrism, and that what he ultimately wants, even more than a heightened sense of his own value, is membership, both mystic and real, in the universal brotherhood? A brotherhood that would consist only of mutually loving adherents of spiritism, free from distinctions of color, and of spirits of light, former *caboclos*, former Negroes, and former whites, all equally luminous.

■ ■ ■

For a sociologist nothing is more exciting than to witness the birth of a new religion before his very eyes, as it were. Arthur Ramos, who watched the beginnings of Umbanda at the very moment when it sprouted from the stem of *macumba*, nevertheless failed, in the second edition of *O Negro Brasileiro*, to detect the difference between the two cults. He saw Umbanda as a new complication of syncretism and summed it up as an Afro-Indo-Catholico-spirito-occultist religion.[127] Here we plainly see the superiority of the sociological viewpoint to the culturalist one. A painting, even an abstract one, is not just a series of dabs of color. Besides creating a new reality through their interaction, each of these dabs has its own meaning. They record on the canvas the artist's feelings and preferences and even the complexes of his libido. Each of the cultural characteristics that are syncretized also has its own significance, and this is what I had in mind when I spoke of valorization, prejudices, resentment, and purification. Syncretism cannot be defined by the mere juxtaposition or merging of civilizations in contact; it is an activity of men united in divergent or cooperative groups. It translates into dogmas or rites the very movement of social structures as they come apart and are reassembled. Civilizations can meet without interpenetrating. When they do interpenetrate, the process is not random; it follows certain laws, the laws of the convergence or clash of the collectivities that sustain these heterogeneous civilizations.

Macumba reflected the initial effects of urbanization on the racial collectivities, the transition from the closed groupings of *candomblé*, *cabula*, and *catimbó* to the atomization of interpersonal relations. The firmly established religions were disintegrating along with social bonds of the communal type. Nonetheless a new kind of solidarity—the solidarity of class—was beginning to emerge within a society that was now a capitalist, industrialized one, regrouping the scattered members of the most diverse "communities." *Macumba* provided this still unorganized class with that indispensable minimum of intellectual or emotional homogeneity without which there can be no communion. But as industrialization cemented proletarian solidarity based on common interests and resistance to certain forms of economic exploitation, and as the black realized that to belong to the proletariat was a step up the social ladder as compared to being just a member of the abandoned, marginal masses, he became more aware of the forces, originating in slavery, that had impeded both this multiracial class coagulation and his own social rise. As Fontenelle says, Umbanda appeals to the poor, and since the majority of its adherents belong to the middle class (a term that is not of course to be taken in the European sense), it made an effort to edify and improve this proletariat.[128]

There is no better way of saying that this emerging spiritism reflects, even for the Umbandists themselves, the second phase of urbanization. That is why, before beginning this study, I had to go to the Negro press to discover in their pure state, so to speak, the claims and demands of Brazilians of color. And indeed the black newspapers and political and social organizations express just the same feelings as Umbanda, the feelings of a social class that strives for solidarity in its struggle yet cannot succeed in getting rid of prejudices inherited from slavery.

However a distinction must be drawn between the world of politics and the mystic world. In politics what is given is a certain pattern of activities, the party struggle to gain control of power, leadership, and the organization of interest groups. In religion, where the important thing is the commemoration of the divine past, what is given is established churches and living traditions. In politics a change of attitudes and values will express itself in the formation of new parties or organizations corresponding to the class shake-up; new emerging needs create their own institutions. In religion, on the other hand, the past resists change because tradition is inherently sacred. The new must therefore insinuate itself into the old—at the risk of breaking it apart. It is more a question of adapting to the modern world, of renovation rather than innovation.

Hence my concepts of purification and upgrading. The Gospels notwithstanding, new wine is always put into old bottles. Purification will consist in eliminating from the social heritage whatever is too incompatible with modern society, whatever shocks people by reminding them too brutally of barbarism. We see it in action in the campaigns of the Negro press against folklore and ancient customs and in its preaching of puritanical mores. The idea is to create a new type of man, quite distinct from the African "savage" and the degraded slave. But in religion it is impossible to create a new kind of faith. Here it is a question not of rejection but merely of purification. And this purification will necessarily take the form of a return to the true original tradition behind these decadent forms—to the primal source. That is why Umbanda traces its roots back to India or Egypt. But this rationalization is of course an illusion. Purification is not a rediscovery of the past but an adaptation to the present. It consists in a dual process of selection. First whatever is compatible with contemporary science and morality is exerpted from the primitive religion. (This accounts for the rejection of bloody sacrifices, long initiations, tattooing, and witchcraft.) Then anything that can be reconciled with the basic elements of the primitive religion is adopted from contemporary science and morality. This explains why Umbanda adopts from science only occultism and not positivist empiricism, why it selects from spiritism the idea of the fluids of nature rather than communication with spirits, why it borrows from ethics the myth of the "good Negro."

But however much one may purify tradition, everything cannot be changed; otherwise one would have to abandon the old religion and found a new one. There is always something that cannot be eliminated, and this calls for upgrading. We have seen this process at work in pantheism, which sanctifies the cult of natural forces and astral bodies, and in Umbanda spiritism, which redefines the *orixás* in so-called scientific terms and sanctifies long-dead slaves by transforming them into gods who mingle with unfortunate humanity to do good and heal the sick. Obviously these two processes of purification and valorization cannot be separated except for the sake of clearer analysis. In fact they are closely linked and their effects merge. Here again we first noted valorization in the Negro press, but it was limited to an apology for great men; it was a history lesson, an appeal for greatness. Religion goes much further. We might say that it gives this apology concrete substance, so that instead of being an ideal to be attained in some vague future if everyone models himself on the heroes of the race, it becomes actual reality. Pai João is deified. Henceforth the line of Africans is composed of spirits of light.

Religion and politics respond to two different attitudes toward the new social structures, although they both rest on the same foundation of resentment. (The analyses of Erich Fromm may have some bearing on this point.)[129] When medieval society collapsed, the institution of capitalism made it possible for the artisan to rise higher on the social scale than when he was restricted by the rules of the trade guilds. But while he could climb higher, he could also fall lower on the wage scale. The trade guild, it is true, confined him to a certain place in society, but at least it offered him security. This accounts for the Protestant Reformation, which was nothing but a reaction to the new social situation. When in the twentieth century capitalist concentration tended to destroy and proletarianize the middle class, it sought in nazism an ideology with which to defend itself. Both cases exemplify the same tendency: fear of the new liberty. The latter one worked itself out in the political sphere, the former in religion, not because the modern world is secular rather than mystical (as is borne out by nazism's attempt to create its own mystique around Wotan) but because the behavior of resignation is different from the behavior of rebellion. We find analogous phenomena in Brazil. While urbanization and industrialization offered the Negro new opportunities, undreamed of under slavery or under the artisanal system of free Africans, the old regime did provide a certain measure of security. Now he found himself in a society in which upward mobility was theoretically possible but where in practice competition from the whites or even from immigrants pushed him down even lower than before. Religion enabled him to show his greatness by hypostatizing it in the world of the phalanxes of *caboclos* or old Negroes, while organizations such as the Black Front helped him to forge weapons for the struggle.

Which offered the sweeter victory? We have seen the ambivalence and hesitation between "mulattoism" and encystment in full swing in the black press, for victory is not certain. The blacks want to rise by assimilating white values, yet at the same time they want to rise as Negroes. Religion presents different conditions because the white has already penetrated the African sects, not as a guest but often as a leader. While black organizations are *ipso facto* closed, the church is open by reason of its catholicism. This undoubtedly accounts for complex developments in which Umbanda spiritism, for example, combines the racial prejudice introduced by the whites with the upgrading of Africa, just as Paulista *macumba* filled the gaps in its forgotten ritual with European occultist elements. But this resulted in a more rigorous "mulattoism." Religion now provides a mystic basis for mulatto or mixed-blood nationalism. It realizes on the "astral" plane the merging of races or at least their fraternal collaboration. Christianity contributes its charitable virtues. Here it may be useful to digress to the word "crossing," which defines Umbanda spiritism. Umbanda "crosses Exús and *caboclos*"—that is to say, it combines under the sign of the cross what remains of the African religions and what remains of the Indian ones.

In this situation we may well ask if by preaching submission, self-sacrifice, and charity this new form of spiritism does not chain the black or poor mulatto more inescapably to his lot rather than help him to rise. The Marxists have long denounced the Afro-American religions as a means of brutalizing the peasant or working-class masses.[130] But we must remember that even if Umbanda were fully accepted by the exploited class, the most violent attacks on it come not from the Marxists but from the capitalists. Umbanda is not a product of the middle class, anxious to maintain its grip on the totality of power. In the underdeveloped countries the law of capitalism is the law of increasing productivity, which, far from requiring the brutalization of the masses, must offer them incentives to rise, to compete, to better their lot. Spiritism is not something imposed on the proletariat from outside; it is a proletarian creation. And in its evolution it follows the changes in the proletarian consciousness. Hence its sacred values are tinged with resentments or hopes, anger or desires. They imperceptibly degenerate into class ideologies or ideologies of ethnic groups within the class.[131]

Formerly the images of the Catholic saints served as masks for the *orixás*. Now the *orixás* serve as masks for the new needs and attitudes of a social group on the rise.

15
The Catholic or Protestant Black: Assimilation or Reinterpretation?

We have seen how, in Umbanda spiritism, the black imbued his most ancient religious symbols with new feelings and attitudes. But the converse problem also arises: in converting to Catholicism and later, in some cases, to Protestantism, did he not introduce archaic values inherited from Africa into his manner of conceiving of or living those religions? The question is especially interesting in the light of Herskovits's insistence on the phenomenon of reinterpretation and his thesis that black Catholicism is merely an extension or generalization of the cult of the *orixás* to the cult of the saints, just as black Protestantism is merely the tenacious pursuit of trance at any price within a ceremonial imposed or accepted from outside.[1]

This concept of reinterpretation is not new; it already occurs in another perspective in the work of Raoul Allier—work undeservedly neglected today. In a study of the process of conversion among noncivilized people[2] Allier shows that while the African is quite capable of being assimilated into Protestantism, black habits or cultural traditions pose obstacles to it. These obstacles—the tendency to regard religion as magic or countermagic, as a source of emotional satisfaction, or as legalism—are actually nothing but reinterpretations of Christianity in terms of African religions (the omnipotence of rite, the stressing of ecstasy, and the importance of taboos in sacred behavior). Allier takes a psychological approach; what interests him most is the transformation in the soul. But if we compare the psychic evolution of the Africans with that of blacks in the United States, where emotional religion typifies the lower class and Puritanism the middle class,[3] we see that Herskovits's reinterpretations or Allier's stages of conversion can furnish an explanation only when they are linked with a sociological theory of structures and social mobility. To some extent each class has its own reinterpretation. If we extend our first comparison to Haiti, where conversion to Protestantism in rural areas is no more than a countermagical expedient to prevent persecution by the *voduns*,[4] we make the interesting discovery that Allier's stages of conversion coincide exactly with the social rise from the still-Africanized rural class to the non-Africanized lower class and finally to the middle class.

This twofold fact—the importance of reinterpretations and the link between the strata of reinterpretations and the social structures—requires that the last chapter of this book be devoted to a study of the Catholicism and Protestantism of Brazilian blacks to determine whether the African religions have not left a sort of watermark upon them.

Note that I said "the Catholicism and Protestantism of blacks" and not "black Catholicism and Protestantism." The two are not identical. A whole chapter in Part I of this book was devoted to showing that in Brazil there were two Catholicisms, black and white, just as in the United States there is a black church and a white church. We are no longer dealing with separate religions that, because they are separate, can more easily preserve their African features; we are dealing with Catholic and Protestant blacks in unified churches in which color discrimination does not exist. Do these black Catholics or Protestants think and feel the dogmas of their faith in the same way as whites or do they reinterpret them in accordance with African sensibilities and habits? This is the question, but before answering it we must see how the transition from black Catholicism to a Catholicism of blacks occurred.

At the end of the nineteenth century Brazilian Catholicism underwent some radical transformations as a result of the separation of church and state. The clergy was no longer recruited from the traditional old families but from foreigners and sons of immigrants—German Franciscans, French Marists, Belgian and Italian priests—who, far from sharing their predecessors' paternalistic attitude toward the blacks, were strongly imbued with the spirit of Rome. Some scholars have spoken in this connection of a denationalization of the church, and it is true that the new religion, devoted exclusively to the service of the faith, was divorced from the old one, focused as it had been on politics and intellectual life and participating in parliamentary debates and even in democratic revolts.[5] But the faith, after all, does not discriminate between races or colors; it brings them all together at one communion table to partake of the same sacred host. This radical change in the composition of the clergy inevitably influenced black Catholicism. The new priests were shocked by anything too reminiscent of the African culture, anything that was too obviously an entertainment or a medieval mystery play. They fought a bitter battle against black Catholic folklore, which all over Brazil was driven out of the churches and relegated to the plaza.

In the twentieth century, however, Brazilian Catholics became disturbed at the drop in religious vocations among native-born Brazilians and at the gulf between the church, closed in upon itself and subsisting entirely on its mystic life, and the indifferent community of a country sinking into materialism. Jackson de Figueiredo and Alceu Amoroso Lima led a revival movement to reunite what had once been united. An intensive propaganda campaign was initiated, using the free schools, the religious press, and the radio to appeal to the masses and transform what had become a Sunday religion into a daily one. The church involved itself in social problems and enlisted young people, Catholic men and women, and finally workers too in the Catholic Action.[6] As I have already said, the blacks constituted the majority of the lower class and were therefore immediately affected by this religious revival. But now they no longer entered the church by the side door to say their prayers in the chapel of Saint Benedict; they entered through the main door, along with the other Catholics. There was now only one people.

Although the dual Catholicism of the colonial era was doomed, it is still not completely dead. Even today the interest of the folklorists and the desire to find, in a return to tradition, a counterbalance to the gradual Americanization of Brazil sporadically resurrect the moribund *congadas*, and the church once more promotes their performance in the shadow of its cross. A study of this black Catholicism in Brazil, which still retains special characteristics, will therefore prove worthwhile. Colored fraternities still exist, with their white or blue robes, black capes, and red Maltese crosses. The principal ones are the Brotherhoods of Our Lady of the Rosary, Saint Iphigeneia, Saint Dominic, Our Lady of Good Parturition, and, above all, Saint Benedict. But the cult of Saint Benedict is now pervaded with resentments that used not to exist, at any rate not to the same degree. The church is supposed to celebrate his feast every year (otherwise the community will suffer for it), and this obligation is justified by a myth that when God told Saint Benedict that he was to become a saint, he replied that he did not want to because he was black. God then assured him that anyone who made fun of him would be punished. Although Saint Benedict's position in the procession is still determined by caste (his statue is carried first in a hierarchical order ranging from the black fraternities to the religious and civil authorities), the blacks claim that he comes first because he is the most important, not the least, and that if his place were changed God would drench the crowds with rain as a punishment.[7] Today, however, although the colored fraternities are often directed by a "king," the successor of the old-time Kings of the Congo, they are no longer restricted to blacks. As the processions emerge from their private chapels, white participants are conspicuous, although blacks are still in the majority.

In rural Brazil the priests tried to put a stop to African entertainments. From the pulpit they attacked not only the religious dancing in the *candomblés* (which would be quite understandable) but even the profane *batuque*.[8] It is true that this dance, which centers on the selection of a sexual partner by a male or female dancer, followed by an enactment of love-making, did originally have a licentious character. Today however the rubbing of navels is usually simulated or, when it is performed, is given an agonizing rather than a voluptuous character. Until comparatively recently the blacks danced their way to the church for the feast of Bom Jesus de Pirapora in a series of carnival-like parades, with bands and flags. After fulfilling their religious obligations, they would spend the night in the shed assigned to them as a dormitory, passionately and joyously dancing the *samba*.[9] Today this dance has been banned by the parish priest and eliminated from the annual procession. In Minas, Mozambique penitents still observe the custom of entering the church, where the priest places a crown on their heads. They then circle the chapel, surrounded by their relatives and friends, as many times as their promise to God requires. On the other hand the *reisados* performed by groups of blacks or *caboclos* (who are often blacks disguised as Indians) have been forbidden by the Archbishop of Diamantina. The Congo dance in the plaza in front of the church before taking to the streets, but they no longer enter the sanctuary.[10] In Cunha, in the state of São Paulo, the parish priest forbade the soliciting of food and money for the big Catholic feasts by groups that covered the whole area and decided to do the soliciting himself, but the custom was so entrenched that his attempt ended in total failure.[11]

These few examples illustrate the clergy's determination to destroy black Catholicism and crush its resistance. The black, however, is not about to abandon his shows just because the priest has driven him out of the temple. If the church will not help him to put them on, he will do it outside the church. These festivals give him a chance to wear gorgeous clothes and display his litheness and agility. He is the center of attraction of the whole community, admired and congratulated. He escapes from the miseries of daily life. He is a king, an ambassador, the dead and resurrected prince. All eyes are upon him; all hearts are set on the medieval mystery; social communion crystallizes around his performance. This explains the survival all over Brazil of Congo societies that hand down the old traditions. The hymns sung in honor of the blacks' Virgin of the Rosary and the *congadas* die out only where the rising generations have acquired, on the school bench or in dance halls, a preference for new collective values. The priest may ban the African dances from the pulpit, but it is not his condemnation that kills them so much as the new ideal of young people who refuse to form separate groups from the whites and to segregate themselves by color.

In Northern Brazil Catholicism long ago rejected the *maracatú* (which certainly contains an African religious element) along with the *calunga*, the divine doll representing the goddess of the sea and of death, although the *maracatú* was originally a Catholic dance performed in front of the church and preceded by the crowning of a king and queen of the blacks. As a result the dance became part of the carnival and today consists of a company of Negroes roaming the streets among the revelers to the music of percussion instruments. But if the *maracatú* was to survive at all, some institution had to become responsible for it, so, since Catholicism rejected it, it looked to the fetishist sects for support and made its way into the *xangôs*. Before taking to the city streets, the black performers elect their *pãe* and *mãe de santo* king and queen and then sing the songs of their *orixás*. The *maracatú* loses its former character of a black tribute to the Virgin and to Christ and becomes a sort of ambulatory *xangô*.[12]

Thus in the north, where African survivals are strongest, whatever Catholicism rejects finds its way into "fetishism." In the south, where the survivals are weaker, what is rejected by Catholicism tries painfully to survive as a recreational society, a kind of amateur theater group, yet no purer form of Catholicism replaces it. On the contrary, each new generation draws further away from both the church and the *congada*, but its rejection of the latter does not stem from any desire to serve the church more faithfully. Rural priests have fully recognized the danger and adopted more flexible tactics. Now they are less concerned with abolishing black Catholicism than with purifying it and eliminating its excessively African, naturalistic, or grotesque elements. This may account for their preference for the *moçambique* over the *congada*.[13] I have already shown in Part I of this book that out of the old struggle between these two ethnic groups a hierarchy emerged in which the Congo constituted the black aristocracy, the Mozambique the common people. Precisely because they were plebeian, the Mozambique dances were less rich, less theatrical, more like a regular procession, just as Mozambique music was less African, being based on European tunes. In any case the clergy uses the *moçambique* as a weapon against "modernism," against the new profane tendencies of the masses. In Cunha the priest uses the Mozambique organizations as a bastion of tradition against the encroachment of urban forms of entertainment —dances and social clubs—and receives them in the parish house when they come to dance at the feast of the patron saint.[14] Where there are no Mozambique, the Congo become the beneficiaries of this policy, but in that case the priest usually does not crown a king and queen but merely blesses the banners and receives in the church the blacks who come to pray before joining the dancing. However the *congada* is blessed only where it has not been totally secularized as a result of the earlier prohibition, where it is still associated with a fraternity such as that of Saint Benedict and there-fore still constitutes a link with the church, and where the participants are united by a vow of religious fidelity.

Thus black Catholicism is not entirely dead, but it no longer occupies its former place in the mystic community. In this chapter we shall be less concerned with black Catholicism itself than with the black's place within Brazilian Catholicism. Merged with the whites, treated like the whites, he still reacts to dogma and rites with a sensibility of his own—a racial or class sensibility.

■ ■ ■

Civilization is interiorized and maintained by education. As we have seen, Africa is handed down in sects such as the *candomblé* far more than in the family. Similarly Catholicism penetrates the spirit only through the teachings of the church. It is therefore linked to ecclesiastical control. Religious assimilation is a function of this control.

Our brief study of the transition from black Catholicism to a Catholi-cism of blacks has also supplied an answer to the question posed in the title of this chapter: assimilation or reinterpretation? The man of African descent, living in a town where there are priests, catechism classes, and Sunday sermons and where he may occasionally be visited by a "home missionary," shares exactly the same Catholicism as his white brother. And the purification of this Catholicism, which is becoming more and more Roman, spiritual, and "engaged," benefits him just as much as the whites. But church control ends when we move from the towns to the rural areas in a country where population dispersal is immense, where its aver-age density is six inhabitants per square kilometer. Counting both the regular and the secular clergy, Brazil has only one priest for every 6,412 Catholics; counting only priests who have a parish or a curacy, the number is one for every 9,200. And even this ratio is deceptive. In fact nearly all the priests are in the towns; in the rural areas parishes exist that are as big as several French departments put together. Particularly in Minas and in the *sertão* of the northeast there are parishes of 150,000 Catholics, and when we remember that they live on farms or in shanties that may be many miles apart, it is easy enough to understand why they see their priest only every year or two.[15] Mass is said in little chapels where the popula-tion is most concentrated. Children are baptized there and couples who are already living together are married, but the rest of the time the people are denied the comfort of the sacraments. To speak of "regular communion" or "catechism" in this context is meaningless. So far as religion goes, the population is thrown back on itself. The only religious education the chil-dren receive comes from the family, and the family, even if it is not illiterate, probably knows nothing about the dogma of the faith. In the absence of all control and education, Catholicism is bound to degenerate and reinterpretations of African religions may crop up.

Having seen in an earlier chapter the importance of the collective memory and its link with the organized social structures, we are in a position to understand how the dispersal and fragmentation of the population into isolated families resulted in a dilution and dwindling of the very substance of the Catholic tradition. A yearly visit from the priest was not sufficient to sustain it. Roman Catholicism degenerated into popular Catholicism. All that has survived is that which meets the needs of people lacking police protection (against the bandits of the *sertão*) and medical care (against malaria and intestinal disorders)—namely the cult of the saints. Each family places itself under the "protection" of a saint and there are also special saints for special purposes: Saints Lucy and Joseph for sending rain in times of drought, Saint Benedict for curing snakebite, Saint Roch for curing poisonous stings, Saint Margaret for safe childbirth, etc. When the highest strata of religion collapsed, nothing seemed to be left but the archaic strata—those of medieval Catholicism. One might suspect that there exists in society a law analogous to Ribot's law of psychology that personality disorders first attack the most recently formed parts of the ego and gradually progress to the older parts. The whites revert to medieval prayers, which they conceive of not as prayers but as magical formulae effective in themselves. The Indians and mixed-bloods, catechized by the Jesuits but abandoned when the Society of Jesus was expelled in the eighteenth century, revert to their ancient superstitions, to their obsession with monsters inhabiting forests and rivers. The Africans, cut off from both the *engenho* chapel and the organized *candomblé*, revert to the African conception of the *orixás*, but now it is integrated into the cult of the saints.

D'Oliveira maintains that African influence is weak in rural Brazil and that the blacks have been absorbed in the *caboclo* civilization.[16] This is true on the whole, first because the population is too dispersed to allow a true African collective memory to survive, and second because here miscegenation is not checked by urban color prejudice associated with racial and class competition. There seems to be no fundamental difference between the popular Catholicism of the Negroes and that of the *caboclos*. Their superstitions draw upon a common stock of beliefs, having to do with the cult of the saints, which is also shared by all the other ethnic groups that make up the rural population. Yet if we look beneath the surface and try to analyze religious behavior, we discover two things. First, the black in the regions closest to the *candomblé-xangô* areas does reinterpret the cult of the saints in terms of the cult of the *orixás*. And second, this distinctive behavior extends to the whole social fabric of which the black is an ethnic part through imitation on the part of the *caboclos*, through the merging of beliefs, and through racial miscegenation (for miscegenation is not a one-way process).

The extension of practices of the African sects to popular Catholicism may take explicitly "fetishist" forms, as when bloody animal sacrifices are offered to the statues of saints. On June 24, 1935, in a little chapel in the back country of Pernambuco, worshipers killed turkeys and chickens. The police official sent out to stop this ceremony, which had been organized in advance, was almost lynched by the angry crowd.[17] Travelers in the northeastern *sertão* say that in village sanctuaries a dish containing animal remains is often seen on a Catholic altar.[18] In the state of Bahia, the Feast of the Children, held under the auspices of Saints Cosmas and Damian, includes the sacrifice of fowls and the mixing of the blood with wine and honey. As the sacrificed fowls are placed near the statues of the saints on the domestic altar, the bowl circulates among the guests and each one drinks. The celebration also includes a communal meal followed until sunrise by Catholic prayers alternating with the profane *samba*.[19]

But reinterpretations may also take less spectacular forms. Although Arthur Ramos usually starts from the African religions and tries to determine which non-African elements have syncretized with them, one of the most interesting chapters in one of his books uses the opposite approach: "I start with popular Catholicism and try to discover what percentage was contributed by Negro religions and cults. I simply want to stress, with the aid of a few examples, that the African black . . . made a decisive contribution to popular polytheism." Ramos then lists the following examples: the favorite saints of the *sertanejos* are precisely the Catholic counterparts of the *orixás*. The prayers written on scraps of paper and hung around the neck in a little bag are called *macumbas*, although they are addressed to the saints. The importance attached by a *soi-disant* Catholic population to prayers addressed to the Devil—also undoubtedly of medieval European origin—can be explained only by the identification of the Devil with Exú.[20] On the other hand the habit of making "promises" to the saints (i.e. of vowing to do a certain thing if they cure someone, grant a good harvest, or give a sterile woman a child), an expression of the *do ut des* law of this essentially practical religion, is completely compatible with the African religion, which is based on the same principle. African-type promises of this sort quite often insinuate themselves into Catholic promises of the European type, such as the promise to dress in a certain color for a whole year. (These colors then become part of the *orixás*-saints-colors table of mystic correspondences.)[21] And the promise to "bathe in the holy water stoup" (there is no indication whether all or only part of the body was to be bathed or whether the bathing was to be done naked or clothed) certainly suggests a Catholic reinterpretation of bathing in the spring of Oxalá.[22]

But in areas where there can be no solidarity, however tenuous, except the ecological solidarity of greater or less proximity, it is clear that these reinterpretations are accepted by the *caboclo*, just as the black in turn accepts the *caboclo*'s Catholicism. In the rural zones assimilation occurs around a Catholicism that is magical rather than religious in character. I will give just one example representing convergence of mentalities rather than transfusion of cultures: the dual persona of the priest. On the one hand the priest is the representative of the church; it is he who administers the host and knows the secrets of God. He therefore has special powers which these simple minds confuse with the power of healers and sorcerers. On the other hand it is he who monopolizes the church, which should belong to the people, and who establishes a kind of hierarchy within Catholicism by separating the Catholicism of the elite from that of the masses. It is he who fights superstitions so firmly rooted in the faith that they seem to be an integral part of the true religion. Hence Catholic devoutness is tinged with anticlericalism. And perhaps even a memory may linger in men's minds of the times—now long gone—when priests were not ashamed to take mistresses and live openly with women, which deprived them of their thaumaturgic powers.

But it is hard for man to live in ambivalence, and he gets out of it by means of a dichotomy—in this case the distinction between the priest endowed with *mana* and the administrator-priest. Whenever a priest works a miracle, restores a blind person's sight, enables a victim of paralysis to walk, or offers the common people some tangible proof that he is in communication with the supernatural, crowds converge upon him, he precipitates fanatical actions, he is worshiped as a thaumaturge or a saint. Yesterday it was Father Cicero, today the curé of Poa.[23] Even after his death his mystic power lives on, either at his grave, which may become a place of pilgrimage, or through the emergence somewhere of a prophet who proclaims himself to be his reincarnation.[24] On the other hand, when a country priest sets himself up as master of his church, when his advice or rebukes cramp the simplistic faith of his flock, they ask by what right this man, who is supposed to be the chief servant of his house, a kind of executive sacristan, keeps the divine treasure under lock and key instead of distributing it to the unfortunate masses. "The priest cannot expel anyone from the church. The church belongs to the people. It is we who can expel the priest. It is our money he lives on."[25] This anticlericalism is clearly illustrated in certain popular dances and in folklore, notably in the *bumba-meu-boi*, where the role of the priest is combined with that of the clown, and in the "selling of the saints," where the priest is swindled by the shopkeeper. Leonardo Motta even cites a virulent satirical verse attacking a priest who buries a dog for money.[26]

Even if the priest's anointment legitimately gives him access to divine powers, when he is reduced to a mere administrator of his parish his thaumaturgic function may naturally pass to others. This explains the mystic epidemics that break out from time to time in remote areas of Brazil. Crowds flock to the new miracle-worker, who may be man, woman (like the "saint of Coqueiros"), or child (like "little Anthony" of São Paulo).[27] Catholic rites and prayers can also be effective without human intervention, through their magical quality, although their potency is increased when the prayer is spoken by a specialist endowed with powers of mediation between the human and the supernatural worlds. Everywhere in Brazil there are "blessers" who are distinct from sorcerers in that they work within Catholicism and for good, not evil, and from ordinary healers in that they use no herbs but only prayers and the sign of the cross. It is the blesser who is sent for when a farm animal falls sick or when the crops are meager. He blesses animals and plants, recites a prayer, and prosperity is miraculously restored.[28]

Here the black is no different from the rural masses. He too is anticlerical. As Tollenare pointed out, he has good reason to be. In the old days the slaves identified Catholicism with white wealth and power and understood and accepted rich, prosperous religious orders and cathedrals gleaming with gold and silver. But the introduction of mendicant orders, whose monks went from village to village, begging, tarnished the white priest's image and reduced him to a social status not much above that of the black himself.[29] On the other hand, the black, like the *caboclo*, regards the priest as endowed with *mana* by virtue of his chastity and his intimacy with the supernatural and believes that his actions have magic power. But the proof of his charisma lies solely in his works, and if some lay anchorite performs miracles or if some prophet roams the *sertão* healing the sick, the black too will turn away from the priest and follow the more powerful layman because the object of his respect is not the servant of God but the bearer of charisma, whether he wears a habit or not.

The assimilation of the Negro into the *caboclo* religion is easier to understand when we remember that this religion does not diverge radically from the conceptions on which the African sects are based. Far removed from the Catholicism of Rome as it may be, it is no less sincere on that account. The peasant thirsts for God and aspires to spiritual life, and since it is beyond the power of the church to provide the priests to guide him, he naturally creates his own ecclesiastical organizations and institutions. This desire for self-education in religion is extremely touching; there is no better illustration of the anguish these abandoned souls must suffer. Many homes, especially the most isolated ones in the back country, have their own little altar consisting of a plank below a color print of some saint, on which a candle flickers all night long. The villages cluster around a rustic chapel. For those who have no domestic altar there are always the wayside crosses[30] marking the place where someone was killed in an accident or murdered—holy ground where people can congregate to pray.

But failing a priest, they need at least a "prayer teller" (commonly called a *sacristão*) to direct the *reza* or religious ceremony. These prayer meetings may be held on fixed dates. In the *sertão*, for instance, the rosary of the Virgin is recited during the month of May,[31] and on Good Friday penitents go from cross to cross and from house to house, chanting hymns for the souls in Purgatory (though never entering the houses, because they are followed by the invisible cohort of the dead).[32] But more often the ceremonies are held on no specific date and consist of "promises" made to a saint to thank him for curing a sick person or finding a husband for an old maid. These religious meetings play an important sociological role as the equivalent of the French *veillée* (the passing of a winter evening in a neighbor's house) but in a form more suited to the equable Brazilian climate. At such times, when people exchange their customary isolation for closeness, a collective spirit may spring to life and forge the kind of bonds that distance destroys. That explains why these "novenas" end with a meal accompanied by brandy and with singing and dancing. The sound of a rustic guitar in the warm darkness creates a climate for love; couples form.[33] Sometimes the whole religious ceremony takes the form of a dance. Indeed in their efforts to evangelize the Indians the Jesuits conceived the idea of making use of their love of dancing by teaching them to dance around an image of a saint. The *catérété*, the *cururú*, the dance of the cross (replacing the maypole), and the dance of Saint Gonçalves (the Portuguese patron saint of marriageable girls) are the last survivals of Luso-Christian folklore.[34] They serve as a rallying point for this secular type of worship, this attempt by simple country people to find a substitute for the office of the mass and to nourish their religious faith in their isolation. Every district has its own *sacristão* or woman "prayer teller" who is called in to preside over the ceremonies since she knows the litanies and songs by heart. She is also called in for *velorios*, night-long wakes during which *excelências* are sung in a fixed order to induce the saints to keep in Paradise the soul that has just left its body.[35]

Strangers are sometimes shocked by the mixture of the profane and the sacred at these wakes, for sometimes stories are told to pass the time, and the *reza* often ends in joking and amorous dancing. But we must bear in mind that social gatherings are few and far between and that for people who live on manioc and dried meat the banquet that precedes the ceremonies, for which a steer is slaughtered, represents a godsend. The essential thing, it seems to me, is the drama of a faith, starved of nourishment by dispersal and distance, that invents its own mystic organs closer to home. The black, being more sociable than the *caboclo*, regularly attends these gatherings, bringing with him his own African concepts and his own exuberant gaiety. In Maranhão, as in Africa, a feature of Negro wakes is the asking of riddles and the playing of games such as "proposal and marriage."[36] In São Paulo the *reza* ends in the triumph of the Negro, who entertains the audience with his grimaces and songs.[37] But above all the black, in his rivalry with the *caboclo*, tries to rise to the rank of *sacristão* and become the master of the Catholic ceremonies. This is one more illustration of his desire to "get even," to wipe out his blackness by drawing as close as possible, in any way open to him, to the supernatural world, whose halo will then surround him, hiding his color in its glory. In any case the *sacristão* is often the blesser too.

Moving from the country to the country town, we find the church exercising a much more rigorous control. It does this through sodalities like the Daughters of Mary and sometimes through the parochial school. Here education is more advanced because the population is concentrated, and education gradually destroys superstition. Hence we are dealing here with a purer religion. But since the towns are still an extension of the fields, Catholicism is still somewhat rural in nature, as is shown by the astonishing gap between the number of baptized Catholics and the number who perform their Easter duty. Festivals have a dual character, both mystic and profane. The climax of the religious part is not the mass but the procession, in which the statues of the saints are carried through the streets surrounded by their devotees. The highlight of the profane part is the banquet and the distribution of food. The latter is performed by *festeiros*, rich or important laymen, nearly always white, who are selected a year in advance. A man may make a "promise" to act as a *festeiro* in acknowledgment of a grace bestowed by divine providence. Of course the *festeiros* are eager for their festival to outshine the previous year's, and their rivalry in providing lavish food becomes a veritable potlatch in which the winners can see their prestige rise within the community. But obviously one *festeiro* alone cannot furnish enough to feed the whole local population, not to mention the peasants who make the pilgrimage to the celebration on foot, on horseback, or by car or truck. So for three to six months beforehand, depending on the density of the population, local organizations known as *folias* go from farm to farm throughout the region soliciting food, money, and resources. In practice, therefore, this is no longer a distribution of food donated by the *festeiro* but rather a compensatory redistribution that takes from the rich to give equitably to the poor.[38]

For us the *folia* is of the utmost importance. Not only does it link the country with the town; it also serves, along with the *reza*, as an instrument of religious life to sustain the faith of people who live remote from any church. The *folia*, like the *festeiro*, is of Portuguese origin. Indeed the *festeiro* was a municipal institution introduced by local governments that lacked sufficient money to organize a proper Catholic festival and therefore decided to appeal to prominent local residents to assume the costs. The *folia* is the equivalent of the groups of boys and girls who until comparatively recently roamed the European countryside during the month of May asking for eggs or chickens. In Brazil, however, the *folia* has been organized as an institution having its own rules, structure, and life members, its musicians and singers, its standard-bearer and spokes-man, and sometimes, if the group is traveling by water, its own boatmen. In the north there are Christmas *folias*, in the south *folias* for the Feast of the Holy Ghost. For us the ceremony they are preparing for is irrelevant. The important thing is what the institution means to the people whom the *folia* visits.

The *folia* might be called a sprig broken off the trunk of the church and carried to all parts of the countryside. Although it consists entirely of laymen, they are surrounded by an ambiance of power, a halo of *mana*; they partake of the sacred and distribute it wherever they go. The rules of the organization forbid its members to derive any personal profit from their enterprise. They accept the food they are given at every stop and a bed overnight in the farmhouse or the barn, and they may pay for this by helping in the fields, but they receive no salary. They announce their arrival with firecrackers so that the more distant neighbors can assemble at their stopping place. Midway through the songs and hymns, the banner is handed to the master of the house, who places it next to the family altar. When night falls, the celebration begins. Like the *reza*, the *folia* is a pretext for a get-together, a momentary gathering in which the profane merges with the religious—a successor of the European *veillée*. The host decorates the banner with ribbons, and each yard of ribbon donated is a token of good luck for the household. The leader of the *folia* may cure the children's intestinal worms. The *folia*'s visit is a benediction for crops and cattle. When it departs, taking along the gifts it has received, it leaves behind its sacred footprints on the fields. It is an instrument of sanctifica-tion.[39]

It is not hard to understand that the black should wish to be a part of this organization—for the same reasons that make him eager to become a blesser or *sacristão*. In any case a life consisting of several months of vagabondage with nightly celebrations and plenty of singing and dancing suits his temperament, his indolence, and his love of social life. But what appeals to him most is the possession of sacred powers. Yet it is in the north that the blacks take the lead in the *folias*;[40] in the south the *caboclos* predominate. But even where they play only a secondary role, blacks will be found at every stop. The black may become a master of the profane ceremonies even if he cannot attain a leading role in the sacred part. Even here, however, the *caboclo* offers him strong competition, for in Brazil folklore still follows the color line, even though political democracy has eliminated it from public life.

In Minas and São Paulo a more popular entertainment, and sometimes the only accepted one, is the *cururú*. This is a dance, or more precisely a literary contest, organized by the Jesuits to teach religion to the Indian or mestizo masses. Each contestant has to improvise a series of verses on a given rhyme and Biblical theme; the winner is the one who shows the

deepest knowledge of the Bible or expresses his knowledge most poeti-
cally. After the expulsion of the Jesuits, the *cururú* survived and its religious function became more important in areas beyond the control of the
church. This oral tradition kept Biblical history and dogma alive (more,
interestingly enough, than the miracles of the saints). The singer became a
lay preacher. But this function, by its very origin, belonged to the *caboclo*.
The black had his *congadas* and *moçambiques*—his colorful, barbaric
rites, his blue or white costumes, his tin crowns gleaming in the sun.
Dressed in his work clothes, the *caboclo* sang outside the chapel or before
the cross, without resonant drums, accompanied only by the twanging of
his guitar. But he explained the Gospels.

It was only by dint of hard struggle that the black forced his way into
the *cururú* and was allowed to play a religious role when the divine *folia*
came by. And he achieved this only comparatively recently and, it seems,
only after immigrants, sons of Spaniards or Italians, had done so—not in
fact until the *cururú* was being eroded by the influence of the towns and
was setting as themes profane subjects, such as the city versus the country,
workers' hardships, and even election contests, instead of Bible stories.[41]
To be sure, the *cururú* has not cut the umbilical cord that links it with the
church. It always begins with a salutation of the saints and of Jesus. The
first contest, preceding the profane themes, is always devoted to Biblical
history. But it was because of this erosion that the Negro, with his remarkable talent for improvisation, was able to compete with the *caboclo*. Thus
it was something of a Pyrrhic victory. In any case, in Catholicism the black
always appears in the same stance: battering down the barriers that exclude him from the sacred and from all that touches it directly or indirectly. He refuses to accept the inferior position of a mere spectator
observing the mysteries from a distance. He wants to force his way into the
forbidden domain, to partake of the mystic values and try to make them
his own. It is more important to him to advance into the domain of the
sacred than to advance economically. He can put up with living in a
miserable hut, with being given nothing but poor land to cultivate, with
being surpassed or downtrodden as a farmer, so long as the community
recognizes him as endowed with power, as a bestower of graces. For he
has sensed—if not understood—that in rural Brazil the supreme value is
not wealth but religion.

■ ■ ■

This religion, for all its weaknesses and debasement, constitutes the
supreme value because it is the only means of communication available to
a scattered population, the only link, the only framework within which the
sertanejos can come together and achieve communion. Yet the Roman
Catholics are intent upon destroying it, as they destroyed black Catholi-

cism, in order to replace it with a purer, more educated Catholicism closer to European models. No wonder the *caboclo* refused to go along with this. It was not just his habits that were at stake; it was the indispensable minimum of social life that stood between him and the hell of solitude. He therefore reacted, and his reaction took the form of messianic movements.

German sociology, with Nietzsche and Max Weber, linked the phenomenon of messianism with resentment or, to use a more contemporary expression, with frustration. This explains the importance Max Weber gives to the concepts of nation, class, and pariah caste in his explanation of messianism.[42] American anthropologists have placed more emphasis on the clash of two heterogeneous civilizations. Their classic example has been the case of the Plains Indians after the extinction of the buffalo, the basis of their diet. Those Indians undoubtedly constituted a pariah class, but they became aware of it only in their struggle against the whites, who destroyed their ancient tribal organizations. In this case messianism is defined by a return to a mythic past and the elimination of the white civilization. The American analysis does not contradict the German one based on the psychology of collective resentment; it merely adds a new element to the sociological explanation, the factor responsible for arousing or crystallizing the resentment—namely the clash of an exploiting and an exploited civilization.[43] Anthropologists interested in messianism have followed this lead. Whether they are dealing with Melanesian, Madagascan, or African messianism, they have invariably seen it as a defensive reaction by the threatened native culture against the new imported culture that is destroying the old values.[44] But they then complicate this counteracculturation interpretation with other elements borrowed either from psychoanalysis or from the theory of alterations in the basic personality (Kardiner's study of the Madagascan *tromba*[45]) or (as in the case of Balandier[46]) from the sociology of colonialism, which by blocking political protest leaves nationalism no outlet except religious messianism. But even if messianism does project the myth of the past into the future, that is no reason to neglect the collective representations that sustain it. The existence of a pariah group or a civilizational clash does not automatically precipitate messianism, even where the basic personality conflicts with the new primary institutions, even where the outlet of political nationalism is blocked by colonialism, if the mythology of the colliding peoples is unable to provide the necessary images for it to build on. Oesterley showed this to be true of the messianism of classical antiquity,[47] and it is equally true of Indian messianism, which is based on the legend of the civilizing hero. However, when the oppressed civilization lacks these indispensable mythic representations (as is usually the case with the African civilizations), it borrows them from the oppressing civilization—i.e. from Christianity. This explains why Negro messianism is more developed in Protestantized settings, where the Bible has familiarized the natives with the notion of the prophet, than in Catholic ones, where the Old Testament and the Apocalypse are of less importance in the education of the faithful.

All the elements I have briefly enumerated appear in the *caboclo* messianism of Brazil: pariah group, civilizational clash, preclusion of a political solution so that religion becomes the only outlet, and the existence of earlier collective representations. The dualism of the seaboard and the *sertão* steadily increased (at least until recently, when better communications between the two parts of the country began to reduce it), turning the *caboclos* into a pariah group. But messianism does not appear until this group becomes conscious of the pressure exerted upon it by the invading seaboard civilization. Messianism is a reaction to that pressure aimed at maintaining the values of the group. Theoretically, of course, this reaction could take a political form, and in fact these messianic movements have always contained political elements—the reaction against the republic after the collapse of the empire, struggles between governors, movements for provincial autonomy—but when pure political protest failed, protest continued in the form of religious revolt.[48] Finally, the *caboclo* group had its own myths to sustain its messianism. Where the Indian element was still strong, though diluted, it had the myth of the Land without Evil;[49] where the Portuguese element was preponderant, it had the myth of Sebastianism —the myth that Dom Sebastian, king of Portugal, did not die but disappeared in the struggle against the Moors and will some day return to restore his country's vanished glory. Sebastianism was transmitted from Portugal to Brazil, where it reinterpreted the myth of the Land without Evil and became the pariah group's dream of a new land where men would no longer have to work and where all would enjoy wealth and happiness.[50] There is no need for us to trace all the phases of Sebastianism in Brazil; it is to be found in all messianic movements and, by infiltrating the popular religion, it opened to the folk culture a channel of protest against Roman Catholicism.

The first point to be made is that urban Roman Catholicism does not accept lay leadership. The priest alone, duly ordained and anointed, may speak for the church, and his value does not derive from his charisma but from his place in the priestly hierarchy. Certainly some priests are dearly loved by the rural people because they heal the crowds by blessing them. (The most famous example is little Father Cicero, whom I have already mentioned, but there are many others.) But the church looks askance at these sporadic movements that arouse whole regions, banning them and transferring the priests involved. Father Cicero was forbidden to say mass. Nevertheless, as I have said, the forsaken inhabitants of the *sertão*, who are beyond the reach of the church, feel a real need to supply their own priests. This explains the emergence of anchorites, prophets, and "prayer tellers" all over Brazil who go from farm to farm preaching the popular faith at the foot of the cross like true itinerant missionaries. These prophets usually lead ascetic lives, never asking for money but simply devoting themselves to charity, but the insistence of the crowd that follows them in their travels, hoping for miracles, sometimes forces them to perform miraculous works of healing against their will. When they become too well known, the Roman church sends regular priests to turn the country people against them. The *caboclos* interpret this interference as an attempt by the people of the seaboard or the big cities to deprive them of their one and only true worldly possession. They see it not as an attempt to lead them back to Catholicism but to deprive them of it, because for them Catholicism is identified with the religious propaganda of these bearers of charisma. If things are going badly for the *sertanejos* economically or politically, their feelings of frustration crystallize around the attacked prophet, who then feels he owes it to his errant flock to become the spokesman of the disinherited.

The messianic explosions of Canudos and the Contestado movement began with a clash of this kind.[51] In the former, Antonio Maciel preached to the peasants of the arid, famine-ridden northeast his apocalyptic message of an overthrow of all values: "In 1896 we shall see the herds return to the *sertão* and the *sertão* will become the seaboard and the seaboard will become the *sertão*. . . . In 1899 the waters will turn to blood and the planet will appear in the East with the rays of the sun and the sun will crash into the sky and . . . from the waves of the sea will emerge Dom Sebastian with his whole army." Under police and ecclesiastial persecution Antonio Maciel was transformed into Antonio the Counselor. The tattered crowds followed him into the *caatinga*, singing hymns and listening to his promises of a world without misery or famine.

In the Contestado revolt the religious preaching of an army deserter who called himself José Maria the Second after a legendary lay monk of that name served as the nucleus for the crystallization of a protest movement of *caboclos* who had been driven off their land to make way for the railroad linking São Paulo to Uruguay. The church sent an Italian priest to denounce this "false monk"—a move that the *caboclos* saw as a disturbing interference with their own Catholicism and that naturally resulted in an intensification of the protest and the triumph of messianism. It was said that the first José Maria was not dead but had retreated to a sacred mountain and that he would come with Saint Sebastian's host of angels to establish the kingdom of the Holy Ghost on earth.

The second point to be made is that this Brazilian messianism takes the mythic form of the restoration of popular Catholicism and its triumph over Roman Catholicism. It may be tragic or joyous depending on local conditions, as if it were assuming the complexion of the land—apocalyptic in the sun-scorched northeast, bristling with spiny vegetation; more clement in the pine forests of the south. But everywhere its aim is to make permanent the rare moments of social communion available to the scattered inhabitants. The world they dream of is not the world of isolation and fragmentation into individual families but the world of the *reza*, the religious celebration or procession that brings people together, uniting them and transforming the sadness of solitude into the exaltation of the reestablished collectivity. At Canudos, Antonio Conselheiro built his new Jerusalem away in the mountains and the *caboclos* came from all over the *sertão* to await the arrival of Heaven on earth with prayers, hymn singing, and interminable processions. But Heaven had already arrived, for solitude had been ended and social communion had become permanent. Yet man cannot live on prayer alone, and in order to eat, the inhabitants of Canudos, along with the bandits who had joined them, pillaged neighboring properties. The army intervened to preserve order, but the Canudos *caboclos* resisted so fanatically that it took four military expeditions to destroy the new Jerusalem, the first three of which ended disastrously for the army.

José Maria the Second also organized his followers into "holy cadres" modeled after the popular fraternities of the Holy Spirit and the Knights of Charlemagne (whose legend is well known in the interior of Brazil, thanks to the fondness of the popular poets for medieval romances) and these developed into a whole series of popular Catholic celebrations—processions, choral singing—that were no longer sporadic but continued day in and day out, as if profane time had been abolished and replaced by a sacred time. They too raided other people's property to obtain food without having to work for it (which would have meant falling back into profane time), once more the army had to intervene, and again it took several bitter military campaigns, in which the army suffered many reverses, to put down the fanatics.

Since Brazilian messianism essentially takes the form of a struggle of popular Catholicism against Roman Catholicism, since the feelings of frustration, of being a pariah group, of civilizational clash, always crystallize around this folklore Catholicism and since, as I pointed out in the first part of this chapter, the rural black was assimilated and integrated into this popular religion, we must now determine his exact place in messianism and see whether he introduced African reinterpretations.

The question is all the more important in view of the fact that black messianism exists in other regions of the Americas, particularly in the United States, and that we have already seen its rudiments emerging in Brazil, within Umbanda spiritism, in conjunction with a psychology of resentment. In the United States the blacks constitute a pariah group, and it is quite understandable that they should dream of liberating heroes and of a new Moses to lead them to the Promised Land. Everything conspired to induce the blacks of the United States to create their own messiahs—their sufferings under slavery, the disintegration of their native cultures as a result of contact with white civilization, then, after the abolition of slavery, the institution of the color line in the south, the existence of ecological or economic discrimination in the north, the poverty of the rural Negro population, the maladjustments of the immigrants of color in the big industrial cities, the riots and the lynchings. And messiahs did emerge, though most of them were local figures whose fame did not extend beyond the radius of their preaching.[52] But it was the interwar Depression that gave the movement its full force, culminating in God's reincarnation in Father Divine. Father Divine's message (which was utilitarian as much as mystical)—the provision of food for the hungry and dormitories for the homeless, building the kingdom of Heaven on earth with the aid of his black angels—gained him over sixty thousand followers, despite police persecution.[53] Two points, however, should be noted. In the first place this is a black, not an African, messianism. In the African religions man is in harmony with nature; the rhythm of his social life is attuned to that of cosmic life; man partakes of the supernatural, a supernatural that does not transcend physical things but whose living presence pervades the whole universe. These are not religions of hope or social protest. They seem unable to furnish the mythic frameworks necessary for prophetic proclamations of civilizing heroes who will reappear in an apocalypse. Their rites do not project the past into future history; they realize it in the present.

Before a messianism offering the blacks revenge upon the whites—a transposition or reinterpretation of the Jews' revenge upon the pagans—can emerge, two conditions are necessary. First, Christianity must have broken with the African religions by preaching the damnation of the sinner and his salvation through rebirth and the dogma of the Cross—tenets that, in killing the old Adam, kill the old native civilization too. Second, to replace what has been destroyed and to fill the gap, Protestantism must have introduced the sense of history, the sense of serial time, the Old Testament of the prophecies of the messiah and the apocalypse in which Christ the Redeemer will return to restore justice. Thus North American messianism is the messianism of a pariah group, not a phenomenon of counteracculturation, and it therefore comes as no surprise to find its equivalent in other countries that are subject to Anglo-Saxon influence, e.g. Jamaica.[54]

In Brazil two factors precluded an authentic black messianism. First, in the *tambores, candomblés, xangôs,* and *batuques* the African religions survived in a pure state, keeping the black attuned to nature, not to a problematical future. Second, the society had no color line and therefore no pariah group. It is true that the disappearance of the African civilizations in the south is creating the conditions of alienation that might provide a basis for a psychology of resentment. It is also true that although there are no official racial barriers, the black usually occupies the lowest positions in society and that this may inspire dreams of divine liberation.

And indeed the only indications we have so far discovered of potential black messianism in Brazil have been among urban Negroes, when their traditional cults have been eroded by urbanization, and within Umbanda spiritism, which is a protest movement against discrimination and against white stereotypes and prejudices intensified by economic competition in the labor market. But although there is no true independent and autonomous Negro messianism, the Brazilian black, as a participant in the *caboclo* culture, could at least participate in the rural messianism described earlier in this chapter. And in fact, although the centers of this messianism are located in areas having the fewest Negro inhabitants— regions such as the arid *sertão* and the cattle-raising country or the border zone between Paraná and Santa Catarina—the black is well represented in the movements I have mentioned. Does he bring to them something new, something specifically Negro or African—modest as such a contribution must be by reason of his small numbers?

In the Canudos uprising one of the prophet's principal counselors was a light-skinned mulatto known as Antonio the Blessed. He would go from shanty to shanty chatting, looking around, and keeping Conselheiro informed of what went on in the holy village. He also played a role in the capitulation. Having been taken prisoner, he was ordered by the government troops to go to the insurgent *caboclos* and ask them to surrender en masse. He did in fact return to the camp but brought along the sick and the women and children—in short, all the noncombatants, so that his mission backfired against the besiegers. Other blacks, mulattoes, and *cafusos* also were involved in the Canudos uprising, but chiefly as soldiers, not as religious leaders.[55]

In the Contestado, *fazendeiros* who shared the folk culture of their hired hands joined up with humble *caboclos*, caboclized Italian and German immigrants, Indians, and a handful of blacks. Here again the blacks were soldiers or subordinates, not leaders. In Joazeiro, Father Cicero's village, one of his followers had given the priest the calf of a cow crossed with a zebu, which was placed in the charge of José Lourenço, a Negro member of the penitent brotherhood. A friend of Lourenço promised the animal a bale of hay if Lourenço would put in a good word for him with the Father. Because of a drought the friend was unable to keep his promise, but Lourenço decided to help himself to the hay, believing that this would not be stealing but merely forcing his forgetful friend to keep his promise. The calf, however, refused the food. Turning its sad eyes on the black, it gently mooed. The plaintive sound made Lourenço fall to his knees. Asking God's forgiveness, he swore never to steal again. The miraculous animal immediately became an object of worship. Pilgrims prostrated themselves before it, decorating its manger with flowers and bringing it the most succulent grass. A therapeutic magic sprang from the cult. The animal's urine cured trachoma and other eye diseases; scrapings from its horns prevented bad luck and healed ulcers. Superstition reached such a pitch that to prevent Father Cicero from becoming a laughing stock it was necessary to kill the calf, despite the frantic resistance of the Negro, who had to be locked up.[56] After the death of the priest, Lourenço became the leader of a group of followers who gave him all they possessed and worked for him free. The police intervened to prevent the exploitation of the poor *caboclos* by "*Beato* Lourenço," the Catholic title by which he was commonly known, and he had to take to the *caatinga* with some of his "believers." The police pursued him, but Lourenço finally escaped, leaving his followers to be massacred.

Clearly when the black is involved in these *caboclo* messianic movements, it is not as an instigator but as a symbol of loyalty to the leader, as a devoted slave. And the element he carries over from his own religion is a tendency toward "fetishism," a tendency to organize the movement as a cult—the very opposite of dynamic hope, of spiritual revolution.

He does not create; he follows. And if he does not follow the *caboclos*, he follows the whites. This was the case with the Negroes of Taubaté in the state of São Paulo. In 1885 a lawyer who had taken up spiritism thought up "the building of Noah's ark," a ceremony that he no doubt conceived of in an apocalyptic vein. The end of the world was at hand, precipitated by human sinfulness. A ship must be built to transport future humanity to the new land. He succeeded in getting his slaves and other members of his spiritist tent to accept this mad idea, and blacks and whites were united in the same dream. The lawyer's house became the scene of strange processions, including barefooted, disheveled women. The ceremony was supposed to end with the sacrifice of a child, reconciled to its fate, whose blood would be drunk by the community. With the help of the police the perturbed local population managed to prevent the ritual murder, and the participants in the ceremony were imprisoned. The arrests were marked by outbursts of madness, particularly on the part of a Negro woman who tried to kill a girl, claiming that she had been ordered to do so by Saint Luke.[57]

In the Serra do Salitré in the state of Minas the Negro again appears in messianism as a collaborator rather than a leader. After seeing visions of angels and hearing celestial voices, the patriarch José Antonio believed himself to be "the living God come down from Heaven" and "the eternal Father." He established a cult centered on the worship of his daughter and began a propaganda campaign that reached as far as Goyaz. Followers were beginning to flock to him when the police were alerted by reports that members of the sect were being tortured. There was a fight in which the prophets of the new religion were killed. Here again the black's contribution was not to develop the messianic element but to lend his organizational talent and introduce certain African survivals. José Antonio's first lieutenant was a Negro named Antonio Rezende, who was believed to be the incarnation of Saint Anthony. It was he who initiated evening services illuminated by candles and torches, amid the smoke of incense and rue, with singing and dancing, Negro bands, etc., as well as elements of animal worship, if not outright totemism. In my opinion these few examples prove that when the black does play a role in messianic prophetic movements it is as the organizer of a ritual order rather than as a messiah or prophet.[58]

In the case of João de Camargo, however, we can actually watch the birth of a religion arising out of a messianic movement. Camargo's mother was a healer in the state of São Paulo and he himself began life as a village healer. In 1905, as he was returning home from the town, drunk, the Virgin appeared to him in a vision and asked him to build a chapel. In a second vision on the road to the Serra São Francisco, a white child, a mulatto woman, and a black man—i.e. Jesus, Our Lady of the Apparition, and Saint Benedict—announced a more important mission: "You are the man of our color chosen to demonstrate the power of God to man."

The color complex underlying this messianism is clearly discernible; the motive is revenge against the whites. We can trace the parallel development of the messianic element and the element of religious organization that, as I have said, is the characteristic contribution of the Negro. At first the prophet receives, in the manner of the spiritist cult he is imitating, only the spirits of Alfredinho, a child who died at the scene of his first vision, and of Monsignor Soares, a great Catholic prelate whose memory was firmly entrenched throughout the area. Later he receives the spirits of the saints, then the Holy Ghost itself, and even God. In the final stage he incarnates the church, which, he believes, stands above God Himself, representing the totality of all the saints, the souls, and the Divinity. This church sends him to Santos, where on a mountain top he will learn "all the secrets of the world and of the church." From then on he is God of the Earth. But as his mystic power grows, his religion is organized on the material plane. The faithful flock to his primitive chapel from all parts of the state and from the rest of Brazil as well. He even receives letters from overseas. Gradually a village grows up. The chapel is replaced by a great church on whose altars the saints are mostly black. Hotels, boarding houses, grocery stores, a medium's house, and a house for the band spring up around it. By 1928 there are eighteen buildings, representing a total cost of 300,000 cruzeiros. Hidden behind the altar of Nosso Senhor de Bomfim, so dear to the hearts of blacks, João de Camargo listens to the requests of his clients, speaks with the spirits, gives prescriptions and advice.

This religion, still in the process of crystallization, includes many African elements along with imitations of Catholicism and spiritist influences. Saint Benedict, for instance, is called Rungondongo. (In the *macumba* of Rio the Negroes call him Lindongo.) The cult of the saints is linked to certain days of the week much as it is in the *candomblés* of Bahia. Friday is dedicated to the Sacred Heart of Jesus (Obatalá), Saturday to Our Lady of Sorrows (Yemanjá), and Sunday to All Saints (all the *orixás*). But the most significant of these African elements is the cult of stones, which João de Camargo brought back from his visit to Santos and which is so characteristic of the Dahoman religion. Polished stones, white at the top, black at the bottom, and chips of rock are placed first on the altar of Bom Jesu, then on a side altar, where finally, through a verbal association, they are dedicated to Saint Peter. It is also possible that the importance attached to certain mysterious numbers such as three and five can be attributed to the influence of *macumba*. Undoubtedly this is a case of black messianism, although it does not involve vast crowds of people, praying, and fighting, as the movements in the *sertão* did. That element is quickly submerged in organization and religious systematization, in the creation of a church. João de Camargo is no itinerant prophet; he waits for the believers to come to him in his church, where they will pray and ask the help of his divine powers.[59]

I believe that these examples suffice to show that we are dealing here with individual messianism, not that of the black group—a messianism that, unlike the *caboclo* movements, tends to create a cult or rites rather than a New Jerusalem ideology.[60]

In any case, returning to the question—assimilation or reinterpretation? —we see that with messianism, as with Catholicism, we never face a real dilemma. Both phenomena occur side by side in messianism and in Catholicism. Reinterpretation is to be seen in animal sacrifices to the saints and in the importance of human sacrifices in messianism. Assimilation is illustrated by the Negro's participation in rural Catholicism as a leader (*sacristão* or blesser) or in the movements of *caboclo* prophets as a soldier. When resentment exists, it shows itself not in the creation of a utopian city, not in dreams of an apocalypse or the promise of better days to come, but in the prosaic, down-to-earth desire to dominate the whites or the *caboclos*, who despise the black for his color. He strives to become the leader of the *reza*, to be accepted in the *folia*, or he is charged by God with the mission of saving the whites as herald of a new religion. When he encounters a stereotype, a prejudice, a barrier, he does not seek escape in daydreams but tries to rise to the top by accepting other people's values and using them as a springboard.

Thus for him mystic compensation, if it exists, is never more than the first step toward practical realization.

■ ■ ■

The problem of the significance of the Protestantism of the blacks is very controversial. Some people believe that in the United States the separation of the two churches by color and the fact that the first Negro preachers were untrained in theology made it possible for the black churches to retain African cultural traits and gave this protestantism certain characteristics that distinguish it from the Protestantism of the whites. These characteristics include emotionalism; the maternal aspect of Christianity or the feminization of God; the greater emphasis in sermons on rebirth and on criticism of the evil rich (the whites); the congregation's participation in the church service through dialogues with the pastor; conversions produced by visions, voices, or dreams; worship seen as a pursuit of ecstasy caused by the descent of the Holy Spirit; hymns sung to the accompaniment of clapping and foot tapping, swaying and convulsive trembling; and literal interpretation of the Bible. According to Herskovits all these features represent African elements reinterpreted in terms of white Christianity. But other sociologists, including Frazier and Palmer, stress the existence of analogous phenomena in the preaching and trances of white religious revivals. In the United States the problem is complicated by racism. In general it is the whites, with their liking for exoticism, who insist on the differences between the white and the black religion, and the blacks, always wanting to deny their African heritage and define themselves in Western terms, who insist on the similarities.[61] It is true that Protestantism made its greatest strides among blacks when revivalism was at its height and that white revivals were characterized by the same type of sermons, hymn singing, testifying, and mystic trance. But white Protestantism has evolved, while that of the blacks has remained the same in the lower class, particularly in the South.[62] The blacks imitated and stuck to revivalist religion rather than nonemotional Protestantism because it suited them better, fitted their own view of man's relations with the supernatural, their love of music, rhythm, and dancing, and their ancient ritual of communion with the divine. So if we were to find an analogous Protestantism of an essentially emotional nature among Brazilian blacks we should have every reason to define it as a reinterpretation of Africa. This, however, is by no means the case. On the contrary the Protestantism of Brazilian blacks is no different from the puritanical, dogmatic, legalist religion of the whites. And when illuministic Protestantism does emerge in Brazil, it draws its followers from the marginal immigrants rather than from the nonwhites, as I shall try to show.

Brazilian Protestantism did not develop until the nineteenth century, largely as a result of North American missionary activity after the constitution of 1823, which provided, if not religious freedom, at least religious tolerance. Methodism was established in 1836, Congregationalism in 1858, Presbyterianism in 1862, and the Baptist denomination in 1882. Protestantism made steady progress under the empire, and after the proclamation of the republic and the separation of church and state it gained ground with disconcerting rapidity, considering the strong Catholic traditions of the country. The number of Protestants rose to almost two million in a total population of fifty-two million. The first Brazilians to be affected were whites of the intermediate class, small landowners or homesteaders in the rural zones, members of the emerging middle class in the towns. Only when Protestantism began to take hold among the big traditional families was the Negro affected, in a sort of chain reaction. I have spoken of the family character of patriarchal Catholicism and we have seen how the slaves attended family worship, listened to the prayers, and joined in the responses to the litanies before going out into the darkness of the *senzala*. So when the masters were converted, the slaves followed suit.

When it came to the evangelization of the blacks, the big Brazilian plantation owner never showed the same hesitation as did his North American counterpart, a hesitation that, when evangelization did begin, led to the founding of black churches separate from the whites ones. The Brazilian tradition was quite different—a domestic tradition that incorporated the slave into the life of the family. Protestantism inevitably strengthened this old established feeling, first because of the role played by family worship but more especially because conversion intensified the master's sense of responsibility and obligation toward his subordinates. There is something of the pastor and the missionary in every Protestant, which explains why, as early as 1879, the Presbyterian community of São Paulo received five black slaves. But it would be wrong to conclude that black Protestantism, still in its infancy, was always imposed from outside. Among those five Negroes in 1879 was at least one, Felismena by name, whose owners had made her wait four years for their permission to embrace the new faith.[63] This case is symptomatic, showing that some nonwhites felt an inner need for a different kind of Christianity, more emotional and less social, more inward and less like a public spectacle. Unless of course they thought that the change of religion would offer a new channel of upward mobility. For Protestantism, a religion of the book, meant learning to read, and this in turn created a new elite among the illiterate rural masses.

Another attraction Protestantism held for the blacks was the antislavery stance it took almost from the outset. This was particularly true of the small Negro and mulatto elite in the towns; although they were free artisans, they were not unmindful of the lot of their enslaved brothers. There seem to have been many of these in certain churches in Bahia and Rio de Janeiro and in some country churches too. In order to explain the great success of Protestantism among these humble workers, the Catholics claimed that pastors were paying people to be converted: twenty cruzeiros (approximately 300 French francs at the time of writing) for whites, fifteen for mulattoes, and ten for blacks.[64] Today in the south, where economic competition has revived prejudice and given rise to discrimination, Protestantism still seems more attractive to blacks than does Catholicism. During my study of race relations in São Paulo, I heard Negroes complain that Catholic girls' schools would not accept black children, that

the boys' schools steered the black students toward vocational rather than humanistic studies in order to keep them separate from the whites, and that in some parishes black girls were discouraged from joining the Children of Mary on the grounds that they had their own sodality of the Rosary. The Protestant churches and schools, however, did not discriminate.[65] Thus Brazilian Protestantism in its various forms still retains its attraction. It is impossible to estimate the number of black Protestants. Judging by the churches I visited in São Paulo and Bahia, I would estimate that it corresponds approximately to the ratio of blacks to the total population of each specific region.

But more important to us than the number of Negro or mulatto Protestants is the character of their faith. Everyone I questioned on this subject agreed that black Protestants are no different from white ones of the same sect, and this is especially true of Methodists and Baptists. Brazilian Protestantism, being of recent origin, assigns a very important place to religious education in the form of Bible study groups and Sunday schools (which are not for children only, as in France, but include adults). Hence, since the church permits no discrimination, the blacks receive exactly the same religious education as the whites, and there is total assimilation of beliefs and feelings. We find indirect evidence of this assimilation in publications by black Protestants such as José da Silva Oliveira, who tried to introduce the Methodist rules of life among the Negroes of São Paulo in an attempt to free the whites of their prejudices (the blacks becoming the equals of the whites through their moral purity) and at the same time to improve the material and social condition of their brothers (a mutual aid society to promote literacy, the will to work, thrift, and a desire for social advancement).[66]

But along with this first type of reformed church there exists in Brazil an illuministic Protestantism into which the black sometimes made his way. There were even some attempts to establish Negro churches. One example is a Negro named Bibiano, who founded the Militant and Triumphant Catholic Church in São Paulo. This was the first Brazilian church established by a black; hence it expressed the inspirations of black Protestantism in a pure state, as distinguished from slavish imitation of the whites. Although its members were preponderantly colored, the new sect attracted whites too. This marked the first major difference from the United States: the impossibility of introducing racial barriers in the churches. In Brazil ecumenism always proved stronger than separatism. While the Protestant church in Rio reflected the religious sensibilities of the whites and imposed them on the blacks, the Militant and Triumphant Catholic Church did just the opposite. "Bibiano enriched the religious ceremonial, creating congregations of men, angelic hierarchies for the women, children's choirs, and organizations for widows and deaconesses."[67]

The prime importance of music in this cult, its adherence to the Bible and to the organization of the primitive Christian church, its establishment of angelic hierarchies (like those of Father Divine in the United States), its liking for pompous ceremonies and titles—these are some of the distinctive features that already existed in North America and that Bibiano unknowingly rediscovered in Brazil, precisely because they corresponded to something specifically black. But an even more striking feature is the separation of religion and morality that sociologists have noted in the black lower class of the United States and that is a survival from the African ancestral religion.[68] Bibiano was arrested for committing indecencies with female members of his congregation under the pretext of satisfying their religious needs. Members of the church accused the police of having acted without valid grounds, purely in response to pressure from white Catholics who wanted to destroy the new sect. They also accused the police of responsibility for Bibiano's death in prison in 1914, which they attributed to poison. But the arrest of Bibiano in 1912 did not destroy the church. It continued to function, from 1914 until 1938 under the direction of Benedito Leite and after that under another Negro, Narciso.

The service consists of hymns of North American origin (which in this black church have taken on the sensual character of Brazilian songs), of sermons, delivered in a state of trance or semitrance, on such subjects as the glorification of the unfortunate and the damnation of the powerful. Narciso divides men into two groups, the pure and the impure, but the impure can be born again through the gift of grace. Science is useless; one must listen to God, who speaks directly to each individual.

We should note, however, that this attempt remains individual rather than collective, reiterating the conclusion we reached about black messianism. Negro protest in southern Brazil takes a political rather than a religious form. The Militant Church now has very few members and is slowly dying out in a small São Paulo suburb. The Protestant black seeks in his faith a means of rising and being assimilated into a white elite, not a means of remaining separate and expressing himself as a man of color. He joins a church in which there is a minimum of superstition and a maximum of Puritanism.

Indeed, one of the facts that observers find most striking is the gradual decline of magic wherever Protestantism is introduced—the substitution of scientific medicine, submission to divine providence, ritual prayers, promises to the saints, and the transition from empiricism to rational thought, from secularization to the supernatural. It is true that in the isolated deserts of the back country the social and cultural climate proves stronger than the dynamism of the reformed religion. Protestant rationalism may clash and struggle with magical collective representations, and where there is struggle there is also the possibility of defeat. Yet such defeats seem to be rare and to involve only recent converts, still incompletely adjusted to the Protestant climate. One might even say that they are a sign that control by the religious community no longer exists. They represent a return to an archaic sensibility, to a repressed past no longer held in check by censorship of any kind, rather than an effect of institutionalized syncretism between Protestantism and magic.

The most significant illustration of this is a mystic crime committed in 1950 in the little village of Belisario in Minas. In 1938 a forty-year-old Negro named João Pedro Gomes, who called himself an Angola but was actually from Rio de Janeiro, arrived in the village, bringing with him an English Bible. Gomes became friendly with the local Methodist pastor, an itinerant minister who went from chapel to chapel preaching the gospel to the scattered rural population. Like many blacks, Gomes was a good speaker and was asked to take charge of the community in the absence of the missionary pastor. By stirring up nationalistic sentiment against this new minister, he succeeded in founding a dissident Methodist community, which he named the Evangelical Apostolic Fraternity of Jesus Christ. But it was not long before Gomes seduced two local girls and was obliged to flee, leaving the new sect without a leader. The wife of a local landowner took his place.

A madwoman named Gloria Fontes Pereira, who was subject to periodic seizures, attended the church. Country people do not regard madness as an ordinary disease to be treated like a regular illness. To them it is the result of demonic possession and the only way to cure it is by exorcism. Gloria was therefore treated by hymn singing, Bible readings, and other supernatural procedures, but the only result was that her madness became so much worse that the poor woman had to be tied up with ropes to prevent her from running away. The members of the congregation walked round and round the bound, howling body, singing and exhorting the Devil to come out. At this point a man of color appeared, a mulatto cowhand from the isolated grazing lands. His nickname was "the Angel" and he was still, after only eight months, incompletely converted to Protestantism. In this atmosphere of mystic turmoil the Angel felt himself entrusted with a divine mission. He knew that the Devil is the serpent that tempted Eve, and that in the country you kill a snake by crushing its head beneath your heel. One day, when the madwoman's contortions and howling were more violent than usual, the two ideas came together, the one Biblical, the other derived from his own experience as a *sertanejo*, and the Angel persuaded the villagers that the only way to deliver the woman from the serpent was to crush its head. With a blow of his heel he crushed Gloria's forehead.[69]

This illustrates the conditions under which the black may introduce superstitious elements and a pathological mysticism into Protestantism: namely in the early stages of his conversion, when the Protestant influence is still superficial and is suddenly suspended because for one reason or another he is no longer under the control of the church. But may this not also represent an institutionalization of mysticism (which would bring us closer to the Negro Protestantism of the United States)? As I have said, blacks turned to the reformed religion under the pressure of emotional needs because they wanted to live their faith more intimately and feel closer to God. It was only later that Protestant rationalization had its effect on them and made the Protestantism of these Brazilian blacks the very opposite of that of their North American brothers. In recent years Pentecostalism has made great gains in Brazil. This religion, based on the preaching of the Holy Spirit and the hope of outward and extraordinary favors through the institutionalization of mystic trance, is more responsive to a certain African cultural trait than the old Methodism or even the Baptist faith. Pentecostalism is enjoying great success in Africa today. How does the Brazilian black react to this new religion?

Pentecostalism in its southern form (the "Christian Congregation," the "Religion of Glory," or the "Fiery Tongues") was founded in Brazil by an Italian-American from the United States named Luis Francescon. At the start he addressed himself to his compatriots, and the first group he formed consisted of Italians. The extraordinary success of the sect stems from the fact that the vast majority of immigrants in the state of São Paulo are Italians or of Italian descent. While some rich industrialists like the Spinas were converted, Pentecostalism remains a proletarian religion, spreading to Portuguese and Spanish immigrant groups and white working-class Brazilians and finally to Negroes and, more especially, to mulattoes. But the colored are always a minority; some churches are one-third black; in others blacks account for only two or three percent of the congregation. Nevertheless this minority plays an important role. Blacks like to talk, and when the time comes for "testifying," making a public confession before their brothers, they are the first to stand up and witness to their conversion.

Conversions seem to result from a direct call from God, who may use extraordinary means such as voices and dreams to save souls. But a first call is not enough. One is received into the "Christian congregation" through a double baptism, baptism by water (in a country stream or a São Paulo swimming pool) and baptism by the Holy Ghost, which is nothing other than mystic trance and manifests itself through the gift of prophecy or speaking in tongues (glossolalia). The two baptisms do not necessarily coincide. With the black Pentecostalist, however, the very opposite is the case: the Holy Ghost descends upon him at the moment the elder, standing in water up to his waist, pronounces a text from the Bible. One cannot help thinking of the connection in the *candomblé* between a certain musical theme and the descent of the *orixá*; one precipitates the other. What the "Religion of Glory" brings to the man of African descent is a feeling of continuous direct contact with the divinity rather than a faith that remains in the background.

The sect is hostile to medicine. Its members refuse to consult surgeons or doctors; illness is cured by holy oil alone. This too may suit the African mentality. But when we compare the "testifying" or the general behavior of black Pentecostalists with that of white Brazilians or immigrants, we find exactly the same phenomena. It therefore seems to me that the black is not seeking in this religion something that will satisfy ancestral tendencies; he is in search of something else. But what? The "Religion of Glory" is a Puritan religion; it prohibits drinking, smoking, and dancing. Negro converts whose histories I was able to document were former drinkers or vagabonds tormented by a desire to give up the "sinner's" life, and indeed after conversion they actually did become respectable citizens. The moral qualities demanded by conversion enabled them to rise on the social ladder. In this religion of mystic trance the most important factor for the man of color is, in my opinion, this puritanical determination, this effort to get out of the lower class and into the bourgeoisie, so to speak. At the very moment when he seems closest to Africa—shaking and trembling, speaking in tongues, possessed by the Holy Ghost—he is actually farthest from it, more Westernized than ever before.[70]

■ ■ ■

The phenomena of assimilation and reinterpretation cannot be treated in a purely "culturalist" perspective, because both of them are conditioned by the social situations in which they occur.

We began by noting the importance of social control either through an official religious group, as in Catholicism, or through a book, the Bible, as in Protestantism. Reinterpretations come into play when this control is relaxed—namely in rural areas beyond the reach of a priest or in sects that pay more heed to the gift of charismas than to "the word of God." But we should note that even though reinterpretations may become more frequent when social censorship is reduced, a minimum of censorship is always necessary. The phenomenon is analogous to one that psychoanalysis discerns in individual psychology. It is the group equivalent of symbolic "transference." The primitive civilization transfers its archaic attitudes to the new one and when they reappear it is only in disguise.

Second, we have seen that reinterpretations are more likely to occur when the believers are segregated by color within the church. The existence during the colonial and imperial eras of a dual Catholicism with its Brotherhoods of the Rosary, black saints, and entertainments like the *congada*, which perpetuated the tribal struggles of Africa by sublimating them, made reinterpretations possible in Brazil, just as even today the existence of a dual Protestantism in the United States preserves features of the African civilizations or at least religious attitudes analogous to the ones those civilizations once produced. The development of racial democracy in Brazil, the clergy's campaign against folkloric Catholicism, and the absence of discrimination in the Protestant sects diminished reinterpretation, if they did not eliminate it, and promoted assimilation instead.

Third, the phenomenon of assimilation cannot be separated from the sociological phenomenon of social integration. We have seen this clearly confirmed so far as rural Catholicism is concerned. Three factors—(a) the dispersal of population, which imposes on the peasants a neighborhood solidarity without regard for color within their own *bairro* or district; (b) the necessity of a minimal homogeneity of beliefs, feelings, and attitudes toward life to permit this ecological (as opposed to ethnic) solidarity to come into play; and (c) the fact that solitude needs to be counterbalanced by moments of togetherness, by gatherings and festivals, moments that re-create the collective consciousness—force blacks caught up in this ecological solidarity or in these moments of communion to accept *caboclo* Catholicism. Of course where people of African descent are in the majority they can enrich that Catholicism, but they are forced to participate in this minimum of religious culture, which is the only cement that can hold this type of rural solidarity together.

In addition to what we might call "horizontal" assimilation, there is also a "vertical" assimilation. We have seen how the rural black not only accepts the *caboclo* civilization but takes advantage of it to attain the office of *sacristão*, a kind of lay priest, or of blesser, a kind of Christian "bone setter." For, as Wagley says, "the existence of preferences as to racial type and even of derogatory attitudes toward people of different racial characteristics within this lower group does indicate that *a mild form of racial prejudice exists on all levels of society in rural Brazil*."[71] This prejudice must of course be slight; that is to say it must not extend beyond the domain of collective representations of the esthetic or folkloric type into discriminatory behavior,[72] or the ecological solidarity that is as precious to the poor white or *caboclo* as it is to the Negro would be impossible. Nevertheless it does exist and determines, as a compensatory mechanism, the black's determination to utilize *caboclo* Catholic values to impose his authority on people who in other contexts might look down on him or pity him because of his color. He needs to destroy the unfavorable collective representations of his rural environment by acquiring a new type of prestige that obliterates the memory of color by enhancing his Catholicism. We have seen this same vertical assimilation in Protestantism. To the black, joining any of the Protestant denominations is in itself an advance. A cultural advance because Protestantism is the religion of the book and therefore of literate people; it is the religion of the United States, of a world power. A social advance because on every level the Protestant tends to rise and enter the middle class. And lastly a religious advance. Yet one should not think that the Protestant Brazilian believes himself to be different from the Catholic Brazilian. On the contrary he thinks he is practicing Christ's teachings, which the Catholic disregards.[73] Thus for the black to accept Protestantism is to enhance his own value as a person.

The problem of white-black race relations dominates the cultural problem of civilizational assimilations or reinterpretations. The phenomena produced when different civilizations clash—i.e. their interpenetrations and fusions or, alternatively, the triumph of one civilization over the other, at least in the domain that concerns us, the domain of religion—depend in the final analysis much more on the prejudices, stereotypes, and possible discrimination that exist in the multiracial society than on the nature of the civilizations in contact. The sociological determines the cultural.

16
Conclusions

Toward a Sociology of Mysticism

Having concluded my analyses, I can now come back to the two problems posed at the start: civilizational interpenetrations and the relationships between social structures and religious values.

For the sake of clearer exposition I can deal with the two subjects separately, but it goes without saying that they are closely linked, at least in the case of the Afro-Brazilian sects. In fact the man of African descent belongs simultaneously to two worlds, different if not mutually opposed: the world of the *candomblé*, which still preserves in a foreign land whole segments of these blacks' original civilizations, and the world of the wider Brazilian community. I say "worlds" because in both cases we are dealing with societies and civilizations, with structured groups and with values, ideals, and more or less coherent systems of collective representations. Thus the same individuals are subjected to two different kinds of influence or pressure, as members of a *candomblé* and as participants in the multiracial Brazilian community. One might say that, broadly speaking, the relations between the substructures and the superstructures are reversed in these two worlds. Where the man of African descent has succeeded in carving out a niche in which the religious values he brought with him across the ocean can flourish, those values secrete the structures. Conversely, where he occupies a position in the structures of the national society, those structures will modify the traditional values. Let us start from the level of individual behavior to find out how this dual dialectic works in practice.

Although the African religion constitutes a rich complex of rites and myth, as has been said, the gods can survive only by incarnating themselves. The existence of sects without mystic trance is certainly conceivable in theory, since certain gods such as Olorun and Ossaim do not descend, but in practice the communion of men is attained only through communion with the gods. It therefore seems to me that a sociology of mysticism can be developed out of our findings. The word "mysticism" may sound exaggerated, for in Christian countries this term has acquired a very specific meaning; some people might prefer to speak of "possession." But I have used it because the Brazilian blacks draw a distinction analogous to the Christian one between mysticism, which is oneness with God, and possession, which is demonic. They clearly separate the mystic trance in which one is inhabited by an *orixá* or a *vodun* from possession by an *egun* or *exú*. The mystic trance itself reminds us in a way of that of Saint Teresa, with its rich diversity of "mansions" and the hierarchy within its unity, ranging from states of beatitude to theopathy, for Afro-Brazilians too distinguish the states of *eré* or *tobossa* (infantile trance) or the states of the *tokhueni* or other guides (transitional trances) from trances of the gods in the strict sense. We are dealing with psychological phenomena of sufficient richness and complexity to justify the use of the term "mystic phenomena."

This trance cannot be explained purely by the facts of psychopathology. It is in fact a cultural trait, normal and obligatory in Negro civilizations. It is part of the religious ritual and is itself a ritual. Far from being a release of an individual's unconscious drives, it follows a fixed ceremonial course. To use Métraux's expression, it is a "comedy" (though I should prefer to call it a liturgical drama) controlled from start to finish, even in its most minute details, by the social group and by ancestral mythic tradition. I have shown that this mysticism has nothing in common with outbreaks of hysteria and related phenomena of contagious imitation, that it is not just a series of autonomous individual trances, but that it is structured. The ecstatic dance is like a language having its own vocabulary and syntax; the vocabulary is provided by the mythological personae of the gods, who "ride" their devotees, and the syntax by these gods' interrelationships, which also are of a mythological nature, by their genealogies, marriages, and quarrels. The individual ecstasies therefore respond to one another, engage in dialogue, and become a statement expressed in mystical action. Our study of the *candomblés* thus confirms the critique of Durkheim's thesis in the early pages of this work in which, to put it briefly, I accused him of confusing the states of intermental communion with mass psychology. It is true that society plays its part in mysticism and that mysticism derives from sociology, as do all the other phenomena of individual psychology, but its part is not to induce trance. (*Orixás* and *voduns* often descend into their daughters to warn them of danger at times when they are not engaged in religious ceremonies.) Society's part is to control and discipline the savage furies of the gods and make them abide by the traditional models. Even the vehemence of the ecstatic episode is dictated by these models, not by personal idiosyncrasies. The outward manifestations of the ecstasy of the children of Ogun, god of war, are much more forceful than those of the children of Oxun, goddess of fresh water. The former have something of the brutality of armies in battle, some of the hardness of steel, while the latter have a liquid, amorous quality—the fascinating sensuality of lazy rivers or still lakes sprinkled with sunlight. Here it is not the facts of social morphology that are uppermost but the values, the collective representations. Durkheim moves from society to religion through the intermediacy of the released collective consciousness. I move from religion to society through the intermediacy of a collective consciousness structured according to the norms of that religion.

Up to now we have confined ourselves to closed sects devoted to maintaining the original, primal civilizations. But the members of these African religious sects are also members of the wider Brazilian community; under the influence of this new environment they acquire new attitudes and habits. What we have called the principle of compartmentalization certainly allows them to live in two different worlds and to avoid the tensions and discords, the clash of values and the conflicting demands of the two societies. But whenever the social structures of this wider community change, the ensuing upheavals inevitably affect the individuals involved in them, and at such moments of crisis the opposite dialectic to the one I have described comes into play. Now the structures act upon values, transforming them or replacing old values with new ones. We have traced three such revolutions in the morphological base of the Afro-Brazilian society. The first was the shift from the system of lineages to that of "nations," the second the shift from the system of slavery to that of free labor, and the third the aftermath of the industrialization and urbanization of the country.

By destroying the lineages, the slave trade made it impossible for the Yoruba and the Dahomans to preserve their family religion and for the Bantu to continue their ancestor cult. Solidarity no longer exists on the domestic level but becomes purely ethnic. This does not necessarily affect religious values; it merely restricts their field of action. The religion is reconstituted in accordance with the individuals' inability to integrate themselves into a kin group and the ease with which they can integrate themselves into an organized "nation"—an alternative recognized and even recommended by the whites. These "nations" have their own "governors," "kings," and *batuques*. Thus the *candomblé* becomes the successor of the African village or country town. On the other hand the transition from slavery to free labor, by destroying the blacks' system of dependence on the whites, destroyed the only system of security they had ever known in America. Religion permitted the blacks, thrown back upon themselves in a hostile—or rather an indifferent—world, to recover their lost security by integrating them into another system of social participations. Here for the first time values begin to be affected, and for this reason we must pause here and take a closer look. But first we must stress that this transition did not occur abruptly on May 13, 1888 (except for the fairly large segment of the population that was immediately affected). It took place over almost a quarter of a century, thus allowing values to change gradually.

White society was based on competition, and every individual's status was determined by his own effort, not dictated by the group. But the free Negroes and many mulattoes were not able to compete successfully against the whites, either because they lacked education or vocational training or because of the unyielding prejudices of descendants of former slaves. A whole group existed that had acquired certain white ideals but could not realize them. They had to find within some community new channels for their new aspirations to leadership, better status, and vertical mobility. Analogous phenomena seem to be occurring in contemporary colonial societies where Africans already imbued with Western values see their desire to rise blocked by the whites, who hold all the key positions, but realize at the same time that religion offers them another channel of vertical mobility since, as the big cities destroy the traditional authorities, they leave room for those of the newcomers. The Bwiti cult, studied by Balandier, is a good illustration of this.[1] That is the only explanation for the increase in the number of African sects in Brazil—from Pôrto Alegre to Bahia, from Amazonas to the *sertão*. Certainly in some cases the traditional *candomblés* reproduce by fission, but this type of growth is slow since it takes at least fourteen years (in some cases twenty-one) after the initiation rites to become a *yalorixá* or *babalorixá*. The proliferation of what we might call small imitative sects is therefore essentially the result of a change of mentality, a kind of cultural whitening or Westernization of people of color. But since these are imitative sects run by poorly or incompletely initiated people, the traditional heritage of myths and rites is impoverished, group control is relaxed, and more scope is given to individual initiative by the leaders of the cult. It becomes easier for the African and the Indian religions to merge and for foreign folkloric elements, such as those I mentioned were borrowed from the *reisados* of Alagoas, to be introduced.

Many relatively large congregations are directed by ad hoc leaders of this kind. Their flocks consist of what might be called victims of the new conditions of life, namely the abandoned population. We have seen how the abolition of slavery quickly fragmented social relations within the black or mixed-blood populations. The *candomblé* offered these populations a solidarity that the multiracial Brazilian society could no longer provide after the disintegration of the patriarchal slave-owning family. And this brings us back to mysticism. Even where trance retains the archaic character of an imitation of the actions of the gods, will it not now assume a different significance? Will it not become a phenomenon of illusory compensation? Will it not be loaded down with feelings of frustration, inferiority complexes, or resentment? We do not have much data on which to base a reply to these questions—the Rorschach tests administered by René Ribeiro in Recife,[2] the life story of a daughter of the gods collected by Pierson in Bahia,[3] and ten or so life stories collected under my direction by students or former students of mine in the *macumbas*.[4] Although this information is too incomplete to furnish a definitive answer, and although the cases are not exactly comparable, being based on variable techniques, the data do suggest that the role played by compensation grows as one passes from the most traditional *candomblés* to Paulista *macumba*. In the first case the content and expression of African mysticism are culturally determined; in the latter, individual complexes tend to play a more important role than tradition. This conclusion is confirmed by participant observation. In its pure form the African religion is in effect, like most religions, an "imitation" of the gods, and this imitation manifests itself not only in the trance, when one is inhabited by the god and cannot help imitating him, but in daily life too. The following quotation from René Ribeiro will indicate what I have in mind. "Believing in the possibility of interaction between the personality of the devotee and that of the *orixá*, they regard the sons of Ogun as good workers, the sons of Shangô as excitable, imperious, and adventurous, the daughters of Oxun as vain, capricious, and fickle, the sons of Ode as austere, those of Orixálá as extremely kind and tolerant, and those of Nanamburucú as equally tolerant but also implacable."[5]

These generalizations may not always be borne out by the facts—but then children of the same father are often quite unlike one another. Nevertheless these ideas do serve as patterns of behavior, and the devotees train themselves in some way to emulate these mythic norms. Thus there is a continuous training or self-training of the individual, which persists even during the episodes of unconsciousness or moments of semiconsciousness during trance, preventing or at any rate severely limiting the play of individual complexes. Here it is the gods who make men and not men who make the gods. Conversely, as the myths are eroded and group control is relaxed, the unconscious ceases to model itself on a tradition that is at the same time a support and merely follows the urges of the individual libido. And this libido will manufacture its own expressive symbols by inventing gods who are merely images of the self.

The last of the three morphological revolutions is that one that accompanied the spread of industrialization in southern Brazil and the resultant proletarianization of the black, leading to his incorporation into the new society. As we have seen, the dogmatics of Umbanda spiritism expresses two things. First, it expresses a desire to merge with the "national" civilization rather than remain confined to closed, "exotic" communities. This desire is defined by the merging of three religions, paralleling the merging of the three constituent races of the nation. Second, it expresses the blacks' and *caboclos'* racial protest against a society culturally dominated by white models. Yet if the frustration of an entire colored class shows itself in the dogmatics of Umbanda spiritism, in ideologies of overcompensation, the mysticism of this sect's adherents also manifests that frustration in the new character of the trance. Umbanda is coming into being in a period when restructuring goes hand in hand with destructuring, when the proletarianization of the blacks and mixed-bloods still remains ambivalent, threatened as they are by the descendants of immigrants, blocked as they are at the level of nonskilled or semiskilled labor. Negro spiritism also will be the product of the reconstruction of old African sects on new bases and the destruction of the old systems of values or social control, of an attempt to create dogmas and rites, and at the same time of anarchy so far as the manifestation of spirits is concerned.

So we can establish a kind of law that wherever group control is relaxed, mysticism ceases to be the expression of collective models and becomes an individual expression of the way people experience the transformations of the social structures. *Macumba* (and Paulista *macumba* even more than the *macumba* of Rio) and Umbanda spiritism are mechanisms for manufacturing new gods, which are more likely to be called by Indian names than African ones because in the white society the Indian is glamorized by certain romantic idealizations. But these new gods—Caboclo Yellow Feather, Black Stone, Michael Shangô, etc.—are nothing but personifications of their devotees' inmost drives or torment. Elemental drives such as eroticism, whether homosexual or heterosexual (one makes love with the spirits to compensate for disillusionment in love in real life). Deep torment such as the guilt complex I have often observed in analyzing what the spirits say through their "media," which is just as likely to stem from an unresolved Oedipus complex as from a setback at work.[6]

Thus ecstatic trance always expresses the degree of cohesion or disintegration that exists in the social environment. Or, to use psychoanalytical terms, the trance of the *candomblé* still represents the triumph of the superego, i.e. of the collective norms, while the trance of syncretistic or improvised sects is the triumph of the self. This does not mean that the *candomblé* does not take into account individual differences. In fact any polytheism provides a set of interchangeable personalities from which one may make a selection, but these personalities are not infinite in number. One might even say that they represent a logical classification of characters correlated with the divisions of nature—earth and fire, fresh water and salt water—or of society—the warrior and the hunter, the healer and the farmer. They are socialized personalities who fix themselves in the unconscious and discipline it instead of allowing it to dissolve into a chaos of unchecked instincts. Not only do syncretism and spiritism increase the number of these interchangeable personalities by offering everyone a multiracial choice of *caboclos*, Negroes and whites, of Catholic saints and disembodied spirits like Joan of Arc or Pedro II; they even obliterate the characteristics of the gods, depersonalize them, turn them into vague concepts that can be filled with anything at all. In the end each individual fills them with his own desires, dreams, illusions, or resentment.

We have reached our first conclusion. There is a sociology of mysticism. And social morphology certainly plays a major role in it. But I cannot conceive of this role in the way Durkheim does. Halbwachs seems to me to come closer to the truth when he sees the church providing Christian mysticism with its conceptual frameworks and substantial images. The structures operate only within this tradition and let only such concepts and images pass as fit contemporary ways of life. An analogous dialectic of values and structures will permit the construction of an objective sociology of other types of mysticism. The one we have briefly sketched for Afro-Brazilian trance has brought out the importance of closed societies and groups open to outside influences, thus leading us into the problem of acculturation. The susceptibility of this trance to infiltration by personal drives seems to me to be associated with the individualization of the black in the industrialized big cities as he has been proletarianized through contact with whites.

The Two "Acculturations"

The problem I posed at the start was this: to what extent have the anthropologists who have studied civilizational clash and interpenetration developed a framework of valid concepts? In this book I have tested out these guiding concepts against the Afro-Brazilian facts—the concepts of resistance and conservation, of adaptation and syncretism, of assimilation and counteracculturation. Let us put aside for the moment the question whether these concepts have proved themselves or have had to be modified; we shall return to that later. We can, however, make one immediate observation: all these classificatory categories are extremely general. Besides being applicable to the case of two civilizations sustained by global societies in confrontation, they also hold good for groups of any kind that meet, form an alliance, imitate each other, or collide, since each group has its own civilization, its distinctive systems of norms and values. This is confirmed by the fact that we speak more and more of "subcultures" and "cultures of social sectors." These may be classes within one country—the proletariat and the bourgeoisie. They may be larger communities—rural and urban ones. They may be strata such as the scientific or technological elite and the broad masses. In every case we find the same phenomena of resistance and counteracculturation, adaptation and assimilation. In these conditions it is not surprising that some anthropologists should drop the term "acculturation" in favor of the wider "cultural change," because the facts remain the same whether or not this change was imposed upon one nation by another. It makes no difference, for example, whether industrialization was imposed on an underdeveloped country from outside or was the result of technological progress independent of external influence. In both cases we find the old values conflicting with the new, individuals trying to adapt to unprecedented conditions of social life without excessively modifying their archaic ways of behaving and thinking—in short, definitive changes of mentality. We can even go further and envisage a microsociology of these subcultural relationships, inasmuch as the family is composed of individuals who, because they participate in different kin groups, form two worlds that conflict, seek a compromise, or finally merge, while the children born of these unions will in turn be caught up in the subcultures of family, school, play group, or gang. In a word, and to summarize my critique, the general concepts of anthropology seem to me undeniably valuable but too wide. The role of the sociologist is to make them more specific, to discern not the common (and therefore commonplace) features in the encounters of "global societies" but their particular features.

I have therefore had to treat certain of those concepts of cultural anthropology in a special way. In fact, I have been forced to pose the problem of the relationships between different civilizations in terms of collective memory. At first sight this change of perspective may not seem particularly helpful in exposing specific phenomena, since any kind of group has its own memory. The family has its collective memory; so does the church. There is a juridical collective memory and there is a national one. Any group, whatever its nature, has its store of memories to which it is piously attached. Nevertheless in moving from the concept of civilization to that of collective memory we have, I think, taken a step forward. The anthropologists were led to differentiate between civilizations and societies (though they would have to go back later and reestablish the connections they had destroyed) on the grounds that cultural traits are mobile and can migrate from one society to another. The concept of collective memory, on the other hand, ties the civilization more closely to the group. It reveals common memories bound up with structures, material objects, a specific space, and temporal landmarks. The phenomena of civilizational interpenetration therefore lead ultimately to an analysis of the destructuring of memories, their ecological displacements, and their reintegration into other social frameworks. In short, social and cultural phenomena prove to be infinitely more interdependent here, inasmuch as this memory can be only a social group memory and collective memories are always articulated in respect to interrelationships within an organized collectivity. Anthropology divides what is whole. Even in the case of the Afro-Brazilians, where the divorce of the cultural from the social seemed most drastic because the Africans were able to bring along their native cultures but not their social organizations, which had been destroyed by the slave trade, memories survived only through the re-creation of space, objects, historic-mythological landmarks, and social structures. Thus, instead of trying to reunify what has been divided, the social and the cultural, we became involved right from the start in the complexity of global realities.

In other words, the merit of the concept of collective memory is that it immediately forces us to take a sociological view of the problem of acculturation. Scholars seem to be increasingly interested in this method. Civilizational clash and interpenetration does not occur in a vacuum but in clearly determined social contexts. Balandier has studied the colonial situation; we have studied the slave situation. When I spoke, for instance, of resistance, what I had in mind was of course primarily religious resistance, since religion was at the heart of my thesis, but I did not separate it from black-white racial resistance or from the economic resistance of slaves against masters. The resistance of the mystics was caught up in a color struggle and a climate of economic oppression. Again, when I spoke of assimilation, I was speaking of assimilation not to a different value system but to values modified by the slave system and injecting certain values into that system at the very time when whole areas of white civilization were being affected by African influences. We certainly need to recognize that integration and assimilation do not necessarily go hand in hand or occur in the same time frame, though they are always to some degree connected. We have therefore studied assimilation within the hierarchical structure of slavery, taking the field hands, house servants, and free negroes and examining their assimilation in relation to white-black ties on these various levels of society. The context of slavery, like the context of colonialism, modifies human relationships, and civilizational exchanges occur through these new types of relationship.

The first task of a sociology of civilizational interpenetration must therefore be to establish a typology of social situations. But we must be careful not to overstress the social at the expense of the cultural. Is it possible, for example, to detach the colonial system entirely from the various ideologies of colonization: from the Anglo-Saxon emphasis on the coexistence of two societies, from the paternalistic ideology of the Portuguese or the French policy of assimilation? The terms we have used may also have been too general, for these policies fluctuate over the years with the interests of the dominant nation. We watch Portuguese colonialism move from paternalism to economic exploitation, French colonialism from assimilation to relative respect for native values. Every social situation is imbued with values, cultural conceptions, and organizational norms that, as I have said, derive partly from different economic interests but also from the specific psychologies of the colonizing nations as they have been shaped by history —political empiricism in one case, impregnation by Jesuit thinking of another, egalitarian revolutionary rationalism in a third. Obviously these ideologies mold behavior and express themselves in different forms and different interpersonal relations, and these in turn are translated into variations in the intensity, speed, or quality of acculturation phenomena. Again, although the slave regime does present some very general characteristics that remain constant whether the ethnic context is Anglo-Saxon or Latin, whether the religious context is Protestant or Catholic, etc., the ideologies vary. This is very evident in Brazil when we compare Dutch colonialism (based on trade) with Portuguese colonialism (based on agriculture). The slave regime differed in the two systems. Apart from the economic conditions—subsistence farming or vast plantations—in the various slave societies (conditions whose importance I do not minimize), we must also bear in mind these ideologies, which are reflected in the black codes, in varieties of Protestantism (Anglicanism or the puritanical denominations), and in ethnic varieties of Catholicism (the tragic type of the Spaniards, the social type of the Portuguese, or the more intellectual type of the French).

While the study of civilizational interrelationships cannot be separated from the study of the social situations in which they occur, the latter also are already in a certain sense civilizational facts. In this work I have therefore tried as far as possible to avoid the Cartesian mind-body dualism that I rejected in the Introduction when discussing Scheler. The problem of the union of the mind and the body is certainly a fascinating topic in the work of the author of the *Traité des Passions*, but its solution is almost impossible because of the radical distinction that Descartes makes between thought and matter from its very beginning in the substantialized *cogito*. The problem of acculturation presents analogous difficulties if it is split up and reassembled. However fine the seams, they will never be invisible. The collective consciousness is always incarnated in structures or situations, just as social material is always culturalized material. This is why I have spoken of encounters between global societies, not just civilizations, even though the slave trade broke up sociocultural complexes and detached the superstructures from the substructures.

But in trying to remain closer to concrete realities, which are always multilevel realities and which act and react upon one another, do we not ultimately rule out all possibility of the sociology we claimed to be placing on a sounder basis? Every society requires a certain measure of abstraction. If we want to set up a sufficiently general theory of "cultural contacts," should we not in fact detach the superstructures from the substructures and confine ourselves entirely to the levels of values as independent even of social situations? Then and only then we might perhaps find "genetic laws" or "functional correlations" that would hold for any intercivilizational contact, whether the encounter be between imperialist civilizations like the Roman and the Asiatic empires, between colonizers and colonized, or between masters and slaves. Again, if we want to discover the overall character of slave or colonial regimes, should we not detach them from correlative ideologies and bracket the latter out? Here I have in mind Talcott Parsons's admission that while his theory of social action can well be applied to static societies, it cannot explain phenomena of social dynamics. Here, he says, we cannot go beyond empirical descriptions of the phenomena of change. Biology offers an example of this type of knowledge. The life cycle, whether of the species or of the individual, can be described, but we have no general theory to explain it.[7] Although Parsons poses the problem in a different context, the context of social equilibrium, we must also ask whether, if we adopt my conception of acculturation, the theory might not prove inadequate and whether we would not be forced to limit ourselves to purely empirical descriptions of phenomena as they occur, with all their specific characteristics. The study undertaken in this book is a monographic one. Not until similar monographs have covered the various types of slave and colonial situations, and not until analyses have been made of the work in the underdeveloped countries of international organizations such as UNESCO (some of which are based on different ideologies) and of the changes that have been effected in the Soviet satellite countries (which are based on differently conceived relationships between civilizations and economies), will it be possible to answer that question and to determine the feasibility of a sociology of the encounter of global societies such as I have defined it.

I believe it is feasible. And I believe that the applicability of certain concepts set forth in this book is wide enough to justify my claim. While I was making my field study of the world of the Brazilian *candomblés*, I was also engaged in a vast bibliographical study of the other forms of Afro-American religion, from Louisiana to Argentina. When I returned to France, I made another field study to test some of the conclusions I had reached concerning "developed" peoples and the problem of acculturation among African students. Since my ideas proved productive enough to elucidate the facts in such widely different cases involving diverse civilizations in contact and diverse social situations, I can at least consider them useful provisional generalizations, even if they cannot yet be regarded as definitive. I should like to present here two of these operative concepts. Others will appear in later discussions—concerning ideologies, for instance.

1. I stressed in the Introduction that different societies can coexist without civilizational interpenetration if the groupings that confront each other are complementary and independent. But it may also happen that two civilizations will coexist within one society without being modified by contact. Conversely, individuals may participate in two separate value systems

without being aware of their opposition and without having to make a choice. The psychology of the marginal man needs to be reexamined, in some of its fundamental aspects at least, to rid him of the pathetic aura in which he is commonly seen. Certainly the man who is torn apart and becomes a battlefield for the two worlds confronting each other inside him does exist, but he is a product of social factors (racial discrimination, caste regime, color hierarchy) more than of cultural ones in the strict sense. I was in fact struck by the contrast in Brazil between the existence of this marginalism, where people of African descent are most completely assimilated but where the social gap between blacks and whites is widest, and on the other hand the admirable psychological balance and *joie de vivre* of *candomblé* members. I suggested the term "compartmentalization" for this way of solving the acculturation problem, and this principle seems to me to possess general validity since I came upon it again, in a slightly different form, among African students living in France. With them Africa is deliberately "put in cold storage." It is not forgotten; they insist that as soon as they return home they will resume their customary behavior and the conventions governing the relations between age groups or occupational castes, but in France, even when they are not in contact with French people, even in relating to other students of the same ethnic origin, they abide by French democratic rules. In Brazil compartmentalization does not take this voluntary form; it is an instinctive or automatic reaction, a defensive posture against anything that might disturb one's peace of mind.

I have mentioned this principle in several chapters so there is no need to go into detail here. Let us just bear in mind that the Brazilian black is a fervent patriot, equally attached to his American homeland and to his ancestral culture. He participates in local party politics just as other citizens do, whatever their color. He takes part in occupational or trade union activities in the labor market or at work exactly as whites do. At the same time, as a member of an African religious sect, he belongs to a world dominated by other values. It may be asked whether we are not dealing here with an extremely general phenomenon going far beyond the field of acculturation phenomena. In any society a given individual belongs in fact to several different circles—family, occupation, political party, trade union, church—and his behavior changes as he moves from one to another. He acts in different ways as a father dealing with his children, as an employer dealing with his workers, or as an employee dealing with the public in his office. Yet the two cases do not seem to me comparable. One is a matter of role playing, the other of interiorized mental worlds. In our society one personality is required by the various capacities in which he functions to follow the behavioral norms those capacities demand, but he plays all these roles (even when they seem to conflict) as himself, and one is quite aware of this, just as one recognizes a certain actor whether he is playing a comic or a tragic role, a sentimental comedy or a historical drama. Of course the personality may compensate for the drab nature of one of his "roles"—e.g. by treating his family sadistically to make up for his lack of prestige at work. But this compensatory behavior is a mark of his character and defines his idiosyncrasy. The case of members of the Afro-Brazilian sects is much closer to that of the very devout scholars (one of whom I quoted earlier) who close the chapel door when they enter the laboratory. Here we are really dealing with two worlds of specific values, one founded on faith, the other on systematic doubt. Yet even here the personality remains one and the same because the scholar is moved to admire the work of God in the natural laws he discovers and he thinks out his faith through rationalizations whose concepts he takes from science. The principle of compartmentalization as I have defined it therefore seems to me to be a characteristic of acculturation phenomena. If we encounter it in the West, it will always be in the context of civilizational contacts. One example might be the individual who as an industrial worker belongs to the world of capitalist values and as a roulette player to the world of magical ones.

The principle of compartmentalization has only limited value. It assumes a certain balance between the African and the Western enculturation movements. That is why it affects chiefly families having traditional connections with the *candomblé*, families in the lower classes of society where the influence of the multiracial school is confined to a few years in early childhood and in communities where color prejudice is at a minimum. On the other hand, when upheavals in the social structures produce ethnic conflict in the labor market leading to the intensification of stereotypes and discrimination, even in a camouflaged form, as a means by which the whites can maintain their hold on the global society, the crisis reveals the contradictions between the coexisting worlds, and black ideologies replace the African religions or permeate them with new values.

2. Of all the concepts cultural anthropology has discovered in its study of civilizational encounters, I believe the most important to be the concept of reinterpretation because it goes beyond the relational sociologies and reverts to Durkheim's crucial idea of the primacy of "internal environments." But two kinds of reinterpretation are possible. For our Afro-Brazilians there is the reinterpetation of Western cultural traits, such as the cult of the saints or concubinage, in terms of the African civilizations, and there is also the reinterpretation of African cultural traits, such as the cult of the dead or of mystic trance, in terms of the Indian or Portuguese civilization. To understand these two opposite movements it seems to me that we must look beneath reinterpretation for an even more fundamental phenomenon that would explain them. That phenomenon is double accul-

turation. And in fact my two studies, the field study in Brazil and the study of African students pursuing their education in France, have led me to distinguish between material and formal acculturation.

We have seen that syncretism could take very different forms depending on whether it occurred in the domain of religious representations or the domain of magical ones, on the ecological or the symbolic level. However all these different syncretisms, to which I have devoted a chapter of this book, still belong to the domain of material acculturation. The Western characteristics borrowed by the Africans to camouflage their sects or to adapt themselves more fully to the surrounding society are reinterpreted in accordance with the African mentality. Catholic communion, for example, is conceived of as a magic rite that may cure a sick person by driving out the evil spirit that is tormenting him. This does not mean that the person takes communion as a bad Catholic. On the contrary, according to the law of magic, if the rite is to be effective it must be performed with the utmost respect for all its implications, and to perform it in a truly Catholic fashion is, paradoxical as this may seem at first sight, one of those implications. The *orixás* are equated with the saints, and this means that all the norms of the church are applied to the African cult—observation of annual celebrations, the reciting of appropriate prayers, participation in processions, etc. But it does not mean that the African "thinks" the saint in the same way as the non-African does—even a non-African peasant who knows nothing but idolatry. The custom I have mentioned of making blood sacrifices to certain saints corroborates this African way of thinking, just as the washing of the Bomfim church recalls the washing of the stones in the *pegi*. As long as acculturation has not penetrated the mentality, or as long as the compartmentalization principle confines the change of mentality to the domains of politics and economics and excludes it from the domain of religion, reinterpretation always occurs in terms of the African values, norms, and ideals.

Blacks studying in France exemplify another kind of acculturation, which, to distinguish it from the one mentioned above, I shall call formal since it affects the mind and modes of feeling and thinking. Nonetheless the nationalism of these students tends more and more to assume the character of counteracculturation. They are concerned with saving the African civilizations, or at least their fundamental values, with upholding the spirit of cooperation against the spirit of competition, with maintaining aesthetic ideals and Negro spirituality. I have no doubt that when this young elite returns to the black continent, it will devote itself to this work of rehabilitation and preservation. But even if this elite refuses to accept, at any rate integrally, the very matter of Western civilization, it has unquestionably been psychically Westernized by its education and university training. Its affectivity, even its mode of experiencing nature and its eroticism, have changed. In building the Africa of tomorrow it may, and

probably will, include bits of archaic Africa, but those bits will be reinterpreted in Western terms.

We find analogous phenomena in Brazil. As people of African descent
acquire new mental habits, new affective attitudes, and are shaped by the
Lusitanian environment and the new industrial conditions of life in their
country, they do not for this reason abandon their sects, but they do
profoundly modify their meaning. Mystic trance, for example, is reinterpreted in terms of spiritism, and instead of being a distinctive characteristic becomes a channel of upward social mobility or a symbolic expression
of the class struggle. The various degrees of initiation cease to be stages of
increasingly intensive mystic participation in the *orixás* and become a
means of improving one's social status. This is borne out by the fact that
people on the rise are no longer mindful of the law of compensation, which
says that the higher one rises, the more one's freedom of action is curtailed
by rigid taboos. These taboos are more or less forgotten; one is in the
West, where power guarantees greater freedom of action, not in Africa,
where power is acquired only at the cost of greater constraints.

In the first case the civilizational exchanges seem to occur on the same
level of depth sociology. On the morphological level the Catholic altar
invades the African sanctuary and sets itself up alongside the *pegi*; candles, statuettes of saints, and crucifixes are placed on the *catimbó* table
beside the Indian bowl of *jurema* or the *orixás'* sacred objects. On the
institutional level the same people belong simultaneously to Catholic
brotherhoods like that of the Rosary and to African organizations like the
samba schools or even the *candomblés*. On the level of crystallized norms
initiation rites conclude with a mass, and the funeral *achêchê* is associated
with the seventh-day mass. Only later are these objects, institutions, or
norms caught up in the new environment they have entered; only then do
they take on the coloration of African values, collective representations,
and acts of communion. In the second case, at its most extreme, all the
superstructures have been abandoned in this depth sociology and replaced
by others. Here the essential dialectical movement is vertical rather than
horizontal; it redefines the lower strata and gives them different kinds of
significance, those which have been learned from the wider society. In both
cases, however, the fundamental level is that of symbolism.

This is by no means surprising when we remember that symbols are
elements of mediation.[8] They are intermediaries between the various levels of social reality, and they serve as intermediaries between societies and
civilizations in contact. Kardiner's work stresses that if institutions join up,
infiltrate one another, or merge to produce original creations, they do so
not simply at the institutional level but by way of the "basic personality"
as an intermediary that gives meaning to these institutional connections,
interpenetrations, or mixtures. To understand why acculturation takes
place by means of intersecting vertical and horizontal dialectics, we need

only substitute the "symbolic level" for the "basic personality," which would take us from the domain of sociology into that of psychology—a domain still poorly determined because the structure of the basic personality is still under discussion precisely in the case of acculturation.[9]

When the saint becomes the symbol of the *orixá*, when communion becomes the symbol of purification from evil, when concubinage becomes the symbol of polygamy, whether simultaneous or serial, then the values of the African religions can infiltrate objects, organized behavior, and institutions and "Africanize" them—i.e. give them a special significance. When *caboclos* and old Negroes become the symbol of a social class, when Kardecite spiritism becomes the symbol of the white's social superiority, when occultism becomes the symbol of the value of magic, then Western values can infiltrate objects (chalk or food offerings), organized behavior (dances and divination), and institutions (such as the *macumba*) and "Aryanize" them, i.e. give them a different significance. In civilizational encounters and in the overthrow of social structures, symbols for the same content may change or the same symbols may come to denote different contents. To avoid persecution by whites the African may for instance have to borrow some of their cultural traits, which from that point on will symbolize or signify his older civilization. On the other hand, in his economic, racial, and cultural struggle against the ruling class he may cling to his religious realities but, already inwardly transformed by his very engagement in a conflict that forces him to use the weapons of his enemies, he will modify the content of his traditions, which will symbolize and signify new values.

This mutation of objects, organized behavior, or institutions into symbols could of course be explained as a general trait of the African civilizations. Griaule has shown the importance of symbolism in these civilizations, whose social structures, present-day dances, and economic system—even the very forms of their houses and musical instruments—are terrestrial replicas of the myths of the gods. However, without wishing to deny or minimize the importance of this assertion, I think a privileged place must be reserved for symbolism in any genuinely sociological interpretation of civilizational interpenetration. If I am not mistaken, Griaule's assertion might enable us to effect a harmonious synthesis of two opposed sociologies (violently opposed since Dilthey)—positivism and the sociology of understanding. By defining social data as things, positivism has given us the only valid methodological rule if we want to avoid the subjectivism of interpretive theories. On the other hand, while positivism cannot be said to forget that these things may be psychic representations, i.e. collective representations, it disregards their significatory values and ultimately tends to dehumanize the social. The sociology of understanding, by contrast, puts significations in the foreground, since the very purpose of understanding is to grasp them. But as I said in the opening pages of this book, it is the sociologist—i.e. a thinker engaged in a dual class and ethnic system—who is supposed to discover them. The danger, pointed out by Lévy-Bruhl, of interpreting data pertaining to other civilizations in terms of our own values remains undiminished.

By relativizing symbolic significations in relation to one of the two societies in contact, my theory of the encounters of heterogeneous civilizations avoids the danger of subjectivism. They can be studied as things within their explanatory frameworks. But at the same time these significations do not lose their human values, because they are not detached from the people involved in the struggle, from their dramas, their efforts to break away or to integrate, for it is through the people who belong to several different societies that symbols are incessantly redefined.

Structures and Values

We cannot, then, regard the facts of acculturation simply as a combination of cultural traits borrowed from two different civilizations that contract a marriage. Discussing colonial societies, Durkheim alludes to the birth of new social species from the union of two preexisting ones, and Malinowski says, also in reference to colonial societies, that the offspring of these encounters are not mere additions but new syntheses in which the syncretized civilizations have been so profoundly fused that they can no longer be recognized. This is certainly the primary aspect of acculturation, but as we have just seen there is much more to it than that. Social matter exists only inasmuch as social agents give it meaning, and this meaning may change in the course of time. Codes, religious institutions, dance steps, and family forms are no more than a language by means of which consciousness, individual or collective, expresses itself. The problem of acculturation is therefore closely linked to the problem of relationships between the substructures and the superstructures. On the one hand the European and African civilizations do not marry in a vacuum. Their contrasts occur in a specific social context, the context of slavery and a society disrupted by the abolition of slave labor, of urbanization, and of industrialization, and they therefore reflect the structural features of these various contexts. On the other hand these changing structures, which might be broadly defined as those of the exploited race, those of the abandoned race, and those of the race in process of reintegrating itself, are in each case reinterpreted in terms of the values of one or the other of the two civilizations in contact, i.e. in terms of either the African values or the European ones. Thus our first problem, acculturation, leads to our second one, the relationship between values and social structures.

Before tackling this problem I should like to recall two conclusions from the Introduction to this book. In the first place, there is no need to discuss the exact nature of these values, not because the question is not interesting in itself, but because it takes us out of the field of science into philosophy. I shall not try to determine the origin of religion or the place of religious values within social values as a whole. I shall confine myself to studying the concrete connections that establish themselves within socio-cultural entities. I have also rejected the idea of privileged causality. If there is any point on which all sociologists seem to agree today, it is that one. One-sided explanations based on climate, race, the economy, or whatever, have no place in science; they too derive from philosophy. Only on condition that we exclude a philosophy of religion and a general phi-losophy of sociological interpretation can we attempt to resolve the problem of the relationships between the substructures and the superstructures.

These terms suggest depth sociology. But in addition to that sociology of superimposed levels there is another that might be called "plane sociol-ogy," which distinguishes a certain number of variables and then tries to discover correlative relationships between them. This school of thought has been strongly influenced by the advances made in contemporary phys-ics. By positing four-dimensional space, the theory of relativity further strengthened it by suggesting that time can be integrated with sociocultural space. This plane sociology at least has the merit of not favoring any one factor at the expense of others; on the contrary it brings out the inter-relationships between the various social, economic, political, and religious phenomena. "Civilization" becomes one of the variables to be considered. Can we, then, deal with the problem of the relationships between social structures and religious values purely on the horizontal plane? Apparently not. For if we take each of the variables in turn—the religious variable and the economic one, for instance—we shall see that they both presuppose the existence of different levels. There are economic values such as price and religious values such as creeds; there are economic institutions such as the market and religious institutions such as churches; there are economic structures and religious structures. The interrelationships between these various phenomena cannot therefore be separated from the vertical dialec-tic between the levels of social reality. Again, depth sociology may show that the substructures are always significant, i.e. imbued with values, and that values in turn always carry some material weight, that streams of collective consciousness tend to crystallize and incarnate themselves in some organized social body, but this does not alter the fact that depth sociology is always in danger of falling back into the dualism that I re-jected earlier. It was precisely to avoid that, that it turned to philosophy, either idealistic or materialistic, depending on whether it sees the crystal-lizations as objectivized spirit or the superstructures as a reflection of economic phenomena. This undoubtedly eliminates the dualism, but it does so by a logical operation rather than by observation of the facts. Thus our second problem is more difficult than the first. I do not claim to offer a

CONCLUSIONS   **393**

complete solution. I simply wish to see to what extent a study of the
history of the African religions in Brazil can help in formulating it more
clearly.

First, if we temporarily adopt the viewpoint of "plane sociology" to see
to what degree the Afro-Brazilian religion varies in response to the variations of certain factors in the global society, such as the demographic
factor or social gaps, we shall see that these factors operate differently in
different historical periods. While the transplantation of Africa to Brazil
required the existence of a fairly large black population, the maintenance
of the African religion did not. In the late eighteenth and early nineteenth
centuries the ratio of slaves to free whites on the seaboard of Rio Grande
do Sul was extremely high, but later European immigration—chiefly
German and Italian—totally reversed the original ratio. Today, even in
towns like Pôrto Alegre or Viamão, the blacks constitute no more than
little enclaves submerged in an essentially white population (pure white,
without any mixed blood). Nevertheless these enclaves have preserved
their ancestral traditions with extraordinary fidelity. We shall also see that
to isolate a variable is to make an artificial abstraction, because everything
hangs together. Observable social phenomena are always a crossroads of
forces that all proliferate under the influence of the others or contradict
one another, so that one can never predict what may happen in a given
situation. At any one point in time or place a multiplicty of causes is
operative, some promoting the development of the African religions, some
their disappearance. Since for the time being none of these forces are
quantifiable, and since, on the other hand, social facts cannot be reduced
to phenomena of the composition of forces analogous to mechanical ones,
this "plane sociology" is not very helpful in solving our problem.

In the course of this book we have also studied the importance of
production systems to changes in religious values. In the beginning the
African religions, linked to an agricultural economy of the communal type,
were transplanted to an environment where production, whether on the
great sugar or coffee plantations or in the gold mines, was of the capitalist
type. We saw how the abolition of slave labor freed capital that was then
used to further the industrialization of Brazil. We have tried to determine
the effect of this change in the production system on the African sects. As
we move on from demographic variables or the social gap between the
races, we leave "plane sociology" behind and enter the domain of depth
sociology in its Marxist form. Here I have made certain assertions.

1. Even though in Africa the African religions may have been no more
than the reflection of a clearly defined type of agricultural production (I do
not believe this, but the subject lies beyond the scope of the present work),
the slave trade cut the civilization off from the society, and the transplanted Africans based their new social structure on religious values. The
first process we observed was therefore not the action of economic factors

on religious ones but the secretion of substructures on the basis of the superstructures. Within the *candomblé* the polygamous family reestablished itself (in the form of the *apetebis*, for instance). To be sure, the clan or lineage was modified into sodalities of sons or daughters of the gods, but these retained the same functions of cooperative work, mutual aid, and communal authority. Lastly, the economy of gifts and return gifts, prestations and counterprestations, survived in the relationship between the devotees and their deities and between priests and initiates.

2. The survival of the African religions must be studied in the context of the situation of free Negroes in the towns of the colonial or the imperial era rather than the context of slavery, and even here in the context of leisure time rather than work. The Marxists could certainly make the point that these free blacks, organized in "nations," were autonomous artisans and that this type of production was more propitious to the development of the African sects than the capitalist system. Nevertheless this family-based skilled working class was not linked to a village community as it was in Africa; in the towns it was caught up in modern competition between trades and races and more particularly between Negro artisans and poor whites. Brazilian history is full of examples of municipalities or urban administrators having to legislate measures to defend poor whites against the ambitions and initiative of the blacks. Thus although the free Negro was still involved in the capitalist system and the competition of the labor market this did not prevent him from preserving his heterogeneous mystic values elsewhere, in his *calundus* or *batuques*, even when these values were incompatible with his new environment. As I have shown, compartmentalization allowed the Negroes to juxtapose two value systems and to participate without inner tension in two different worlds shaped by the capitalist spirit and the communal one. That is to say, the economic substructures do not always or immediately affect the superstructures. The dialectic inherent in our earlier depth sociology must assign an important place to the phenomena of breaks and gaps; we must not forget the reality of social discontinuities. Even if we were to establish cause-and-effect connections between economic systems and religious values, such connections can be broken. In certain historical situations the tide of actions and reactions may be halted and come into play only later or not at all.

3. Continuity between production systems and religions can be reestablished only through the intermediary process of what Marx called the rise into consciousness. That is to say, modifications in economic structures or in technology do not become operative until living men perceive or experience them. As we have seen, it was not until the twentieth century that this happened, and then only within certain segments of the population in metropolitan cities.

Be that as it may, the Afro-Brazilian religions illustrate the importance of breaks as a factor in the sociological explanation. Neither civilizations nor societies are homogeneous entities. As I have said, Brazil is less a stratification of classes than a series of historical moments; some areas live in a slow-moving time frame, others in a fast-moving one. I would add that as a result of this dualism, which still prevails despite the growth of the real middle class, the economic systems interpenetrate the historical strata, so that history is able to dominate the economy. It is simplistic to link a global production system directly with a value system. Indeed I have felt obliged to distinguish between field hands and house slaves, slaves and free Negroes or mulattoes, dispersed populations and concentrated ones, and we have seen that their different situations are reflected in attachment to heterogeneous values. I also defined Brazilian civilization as a set of subcultures, a kind of mosaic of life styles derived from its geographic and ethnic diversity, the ubiquitous influence of Lusitanian Catholicism notwithstanding. Psychiatrists have brought to light the conflicts in modern civilization, which juxtaposes the most contradictory values—Christian values preaching altruism and sacrifice and capitalist values invoking the struggle for existence and the necessity of proving oneself one of the fittest. Even more contradictions exist within the component elements of the Brazilian civilization. What makes the problem of the relationship between social structures and religious values so difficult to resolve is that in Brazil one is always confronted with multiple structures and different subcultures.

I have just spoken of historic strata side by side with economic ones. These seemed to me so important that I devoted a whole chapter to the problem of collective memory. The conclusions I reached also help to formulate my conception of the interrelationships between values and structures.

Collective representations, group mental images, cannot survive without material substrata, without well-organized interaction between the members of the groups. Forgetting is always the result of a destructuring of the transplanted society. But the fact that traditional values can survive only by reincarnating themselves in a set of institutionalized interrelationships does not mean that it is those structures that produce the values. While I obviously do not wish to identify social with biological phenomena and stipulate that what I am about to say is no more than an analogy, one might conceive of the action of the social structures somewhat as Bergson conceives of the role of the structures of the nervous system in psychic memory. According to this theory, the body's function is to transpose memories from the level of pure images to the level of action, not to preserve the images themselves, and still less to produce them. The body, with its impulse-conducting nerve cells, its complicated communication networks, is "the passageway for received and transmitted impulses," a "center of action" that actualizes essential memories. Similarly, the social structures form a system of organs that permits values to function effectively and to actualize themselves in coordinated action and lived sig-

nificances—in short, to remain in being. The reason why I have laid so
much stress on completing Halbwachs's theory and on interposing, between collective memory and the individuals, the totality of the relationships that these individuals maintain among themselves, is that I consider
the latter to be essential. And indeed when some of those relationships
could no longer function within the transplanted African religions because
the slave trade had created gaps in the specialized cast of actors or agents,
the corresponding values could not be handed on, since their routes of
actualization had been cut. They therefore disappeared unless substitute
communication routes could be created—as happened when the practice
of divination passed from the *babalaô* to the *babalorixá*. Conversely,
whenever the African religious society was able to restructure itself by
restoring these interdependent "roles," the traditional collective representations survived because they were able to infiltrate Afro-Brazilian reality.

But the importance of the collective memory should not lead us to
underestimate the existence of creative activity. Alongside the preserved
values, new ones emerge. We are in the habit of defining religions by
tradition and constant imitation of the past, but religions, like other social
realities, are living things. How did we explain these creative phenomena?
Are they a product of streams of collective consciousness? Or do they
reflect the changes that appear in the substructures? So far as the substructures are concerned, our analysis led us to adopt the concept of alternative
responses. We first saw this in action in the slave system and in the
struggle against the exploitation of one race by another. The slave had two
ways of escaping from this exploitation. One was open resistance (suicide,
abortion, running away, murdering his master, or armed revolt organized
by the "nations"). The other was to accept the system of slavery instead of
resisting it violently and to take advantage of all the channels of upward
mobility that it left open to him—the Portuguese predilection for the dark
Venus, the possibility of moving from the fields into the *casa grande*, for
men marriage with free Negroes abandoned by their former lovers (because children assumed the mother's status), *compadrismo*, organizations
that collected money to buy "freedom tickets," etc. In the first case resistance usually crystallized around the African priests; in the second a man
rose by accepting Christianity—or at least by seeming to accept it—and
hence by changing his values. We then saw how the capitalist regime
offered people of color behavioral options. The transition from caste to
class; the fact that in certain regions of Brazil the class hierarchy largely
follows the color line, from white to light and dark mulattoes down to pure
Negroes; the frustrations resulting from the changed function of the old
stereotypes, which had become a tactical resource in the class struggle; and
the whites' justification of certain forms of economic discrimination—all
these factors inevitably provoked defensive reactions in the blacks.

These reactions could be either political or religious. Hence the simultaneous emergence of Brazilian Negro organizations modeled on the political parties and having clearly defined programs (including the prohibition of overt discrimination [the only type the law can control], the improvement of the economic and social status of "nationals of color," protection for the Negroes against the immigrants, and self-education—in other words total assimilation of the blacks into Western civilization) and Umbanda spiritism, which may even in some respects become messianic in character. The preservation, maintenance, or elimination of the old mystic values does not follow automatically from changes in the social situations. In the first place the people affected by these structural upheavals must become conscious of them. In the second place each of these upheavals admits of multiple solutions, and to determine which solution will ultimately be chosen requires consideration of both the orienting structures and the relative strength of the archaic values and the mental or affective habits of the people who will make the choice. The failure of the Black Front in Bahia, the successive acceptance in Minas Gerais of both the Black Front and Umbanda spiritism, and on the other hand the difficulties encountered by Umbanda spiritism in establishing itself in São Paulo as strongly as it did in Rio or in southern Brazil clearly show that the solutions adopted vary in response to the existing superstructures as much as to the substructures. It is always easy enough to see through hindsight how economic or social systems are reflected in religion, but one forgets that there was a factor of creative freedom, that substructural upsets are determinative but not compelling, and that the people confronted with them can either reject the old values that no longer seem to fit the new social situations or invent new meanings for the old symbols they do not wish to reject completely and thus be forced to find an original solution.

Up to now I have spoken only of religion. But my thesis also generates similar ideas about the relationships between magic and the social structures. It has often been noted that when an invading people imposed its religion on the people it conquered, a shift of value levels followed the transition from a more or less egalitarian society to a more or less stratified one. The religion of the conquering nation becomes the only official religion available to the masses, while the conquering religion (where options in collective behavior again come into play) deteriorates into magic or is transformed into a mystery religion based on initiation and the secret. Both phenomena occur in Brazil, as they do throughout black North and South America. The *candomblé* withdraws into secrecy, holding its ceremonies on the outskirts of the cities, in isolated houses, or in retreats in the tropical forest. It tends to become a mystery cult. Membership in a sect is conferred by voluntary initiation, not automatically by lineage. But the white man finds this secrecy disquieting. He is aware that within these closed sects formidable forces are manipulated, and since his conscience is not always clear where blacks are concerned, he is afraid that these forces may be used against him. His fear is not entirely unfounded. The slaves did in fact use Exú and Ogun and the herbs of Ossaim in their struggle against the economic and racial oppression of the ruling class. Nevertheless the *candomblés* were never completely closed to the whites' curiosity, sadism, or eroticism. We have seen that African religion imposed upon the sexuality of the black a control different from the control of Western societies but no less binding. The Portuguese and even certain Catholic priests of the seventeenth and eighteenth centuries took the non-existence of conventional white restrictions within the doors of the African sects for the nonexistence of any sexual taboos at all. For them the sects had the appeal of a beckoning abyss, and they yielded to it sensuously. Be that as it may, the whites could not attend the great *candomblé* ceremonies without recognizing their essentially religious character. This is why the dualism between magic and mystery cults was reflected structurally in a dualism between the various African "nations." The Mussulman and particularly the Mandingo Negroes were considered the master magicians, probably because of their stronger hostility to the new environment and their more tenacious resistance. And when black Islam disappeared from Brazil, the Bantu, especially the Congo, took its place. The Ketu and Jesha sects, on the other hand, are believed not to practice magic, or at least to restrict themselves to white magic. Similar situations occur in Cuba (the religion of the Lucumi and the magic of the Congo), in Haiti (Arada religion and Petro witchcraft), in the extreme south of the North American continent, and in Uruguay and Argentina in the early days of independence (where the Mandingo were generally feared). In short—and this is my first point—there is a tendency to structure magical collective representations, like religious ones, within the frameworks of institutionalized organizations.

But the social structures of the slave era affected even religious representations, orienting them toward magic, as I have just mentioned with reference to Exú and Ogun. The sinister character of certain deities was continually intensified, though without completely destroying traditional personae such as Exú the godfather or Ogun the blacksmith. The gods, as well as mortals, were caught up in the economic and racial struggle. Saint Anthony became the supernatural bush captain who helped whites find their runaway slaves. Ossaim put his knowledge of the virtues of plants at the disposal of his black children to "soften" the harshness of their masters (as the charming euphemism put it). These modifications of collective representations under the influence of the new social structures have been dealt with fully, and there is no need to dwell on them here. It is sufficient to note that any society that distinguishes between the "strong" and the "weak" tends to set great store by magic, which is of course one of the few weapons available to the "weak."

The Marxist assertion that religion is a response to contradictions in the production system, whether it be agricultural or industrial, communal or capitalist, seems to me infinitely more applicable to magic. When there appears to be no rational way of resolving these contradictions—a man may plant, but he can never count on the crop, because it depends not on his own will but on many other factors such as the weather, which is beyond his control; a man may be a reliable, diligent white-collar worker, but he may be out of a job tomorrow because unemployment depends on the capitalist market, which is beyond his control—the only alternative is a mystic one. But in my opinion this mystic solution is magical rather than religious because, while it is certainly quite different from a rational solution, it must be of a very similar nature. Magic, like science, is a matter not of prayers but of procedures that are effective in themselves. It follows the same law of causality, even though the magic causality may shock our Western mentality. Again, religion differs from magic in that the purpose of the latter is merely to restore threatened security, while the purpose of religion is to strengthen the communion of individuals by allowing them all to participate in the same supernatural world. This being so, changes in the social structures will at times tend to intensify magic, at other times religion. Slavery oriented values toward magic, no matter which of the two possible responses to his social situation the slave adopted—harmful magic used against the master if he chose the solution of revolt, love philters if he preferred to rise in society by way of the channels open to him. In the case of the free Negroes in the colonial or imperial era and of the masses liberated by the law of May 13, 1888, the abolition of slave labor oriented values toward religion because bonds of solidarity had been shattered and reduced to a chaotic scattering of interpersonal relationships, and ethnic or racial communion had to be restored in the country of exile by consolidating it around the *orixás*.

The distinction between Quimbanda and Umbanda—i.e. between witchcraft and the new African occultism—represents the latest phase in the impact of the social structures on religious values, the phase of the more or less complete integration of the blacks into the class society. We find analogous phenomena in colonies, where the two phases of urbanization, the disintegrative and the reconstructive, are typified by the development of black magic as a response to "the proliferation of antagonisms that cannot be controlled or compensated" and later by the emergence of messianic movements whose first tasks are, by contrast, to fight witchcraft and to "transcend clan affiliations" in order to regroup the dispersed individuals according to new forms of solidarity.[10] Although in both cases the social reconstruction is directed against magic, the Brazilian phenomena are quite different from the colonial ones because they occur in a different social context. One case represents integration *against* something, the other integration *into* the overall multiracial community. Here rejection of black magic becomes a rejection of African "barbarity," and whatever is preserved of the ancestral traditions is regarded as a valid equivalent of Western values—an equivalence that then permits the fusion of all colors in a single national communion.

Before leaving the field of magic, I should like to make one important observation. In moving from Africa to America, magic breaks the bonds that linked it to a certain form of social organization. To quote Meyer Fortes: "It is of great significance, too, that witchcraft (*bayi*) is believed [among the Ashanti] to be effective only within the lineage. It is only within the lineage that amity and solidarity are binding. . . ."[11] Among the Fanti black magic (*anyen*) is again inextricably linked to maternal descent and is effective only within the framework of the *abusua*, the matrilineal clan.[12] Among the Nuba "the power of *kamerge* [witchcraft] is . . . powerful only within the clan" and does not extend to other clans, even though they may belong to the same tribe.[13] Many more examples could be cited. Africans often insist to interrogators that their "magics" are effective for them but do not work for whites. The reason is that blacks and whites are not linked by common participations through which the magical activity could flow. The same is true of blacks of different ethnic origin and different lineages. But in America the effectiveness of witchcraft is not determined by affiliation with a lineage or clan or even a "nation"; the formidable power of the witch doctor serves the struggle of one entire race against another, and the white man is trapped in a net of sympathetic magic, magic knots, and the ritual of "changing heads" (which consists in transferring the ailment of the suffering black to the healthy white).[14]

Thus magic was detached from its social frameworks, and the detachment was certainly facilitated by the disappearance of the lineages and clans and by the creation of a new solidarity, the solidarity based on the slaves' dependence on their white masters. But was the detachment total? We have seen that the process of acculturation was not the same in religion as in magic. In the one it follows the law of analogy, in the other the law of accumulation, according to which the techniques of Western demonic magic were added to those of African magic. We have also noted that the principle of addition, which is also found in ancient witchcraft, might be explained by the necessity of taking all necessary precautions to ensure success. Without rejecting this factor, we may now ask whether still another cause may not have been at work in this cumulative process. When a rite was extended from one ethnic group to another, no one could be sure that it would be as effective against whites as it was against blacks since the whites did not belong to the same participatory system as the Africans. It was therefore advisable to add to the African rite the techniques of medieval witches and sorcerers, which were known to be effective against whites because they themselves made use of them.

On the basis of these facts, we are now in a position to bring together the relationships between social structures and religious values, at least for the Afro-Brazilian context. These are not one-way but two-way influences; values influence structures and structures influence values. Strictly speaking, it is a matter not so much of causality as of dialectics—i.e. of chain reactions, influences, or directions. Certainly acculturation complicates the problem since it is sometimes the structures of the global society that affect the values of the African group, while in other cases African values may be transmitted via the "black mammy" or the colored mistress from the slave group to the master group and thus subsequently affect white society. But even though acculturation complicates the problem, the general pattern holds. Sociology has to work on two fronts; it must take into account modifications of the lower levels by values as well as changes in those values resulting from pressure emanating from the morphological stratum or from the stratum of intergroup relationships.

While economic phenomena and especially production systems are of undeniable importance, we may accept them only on condition that we do not confine ourselves to "plane sociology" but also take into consideration the superimposed levels in an economic depth sociology. Production systems do not act on religious values directly but through the intermediacy of economic values. Capitalism, for instance, modifies the attitudes of blacks by making them aware of the value of personal effort, by removing them from the world of prestations and counterprestations, and by helping them to understand that money is the most effective means of improving their social status. "A rich Negro is a white; a poor white is a Negro," according to a Brazilian proverb. And it is because these new values conflict with those of the *candomblés* that after a first phase of compromise and a second phase of internal tensions (compartmentalization followed by mental assimilation) the black is led to modify his mystique, as he has done in Umbanda spiritism.

Finally, relationships between the two constantly interacting poles are not necessarily continuous. Influences may be intermittent; breaks may occur in their movement, interrupting chain reactions on one level or another. New relationships may be created, since the overthrow of structures permits alternative responses and offers multiple options to the activities of individuals and organized groups.

Religion and Ideology

Marx wavered between two different conceptions of ideology. Sometimes he used the term in the widest possible sense to cover all superstructures, all products of culture, where every production system has its conscious correlate in a system of concepts that is merely its psychic expression. Sometimes ideology really appears only with the class struggle. While it is still the same conceptual apparatus just described, it is caught up in conflicts of interest and becomes an offensive weapon in a shattered world and a climate of mutual hostility. Ideology is then connected with the theory of the "unhappy consciousness" or the theories of "alienation" and "mystification." In the first case we are dealing with historical materialism. Religion is the expression of a certain economic and social state; it is the problem—or part of the problem—discussed in the previous section, and there is no need to revert to it. In the second case religion, though still a reflection of the substructures, hovers above objective reality rather than expressing it and ultimately becomes a kind of pathological excrescence utilized by one class to ensure its dominance or reflecting in an illusory way the traumatized consciousness of a proletariat seeking escape from painful reality into an imaginary world. I use the term only in this second sense because my study of the metamorphoses of African sects seems to me to show that at a certain point religion was transformed into ideology. We must ask how religion as the manipulation of the sacred differs from ideology as an expression of the class struggle and how the sacred can be distorted into ideology.

I have declined to move out of the field of science into philosophy—i.e. to become involved in a theory of values. Values must always be seen in their sociological perspective and regarded simply as objective facts discernible at a given level of depth sociology. Values in fact constitute one of these levels, one that manifests itself in human behavior at this level by affective attachments and emotional participations, reaching down to a lower level through behavioral norms, obligatory orientation of activity, and social constraint, and up to a higher one through acts of communion or the formation of what might be called "axiological communities." Religious values are no exception; on the contrary, it is here that my definition attains its widest scope.

Religious values in fact wither away and ultimately disappear if they are not incarnated in a specific social situation to which they can give direction through norms or action models. Again, these active values enable individuals to come together not just in a group in an "axiological community." The latter point is so evident that some people have even defined religion by this community, confusing the religious bond with the social one and forgetting that all values realize communions—aesthetic and moral values just as much as mystic ones. To assimilate religion to the collective consciousness is to forget the pluralism of values and to mistake an extremely general phenomenon for the characteristic of a single type of value. In fact, as I said at the outset, what distinguishes religious values from other values is the utilization of "the sacred," transcendence in respect to the social, the participation of the human in something that goes beyond it. This does not of course prevent individuals from achieving communion with one another in this category of the sacred and thus realizing "axiological community."

But this axiological community is located in a certain social context that may influence it, causing distortions of collective ideals, introducing foreign elements such as class interests and other impurities into the sacred. However, these distortions occur only when society is fragmented into antagonistic classes or when religion for some reason begins to "hover above" social reality instead of orienting it and incarnating itself in it. In the first case we are dealing with one of the aspects of relationships between social structures and values, in the second with a new aspect of the problem of acculturation.

The difference between the church and the sect is certainly that the former tends to be ecumenical or catholic while the latter functions as a separate clan. The church transcends class and race, bringing them together in one and the same world of beliefs and collective feelings, but when society breaks up into divergent and sometimes hostile groups, this universal communion becomes more difficult. It is at this point that small sects emerge on the margin of the wider society; their members are drawn from the same class and, in countries with an immigrant population, from the same ethnic group, and their religious preoccupations often reflect other, more profane ones. I used the term *sects* when referring to Afro-Brazilian fraternities precisely because these fraternities also grew up on the margins of the Luso-Catholic civilization and because within them race was confused with caste or class. Thus religious values, the basis of axiological communion, were subjected to external pressures resulting in a compromise moving between the sacred and the ideological. As long as the *candomblé* restores African civilization, the sacred remains dominant; individual consciousnesses are merged in a single system of beliefs; everyone shares the same values, irrespective of the social position of the *candomblé* members, free or enslaved, rich or poor. The metamorphoses of the gods merely accentuate certain magical or sinister traits and efface others; the system itself is not affected. But when the overthrow of the social structures resulting from the industrialization of the country creates new forms of solidarity that are incompatible with the old norms, the interests of economic classes, tensions between social groups, and racial frustrations can make their way in. The result is Umbanda spiritism.

As I have tried to show, this spiritism reflects the vertical mobility of people of African descent and the obstacles that racial groups place in its way. This mobility poses the problem of acculturation. Mannheim, starting from the sociology of knowledge, reaches similar conclusions. When the peasant moves to the city, he says, he acquires a certain detachment from the village way of thinking; he can judge it from the level of his new urban values, and rural "truth" no longer seems as axiomatic as it did before.[15] Similarly, every time two civilizations, with their different value systems, meet, the validity of principles that had formerly seemed self-evident is destroyed and the relativity of ideals is laid bare. We have seen this "detachment syndrome" occurring in the big cities in connection with the old African traditions, making it possible to appraise them from outside, to select or reject cultural traits, to turn inherited norms around rather than passively accept them. Blood sacrifices are prohibited and replaced by vegetable offerings. The old gods are transformed into administrators of justice and upholders of morality. The *orixás* merge with the *caboclos* and the saints to consolidate multiracial communion. But all these transformations are more or less conscious and, as has been brought out, although they express the new interests of a colored proletarian class, they are the work of mulatto or even white leaders.

Besides promoting the distortion of sacred values into ideologies, the facts of acculturation may also help to show up these emerging ideologies for what they are. The linking of values to different group interests is more obvious to a critical mind, and the mind of the man who is straddling two heterogeneous civilizations is bound to be critical. The role Marx assigned to work—putting the mind in touch with objective reality and de-alienating it so that it may construct itself in the process of constructing the world—may to some extent be assigned to acculturation, which relativizes all values, to horizontal mobility (from ethnic group to class), and to vertical mobility (from one life style to another), all of which end up destroying values by opposing them in the very process of transition. Thus Umbanda spiritism is threatened even as it constructs itself, as is any religion that events have transformed into an ideology. This is what I was trying to express when I said that although values are born of the substructures, they "hover." They are a reflection playing above the substructures; they no longer "signify" them. To understand this hovering, we must remember that it occurred when the African civilizations were transplanted to Brazil. Here too the world of values had been cut off from social reality by the slave trade, but it had secreted a structure in which it could incarnate itself to make a signifying substance effective. Continuity had been reestablished between the levels of black society, inasmuch as the values were structured, while the structures were given value. In Umbanda spiritism, on the other hand, the superstructures no longer constitute the norms that govern social life and bring into play interpersonal or intergroup relationships. They are no longer the living models of the substructures but simply an expression of the trauma of a colored class, an impassioned phantasmagoria playing above the structural upheavals that no longer depend upon those values but on other causalities or dialectics. In short, in religion, values give a meaning to reality; in ideology they are merely a subjective expression of the interests or frustrations of a social group.

Nevertheless any religious ideology is still a religion—i.e. it still tends to create an axiological community. This is precisely why the sects are so much like clans or tribes, constituting small closed worlds defined by a different "civilization," by homogeneity of beliefs and feelings, by the transition from values to norms or models and then to structures. This also explains why the sects are usually recruited within one social class, for this promotes homogeneity of beliefs and feelings and the mystic solidarity that is the reverse side of material solidarity. Communion of values tends to become the significant language again, to reestablish continuity of interaction between the sect's levels of social reality, just as it produced it in Africa in the clans, tribes, and ethnic groups. Although Umbanda spiritism is very far removed from *candomblé* and although it has broken with *macumba*, which it contemptuously rejects as witchcraft, it still defines a civilization and expresses the collective subjectivity of a social class within the Brazilian community. In my opinion, then, religious ideology can be differentiated from other forms of ideology—political ones, for instance— by the fact that however much these other forms may degrade the sacred, they can never completely obliterate its distinctive character. Mystic values may bear the obvious scars of social tensions, but inasmuch as they are mystic, not political, values, they always retain a certain specificity that the sociologist is obliged to describe or at any rate to acknowledge.

Notes

The almost 1,200 footnotes to Roger Bastide's *African Religions of Brazil* cite sources spanning four centuries, from as many languages and continents. In their original form Bastide's bibliographic references present many difficulties. In some cases the names of authors cited by him are given here in a slightly different form in order to conform to the Library of Congress Catalogue or to another standard catalogue. When an edition cited by Bastide was unavailable, another has been substituted. References to English translations of works cited have been added. In the case of books published in both United States and Great Britain, the North American edition has been used. Since Bastide himself did not always indicate which edition he was citing, many problems of pagination arose, some of which could be resolved only by guesswork. Finally, some bibliographic information (author, title, or publisher) proved to be irretrievable. In those cases Bastide's reference has been reproduced verbatim.

References to journals and newspaper articles were difficult to check because many of the Brazilian and Portuguese journals are unavailable in the United States. Where checking was impossible, Bastide's citations have been given as they stand in the original.

The abbreviations for journal titles are Bastide's; a list follows this note.

For a selective bibliography on the Afro-Brazilian religions the reader is referred to Roger Bastide, *Le Candomblé de Bahia (Rite Nagô)* (Paris: Mouton & Co., 1958).

EUGENE K. GALBRAITH

Abbreviations

IBECC   Instituto Brasileiro de Educação, Ciência e Cultura
IBGE   Instituto Brasileiro de Geografia e Estatística
IFAN   Institut Français d'Afrique Noire
JRAI   Journal of the Royal Anthropological Institute of Great Britain and Ireland
RAM de SP   Revista do Arquivo Municipal de São Paulo
RIAGP   Revista do Instituto Arqueológico e Geográfico Pernambucano
RIAHGP   Revista do Instituto Archeológico, Histórico e Geográfico Pernambucano
RIH de Alagoas   Revista do Instituto Histórico de Alagoas
RIH de Pernambuco   Revista do Instituto Histórico de Pernambuco
RIHGB   Revista do Instituto Histórico e Geográfico Brasileiro
RIHG de Rio Grande do Sul   Revista do Instituto Histórico e Geográfico de Rio Grande do Sul
RIHG de SP   Revista do Instituto Histórico e Geográfico de São Paulo

Foreword

1. These data, as well as much of the biographical information used in preparing this foreword, were generously provided by Françoise Morin, who is currently completing an obituary on Bastide for the *American Anthropologist*. All errors and incorrect interpretations are, of course, my own responsibility. An exhaustive bibliography of Bastide's work is in preparation, to be published in 1978 by the Centre Charles Richet d'Étude des Dysfonctions de l'Adaptation (CREDA), Paris.

2. *Les Problèmes de la Vie Mystique* (Paris, 1931) and *Eléments de Sociologie Religieuse* (Paris, 1936).

3. Some of these works, including his book *A Poesia Afro-Brasileira* (São Paulo, 1943), have been collected and published as *Estudos Afro-Brasileiros* (São Paulo: Editôra Perspectiva, 1973). See also his *Arte e Sociedade* (São Paulo, 1945, 1971), reprinted as *Art et Société* (Paris, 1977).

4. M. I. Pereira de Queiroz, "Roger Bastide et les Études Sociologiques au Brésil," *TILAS* (Strasbourg), 13e–14e année (1973–1974), pp. 96–102. On Bastide's activities in Brazil see also her "Les Années Brésiliennes de Roger Bastide," *Archives des Sciences Sociales des Religions* 40 (1975): 79–87, and Gilberto Freyre, "Un Sociologue Français Particulièrement Lié aux Études Sociales du Brésil," in *L'Autre et l'Ailleurs: Hommage à Roger Bastide*, ed. Jean Poirier and François Raveau (Paris, 1976).

5. Introduction to *Estudos Afro-Brasileiros*. Françoise Morin kindly provided me with Bastide's French typescript of this introduction, from which my quotations are translated.

6. *Brésil, Terre de Contrastes* (Paris: Hachette, 1957), p. 9, cited by Pereira de Queiroz in "Les Années Brésiliennes," pp. 82–83.

7. "The Present Status of Afro-American Research in Latin America," *Daedalus*, Spring 1974, p. 113.

8. Introduction to *Estudos Afro-Brasileiros*.

9. Ibid.

10. Ibid. and "The Present Status of Afro-American Research," pp. 115–16.

11. "Roger Bastide ou l'Anthropologie des Gouffres," *Archives des Sciences Sociales des Religions* 40 (1975): 99–106.

12. "Anthropologie Religieuse," *Encyclopedia Universalis*, 1: 65, 68, cited by Morin in "Roger Bastide," p. 103.

13. Morin, "Roger Bastide," pp. 104–5.

14. See, in particular, his critical essay "La Pensée Obscure et Confuse," *Le Monde Non Chrétien* 75–76 (1965): 137–56.

15. "L'Ethnologie et le Nouvel Humanisme," *Revue Philosophique*, October–December 1964, p. 447, cited by Morin in "Roger Bastide," p. 102.

16. "Pour Roger Bastide," *Cahiers Internationaux de Sociologie* 57 (1974): 293.

17. To mention only a few titles: *Sociologie de Maladies Mentales* (1965); *Le Prochain et le Lointain* (1970); *Anthropologie Appliqué* (1971); *La Rêve, la Transe et la Folie* (1972); *Sciences de la Folie* (1972); *Sociologie et Psychanalyse* (rev. ed., 1972); and *Anatomie d'André Gide* (1972). Bastide's collected essays on religion were published posthumously as *Le Sacré Sauvage* (1975); see also Poirier and Raveau, eds., *L'Autre et l'Ailleurs: Hommage à Roger Bastide*.

18. Introduction to *Estudos Afro-Brasileiros*.

19. *Le Candomblé de Bahia: Culte Nagô* (Paris and The Hague 1958).

20. Introduction to *Estudos Afro-Brasileiros*.

21. "Ultima Scripta" (collected and presented by Henri Desroches), *Archives des Sciences Sociales des Religions* 38 (1974): 3–47.

22. Introduction to *Estudos Afro-Brasileiros*.

23. "Mémoire Collective et Sociologie du Bricolage," *Année Sociologique* 21 (1970): 65–108.

24. "Acculturation," *Encyclopedia Universalis* (1968), 1: 106–7, cited by Sélim Abou in "Roger Bastide, ou Comment le Lointain Peut Devenir le Prochain," *SAFA* (Lebanon) 2, no. 631 (April 20, 1974).

25. Introduction to *Estudos Afro-Brasileiros*.

26. "Du Syncrétisme à la Synthèse: Umbanda, une Religion Brésilienne," *Archives des Sciences Sociales des Religions* 40 (1975): 96. On developments in Umbanda, see also Monteiro's introduction to this volume.

27. "The Present Status of Afro-American Research." Among the many important works since the publication of *The African Religions of Brazil* one might cite: Candido Procópio de Camargo, *Kardecismo e Umbanda: Uma Interpretação Sociológia* (São Paulo, 1961); M. I. Pereira de Queiroz, *O Messianismo no Brazil e no Mundo* (São Paulo, 1965); Deoscoredos M. dos Santos, *West African Sacred Art and Ritual in Brazil* (1967); Seth and Ruth Leacock, *Spirits of the Deep* (New York, 1971); Rainer Flasche, *Geschichte und Typologie afrikanischer Religiosität in Brasilien* (Marburg an der Lahn, 1973); Renato Ortiz, *La Mort Blanche du Sorcier Noir* (Paris, 1975); Juana Elbein dos Santos, *Os Nagô e a Morte: Pàde, àsèsè e o Culto Egun na Bahia* (Petrópolis, 1976).

28. See "Ultima Scripta," pp. 10–11. In another publication, he announced the new title as *The African Religions of Brazil During the Industrial Era* (see "The Present Status of Afro-American Research," p. 122).

29. It is worth underlining, in a comparative Afro-American context, that the approximately three and a half million Africans who were brought as slaves to Brazil represented more than twice the total number brought to the British Caribbean, the French Caribbean, or the whole of the Spanish Americas, and some nine times the number brought to North America (see Philip D. Curtin, *The Atlantic Slave Trade: A Census* [Madison, Wis., 1969], p. 268).

30. Introduction to *Estudos Afro-Brasileiros*.

Introduction to the Translation

1. P. 28. Unless otherwise identified, page numbers in the notes to this Introduction refer to the present volume.

2. P. 70.

3. Roger Bastide and Floristan Fernandes, *Relações Raciais entre Negros e Brancos em São Paulo* (São Paulo: Editora Anhembi, 1955); or idem, *Brancos e Negros em São Paulo* (São Paulo: Cia. Editora Nacional, 1959).

4. P. 194. *Le Candomblé de Bahia (Rite Nagô)* (Paris: Mouton & Co., 1958) is his most important anthropological study on Afro-Brazilian sects.

5. P. 16.

6. P. 157.

7. Ibid.

8. P. 142.

9. Pp. 398–99.

10. P. 399.

11. Pp. 401–5.

12. P. 402. Bastide's term is *mauvaise conscience*. Lalande's *Vocabulaire Technique et Critique de la Philosophie* (Paris: Presses Universitaires de France, 1962) relates *mauvaise conscience* to *conscience malheureuse* and to "Unglückseliges Bewusstsein. . . . Expression crée par Hegel et qui s'est récemment répandue en français, pour marquer le caractère qu'a, selon lui, toute conscience psychologique d'être en principe en souffrance, en raison de l'antinomie qu'elle contient entre son pôle subjectif et son pôle objectif . . ." (p. 1233).

13. A detailed description of this "social situation" in relation to *candomblé* can be found on pp. 231 ff. In contrast, see pp. 404–5 on Umbanda.

14. P. 3; cf. pp. 26–27 (critique of Tullio Seppilli's analysis).

15. On p. 27 of this book the author refers to an article published in *Renaissance*, nos. 2–3 (January 1946), pp. 13–29, where the "conceptual framework of the research" undertaken had been outlined. In fact, however, it deals with the definition of the lines of investigation to be followed rather than with the theoretical frame of reference to be adopted.

16. P. 227.

17. P. 293.
18. P. 403.
19. P. 231; cf. p. 401.
20. Pp. 404–5.
21. P. 404.
22. Ibid.
23. Ibid. and p. 322.
24. Pp. 157 and 399.
25. P. 280.
26. P. 295.
27. P. 398.
28. Ibid.
29. P. 392.
30. P. 402.
31. Ibid.
32. Ibid.
33. P. 403.
34. In contrast, most classical analyses of "the sacred" are based on more or less definite polarizations. Compare Durkheim's "De la Définition des Phénomènes Religieuses," in *L'Année Sociologique* (Paris, 1898), and his *Elementary Forms of the Religious Life* for the opposition between "repression" and "aspiration," and see R. Otto's *Le Sacré* (Paris: Payot, 1949) for his formulation—*mysterium tremendum* vs. *mysterium fascinans*.
35. G. Gurvitch, *La Vocation Actuelle de la Sociologie: Vers une Sociologie Différentielle* (Paris: Presses Universitaires de France, 1950).
36. P. 403.
37. Pp. 168–69, 302–3, 385–86, 394.
38. P. 403.
39. Pp. 404–5.
40. P. 2.
41. P. 404.
42. Gurvitch, *La Vocation Actuelle de la Sociologie*.
43. Pp. 392–93.
44. P. 11.
45. Ibid.
46. Pp. 12–15.
47. P. 159.
48. Ibid.
49. Ibid.
50. P. 160.
51. P. 96.
52. P. 108.
53. Pp. 106–7.
54. Pp. 156–57.
55. G. Lukács, *História y Consciencia de Clase* (Mexico, D. F.: Editora Grijalbo, 1969), p. 64.
56. Bastide and Fernandes, *Relações Raciais*, p. 142.
57. P. 303.
58. Roger Bastide, *Anthropologie Appliquée* (Paris: Payot, 1971), pp. 212ff.
59. The liveliness of these nuclei is attested, for instance, in recent studies such as that by Juana Elbein dos Santos, *Os Nagô e a Morte: Pàde, Àsèsè e o Culto Egun na Bahia* (Paris: Editora Vozes, Petrópolis, 1976).
60. The statements made by Bastide in the first lines of Chapter 13 in Part II, although true at the time they were made, are no longer valid. Even the great contingents of the population that are still today devoted to agrarian work and cattle raising live under conditions that reflect on the one hand the expansion of modern capitalist enterprise forms and on the other the influence of urban life transmitted through greater transport and communications facilities.

61. Cf. Renato Ortiz, "La Mort Blanche du Sorcier Noir" (thesis presented at the École des Hautes Études en Sciences Sociales, Paris, in 1975), which contains an excellent bibliography on Umbanda (to be published shortly by Editora Vozes, Petrópolis).

62. Cf. C. Procópio F. de Camargo, *Kardecismo e Umbanda* (São Paulo: Pioneira, 1961).

63. C. Procópio F. de Camargo et al., *Católicos, Protestantes e Espíritas* (Paris: Editora Vozes, Petrópolis, 1973), pp. 159ff.

64. F. C. Rolim, "Pentecostalismo: Gênese, Estrutura e Função" (Rio de Janeiro, 1976), manuscript.

65. Cf. Duglas Teixeira Monteiro, "A Cura por Correspondência," *Religião e Sociedade*, no. 1 (May 1977), pp. 61–79.

66. See P. Berger, *The Sacred Canopy: Elements of a Sociological Theory of Religion* (New York: Doubleday, 1969).

Introduction

1. Karl Marx, "Zur Kritik der Hegelschen Rechtsphilosophie," *Werke, Schriften, Briefe* (Stuttgart, 1962), 1:488.

2. Jean Piaget, *Introduction à l'Epistémologie Génétique* (Paris: Presses Universitaires de France, 1950), vol. 3, chap. 12.

3. Lucien Henry [Charles Hainchellin], *Les Origines de la Religion* (Paris: Éditions Sociales Internationales, 1935), p. 21.

4. Gerardus Van Der Leeuw, *L'Homme Primitif et la Religion: Étude Anthropologique* (Paris: F. Alcan; Presses Universitaires de France, 1940), p. 189.

5. See Georges Gurvitch, *La Vocation Actuelle de la Sociologie*, 3d ed. (Paris: Presses Universitaires de France, 1969), 2:258–65 and 285–88, on the distinction between cultural products and ideologies. See also his *Déterminismes Sociaux et Liberté Humaine* (Paris: Presses Universitaires de France, 1955), p. 136, n. 1 [2d ed., 1963, p. 146], on the various meanings of ideology in Marx.

6. Émile Durkheim, *Les Formes Élémentaires de la Vie Religieuse*, 2d ed. rev. (Paris: F. Alcan, 1925), pp. 121–22 [*The Elementary Forms of the Religious Life*, trans. J. W. Swain (Glencoe, Ill.: The Free Press, 1965), p. 86].

7. Ibid., p. 98 [English trans., p. 69].

8. Émile Durkheim, *Le Suicide* (Paris: F. Alcan, 1897), p. 245 [*Suicide*, trans. J. A. Spaulding and G. Simpson (Glencoe, Ill.: The Free Press, 1950), p. 227].

9. Talcott Parsons, *Éléments pour une Sociologie de l'Action*, with an introduction by F. Bourricaud, pp. 28–31. [See also Parsons, Bales, and Shils, *Working Papers in the Theory of Action* (Glencoe, Ill.: The Free Press, 1953), p. 44, and note 11 below.]

10. Gaston Richard, "L'Athéisme Dogmatique en Sociologie Religieuse," *Cahiers de la Revue d'Histoire et de la Philosophie Religieuse* (Strasbourg, 1923); Georges Gurvitch, "Le Problème de la Conscience Collective dans la Sociologie de Durkheim," in his *La Vocation Actuelle*, 3d ed., 2:1–58; Talcott Parsons, *The Structure of Social Action* (New York: McGraw-Hill & Co., 1937), pp. 409ff.

11. Parsons, *The Structure of Social Action*, pp. 409ff.; Durkheim, *Formes Élémentaires*, pp. 566–68 [English trans., 396–97].

12. E.g. Durkheim, *Formes Élémentaires*, p. 359 [English trans., pp. 250–51].

13. Claude Lévi-Strauss, "French Sociology" in *Twentieth Century Sociology*, ed. G. Gurvitch and W. E. Moore (New York: The Philosophical Library, 1946), pp. 517ff.

14. Ernst Cassirer, *Philosophie der Symbolischen Formen* (Berlin: B. Cassirer, 1924), pt. 2, "Das Mythische Denken" [*The Philosophy of Symbolic Forms*, trans. Ralph Mannheim (New Haven: Yale Univ. Press, 1960–1963)]. [On the use of the terms *pensée mystique, le mystique*, etc., from Lévy-Bruhl on, see Maurice Leenhardt's preface to Lucien Lévy-Bruhl, *Les Carnets* (Paris: Presses Universitaires de France,

1949), and Georges Gurvitch, *The Social Framework of Knowledge*, trans. M. A. and K. A. Thompson (Oxford: Oxford Univ. Press, 1971), p. 5, n. 1.]

15. Raymond Aron, *German Sociology*, trans. Mary and Thomas Bottomore (Glencoe, Ill.: The Free Press, 1957), pp. 95–97.

16. Max Weber, *Wirtschaft und Gesellschaft* (Tübingen: Mohr, 1922), pt. 2, chap. 4, sec. 7: "Stände, Klassen und Religion" [*Economy and Society: An Outline of Interpretive Sociology*, ed. Guenther Roth and Claus Wittich, trans. Ephram Fischoff (New York: Bedminster Press, 1968), vol. 2, chap. 6, secs. 5–7].

17. Max Scheler, "Probleme einer Soziologie des Wissens," in *Gesammelte Werke*, vol. 8, *Die Wissensformen und die Gesellschaft* (Bern and Munich, 1960), p. 21.

18. Ibid., esp. pp. 17–51.

19. The character of Lévy-Bruhl's theory considered as a "sociology of understanding" has been brought out by Florestan Fernandes, "Lévy-Bruhl e o Espírito Científico," *Revista de Antropológia* (São Paulo) 2, no. 2 (1954): 121–42.

20. Lévy-Bruhl, *Les Carnets*, p. 214.

21. E.g., A. R. Radcliffe-Brown, *Structure and Function in Primitive Society* (London: Cohen & West, 1952).

22. E.g., Raymond Firth, "Social Organization and Social Change," *Essays on Social Organization and Values*, London School of Economics Monographs on Social Anthropology, no 28 (London: The Athlone Press, 1964), pp. 30–58.

23. As does Lévi-Strauss, for example, in his *The Elementary Structures of Kinship*, trans. James H. Bell, John R. von Sturmer, and Rodney Needham (Boston: Beacon Press, 1969). See also his *Tristes Tropiques* (Paris: Plon, 1956), chap. 28 [*Tristes Tropiques*, trans. John Russell (New York: Atheneum, 1961)], where the problem of the search for models is arbitrarily linked to the overcoming of ethnocentrism.

24. See Mikel Dufrenne, *La Personalité de Base: Un Concept Sociologique* (Paris: Presses Universitaires de France, 1953).

25. Abraham Kardiner, *The Psychological Frontiers of Society* (New York: Columbia Univ. Press, 1945), pp. 240–51.

26. Claude Lévi-Strauss, preface to Marcel Mauss, *Sociologie et Anthropologie* (Paris: Presses Universitaires de France, 1950), pp. xxxviii–xl.

27. Marcel Granet, *Études Sociologiques sur la Chine* (Paris: Presses Universitaires de France, 1953), pp. 84, 166, 184, 186, etc.

28. Maurice Leenhardt, *Do Kamo* (Paris: Gallimard, 1947).

29. Georges Gurvitch, *The Spectrum of Social Time*, trans. M. Korenbaum and P. Bosserman (Dordrecht: D. Reidel Publishing Co., 1964), p. 3. [See also K. A. Thompson's introduction to Gurvitch, *The Social Framework of Knowledge*, trans. Margaret A. and Kenneth A. Thompson (Oxford: Blackwell, 1971), pp. xivff.]

30. Marcel Griaule, "Réflexions sur les Symboles Soudanais," *Cahiers Internationaux de Sociologie* 13 (1952): 9 and 29–30.

31. Gurvitch, *La Vocation Actuelle*, 3d ed., 2: 260ff. on Marx, 2:4 on Durkheim.

32. Georges Gurvitch, *La Vocation Actuelle*, 1st ed. (Paris: Presses Universitaires de France, 1950), p. 101.

33. Émile Durkheim, *Les Règles de la Méthode Sociologique* (Paris: Alcan, 1895), p. 108 [*The Rules of the Sociological Method*, 8th ed., trans. Sarah A. Salovay and John H. Mueller, ed. George E. G. Catlin (Glencoe, Ill.: The Free Press, 1968)].

34. Henry, *Les Origines*, p. 190.

35. Roger Bastide, *Initiation aux Recherches sur l'Interpénétration des Civilisations* (Paris: Centre de Documentation Universitaire, 1948), pp. 28–29.

36. R. Redfield, R. Linton, and M. J. Herskovits, "A Memorandum for the Study of Acculturation," *American Anthropologist* 38 (1936): 149–52.

37. On this development and the current state of the problem see M. J. Herskovits, *Man and His Works* (New York: Alfred A. Knopf, 1948), chaps. 27–32.

38. Gregory Bateson, "Culture Contact and Schismogenesis," *Man* 35, no. 199 (1937): 178–83.

39. Lévi-Strauss, reviews of works on acculturation in *L'Année Sociologique*, 3d ser., 1940–1948, 1: 335–36.

40. M. J. Herskovits, "The Significance of the Study of Acculturation for Anthropology," *American Anthropologist* 39, no. 2 (1937): 260–63; "Some Comments on

the Study of Cultural Contact," ibid. 43, no. 1 (1941): 3–5; and *The Myth of the Negro Past* (New York: Harper & Bros., 1941).

41. Tullio Seppilli, *La Acculturazione come Problèma Metodologico*, pp. 15–18.

42. The "memorandum" of Redfield, Linton, and Herskovits had already called for the study of the psychological mechanisms. See Herskovits, "Some Psychological Implications of Afro-American Studies," in *Proceedings and Selected Papers of the Twenty-ninth International Congress of Americanists* (1948) (Chicago: Univ. of Chicago Press, 1952), 3: 152–60, and his *Man and His Works*.

43. Roger Bastide, "Sociologie et Littérature Comparée," *Cahiers Internationaux de Sociologie* 17 (1954): 94–95; Seppilli, *Acculturazione*, pp. 15–18.

44. Roger Bastide, "La Causalité Externe et la Causalité Interne dans l'Explication en Sociologie," *Cahiers Internationaux de Sociologie* 21 (1956).

45. Seppilli, *Acculturazione*, p. 17.

46. Rémy Guérin, "Un Futur pour les Antilles?" *Présence Africaine*, n.s., February-March 1956, pp. 20–27.

47. On the connection between history and sociology in the specific case of colonization see Georges Balandier, "La Situation Coloniale: Approche Théorique," *Cahiers Internationaux de Sociologie* 11 (1951): 47–61.

48. Georges Balandier, *Sociologie Actuelle de l'Afrique Noire: Des Changements Sociaux en Afrique Centrale* (Paris: Presses Universitaires de France, 1955), pp. 3–36 [*The Sociology of Black Africa: Social Dynamics in Central Africa*, trans. Douglas Garman (New York: Praeger, 1970)].

49. See Pedro Calmon, *História Social do Brasil*, 2d ed. (São Paulo: Cia. Editora Nacional, 1937–1939): "Socially Brazil is a stratification not of classes but of epochs. It is not divided into human levels but into a juxtaposition of centuries." See also Fernando de Azevedo, "Para a Análise e Interpretação do Brasil," *Revista Brasileira de Estudos Pedagógicos* 24, no. 60 (1955): 12–14.

50. J. Lambert, *Le Brésil: Structure Social et Institutions Politiques* (Paris: A. Colin, 1953), pp. 64ff.

51. Nina Rodrigues, *L'Animisme Fétichiste des Nègres de Bahia* (Bahia, 1900) [published first in French, later in Portuguese as *O Animismo Fetichista dos Negros Bahianos* (Rio de Janeiro: Civilização Brasileira, 1935)].

52. Almost contemporaneously with Nina Rodrigues, Manoel Querino, a man of color from Bahia who wished to glorify his "race" and its contribution to Brazilian culture, wrote a series of articles on Negro religion and folklore. Although these articles stand in an isolated position, outside the mainstream, the documentary material is, in my opinion, usually interesting and its importance has been underestimated.

53. I have attempted a critique of this aspect of the work of Arthur Ramos in *Sociologie et Psychanalyse* (Paris: Presses Universitaires de France, 1950).

54. René Ribeiro, *Cultos Afro-Brasileiros de Recife: Um Estudo de Adjustamento Social* (Recife: Boletim do Instituto Joaquim Nabuco de Pesquisa Social, Numero Especial, 1952), pp. 142–43.

55. Donald Pierson, *Negroes in Brazil* (Carbondale, Ill.: Southern Illinois Univ. Press, 1967).

56. Roger Bastide, "Structures Sociales et Religions Afro-Brésiliennes," *Renaissance: Revue de l'École Libre des Hautes Études de New York*, 2 and 3: 13–29, published in 1945 but written earlier.

57. It is to be hoped that Pierre Verger will some day publish the results of his ethnographic studies, which are more extensive than my own.

58. Guerreiro Ramos, "O Problema do Negro na Sociologia Brasileira," *Cadernos do Nosso Tempo* 2 (1954): 207–15.

Chapter 1

1. On this earliest form of Brazilian colonization see Alexander Marchant, *From Barter to Slavery* (Baltimore: The Johns Hopkins Univ. Press, 1942). On the fusion of the earlier explorers with the Indian civilization see Gilberto Freyre, *Casa Grande*

414 NOTES TO CHAPTER 1

e Senzala (Rio de Janeiro: Schmidt, 1936) [*The Masters and the Slaves*, trans. Samuel Putnam (New York: Knopf, 1966)].

2. At first sight the *bandeiras*, which set out from São Paulo, may seem to have been more spontaneous than the *entradas*, which originated in the northeastern cities. However, Jaime Cortesão has shown, in a series of articles in *Estado de S. Paulo*, 1948, that the government secretly controlled the *bandeira* movement too.

3. Caio Prado, Jr., *História Econômica do Brasil* (São Paulo: Editora Brasiliense, 1953), pp. 21–31.

4. Freyre, *Masters and Slaves*, pp. 18, 84–85.

5. Fernando de Azevedo, *A Cultura Brasileira* (São Paulo: Cia. Editora Nacional, 1944), p. 89 [*Brazilian Culture*, trans. Rex Crawford (New York: Macmillan Co., 1950)]; F. J. Oliveira Vianna, *Pequenos Estudos de Psicologia Social* (São Paulo: Cia. Editora Nacional, 1942), and *Instituções Politicas Brasileiras* (Rio de Janeiro: J. Olympio, 1949), vol. 1, chap. 9; Caio Prado, Jr., *Evolução Politica do Brasil* (São Paulo: Emprêsa Gráfica "Revista dos Tribunais," 1933); Arthur Ramos, *Introdução a Antropologia Brasileira* (Rio de Janeiro, 1951), 2: 120; Roberto C. Simonsen, *História Econômica do Brasil, 1500–1820* (São Paulo: Cia. Editora Nacional, 1937), 1: 124–27.

6. Caio Prado, Jr., *História Econômica*, p. 41.

7. Freyre, *Masters and Slaves*, pp. 250–52.

8. João Pandiá Calogeras, *A Politica Exterior do Imperio* (Rio de Janeiro: Imprensa Nacional, 1927–1933), chap. 9, pp. 283ff. and 302.

9. Pedro Calmon, *História Social do Brasil* (São Paulo: Cia. Editora Nacional, 1934), cited by Affonso de E. Taunay in *Subsidios para A História do Trafico Africano no Brasil* (São Paulo: Imprensa Oficial do Estado, 1941), p. 239.

10. Taunay, *Subsidios*, p. 247, and Mauricio Goulart, *A Escravidão Africano no Brasil* (São Paulo: Livraria Martins, 1949), p. 275. The following points should be noted: (1) Calogeras overestimates the clandestine traffic. Although it certainly existed, it could not have accounted for twice the volume of the regular trade. (2) Calogeras disregards black reproduction in Brazil, relying on the evidence of Eschwege, who asserts that the blacks had a negative population growth rate. This, however, conflicts with known statistics, and in any case Eschwege's arithmetic is faulty. He assumes a rate of −2.19 percent for mulattoes and −3.95 percent for Negroes. From this Calogeras concludes that after 20–25 years all the imported blacks would have disappeared and therefore, "to maintain a constant level, their number would have to be renewed four or five times every century." But these negative rates apply only to Minas and to the eighteenth century. For other regions and other periods Maurice Goulart cites positive coefficients ranging from 0.05 percent to 0.2 percent. My own research in the São Paulo archives shows that the negative rates of the eighteenth century become positive in the nineteenth (ranging from +7.6 percent to +18 percent). And even so far as the eighteenth century is concerned, Calogeras's figures are obviously wrong. If we take 100 slaves and deduct 4.5 percent, we are actually deducting 4.5 persons. But the second diminution of 4.5 percent from a total of only 95.5 amounts to only 4.03 persons. At this rate, after 25 years 32 of the original 100 Negroes would still be left. In addition to these major errors, Calogeras commits several others. For example, to the 92,128 slaves on whom head tax was collected in Minas in the first semester he adds 92,740 for the second semester, although these represent the same individuals, since the head tax was paid in two installments. Again, Calogeras assumes that all of the 52,053 Negroes who left the Portuguese colony of Angola between 1572 and 1591 went to Brazil, although at that time Portugal also supplied slaves to the Spanish Indies (ibid., p. 155).

11. *Arroba* is the Portuguese measure of weight equivalent to 32 pounds.

12. Roberto S. Simonsen, *História Econômica do Brasil, 1500–1880* (São Paulo: Cia. Editora Nacional, 1937), 1: 201–5.

13. Taunay, *Subsidios*, pp. 304–5.

14. Goulart, *A Escravidão Africana*, 149.

15. Ibid., pp. 114–15. (M. Frezier, for example, estimated that in Bahia there were twenty Negroes to every white. *Relation d'un Voyage à la Mer du Sud* [Paris, 1716], pp. 271, 275, 279.)

16. Goulart, *A Escravidão Africana*, p. 272.
17. On the slave trade and its horrors see Taunay, *Subsidios*, pp. 123–31; J. F. de Almeida Prado, *Pernambuco e as Capitanias do Norte do Brasil, 1530–1630* (São Paulo: Cia. Editora Nacional, 1939–1941), pp. 246ff.; João Dornas, *A Escravidão no Brasil* (Rio de Janeiro: Civilização Brasileira, 1939), pp. 57–61; Charles de la Roncière, *Nègres et Négriers* (Paris, 1933), chap. 3.
18. In addition to works on the slave trade in general there are others that deal with it in one particular region. These include Luiz Vianna Filho, *O Negro no Bahia* (Rio de Janeiro: J. Olympio, 1946), and Ciro T. de Padua, *O Negro no Planalto* (São Paulo: Imprensa Oficial, 1943), pp. 127–228. I have deliberately left out any study of the slave trade and black slavery in Dutch Brazil because the influence of the Dutch on the later history of the country cannot be adequately traced. On this see E. Hermann Wätjen, *Das Holländische Kolonialreich in Brasilien* (Gotha: 1921), pp. 378ff. and 487. José Antonio Gonçalves de Mello Neto, *Tempo dos Flamengos: Influência da Ocupação Holandesa no Vida e na Cultura do Norte do Brasil* (Rio de Janeiro: J. Olympio, 1947), pp. 208, 222, 229.
19. Perdigão Malheiro, *A Escravidão no Brasil* (Rio de Janeiro, 1867); F. Contreieras Rodrigues, *Traços da Economia Social e Politica do Brasil Colonial* (Rio de Janeiro: Ariel Editora, 1935), pp. 93–94.
20. Giorgio Mortara, *O Desenvolvimento da População Preta e Parda no Brasil*, IBGE, Estudos Demograficas no. 18 (n.d.), p. 2.
21. *Recenseamento da População do Imperio do Brasil a Que Se Proceden no Dia 1° de Agosto de 1872.*
22. Souza Silva Costa Lobo, *História da Sociedade em Portugal no Seculo XV* (Lisbon, 1903), pp. 427–28.
23. On Indian influence see Sérgio Buarque de Hollanda, "Indios e Mamelucos na Expansão Paulista," *Anais do Museu Paulista* 13 (1949):177–290, and his *Raizes do Brasil* (Rio de Janeiro: J. Olympio, 1936), p. 42, as well as Freyre, *Masters and Slaves*, pp. 81–158.
24. Oliveira Vianna, *Instituições Politicas Brasileiras*, 1: 119–20.
25. From the evidence of books on family geneology, so highly prized in Brazil, Alfredo Ellis, Jr., estimates the index of consanguinity at 23.3 percent. For the province of São Paulo he gives it as 42.1 percent, as compared to 2 percent in France and 7 percent in Norway (the European country with the highest index). See his *Capitulos da História Social de São Paulo* (São Paulo: Cia. Editora Nacional, 1944), p. 121.
26. Vianna, *Instituições*, chaps. 9 and 10, and *Populações Meridionaes do Brasil* (São Paulo: Cia. Editora Nacional, 1933–), chap. 9.
27. Luiz Aguiar da Costa Pinto, *Lutas de Familias no Brasil (Introdução ao Seu Estudo)* (São Paulo: Cia. Editora Nacional, 1949); Affonso de E. Taunay, *Sob el Rey Nosso Senhor: Aspectos da Vida Setecentista Brasileira, Sobretudo em Brasil* (São Paulo: Oficinas do "Dairo Oficial," 1923), chap. 19.
28. On *compadrismo* see Vianna, *Populações Meridionaes*, pp. 263ff. Vianna quotes a typical observation by the traveler Sir Richard F. Burton to the effect that in small communities all the inhabitants are related by baptism, if not by birth. See also Luis da Câmara Cascudo's good survey article in *Dicionário do Folclore Brasileiro* (Rio de Janeiro: Ministério da Educação e Culturo, Instituto Nacional do Livro, 1954).
29. Gilberto Freyre, *Sobrados e Mucambos* (São Paulo: Cia. Editora Nacional, 1936) [*The Mansions and the Shanties*, trans. Harriet de Onís (New York: A. Knopf, 1963), pp. 94–96].
30. Freyre, *Masters and Slaves*, pp. xxxvi–vii, 372.
31. Hollanda, *Raizes*, pp. 179–93.
32. Ramos, *Introdução*, 2: 123.
33. See the wills published by the archives of São Paulo, Recife, and Bahia.
34. Affonso de E. Taunay, *História da Cidade de S. Paulo no Seculo XVIII* (São Paulo: Edições Melhoramentos, 1953), 1: 182–88, etc.
35. Freyre, *Mansions and Shanties*, pp. 61–64.
36. Azevedo, *A Cultura Brasileira*, pp. 298–309.
37. Nelson Werneck Sodre, *Formação da Sociedade Brasileira* (Rio de Janeiro: J. Olympio, 1944), pp. 244–45; Hollanda, *Raizes*, pp. 62–65. Hollanda cites one par-

ticularly significant text, a letter from the viceroy of Brazil dated 1767 complaining
that the population of Rio consists entirely of small artisans, fishermen and seamen,
mulattoes, "naked, barbarian blacks," and merchants, "very few of whom deserve the
name." He also complains that it is impossible to find city councillors or candidates for
public office because the "noble, distinguished" people all live on their country estates (ibid., p. 124).

38. Freyre, *Mansions and Shanties*, pp. 251–53.

39. Azevedo, *A Cultura Brasileira*, pp. 65–72, 86–89; Sodre, *Formação*, pp. 173ff.
and 224–34.

40. Ramos, *Introdução*, pp. 91–96. At first, colonization was open to foreigners and
Portuguese on equal terms. The only condition for land grants was that the recipients
be good Catholics. But in the seventeenth century restrictions were imposed, preventing
the development of a Brazilian culture more cosmopolitan than Portuguese (ibid., p.
98; Sodre, *Formação*, p. 113; Caio Prado, Jr., *História Econômica*, pp. 60–61).

41. Simonsen, *História Econômica*, chap. 8.

42. Chap. 2 of M. J. Herskovits's *The Myth of the Negro Past* (New York: Harper
& Bros., 1941) disputes the importance of central Africa in the slave trade. Francis de
Castenau questioned slaves in Bahia to obtain a geographical and ethnological descrip-
tion of the interior of Africa (*Renseignements sur l'Afrique Centrale* [Paris, 1851]).

43. Henry Koster, *Travels in Brazil*, 2d ed. (London: Longman, Hurst, Rees, Orme
& Brown, 1817), 2: 251; Johann Moritz Rugendas, *Viagem Pitoresca Através do
Brasil*, trans. Sergio Milliet (orig. pub. in German in the nineteenth century; Rio de
Janeiro: A Casa do Livro, 1972), p. 176.

44. Silvio Romero, *História da Litteratura Brasileira*, 2d ed. (Rio de Janeiro:
H. Garnier, 1902–1903), 1: 74. See also J. B. von Spix and C. F. P. von Martius,
Reise in Brasilien (Munich: M. Lindauer, 1823–1831), pt. 2 [*Travels in Brazil in the
Years 1817–1820*, trans. H. E. Lloyd (London: Longman, Hurst, Rees, Orme, Brown
& Green, 1824)]. This is inexcusable on the part of Silvio Romero and João Ribeiro be-
cause they well knew that in the war against the Dutch Henrique Dias had four regi-
ments of Negroes differentiated according to their "nations"—Mina, Arda (Daho-
mans), Angola and Creoles.

45. Braz do Amaral, *Os Grandes Mercados de Escravos Africanos: As Tribus Importadas, sua Distribuição Regional* (Rio de Janeiro: Livaria J. Leite, 19—), pp.
437–96.

46. Nina Rodrigues, *Os Africanos no Brasil* (São Paulo: Cia. Editora Nacional,
1932), chaps. 4 and 5, 188–229.

47. Arthur Ramos, *Las Poblaciónes del Brasil* (Mexico: Fondo de Cultura Econó-
mica, 1944), chap. 12, and *Introdução*, vol. 1, esp. chaps. 11, 12, 14, 15, 16, and 18.

48. The cultural heterogeneity of the peoples who furnished slaves to Brazil becomes apparent when we compare the list of imported tribes with the "cultural areas"
of Africa as enumerated by Frobenius in *Der Ursprung der Afrikanischen Kulturen*
(Berlin 1898) and "Der Westafrikanische Kulturkreis," in *Petermanns Mitteilungen*,
vols. 43–44 (1897–1899); by M. J. Herskovits in "Social History of the Negro," in
Handbook of Social Psychology (Worcester: Clark Univ., 1935), pp. 214ff.; and by
H. Baumann, *Les Peuples et les Civilisations de l'Afrique*, followed by D. Westermann,
Les Langues et l'Education, trans. L. Homberger (Paris: Payot, 1948).

49. In this paragraph I am following the ideas of Luiz Vianna Filho in *O Negro na
Bahia*. Although Vianna was writing of Bahia, what he says is applicable to Brazil as
a whole.

50. *Primeira Visitação do Santo Oficio às Parte do Brasil pelo Licenciado Heitor
Furtado de Mandoça: Denunciações da Bahia, 1591–1593* (São Paulo: P. Prado,
1925), pp. 406–8.

51. E. Hermann Wätjen, *Das Holländische Kolonialreich in Brasilien* (The Hague:
M. Nijhoff, 1921).

52. See Affonso Claudio, "As Tribus Negras Importadas," and Braz do Amaral,
"Os Grandes Mercados de Escravos," *RIHGB*, special issue, First National History
Congress, pp. 597–655 and 437–96. See also Koster, *Travels*; R. Walsh, *Notices of
Brazil in 1828 and 1829* (Boston: Richardson, Lord & Holbrook, 1831), 2: 331; João

P. de Mello Barreto and Hermeto Lima, *História da Policia do Rio de Janeiro: Aspectos da Cidade e da Vida Carioca* (Rio de Janeiro: A. Noite, 1939).
53. [Throughout this work the form *Shangô* will be used to denote the god, the form *xangô* (pronounced *shango*) to denote the sanctuary or the ceremonies in which the god is worshiped.]
54. Verger discusses the possibility that the *vodun* cult of Abomey may have been brought to São Luiz do Maranhão by the mother of King Ghézo (Pierre Verger, ed., *Les Afro-Américains*, Mémoires de l'Institut Français d'Afrique Noire, no. 27 [Dakar, Senegal, 1953], pp. 157–60).
55. Nunes Pereira, *A Casa das Minas* (Rio de Janeiro: Publ. da Sociedade Brasileira de Antropologia e Etnologia, no. 1, 1947), p. 22.
56. Edison Carneiro, *Candomblés da Bahia* (Bahia: Secretaria de Educação e Saúde, 1948), p. 31.
57. Herskovits, *Myth of the Negro Past*, pp. 112ff. See also Hope Franklin, *From Slavery to Freedom* (New York: A. Knopf, 1947), chap. 13, and E. Franklin Frazier, *The Negro in the United States* (New York: Macmillan Co., 1949), chaps. 2 and 3.
58. Fernando de Azevedo, *Canaviais e Engenhos na Politica do Brasil* (Rio de Janeiro: Instituto do Açucar e do Alcool, 1948), p. 57.
59. Walsh, *Notices*, 2: 187–88; L. F. de Tollenare, "Notas Dominicales," *RIAGP* 61 (1905): 110.
60. João Antonio Andreoni [André João Antonil], *Cultura e Opulência do Brasil* (São Paulo: Cia. Melhoramentos de São Paulo [Weiszflog Irmãos], 1923), p. 96.
61. On these dances see: Arthur Ramos, *O Folclore Negro do Brasil* (Rio de Janeiro: Civilização Brasileira, 1935), pp. 129–58; Luciano Gallet, *Estudos de Folclore* (Rio de Janeiro: C. Wehrs & Cia., 1934), pp. 61ff.; Edison Carneiro, *Negros Bantus* (Rio de Janeiro: Civilização Brasileira, 1937), pp. 131–45 and 161–65; Manuel Diegues, Jr., "Dansas Negras no Nordeste," in *O Negro no Brasil*, [n.d.], pp. 293–302; Oneyda Alvarenga, *Música Popular Brasileira* (São Paulo: Editôra Globo, 1950), pp. 130–58; Mario de Andrade, "O Samba Rural Paulista," *RAM de SP* 41 (November 1937): 37–116; Maynard Araujo, *Documentário Folclórico Paulista* (São Paulo: Prefeitura do Municipio de São Paulo, Departamento de Cultura, Divisão do Arquivo Histórico, 1952), pp. 11–13 and 31–33; Câmara Cascudo, *Dicionário do Folclore Brasileiro* (Rio de Janeiro: Ministero da Educação e Cultoro, Instituto Nacional do Livro, 1954).
62. On conditions of slavery in the mines see: W. L. Eschwege, *Pluto Brasiliensis* (Berlin: G. Reimer, 1833); J. Lucio de Azevedo, *Epócas de Portugal Econômico: Esboços de História* (Lisbon: Livraria Clássica Editora, A. M. Teixeira & Cia. [Filhos], 1947), pp. 364–65; Antonil, *Cultura*, pt. 3; Auguste de Saint-Hilaire, *Voyage dans les Provinces de Rio de Janeiro et de Minas Geraes* (Paris: Grimbert & Dorez, 1830), and *Voyage dans le District des Diamants et sur le Littoral du Brésil* (Paris, 1833); E. Pohl, *Reise im Innern von Brasilien*; J. P. Oliveira Martins, *O Brazil e as Colonias Portuguezas* (Lisbon: Parceria A. M. Pereira, 1920), bk. 2, chaps. 6 and 7; Miran M. de Barros Latif, *As Minas Gerais* (Rio de Janeiro: A. Noite, 1939), pp. 165ff.; Richard F. Burton, *Explorations of the Highlands of Brazil* (London: Tinsley Bros., 1869), 1: 270–78; Spix and Martius, *Travels in Brazil*.
63. The story of Chico Rei, who finally became owner of the Palacio Velho mine and organized what has been called the first effort toward "Christian socialism" (see Freyre, *Mansions and Shanties*, p. 40), is a famous one. Chico Rei, an African king, was taken prisoner and enslaved but succeeded in saving enough money to buy the freedom of his son, with whose help he liberated first himself, then his whole family, and finally "the entire tribe." In the end they bought the freedom of slaves from other tribes (no doubt belonging to the same ethnic group) and established "a veritable state within a state," with a king (Chico), a queen (his second wife), a prince and a princess, and a Brotherhood of Saint Iphigenia, the brotherhood that built one of the most beautiful churches in Ouro Preto, the Church of the Rosary. See Diogo de Vasconcellos, *História Antiga das Minas Gerais* (Rio de Janeiro: Imprensa Nacional, 1948), pp. 324ff., and Alcibiades Delamare, *Vila Rica* (Rio de Janeiro: Livraria Clássica Brasileira, 1955), pp. 25ff.

64. On conditions of slavery in the *sertão* see Câmara Cascudo, "A Escravidão na Evolução Econômica do Rio Grande do Norte," *Revista Nova* 1 (1931); Vianna Filho, *O Negro na Bahia*, pp. 126–32; and Caio Prado, Jr., *Evolução Política*, pp. 52–54. On conditions in the pampas see Auguste de Saint-Hilaire, *Voyage au Rio Grande do Sul (1820–1821)*, trans. Azeredo Pena (São Paulo: Cia. Editora Nacional, 1939), and Louis Couty, *L'Esclavage au Brésil* (Paris: Librairie de Guillaumin, 1881), p. 24. On the cattle-raising areas of Minas see Caio Prado, Jr., *Formação de Brasil Contemporâneo* (São Paulo: Editora Brasiliense, 1945) [*The Colonial Background of Modern Brazil*, trans. Suzette Macedo (Berkeley: Univ. of California Press, 1967)].

65. Roger Bastide and Florestan Fernandes, *Relações Raciais entre Negros e Brancos em São Paulo: Ensaio Sociológico sôbre as Origens, as Manifestações e os Efeitos do Preconceito de Côr no Municipio de São Paulo* (São Paulo: Editôra Anhembi, 1955), pp. 16–105.

66. Sud Menucci, *O Precursor do Abolicionismo no Brasil, Luiz Gama*.

67. On the *negros de ganho* see: Taunay, *História da Cidade de S. Paulo*, 2: 87; Donald Pierson, *Negroes in Brazil* (Chicago: Univ. of Chicago Press, 1942), pp. 38–39; James Wetherell, *Brazil: Stray Notes from Bahia* (Liverpool: Webb & Hunt, 1860), p. 53; Charles Ribeyrolles, *Brazil Pittoresco* (São Paulo: Livraria Martins, 1941), 2: 60–65; and esp. Charles Expilly, *Le Brésil Tel qu'Il Est* (Paris: Charlieu et Huillery, 1863), and Jean Baptiste Debret, *Voyage Pittoresque et Historique au Brésil* (Paris: Firmin Didot Frères, 1835), which contains a whole series of illustrations of Negro artisans, with commentaries. See also Thomas Ewbank, *Life in Brazil; or A Journal of a Visit to the Land of the Cocoa and the Palm* (New York: Harper Bros., 1856).

68. Manoel R. Querino, *Costumes Africanos no Brasil* (Rio de Janeiro: Civilização Brasileira, 1938), pp. 94–96 .

69. João Dornas Filho, *Escravidão no Brasil*, p. 243.

70. John Thrunbell, *A Voyage round the World in the Year 1800*, cited by Dornas in *Escravidão no Brasil*, p. 244.

71. Freyre, *Masters and Slaves*, pp. 138–53.

72. Serafin Leite, *História da Companhia de Jesus ao Brasil* (Lisbon: Livraria Portugalia, 1938–1950), 2: 353–54; chap. 3, on religious help to Negro slaves, is also well worth reading.

73. Diogo de Vasconcellos, *Marianna e seus Templos*, pp. 89–94 and 107.

74. See, for example, Vincente Rossi, *Cosas de Negros* (Cordoba: Imprenta Argentina, 1926); I. Pereda Valdes, *Negros Esclavos y Negros Libros* (Montevideo, 1941); Ed. Enece, *Los Morenos* (Buenos Aires, 1942); Fernando Romero's articles on blacks in Peru; J. Pablo Sojo, "Confrarias Etnoafricanas en Venezuela," *Cultura Universitaria* (Caracas) 1 (1947); M. Acosta Saignes, "Las Confrarias Coloniales y el Folclore," ibid. 47 (1955).

75. *Ordenações Filipinas*, II, tit. V, no. 6, cited by F. Mendes de Almeida in "O Folclore nas Ordonações do Reino," *RAM de SP* 56 (April 1939): 31; Taunay, *História da Cidade de S. Paulo*, 1: 107.

76. João Pandiá Calogeras, *Formação Histórica do Brasil*, 7th ed. (São Paulo: Cia. Editora Nacional, 1972) [*A History of Brazil*, trans. and ed. Percy Alvin Martin (Chapel Hill: Univ. of North Carolina Press, 1939)]; Hollanda, *Raizes*, p. 60.

77. J. Alvarès do Amaral, *Resumo Chronológico*, p. 403; Xavier da Veiga, *Ephemerides Mineiras*, 1: 208 and 2: 293.

78. Braz do Amaral, *Os Grandes Mercados*, p. 467.

79. Cited by Nina Rodrigues, *Os Africanos*, pp. 234–35. It is also true that when the king of Dahomey sent an embassy to Bahia asking for a monopoly in the slave trade, the governor submitted a report to the king of Portugal ending on this negative note: ". . . because it is not right that a great number of slaves from one single nation should be assembled in this *capitania*. The consequences might be pernicious" (letter from the Captain General of Bahia, 1795, cited by Taunay in *História da Cidade de S. Paulo*, 1: 215). We may note that these two policies were not contradictory. On the contrary, increasing the number of "nations" in any one locality and setting one against the other served one and the same purpose: to prevent the development of class consciousness.

80. At the end of the eighteenth century, for example, the Count of Pevolide asked

that the dances of the "nations" be preserved since they were no more immoral than those of the whites. But at the same time he condemned the dances performed "in the secrecy of their homes or in clearings, with a black mistress of ceremonies, an altar to idols, adoring live buck goats, and other fetishes of clay, anointing their bodies with oils and cocks' blood" (from a manuscript in the state library, Pernambuco, cited by Freyre in *Mansions and Shanties*, p. 264).

81. *Ordenações Filipinas*, LIV, tit. LXXX, VIII, nos. 7 and 8, cited by Mendes de Almeida in "O Folclore nas Ordonações do Reino," p. 58.

82. See Chapter 6.

83. Robert E. Park and Ernest W. Burgess, *The City* (Chicago: Univ. of Chicago Press, 1925), pp. 130–41.

Chapter 2

1. The literature on African religions is too extensive to be cited here. On the Bantu, the reader is referred to H. Baumann, *Les Peuples et les Civilizations de L'Afrique*, followed by D. Westermann, *Les Langages et l'Education*, trans. L. Homberger (Paris: Payot, 1948). On the blacks from the west coast of Africa see Geoffrey Parrinder, *West African Religion* (London: Epworth Press, 1949).

2. Leo Frobenius, *Atlantis*, vol. 10, *Die Atlantische Götterlehre* (Jena, 1926), pp. 122–23.

3. Henry Koster, *Travels in Brazil*, 2d ed. (London: Longman, Hurst, Rees, Orme & Brown, 1817); L. F. de Tollenare, *Notas Dominicals Tomadas durante uma Viagem em Portugal e no Brasil em 1816, 1817 e 1818* (Salvador: Livraria Progresso Editor, 1956), pp. 79, 139. Charles Expilly cites many examples in *Mulheres e Costumes do Brasil*, trans. Gustão Penalua (São Paulo: Cia. Editora Nacional, 1935), pp. 385–96.

4. To take one example, in 1811 the Freguezia *engenho* had 13 Creoles, 32 mulattoes, 16 unspecified Africans, 7 Dahomans, 3 Nagô, 2 Angola, 1 Mina. In 1832 it had 15 Creoles, 13 mulattoes, 9 *cabras*, 4 Hausa, 4 Dahomans, 1 Mina, 1 Mendobi. In 1853 it had 102 Nagô, 15 Creoles, 14 Hausa, 1 Calabar, 1 Mozambique, 3 Cabinda, 1 mulatto, 27 unspecified Africans. See Wanderley Pinho, *História de um Engenho do Reconcavo*, pp. 163–64.

5. On this first solution see A. d'Assier, *Le Brésil Contemporain* (Paris, 1867), pp. 26–28.

6. P. Nobrega, *Carlas do Brasil, 1549–1560* (Rio de Janeiro: Oficina Industrial Gráfica, 1931), pp. 99–100.

7. See Chapter 9.

8. Alexander Caldeleuch, *Travels in South America* (London, 1825), 1: 25; Koster, *Travels*, 2: 245–46.

9. Koster, *Travels*, 2: 243, 264. On the tendency to marry mulatto slaves to darker individuals to prevent "passing" see ibid., p. 266, and Affonso de E. Taunay, *História do Café no Brasil* (Rio de Janeiro: Departamento Nacional do Café, 1939), vol. 4, chap. 63, and vol. 8, p. 174. See Debret, *Voyage Pittoresque et Historique au Brésil* (Paris: Firmin Didot Frères, 1835), vol. 3, pl. 15, for an excellent engraving of a slave marriage.

10. Couty, *L'Esclavage au Brésil* (Paris: Librairie de Guillaumin, 1881), pp. 74–75.

11. Charles Expilly, *Le Brésil Tel qu'Il Est* (Paris: Charlieu & Huillery, 1863), chap. 6; Koster, *Travels*; V. Coaracy, *O Rio de Janeiro no Seculo XVII* (Rio de Janeiro: J. Olympio, 1944), p. 201.

12. The split between the two religions as it affects the organization of the *candomblés* has been well treated by M. J. Herskovits in "The Social Organization of the *Candomblé*," *Anais XXXI Congresso de Americanistas* (Nendeln, Lichtenstein: Kraus Reprints, 1976), p. 521, and, from the viewpoint of enculturation, by E. F. Frazier in "The Negro Family in Bahia, Brazil," *American Sociological Review* 7, no. 4 (1942): 471.

13. On these three families and their present-day theological similarity see Nunes Pereira, *A Casa das Minas* (Rio de Janeiro: Publ. da Sociedade Brasileira de Antro-

420   NOTES TO CHAPTER 2

pologia et Etnologia, no. 1, 1947), pp. 31–32; Octavio da Costa Eduardo, *The Negro in Northern Brazil* (Seattle and London: American Ethnological Society; University of Washington Press, 1948), pp. 76–80; and Verger, *Les Afro-Américains*, pp. 159–60.

14. Alexander Marjoribanks, *Travels in North and South America* (London: Simpkin, Marshall & Co., 1854), p. 73; A. R. Wallace, *A Narrative of Travels on the Amazon and Rio Negro* (London: Reeve & Co., 1853), p. 120; Hamlet Clark, *Letters Home from Spain, Algeria, and Brazil during the Past Entomological Rambles* (London: J. Van Voorst, 1867), p. 160; S. W. H. Webster, *Narrative of a Voyage of the South Atlantic Ocean*, p. 43; George Gardner, *Travels in the Interior of Brazil, 1836–1841* (London: Reeve, Benham & Reeve, 1849), p. 14; Hastings Charles Dent, *A Year in Brazil, with Notes on the Abolition of Slavery* (London: K. Paul, Trench & Co., 1886), p. 28; Frank Bennett, *Forty Years in Brazil* (London: Mills & Boon, 1914), p. 111; James William Wells, *Exploring and Travelling Three Thousand Miles through Brazil from Rio de Janeiro to Maranhão* (London: S. Low, Marston, Searle, & Rivington, 1886), 2: 187.

15. Auguste de Saint-Hilaire, *Voyage dans les Provinces de Rio de Janeiro et de Minas Geraes* (Paris: Grimbert & Dorez, 1830), chap. 4. Accounts by other French travelers agree: Couty, *L'Esclavage*, pp. 3–9; Ferdinand Denis, *Brésil* (Paris: Firmin Didot Frères, 1837), p. 142. Koster (*Travels*, 2: 207) even stresses that slaves belonging to foreigners are treated more harshly than those of Brazilian nationals. Although he opposed slavery, Ribeyrolles admitted that the slaves were better off than European laborers, (*Brasil Pittoresco* [São Paulo: Livraria Martins, 1941]). See also Ida Pfeiffer, *Voyage d'une Femme autour du Monde* (Paris: L. Hachette, 1865), p. 18.

16. Two examples are Abbé Lallemant and the anonymous author of *Brasilienische Zustände*. Other German travelers, however, stress the relatively humane character of Brazilian slavery. See J. B. von Spix and C. F. P. von Martius, *Travels in Brazil in the Years 1817–1820* (London: Longman, Hurst, Rees, Orme, Brown & Green, 1824); J. Emmanuel Pohl, *Reise im Innern von Brasilien*; and Johann Moritz Rugendas, *Viagem Pitoresca Através do Brasil*, trans. Sergio Milliet (orig. pub. in German in the nineteenth century; Rio de Janeiro: A Casa do Livro, 1972).

17. Auguste de Saint-Hilaire, *Voyage aux Sources du Rio São Francisco et dans la Province de Goyaz* (Paris: A. Bertrano, 1847–1848), p. 110; Koster, *Travels*.

18. Auguste de Saint-Hilaire, *Viagem ao Rio Grande do Sul*, trans. Azeredo Pena (São Paulo: Cia. Editora Nacional, 1939), p. 87.

19. Couty, *L'Esclavage*, pp. 83–84.

20. The profit realized from the sale of a slave, which had ranged from 20 percent to 30 percent, went up to 200 or even 300 percent (João Dornas Filho, *A Escravidão no Brasil* [Rio de Janeiro: Civilização Brasileira, 1939], p. 63*n*).

21. Taunay, *História do Café no Brasil*, vol. 3, chaps. 62–69; vol. 6, chaps. 9 and 10; vol. 8, chap. 17.

22. On the religious factor see Castelnau, cited by Taunay in *No Brasil do 1840* (São Paulo: Imprensa Oficial do Estado, 1936), p. 311. D'Assier clearly recognized the economic reason for the white masters' change of policy (*Le Brésil Contemporain* (Paris, 1867), p. 160).

23. Gardner agrees (*Travels*, p. 12).

24. Gilberto Freyre, *The Masters and the Slaves*, 2d ed., trans. Samuel Putnam (New York: A. Knopf, 1966), pp. 75–77, 330–31.

25. Arthur Ramos, *A Aculturação Negra no Brasil* (São Paulo: Cia. Editora Nacional, 1942), pp. 103–14. On the punishment of slaves in Brazil see also: d'Assier, *Brésil Contemporain*, p. 96; Nuto Sant'Anna, *São Paulo Histórico*, 2: 185–92; José Tavares Bastos, *Cartas do Solitario* (São Paulo: Cia. Editora Nacional, 1938); Denis, *Brésil*, p. 156; François Auguste Biard, *Deux Années au Brésil* (Paris: L. Hachette, 1862), p. 180. V. Coaracy (*O Rio de Janeiro no Seculo XVII* [Rio de Janeiro: J. Olympio, 1944], p. 204) recounts that in 1688 the king of Portugal introduced measures against the cruelty of slaveowners. When the slaves learned of them, a series of revolts occurred and the governor requested that the royal recommendations be withdrawn. The laws governing punishment inflicted on Negroes can be found in *Coleção das Leis do Imperio do Brasil do 1835* (Rio de Janeiro, 1864), 1: 5ff. Newspaper ad-

vertisements for runaway slaves often mention as identifying features scars left by corporal punishment.
  26. Gardner, *Travels*, p. 14; Spix and Martius, *Travels*, 1: 179.
  27. Koster, *Travels*, 2: 233–34; Ramos, *Introdução*, p. 121.
  28. A. Comte, *Cours de Philosophie Positive*, [edition not cited], vol. 5, lesson 53.
  29. Couty, *L'Esclavage*; Johann von Tschudi, *Reise durch Süd-Amerika* (Leipzig: F. A. Brockhaus, 1866–1869), 2: 76–79.
  30. Fernando de Azevedo, *Canaviais e Engenhos na Politica do Brasil* (Rio de Janeiro: Instituto do Açucar e do Alcool, 1948). The opinion of Max Weber to which Avevedo refers is in *Wirtschaft und Gesellschaft* (Tübingen: Mohn, 1922), chap. 2, par. 30, p. 95 [*Economy and Society: An Outline of Interpretive Sociology*, ed. Guenther Roth and Claus Wittich, trans. Ephraim Fischoff (New York: Bedminster Press, 1968)].
  31. On the black child as the white child's whipping boy see Freyre, *Masters and Slaves*, pp. 75, 349–50, 390–94; on female jealousy see p. 351.
  32. João Antonio Andreoni [André João Antonil], *Cultura e Opulência do Brasil* (São Paulo: Cia. Melhoramentos de São Paulo [Weiszflog Irmãos], 1923).
  33. Roger Bastide, "Introduction à l'Étude de Quelques Complexes Afro-Brésiliens," *Bulletin du Bureau d'Ethnologie* (Port-au-Prince, Haiti) 2, no. 5 (1948): 26–27, and *Sociologie et Psychanalyse* (Paris: Presses Universitaires de France, 1950), pp. 242–43.
  34. Gilberto Freyre devoted a whole book, *Sobrados e Mucambos* (São Paulo: Cia. Editora Nacional, 1936) [*The Mansions and the Shanties: The Making of Modern Brazil*, trans. Harriet de Onís (New York: A. Knopf, 1968)], to this problem as well as a major chapter in *Região e Tradição* (Rio de Janeiro: J. Olympio, 1941), pp. 107–94 ("Aspectos de um Seculo de Transição no Nordeste do Brasil").
  35. Freyre, *Mansions and Shanties*, chap. 5.
  36. A. Arinos de Mello Franco, *Conceito de Civilisação Brasileira* (São Paulo: Cia. Editora Nacional, 1936).
  37. See, for example, Parrinder, *West African Religion*.
  38. *Revista de Archivo Publico* (Recife), 2d semester, 1946, documents from the archives, pp. 231ff.
  39. Arthur Ramos, *O Negro Brasileiro* (Rio de Janeiro, 1934), pp. 192–96.
  40. The whites encouraged their slaves to breed. Any woman who produced ten children was freed, and this number was later reduced to seven. In spite of such inducements, the birth rate was quite low, partly because of contraception and even voluntary abortion, which were practiced as gestures of resistance.
  41. Tullio Seppilli, *Il Sincretismo Religioso Afro-Cattólico*, p. 35.
  42. The reader seeking more extensive information on this subject is referred to Freyre, *Masters and Slaves*.
  43. See, for example, Mary H. Kingsley, *West African Studies* (New York: Macmillan, 1899), p. 318.
  44. This is confirmed by the fact that in present-day industrial society the black does not hesitate to give up these professions, if they do not pay well enough, in favor of better-paid "dirty" or "hard" jobs such as mechanics' positions. See Roger Bastide and Florestan Fernandes, *Relações Raciais entre Negros e Brancos em São Paulo* (São Paulo: Editôra Anhembi, 1955), pp. 57–60, 224–26.
  45. Nina Rodrigues compared some of these African animal stories collected by Sylvio Romero in Bahia (*Contes Populares do Brésil* (Lisbon: Nova Livraria Internacional, 1883) with their African counterparts collected by A. Ellis (*The Yoruba-speaking Peoples of the Slave Coast of West Africa* (London: Chapman & Wall, 1894), pp. 258ff.). See Nina Rodrigues, *Os Africanos no Brasil* (São Paulo: Cia. Editora Nacional, 1932). Arthur Ramos devoted a whole chapter (chap. 6) of his book *O Folclore Negro do Brasil* (Rio de Janeiro: Civilização Brasileira, 1935) to these popular animal tales. See also L. da Câmara Cascudo's comments on Charles Hartt's *Os Milos Amazonicos de Tartaruga* and Octavio da Costa Eduardo's *Aspectos do Folclore de uma Communidade Rural* (São Paulo: Departamento de Cultura, 1951) in his *Geografia dos Milos Brasileiros* (Rio de Janeiro: J. Olympio, 1947).
  46. On the Father John cycle see Arthur Ramos, *Introdução a Anthropologia Bra-*

NOTES TO CHAPTER 2

sileira (Rio de Janeiro, 1950), chap. 9. See also the collection by G. Freyre et al., *Novos Estudos Afro-Brasileiras* (Rio de Janeiro: Biblioteca de Divulgação Científica, IX, Civilização Brasileira, 1937), p. 60; Theo Brandão, *Folclore de Alagoas* (Maceió, Alagoas: Oficina Gráfica de Casa Romalho, 1949), pp. 121–33; Osmar Gomes, "Tradições Populares Colhidas no Baixo São Francisco," *IBECC, 1° Congresso, Anais II* (1951), pp. 175ff.

47. On the Quibungo tales see Ramos, *Introdução*, chap. 7, and Camara Cascudo, *Geografia*, pp. 272–77. For the story of the little girl in the sack see Nino Rodrigues, *Os Africanos*, pp. 285–87, and for its African counterpart, pp. 288–90. For the story of Calunga see J. da Silva Campos, "Cantos e Fabulas Populares da Bahia," in *O Folclore no Brasil*, ed. Basilio de Magalhães (Rio de Janeiro: Imprensa Nacional, 1939), pp. 244–46.

48. Roger Bastide, *Psicanálise do Cafuné e Estudos de Sociologia Estética Brasileira* (Curitiba: Guaíra, 1941).

49. Arthur Ramos quotes the saying of Nina Rodrigues: "In Bahia all classes, even the upper class, have a tendency to become Negro," and adds: "The gradual de-Africanization of the Negro in Brazil is accompanied by its counterpart, a de-Europeanization of the white" (*A Aculturação Negra no Brasil* [São Paulo: Cia. Editora Nacional, 1942], pp. 11–12).

50. Freyre, *Masters and Slaves*, pp. 363–68.

51. Daniel P. Kidder, *Sketches of Residence and Travels in Brazil* (London: Wiley & Putnam, 1845), p. 203; Alvin Percy, *La Esclavitud e su Abolition*, p. 1213.

52. Antonio Candido, "L'État Actuel et les Problèmes les Plus Importants des Études sur les Sociétés Rurales du Brésil," *Proceedings and Selected Papers of the Twenty-first International Congress of Americanists*, p. 322. Tollenare sensed the importance of this middle class and regretted its neglect, since it might have provided a foundation for a better-balanced Brazil. See L. F. de Tollenare, *Notes Dominicales* (Paris: Presses Universitaires de France, 1971).

53. F. J. de Oliveira Vianna, *Populações Meridionães do Brasil* (São Paulo: Cia. Editora Nacional, 1933), chap. 4.

54. On the connection between this interstitial class and the development of subsistence cultures see Caio Prado, Jr., *História Econômica do Brasil* (São Paulo: Editora Brasiliense, 1953), pp. 49–52.

55. Oliveira Vianna, *Populações*, chaps. 7 and 8.

56. Osvaldo Orico, *Patrocinio: Segundo Edição d' "O Tigre da Abolição"* (Rio de Janeiro: Irmãos Pongetti, 1935).

57. *Anais de Biblioteca Nacional* 38 (1913): 85.

58. Freyre, *Mansions and Shanties*, pp. 251–52.

59. On shoes as a status symbol see Freyre, Mansions and Shanties, pp. 376–78; Louis A. Gaffre, *Vision du Brésil* (Rio de Janeiro: F. Alves & Cia., 1912), p. 203; Karl F. G. Seidler, *Dez Anos no Brasil*, trans. Bertoldo Klinger (São Paulo: Livraria Martins, 1941), p. 237; Debret, *Voyage*, p. 205; Daniel P. Kidder and James C. Fletcher, *Brazil and the Brazilians* (Philadelphia: Childs & Peterson, 1857), p. 148.

60. On the rise of the mulatto see Freyre, *Mansions and Shanties*, chap. 11; Donald Pierson, *Negroes in Brazil* (Chicago: Univ. of Chicago Press, 1942), chap. 7; J. F. Oliveira Vianna, *Evolução do Povo Brasileiro* (São Paulo: Cia. Editora Nacional, 1933), pp. 157ff.; Pedro Calmon, *História Social do Brasil* (São Paulo: Cia. Editora Nacional, 1934), 1: 187 and 2: 116ff.

61. This explains the importance attached to art and literature by mulattoes and free Negroes as an expression of their total assimilation (Roger Bastide, *A Poesia Afro-Brasileira* [São Paulo: Livraria Martins Editora, 1943]).

62. Bastide and Fernandes, *Relações Raciais*, pp. 124, 141, etc.

63. In Brazil straight, shiny hair and a thin, pointed nose are often more important than skin color. See Pierson, *Negroes in Brazil*, p. 140 and p. 228, n. 49, and Charles Wagley, ed., *Race and Class in Rural Brazil* (Paris: UNESCO, 1952), p. 94.

64. Bonifacio's proposals can be found in Edison Carneiro's *Antologia do Negro Brasileiro* (Rio de Janeiro: Editora Globo, 1950); see esp. articles 10, 27, and 28. On the positivists' campaign see my article "O Positivismo Brasileno y la Incorporación do Homem de Côr," in *Revista Mexicana de Sociologia* 8, no. 3 (1947): 371–88.

65. Nelson W. Sodre, *Formação da Sociedade Brasileira* (Rio de Janeiro: J. Olympio, 1944).
66. I shall mention only Gordon W. Allport, *The Nature of Prejudice* (Reading, Mass.: Addison Wesley Publishing Co., 1954); Otto Klineberg, *Tensions Affecting International Understanding* (New York: Social Science Research Council, Bulletin no. 62, 1950), p. 208; and esp. John Dollard, *Caste and Class in a Southern Town* (New Haven: Yale Univ. Press, 1937).
67. Saint-Hilaire, *Voyage dans les Provinces de Rio et Minas*, vol. 2, chap. 11. On rich Negroes see Wanderley Pinho, *História*, p. 166.
68. Freyre, *Mansions and Shanties*, p. 418.

Chapter 3

1. E. T. Bosche, *Quadros Alternados*, p. 116.
2. Charles Expilly, *Le Brésil Tel qu'Il Est* (Paris: Charlieu & Huillery, 1863).
3. For other examples see Johann J. von Tschudi, *Reisen durch Südamerika* (Leipzig: F. A. Brockhaus, 1866–1869), 2: 76; Louis Couty, *L'Esclavage au Brésil* (Paris: Librarie de Guillaumin Éditeurs, 1881), p. 78; *RIHG de SP* 35: 145; Luiz do Santos Vilhena, *Recopilação de Noticias Soteropolitanis e Brasilicas: Contidas em XX Cartas* (Bahia: Imprensa Oficial do Estado, 1921), 1: 138; Affonso de E. Taunay, *Em Santa Catarina Colonial: Capitulo da História do Povoamento* (São Paulo: Imprensa Oficial do Estado, 1936), p. 380; A. d'Assier, *Le Brésil Contemporain* (Paris, 1867), pp. 97–98; Roger Bastide, *Estudos Afro-Brasileiros* (São Paulo: Editora Perspectiva, 1973), p. 125; Gilberto Freyre et al., *Novos Estudos Afro-Brasileiros* (Rio de Janeiro: Biblioteca de Divulgação Científica, IX, Civilização Brasileira, 1937), pp. 73–74; João Dornas, *A Escravidão no Brasil* (Rio de Janeiro: Civilização Brasileira, 1939), pp. 148, 224–26; Robert Walsh, *Notices of Travel in Brazil in 1828 and 1829* (Boston: Richardson, Lord & Holbrook, 1831), 2: 360; Auguste de Saint-Hilaire, *Voyage dans les Provinces de Rio de Janeiro et de Minas Geraes* (Paris: Grimbert & Dores, 1830), 1: 567 and 2: 454; João P. de Mello Barreto and Hermeto Lima, *História da Policia do Rio de Janeiro: Aspectos da Cidade e da Vida Carioca* (Rio de Janeiro: A. Noite, 1939); etc.
4. Jesuino was a Moslem. Langsdorff (cited by Taunay in *Em Santa Catarina*, p. 380) states that in Rio all slaves were affiliated with secret societies whose presidents were free Negroes and that this Negro freemasonry explains some mysterious homicides. This, however, has been disproved. See also J. Wetherell, *Brazil: Stray Notes from Bahia* (Liverpool: Webb & Hunt, 1860), p. 138, and Abbé Lallemant, *Reise*, p. 47.
5. John Dollard, *Caste and Class in a Southern Town* (New Haven: Yale Univ. Press, 1934), chap. 14.
6. Daniel P. Kidder and James C. Fletcher, *Brazil and the Brazilians* (Philadelphia: Childs & Peterson, 1852), p. 124; Daniel P. Kidder, *Sketches of Residence and Travels in Brazil* (London: Wiley & Putnam, 1845), 2: 45; Henry Koster, *Travels in Brazil*, 2d ed. (London: Longman, Hurst, Rees, Orme & Brown, 1817), 1: 58 and 2: 29, on conflict between slaves from different *fazendas* and conflict between slaves and free negroes; Luis Edmundo da Costa, *O Rio de Janeiro no Tempo dos Vice-Reis* (Rio de Janeiro: Imprensa Nacional, 1932), p. 24. Ferdinand Denis, *Brésil* (Paris: Firmin Didot Frères, 1837), p. 113 [*Brazil*, trans. B. Miall (New York: C. Scribner's Sons, 1911)]; A. d'Assier, *Le Brésil Contemporain* (Paris, 1867), p. 199; Santos Vilhena, *Recopilação*, p. 136 (on clashes between different nations and between Creoles and Africans); José Francisco da Rocha Pombo, *História do Brasil*, 12th ed. (São Paulo: Edições Melhoramentos, 1964), 2: 542.
7. Auguste de Saint-Hilaire, *Viagem ao Rio Grande do Sul, 1820–1821*, trans. Azeredo Pena (São Paulo: Cia. Editora Nacional, 1939), p. 367, and *Voyage aux Sources du Rio São Francisco et dans la Province de Goyaz* (Paris: A. Bertrand, 1847–1848), 2: 354–59. Cross-breeding between Indian men and Negro women also occurred but usually not spontaneously (see Johann M. Rugendas, *Viagem Pitoresca Através do Brasil*, trans. Sergio Milliet [orig. pub. in German in the nineteenth century: Rio de Janeiro: A Casa do Livro, 1972], p. 127). It was more likely to be the

result of the white slaveowner's desire to increase his labor force; the child's status was determined by its mother's (*RIHG de SP* 35 (1939): 112; Mello Moraes Filho, Quadros, p. 382).

8. On the capture of Negroes by Indians see: J. F. de Almeida Prado, *Pernambuco e as Capitanias do Norte do Brasil (1530–1630)* (São Paulo: Cia. Editora Nacional, 1939), p. 286; Padre Vicente do Salvador, *História do Brasil, 1500–1627*, 6th ed. (São Paulo: Edições Melhoramentos, 1975), p. 369; João Dornas, *Escravidão*, pp. 208, 244–45, 322, 389, 397.

9. On the Negro's role in the military defense of Brazil see: Rocha Pombo, *História do Brasil*, 2: 55; Francisco de Brito Freyre, *Nova Lusitania* (Lisbon: J. Gabram, 1675), pp. 244–45, 322, 389, 397; Dante de Laytano, "O Negro e o Espirito Guerreiro nas Origens do Rio Grande do Sul," *RIHG de Rio Grande do Sul* 17 (1937): 95, 117; [Laytano?], "Como Saint-Hilaire Viu o Negro no Rio Grande do Sul," *Congresso Sul Rio Grandenso de História* 3: 22; Freyre et al., *Novos Estudos*, p. 37; Nelson Coehlo de Senna, *Africanos no Brasil* (Belo Horizonte: Oficinas Gráficas Queiroz Breyner, 1938), pp. 45–46.

10. Diogo de Vasconcellos, *História Antiga das Minas* (Rio de Janeiro: Imprensa Nacional, 1948), p. 325.

11. Nestor Ericksen, "O Negro na Revolução dos Farrapos," *Planalto*, November 15, 1942, p. 12; Aydano do Couto Ferraz, "O Escravo Negro na Revolução da Independencia da Bahia," *RAM de SP* 56 (1939): 195–202.

12. G. Pereira da Silva, *Prudento de Moraes, O Pacificador* (Rio de Janeiro: Z. Valverde, 1937), pp. 216–18; Braz do Amaral, *História de Bahia do Imperio a Republica* (Bahia: Imprensa Oficial do Estado, 1923).

13. Couty, *L'Esclavage*, p. 84; Mello Moraes, *Crônica Geral* 11: 178.

14. Roger Bastide, "Introduction à l'Étude de Quelques Complexes Afro-Brésiliens," *Bulletin du Bureau d'Ethnologie* (Port-au-Prince, Haiti) 2, no. 5 (1948): 22–31.

15. Couty, *L'Esclavage*, p. 84. This explains why a Negro who had killed a *feitor* might make an excellent slave on a different *fazenda* (ibid., p. 79). See also Koster, *Travels; Documentos Interessantes*, 57: 147; M. M. de Barros Latif, *As Minas Gerais* (Rio de Janeiro: A. Noite, 1939), p. 169; Rugendas, *Viagem*, pp. 181–82.

16. Koster, *Travels*; Denis, *Brésil*, pp. 142, 146; Charles Ribeyrolles, *Brésil Pittoresque* (Paris: Imp. Lemercier, 1861), p. 45; Expilly, *Brésil*, chap. 6.

17. On slavery in monasteries and dualism in the master-figure see Koster, *Travels*, 2: 265–66; *Brasilianische Zustände*, p. 50; Kidder, *Sketches*; G. H. Handelmann, *História do Brasil* (Rio de Janeiro: Imprensa Nacional, 1931), p. 104; Dornas, *Escravidão*, p. 243; Andrew Grant, *History of Brazil* (London: H. Colburn, 1809); Gilberto Freyre, *The Masters and the Slaves*, trans. Samuel Putnam (New York: A. Knopf, 1966), p. 442 (slaves treated better by some religious orders than by others; fast days increased for economic, not religious, reasons), and *The Mansions and the Shanties*, trans. Harriet de Onís (New York: A. Knopf, 1968), p. 384 (on the Benedictines' genetic experiments); F. Contreiras Rodrigues, *Traços da Economia Social e Politica do Brasil Colonial* (Rio de Janeiro: Ariel Editora, 1935), pp. 62–63. For the Catholic point of view see Serafim Leite, *História da Companhia de Jesus no Brasil* (Lisbon: Livraria Portugalia, 1938–1950), 2: 357–59.

18. On the mentality of the *fazendeiro*, who regarded new immigrants as substitutes for slaves, see Thomas Davatz, *Les Mémoires d'un Colon*, pp. 84, 114, 123, 215, 262 [*Die Behandlungen der Kolonisten in der Provinz St. Paulo in Brasilien* . . . (Chur: Druck von L. Hitz, 1858)]. On appeals to blacks to resist the colonists see ibid., p. 269. On massacres of German troops by Negroes see E. T. Bosche, *Quadros Alternados*, p. 102, and Denis, *Brésil*, p. 154.

19. *RAM de SP* 66: 70. Originally this custom represented an *auto-da-fé* of a Jew (*queimamento em estatua*). After the Jews were converted to Catholicism or had left Portugal, the effigy of the Jew became an effigy of Judas. Marianne Baille (*Lisbon in the Years 1821, 1822, and 1823* [London: J. Murray, 1825], 1: 67) gives a description of this ceremony in Lisbon.

20. Jean Baptiste Debret (*Viagem Pitoresca e Histórica ao Brasil*, trans. Sergio Milliet [São Paulo: Livraria Martins, 1940], 2: 198) contrasts the court, middle-class,

and poor people's Judas. On the Negroes' Judas see Kidder and Fletcher, *Brazil*, p. 154. Debret (*Voyage Pittoresque et Historique au Brésil* [Paris: Firmin Didot Frères, 1834–1839], plate 21) shows the segregation of Negroes and Whites at the Judas festival. See also Auguste de Saint-Hilaire, *Voyage dans les Provinces de Saint-Paul et de Sainte-Catherine* (Paris: A. Bertrand, 1851), 2: 195–96.

21. Debret cites a prohibition from 1863: "Anyone who on Hallelujah Saturday makes a Judas resembling an individual will be punished by a fine of 30 milreis" (see *RAM de SP* 56: 70). Writing in 1837, Denis said: "Sometimes the allusion is a general one, addressed to a whole class; sometimes it is personal. Often it is a political warning to important personages" (*Brésil*, p. 135).

22. Gustavo Barroso, *Através dos Folclores* (São Paulo: Cia. Melmoramentos de São Paulo [Weiszflog Irmãos], 1927), pp. 40–42.

23. Debret, *Voyage*, plates 21 and 197.

24. Walsh, *Notices*, pp. 189–90; Koster, *Travels*; Rocha Pombo, *História do Brasil*, 1: 562; Affonso de E. Taunay, *História da Vila de São Paulo (Anais Museu Paulista 7:* 121) [perhaps *História da Cidade de São Paulo* (São Paulo: Edições Melhoramentos, 1953)]; Diogo de Vasconcellos, *História Média de Minas Gerais* (Rio de Janeiro: Imprensa Nacional, 1948), p. 164; d'Assier, *Brésil Contemporain*, p. 99; L. F. de Tollenare, *Notas Dominicaias* (Salvador: Livraria Progresso Editor, 1956), p. 55. Auguste de Saint-Hilaire (*Voyage dans le District des Diamants et sur le Littoral du Brésil* [Paris, 1833], p. 242) says that the Portuguese call these isolated Negroes "ribeirinhos." See also Walsh, *Notices*, p. 342; *RIHGB* 56 (1893): 164–65.

25. On suicides among the Gallina, Braz do Amaral, *História de Bahia*, p. 479; among Gabon Negroes, Koster, *Travels*, 2: 255, and Affonso de E. Taunay, *História do Café no Brasil* (Rio de Janeiro: Departmento Nacional do Café, 1939), 3: 232; among the Mozambique, Koster, *Travels*, 2: 256–57, and J. B. von Spix and C. F. P. von Martius, *Através da Bahia: Excerptos da Obra Reise in Brasilien* (São Paulo: Cia. Editora Nacional, 19–), p. 99*n*; among the Mina, Taunay, *História do Café*, 2: 240.

26. Émile Durkheim, *Le Suicide* (Paris: F. Alcan, 1897) [*Suicide: A Study in Sociology*, trans. John A. Spaulding (New York: The Free Press, 1968)].

27. The suicide rate was high until the end of slavery. The report of the Rio chief of police for 1866 states that out of 23 persons who committed suicide 16 were slaves. On the suicide rate among slaves see Armand Corre, *L'Ethnographie Criminelle d'apres les Observations et les Statistiques Judiciaires Recueillies dans les Colonies Françaises* (Paris: C. Reinwald & Cie., 1894), chap. 9, p. 26. According to Kidder and Fletcher, although Brazilian slaves were treated better than those in the United States, their suicide rate was much higher (*Brazil*, p. 132).

28. Koster, *Travels*, 2: 256–57.

29. Johann J. von Tschudi, *Reisen durch Südamerika* (Leipzig: F. A. Brockhaus, 1866–1869), 2: 76–79.

30. D'Assier, *Brésil Contemporain*, pp. 26–28.

31. George Wilhelm Freyreiss, *Beiträge zur Nähren Kenntniss des Kaiserthums Brasilien nebst einer Schilderung der Neuen Colonie Leopoldina . . .* (Frankfurt am Main: J. D. Sauerländer, 1824), p. 160.

32. Rocha Pombo, *História*, p. 561; Spix and Martius, *Através da Bahia*, p. 99*n*; Paulo Prado, *Retrato do Brasil: Ensaio sôbre a Tristeza Brasileira* (Rio de Janeiro: F. Briguiet & Cia., 1931), chap. 3.

33. On the difficulty of localizing Palmares geographically and in time see Nina Rodrigues, *Os Africanos no Brasil* (São Paulo: Cia. Editora Nacional, 1932), pp. 115, 126, 150, and Alfredo Brandão, "Os Negros na História de Alagôas," in *Estudos Afro-Brasileiros* (Rio de Janeiro, 1935), pp. 61–63, 64, 66, 68, 73, 75.

34. Figures from Kaspar van Baerle [Barleus], *Res Gestae Mauriti*, p. 270. These figures are probably exaggerated. Jean Laert estimates the population of Palmares Grandes at 1,500, Brito Freyre at 30,000 (*Nova Lusitania* [Lisbon: J. Gabram, 1675], p. 281)!

35. *Brieven en Pepieren in Brasilien*, Portuguese translation by Alfredo de Carvalho, *RIAGP* 10 (March 1902): 87.

36. *RIHGB* 47. Benjamin Peret ("Que Foi o Quilombo de Palmares," *Anhembi* 66

[May 1956]) rejects the idea that the Palmares monarchy always had the same character and attempts to prove hypothetically an evolution in the form of government in the course of the *quilombo*'s sixty years of existence.

37. E. Ennes, *As Guerras nos Palmares* (collection of unpublished documents) (São Paulo: Cia. Editora Brasiliana, vol. 127, 1938), pp. 44, 161.

38. Edison Carneiro, *O Quilombo de Palmares* (São Paulo: Editora Brasiliense, 1947), pp. 102ff.

39. S. da Rocha Pitta, *História da America Portuguesa*, 2d ed. (orig. pub. 1730; Lisbon: F. A. da Silva, 1880), pp. 45–46; Joaquim P. Oliveira Martins, *O Brasil e as Colônias Portuguesas*, 5th ed. (Lisbon: Parceria A. M. Pereira, 1929), pp. 65–66; Rocha Pombo, *História*, 5: 359–63; Nina Rodrigues, *Os Africanos no Brasil* (São Paulo: Cia. Editora Nacional, 1932), p. 132.

40. Mario Behring, "A Morte de Zumbi," *Don Casmurro*, February 8, 1941.

41. DOCUMENTS ON THE PALMARES WARS: Barleus, *Res Gestae*, pp. 270–73; *RIHGB* 2: 153 and 14: 491; "Dezenove Documentos sobre os Palmares," *Revista do Instituto do Ceara* 16: 161–91; Brito Freyre, *Nova Lusitania*; Johann Nieuhof, *Voyages and Travels into Brazil, with a particular account of all the remarkable passages that happened during the author's stay in Brazil . . . 1640–1649*, cited in *A General Collection of the Best and Most Interesting Voyages and Travels*, ed. John Pinkerton (London, 1808–1814), 14: 8; Rocha Pitta, *História de America Portuguesa*, 1st ed. (1730); João Blauer, "Diario de Viagem aos Palmares," *RIH de Pernambuco* (March 1902); Ennes, *As Guerras*; "Relação das Guerras Feitas aos Palmares de Pernambuco no Tempo de Governador D. Pedro de Almeida de 1675 a 1677," *RIHGB* 22: 303; Alfredo Brandão, "Documentos Antigos sôbre a Guerra dos Negros Palmarinos," in *O Negro no Brasil*, pp. 275–89.

HISTORICAL AND SOCIOLOGICAL STUDIES: Handelmann, *História*, conclusion of chap. 8; Mario Melo, *Dentro da História* (São Paulo: Cia. Editora Nacional, 1931), pp. 101–16; Francisco A. de Varnhagen, *História Geral do Brasil* (São Paulo: Laemmert & Cia., 1907), 3: 319; Pedro Paulino da Fonseca, "Memorias dos Feitos que se Deram durante os Primeiros Anos da Guerra com os Negros Quilombolas dos Palmares, seu Destroço em Junho de 1718," *RIHGB* 39: 193–322; Dias Cabral, "Narracão de Alguns Successos Relativos a Guerra com os Negros Quilambolas dos Palmares de 1668–1680," in *RIH de Alagoas* (1875); Nina Rodrigues, *Os Africanos*, pp. 115–45.

MISCELLANEOUS: *Estudos Afro-Brasileiro*, preface by E. Roquette Pinto (Rio de Janeiro, 1935), pp. 60–77; Edison Carneiro, *O Quilombo de Palmares* (São Paulo: Editora Brasiliense, 1947); Benjamin Peret, "O Que Foi o Quilombo de Palmares," *Anhembi* 66 (May 1956): 467–68 and 65 (1955): 230–49. Jayme de Altavilla's novel *O Quilombo dos Palmares* (São Paulo: Cia. Melhoramentos de São Paulo [Weiszflog Irmãos], 1931), must be read with caution. It fails to distinguish between historical periods and even confuses the *quilombo* priests with Mohammedan *alufas*!

42. A. Vidal, "Tres Seculos de Escravidão na Parahyba," in *Estudos Afro-Brasileiros*, pp. 109–10.

43. Ayres de Casal, *Chorografia Brasileira*, cited by Nina Rodrigues in *Os Africanos*, p. 138.

44. Nina Rodrigues, *Os Africanos*, pp. 139–45.

45. Ennes, *As Guerras*, p. 325.

46. Brandão, "Os Negros na História," p. 67.

47. Altavilla, *O Quilombo*, p. 35.

48. Barleus, *Res Gestae*, pp. 270–71; Nina Rodrigues, *Os Africanos*, p. 122.

49. On costume see Rocha Pitta, *História da America Portuguesa*, 2d ed., p. 237.

50. On the agrarian economy see Barleus, *Res Gestae*, p. 270; Rocha Pitta, *História da America Portuguesa*, 2d ed., p. 240; Brito Freyre, *Nova Lusitania*, p. 280. According to Peret ("Que Foi O Quilombo," pp. 469–86), the economy evolved from collective labor performed by the runaway Negroes in the early days of the *quilombo* into an economy based on slavery in which women and enslaved men did the agricultural work and the free men devoted themselves to hunting or war.

51. On trading see Altavilla, *O Quilombo*, p. 32n; Barleus, *Res Gestae*, p. 270; Rocha Pitta, *História da America Portuguesa*, 2d ed., p. 238; Nina Rodrigues, *Os Africanos*, p. 120; Carneiro, *O Quilombo*, pp. 59–60.

52. This actually did happen in the declining years of Palmares, possibly as a result of the disorganization that the continuous struggle against the whites inevitably produced in domestic affairs.

53. Text by Fernandes Gama as cited by Altavilla in *O Quilombo*, p. 114. Cf. Nina Rodrigues, *Os Africanos*, p. 121, and Brito Freyre, *Nova Lusitania*, p. 282.

54. On the stealing of women see Nina Rodrigues, *Os Africanos*, p. 120.

55. Document of February 4, 1678, cited by Brandão in "Documentos Antigos," p. 283. Concerning marriage among the *quilombolas* Blauer wrote in 1645: "To baptize and marry them they choose one of their most educated men, whom they revere like a priest. Baptism, however, does not take the form prescribed by the church, and marriage ignores the singularities required by the law of nature. . . . Their appetites govern their choice" (Carneiro, *O Quilombo*, pp. 43 and 189).

56. José Honorio Rodrigues and Joaquim Ribeiro (*Civilização Holandesa no Brasil* [São Paulo: Cia. Editora Nacional, 1940], p. 375) are particularly perceptive on this point. See also Affonso Arinos de Melo Franco, *Conceito de Civilização Brasileira* (São Paulo: Cia. Editora Nacional, 1936), pp. 121–29, and Arthur Ramos, *Culturas Negras* (Rio de Janeiro, 19–), p. 363.

57. M. J. and F. S. Herskovits, *Rebel Destiny* (New York: McGraw-Hill & Co., 1934); Willem F. van Lier and C. H. de Goeje, "Aantekeningen over het Geestelijk Leven en de Samenleving der Djoekas in Suriname," *Bijdragen Tot de Taal, Land- en Volkenkunde* 99, no. 2: 129–294; Morton Charles Kahn, *Djuka: The Bush Negroes of Dutch Guyana* (New York: The Viking Press, 1931).

58. Barleus, *Res Gestae*, p. 270. See also J. Blauer, "Diario de Viagem aos Palmares."

59. Brito Freyre, *Nova Lusitania*, p. 281.

60. Rocha Pitta, *História da America Portuguesa*, 2d ed., p. 237.

61. Malinowski's preface to L. Shapera, *The Contributions of Western Civilizations to Modern Kratla Culture*, from the review in *Revista Bimestre Cubana* 49, no. 2 (1942): 375–87.

62. Barleus, *Res Gestae*, p. 271.

63. Agostinho M. Perdigão Malheiro, *A Escravidão Africano no Brasil* (São Paulo: Editôra Obelisco, 1964), p. 37. Similar place names are found even in the southern states, where there were fewer Africans, as, for instance, in Santa Catarina. The municipalities of Florianopolis, Tijucas, Imaruhy, and Chapoco have a total of six such names (Boiteux, *Dicionário Histórico e Geográfico do Estado de Santa Catarina* [Rio de Janeiro, 1915–1916]). They are even more common in the central and northern states. The *Guia Postal do Brasil* for 1930 lists no less than 101 post offices under this name, 35 in Minas, 22 in São Paulo, 19 in Rio. There are 28 places named Mucambo in Bahia, 10 in Piaui, 8 in Sergipe, and 5 in Pernambuco. Fifty mountains or rivers also bear these names (Alfredo Moreira Pinto, *Apontamentos para o Dicionário Geográfico do Brasil* [Rio de Janeiro: Typ. de G. Leuzinger & Filhos, 1887–1889]). Cf. Affonso de E. Taunay, *Subsidios para a História do Tráfico Africano no Brasil* (São Paulo: Imprensa Oficial do Estado, 1941), pp. 51–52. The earliest documents date from the beginning of the seventeenth century. They can be found in *Documentos Históricos do Arquivo Municipal do Salvador*, vol. 1.

64. Handelmann, *História*, conclusion of chap. 8.

65. Cited by Leite, *História da Cia do Jesus*, 2: 358.

66. Felte Bezerra, *Etnias Sergipanas: Contribuição ao Seu Estudo* (Aracaju, 1950), p. 154.

67. On the events of 1617 and 1650 see the article by A. Ramos in *Boletin da Sociedade Luso-Americana*, no. 24 (December 1938), p. 15.

68. Bezerra, *Etnias Sergipanas*, p. 178.

69. A. Vianna, *Bandeiras e Sertanistas Baianos*, p. 65.

70. Nuto Sant'Anna cites documents concerning this *quilombo* in "O Ribeirao da Traição," *Actas* 11: 79, 12: 17, and 18: 116, 455; cf. Taunay, *História da Cidade de S. Paulo*, p. 123.

71. Barros Lestif, *As Minas Gerais*, p. 169.

72. Diogo de Vasconcellos, *História Antiga de Minas Gerais*, p. 326.

73. Diogo de Vasconcellos, *História Media de Minas Gerais*, pp. 164–75; Xavier da Veiga, *Efemerides Mineiras*, p. 77.

74. Nina Rodrigues, *Os Africanos*, p. 148.

75. J. Resende Silva, "A Formação Territorial de Minas Gerais," *Anais do III° Congresso Sul-Riograndense de História e Geografia* 3; João Dornas Filho, "Povoamento do Alto S. Francisco," *Sociologia* 18, no. 1 (1956): 70–109; Vasconcellos, *História Media*, p. 164; Edison Carneiro, "O Quilombo de Carlota" (unpublished manuscript); Conego R. Trindade [perhaps Raymundo Octavio da Trindade, *S. Francisco de Assis de Ouro Prêto: Crônica Narrada Pelos Documentos da Ordem* (Rio de Janeiro: Directoria do Patrimônio Histórico e Artístico Nacional, 1951)], p. 227; Aires da Mata Machada Filho, "O Negro e o Garimpo em Minas Gerais," *RAM de SP* 61 (1939): 277; J. Eugenio do Assis, "Levante de Escravos no Distrito de S. José des Queimades, Estado de Espirito Santo," *Museu Paulista* (1948); Ivaldo Falconi, "Um Quilombo Esquecido," *Correio das Artes* (João Pessoa), September 25, 1949, pp. 8–9. The Minas *quilombos* survived very late, until well into the nineteenth century, as shown by the books of Rezende, *Recordações*, p. 43, and Bernardo J. da Silva Guimarães, *Lendas e Romances: Uma História de Quilombolas* (orig. pub. 1870[?]; São Paulo: Livraria Martins, 194–).

76. Vasconcellos, *História Media*, p. 168.

77. Resende Silva, "A Formação Territorial," p. 707.

78. Nina Rodrigues, *Os Africanos*, p. 149.

79. Eduardo Roquette Pinto, *Rondonia* (orig. pub. 1817; São Paulo: Cia. Editora Nacional, 1975), pp. 31–45.

80. *Documentos Interessantes*, 59: 319.

81. J. E. Pohl, *Reise*, 2: 307–8.

82. Pereira da Costa, "Folclore Pernambucano," *RIHGB* 40.

83. Debret, *Voyage*, 1: 56; *RIHGB* 90 & 144: 512–13; F. Dabadie, *Récits et Types Américains* (Paris: F. Sartorius, 1860), p. 34; Walsh, *Notices*, p. 342. Walsh notes instances of the survival of African religion, in the use of cowrie shells, for instance.

84. Padre Protasio Frikel, "Tradições Histórico-Lendarias dos Kachuyana e Kahyana," *Rev. do Museu Paulista*, n.s. (1955), pp. 227–29.

85. Perdigão Malheiro, *A Escravidão no Brasil*, chap. 2.

86. Richard F. Burton, *Exploration of the Highlands of Brazil* (London: Tinsley Bros., 1869), 2: 97.

87. D'Assier, *Brésil Contemporain*, p. 80.

88. Cited by Roquette Pinto, *Rondonia*, p. 32; cf. *Anais Museu Paulista* 5 (1931): 703.

89. Roquette Pinto, *Rondonia*, p. 38n.

90. Raymundo Moraes, *Amfiteatro Amazônicô* (São Paulo: Cia. Melhoramentos de São Paulo [Weiszflog Irmãos], 1936), pp. 135–49; Nunes Pereira, "Negros Escravos na Amazonas," *Anais do X° Congresso Brasileiro de Geografia* 3 (1952): 178.

91. Saint-Hilaire, *Voyage dans les Provinces de Rio et Minas*, 1: 413.

92. Ibid., p. 424.

93. Saint-Hilaire, *Voyage aux Sources du Rio São Francisco*, 2: 253–71.

94. Saint-Hilaire, *Voyage dans les Provinces de Rio et Minas*, 1: 49.

95. Carlos Lacerda Marcos, *O Quilombo de Marcel Congo* (Rio de Janeiro, 1935). An unpublished document sent to the present writer by P. de Carvalho Neto contains information found in the archives of Marina about a *quilombo* in Rio.

96. A. Brandão, *Viçosa de Alagôas*, pp. 95–98, and "Os Negros na História do Alagôas," pp. 89–90.

Chapter 4

1. Gustavo Barroso, *História Secreta do Brasil* (São Paulo: Cia. Editôra Nacional, 1937); Viriato Correa, *Mata Galego: História da "Noite das Garrafadas" e Outras Histórias* (São Paulo: Cia. Editôra Nacional, 1933); Alvarès do Amaral, *Résumé Chronologique*, p. 324; and esp. Affonso Ruy de Souza, *A Primeira Revolução Social Brasileira* (orig. pub. 1798; São Paulo: Cia. Editôra Nacional, 1942).

2. "Inconfidencia de 1789," M.2, no. 20, Archives of Bahia, cited by Ruy de Souza in *A Primeira Revolução*.

3. Ferdinand Denis, *Brésil* (Paris: Firmin Didot Frères, 1837), p. 258; Muniz Tavares, *História da Revolução Pernambucana*; Pedro Calmon, *História do Brasil na Poesia do Povo* (Rio de Janeiro: A. Noite, 1943), pp. 96–100.

4. Alfredo de Carvalho, *Estudos Pernambucanos* (Recife: Cultura Academica, 1907), p. 259; Mario Melo, *Dentro da História* (São Paulo: Cia. Editora Nacional, 1931), pp. 117ff.; Francisco Pacifico do Amaral, *Escavações: Fatos da História de Pernambuco* (orig. pub. 1884; Recife: Arquivo Publico Municipal, 1974), p. 230.

5. Frei Canaca, *Obras Politicas*, p. 159.

6. "Sailors" was a contemptuous nickname for the Portuguese, and *caidos* ("the whitewashed") a pejorative name for whites.

7. Gilberto Freyre, *Região e Tradição* (Rio de Janeiro: J. Olympio, 1941), pp. 189–90.

8. F. P. do Amaral, *Escavações*, p. 427.

9. Viriato Correa, *A Balaiada: Romance do Tempo da Regencia* (São Paulo: Cia. Editora Nacional, 19–) [a fictional account]; José Gonçalves de Magalhães, "Memoria Histórica e Documentada da Revolução da Provincia de Maranhão," *RIHGB* 10 (1848): 263–362.

10. Caio Prado, Jr., *Evolução Politica do Brasil* (São Paulo: Emprêsa Gráfica, "Revista dos Tribunais," 1933), chap. 12.

11. Amaro Soares Quintas, *A Revolução Praieira* (Recife, 1949), p. 39, and *O Sentido Social da Revolução Praieira: Ensaio de Interpretação* (Recife: Imprensa Universitária, 1961), p. 34.

12. Bernadino José de Souza, *Dicionário do Terra e da Gente do Brasil* (São Paulo: Cia. Editora Nacional, 1939), pp. 204–5.

13. João Dornas, *A Escravidão no Brasil* (Rio de Janeiro: Civilização Brasileira, 1939), pp. 120–22 (account based on documents published in *Revista do Arquivo Mineira* 5: 158.

14. Noël Baudin, *Fétichisme et Féticheurs* (Lyon, 1884), p. 67; Leo Frobenius, *Die Atlantische Götterlehre* (Jena, 1926); [Edward Geoffrey Parrinder, *West African Religion* (London: Epworth Press, 1949)]; and esp. William R. Bascom, *The Sociological Role of the Yoruba Cult Group*, Am. Anthropol. Assn. Memoir Series, no. 46 (Washington, D.C., 1944), pp. 65ff., and M. J. Herskovits, *Dahomey: An Ancient West African Kingdom* (New York: J. J. Augustin, 1938), 2: 178–79. On the term *Ohogbo* see R. E. Dennett, *Nigerian Studies; or the Religious and Political System of the Yoruba* (London: Macmillan & Co., 1910), chap. 3, and P. A. Talbot, *Peoples of Southern Nigeria* (London: Oxford Univ. Press, 1928), 2: 91.

15. On these insurrectionaries see Alvarès do Amaral, *Resumo Cronológico*, p. 147; Braz do Amaral, *História da Bahia do Imperio a Republica* (Bahia: Imprensa Oficial do Estado, 1923), pp. 119–21; E. I. Brasil, "Os Malês," *RIHGB* 72: 67–126; G. Heinrich Handelmann, *História do Brasil* (Rio de Janeiro: Imprensa Nacional, 1931), p. 1813; Nina Rodrigues, *Os Africanos no Brasil* (São Paulo: Cia. Editora Nacional, 1932), pp. 65–98; Aderbal Jurema, *Insurreições Negras no Brasil* (Recife: Casa Mozart, 1935), pp. 17–32 (and the response by Arthur Ramos, "Levantes de Negros Escravos no Brasil," *Boletim da Sociedade Luso-Africana do Rio de Janeiro*, no. 24 [December 1938], pp. 15–17); Manoel R. Querino, *Costumes Africanos no Brasil* (Rio de Janeiro: Civilização Brasileira, 1938), pp. 121–24; Luiz Vianna Filho, *O Negro na Bahia* (Rio de Janeiro: J. Olympio, 1946), p. 108.

16. This custom of attracting good luck by copying verses from the Koran on a wooden tablet, then rinsing the tablet and drinking or washing in the water, still exists in Moslem Africa. See, for example, D. W. Ames, "The Selection of Mates, Courtship, and Marriage among the Wolof," *BIFAN* 18, nos. 1–2 (1956): 160.

17. Jurema, *Insurreições*. Djacir Menezes (*O Outre Nordeste: Formação Social do Nordeste* [Rio de Janeiro: J. Olympio, 1937]) and João Ribeiro (*O Elemento Negro: História, Folclore, Linguistica* [Rio de Janeiro: Record, 19–], pp. 33–38) take a similar position.

18. Ramos, "Levantes de Escravos," pp. 15–17.

19. James Wetherell (*Brazil: Stray Notes from Bahia* [Liverpool: Webb & Hunt

1860], p. 138) notes the intractable character of the Moslem Negroes of Brazil and their perennial spirit of rebellion. When one of them killed his master, his religious faith was always an incentive. Abbé Lallemant (*Reise*, p. 47) also notes that in the powerful "freemasonry" of the Moslem Mina, political and social resistance cannot be separated from religious resistance to the Christianity the whites were trying to impose upon them.

Chapter 5

1. Gilberto Freyre, *The Masters and the Slaves*, trans. Samuel Putnam (New York: A. Knopf, 1966), pp. 532–35.
2. Hortense Powdermaker, *After Freedom: A Cultural Study in the Deep South* (New York: The Viking Press, 1939), esp. pp. 221–96; Bertram W. Doyle, *The Etiquette of Race Relations in the South* (Chicago: Univ. of Chicago Press), esp. chap. 4; W. E. B. Du Bois, *The Negro Church*, Atlanta Univ. Publications, no. 8 (Atlanta: The Atlanta Univ. Press, 1903); Caster G. Woodson, *The History of the Negro Church* (Washington, D.C.: Associated Publishers, 1921); Jerome Dowd, *The Negro in American Life* (New York: The Century Co., 1926), chap. 25; etc.
3. Louis Gillet, "L'Art dans l'Amerique Latine," in *Histoire de l'Art depuis les Premiers Temps Chrétiens jusqu' à Nos Jours*, ed. André Michel (Paris: A. Colin, 1905–1929), vol. 3.
4. Luiz Saia, "O Alpendre nas Capelas Brasileiras," *Revista do Serviço do Património Histórico* 3 (1939): 235–49.
5. Serafim Leite, *História da Companhia de Jesus* (Lisbon: Livraria Portugalia, 1938–1950), 2: 355.
6. L. F. de Tollenare, *Notas Dominicais Tomadas durante uma Viagem em Portugal e no Brasil em 1816, 1817 e 1818* (Salvador: Livraria Progresso Editor, 1956), p. 159.
7. Gilbert Farquhar Mathison, *Narrative of a Visit to Brazil, Chile, Peru, and the Sandwich Islands* . . . (London, C. Knight, 1825), p. 159. But the mulatto priest served only his own class. See Robert Walsh, *Notices of Brazil in 1828 and 1829* (Boston: Richardson, Lord & Holbrook, 1831), 1: 204: ". . . negroes . . . officiate in churches indiscriminately with whites. . . . In Brazil a black is seen as the officiating minister, and whites receiving [the sacrament] from his hands." Nevertheless Victor Jacquemont, who visited Brazil in 1828, noted that the Negroes preferred mulatto priests to white ones (Affonso de E. Taunay, *Rio de Janeiro ed Antanho: Impressões de Viajantes Estrangeiros* [Rio de Janeiro: Cia. Editora Nacional, 1942], p. 513). During the colonial period a mulatto needed authorization from the church before he could take orders; such authorization was granted by the pope (Caio Prado, Jr., *Formação de Brazil Contemporâneo* [São Paulo: Editora Brasiliense, 1945], p. 278 [*The Colonial Background of Modern Brazil*, trans. Suzette Macedo (Berkeley: Univ. of California Press, 1967)]). Under the monarchy, on the other hand, a light, almost white mulatto could attain the highest levels of the ecclesiastical hierarchy, to become archbishop, like Dom Silveira Pimenta, or bishop, like Dom Prudencio Gomes and Dom Modesto Vieiro. See Nelson Coelho de Senna, *Africanos no Brasil* (Belo Horizonte: Oficinas Gráficas Queiroz Breyner, 1938), pp. 45–46.
8. W. Lloyd Warner, Buford H. Junker, and Walter A. Adams, *Color and Human Nature: Negro Personality Development in a Northern City* (Washington, D.C.: American Council on Education, 1941), chap. 4.
9. James Wetherell, *Brazil: Stray Notes from Bahia* (Liverpool: Webb & Hunt, 1860), p. 7.
10. Doyle, *Etiquette*; John Dollard, *Caste and Class in a Southern Town* (New Haven: Yale Univ. Press, 1937).
11. Walsh, *Notices*, 2: 188.
12. Maria [Dundas] Graham [Calcott], *Journal of a Voyage to Brazil and Residence There during Part of the Years 1821, 1822, 1823* (orig. pub. 1824; New York: Praeger, 1969).

13. Tollenare, *Notas Dominicais*, p. 81; Charles Ribeyrolles, *Brasil Pitoresco: História-Descrições-Viagems-Colonização-Instituições* (orig. pub. 1859; São Paulo: Livraria Martins, 1941), pp. 83–84.

14. Kidder, *Sketches*, p. 246. Cf. Alfredo Brandão, "Os Negros na História de Alagõas," in *Estudos Afro-Brasileiros* (Rio de Janeiro, 1935), p. 80.

15. A. d'Assier, *Le Brésil Contemporain* (Paris, 1867), p. 150.

16. Koster, *Travels in Brazil*, 2d ed. (London: Longman, Hurst, Reese, Orme & Brown, 1817), 1: 394–95.

17. Alexandre José de Mello Moraes, *Festas e Tradições Populares do Brasil* (orig. pub. 1888; Rio de Janeiro: F. Briguiet, 1946), pp. 227–90.

18. Tollenare, *Notas Dominicais*, p. 134.

19. Koster, *Travels*, 1: 357.

20. João Antonio Andreoni [André João Antonil], *Cultura e Opulência do Brasil* (São Paulo: Cia. Melhoramentos de São Paulo [Weiszflog Irmãos], 1923), p. 96.

21. Luis da Câmara Cascudo, *Dicionário do Folclore Brasileiro* (Rio de Janeiro: Ministério da Educação e Culturo, Instituto Nacional do Livro, 1954), p. 97; João da Silva Campos, *Processões Tradicionais da Bahia* (Salvador: Secretaria de Educação e Saúde, 1941), p. 205. The tendency to give Negroes colored saints dates far back beyond the period of slavery to the Middle Ages (Seiferth, "St. Mauritius, African," *Phylon* 4 [1941]: 370–76).

22. Dante de Laytano, *Festa de Nossa Senhora dos Navegantes* (Pôrto Alegre, 1955), pp. 39–51; Charles de la Roncière, *Nègres et Négriers* (Paris, 1933), p. 118.

23. Ribeyrolles, *Notas*, pp. 43–45 [perhaps Tollenare, *Notas Dominicais*, or Ribeyrolles, *Brasil Pitoresco*].

24. Gilberto Freyre, *Sobrados e Mucambos* (São Paulo: Cia. Editôra Nacional, 1936), p. 179, n. 41.

25. Alfonso de E. Taunay, *Sob El Rey Nosso Senhor: Aspectos da Vida Setecentista Brasileira, Sobretude em Brasil* (São Paulo: Oficinas do "Diario Oficial," 1923), p. 361.

26. Caio Prado, Jr., *Formação*, p. 352.

27. One example is the dispute over the route of a procession between the black Brotherhood of the Rosary and the (white) Fraternity of the Passion of Christ (*Instituições de Igrejas no Bispado de Mariana*, pp. 156ff).

28. Raymundo Octavio da Trindade, *S. Francisco de Assis de Ouro Prêto: Crônica Narrada Pelos Documentos da Ordem* (Rio de Janeiro: Directoria do Patrimônio Histórico e Artístico Nacional, 1951), pp. 90–101.

29. Adalberto Ortman, *História da Antiga Capela da Ordem Terceira da Penitência de São Francisco em São Paulo, 1676–1873* (Rio de Janeiro: Directoria do Patrimônio Histórico e Artístico Nacional, 1951), p. 27.

30. On the principal fraternities of Minas and their composition see Luiz Jardin, "A Pintura Decorativa em . . . Minas," *Revista do Sphan* 3: 67–71. This class distinction is linked with racial distinctions. The Franciscans did not accept men married to mulatto women; the Carmelites did.

31. Aires da Mato Machado Filho, *Arraial do Tijuco, Cidade de Diamantina* (Rio de Janeiro: Imprensa Nacional, 1944), pp. 51, 162ff. Originally the Creoles and mulattoes joined the black Brotherhood of the Rosary, but in 1771 they left it on the grounds that it was a Negro fraternity. They succeeded in obtaining a chapel of their own in a "white" church, but this arrangement apparently did not work. They felt slighted there and later applied for reinstatement in the black Brotherhood of the Rosary. This was refused "because there would be constant discord between blacks and Creoles." In addition to this schizogenic trend we should note that some fraternities tried to include all colored males, without regard for the lightness or darkness of their skin, and to create a race consciousness as opposed to differentiation by "nation." The mulatto Brotherhood of Mercy in Minas, for example, admitted "everybody, even captive blacks and natives of the Guinea coast" (ibid., p. 162). On analogous phenomena in the northeast see Gilberto Freyre, *The Mansions and the Shanties*, trans. Harriet de Onís (New York: A. Knopf, 1968), pp. 252–53.

32. Auguste de Saint-Hilaire, *Voyage dans le District des Diamants et sur le Littoral du Brésil* (Paris, 1833), 1: 48.

33. Daniel P. Kidder and James C. Fletcher, *Brazil and the Brazilians* (Philadelphia: Childs & Peterson, 1857), p. 152.

34. Sylvio Romero, *Contos Populares do Brasil* (Lisbon: Nova Livraria Internacional, 1833), p. 295.

35. Affonso de E. Taunay, *Na Bahia Colonial, 1610–1774* (Rio de Janeiro, 1925), chap. 2 (Padre Correal).

36. Fernando Mendes de Almeida, "O Folclore nas Ordenações do Reino," *RAM de SP* 56 (1939): 75.

37. Ibid.

38. Koster, *Travels*, 2: 240.

39. *Archives of the State of São Paulo*, bk. 90 on the Brotherhood of the Rosary of Meias Arino (1861).

40. Alcibiades Delamare, *Vila Rica* (Rio de Janeiro: Livraria Clássica Brasileira, 1955), p. 71.

41. Nuto Sant'Anna, "O Templo dos Homens Pretos," *Estado de S. Paulo*, 1940.

42. Silva Campos, *Processões*, p. 168.

43. Laytano, *Festa*, pp. 39–51.

44. Auguste de Saint-Hilaire, *Segunda Viagem do Rio de Janeiro a Minas Gerais e a São Paulo*, trans. Affonso de E. Taunay (São Paulo: Cia. Editora Nacional, 1932), p. 186. Cf. Gobineau: "On Maundy Thursday . . . the churches were filled to overflowing. One white or half-white to every twenty mulattoes or Negroes" (G. Raeders, *Gobineau au Brésil*, p. 38).

45. Nuto Sant'Anna, "Serpe et Pelle," *Estado de S. Paulo*, November 17, 1940.

46. Auguste de Saint-Hilaire, *Voyage dans les Provinces de Rio de Janeiro et de Minas Geraes* (Paris: Grimbert & Dorez, 1830), 1: 347–48.

47. Auguste Saint-Hilaire, *Voyage aux Sources du Rio São Francisco et dans la Province de Goyaz* (Paris: A. Bertrand, 1847–1848), 1: 100.

48. Simão Ferreira Machado, "Triunfo Eucaristico, Exemplar da Cristandade Lusitania em Publica Exaltação da Fé no Solene Transladação do Divinissimo Sacramento dal Greja de N.S. do Rosário para um Novo Templo da Senhora de Pilar em Vila Rica, côrte de Capitania das Minas, aos 24 de Maio de 1733, Lisboa 1734" (entirely retranscribed by Gastão Penalva in *O Aleijadinho de Vila Rica* (Rio de Janeiro: Renascença Editora, 1933), pp. 126–51.

49. Mello Moraes Filho, *Festas*, pp. 229–36; Silva Campos (*Processões*) give the traditional order of the great old processions in Bahia.

50. Freyre, *Sobrados e Mucambos* (São Paulo: Cia. Editora Nacional, 1936), pp. 250–51; Graham, *Journal*, p. 127; Tollenare, *Notas Dominicais*, p. 51.

51. Affonso de E. Taunay, "Na Bahia Colonial," *RIHGB*, tit. 90, vol. 144, p. 484.

52. Kidder and Fletcher, *Brazil*, pp. 170–74.

53. Thomas Ewbank, *Life in Brazil; or a Journal of a Visit to the Land of the Cocoa and the Palms* (New York: Harper Bros., 1856), pp. 182–83. [Ewbank does not mention a decline in the prestige of urban religion but states that the blacks were so enthusiastic in their devotions that these street shrines became "a municipal nuisance" and were therefore removed.] The mendiant orders, however, fell into disrepute because "it is impossible for a Negro to look up to a white who humiliates himself to obtain alms" (Denis, *Brésil*, p. 257).

54. Tollenare, *Notas Dominicais*, p. 110.

55. Leite, *História da Companhia de Jesus*, 2: 359; Freyre, *Masters and Slaves*, p. 262.

56. Silvo Campos, *Processões*, pp. 168, 243, 206.

57. Leite, *História da Companhia de Jesus*, p. 358.

58. Guilherme Pereira do Melo, *A Música no Brasil desde os Tempos Coloniaes até o Primeiro Decenio de Republica* (Bahia: Typ. de S. Joaquim, 1908), p. 49.

59. Frederico J. de Sant'Anna Nery, *Folklore Brésilien* (Paris: Perrin, Cie., 1889), p. 48; Pereira do Melo, *A Música no Brasil*, p. 49.

60. On the relationship of white Brazilians to the saints see Freyre, *Masters and Slaves*, pp. 254–59, 334, 434–35.

61. Pereira da Costa, "Rei do Congo," *Journal do Brasil*, April 21, 1901.

62. For instance, the embassy, one of the fundamental parts of the *congada*. Cf. Kaspar van Baerle [Barleus], *O Domínio Holandês* (São Paulo: Difusão Nacional do Livro, 19–), p. 272.

63. Cascudo, *Dicionário do Folclore Brasileiro*, pp. 191–94.

64. Dante de Laytano, *As Congadas do Município de Osório* (Pôrto Alegre: Associação Rio Grandense de Música, 1945), pp. 41, 55, 65; João Dornas Filho, "A Influencia Social do Negro," *RAM de SP* 51 (1938): 95–134.

65. Cascudo, *Dicionário do Folclore Brasileiro*, p. 402, and Folclore Nacional (Centre de Pesquisas Folclóricas, 1946), p 4.

66. Mello Moraes Filho, *Festas*, pp. 343–49.

67. Debret, *Viagem Pitoresca e Histórica ao Brasil*, trans. Sergio Milliet (São Paulo: Livraria Martins, 1940), 2: 225.

68. Koster, *Travels*, 2: 25–28; J. E. Pohl, *Reise im Innern von Bresilien*, 1: 157 and 2: 81–86; Adhemar Vidal, "Congos," *Revista do Brasil* (February 1939): 53–62; etc.

69. Mario de Andrade, "Os Congos," *Lanterna Verde* 2 (1935): 36–53.

70. Luis da Câmara Cascudo, "Festas de Negros," *A Republica* (Natal), February 20, 1942.

71. J. B. von Spix and C. F. P. von Martius, *Travels in Brazil in the Years 1817–1820* (London: Longman, Hurst, Rees, Orme, Brown & Green, 1824).

72. Koster, *Travels*, 2: 25–28.

73. Cascudo, *Dicionário*, pp. 191–94, 243, 611, 623.

74. This description of the *congada* is based on the two oldest versions available, that of Mello Moraes Filho (*Festas*, pp. 159–64) which dates back to about 1850, and that of Luiz Edmundo da Costa (in Gilberto Freyre et al., *Novos Estudos Afro-Brasileiros* [Rio de Janeiro: Biblioteca de Divulgação Científica, IX, Civilização Brasileira, 1937], pp. 227–30), dating from 1811. I have interposed the embassy of Queen Ginga because of its essentially archaic character (Mario de Andrade, "Os Congos," pp. 36–53). I have also referred to Gustavo Barroso, *A Som da Viola* (Rio de Janeiro: Leite Ribeiro, 1921), pp. 213–55, since the crustacean dance is certainly a very ancient survival, possibly totemic in character.

75. Mario de Andrade, "Os Congos," pp. 50–53.

76. Arthur Ramos, *O Folclore Negro do Brasil* (Rio de Janeiro: Civilização Brasileira, 1935), p. 60.

77. R. A. Dias do Carvalho, *Etnografia e História Tradicional dos Povos de Lunda* (Lisbon, 1890), cited by Mario de Andrade in "Os Congos."

78. Mello Moraes Filho, *Festas*, p. 127.

79. Texts cited by F. Mendes de Almeida in "O Folclore nas Ordenações do Reino," *RAM de SP* 56 (1939): 64–69.

80. Le Gentil de la Barbinais, *Nouveau Voyage autour du Monde* (Amsterdam: P. Mortier, 1728), cited by Freyre in *Masters and Slaves*, p. 256, and paraphrased by Taunay in *Na Bahia Colonial*, chap. 7.

81. Debret, *Viagem*, p. 225.

82. Mathison, *Narrative*, pp. 157–59.

83. Arthur Ramos, *O Negro Brasileiro* (Rio de Janeiro: Civilização Brasileira, 1934,) pp. 106–7, 110.

Chapter 6

1. A. d'Assier, *Le Brésil Contemporain* (Paris, 1867), pp. 77–79.

2. Henry Koster, *Travels in Brazil*, 2d ed. (London: Longman, Hurst, Rees, Orme & Brown, 1817), 2: 239–40. Cf. L. F. de Tollenare, *Notas Dominicais Tomadas durante uma Viagem em Portugal e no Brasil em 1816, 1817 e 1818* (Salvador: Livraria Progresso Editor, 1956), p. 140.

3. Serafim Leite, *História da Companhia de Jesus no Brasil* (Lisbon: Livraria Portugalia, 1938–1950), pp. 353–54 (on catechization in the Angola language in Bahia) and p. 357 (on catechization in monasteries).

4. Nina Rodrigues, *O Animismo Fetichista dos Negros Bahianos* (Rio de Janeiro: Civilização Brasileira, 1935), p. 199.

5. Cited by Manoel R. Querino in *Costumes Africanos no Brasil* (Rio de Janeiro: Civilização Brasileira, 1938), p. 35.

6. Charles Ribeyrolles, *Brasil Pitoresco: História-Descrições-Viagens-Colonização-Instituições* (São Paulo: Livraria Martins, 1941), pp. 43–45.

7. L. Couty, *L'Esclavage au Brésil* (Paris: Librairie de Guillaumin, 1881), p. 76.

8. Thomas Lindley, *Narrative of a Voyage to Brazil* (London: J. Johnson, 1805).

9. Affonso de E. Taunay, *Santa Catarina nos Anos Primevos* (São Paulo: Typ. "Diario Oficial," 1931).

10. Koster *Travels* 1: 133. João Pandiá Calogeras (*Formação Histórica do Brasil* [São Paulo: Cia. Editora Nacional, 1972], p. 78 [*A History of Brazil*, trans. and ed. Percy Alvin Martin (Chapel Hill: Univ. of North Carolina Press, 1939)]) also mentions the difficulty of christianizing the rural African masses owing to the vast distances. See also J. Abreu Filho, "A Influencia Negra," *Problemas* 1, no. 5 (1938): 32–33; Leite, *História da Companhia de Jesus no Brasil*, 2: 355; Charles Blachford Mansfield, *Paraguay, Brazil, and the Plate* (orig. pub. 1856; New York: AMS Press, 1971), p. 93; Johann Moritz Rugendas, *Viagem Pitoresca Através do Brasil*, trans. Sergio Milliet (orig. pub. in German in the nineteenth century; Rio de Janeiro: A Casa do Livro, 1972), pp. 43, 46; Jean Baptiste Debret, *Viagem Pitoresca e Histórica ao Brasil*, trans. Sergio Milliet (orig. pub. 1834–1839; São Paulo: Livraria Martins, 1940), 2: 100; Daniel P. Kidder, *Sketches of Residence and Travels in Brazil* (London: Wiley & Putnam, 1845); Louis and Elizabeth Agassiz, *Viagem ao Brasil*, p. 85 [*A Journey in Brazil* (Boston: Ticknor & Fields, 1868]; Johann Jakob von Tschudi, *Reisen durch Südamerika* (Leipzig: F. A. Brockhaus, 1866–1869), 3: 134.

11. Tollenare, *Notas Dominicais*, p. 79n.

12. Agostinho M. Perdigão Malheiro (*A Escravidão Africano no Brasil* [São Paulo: Editôra Obelisco, 1964], vol. 2, chap. 3) notes that while religious education was possible in the country, it was nonexistent in the city.

13. Auguste de Saint-Hilaire, *Voyage dans les Provinces de Rio de Janeiro et de Minas Geraes* (Paris: Grimbert & Dorez, 1830), chap. 8, and *Voyage aux Sources du Rio São Francisco et dans la Province de Goyaz* (Paris: A. Bertrand, 1847–1848), p. 338 and chap. 16. Cf. Diogo de Vasconcellos, *História Antiga das Minas Gerais* (Rio de Janeiro: Imprensa Nacional, 1948), p. 300, on the clergy in Minas (reform was attempted, however, under D. Pedro de Almeida), and Andrew Grant, *History of Brazil* (London: H. Colburn, 1809).

14. Luiz dos Santos Vilhena, *Recopilação de Noticias Soteropolitanis e Brasilicas Contidas em XX Cartas* (Bahia: Imprensa Oficial do Estado, 1921), p. 137.

15. L. Vianna Filho, *O Negro na Bahia* (Rio de Janeiro: J. Olympio, 1946), p. 108.

16. Cited by M. Bandeira in "De Vila Rica de Albuquerque a Ouro Preto," in the special issue of *O Jornal* commemorating the centenary of Ouro Preto.

17. Daniel P. Kidder and James C. Fletcher, *Brazil and the Brazilians* (Philadelphia: Childs & Petersen, 1857), p. 136. Cf. *RIHGB* 90 (1921): 513 and Gilbert F. Mathison, *Narrative of a Visit to Brazil, Chile, Peru, and the Sandwich Islands* (London: C. Knight, 1825), p. 157.

18. As was the case with Nuno Marques Pereira, for example, cited by Luis de Câmara Cascudo in *Meleagro* (Rio de Janeiro: AGIR, 1951), p. 180.

19. L. Vianna Filho, *O Negro na Bahia*, p. 107. When a *mocambo* of runaway Negroes was destroyed in 1637, it was immediately reported that the "governor" (i.e. the military commander) and the "bishop" (i.e. the high priest) had been taken prisoner.

20. Ildefonso Pereda Valdes, *El Negro Rioplatensa y Otros Ensayos* (Montevideo: C. García & Cia., 1937), p. 107; M. J. Herskovits, *Life in a Haitian Valley* (New York: A. Knopf, 1938), chap. 10; Martha Warren Beckwith, *Black Roadways: A Study of Jamaican Folk Life* (Chapel Hill: Univ. of North Carolina Press, 1929), chaps. 6 and 7; etc.

21. M. J. Herskovits, *The Myth of the Negro Past* (New York: Harper Bros., 1941), chap. 6.

22. Card from the king to the governor of Pernambuco dated March 17, 1693, cited

by Jayme de Altavilla in *O Quilombo dos Palmares* (São Paulo: Cia. Melhoramentos de São Paulo [Weiszflog Irmãos], 1931), p. 110.
23. José Lins de Rego, *Banguê* (Rio de Janeiro: J. Olympio, 1934), p. 258.
24. Luis de Câmara Cascudo, *Vaqueiros e Contadores: Folclore Poético do Sertão de Pernambuco, Paraíba, Rio Grande do Norte e Ceara* (Pôrto Alegre: Livraria do Globo, 1939), p. 113.
25. Gilberto Freyre et al., *Novos Estudos Afro-Brasileiros* (Rio de Janeiro: Biblioteca de Divulgação Científica, IX, Civilização Brasileira, 1937), p. 56.
26. Florestan Fernandes, "O Negro na Tradição Oral," *Estado de S. Paulo*, July 7, 1943.
27. Maria Graham recounts that some English gentlemen found a Negro woman dying by the side of the road. They asked their Portuguese companions to comfort her, but they replied: "Oh, 'tis only a black: let us ride on." (Maria [Dundas] Graham [Calcott], *Journal of a Voyage to Brazil and Residence There during Part of the Years 1821, 1822, 1823* (orig. pub. 1824; New York: Praeger, 1969), pp. 144–45.
28. D'Assier, *Brésil Contemporain*, p. 157.
29. L. Vianna Filho, *O Negro na Bahia*, p. 108.
30. Letter printed in 1639, cited by G. de Mello Neto in "A Situação de Negro sob o Dominio Holandes," in Freyre et al., *Novos Estudos*, p. 220.
31. Debret, *Viagem*, pp. 184–85.
32. Ibid., pp. 185–86.
33. Kidder, *Sketches*, p. 177.
34. A. J. de Mello Moraes Filho, *Festas e Tradições Populares do Brasil* (orig. pub. 1888; Rio de Janeiro: F. Briguiet, 1946), pp. 379–84.
35. Spencer Vampré, *Memorias para a História da Academia de São Paulo* (São Paulo: Saraiva & Cia., 1924), 1: 75. Cf. Lallemant, *Reise*, p. 36, for analogous customs in northern Brazil in the same period.
36. Rocha Pombo, *História do Brasil* (orig. pub. 1905; São Paulo: Edições Melhoramentos, 1964), 2: 543.
37. José de Alcantara Machado, *Vida e Morte do Bandeirante* (São Paulo: Livraria Martins Editora, 1953), p. 97.
38. Gregorio de Mattos Guerra, *Obras de Gregorio de Mattos, 4, Satirica* (Rio de Janeiro: Oficina Industrial Gráfica, 1930), 1: 345.
39. Gilberto Freyre, *The Masters and the Slaves*, trans. Samuel Putnam (New York: A. Knopf, 1966), pp. 335–36.
40. On magic as a weapon against the white man see Antonil, *Cultura*, pp. 95–96. On magic used to help slaves see Koster, *Travels*, 2: 94–95.
41. Xavier da Veiga, *Efemerides Mineiras*, p. 511.
42. *O Guaripocaba* (Campinas, São Paulo), December 12, 1886.
43. L. Edmundo da Costa, *O Rio de Janeiro no Tempo dos Vice-Reis (1763–1808)* (Rio de Janeiro: Imprensa Nacional, 1932), p. 472.
44. Robert Walsh, *Notices of Brazil in 1828 and 1829* (Boston: Richardson, Lord & Holbrook, 1831).
45. Saint-Hilaire, *Voyage dans les Provinces de Rio et Minas*, p. 305.
46. A. de Carvalho, "A Magia Sexual no Brasil," *RIAHG* 21: 406.
47. Alvarès do Amaral, *Resumo Chronológico*, p. 277. I speak of probable Bantu influence because in Cuba, where African religious survivals are closer (than anywhere else in America) to those found in Brazil, magic using bones, especially skulls, stolen from graveyards is still practiced by the Congo. See Lydia Cabrera, *El Monte, Igbo Finda, Ewe Orisha, Vititinfinda* (Havana: Ediciones, 1954), p. 147.
48. The custom of sending the hat still survives. One of my Brazilian students encountered it in the state of São Paulo in 1938.
49. Tollenare, *Notas Dominicais*, pp. 107–8.
50. Saint-Hilaire, *Voyage aux Sources du Rio São Francisco*, p. 98.
51. Ibid., p. 152.
52. Koster, *Travels*, 1: 253.
53. D'Assier, *Brésil Contemporain*, pp. 45 and 285.
54. M. J. and F. S. Herskovits, *Rebel Destiny* (New York: McGraw-Hill, 1934), p. 72.

436 NOTES TO CHAPTER 6

55. *Codex Felepino* (Rio de Janeiro, 1870), cited by F. Mendes de Almeida in "O Folclore nas Ordenações do Reino," *RAM de SP* 56 (1939): 85.
56. Charles Expilly refers to this elusive book in *Mulheres e Costumes do Brasil*, trans. Gustão Penalva (São Paulo: Cia. Editora Nacional, 1935). The snake cult does exist among the Bantu. See Richard E. Dennett, *At the Back of the Black Man's Mind: Notes on the Kingly Office in West Africa* (New York: Macmillan Co., 1906), p. 140. On the snake cult in Africa in general see W. D. Hambly, "The Serpent in African Belief and Custom," *American Anthropologist* 31, no. 4 (1929): 655–66.
57. Alfredo de Carvalho, "O Zoobiblion de Zacharias Wagner," *RIAHGP* 11: 181–95.
58. René Ribeiro, *Cultos Afro-Brasileiros de Recife: Um Estudo de Adjustamento Social* (Recife: Boletim do Instituto Joaquim Nabuco de Pesquisa Social, 1952), p. 27. Even before this, G. de Mello Neto had made a similar observation in "A Situaçao," in Freyre et al., *Novos Estudos*, p. 221.
59. Gregorio de Mattos, *Satirica*, pp. 186–88.
60. Arthur Ramos, *O Negro Brasileiro* (Rio de Janeiro: Civilização Brasileira, 1934), p. 113.
61. A. J. de Mello Moraes Filho, "O Condomblé," in *Cantos de Equador* (Rio de Janeiro: Typ. de G. Leuzinger and Filhos, 1881).
62. Almeida, "O Folclore," pp. 85–86.
63. Informação do Conde de Pavoide a Martinho de Mello e Castro," from a manuscript in the Coleção Pereira da Costa of the state library, Pernambuco, cited by Freyre in *Mansions and Shanties*, pp. 264–65 (where the Count's name is given as Pevolide), and by Ribeiro, *Cultos*, pp. 27–28.
64. On the question of the legitimacy of the African religions see Diario de Bittencourt, "A Liberdade Religiosa no Brasil: A Macumba e o Batuque em Face da Lei," in *O Negro no Brasil* (n.d.), pp. 173–86.
65. Almeida, "O Folclore," pp. 85–86.
66. See also *O Guaripocaba*, December 12, 1886.
67. Querino, *Costumes Africanos*, p. 45.
68. Historians like Mello Moraes Filho and Pereira da Costa and contemporary newspapers report many such cases.
69. Cited by Luis da Câmara Cascudo, *Dicionário do Folclore Brasileiro* (Rio de Janeiro: Ministerio de Educação e Culturo, Instituto Nacional do Livro, 1954), p. 147.
70. Maria Graham [Calcott], *Voyage*, pp. 198–99.
71. Braz do Amaral's contrary opinion notwithstanding (*Os Grandes Mercados de Escravos Africanos* [Rio de Janeiro: Livraria J. Leite, 19–], p. 478).
72. Gastão Penalva, *O Aleijadinho de Vila Rica* (Rio de Janeiro: Renascença Editora, 1933), p. 373.
73. Kidder and Fletcher, *Brazil*, pp. 136–37.
74. Koster, *Travels*, 1: 352.
75. Tollenare, *Notas Dominicais*, p. 234.
76. Proteaux, "Premiers Essais de Théâtre chez les Indigènes de la Haute-Côte-d'Ivoire," *Bulletin du Comité d'Études Historiques de l'A.O.F.* 2 (1929): 448–75.
77. Ruy Coelho, "As Festas dos Caribes Negros," *Anhembi* 25 (1952): 54–72.
78. Nina Rodrigues, *Os Africanos no Brasil* (São Paulo: Cia. Editora Nacional, 1932), pp. 262–69; Arthur Ramos. *O Folclore Negro no Brasil* (Rio de Janeiro: Civilização Brasileira, 1935), pp. 80–85.
79. On the *bumba-meu-boi* see Cascudo's survey article in his *Dicionário*, pp. 124–27. A. Ramos has investigated (perhaps in a somewhat exaggerated way) the African sources of this ballet-drama (*O Folclore Negro*, pp. 103–28).
80. Leonardo Motta, *Cantadores (Poesia e Linguagem do Sertão Ceaŕense)* (Rio de Janeiro: Castilho, 1921), pp. 90ff.
81. *Estudos Afro-Brasileiros* (Rio de Janeiro, 1935).
82. F. J. de Sant'Anna Nery, *Folklore Brésilien* (Paris: Perin, Cie., 1889), p. 40.
83. Saint-Hilaire, *Voyage aux Sources du Rio São Francisco*, 2: 59.
84. Freyre gives an example in *The Mansions and the Shanties* (New York: A. Knopf, 1968), p. 324.
85. Fernando Ortiz, [title not given], p. 34.

Chapter 7

1. João de Rio, *As Religôes no Rio* (Rio de Janeiro: Editora Nova Aguilar, 1976), p. 16; Arthur Ramos, *O Negro Brasileiro* (Rio de Janeiro: Civilização Brasileira, 1934), pp. 90–92.

2. Arthur Ramos, *As Culturas Negras* (Rio de Janeiro, 19–), p. 349.

3. Nina Rodrigues was the first to connect the words *malê* and *malenké* (*O Animismo Fetichista dos Negros Bahianos* [Rio de Janeiro: Civilização Brasileira, 1935], p. 30). He discusses this etymology again in *Os Africanos no Brasil* (São Paulo: Cia. Editora Nacional, 1932), pp. 109–12. Arthur Ramos follows his lead in *O Negro Brasileiro*, pp. 77–79, and *Culturas Negras*, pp. 333–35. In the latter context Ramos notes that the root *malê* means "hippopotamus," indicating that the name designated a primitively totemic people (Louis Tauxier, *La Religion Bambara* [Paris: Librarie Orientaliste Paul Guenther, 1927], p. xviii). Étienne Brasil states that the word *malê* means "pedagogue" ("La Secte Musulmane de Malês du Brésil," *Anthropos* 4 [1909]: 95). This is probably a derivative meaning, since the Mussulmans in Brazil had schools and an erudite culture. The Soilma Negroes told Nina Rodrigues that the word *malê* meant "learned nation" or "people who go to school" (*Os Africanos*, p. 112). Jacques Raimundo derives it from the Yoruba word *imalé*, meaning "renegade, one who has embraced Islam" (*O Negro no Brasil* [n.d.], p. 361). Braz do Amaral believes it to be a contraction of the Portuguese *mâ lei* ("the false law"), the Malê being those who do not follow the true law of God. Both of these etymologies, which are based on the derivative meaning that the word *malê* acquired in Brasil, are false. Because of the Mussulman-fetishist syncretism of the Malinke and their pagan origin, the Hausa used the word *malê* as a term of contempt. The French traveler Francis de Castenlau wrote in 1851: "The name *Malais* is used for all infidels, that is, for all those who are not Mohammedans" (*Renseignements sur L'Afrique Centrale* [Paris: Bertrand, 1851], p. 12).

4. Nina Rodrigues, *Os Africanos*, pp. 167–75; Romos, *Culturas Negras*, pp. 335–41.

5. Joseph de Crozals, *Les Peuhls: Étude d'Ethnologie Africaine* (Paris: Maisonneuve, 1883); P. Henry, *Les Bambara* (Münster, 1910); H. Labouret, *Les Tribus du Rameau Lobi* (Paris: Institut d'Ethnographie, 1931), 2: 510; E. F. Gautier, *L'Afrique Noire Occidentale* (Paris: Librairie Larose, 1935); G. Cheron, "La Circoncision et l'Excision chez les Malenke," *Journal de la Société des Africanistes* 3, no. 2 (1933): 297–303; etc.

6. Raeders, *Le Comte de Gobineau au Brésil*, pp. 75–76.

7. Sud Menucci, *O Precursor de Abolicionismo no Brasil, Luis Gama*, p. 117n. My own research, as was the case in Rio, shows that no real mosque existed in São Paulo and that the black Mussulmans celebrated their cult in a private house. As Richard rightly says, with reference to Brazilian texts, "the word *machachali* denotes simply chapels," not mosques ("L'Islam Noir au Brésil," *Hesperis*, 1948, nos. 1 and 2, p. 3).

8. Alex J. de Mello Moraes Filho, *Festas e Tradições Populares do Brazil* (orig. pub. 1888; Rio de Janeiro: F. Briguiet, 1946), p. 333; Ramos, *O Negro Brasileiro*, pp. 90–91; F. Mendes de Almeida, "O Folclore nas Ordenações do Reino," *RAM de SP* 56 (1939): 53.

9. The writer mentions seven marabouts in Bahia, five of whom were Hausa, two Nagô.

10. Nina Rodrigues, *Os Africanos*, pp. 99–101. To this information may be added Querino's mention of the existence in Bahia of a shereef or kind of prophet (usually an old man), a *lemano* or bishop, a *ladano*, his secretary, and an *alufa* or regular priest (*Costumes Africanos no Brasil* [Rio de Janeiro: Civilização Brasileira, 1938], p. 113). Étienne Brasil also mentions the *iman* (known as the *sogabamu* when he was celebrating the cult), the *ladano*, who served as secretary, muezzin, and deacon, the *achuaju* or master of ceremonies, and the *alikalya* or judge. Brasil, however, seems to exaggerate the unity and systematization of this Mussulman church when he states that there was a supreme *iman* in Bahia (called, after his death, the "universal *iman*") who was in charge of the faithful in Bahia, Rio, Ceara, and Pernambuco and who set the date of feasts ("La Secte Musulmane," p. 103).

11. João de Rio, *As Religôes no Rio*, p. 16.
12. João de Rio, "O Natal dos Africanos," *Kosmos*, December 1904. For the opposite view see Nina Rodrigues, *Os Africanos*, p. 108: "The *iman* tells me . . . that in Rio too there is a regularly organizedMussulman church which, unlike the one in Bahia, is not subject to the ban on high church holidays and which celebrates them with great pomp. But so far as I can make out this is actually a church of Arab Mussulmans that admits Malê Negroes."
13. Almeida, "O Folclore," p. 53. See also the anonymous article "Reminiscencias dos Cultos Africanos" in *RIAHGP* 30 (1930): 49–50.
14. Ramos, *O Negro Brasileiro*, pp. 90–92.
15. Ramos, *Culturas Negras*, p. 337.
16. Ibid., p. 345.
17. Querino, *Costumes*, pp. 111–12.
18. Nina Rodrigues, *Os Africanos*, p. 101; cf. *L'Animisme Fétichiste*, pp. 28–29 [*Animismo Fetichista*].
19. Querino, *Costumes*, p. 110. Étienne Brasil, however, says that the Mussulmans had plenty of faults. Since this is a Catholic priest speaking, he was probably thinking chiefly of polygamy.
20. This, of course, refers to free Negroes; slavery precluded the observation of these sacred times. The slave's inability to make the rhythm of his day conform to the rules of his faith must be regarded as one of the reasons for revolts against the slave regime. This confirms our already stated thesis that the black Mussulman revolts were religious in nature.
21. Ademar Vidal, "Costumes e Praticas do Negro," in *O Negro no Brasil* (n.d.), p. 49.
22. Querino, *Costumes*, p. 111.
23. Ibid.
24. Nina Rodrigues, *Os Africanos*, pp. 89, 93, 98.
25. Raeders, *Comte de Gobineau*, p. 76.
26. Querino, *Costumes*, pp. 117–18.
27. Ibid., p. 111.
28. Ibid., p. 118. An article by Mariza Lira in *IBECC*, June 18, 19[?]8, states that according to legend the costume of the women of Bahia originated in a punishment. A *limano* had a very pretty but flighty daughter who became pregnant. To punish her, he turned her out of the house to sell pastries in the streets, "dressed in a humiliating costume—the one which was later introduced into Brazil" under the name *vestimenta bahiana*.
29. Querino, *Costumes*, p. 111.
30. Brasil, "La Secte Musulmane," p. 104 (on Malê costumes).
31. Querino, *Costumes*, pp. 111–12.
32. Ramos, *O Negro Brasileiro*, p. 92. Brasil says that the dead body was dressed in five garments if it was a man, seven in the case of a woman ("La Secte Musulmane," p. 105).
33. Querino, *Costumes*, p. 120.
34. Mello Moraes Filho, *Festas*, pp. 335–42.
35. R. Ricard, "L'Islam Noir," p. 12, n. 2. In Africa the *egun* cult (the cult of the dead) is practiced chiefly by Yoruba.
36. Brasil, "Le Secte Musulmane," p. 103.
37. Querino, *Costumes*, p. 113; Brasil, "Le Secte Musulmane," pp. 103–5.
38. Nina Rodrigues, *Os Africanos*, p. 102.
39. Querino, *Costumes*, pp. 115–16.
40. Nonetheless Nina Rodrigues saw a map of Mecca hanging on the wall in the house of the *limano* Luis (*Os Africanos*, p. 102). Did the priest perhaps accomplish his pilgrimage in the fond hopes of his imagination?
41. Querino, *Costumes*, pp. 120–21.
42. Ibid., p. 119.
43. Ibid.
44. Nina Rodrigues lists some of these talismans. One, for instance, is inscribed with sura 106 of the Koran and with verses 129 and 130 of the second sura. Each

verse is repeated several times—in one case 36 times—since reiteration of the text enhanced its magic power (*Os Africanos*, pp. 102–7).

45. Ibid., p. 107.
46. Querino, *Costumes*, p. 118.
47. Ibid., p. 110.
48. Ibid., p. 115.
49. João de Rio, *As Religôes*, pp. 16–18.
50. Arthur Ramos, *Introdução a Antropologia Brasileira* (Rio de Janeiro, 1951), 1: 248.
51. João de Rio, pp. 53–60.
52. Ramos, *O Negro Brasileiro*, p. 82, n. 96. Aydano de Couto-Ferraz also mentions a "Mussurumin" sect at no 26, rue Orientale du Japon ("As Culturas Negras no Novo Mundo," *Boletim d'Ariel*, no. 8 [1938], p. 340).
53. Edison Carneiro, *Negros Bantus*, p. 37.
54. Ramos, *O Negro Brasileiro*, pp. 88–89.
55. Ibid., p. 90.
56. Ibid., p. 83.
57. Roger Bastide, *Imagens do Nordeste Místico em Branco e Preto* (Rio de Janeiro: O Cruzeiro, 1945), p. 57, and "Le Batuque de Porto Alegre," in *Acculturation in the Americas: Proceedings and Selected Papers of the Twenty-ninth International Congress of Americanists*, ed. Sol Tax (New York: Cooper Square Publishers, 1967), p. 202; Oneyda Alvarenga, *Arquivo Folclórico da Discoteca Municipal II: Catálogo do Museu Folclórico* (São Paulo: Discoteca Pública Municipal, 1950), pp. 78–83.
58. Geoffrey Parrinder, *West African Religion* (London: Epworth Press, 1949).
59. On the Arabian origin of geomancy see Bernard Maupoil, *La Géomancie à l'Ancienne Côte des Esclaves* (Paris: Institut d'Ethnographie, 1943), pp. 35–43. See also R. F. A. Trautman, *La Divination à la Côte des Esclaves et à Madagascar* (Paris: Larose, 1940), pp. 36, 143.
60. Roger Bastide, "L'Islam Noir au Brésil," *Hesperis*, 1952, nos. 3 and 4, p. 7.
61. Protasius Frikel, "Die Seelenlehre der Gêge und Nago," *Santo Antonio*, 1940–1941, pp. 203–4.
62. Edison Carneiro, *Candomblés da Bahia* (Bahia: Secretaria de Educação e Saúde, 1948), p. 105, n. 4. Cf. P. A. Talbot, *Peoples of Southern Nigeria* (London: Oxford Univ. Press, 1928), 3: 477–760.
63. Letter from Pierre Verger dated October 21, 1955.
64. Conversation with Pierre Verger.
65. Fernando Ortiz, *Los Bailes y el Teatro de los Negros en el Folklore de Cuba* (Havana: Ministerio de Educación Dirección de Cultura, 1951), pp. 342ff.
66. A. Almeida, Jr., "Sobre o Aguardentismo Colonial," *RAM de SP* 72 (1940): 155–64. This Moslem puritanism in Brazil is to be contrasted with the tolerance extended to black customs in Africa. See Richard L. Thurnwald, *Black and White in East Africa: The Fabric of a New Civilization* (London: G. Routledge & Sons, 1935), chap. 5.

Chapter 8

1. Georges Balandier, *Sociologie Actuelle de l'Afrique Noire: Dynamique des Changements Sociaux en Afrique Centrale* (Paris: Presses Universitaires de France, 1955), p. 496 [*The Sociology of Black Africa: Social Dynamics in Central Africa*, trans. Douglas Garman (New York: Praeger, 1970)].
2. Maria Isaura P. de Queiroz, *La "Guerre Sainte" au Brésil* (São Paulo, 1957).
3. Luis da Câmara Cascudo, *Dicionário do Folclore Brasileiro* (Rio de Janeiro: Ministério de Educação e Culture. Instituto Nacional do Livro, 1954), pp. 49–52.
4. A. d'Assier, *Le Brésil Contemporain* (Paris, 1867), p. 202.
5. Gilberto Freyre, *The Mansions and the Shanties*, trans. Harriet de Onís (New York: Knopf, 1968), p. 315.
6. Gilberto Freyre, *The Masters and the Slaves*, trans. Samuel Putnam (New York: Knopf, 1966), p. 31.

440	NOTES TO CHAPTER 8

7. Louis Couty, *L'Esclavage au Brésil* (Paris: Librairie de Guillaumin Editeurs, 1881), p. 86. This was so notwithstanding the numerical size of the intermediate class, which greatly surpassed the other two classes in number. In the intermediate class between the 500,000 members of the aristocracy and the 1,500,000 slaves, some six million inhabitants were born, vegetated, and died without making any contribution to the country.

8. L. F. de Tollenare, *Notes Dominicales* (Paris: Presses Universitaires de France, 1971).

9. On social distance as a factor parallel to, but quite different from, geographical distance in the preservation of folklore see Sidney W. Mintz, "El Continuum Folk-Urbano y a Comunidad Rural Proletaria," *Ciencias Sociales* (Pan American Union, Washington, D.C.) 4, no. 23 (October 1953): 194–204 ["The Folk-Urban Continuum and the Rural Proletarian Community," *American Journal of Sociology* 59 (1953): 136–43].

10. Pierre Verger, "l'Influence du Brésil au Golfe du Bénin," in *Les Afro-Americains*, Mémoires de l'Institut Français d'Afrique Noire, no. 27 (Dakar, Senegal, 1953), pp. 11–101.

11. M. J. Herskovits, "Les Noirs du Nouveau Monde," *Journal de la Société des Africanistes* 8 (1938): 80.

12. This is, in part, the basis of the position taken by Gonçalves Fernandes (see note 13).

13. Gonçalves Fernandes, "O Sincretismo Gêge-Nago-Catolico como Expressão Dinamica dum Sentimento de Inferioridade," in *Les Afro-Américains*, pp. 125–26.

14. René Ribeiro's article in *RIH de Alagoas* 26: 14.

15. M. J. Herskovits, "Some Psychological Implications of Afro-American Studies," in *Acculturation in the Americas: Proceedings and Selected Papers of the Twenty-ninth International Congress of Americanists*, ed. Sol Tax (New York: Cooper Square Publishers, 1967), p. 158. On the persistence of African attitudes, not merely their organization, see the life story of a young black woman in Donald Pierson, *Negroes in Brazil* (Chicago: Univ. of Chicago Press, 1942), pp. 263–70. See also René Ribeiro, "Projective Mechanisms and the Structuralization of Perception in Afro-Brazilian Divination, *Revue Internationale d'Ethnopsychologie Normale et Pathologique* 1, no. 2 (1956).

16. E. Franklin Frazier, "The Negro Family in Bahia, Brazil," *American Sociological Review* 7, no. 4 (1942): 471, 478. I cannot accept this point of view without strong reservations. Although it is certainly the *candomblé* that Africanizes the black, the fact remains that his family provides the spiritual climate in which this action by the religious sect can occur.

17. The doctrine of the church with regard to *candomblés* and an anlysis of the pastorals in question can be found in *X*. [sic] *Candomblé (Santo Antonio* 15, no. 1 [April 1937]: 15–29).

18. Alfredo Brandão, "O Negro na História de Alagôas," in *Estudos Afro-Brasileiros*, (Rio de Janeiro, 1935), p. 60.

19. Or else to camouflage themselves as spiritist sects (which were tolerated by the police) or carnival societies. Reporting a police visit to the spiritist center known as Charity and the Love of Jesus Christ, the Recife *Diario da Tarde* of April 12, 1934, said: "The spiritist centers operate freely once they obtain police authorization. Taking advantage of this, the worshipers of Exú proceeded to declare themselves spiritists, with the result that what used to go on in deserted places or outlying districts now occurs in the very heart of the city." On this point see Albino Gonçalves Fernandes, *Xangôs do Nordeste* (Rio de Janeiro: Civilização Brasileira, 1934), pp. 7–17.

20. Gonçalves Fernandes, *O Sincretismo Religioso no Brazil* (Curitiba: Editora Guaíra, 1941), pp. 29ff.

21. Edison Carneiro, *Candomblés de Bahia* (Bahia: Secretaria de Educação e Saúde, 1948), p. 31.

22. On this trade see Pierson, *Negroes in Brazil*, p. 239. Members of Pôrto Alegre *batuques* have told me that a similar trade existed between Africa and southern Brazil, but I have not been able to verify this from historical documents or newspaper files.

23. I am alluding to the introduction of the twelve ministers of Shangô. And I say

"thought he had seen" rather than "had seen" because, although some writers do state that there were twelve *Obas*, the names of these ministers include extremely heterogeneous titles (letter from Pierre Verger dated December 21, 1953).

24. Pierson, *Negroes in Brazil*, pp. 240–42.

25. Gilberto Freyre, *Sobrados e Mucambos* (São Paulo: Cia. Editôra Nacional, 1936), 1: lii.

26. Felte Bezerra, *Etnias Sergipanas* (Aracaju, 1954), p. 160.

27. Emilio Willems, "Mobilidade e Fluctuação das Profissôes no Brasil." Cf. Caio Prado, Jr., *História Econômica*, pp. 217–308, which contrasts modern Brazil with Brazil in the era of slavery.

28. On the Recife *mucambos* or *mocambos* see Josué de Castro, *Documentario de Nordeste* (Rio de Janeiro: J. Olympio, 1937), and Gilberto Freyre, *Mucambos do Nordeste* (Rio de Janeiro: Ministerio de Educação e Saúde, 1937).

29. On the Rio *favelas* see *Censo da Favelas* (Rio de Janeiro: Departamento de Geografia e Estatística, 1949) and Luiz Aguiar da Costa Pinto, *O Negro no Rio de Janeiro: Relações de Raças numa Sociedade em Mudança* (São Paulo: Cia. Editora Nacional, 1953), pp. 129–37.

30. On the São Paulo *cortiços* see Roger Bastide and Florestan Fernandes, *Relações Raciais entre Negros e Brancos em São Paulo: Ensaio Sociológico sôbre as Origens, as Manifestações e os Efeitos do Preconceito de Côr no Municipio de São Paulo* (São Paulo: Editôra Anhembi, 1955), p. 137.

31. Costa Pinto, *O Negro no Rio de Janeiro*, pp. 122ff.

32. Tullio Seppilli (*Il Sincretismo Religioso Afro-Cattólico*, p. 40) recognizes the blacks' difficulty in securing a place in the new production cycle of republican Brazil as an important factor in the survival of the African cults.

33. F. J. Oliveira Vianna, *Populações Meridionães no Brasil* (São Paulo: Cia. Editora Nacional, 1933), chap. 10. In 1882 there were 2,822, 583 persons with no regular occupation in Brazil—more than 50 percent of the free population.

34. Pierre Denis, *Le Brésil au XXᵉ Siecle* (Paris: A. Colin, 1909), chap. 12 (on Negro populations).

35. The best account of the life of the common people of northeastern Brazil is to be found in novels such as those of José Lins do Rego describing the Pernambuco region and the sugar cane cycle from *banguê* to refinery, and those of Jorge Amado dealing with the region of Bahia or Ilhéus. For the sociological aspects and studies of the cultural geography of this region see Gilberto Freyre's preface to Julio Bello, *Memórias de um Senhor de Engenho* (Rio de Janeiro: J. Olympio, 1938); Aurelio de Limeira et al., *Brejos e Carrascães do Nordeste: Documentario* (São Paulo: Edições Cultura Brasileira, 1937), pp. 35–79; Clovis Amorim, "O Moleque de Canavial," in *O Negro no Brasil* (n.d.), pp. 71–74; Jovino de Raiz, "O Trabalhador Negro no Tempo do Banguê Comparado com o Trabalhador Negro no Tempo das Uzinas de Açucar," in *Estudos Afro-Brasileiras* (Rio de Janeiro, 1935), pp. 191–94.

36. Costa Pinto, *O Negro no Rio de Janeiro*, p. 244.

37. To cite one example, at the time of writing, the *ialorixá* of Engenho Velho was the granddaughter of an Egba married to a Gêgê-Mahum. An Egba of the same sect was about to marry a Yoruba woman according to both the Catholic and the Moslem rites. (Frazier, "The Negro Family," pp. 473–75).

38. A. de Couto Ferraz, "As Culturas Negras no Novo Mundo," *Boletim d'Ariel*, no. 8 (1938), p. 340.

39. Herskovits justifiably deplores the lack of studies of recruitment in the present-day *candomblés*. See "The Social Organization of the *Candomblé*," in *Proceedings and Selected Papers of the Thirty-first International Congress of Americanists* (Nendeln, Lichtenstein: Kraus Reprints, 1976), p. 508.

40. Roger Bastide, "Le Principe de Coupure et le Comportement Brésilien," in *Thirty-first International Congress of Americanists*, pp. 497–98.

41. Everett V. Stonequist, *The Marginal Man* (orig. pub. 1937; New York: Russell & Russell, 1961).

42. P. Oschwald, "Defense de la Jeunesse Gabonaise," *Le Christianisme au XXᵉ Siècle*, January 20, 1949, p. 21.

43. A. de Couto Ferraz, "Volta a Africa," *RAM de SP* 54 (1939): 175–78.

44. The goal of this federation is "to maintain and orient the Afro-Brazilian religion within the ritual handed down by the ancestors . . . to discourage affiliated societies from directly participating, using objects associated with the Afro-Brazilian cult, in carnival celebrations. . . . The federation shall exercise authority over affiliated societies to prevent abuses in the cult as well as practices that diverge from the rite established by the ancestors." The federation threatens not only to expel offending groups but also "to terminate their right to practice the cult," but it is difficult to see how this sanction could be imposed.

45. H. W. Huchinson, "Race Relations in a Rural Community of the Bahian *Recôncavo,*" in *Race and Class in Rural Brazil,* ed. Charles Wagley (Paris: UNESCO, 1952), pp. 41–42.

46. Donald Pierson, "The Educational Process and the Brazilian Negro," *American Journal of Sociology* 48, no. 6 (1943): 692ff.

47. Pierson, *Negroes in Brazil,* pp. 314–17.

48. Carneiro, *Candomblés de Bahia,* pp. 79–81.

Chapter 9

1. *Primeira Visitação do Santo Oficio ás Partes do Brasil pelo Licenciado Heitor Furtado de Mendoça: Denunciações da Bahia, 1591–1593* (São Paulo: P. Prado, 1925), p. xviii. The phenomenon of *santidade* occurs all over Brazil as an effect of Jesuit evangelization and as a reaction against it. For São Paulo, for example, see José de Alcantara Machado, *Vida e Morte do Bandeirante* (São Paulo: Livraria Martins Editora, 1953), p. 212 (known here as Caramoinhaga).

2. Alcantara Machado, *Vida e Morte,* pp. 28–29, 64–65, 78–79, 104–9, 121–23, 167–73.

3. On the use of smoke for magical and religious purposes among the Indians see Hans Staden, *Duas Viagens e Captiveiro entre os Selvagens do Brasil* (edition commemorating the 4th centenary of São Paulo, 1900, vols. 8–35), p. 23 [*The Captivity of Hans Staden of Hesse, in A.D. 1547–1555, among the Wild Tribes of Eastern Brazil,* trans. A. Tootal (New York: B. Franklin, 1963)]; Francisco S. G. Schaden, "Erva Santa," *Estado de S. Paulo,* May 4, 1946; Thales de Azevedo, "O Vegetal como Alimento e Medicina do Indio," *RAM de SP* 76 (1941), p. 268; Charles Wagley, "Xamanismo Tapirapé," *Bol. Museu Nacional, N. Sie, Antropologia,* no. 3 (1943), pp. 17–18, 33.

4. Luis da Câmara Cascudo, *Meleagro: Depoimento e Pesquisa sôbre a Magia no Brasil* (Rio de Janeiro: AGIR, 1951), p. 20; Albino Gonçalves Fernandes, *O Folclore Mágico do Nordeste* (Rio de Janeiro: Civlzação Brasileira, 1938), p. 7.

5. C. Estevão de Oliveiro, "O Ossuário de Gruta do Padre," *RIAHGP* 38 (1943): 157–59.

6. Cited by Cascudo in "Notas sôbre o Catimbó," in Gilberto Freyre et al., *Novos Estudos Afro-Brasileiros* (Rio de Janeiro: Biblioteca de Divulgação Científica, IX, Civilização Brasileira, 1937), p. 87.

7. On *pagelança* (from *pagé,* the native Indian priest) se Cascudo, *Meleagro,* p. 77, and *Dicionário de Folclore Brasileiro* (Rio de Janeiro: Min. da Eduação e Culturo, Instituto Nacional do Livro, 1954), p. 466. On the *encantado* cult in Piaui see ibid., p. 245. On *catimbó* (from *cachimbo,* meaning "pipe," which plays an important role in the cult) see Cascudo's *Meleagro* in its entirety and "Notas sôbre o Catimbó," pp. 75–129. See also Fernandes, *O Folclore Mágico,* chaps. 1, 7, 10; Mario de Andrade, *Música de Feiticaria no Brasil;* Alfredo de Carvalho, "A Magia Sexual no Brasil," *RIAHGP* 21 (1914): 406–22; Roger Bastide, *Imagens do Nordeste Místico em Branco e Preto* (Rio de Janeiro, 1945), pp. 202–22. While I am indebted to these sources, the description that follows is based chiefly on my own research in Paraíba.

8. On the depth of these beliefs see Xavier de Oliveira, *Espiritismo e Loucura.*

9. A. Vidal, "Costumes e Praticas do Negro," in *O Negro no Brasil* (n.d.), pp. 51–53.

10. Letter to the author from Joaquim Alves dated March 12, 1945.

11. Fernandes, *O Folclore Mágico*, pp. 108–9.

12. Bastide, *Imagens*, pp. 206–7 and 221–22.

13. Cascudo, "Notas sôbre o Catimbó," p. 101, and *Meleagro*, p. 155.

14. Cascudo, "Notas sôbre o Catimbó," p. 102.

15. José Carvalho, *O Matuto Cearense e o Caboclo do Para* (Belem: Oficinas Gráficas do "Jornal de Belem," 1930), p. 34.

16. See, for example, Gustavo Barroso, *Através dos Folclores* (São Paulo: Cia. Melhoramentos de São Paulo [Weiszflog Irmãos], 1927), p. 108, and Leonardo Motta, *Sertão Alegre* (Belo Horizonte: Imprensa Oficial de Minas, 1928), pp. 218–21.

17. Aurelio de Limeira Tejo, *Brejos e Carrascais do Nordeste* (São Paulo: Edições Cultura Brasileira, 1937), pp. 151–56.

18. Cascudo, "Notas sôbre o Catimbó," p. 103.

19. Ibid., p. 106.

20. Gustavo Barroso, Câmara Cascudo, and Cariolano de Medeiros, however, report the existence of choreographic elements in certain *catimbós*. Some of these may be of African origin, like the ones reported by Medeiros in his preface to Edmundo Krug's "Curiosidades da Superstição Brasileira," *RIHG de SP* 35: 223–33, and by Cascudo in *Dicionário*, p. 245. Others are reminiscences of Indian dances (Gustavo Barroso, *Terra do Sol* [Rio de Janeiro: F. Alves, 1930], chap. 3).

21. On *maconha* and its introduction into the *catimbós* see C. Tschauer, *Avifauna e Flora nos Costumes: Superstições e Lendas Brasileiras e Americanas* (Pôrto Alegre, 1925), pp. 222–24.

22. Andrade, *Música*.

23. Bastide, *Imagens*, pp. 206, 209, 210, 220.

24. J. Froès Abreu, *Na Terra das Palmeiras*, p. 249.

25. Raymundo Lopes refers to this research in *O Terrão Maranhense* (Rio de Janeiro: Typ. do "Jornal do Commercio," 1916), p. 80.

26. Nina Rodrigues, *Os Africanos no Brasil* (São Paulo: Cia. Editora Nacional, 1932), pp. 344–47; Arthur Ramos, *Introdução a Antropologia Brasileira* (Rio de Janeiro, 1951), pp. 394–95; Edison Carneiro, *Candomblés da Bahia* (Bahia: Secretaria de Educação e Saúde, 1948), p. 51; Aydano de Couto Ferraz, "Vestigos de um Culto Daomeano no Brasil," *RAM de SP* 76 (1941): 271–74; Abelardo Duarte, "Sobrevivencias do Culto da Serpente (Dânh-gbi) na Alagoas," *RIH de Alagoas* 26 (1952): 66–67; Albino Gonçalves Fernandes, *Xangôs do Nordeste* (Rio de Janeiro: Civilização Brasileira, 1937), p. 75; Waldemar Valente, *Sincretismo Religioso Afro-Brasileiro* (São Paulo: Cia. Editora Nacional, 1955), pp. 77–78 and plate 39.

27. Bernard Maupoil, "Le Culte du Vodou," *Outre-Mer*, 1939, no. 3.

28. The snake is linked with Ogun (René Ribeiro, "Projective Mechanisms and the Structuralization of Perception in Afro-Brazilian Divination," *Revue Internationale d'Ethnopsychologie Normale et Pathologique* 1, no. 2 [1956] and it is perhaps more likely that the iron necklaces in the form of a snake found by Ramos and Duarte belong to Ogun than to a Dahoman deity. I have already mentioned (in connection with Expilly) the importance of the snake in the Bantu religion. On the connection between Ogun and the snake see P. A. Talbot, *The Peoples of Southern Nigeria* (London: Oxford Univ. Press, 1928), p. 88, and Oneyda Alvarenga, *Xangô*, p. 11.

29. Carneiro and Couto Ferraz find traces of the snake cult in the Bantu–*caboclo terreiro* of Joasinho da Gomea. Valente finds them in the *terreiro* of Apolinario, which, although nominally Yoruba, is, as Valente rightly points out, permeated with Bantu— and particularly Congo—traits.

30. Edmundo Correia Lopes, "O Kpoli da Mãe Andresa," *O Mundo Português* (Lisbon) 9, no. 99 (1942): 139–44; this article is to be used cautiously because it rests entirely on a confusion between Poli-Bogi, one of the names for the god of smallpox, with the Kpoli of the Fa or Ifá people. See also the same author's "A Proposito de 'A Casa das Minas,'" *Atlantico* (Libson), n.s., 5 (1947): 78–82, and "O Pessoal Gêge," *Revista do Brasil*, February 1940, pp. 44–47.

31. Oneyda Alvarenga, *Tambor de Mina e Tambor de Crioulo*. This book appeared before the works of Nunes Pereira and Octavio da Costa Eduardo. The interpretation of the documents of the folkloric expedition should be corrected as follows: The texts of *tambor de mina* songs belong to a degenerate "Nagô" sect, not to a Dahoman

one, although they do show Dahoman influences. The *tambor de crioulo* is a purely recreational society with no religious element whatever. It might be compared, *mutatis mutandis*, with the "samba schools" of Rio de Janeiro.

32. Nunes Pereira, *A Casa das Minas* (Rio de Janeiro: Publ. da Soc. Bras. de Antropologia e Ethnologia, no. 1, 1947); Octavio da Costa Eduardo, "Three-Way Religious Acculturation," in *Afro-America: Journal de l'Institut International des Études Afro-Américaines* (Mexico: Fondo de Cultura Economica, II, 1946), pp. 81–90; and esp. Octavio da Costa Eduardo's *The Negro in Northern Brazil* (Seattle: Univ. of Washington Press, 1948).

33. Pierre Verger, "Le Culte des Vodoun d'Abomey Aurait-Il Été Apporté à Saint-Louis de Maranhon par la Mère du Roi Ghézo?" in *Les Afro-Américains, Mémoires de l'Institut Français d'Afrique Noire*, no. 27 (Dakar, Senegal, 1952), pp. 157–60. See also Verger, "Influence du Brésil au Golfe du Benin," in *Les Afro-Américains*, pp. 11–101.

34. The folklore expedition obtained its information from 7 *filhos* and 10 *filhas* of the "Faith in God" sect. Seven of them were black, 10 mulatto, 6 illiterate; several did not known their fathers' names, indicating that they came from broken or matriarchal families. They included 3 cooks, 1 laborer, 1 seaman, 1 domestic servant, 1 ironer, 1 peddler, 1 watchman, 1 painter, 1 stevedore; four had no occupation.

35. Alvarenga, *Tambor de Mina*, p. 64.

36. Ibid., p. 28.

37. Ibid., p. 26.

38. Costa Eduardo, *The Negro in Northern Brazil*, p. 84.

39. Ibid., p. 98.

40. Ibid.

41. The rural sects know nothing about the "sacred stones," the receptables of divine power. In this respect the suburban cult centers present a transitional form. Instead of having a stone for each god, they have a single one, known as the "punishment stone," on which the tranced children of the gods place their hands to seek pardon when they have violated a taboo.

42. Nunes Pereira, *A Casa das Minas*, pp. 31–36; Costa Eduardo, *The Negro in Northern Brazil*, pp. 67–82. Cf. the Fon theology as outlined by M. J. Herskovits in *Dahomey: An Ancient West African Kingdom* (New York, J. J. Augustin, 1938), vol. 2. Nunes Pereira uses the spellings *tobossa*, *tôbôssi* and *tôbôci*. It will be noted that this list of gods does not include the Dahoman deity Legba, who nevertheless survives, as we have seen, in rural areas and who generally "opens the ways" and serves as an intermediary between man and the *voduns*. He is replaced by the *tokhueni*. But this does not mean that Legba is unknown here. Correia Lopes has noted a mention of him in a song, and when I visited Mãe Andresa, she told me with a smile that Legba was very well known to her but that she was not going to tell me anything else about him. One of her *filhas* told me that he was consulted prior to a marriage.

43. Curiously enough, the worship of the *voduns* in Haiti is also carried out on a veranda. As we shall see, the sects of Recife, Bahia, Rio, and Pôrto Alegre hold their ceremonies in pavilions known as *barraçaos*.

44. Costa Eduardo, *The Negro in Northern Brazil*, p. 88.

45. Nunes Pereira, *A Casa das Minas*, p. 39.

46. Octavio da Costa Eduardo, "O Tocador de Atabaques nas Casas de Culto Afro-Maranhense," in *Les Afro-Américains*, pp. 119–24.

47. In this work I shall leave aside the *xangôs* of Alagoas, which have not yet been treated in adequate depth, and those of Sergipe, which have been totally changed by the influence of *catimbó*. On the Sergipe *xangôs* see Felte Bezerra, *Etni as Segipanas* (Aracajo, 1954), pp. 187–91 (description of the Lambe *xangô*). On those in Alagoas see Fernandes, *Sincretismo Religioso*, pp. 9–28, and Abelardo Duarte, "Pantheon Afro-Brasileiro," *RIH de Alagoas* 26: 70–77.

48. The *xangô* was given this name by the whites because of the important role the god Shangô plays in it. The word *candomblé* was originally used for any of the dances of the blacks, whether profane or religious. In the extreme south of Brazil and in Uruguay and Argentina, the profane meaning is the only one that survives. As I

have explained, in early times the blacks probably camouflaged their cult behind these profane dances.

49. René Ribeiro, "Novos Aspectos do Processo de Reinterpretação nos Cultos Afro-Brasileiros do Recife," *Thirty-first International Congress of Americanists*, pp. 481–86.

50. René Ribeiro, *Cultos Afro-Brasileiros do Recife: Um Estudo de Adjustamento Social* (Recife: Boletim do Instituto Joaquim Nabuco de Pesquisa Social, 1952), p. 42.

51. Ibid.

52. Manuscript notes by Luiz Saia.

53. Unlike Ribeiro, I find no difference between Bahia and Recife as regards the existence of two types of god: those "fixed" in stones and those "fixed" in iron. This distinction also exists in Bahia; here the only difference may well be that Obaluayé moves from one town to another, from the "iron" to the "stone" group (*Imagens*, p. 135). Neither do I find any difference in the structure of the public ceremonies. In both cases there is undoubtedly a division into two phases: the invocation and the ecstasy.

54. There is a description of the *ile-sahim* of Bahia in Henri Georges Clouzot, *Le Cheval des Dieux* (Paris: Julliard, 1951), pp. 103–9, and one of the "house of Balé" in Ribeiro, *Cultos*, pp. 38 and 133.

55. On the assets of the *xangôs* see Ribeiro, *Cultos*, p. 60. The figures he cites are far below the value of the houses and grounds of Bahian centers such as Engenho Velho, Gantois, Afonja, Bate-Folha, etc.

56. Bastide, *Imagens*, p. 70.

57. Ribeiro, *Cultos*, pp. 35 and 75. The ethnic origin of the Chamba "nation" is unknown. Two tribes of this name exist in Africa, one to the north of the Ashanti, the other on the Nigerian-Cameroon frontier. On the *xangôs* see, in addition to Vicente Lima's short, polemical work *Xangô* (Recife: Jornal do Commercio, 1937), Borges Cavalcanti and Denice C. Lima, "Investigações sôbre as Religiões no Recife," *Arquivos da Assistencia a Psicopatos de Pernambuco* 2 (1932). Fernandes, *Xangôs do Nordeste*; Ribeiro, *Cultos*; Valente, *Sincretismo*; Oneyda Alvarenga, *Xangô* (data and songs collected by the folkloric mission of São Paulo); and *Melodias Registradas por Meios Não-Mecânicos* (São Paulo: Prefeitura do Muncípio de São Paulo, Departamento de Cultura, 1946), pp. 348–49.

58. For a list of these houses (incomplete because it does not include the Malê centers, which I was unable to locate) see Bastide, *Imagens*, pp. 241–47.

59. Nonetheless, specialized research on the Bantu, as distinct from the Nagô, religion has already produced significant studies, such as those of Reginalde Guimarães, "Contribuições Bantus para o Sincretismo Fetichista," in *O Negro no Brasil*, pp. 129–37, and Edison Carneiro, *Negros Bantus* (Rio de Janeiro: Civilização Brasileira, 1937). On the Dahomans (Gêgê) the only study I know of is the article by E. Correia Lopes, "Exéquias no Bôgum do Salvador," *O Mundo Português* 109 (1943): 539–65.

60. Roger Bastide, *Estudos Afro-Brasileiros*, 3d ser. (São Paulo: Editora Perspectiva, 1973), pp. 75–104.

61. This is brought out very clearly in Carneiro's *Negros Bantus*. This is why I remarked that the subject has not yet been adequately studied—at least insofar as ethnic differentiations and contrasts are concerned.

62. Table based on Carneiro, *Negros Bantus*; Guimaraes, "Contribuições"; Manoel R. Querino, *Costumes Africanos no Brasil* (Rio de Janeiro: Civilização Brasileira, 1938); Thomas Kockmeyer, "Candomblé," *Santo Antonio*, January 14, 1936; and Pierre Verger, *Notes sur le Culte des Orisa et Vodun à Bahia, la Baie de Tous le Saints, au Brésil et a l'Ancienne Côte des Esclaves en Afrique* (Dakar, Senegal: IFAN, 1957).

63. I omit a detailed description of these rituals, having devoted a whole book to the subject: *Le Candomblé de Bahia (Rite Nagô)* (Paris: Mouton & Co., 1958).

64. In addition to the work cited in the preceding note, see the two most recent accounts of this hierarchy: Carneiro, *Candomblés da Bahia*, pp. 91–99, and M. J. Herskovits, "The Social Organization of the Candomblé," in *The New World Negro* (Bloomington, Ind: Minerva Press), pp. 226–47.

65. Ruth Landes, "A Cult Matriarchate and Male Homosexuality," *Journal of Abnormal and Social Psychology* 35, no. 3 (1940): 386–97.

66. Querino, *Costumes*, pp. 125–27; Arthur Ramos, *O Negro Brasileiro* (Rio de Janeiro: Civilização Brasileira, 1934), pp. 159–62; Carneiro, *Negros Bantus*, pp. 28, 30, 103ff., 181–86, and *Candomblés da Bahia*, pp. 52–55, 64–66.

67. Carneiro, *Candomblés da Bahia*, p. 66.

68. On the Yoruba see: C. Daryll Forde, *The Yoruba-speaking Peoples of South Western Nigeria* (London: International African Institute, 1951), p. 29; R. James Johnson, *Yoruba Heathenism*, cited by Richard E. Dennett in *At the Back of the Black Man's Mind; or, Notes on the Kingly Office in West Africa* (New York: Macmillan Co., 1906); Pierre B. Bouche, *Sept Ans en Afrique Occidentale: La Côte des Esclaves et le Dahomey* (Paris: E. Plon, Novritt & Cie., 1885), p. 106; Noel Baudin, *Fétichisme et Féticheurs* (Lyon, 1884), pp. 5–7 on monotheism, the rest of the book on the *orixás*. (I cite Baudin in preference to Ellis, who seems merely to paraphrase Baudin insofar as religious topics are concerned.) On the Afro-Brazilians see Ramos, *O Negro Brasileiro*, p. 41, n. 33.

69. For examples see Bastide, *Le Candomblé de Bahia*.

70. On the Yoruba see J. D. Clarke, "Ifá Divination," *JRAI* 69 (1939): 235; William R. Bascom, "The Sanctions of Ifa Divination," ibid. 71 (1941): 43–54; Talbot, *Peoples of Southern Nigeria*, pp. 185ff.; and Bernard Maupoil, *La Géomancie sur l'Ancienne Côte des Esclaves* (Paris: Institut d'Ethnologie, 1943). On its Brazilian counterparts see Roger Bastide and Pierre Verger, "Contribuição ao Estudo da Adivinhação," *Revista do Museu Paulista* 7 (1952): 357–80, for Bahia, and Ribeiro, *Cultos*, pp. 84–97, for Recife.

71. The singing and dancing may last three days (see Baudin, *Fétichisme*, p. 97) or seven (see M. Prouteaux, "Le Culte de Seko," *Revue d'Ethnographie et des Traditions Religieuses*, 1921, p. 167), just as it varies in Brazil from one *terreiro* to another (see Bastide, *Imagens*, p. 56).

72. Baudin, *Fétichisme*, p. 97, on Africa; Bastide, *Candomblé*, p. 103, on Brazil.

73. The name *achêchê* apparently comes from the Yoruba word *adjêjê*, designating the moment in the funeral ceremony when the remains of the dead man's clothing and belongings are about to be carried away into the bush (letter from P. Verger dated March 26, 1954).

74. On the Yoruba homelands see R. P. Le Port, "Le Culte des Morts chez les Yorouba (Nagô)," *Echo des Missions Africaines de Lyon*, April and May, 1938, and Geoffrey Parrinder, *West African Religion* (London: Epworth Press, 1949). On Bahia see Clouzot, *Le Cheval des Dieux*, pp. 102–8, and José Lima, *A Festa de Egun e Outros Ensaios* (Bahia: Oficina Tipográfica Manú, 1952). It should be noted that in Bahia, as in Africa, the dead man appears on the seventh day after death.

75. Baudin, *Fétichisme*, pp. 75–80; Leo Frobenius, *Die Atlantische Götterlehre* (Jena, 1926), pp. 128–29, 242; Carneiro, *Candomblés da Bahia*, pp. 91–99. The correspondence extends to priests' wives who perform priestly functions, for instance the *apetebi*. See Dennett, *At the Back of the Black Man's Mind*; Maupoil, *Géomancie*, chap. 4. Cf. Bastide and Verger, "Contribuição ao Estudo da Advinhação," pp. 363–64, on Bahia, and Ribeiro, "Novos Aspectos," p. 481–86. The *apetebi* also exist in Cuba. See Fernando Ortiz Fernández, *Hampa Afro-Cubana: Los Negros Brujos* (Madrid: Editorial-América, 1917), pp. 117–82.

76. Compare Parrinder's description of the African ritual (*West African Religion*) with Carneiro's account of the Bahian one (*Candomblés da Bahia*, pp. 74–77)—the two most complete descriptions.

77. This part of the ritual is rarely mentioned by Africanists. It is performed in two slightly different ways. Among the Yoruba it occurs at the moment of the triple bathing of the head. If the girl falls into trance on the third bathing, this means that the god has accepted her (Baudin, *Fétichisme*, p. 81). In Bahia it consists in drumming. The *alabé* plays seven, fourteen, or twenty-one songs in honor of the candidate's *santo* until the *orixá* manifests itself, thus reconfirming the identity of her *orixá* (Carneiro, *Candomblés da Bahia*, p. 75). It must be noted, however, that confirmation by a combination of trance and certain music also exists in Africa (Pierre Verger, *Dieux d'Afrique* [Paris: P. Hartmann, 1954], p. 166).

78. On the possible existence of the Oro in Brazil see Nina Rodrigues, *Os Africanos*, p. 353.

79. See Verger, *Dieux d'Afrique*, with its photographs of Bahian and African liturgical costumes or clothing; see also the commentaries and photographs at the end of the book.

80. Richard E. Dennett, *Nigerian Studies; or the Religious and Political System of the Yoruba* (London: Macmillan & Co., 1910), chap. 7; Frobenius, *Die Atlantische Götterlehre*, pp. 126, 255; cf. Ramos, *O Negro Brasileiro*, p. 74.

81. William R. Bascom, *The Sociological Role of the Yoruba Cult Group* (Menasha, Wis.: American Antropological Assn. Memoir Series, no. 46, 1944), p. 34. Herskovits ("Social Organization") discusses the term *slave* used by Carneiro to designate the *ekedi*. The Yoruba word *ekedi* means "messenger." But Carneiro may have hit upon the right word without being aware of the capital distinction between slaves and brides, which, according to M. Tardits, also occurs in the Dahoman *vodun* cult.

82. On the *irôkô* cult see P. Victor Rublon, "Le Fétiche Montani," *Echo des Missions Africaines de Lyon*, March 2, 1951. Cf. Nina Rodrigues *O Animismo Fetichista dos Negros Bahianos* (Rio de Janeiro: Civilização Brasileira, 1935), pp. 53–57.

83. Cf. Herskovits (*Dahomey*, chap. 31) on the soul's sixteen visits to the earth to reincarnate itself, after which it returns to its tribe or, if it has failed to find descendants, takes to a tree, particularly the *lôkô* tree, with R. P. Frikel's discussion of the subject in "Die Seelenlehre der Nagô und der Gêge," *Santo Antonio*, nos. 18–19 (1940–1941), pp. 199 and 209.

84. Baudin, *Fétichisme*, p. 78, and Martiano de Bomfim, "Os 12 Ministros de Xangô," in *O Negro no Brasil* (n.d.), pp. 233ff.

85. Bascom, *Sociological Role of the Yoruba Cult Group*, p. 24; S. Johnson, *The History of the Yoruba* (London: Routledge, 1921), p. 27; Ribeiro, *Cultos*, p. 124.

86. On the festival of the new yams see Parrinder, *West African Religion*; Quernio, *Costumes*, p. 55; and Valente, *Sincretismo*, pp. 79–86. Obviously this list of parallels could be expanded to include details such as the seven-day duration of the festivals (Bascom, *Sociological Role of the Yoruba Cult Group*, p. 21; Ramos, *O Negro Brasileiro*, p. 74) or the relatively secret Bahian rite of sprinkling the toes of the *filhos* with blood, the African explanation of which is given by Baudin (*Fétichisme*, p. 43).

87. Bascom, *Sociological Role of the Yoruba Cult Group*, pp. 68–69.

88. Cf. the calendar of Yoruba festivals in Parrinder, *West African Religion*, with the one given by Fernandes in *Xangôs do Nordeste*, pp. 28ff. Also cf. *Novos Estudos Afro-Brasileiros*, pp. 252–54.

89. Bastide, *Imagens*, p. 107.

90. Bouche, *Sept Ans en Afrique Occidentale*, p. 113. The solutions were analogous but not necessarily identical. Sunday is Obatalá's day, Saturday is Shangô's, etc. But in Brazil the assignment of days varies from one region of African culture to another.

91. Verger, *Dieux d'Afrique*, photograph 84, and letter dated June 30, 1955.

92. Forde, *Yoruba-speaking Peoples*, pp. 35ff., deals with the distribution of the gods according to the principal territorial groups. See also Bascom, *Sociological Role of the Yoruba Cult Group*, pp. 37–40.

93. Forde, *Yoruba-speaking Peoples*, p. 37.

94. In Recife, for instance, Afréquété, Obá, and Dada no longer descend, although their names are remembered (Alvarenga, *Tambor de Mina*, pp. 6, 14, 15).

95. Talbot, *Peoples of Southern Nigeria*, p. 92; Bascom, *Sociological Role of the Yoruba Cult Group*, pp. 21–22 and 65.

96. Parrinder, *West African Religion*.

97. Cf. Herskovits, *Dahomey*, chap. 29, and "Social Organization," p. 232.

98. Renato Mendonça, *A Influencia Africana no Portugûes do Brasil* (São Paulo: Cia. Editora Nacional, 1935), p. 95; Jacques Raimundo, *O Negro Brasileiro* (Rio de Janeiro: Record, 1936), pp. 55, 58.

99. Aires da Mata Machado Filho, "O Negro e o Garimpo em Minas Gerais," *RAM de SP* 63 (1940): 284, 288.

100. Machado Filho, *RAM de SP* 62 (1939): 317, and "O Negro," ibid. 63 (1940): 275–80 and 295.

101. Ibid., 62: 311.

102. Extract from the pastoral letter of Dom João Nery on leaving the diocese of Espírito Santo, Campinas, São Paulo, 1901, cited by Rodrigues, Ramos, and others.

Some of the terms used in this letter need explaining. *Enba* is a magic powder made of leaves. *Santé* is an abbreviation of *santidade*, a term we have already encountered designating the mystic trance produced by the *santos*, the gods or spirits. It is interesting to note that, although the assistants spoke Portuguese, they were in the habit of attaching the classificatory Bantu prefix *ka* to Portuguese words.

103. Duglas Teixera Monteiro, "A Macumba de Vitoria," in *Thirty-first International Congress of Americanists*, pp. 463–72.

104. Armando Magalhães Corrêa, *O Sertão Carioca* (Rio: Imprensa Nacional, 1936), p. 206.

105. João do Rio, *As Religões no Rio* (Rio de Janeiro: Ed. Nova Aguilar, 1976), pp. 182–86.

106. Magalhães Corrêa, *O Sertão Carioca*, p. 206 This name, which is not used in Bahia, is used in other Yoruba areas to designate the divinities (Dennett, *At the Back of the Black Man's Mind*, p. 192).

107. Magalhães Corrêa, *O Sertão Carioca*, p. 209.

108. Ibid., pp. 209–10; João do Rio, *As Religões*, pp. 36–38.

109. Magalhães Corrêa, *O Sertão Carioca*, pp. 210–11; João do Rio, *As Religões*.

110. Magalhães Corrêa, *O Sertão Carioca*, p. 211.

111. João do Rio, *As Religões*, pp. 53–56.

112. Ibid., pp. 93–98.

113. João do Rio, "O Natal dos Africanos," *Kosmos*, December 1904.

114. João do Rio, *As Religões*, pp. 25–32.

115. All we know about it is that the Djé-djé called their *babalaôs ogans*. In Gabon they were known as *ugangas*. See Magalhães Corrêa, *O Sertão Carioca*, p. 210.

116. Magalhães Corrêa, *O Sertão Carioca*, pp. 217–21.

117. On this earliest syncretism, the first of many, see ibid., pp. 217–18, 220–21.

118. Achylles Porto-Alegre, *Jardim de Saudades*, pp. 160–63. The author gives no information on the cult itself, merely remarking that brandy is drunk, but no one gets intoxicated, and that the ceremonies are always conducted in an extremely orderly manner.

119. The name *batuque* is of course the one used by the whites. The blacks' own name for their ceremonies is *pará*.

120. Ramos, *O Negro Brasileiro*, pp. 169–74. Ramos's data consists essentially of an article he cites from *Folha da Tarde*, May 28, 1936.

121. M. J. Herskovits, "The Southernmost Outpost of New World Africanisms," in *New World Negro*, pp. 199–216.

122. Dante de Laytano, *Festa de Nossa Senhora dos Navegantes* (Pôrto Alegre, 1955).

123. Roger Bastide, "Le Batuque de Porto-Alegre," in *Acculturation in the Americas*, ed. Sol Tax, pp. 195–206.

124. Data furnished by the Pôrto Alegre police.

125. The growth rate was as follows: 1937, 13 cult centers; 1938, 23 cult centers; 1939, 27 cult centers; 1940, 37 cult centers (891 ceremonies performed); 1941, 42 cult centers (1,160 ceremonies performed); 1942, 57 cult centers (637 ceremonies performed). See *Estatísticas Culturães*, Secretaria da Educação e Cultura, Rio Grande do Sul.

126. Data from police records.

127. Herskovits, "Southernmost Outpost," pp. 200–201.

128. Judging by the names of the *batuques*, the most popular deities in Pôrto Alegre seem to be Oxun Pandá (7 centers), Bara (5), Shangô (4), Oxalá (4), Yemanjá (3), Oiâ (3), Shangô Dada (1, and Orunmila (1).

129. Cited by Ramos, *O Negro Brasileiro*, p. 171.

130. Herskovits, "Southernmost Outpost," pp. 209–10.

131. In 1941 there were 6 adult baptisms, 5 funeral ceremonies; in 1942, 6 infant baptisms, 15 adult baptisms, 2 funeral ceremonies.

132. Herskovits, "Southernmost Outpost," p. 206. According to my informants, the average duration is 16 days.

133. Ibid., p. 212. The old name for this funeral ceremony seems to have been *Houtambi* (Dante de Laytano, *Os Africanismos do Dialeto Gaucho* [Pôrto Alegre:

Oficinas Gráficas da Livraria do Globo; Barcellos, Bertaso & Cia., 1936], p. 57).
134. Ribeiro, *Cultos*, p. 126.
135. Bastide, *Imagens*, p. 49.
136. Herskovits also mentions this point ("Southernmost Outpost," pp. 202–3) but attributes it primarily to climatic conditions. In my opinion the economic factor is the major one since this spatial confinement also typifies the proletarian *candomblés* of Bahia, which I have mentioned.
137. These figures are from *Estatísticas Culturães*.
138. Herskovits, "Southernmost Outpost," p. 204.
139. Roberto C. Simonsen, *Recursos Econômicos e Movimentos das Populações* (Rio de Janeiro: Instituto Brasileiro de Geografia e Estatística, 1940).
140. On contemporary domestic migration see the official statistics. For the sociological aspect see Costa Pinto, *Migrações Internas no Brasil* (Rio de Janeiro: Instituto de Economia, 1952).
141. Donald Pierson, *Negroes in Brazil* (Chicago: Univ. of Chicago Press, 1942).
142. There is a "branch" of the Opo Afonja *candomblé* in Rio.
143. J. Lambert, *Le Brésil: Structure Sociale et Institutions Politiques* (Paris: A. Colin, 1953), pp. 64–82. Pierre Monbeig (*Le Brésil* [Paris: Presse Universitaires de France, 1954], pp. 85–87), approaches the subject more subtly.
144. Mario de Andrade, "Geografia Religiosa do Brasil," *Publicações Médicas*, August 1941, p. 796.
145. Mario de Andrade, *Música*.
146. Oneyda Alvarenga, *Babassuê* (São Paulo: Discoteca Pública Municipal, 1950), pp. 9, 21.
147. Ibid., p. 113.
148. Ibid., pp. 32–33.
149. Ibid., p. 31.
150. Ibid., pp. 22–24.
151. In his letter to me of February 7, 1951, Geraldo Pinheiro mentions a *yalorixá* of Amazonas who, having been "made" in Alagoas, introduced yet another form of religious sect, differing from the *tambor* of Maranhão and from the *xangô*. Pinheiro also mentions divination by shells, which is common to all the Yoruba-Dahoman sects, and the existence of the "punishment of the *bié-é*" in Manaus. From his description this is obviously a characteristic rite of the Nagô sects of Maranhão. "A *filha* or *filho* who recognizes that he has been guilty of some fault during the ceremonies, or even outside the sect, will go to the *pegi* and strike the *bié-é* stone violently with his hands until a lighted candle has burned down. During this sacrifice he sings a hymn 'in language.' When he comes out again, his hands are always bleeding." Other letters deal with the place assigned to Exú and included transcriptions of songs.
152. Of the seventeen informants from the Babassuê sect, four were born in Maranhão and one was a former member of Mãe Andresa's *Casa das Minas* (Alvarenga, *Babassuê*, p. 49).
153. Ibid., pp. 33–34.
154. Ibid., p. 30. On the other hand the language shows obvious syncretism: 51.51 percent of the collected songs are in Portuguese, 34.85 percent are in African languages, but in 13.65 percent of the songs, the two idioms are mixed. It is true that Portuguese is preferred for hymns to *caboclo* spirits (70.59 percent), African languages for those to the *orixás* or *voduns* (78.26 percent).

Chapter 10

1. Jean Price-Mars, *Ainsi Parla l'Oncle* (Paris: Compiègne, 1928), pp. 48–49, 65; Lorimer Denis and François Duvalier, "L'Evolution Stadiale du Vodou," *Bulletin du Bureau d'Ethnologie* (Port-au-Prince, Haiti), no. 3 (1944), pp. 9–32.
2. L. Derrigny, *U.S.A.*, pp. 49–66.
3. M. J. Herskovits, *Pesquisas Etnológicas na Bahia* (Salvador: Publicações do Museu de Bahia, no. 3, 1943), pp, 21–23.
4. René Ribeiro, *Cultos Afro-Brasileiros de Recife: Um Estudo de Adjustamento*

Social (Recife: Boletim do Instituto Joaquim Nabuco de Pesquisa Social, 1952), pp. 142–43.

5. Roger Bastide, *Sociologie et Psychanalyse* (Paris: Presses Universitaires de France, 1950), pp. 252–57.

6. Jorge Amado, *Bahia de Todos os Santos* (São Paulo: Livraria Martins, 1945).

7. In discussing acculturation as it applies to the world of the *candomblés* and the *xangôs*, Herskovits and Ribeiro have shown the power the African religious organization exercises over individuals. See M. J. Herskovits, "The Social Organization of the Candomblé," in *The New World Negro* (Bloomington, Ind.: Minerva Press, 1969), pp. 226–47, and Ribeiro, *Cultos*, pp. 99–129. These writers, however, juxtapose the Africanization of the individual and the functions of the cult instead of stressing their close interdependence. While *candomblé* or *xungô* certainly satisfy many individual needs, these are needs that have already been "Africanized."

8. On the discussion of this subject by Herskovits and Frazier see Roger Bastide, "Dans les Amériques Noires: Afrique ou Europe?" in *Annales: Economies—Sociétés—Civilisations*, 1948, pp. 3–20.

9. Octavio da Costa Eduardo, *The Negro in Northern Brazil* (Seattle: Univ. of Washington Press, 1948), pp. 34–38.

10. Ibid., p. 22.

11. Ibid., p. 23.

12. On all these points see René Ribeiro, "Novos Aspectos do Processo do Reinterpretação," in *Proceedings and Selected Papers of the Thirty-first International Congress of Americanists* (Nendeln, Lichtenstein: Kraus Reprints, 1976), pp. 481–86.

13. E. Franklin Frazier gives several examples in "The Negro Family in Bahia, Brazil," *American Sociological Review* 7, no. 4 (1942): 474–75. They include the case of a *babalaô* with five wives, one of whom was his principal spouse.

14. The difference can easily be grasped by comparing, for example, ritual polygamy as described by Ribeiro (see note 12 above) and the type he deals with in his article "On the Amaziado Relationship and Other Aspects of the Family in Recife," *American Sociological Review* 10, no. 1 (1945): 44–51.

15. See the account of this myth in Roger Bastide, *Le Candomblé de Bahia (Rite Nagô)* (Paris: Mouton & Co., 1958).

16. See the account of myths about Shangô's loves (ibid.).

17. Variations occur, of course, from one religious area to another, but they remain within the general norm I have described. On Bahia see Bastide, *Imagens do Nordeste Místico em Branco e Preto* (Rio de Janeiro, 1945), p. 49. On Recife see Ribeiro, *Cultos*, pp. 126–27.

18. E. Franklin Frazier, *The Negro in the United States* (New York: Macmillan Co., 1949), chaps. 5–8. On the important position occupied by Yoruba women, of which this matriarchal type of family is an extension, see H. V. Beier, "The Position of Yoruba Women," *Présence Africaine*, April–July 1957, pp. 39–46.

19. Lucila Hermann, *Evolução da Estrutura Social de Guaratingueta num Periodo de Tresentos Anos*, pp. 30, 157ff., 274–75.

20. On sexual magic in connection with the *catimbós* and other African sects see Alfred de Carvalho, "A Magia Sexual no Brasil," *RIAHGP* 21, no. 106 (1914): 406–22.

21. On these "punishment songs," called *toados de couro* in Portuguese, *telebé* in African, see Ribeiro, *Cultos*, p. 116.

22. In his Bahia lecture Herskovits called for a study of the economy of the *candomblé* (*Pesquisas Etnologicas*, pp. 12–14). So far the only response has been Ribeiro's brief account in *Cultos*, pp. 59–61. [In 1958 Herskovits himself published an article on this subject, "Some Economic Aspects of the Afro-Bahian Candomblé," in *Paul Rivet Octogenario Dictata*, vol. 2 (Mexico: Universidad Autonoma de Mexico, 1958), pp. 227–47 (reprinted in his *New World Negro*, pp. 248–66.]

23. Roger Bastide and Pierre Verger, "Contribução ao Estudo da Advinhação," *Revista de Museu Paulista* 7 (1952): 365–66; Roger Bastide, *Estudos Afro-Brasileiros*, 3d ser. (São Paulo: Boletim da Faculdade de Filosofia, Ciências e Letras da Universidade de São Paulo, 1953), pp. 69–73.

24. E. G. Léonard, "O Protestantismo Brasileiro, I" *Revista de História* 2, no. 5 (1951): 130.

25. Waldemar Valente, *Sincretismo Religioso Afro-Brasileiro* (São Paulo: Cia. Editora Nacional, 1955), p. 162, n. 7.

26. On these sociopolitical organizations for the defense of the "black race" see Roger Bastide, "A Imprensa de Côr em São Paulo," in *Estudos Afro-Brasileiros*, 2d ser. [probably "A Imprensa Negra do Estado de São Paulo," in *Estudos Afro-Brasileiros*, 2d series (São Paulo: Editora Perspectiva, 1973), pp. 129–56], and Roger Bastide and Florestan Fernandes, *Relações Raciais entre Negros e Brancos em São Paulo* (São Paulo: Editôra Anhembi, 1955), pp. 193–222.

27. On these attempts and failures see Thales de Azevedo, *Les Élites de Couleur dans une Ville Brésilienne* (Paris: UNESCO, 1953), pp. 98–102.

28. Bastide, *Sociologie et Psychanalyse*, pp. 252ff.

29. J. Ingeneiros, *A Loucura em Argentina* [see *La Locura en la Argentina* (Buenos Aires: Cooperative Editorial, 1920)].

30. Ribeiro, *Cultos*, p. 118.

31. Bastide, *Le Candomblé de Bahia*.

Chapter 11

1. I believe that I was the first to call attention to the importance of myth in Afro-Brazilian research (*Imagens do Nordeste em Branco e Preto* [Rio de Janeiro, 1945], chap. 3). Since then many myths have been collected, notably by René Ribeiro (*Cultos Afro-Brasileiros de Recife: Um Estudo de Adjustamento Social* [Recife: Boletim do Instituto Joaquim Nabuco de Pesquisa Social, 1952]) and Pierre Verger (*Dieux d'Afrique* [Paris: P. Hartmann, 1954]).

2. Seppilli is misleading on this point because he relied largely on already outdated works (*Il Sincretismo Religioso Afro-Cattólico*, pp. 29–30).

3. An analogous phenomenon occurred in the early Christian church, where the Halakah, the laws of the cult and the stories explaining them (the Last Supper, the Crucifixion, etc.), was preserved, while the Haggadah, the purely historical traditions such as anecdotes from the childhood of Jesus, was gradually forgotten.

4. *Psyché*, no. 17 (March 1948), pp. 310–23.

5. Roger Bastide, "Groupes Sociaux et Transmission des Légendes," ibid., no. 34 (August 1949), pp. 716–55.

6. Maurice Halbwachs, *Les Cadres Sociaux de la Mémoire* (Paris: Presses Universitaires de France, 1952), p. 401.

7. Roger Bastide, *Sociologie et Psychanalyse* (Paris: Presses Universitaires de France, 1950), pp. 249–50.

8. From a series of newspaper clippings Ramos strikingly illustrates Yemanjá's role as a consoling mother in the life of Afro-Brazilians and even of the half-whites and whites who worship her (*O Negro Brasileiro* [Rio de Janeiro: Civilização Brasileira, 1934], pp. 306–14 and 320). His interpretation of the phallic fathers and heroes, on the other hand, is based entirely on Afro-American elements.

9. Henri A. Junod, *The Life of a South African Tribe* (London: D. Nutt, 1912–1913), 2: 201.

10. Octavio da Costa Eduardo, "Aspectos do Folclore de uma Comunidade Rural," *RAM de SP* 140 (1951): 13–60.

11. Ibid., p. 35.

12. Maurice Halbwachs, "La Mémoire Collective chez les Musiciens," *Revue Philosophique* 3–4 (1939): 136–65.

13. This impression was created to some extent by Durkheim but more particularly by Roger Caillois, *L'Homme et le Sacré* (Paris: Leroux; Presses Universitaires de France, 1939).

14. M. Varagnac presents an analogous case in another field—folklore (*Civilisations et Genres de Vie*).

15. Leo Frobenius, *Die Atlantische Götterlehre* (Jena, 1926).

452   NOTES TO CHAPTER 11

16. Verger, *Dieux d'Afrique*, pp. 186–87.
17. There is a description of the ceremony of presentation of gifts to Yemenjá in Ramos, *O Negro Brasileiro*, pp. 306–7 and 310–14; Edison Carneiro, *Religiões Negras: Notas de Etnografia Religiosa* (Rio de Janeiro: Biblioteca de Divulgação Científica, VII, Civilização Brasileira, 1936), pp. 171–78; José Pereira, *Festa de Yemanjá* (Salvador, 1951); Bastide, *Imagens*, pp. 122–28; Odorico Tavares, *Bahia: Imagens da Terra do Povo* (Rio de Janeiro: J. Olympio, 1951), pp. 67–81.
18. Halbwachs, "La Mémoire," pp. 130–39.
19. Maurice Halbwachs, *La Topographie Légendaire des Évangiles en Terre Sante* (Paris: Presses Universitaires de France, 1941).
20. Nunes Pereira, *A Casa das Minas* (Rio de Janeiro: Publ. da Sociedade Brasileira de Antropologia e Etnologia, no. 1, 1947), pp. 29–30.
21. Roger Bastide, "Magia e Medicina no Candomblé," *Boletim Bibliográfico* (São Paulo), 16 (1950): 7–33.
22. This taboo is of African origin. See P. A. Talbot, *The Peoples of Southern Nigeria* (London: Oxford Univ. Press, 1928), 3: 735.
23. Bernard Naupoil, *La Géomancie sur l'Ancienne Côte des Esclaves* (Paris: Institut d'Ethnographie, 1943), p. 374; J. D. Clarke, "Ifá Divination," *JRAI* 69 (1939): 325ff.
24. Halbwachs, *Cadres Sociaux*, p. 401.
25. Cf. Noel Baudin, *Fétichisme et Féticheurs* (Lyon, 1884), pp. 8–12. Richard E. Dennett, *Nigerian Studies* (London: Macmillan & Co., 1910), chap. 7; Pierre B. Bouche, *Sept Ans en Afrique Occidentale: La Côte des Esclaves et le Dahomey* (Paris: E. Plon, Novritt & Cie., 1885), pp. 111–14; Talbot, *Peoples of Southern Nigeria*, pp. 30–31; Bastide, *Imagens*, pp. 117–19.
26. Ramos, *O Negro Brasileiro*, p. 43.
27. Baudin, *Fétichisme*, p. 12.
28. Edison Carneiro, *Candomblés da Bahia* (Bahia: Secretaria de Educação e Saúde, 1948), p. 42; also mentioned by Ramos in *O Negro Brasileiro*, p. 44.
29. Nina Rodrigues, *O Animismo Fetichista dos Negros Bahianos* (Rio de Janeiro: Civilização Brasileira, 1935), p. 40.
30. On Exú in Brazil see Roger Bastide, "Immigration et Métamorphose d'un Dieu," *Cahiers Internationaux de Sociologie* 20 (1956): 45–60.
31. A. Le Herissé, *L'Ancien Royaume du Dahomey* (Paris, 1911), pp. 137–39.
32. Milo Marcelin, *Mythologie Vodou* (Port-au-Prince: Éditions Haïtiennes, 1949–1950), 1: 16; J. Roumain, *Le Sacrifice du Tambour-Assoto(r)* (Port-au-Prince: Imprimerie de l'État, 1943), p. 19. For the psychoanalytical explanation of this change see M. S. Wolff, "Notes on the Vodoun Religion," *Revue Internationale d'Ethnologie Normale et Pathologique*, vol. 1, no. 2, pp. 238–40.
33. On the representation of Exú in Africa see, among others, Bouche, *Sept Ans*, pp. 120–21 (on his phallic character); Baudin, *Fétichisme*, p. 49 (on his "bad boy" persona); Verger, *Dieux d'Afrique*, p. 183 (on his pranks); Clarke, "Ifá Divination," p. 235; Frobenius, *Atlantische Götterlehre* (particularly on Exú as a god of orientation); Parrinder, *West African Religion* (on his characteristics in general); and Dennett, *Nigerian Studies*, chap. 9. On the representation of Exú in Brazil cf. Nina Rodrigues, *O Animismo*, pp. 39–42; Étienne Brasil, "O Fetichismo dos Negros de Brazil," *RIHGB* 74, pt. 2 (1911): 195, 260; and Ramos, *O Negro Brasileiro*, pp. 45–46. There are the older, classical works on the subject. Other references will be found in subsequent notes.
34. Personal letter to the author from an *obá* of Opo Afonja.
35. Ramos, *O Negro Brasileiro*, pp. 208–9.
36. For Bahia see Carneiro, *Candomblés da Bahia*, pp. 46–49; for Recife see Ribeiro, *Cultos*, pp. 53–54.
37. Edison Carneiro, *Negros Bantus: Notas de Etnographia Religiosa e Folclore* (Rio de Janeiro: Civilização Brasileira, 1937), pp. 43–50.
38. Talbot, *Peoples of Southern Nigeria*, 2: 37.
39. Frobenius, *Atlantische Götterlehre*; Dennett, *Nigerian Studies*, chap. 13.
40. Frobenius, *Atlantische Götterlehre*.
41. Ramos, *O Negro Brasileiro*, p. 47.

42. See the myth of Ogun the warrior in Verger, *Dieux d' Afrique*, p. 179.
43. Parrinder, *West African Religion*.
44. Dennett, *Nigerian Studies*, p. 123.
45. Carneiro, *Negros Bantus*, pp. 61–68.
46. Ramos, *O Negro Brasileiro*, p. 124.
47. Waldemar Valente, *Sincretismo Religioso Afro-Brasileiro* (São Paulo: Cia. Editora Nacional, 1955), p. 133.
48. Albino Gonçalves Fernandes, *O Sincretismo Religioso no Brasil* (Curitiba: Editora Guaíra, 1941), pp. 107–8.
49. Le Herissé, *L'Ancien Royaume*, p. 128; M. J. Herskovits, *Dahomey: An Ancient West African Kingdom* (New York: J. J. Augustin, 1938), chap. 27.
50. Frobenius distinguishes two Shankpannas: Shankpanna-Boku, the malevolent god of smallpox; and Shankpanna-Airo, a benevolent god (*Atlantische Götterlehre*, p. 193). Manoel R. Querino distinguishes Humolu, the god of smallpox, and Aruaru, the god of measles, who is now extinct in Brazil (*Costumes Africanos no Brasil* [Rio de Janeiro: Civilização Brasileira, 1938], p. 51). One wonders whether this Aruaru may not be the Airo of Frobenius.
51. Frobenius, *Atlantische Götterlehre*. It is interesting to note that in Yoruba countries those possessed by Xapanan speak the language of the Dahoman *eguns* when they are in trance.
52. Herskovits, *Dahomey*, chap. 27.
53. Baudin, *Fétichisme*, p. 28.
54. Parrinder, *West African Religion*; Verger, *Dieux d'Afrique*, p. 184.
55. On smallpox epidemics in Bahia see Thalès de Azevedo, *Povoamento da Cidade do Salvador* (Salvador: Editôra Itapuã, 1969), pp. 122, 131, 143, and Octavio de Freitas, *Doenças Africanas no Brasil* (São Paulo: Cia. Editora Nacional, 1935).
56. On the association of Exú and Omolú in Bahia see Ramos, *O Negro Brasileiro*, pp. 49–50. On Omolú's association with black magic in Rio see Lourenço Braga, *Umbanda e Quimbanda* (Rio de Janeiro: Livraria Jacintho, 1942).
57. Reginaldo Guimarães, "Contribuições Bantus," in *O Negro no Brasil* (n.d.), p. 135.
58. Carneiro, *Negros Bantus*, pp. 85–92 (the poor people's doctor).
59. Valente, *Sincretismo*, pp. 135–36.
60. This seems to have had a scientific counterpart in the Africans' discovery of antismallpox vaccination. They would vaccinate healthy people with a small amount of pus from the lesions of those suffering from the disease (Parrinder, *West African Religion*).
61. Fernando Ortiz Fernández, *Hampa Afro-Cubana: Los Negros Brujos* (Madrid: Editorial-América, 1917), p. 132.
62. Cf. Frobenius, *Atlantische Götterlehre*, and Martiniano do Bomfim, "Os 12 Ministros de Xangô," in *O Negro no Brasil* (n.d.), pp. 233–38.
63. Cf. Frobenius, *Kulturgeschichte Afrikas*, and Baudin, *Fétichisme*, p. 25, with Ogosse Nabeji, *Xangô* (Rio de Janeiro, 1949).
64. Cf. Frobenius, *Kulturgeschichte Afrikas*, and Baudin, *Fétichisme*, p. 21, with Ribeiro, *O Animismo*, p. 51.
65. On the quarrels between Shangô and Ogun see Dennett, *Nigerian Studies*, pp. 171–74, for Africa, and Lydia Cabrera, *El Monte, Igbo Finda, Ewe Orisha, Vititinfinda: Notas sobre las Religiones, la Magia, las Supersticiones y el Folklore de los Negros Criollos y del Puebla de Cuba* (Havana: Ediciones C.R., 1954), pp. 232–34, for Cuba. On Oxun's passage from Ogun to Shangô see Oneyda Alvarenga, *Xangô*, p. 101.
66. Verger, *Dieux d'Afrique*, pp. 185–86.
67. Cf. L. R. Meyerowitz, "Note on the King-God Shangô and His Temple at Ibadan, Southern Nigeria," *Man* 46 (1946): 29–31, and Ramos, *O Negro Brasileiro*, pp. 345–46.
68. Frobenius (*Kulturgeschichte Afrikas*) distinguishes two Shangôs, the ram and fire-thrower, and the hero and chivalrous upholder of morality. In fact these two deities merged, and Shangô is conceived of as *Jupiter tonans* hurling his thunderbolt at the ungodly—and especially at thieves. See Baudin, *Fétichisme*, p. 27; Frobenius,

Kulturgeschichte Afrikas; and Verger, *Dieux d'Afrique*, p. 174, on Shangô's Dahoman counterpart, Sobo.

69. Verger, *Dieux d'Afrique*, p. 173.

70. See Bastide, *Imagens*, p. 101, on Bahia; Ribeiro, *O Animismo*, pp. 40 and 128, for Recife; Verger, *Dieux d'Afrique*, pp. 173–74, on Africa.

71. Alvarenga, *Xangô*, pp. 5–6.

72. Ribeiro, *O Animismo*, p. 45.

73. Alvarenga, *Xangô*, p. 101.

74. Ribeiro, *O Animismo*, p. 48.

75. Baudin, *Fétichisme*, p. 13; Alfredo Ellis, *Yoruba-speaking Peoples of the Slave Coast of West Africa* (London: Chapman & Hall, 1894), pp. 43ff. Cf. Talbot's more recent work, *Peoples of Southern Nigeria*, 2: 31.

76. Ribeiro, *O Animismo*, p. 48.

77. Ibid., p. 49.

78. M. Dowell, "O Candomblé da Bahia," *A Mascara* (Bahia) 11 (May 5, 1942).

79. Carneiro, *Negros Bantus*, pp. 53–54.

80. Ribeiro, *O Animismo*, p. 127.

81. Bastide, *Imagens*, p. 76, and more especially Edison Carneiro, "Una Revisão na Etnografia Religiosa," in *O Negro no Brasil* (n.d.), p. 65.

82. On Recife see Ribeiro, *O Animismo*, p. 44. On Maranhão see Octavio da Costa Eduardo, *The Negro in Northern Brazil* (Seattle: Univ. of Washington Press, 1948). On Pará see Oneyda Alvarenga, *Babassuê* (São Paulo: Discoteca Pública Municipal, 1950), p. 21.

83. Her cult is growing in Rio, along the beaches of Santos in the state of São Paulo and in Pôrto Alegre. See Bastide, *Le Candomblé de Bahia (Rite Nagô)* (Paris: Mouton & Co., 1958).

84. Albino Gonçalves Fernandes, *Xangôs do Nordeste*, p. 83.

85. Donald Pierson, *Negroes in Brazil* (Chicago: Univ. of Chicago Press, 1942), pp. 308–9.

86. Roger Bastide, "Le Batuque de Porto Alegre," in *Acculturation in the Americas: Proceedings and Selected Papers of the Twenty-ninth International Congress of Americanists*, ed. Sol Tax (New York: Cooper Square Publishers, 1952), pp. 195–206.

87. Ribeiro, *O Animismo*, p. 90.

Chapter 12

1. Nina Rodrigues, *O Animismo Fetichista dos Negros Bahianos* (Rio de Janeiro: Civilização Brasileira, 1935), p. 171.

2. Arthur Ramos effectively exposed the importance of these two movements: counteracculturation, which promotes separation, and police persecution, which promotes assimilation. He mentions the former in discussing Nina Rodrigues's thesis (*A Aculturação Negra no Brasil* [São Paulo: Cia. Editora Nacional, 1942], p. 8) and the latter later in the same book (pp. 223–24). Cf. Waldemar Valente, *Sincretismo Religioso Afro-Brasileiro* (São Paulo: Cia. Editora Nacional, 1955), p. 114.

3. I would add that Christian mysticism is always defined as a merging with God. But it should be noted that even though the saints do not inspire mystic trance, phenomena do occur which suggest a type of trance closer to the African type than the classical rapture of oneness with God. I am referring to those that mime the passion of Christ or the suckling of Jesus by the Virgin. In these cases mysticism appears as an "imitation of sacred history" recalling, *mutatis mutandis*, the link between myth and ecstatic rite in the *candomblés*. See Roger Bastide, *Les Problèmes de la Vie Mystique* (Paris: A. Colin, 1931), pp. 177–83.

4. M. Lamartinière Honorat, *Les Danses Folkloriques Haïtiennes* (Port-au-Prince: Imprimerie de l'État, 1955), p. 105.

5. For Cuba see the books of Fernando Ortiz and Lydia Cabrera, for Haiti those of Milo Marcelin, Alfred Métraux, Louis Maximilien, Jean Price-Mars, M. J. Herskovits, etc. For Louisiana see Newbell Niles Puckett, *Folk Beliefs of the Southern Negro* (Chapel Hill: Univ. of North Carolina Press, 1926), chap. 3. For Trinidad see M. J.

and F. S. Herskovits, *Trinidad Village* (New York: Knopf, 1947), appendix. For America as a whole see M. J. Herskovits, *The Myth of the Negro Past* (New York: Harper & Bros, 1941).

6. On these parallels see Roger Bastide, "Contribuição ao Estudo do Sincretismo Catolico-Fetichista," in *Estudos Afro-Brasileiros* (São Paulo: Editora Perspectiva, 1973).

7. René Ribeiro, *Cultos Afro-Brasileiros do Recife* (Recife: Boletim do Instituto Joaquim Nabuco de Pesquisa Social, 1952), pp. 65–67.

8. See (especially for Haiti) M. Leiris, "Note sur l'Usage des Chromolithographies Catholiques par les Vodouisants d'Haïti," in *Les Afro-Américains,* Mémoires de l'Institut Français d'Afrique Noire, no. 27 (Dakar, Senegal, 1953), pp. 201–8.

9. Ribeiro, *Cultos,* p. 56.

10. Ribeiro, it is true, gives another reason. "Local variations in the prestige of certain saints, so common in Catholic countries, explain the differing identifications of the Afrcan deities. Obá presents a typical case. In Recife this warrior god is equated with Our Lady of Pleasures, who is said to have been responsible for the Portuguese victory over the Dutch in the Guararapes mountains, while in Bahia he is identified wth Joan of Arc" (ibid., p. 57).

11. Nina Rodrigues, *O Animismo,* p. 56.

12. Cf. Albino Gonçalves Fernandes, *Xangôs do Nordeste* (Rio de Janeiro: Civilização Brasileira, 1937), pp. 25 and 128, and Waldemar Valente, *Sincretismo Religioso Afro-Brasileiro* (São Paulo: Cia. Editora Nacional, 1955), pp. 134 and 142–44.

13. M. J. Herskovits, "African Gods and Catholic Saints," in *The New World Negro* (Bloomington, Ind.: Minerva Press, 1969), p. 328.

14. Dante de Laytano, *Festa de Nossa Senhora dos Navigantes* (Pôrto Alegre, 1955).

15. Fernandes, *Xangôs do Nordeste,* pp. 25–26 (Joana Batista's Santana sect) and p. 27 (Eloy *terreiro*); Bastide, "*Contribuição,*" p. 19 (Master Apolinário's *terreiro*); P. Cavalcanti, in *Estudos Afro-Brasileiros,* p. 252 (African Center of Saint Barbara, where Obaluayê is identified with the Savior, not with Saint Sebastian as in the other centers); and ibid., pp. 254–55 (African Center of Saint George).

16. Laytano, *Festa,* p. 59.

17. Thomas Kockmeyer, "Candomblé," *Santo Antonio,* 1936, p. 32; Laytano, *Festa,* p. 59.

18. Bastide, "Contribuição," pp. 12 and 27–33.

19. Ribeiro, *Cultos,* p. 134.

20. Valente, *Sincretismo,* pp. 124–25 and 116.

21. Ribeiro's study of the same *xangôs* during the same period confirms this (*Cultos,* p. 134).

22. See, for example, the photographs of *pegis* in Bantu *candomblés* in Arthur Ramos, *O Negro Brasileiro* (Rio de Janeiro: Civilização Brasileira, 1934), pp. 20, 22, 39.

23. Fernandes, *Xangôs do Nordeste,* pp. 30–34.

24. René Ribeiro, "Novos Aspectos do Processo de Reinterpretação nos Cultos Afro-Brasileiros de Recife," *Proceedings and Selected Papers of the Thirty-first International Congress of Americanists* (Nendeln, Lichtenstein: Kraus Reprints, 1976), pp. 478–81. A description of the ceremony, signed by Ribeiro and with photographs by Pierre Verger, was published in *O Cruzeiro,* November 19, 1949, pp. 50–59.

25. Fernando Ortiz, "A Poesia Mulata," *Estudos Afro-Cubanos,* vol. 1, no. 6, p. 49, n. 64.

26. Leo Frobenius, *Die Atlantische Götterlehre* (Jena, 1926).

27. Ribeiro, "Novos Aspectos," pp. 473–77.

28. See the description by Carlos Alberto de Carvalho, *Tradições e Milagres de Bomfim* (Bahia, 1915), pp. 50ff., cited by Ramos in *O Negro Brasileiro,* pp. 153–55.

29. There is a description of this ceremony in Bastide, *Le Candomblé de Bahia (Rite Nagô)* (Paris: Mouton & Co., 1958).

30. Bastide, "Contribuição," pp. 22–23.

31. Valente, *Sincretismo,* p. 117.

32. Rodrigues, *O Animismo,* p. 176.

33. Fernando Ortiz, *Hampa Afro-Cubana: Los Negros Brujos* (Madrid: Editorial-América, 1917), p. 307.

34. Kockmeyer, "Candomblé," p. 135.

35. Ramos, *Aculturação*, pp. 253–71; Getulio Cesar, *Crendices do Nordeste* (Rio de Janeiro: Irmãos Pongetti, 1941), pp. 143–67; Eduardo Campos, *Medicina Popular: Superstições, Crendices e Meizehnas* (Rio de Janeiro: Livraria-Editôra da Sasa do Estudante do Brasil, 1955), pp. 139–81; José A. Teixeiro, *Folclore Goiano: Cançioneiro, Lendas, Superstições* (São Paulo: Cia Editora Nacional, 1941), pp. 413–19; G. Santos Neves, *Alto Está e Alto Mora*, pp. 49–57, 87–91, etc.

36. Luiz Saia, *Escultura Popular Brasileira* (São Paulo: Edições Gaveta, 1944); Oneyda Alvarenga, *Catálogo do Museu Folclórico*, pp. 202–4; Luis da Câmara Cascudo, *Dicionário do Folclore Brasileiro* (Rio de Janeiro: Ministério de Educação e Culturo, Instituto Nacional do Livro, 1954), p. 399.

37. P. Ildefonso, "Candomblé," *Santo Antonio*, 1938, p. 11.

38. Article by P. Ildefonso, ibid., 1937, pp. 64–65.

39. On the *balagandan* and the *penca* see F. Oliveira Neto, "A Penca e o Balangandan," *Dom Casmurro*, May 16, 1942, p. 8; E. Tourinho, *Alma e Corpo da Bahia* (Rio de Janeiro: J. Olympio, 1950), pp. 306ff.; Afranio Peixoto, *Breviário da Bahia* (Rio de Janeiro: Livraria Agir, Editôra, 1946), pp. 318–21. Some of the charms are controversial. What some interpret as African drums others see as the wood blocks in which blacks used to cut a notch to record payment of their monthly dues to a society for slave emancipation. On the *figa* and its origins see Leite de Vasconcellos, *A Figa* (Pôrto Alegre, 1925).

40. Mandelbaum, quoted by M. J. Herskovits in *Les Bases de l'Anthropologie Culturelle*, trans. François Vaudou (Paris: Payot, 1952), p. 249 [*Man and His Works* (New York: A. Knopf, 1947)]. Other cases could be cited, including those of the Guaycuru and Guaná Indians (see Guido Baldus, *Os Caduveo* [São Paulo: Martins, 1945], and the introduction by H. Baldus).

41. I myself was deeply struck by this phenomenon, to which Victor Vianna had already called attention in his reply to an inquiry about the feasibility of Negro immigration to Brazil as proposed by the Society for Agriculture (*Sociedade Nacional de Agricultura: Imigração*, pp. 300–301).

42. Donald Pierson, *Negroes in Brazil* (Chicago: Univ. of Chicago Press, 1942), p. xlviii.

43. The table of correspondences presented here shows the only existing equivalents for some forty *voduns* worshiped in Maranhão.

44. Nunes Pereira, *A Casa das Minas* (Rio de Janeiro: Publ. da Sociedade Brasileira de Antropologia e Etnologia, no. 1, 1947), p. 38; Octavio da Costa Eduardo, *The Negro in Northern Brazil* (Seattle: Univ. of Washington Press, 1948), pp. 53–54.

45. Tullio Seppilli, *La Acculturazione come Problèma Metodológico*, p. 14.

Chapter 13

1. Luis Amaral, *Aspectos Fundamentães da Vida Rural Brasileira* (São Paulo: E. G. "Revista dos Tribunaes," 1936), p. 87.

2. Statistics (dating from 1940) from L. A. da Costa Pinto, "A Estrutura da Sociedade Rural Brasileira," *Sociologia* 10, nos. 2–3 (1948): 156–93.

3. Oswaldo Elias Xidieh, "Elementos Mágicos no Folk Mogiano," ibid. 5, no. 2 (1943): 132.

4. Ferdinand Denis, *Le Brésil au XXᵉ Siecle* (Paris: A. Colin, 1909), pp. 262–263.

5. Antonio Candido, "L'État Actuel et les Problèmes les Plus Importants des Études sur les Sociétés Rurales du Brésil," *Proceedings and Selected Papers of the Thirty-first International Congress of Americanists* (Nendeln, Lichtenstein: Kraus Reprints, 1976), pp. 330–31.

6. C. d'Oliveira, *O Trabalhador Brasileiro* (Rio de Janeiro: Tip. da A. Balança, 1933), pp. 73–75.

7. See the chapters by Marvin Harris and Charles Wagley in *Race and Class in Rural Brazil*, ed. Charles Wagley (Paris: UNESCO, 1952), pp. 65 and 142–45.

8. Octavio da Costa Eduardo, *The Negro in Northern Brazil* (Seattle: Univ. of Washington Press, 1948), p. 58.

9. Letter from Octavio da Costa Eduardo dated June 17, 1948.

10. Costa Eduardo, *The Negro in Northern Brazil*, pp. 60–65.

11. H. W. Hutchinson in *Race and Class*, ed. Wagley, p. 42.

12. Luis da Câmara Cascudo, *Meleagro: Depoimento e Pesquisa sôbre a Magia Branca no Brasil* (Rio de Janeiro: AGIR, 1951), p. 77.

13. Information from Dr. Pidoux.

14. Ben Zimmerman in *Race and Class*, ed. Wagley, p. 92.

15. H. W. Hutchinson in ibid., p. 42.

16. Information from Octavio da Costa Eduardo after a field trip to the São Francisco region.

17. Armando Magalhães Corrêa, *O Sertão Carioca* (Rio de Janeiro: Imprensa Nacional, 1936), p. 206.

18. H. Silvestre, "Cousas de Negro," *Jornal do Commercio*, November 1935.

19. Oswaldo Elias Xidieh: "Elementos Mágicos no Folk Paulista, o Intermediario," *Sociologia* 7, nos. 1–2 (1945): 11–29; "Elementos Mágicos no Folk Mogiano," ibid. 5, no. 2 (1943): 116–33; and "Um Elemento Italo-Afro-Brásileiro no Mágica Mogiana," ibid. 6, no. 1 (1944): 5–18.

20. Unpublished material from Oswaldo Elias Xidieh.

21. Roger Bastide, "A Macoumba Paulista," in *Estudos Afro-Brasileiros*, 1st ser. (São Paulo: Editora Perspectiva, 1973), pp. 80–89.

22. Xidieh, "Elementos Mágicos no Folk Paulista," p. 16.

23. Amaral Carvalho, "A Prática da Macoumba na Região de Santo Amaro," *Folha de S. Paulo*, September 16, 1950.

24. Bastide, "A Macoumba Paulista," pp. 97–102.

25. *Statistical Yearbook*.

26. Writ of January 5, 1785, ordering the destruction of factories in Brazil (*Documentos Interessantes* [São Paulo], vol. 25).

27. Roberto C. Simonsen, *A Evolução Industrial do Brasil* (São Paulo: Emprêsa Gráfica da "Revista dos Tribunaes," 1939), pp. 18–34 [*Brazil's Industrial Evolution* (São Paulo: Escola Livre de Sociologia e Politica, 1939)].

28. L. A. da Costa Pinto, *Migrações Internas no Brasil*, pp. 4 and 12.

29. Tullio Seppilli, *La Acculturazione come Problèma Metodológico*, p. 14.

30. Arthur Ramos, *O Negro Brasileiro* (Rio de Janeiro: Civilização Brasileira, 1934), p. 113. In Angola the *kimbanda kia dihamba*, who evokes the spirits, is distinguished from the *kimbanda kia kusaa*, the healer. In Brazil the same *embanda* fulfills both functions. It should also be noted that the title of the supreme priest varies from one *macumba* to another; this may represent a last vestige of the "nations" of bygone days. I have even encountered the term *babalaô*. Since a *babalaô* is actually a diviner who uses the necklace of Ifá, this name has obviously been confused with that of the *babalorixá*. The more common expressions *pai* and *mai de santo* also are frequently used.

31. In some of the more traditional *macumbas* the *mãe pequena* is known as the *jibanan*.

32. On Rio *macumba* see Ramos, *O Negro Brasileiro*, pp. 121–73, and *A Acultuação Negra no Brasil* (São Paulo: Cia. Editora Nacional, 1942), pp. 145–57. See also Albino Gonçalves Fernandes, *O Sincretismo Religioso no Brasil* (Curitiba: Editora Guaíra, 1941), p. 95–111, and several articles in *O Cruzeiro*. For the information on the dishes hidden below the altar I am indebted to the article of Newton Freitas, "Macoumba," *Guaira*, September 1949, pp. 43–46.

33. There is an account of the initiation ritual, with supporting material drawn from European occultism, in Waldemar L. Bento, *A Magia no Brasil* (Rio de Janeiro: Oficinas Gráficas do "Jornal do Brasil," 1939), pp. 90–97. This is the first indication, chronologically, of the status-raising process that will reach its peak in Umbanda spiritism.

34. On these *vêvê* or *vevers*, see the drawings of Milo Marcelin and L. Maximilien in their books on voodoo.

35. Roger Bastide, "Os Pontos Riscados," *Estado de S. Paulo*, December 22 and 29, 1941.

36. On the location of the *macumbas*, past and present, see Ramos, *O Negro Brasileiro*, p. 134 (past), and Luiz Aguiar da Costa Pinto, *O Negro no Rio de Janeiro* (São Paulo: Cia. Editora Nacional, 1953), p. 245 (their locations in recent years, as determined by the prohibition of drum playing within city limits). Nonetheless *macumbas* still exist in the city and in the inner suburbs. See the list of 62 *terreiros* inspected by the police in *Diario da Noite*, April 1, 1941.

37. Costa Pinto, *O Negro no Rio*, pp. 244–45.

38. On the commercialization of *macumba* see Ramos, *O Negro Brasileiro*, p. 183, and Fernandes, *Sincretismo*, p. 117.

39. Fernandes, *Sincretismo*, pp. 97 and 101.

40. On the degeneration of religion into magic in the *macumba* see Ramos, *O Negro Brasileiro*, pp. 176ff. and 205ff. (Ramos lists the prices charged). See also Fernandes, *Sincretismo*, pp. 111ff.

41. Duglas Teixeira Monteiro, "A Macoumba de Vitoria," in *Proceedings and Selected Papers of the Thirty-first International Congress of Americanists*, pp. 463–72.

42. Dalmo Belfort de Mattos, "As Macoumbas de S. Paulo," *RAM de SP* 49 (1938): 151–60; Bastide, "A Macoumba Paulista," pp. 51–112.

43. Jorge Stamato, "A Influencia Negra na Religião do Brasil," *Planalto*, July 2, 1941; Paulo Pinto Machado, *Joaquim Matteus, O Feiticeiro* (São Paulo, 1930.)

44. Between 1938 and 1941 the figures for *macumbeiros* were as follows: 387 men and 172 women; 271 whites, including 156 foreigners; 73 blacks and 21 mulattoes. Those arrested as healers numbered 321; as *feiticeiros*, 137, including 26 blacks; as *macumbeiros*, 5, including 1 black; as "low spiritists," 50, including 20 blacks; overlapping categories, 46. The occupational breakdown was as follows: farm workers, 55; domestic servants, 54; artisans, 33; office workers, 17; laborers, 15; street hawkers, 6; others, 22; no occupation, 15.

45. On the connection between the *macumba* and criminality, which becomes closer as one moves from collective to individual forms, see Fernandes, *Sincretismo*, pp. 121–27, for Rio; and Bastide, "A Macoumba Paulista," pp. 97–102, for São Paulo.

46. Ramos, *O Negro Brasileiro*, pp. 221–22.

47. Julian H. Steward, *Teoría y Práctica del Estudio de Areas* (Washington, D.C.: Oficina de Ciências Sociales, Departamento de Asuntos Culturales, Unión Panamericana, 1955), p. 19 [*Area Research: Theory and Practice* (New York: Social Science Research Council, 1950)].

Chapter 14

1. S. H. Lowrie, *Imigração e Crescimento da População no Estado de S. Paulo* (São Paulo, 1938), p. 29, and "A Origem da População da Cidade de S. Paulo e Deferenciação das Clases Sociais," *RAM de SP* 48 (1938): 32.

2. H. Lobo and I. Aloisi, *O Negro na Vida Social Brasileira*, pp. 27–29; S. H. Lowrie, "O Elemento Negro na População de S. Paulo," *RAM de SP* 48 (1938).

3. Vicente Lima, *Xangô* (Recife: "Jornal do Commercio," 1937), p. 21.

4. Oracy Nogueira, "Atitude Desfavoravel de Alguns Anunciantes de S. Paulo en Relação aos Empregados de Côr," *Sociologia* 4, no. 4 (1942): 328, 358.

5. G. Mortara, "Os Empregados Domesticos no Distrito Federal," *Publications of the National Census Service*, no 296.

6. René Ribeiro, "On the Amaziado Relationship," *American Sociological Review* 1, no. 1 (1945): 14 and 49.

7. G. Mortara, *Estudos sôbre a Natalidade e a Mortalidade no Brasil*, pp. 42–43.

8. Alfredo Ellis, Jr., *Populações Paulistas* (São Paulo: Cia. Editora Nacional, 1934), pp. 90ff., and *A Evolução da Economia Paulista* (São Paulo: Cia. Editora Nacional, 1937), pp. 89–101; Sergio Milliet, *Roteiro do Café e Outros Ensaios* (São Paulo, 1939), pp. 145–60; Rubens do Amaral, "O Aniquilamento dos Negros em

NOTES TO CHAPTER 14

S. Paulo," *Planalto,* November 1, 1941. See also Souza Soares and Ferrera Faris, "Tuberculose e Raça," *Rev. Paulista de Fisiologia* 11, no. 3 (May–June 1943) (tuberculosis mortality rate: 26.6–70.5 percent for blacks as against 18.7–39.9 percent for whites, owing to differences between sanatoriums), and Alvaro de Faria, "O Problema do Tuberculose no Preto e no Branco," in *Estudos Afro-Brasileiros* (Rio de Janeiro, 1935), pp. 215–25.

9. Franco da Rocha, "Contribution à l'Étude de la Folie dans la Race Noire," *Rev. Med. de S.P.* 14 (1904), for São Paulo; Romeu de Mello, "Pertabações Mentais dos Negros do Brasil do Dr. Roxo," ibid., for Rio de Janeiro; U. Pernambucano, "As Doenças Mentais entre os Negros de Pernambuco," in *Estudos Afro-Brasileiros,* pp. 93–98.

10. G. Mortara, "Alguns Dados sôbre a Alfabetisação da População do Brasil," *Publications of the National Census Service,* no. 357, pp. 5–9.

11. Luiz Aguiar da Costa Pinto, *O Negro no Rio de Janeiro* (São Paulo: Cia. Editora Nacional, 1953), p. 149.

12. Roger Bastide, "A Imprensa de Côr no Estado de São Paulo," in *Estudos Afro-Brasileiros,* 2d ser., pp. 50ff. [probably "A Imprensa Negra do Estado de São Paulo," in *Estudos Afro-Brasileiros* (São Paulo: Editora Perspectiva, 1973), pp. 129–56]; Roger Bastide and Florestan Fernandes, *Relações Raciais entre Negros e Brancos em São Paulo* (São Paulo: Editôra Anhembi, 1955), pp. 159ff.

13. *Getulino* 2: 59; *Voz da Raça* 1: 33.

14. *Clarim* 1: 1; *Voz da Raça* 1: 4, 15, 27, 31, etc.

15. *Voz da Raça* 3: 64.

16. Ibid. 1: 6.

17. *Senzala* 1, no. 2: 21.

18. *Voz da Raça* 3: 52.

19. Ibid. 2: 36-II, 44-III, 56-I, 31-II, 44-I, 15, etc.

20. Ibid. 3: 52.

21. P. Duarte, "Negros do Brasil," *Estado de S. Paulo,* April 16 and 17, 1943.

22. *Voz da Raça* 1: 33.

23. Ibid. 1: 27 and 3: 46-II, 34-I, 22; *Progresso* 4: 37; *Kosmos* 1: 22, etc.

24. *Voz da Raça* 1: 22, 29, 30; 2: 35, 46.

25. On this problem, tendencies in the urbanized Negro, see V. Leone Bicudo, "Atitudes Raciais de Pretos et Mulatos em S. Paulo," *Sociologia* 9, no. 3 (1947): 195–219.

26. *Alfinete* 1: 2; *Getulino* 1: 45; *Voz da Raça* 3: 60.

27. Gilberto Freyre, *The Masters and the Slaves,* trans. Samuel Putnam (New York: A. Knopf, 1966), p. 316, n. 105.

28. P. Cavalcanti, *Arquivos da Assistencia a Psicopatas de Pernambuco* 3, no. 1 (1953): 59ff.; Albino Gonçalves Fernandes, *O Sincretismo Religioso no Brasil* (Cruiitiba: Editora Guaíra, 1941), pp. 57–77.

29. Leandro Gomes de Barros, *Bento, o Milagroso de Beberibe,* cited by Fernandes in *Sincretismo,* p. 41. See also the little work in verse by Francisco das Chagas, *Os Milagres de Bento de Beberibe e o Enterro da Medicina* (Paraíba do Norte, 1913).

30. Fernandes cites these bylaws in *Sincretismo,* pp. 68–76.

31. Ibid., p. 63.

32. Cl. Camarão, "O Panteismo dos Negros do Recife," *Seiva* 2, no. 7 (1940).

33. See L. Ribeiro and Murillo de Campos, *O Espiritismo no Brasil* (São Paulo: Cia. Editora Nacional, 1931), on spiritism in general. On its origins in Brasil see João do Rio, *As Religiõs no Rio* (Rio de Janeiro: Editora Nova Aguilar, 1976), chap. 21.

34. *Anuario Estatístico do Brasil* 8 (1947): 49.

35. V. Torres, *Ensaio de Sociologia Rural Brasileira,* pp. 69–70.

36. Roger Bastide, "Religion and the Church," in *Brazil: Portrait of Half a Continent,* ed. T. Lynn Smith and Alexander Marchant (New York: Dryden Press, 1951), pp. 353–54.

37. Roger Bastide, "Structures Sociales et Religions Afro-Brésiliennes," *Renaissance* 2, no. 3 (1945): 20–21.

38. S. Romero, *História da Literatura Brasileira* (Rio de Janeiro: H. Garnier, 1902–1903), vol. 3.

39. L. Motta, *Violeiros do Norte* (São Paulo: Cia. Gráfica–Editora Monteiro Lobato, 1925), p. 92. See also Gustavo Barroso, *Terra do Sol: Naturezas e Costumes do Norte* (Rio de Janeiro: F. Alves, 1930); Arthur Ramos, *O Folclore Negro do Brasil* (Rio de Janeiro: Civilização Brasileira, 1935), pp. 267–71; Roger Bastide, *Psicanálise do Cafuné e Estudos de Sociologia Estética Brasileira* (Curitiba: Editora Guaíra, 1941), pp. 34–35.

40. John Dollard, *Caste and Class in a Southern Town* (New Haven: Yale Univ. Press, 1937); Hortense Powdermaker, *After Freedom: A Cultural Study in the Deep South* (New York: Viking Press, 1939), p. 3; Charles S. Johnson, *Patterns of Negro Segregation* (New York: Harper & Bros., 1943), chap. 10, etc.

41. Richard Wright, for example, in his novel *Native Son* (New York: Harper & Bros., 1940).

42. Cited by João de Freitas in *Umbanda em Revista*, pp. 41–42 [perhaps *Umbanda: Reportagens, Entrevistas, Commentarios, Rituais, etc.* (Rio de Janeiro: Edições Cultura Afro-Aborigene, 1941)].

43. Lourenço Braga, *Umbanda e Quimbanda* (Rio de Janeiro: Livraria Jacintho, 1942), pp. 54–55.

44. Reply to a survey by *Radical*, cited by Alfredo d'Alcantara in *Umbanda em Julgamento* (Rio de Janeiro: Edições "Mundo Espirita," 1949).

45. Cf. Oliveira Magno, *Ritual Prático de Umbanda*, p. 11 [perhaps *Práticas de Umbanda* (Rio de Janeiro: Editôra Espiritualista, 1969)].

46. The papers presented at this congress were published in 1942 in *Primeiro Congresso Brasileiro de Espiritismo de Umbanda*, commemorating the emergence or founding of a "Spiritist Federation of Umbanda," as distinct from the "Kardecite Spiritist Federation." Later Emmanuel Zespo tried to unite the two, but the Kardecites persistently refused: see Emmanuel Zespo, *O Que É a Umbanda?; Saravá! Agô!* (Rio de Janeiro: Borsol, 1953).

47. Leal de Souza, "Espiritismo: Magia e as Sete Linhas de Umbanda," in *Mundo Espirita* (1925), etc.; Freitas, *Umbanda*; E. Morel, "Eu Fui Girar na Linha de Umbanda," *O Cruzeiro*, April 29, 1944.

48. Samuel Ponze, *Lições de Umbanda*, pp. 20 and 23; Zespo, *O Que É a Umbanda?*, p. 63; Aluizio Fontenelle, *Exú* (Rio de Janeiro: Editôra Espiritualista, 1966), p. 60.

49. Byron Tôrres de Freitas and Tancredo da Silva Pinto, *Doutrina e Ritual de Umbanda* (Rio de Janeiro: Editôra Espiritualista, 1970), p. 152.

50. Byron Tôrres de Freitas and Tancredo da Silva Pinto, *As Mirongas de Umbanda* (Rio de Janeiro: Gráfica Editora Aurora), pp. 77–79.

51. Ponze, *Lições*, p. 24.

52. Arthur Ramos, *Introdução a Antropologia Brasileira* (Rio de Janeiro, 1951), 1: 471.

53. Reply to the survey conducted by *Radical*, cited by Alcantara in *Umbanda*, p. 161; Ponze, *Lições*, p. 9.

54. Valdemar L. Bento, *A Magia no Brasil* (Rio de Janeiro: Oficinas Gráficas do "Jornal do Brasil," 1939), p. 111.

55. Paper by Dr. Baptista de Oliveira in *Primeiro Congresso Brasileiro de Espiritismo de Umbanda* (1942), pp. 114–17.

56. Paper by A. Fl. Nogueira, ibid., pp. 257–58.

57. Paper by M. D. Coelho Fernandes, ibid., pp. 21–23. Silvio Perreiro Maciel divides the word *Umbanda* into three words: *Um* = the Father; *Ban* = the Son; and *Da* = the Holy Spirit.

58. Reply to the survey conducted by *Radical*, cited by Alcantara in *Umbanda*, pp. 167–68.

59. Alcantara, *Umbanda*, p. 126.

60. The Yoruba god of the hunt, Oxóssi.

61. Corruption of Yansan, the wife of Shangô.

62. Alcantara, *Umbanda*, pp. 162–63.

63. Braga, *Umbanda*, pp. 15–23.

64. Freitas, *Umbanda*, p. 120.

65. Bento, *A Magia*, p. 15.

66. Ibid., p. 106.
67. Zespo, *O Que É a Umbanda?* pp. 33–34.
68. Annie W. Besant, *The Ancient Wisdom* (orig. pub. 1897; London: Theosophical Publishing Society, 1904).
69. Zespo, *O Que É a Umbanda?* p. 41.
70. On this spiritism see H. Roxo, *Filhos da Estrela d'Alva; Livro dos Mediums de Umbanda; Missionarios;* and *O Que Se Aprende em Estrela d'Alva.* My account is based largely on the last work.
71. Magno, *Ritual Prático,* pp. 15–16 and 38–39; Aluizio Fontenelle, *O Espiritismo no Conceito das Religões e a Lei de Umbanda* (Rio de Janeiro: Gráfica Editora Aurora, 195–), p. 63.
72. Freitas and Silva Pinto, *Doutrina,* pp. 97, 104, 108–10, 115–16.
73. Fontenelle, *Exú,* pp. 61–89. Ponze (*Lições,* p. 12) takes a different point of view but follows the same line.
74. Fontenelle, *Exú,* p. 124.
75. Paper by M. Josué Mendes in *Primeiro Congresso Brasileiro de Espiritismo de Umbanda,* pp. 246–49.
76. Ibid., pp. 249–52.
77. Fl. Maria de Souza Franco, [title not given], pp. 17 and 25.
78. Heraldo Meneses, *Iára, a Deusa do Mar: Iniciação, Magia, Ritual, Ponto, Fétiches* (Rio de Janeiro, 1946).
79. Heraldo Meneses, *Aimoré, o Deus da Caça: Iniciação, Magia, Ritual, Ponto, Fétiches* (Rio de Janeiro, 1946).
80. O. Nabeji, *Xangô.*
81. Heraldo Meneses, *Urbatão, Deus da Guerra: Iniciação, Magia, Ritual, Ponto, Fétiches, Magia* (Rio de Janeiro, 1946).
82. Edison Carneiro, "Xangô," in Gilberto Freyre et al., *Novos Estudos Afro-Brasileiros* (Rio de Janeiro: Biblioteca de Divulgação Scientifica, IX, Civilização Brasileira, 1937), p. 139n.
83. Fontenelle, *Exú,* pp. 123–26.
84. Fontenelle, *Espiritismo,* p. 73. In other tents Omolú appears in the line of both the Souls (Umbanda) and the Exús (Quimbanda), but in the former case under the command of Saint Michael and in the latter, of Exú (Oliveiro Magno, *Umbanda e Ocultismo* (Rio de Janeiro: Gráfica Editora Aurora, 1952), pp. 22–24.
85. Fontenelle, *Espiritismo,* p. 73.
86. Benedicto Ramos da Silva, *Ritual de Umbanda* (Rio de Janeiro, 1948), p. 37.
87. Fl. Maria de Souza Franco, [title not given], p. 32.
88. Ramos da Silva, *Ritual,* p. 38; Fontenelle, *Espiritismo,* p. 94.
89. Oliveiro Magno, *A Umbanda Esotérica e Iniciática* (Rio de Janeiro: Editora Espiritualista, 1962), pp. 30–48.
90. Magno, *Umbanda e Ocultismo,* pp. 25, 29, 34. For H. Roxo's theory on the various planes see note 70 above.
91. Magno, *Umbanda e Ocultismo,* p. 24.
92. Fontenelle, *Espiritismo,* p. 81; see also p. 96. Fontenelle even offers a precise formulation of the phenomenon when he says that while Umbanda does accept the theogony and liturgy of the Negroes, it does so "in an attempt to incorporate them and elevate them to the level of contemporary civilization without adulterating the basic principles on which they rest."
93. Deolindo Amorim, *Africanismo e Espiritismo,* trans. Cristoforo Postiglione (Buenos Aires: Editorial Constancia, 1958), pp. 73–74.
94. Ramos da Silva, *Ritual,* p. 109.
95. Braga, *Umbanda,* pp. 36–39.
96. Lourenço Braga, *Trabalhos de Umbanda: Ou Magia Prática* (Rio de Janeiro: Editora Moderna, 1946), pp. 21–22.
97. Ibid., pp. 32–40 and 45–59.
98. Fl. Maria de Souza Franco, [title not given], pp. 25, 11, 38–39, 16, 109.
99. My own experience of Umbanda suggests that the percentage of colored men may range from 20 to 99, depending on the tent and the day of the week.

100. Leal de Souza, *Espiritismo*, p. 73.

101. I have not studied the spiritism of Christ the Redeemer, which Kardecism also opposes, because according to my informants it is more significant outside Brazil—in the Cape Verde Islands, for instance—than in Rio, where it originated.

102. Alcantara, *Umbanda*, pp. 15, 173, 194.

103. Fl. Maria de Souza Franco, [title not given], p. 37.

104. Ibid., pp. 40–41.

105. Braga, *Trabalhos*, p. 37.

106. Braga, *Umbanda*, p. 31; see also Emmanuel Zespo's preface to *Pontos Cantados e Pontos Riscados da Umbanda* (Rio de Janeiro, 1951). An Umbandist explanation of some of these drawings will be found in Osorio Cruz, *O Esoterismo de Umbanda*, pp. 21–22.

107. Zespo, *O Que É a Umbanda?* p. 61.

108. Ibid., p. 61; Braga, *Trabalhos*, p. 41.

109. Braga, *Trabalhos*, pp. 42, 77–79; Zespo, *O Que É a Umbanda?* p. 62; Braga, *Umbanda*, pp. 30–31.

110. Braga, *Trabalhos*, p. 43, and *Umbanda*, p. 31.

111. Braga, *Trabalhos*, p. 80.

112. On these purifying fluidic baths and their connection with the African *orixás* see Emmanuel Zespo, *Banhos de Descarga*, p. 24.

113. Zespo, *Banhos*, pp. 64–65.

114. *Primeiro Congresso Brasileiro de Espiritismo de Umbanda*, pp. 88–89.

115. Braga, *Umbanda*, pp. 54–55.

116. Fl. Maria de Souza Franco, [title not given], pp. 15 and 64.

117. Ibid., p. 56.

118. Ibid., pp. 55–57, 65–66.

119. Ibid., p. 43.

120. [Author not given], *O Culto de Umbanda*, pp. 22–23.

121. *Primeiro Congresso Brasileiro de Espiritismo de Umbanda*, pp. 118–20; S. Pereira Maciel, *Alquimia*, p. 55.

122. Jacy Rego Barros, *Senzala e Macumba* (Rio de Janeiro: "Jornal do Commercio," Rodrigues & Cia., 1939), pp. 78–79, 128.

123. Max Weber, *Gesammelte Aufsätze zur Religionssoziologie* (Tübingen: Mohr, 1922–1923), 2: 142–43.

124. Braga, *Umbanda*, p. 7.

125. H. Roxo, *Livro dos Mediums*, p. 19.

126. Fl. Maria de Souza Franco, [title not given], p. 47.

127. Arthur Ramos, *O Negro Brasileiro* (Rio de Janeiro: Civilização Brasileira, 1934), pp. 168, 175–76.

128. Fontenelle, *Espiritismo*, p. 75.

129. Erich Fromm, *The Fear of Freedom* (London: K. Paul, Trench, Trubner & Co., 1942).

130. See particularly the articles of Americo Albuquerque, "Como Compreendo a Religião Negra," and Luiz Bastos, "Para onde Vae a Afrologia?" in *Seiva* April 1, 1939.

131. When a friend of Fontenelle remarked that Umbanda was a "garbage can," Fontenelle replied that while it is true that it takes in all the riffraff of humanity, all the victims of society, all the unfortunate, it does so in order to save them from "moral putrefaction" and to restore their sense of dignity.

Chapter 15

1. M. J. Herskovits, *The Myth of the Negro Past* (New York: Harper & Bros., 1941), chap. 7.

2. Raoul Allier, *La Psychologie de la Conversion chez les Peuples Non-Civilisés* (Paris: Payot, 1925), vol. 1, pt. 2, chaps. 5–7, and vol. 2, chaps. 2–3.

3. See, for example, John Dollard, *Caste and Class in a Southern Town* (New Haven: Yale Univ. Press, 1937), chap. 11.

4. A. Metraux, "Vodou et Protestantisme," *Revue d'Histoire des Religions* 144 (1953): 198–216.

5. Fernando de Azevedo, *A Cultura Brasileira* (Rio de Janeiro: Serviço Gráfico do Instituto Brasileiro de Geografia e Estatística, 1943), pp. 146–47 [*Brazilian Culture*, trans. William Rex Crawford (New York: Macmillan Co., 1950)]; Roger Bastide, "Religion and the Church," in *Brazil: Portrait of Half a Continent*, ed. T. Lynn Smith and Alexander Marchant (New York: Dryden Press, 1951), pp. 340–41.

6. Azevedo, *Cultura*, pp. 167–68; Bastide, "Religion and the Church," p. 343.

7. A. Maynard Araujo, *Ciclo Agricola, Calendário Religioso e Magias Ligadas à Plantação* (São Paulo: Departamento de Educação e Cultura, 1957).

8. Antonio Candido, "Opiniões e Clases Sociais em Tieté," *Sociologia* 9, no. 2 (1947): 109–10; L. Hermann, *Guaratinguetá*, p. 174.

9. Mario W. V. de Cunha, "A Festa de Bom Jesus de Pirapora," *RAM de SP* 41 (1937): 5–36.

10. João Dornas Filho, *A Influência Social do Negro Brasileiro* (Curitiba: Editora Guaíra, 1943), pp. 19–40.

11. Emilio Willems, *Cunha: Tradição e Transição em uma Cultura Rural do Brasil* (São Paulo: Secretaria da Agricultura do Estado de São Paulo, Directoria de Publicidada Agrícola, 1947), p. 155.

12. Ascenso Ferreira, "O Maracatú," *Arc. de Recife* 1, no. 2: 156–59; Bastide, *Imagens*, pp. 176–78, and "O Carnaval de Recife," *Rev. no Brasil*, n.s., April 1, 1944, pp. 50–51; Mario de Andrade, "A Calunga dos Maracatús," in *Estudos Afro-Brasileiros* (Rio de Janeiro, 1935), pp. 39–48.

13. In Minas the two were opposed in a sort of religious rivalry. The Mozambique say that the statue of Our Lady of the Rosary once appeared on the ocean and the people gathered to take it back to the church. The priest (white) asked her to come back, but she refused. The Congo came and sang and danced to attract her, but to no avail. The Mozambique came and beat their drums and sang. Then Our Lady of the Rosary smiled and accompanied them back to the church, where she has remained to this day (Dornas Filho, *Influência*, p. 25).

14. Willems, *Cunha*, pp. 65, 151.

15. See particularly P. Kapistran, "Warum Ist das Gebiet des Amazonas So Menschenleer?" *Santo Antonio* 16: 90–108; Fr. L.[?], "Zum Priesterproblem in Brasilien," *ibid.*, 1933, p. 20; and E. G. Léonard, "O Protestantismo Brasileiro," *Revista de História* 2, no. 5 (1951): 118–24.

16. C. d'Oliveira, *O Trabalhador Brasileiro* (Rio de Janeiro: Tip. da A. Balança, 1933), pp. 73–75. Discussing a stratified rural society, Thomas Davatz makes an analogous observation: the Negroes are strongly attached to a few of the dogmas of Catholicism and have a religion as shoddy as that of their white masters (*Memorias de um Colono no Brasil* [see *Die Behandlungen der Kolonisten in der Provinz St. Paulo in Brasilien* (Chur: Druck von L. Hitz, 1858)]).

17. Article in the Recife *Diario da Tarde* cited by Gonçalves Fernandes in *Xangôs do Nordeste* (Rio de Janeiro: Civilização Brasileira, 1937), pp. 131–32.

18. Arthur Ramos, *A Aculturação Negra no Brasil* (São Paulo: Cia. Editora Nacional, 1942), p. 273.

19. Cecilia Meirelles, "Festa de S. Cosme no Arraial" (paper presented at the First National Folklore Congress).

20. Ramos, *Aculturação*, pp. 237–76.

21. Gilberto Freyre, *The Masters and the Slaves*, trans. Samuel Putnam (New York: A. Knopf, 1966), p. 334 and n. 162.

22. L. A. Gaffre, *Visions du Brésil* (Rio de Janeiro: F. Alves & Cia., 1912), p. 252.

23. Manoel Bergström Lourenço, *O Joazeiro do Padre Cicero* (São Paulo: Cia. Melhoramentos de São Paulo [Weiszflog Irmãos], 193–). On the curé of Poa see "A Vida Intima do Padre Antonio," *O Cruzeiro*, October 18, 1947, pp. 16ff.

24. On the reincarnations of Father Cicero and the continuation of his movement after his death see José Lucena, "Uma Pequena Epidemia Mental em Pernambuco,"

Neurobiologia 3, no. 1 (1940): 41–91, and Francisco de Barros, Jr., *Caçando e Pescando por Todo o Brasil*, 3d ser. (São Paulo: Cia. Melhoramentos de São Paulo, 1947), pp. 188–93. [For a general account of the movement see Ralph Della Cava, *Miracle at Joaseiro* (New York: Columbia Univ. Press, 1970).]

25. Willems, *Cunha*, p. 64.

26. Arthur Ramos, *O Folclore Negro do Brasil* (Rio de Janeiro: Civilzação Brasileira, 1935), pp. 112–13; A. Amaral, "Reisado, Bumba-Meu-Boi e Pastoris," *RAM de SP* 64 (1940): 293; Leonardo Motta, *Violeiros do Norte: Poesia e Linguagem do Sertão Nordestino* (São Paulo: Cia. Gráfico-Editora Monteiro Lobato, 1925), pp. 151ff.

27. *A Santa de Coqueiros* (Rio de Janeiro, 1931), a collection of pieces by devotees of the saint; G. Ribeiro, "Investigação sôbre o Culto de Santo Antonio," *Sociologia* 3, no. 1 (1941): 20–28; and an anonymous article, "A Formação da Santidade: Investigação sôbre o Caso de Antoninho da Rocha Marmo," *Sociologia* 2, no. 3 (1940): 278–92.

28. O. Elias Xidieh, "O Intermediaro," *Sociologia* 7, nos. 1–2 (1945): 11; Florestan Fernandes, "Aspectos Mágicos de Folclore Paulistano," ibid. 6, no. 2 (1944): 85–88; and Willems, *Cunha*, p. 104; Galvão de Franca, "Benzimentos," *Filosofia, Ciências e Letras* 7 (1940): 74–81.

29. Ferdinand Denis, *Brésil* (Paris: Firmin Didot Frères, 1837), p. 257; Roger Bastide, "Estudos Afro-Brasileiros: O Lundum do Padre," *RAM de SP* 98 (1944): 101–3.

30. Information from an unpublished study by Mr. Galvão, a student of mine.

31. Getulio Cesar, *Crendices de Nordeste* (Rio de Janeiro: Irmãos Pongetti, 1941), pp. 117–25; G. Brandão, *Notas sôbre a Dança de S. Gonçalves de Amarante* (São Paulo, 1953); Marciano dos Santos, "A Dança de S. Gonçalo," *RAM de SP* 33 (1936): 85–116.

32. J. Nascimento de Almeida Prado, "Trabalhos Fúnebres na Roça," in *RAM de SP* 115 (1947): 72–80; O. Elias Xidieh, "Semana Santa Cabocla," *Estado de S. Paulo,* December and January 1948; A. Maynard Araujo, "Recomendação das Almas," *Correio Paulistano,* April 30, 1950, etc.

33. Gaffre, *Visions,* pp. 252ff.; Marciano dos Santos, "A Dança," pp. 98–101.

34. O. Alvarenga, *Música Popular Brasileira* (São Paulo: Editora Globo, 1950), pp. 112–72; Marciano dos Santos, "A Dança," pp. 85ff.; A. Maynard Araujo, "Dança de Santa Cruz," *Correio Paulistano,* February 12, 19, and 26, 1950; Aluiso de Almeida, "Dança de S. Gonçalo," *Estado,* October 26, 1947.

35. Almeida Prado, "Trabalhos," for São Paulo; Fernandes, *Xangôs do Nordeste,* chap. 5, for the northeast.

36. Octavio da Costa Eduardo, *The Negro in Northern Brazil* (Seattle: Univ. of Washington Press, 1948), pp. 117–18.

37. Gaffre, *Visions,* pp. 252ff.

38. Roger Bastide, "Sociologie du Folklore Brésilien," *Revue de Psychologie des Peuples* 5, no. 9 (1950): 377–412.

39. O. Elias Xidieh, "A Promessa," *Estado,* January 19, 1949; Pires de Almeida, "A Festa do Divino," *RAM de SP* 59 (1939): 39–62; Roger Bastide, "O Folclore Brasileiro e a Geografia," *Bol. Paulista de Geografia* 8 (1951): 19–34.

40. Dalcidio Jurandir, *Marajó* (Rio de Janeiro: J. Olympio, 1947).

41. A. Maynard Araujo, *Cururú* (São Paulo: Publicações do Instituto de Administração, no. 18, 1948). On the urbanization of the *cururú* see Chiarini, "Cururú," *RAM de SP* 115 (1947): 81–198, (including a critique of the miracles of the saints, pp. 154–55). On the sociological history of this contest see Roger Bastide, "O Cururú: Expressão da Alma Paulista," *Estado do S. Paulo,* July 5, 1951.

42. Max Weber, *Gesammelte Aufsätze zur Religionssoziologie* (Tübingen: Mohr, 1922–1923), vol. 3.

43. For a résumé of Indian messianism and of works on the subject see R. H. Lowie, *Primitive Religion* (New York: Liveright, 1948). For an exposé of the American approach see H. Kohn, "Messianism," *Encyclopedia of the Social Sciences* 10, and B. Barber, "Acculturation and Messianic Movements," *American Sociological Review* 6 (1941): 664ff.

44. G. Eckert, "Prophetentum in Melanesien," *Zeitschrift für Ethnographie* 69 (1937): 135–40; E. F. Hanneman, "Le Culte du Cargo en Nouvelle-Guinée," *Le Monde Non-Chrétien* 8 (1948): 937–62; H. Rusillon, *Un Culte Dynastique avec Evocation des Morts chez les Sakalaves de Madagascar: Le Tromba* (Paris, 1922); Katesa Schlosser, *Propheten in Afrika* (Brunswick: A. Limbach, 1949); etc.

45. Abram Kardiner, *The Individual and His Society* (New York: Columbia Univ. Press, 1939), pp. 270, 301–3.

46. G. Balandier, "Messianismes et Nationalismes en Afrique Noire," *Cahiers Internationaux de Sociologie* 14 (1953): 41–65.

47. W. O. E. Oesterley, *The Evolution of the Messianic Idea* (London: Sir I. Pitman & Sons, 1908).

48. M. I. Pereira de Queiroz, "Un Mouvement Messianique dans le Sud du Brésil," *Fac. Filos. S. Paulo.*

49. C. Ninuendaju Unkel, "Die Sagen von der Erschaffung und Vernichtung der Welt als Grundlagen der Religion der Apapacua-Guarani," *Zeitschrift für Ethnologie* 46 (1914): 284–403; A. Metraux, *La Religion des Tupinamba et Ses Rapports avec Celles des Autres Tribus Tupi-Guarani* (Paris: E. Leroux, 1928); E. Schaden, *Ensaio Etno-Sociológico sôbre a Mitologia Heróica de Algumas Tribos Indigenos do Brasil* (São Paulo: Boletim da Fac. de Filosofia, Ciências e Letras, LXI, 1946), pp. 156–57.

50. On Sebastianism in Brazil see G. Barroso, *Almas de Lama e de Aco* (São Paulo, 1930); Johann B. von Spix and Carl F. P. von Martius, *Viagem pelo Brazil* (Rio de Janeiro: Imprensa Nacional, 1938), 2: 168ff.; and Denis, *Brésil*, pp. 130ff.

51. On the Canudos episode see Nina Rodrigues, *As Colectividades Anormais*, pp. 50–57, a primarily psychiatric interpretation; and Euclides da Cunha, *Os Sertões* (Rio de Janeiro: F. Alves & Cia., 1902) [*Rebellion in the Backlands*, trans. Samuel Putnam (Chicago: Univ. of Chicago Press, 1944)], a social and geographic interpretation in the manner of Taine. Abelardo F. Montenegro, *Antonio Conselheiro* (Fortaleza, 1954), shows the influence of collective representations of Catholic origin. On the Contestado episode see M. I. Pereira de Queiroz, "Un Mouvement Messianique," and Oswaldo R. Cabral, *Santa Catarina* (São Paulo: Cia. Editora Nacional, 1937), pp. 377–426.

52. W. Dowson, *Le Nègre aux États-Unis*, pp. 205ff.; Theodore Schraeder, "A Living God Incarnate," *Psychoanalytic Review* 19 (1922): 36ff.; E. Dianne Benyon, "The Voodoo Cult among Negro Migrants in Detroit," *American Journal of Sociology* 43 (1938): 894–907.

53. Roi Ottley, *New World A-Coming: Inside Black America* (Boston: Houghton Mifflin & Co., 1943), chap. 8; Hadly Cantril, *The Psychology of Social Movements* (Huntington, N.Y.: R. E. Krieger, 1941), chap. 5.

54. Martha W. Beckwith, *Black Roadways: A Study of Jamaican Folk Life* (Chapel Hill: Univ. of North Carolina Press), chap. 10.

55. On *Beato* Antonio and his role in the Canudos drama see Cunha, *Rebellion*, pp. 159 and 468–71. On other Negroes involved in the movement see ibid., pp. 156–58 and 440–41.

56. Lourenço Filho, *O Joazeiro*, chap. 8. For the end of the story of Lourenço see Barros, Jr., *Caçando*, pp. 188–93.

57. Nina Rodrigues, *As Colectividades*, pp. 113–14.

58. Martin de Oliveira, *Sangue Morte* (Rio de Janeiro, 1934), pp. 106–12.

59. Generio Machado, *João de Camargo e Seus Milagres* (São Paulo: 1928); Antonio Francisco Gaspar, *O Mistério da Agua Vermelha* (Sorocaba, 1941). For one interpretation see Floristan Fernandes, "Contribuição para o Estudo de um Lider Carismatico," *RAM de SP* 138 (1951): 19–34.

60. See Roger Bastide, "Le Messianisme chez les Noirs du Brésil," *Le Monde Non-Chrétien* 15 (1950): 301–8, for a survey of the problem.

61. Newbell Niles Puckett, *Folk Beliefs of the Southern Negro* (Chapel Hill: Univ. of North Carolina Press, 1926), chap. 8; Hortense Powdermaker, *After Freedom: A Cultural Study in the Deep South* (New York: Viking Press, 1939), chap. 4; M. J. Herskovits, *The Myth of the Negro Past* (New York: Harper & Bros., 1941), chap. 7. For the other view see E. Franklin Frazier, *The Negro in the United States* (New

York: Macmillan Co., 1949), chap. 16, and E. N. Palmer, "The Religious Acculturation of the Negro," *Phylon* 5, no. 3 (1944): 260–65.

62. Nevertheless Powdermaker states that in these white revivals trance is an individual phenomenon and most of the members of the congregation are merely spectators, while in black churches it is collective and organized.

63. E. G. Léonard, "L'Eglise Presbytérienne au Brésil et Ses Expériences Ecclésias-
tiques," *Études Évangéliques* 9, no. 1 (1949): 12–14.

64. Ibid., p. 14. Furthermore the propaganda of certain sects was especially appealing to the blacks because the North American missionaries were Negroes themselves.
Darbyism, for instance, was propagated by a Jamaican Negro (Léonard, "Protestantismo," p. 331).

65. Roger Bastide and Florestan Fernandes, *Relações Raciais entre Negros e
Brancos em São Paulo* (São Paulo: Editôra Anhembi, 1955).

66. See the journal of José da Silva Oliveira, *Cruzada Cultural e Social* (São Paulo),
from 1950 on.

67. O. Elias Xidieh, "Suburbio," *RAM de SP* 114 (1947): 181.

68. See, for example, John L. Dollard, *Caste and Class in a Southern Town* (New
Haven: Yale Univ. Press, 1937), chap. 11.

69. Alvares da Silva, "Por Quem os Sinos Dobram," *Cruzeiro*, June 10, 1950, and
accounts in the São Paulo *Diario da Noite*, May 16 and 19, 1950. We may add that
the behavior of incompletely evangelized *caboclos* not under the control of their
pastor is absolutely identical to that of blacks. Cf. Carlo Castaldi, "O Demonio no
Catulé," *Anhembi* 65 (April 1956): 250–68.

70. My study of the Christian Congregation of Brazil is based on its statutes, annual
reports, and tracts and on a series of interviews with Negroes and monographs on
temples undertaken by my students in 1948. See also Léonard, "Protestantismo."

71. Charles Wagley, ed., *Race and Class in Rural Brazil* (Paris: UNESCO, 1953),
p. 149 (author's italics).

72. Ibid., p. 154.

73. Eunice T. Ribeiro, "O Diablo no Catulé," *Anhembi* 64 (March 1956): 37.

Chapter 16

1. Georges Balandier, *Sociologie Actuelle de l'Afrique Noire: Dynamique des
Changements Sociaux en Afrique Centrale* (Paris: Presses Universitaires de France,
1955), pp. 271–75 [*The Sociology of Black Africa: Social Dynamics in Central Africa*,
trans. Douglas Garman (New York: Praeger, 1970)].

2. René Ribeiro, "O Teste de Rorschach no Estudo da 'Aculturação' e da 'Posses-
são' dos Negros do Brasil," *Boletim do Instituo J. Nabuco* 1: 44–50.

3. Donald Pierson, *Negroes in Brazil* (Chicago: Univ. of Chicago Press, 1942), pp.
263–70.

4. Only one of these studies has been published so far, an autobiography in *Estudos
Afro-Brasileiros*, 1st ser. (Rio de Janeiro, 1935), pp. 78–80.

5. René Ribeiro, *Cultos Afro-Brasileiros do Recife: Um Estudo de Adjustamento
Social* (Recife: Boletim do Instituto Joaquim Nabuco de Pesquisa Social, 1952), p.
125.

6. Many examples will be found in the transcriptions of mediums' trances in Leal
de Souza's *No Mundo dos Espiritos*.

7. Talcott Parsons, *The Social System* (Glencoe, Ill.: The Free Press, 1951), p. 487.

8. Georges Gurvitch, *La Vocation Actuelle de la Sociologie* (Paris: Presses Universitaires de France, 1950), p. 174.

9. A. Irving Hallowell, "Ojibwa Personality and Acculturation," in *Acculturation in
the Americas: Proceedings and Selected Papers of the Twenty-ninth International Congress of Americanists*, ed. Sol Tax (New York: Cooper Square Publishers, 1952), pp.
105–12.

10. Balandier, *Sociologie Actuelle*, pp. 428–29.

11. Meyer Fortes, "Kinship and Marriage among the Ashanti," in *African Systems*

of Kinship and Marriage, ed. A. R. Radcliffe-Brown and Daryll Forde (London: International African Institute, Oxford Univ. Press, 1950), p. 258.

12. J. B. Christensen, *Double Descent among the Fanti* (New Haven: Human Relations Area File Press, 1954), pp. 74–75.

13. S. F. Nadel, "Dual Descent in the Nuba Hills," in *African Systems of Kinship and Marriage*, ed. Radcliffe-Brown and Forde, p. 345.

14. Manoel R. Querino, *Costumes Africanos no Brasil* (Rio de Janeiro: Civilização Brasileira, 1938), pp. 83–84; Arthur Ramos, *O Negro Brasileiro* (Rio de Janeiro: Civilização Brasileira, 1934), p. 209.

15. Karl Mannheim, *Ideology and Utopia: An Introduction to the Sociology of Knowledge* (New York: Harcourt, Brace & Co., 1936), p. 252.

Glossary

abada. Drum used in the Babassuê African sect in Belem (Para).

Abaluayé or *Obaluayé*. Yoruba god of smallpox (as a young god).

abará. Fritter of black bean flour, chopped shrimp, and pimento fried in palm oil and served rolled in a banana leaf.

Abe. Dahoman goddess (Agbê in Africa), daughter of Sogbo, one of the names of Mawu, the supreme deity.

abêbê. Fan.

abian. Novice; girl whose initiation has not yet begun.

aboshe. Yoruba family priest.

acarajé. Fritters of bean flour, salt, onions, and dried shrimp fried in palm oil.

aché. Mystic forces which may inhabit certain objects. For this reason the term is also applied to magical preparations deposited in the foundations of the *candomblé* house (plants having medicinal or other properties, etc.).

achêchê (*axêxê*). Funerary ritual in the Bahian cult.

achôgún (*axôgún*). Priest who performs animal sacrifices.

adjá. Small metal bell used by African religious sects.

adje. Community or fraternity priest in Yoruba areas.

administrados. The "help" on a plantation.

adufo. Square drum.

afoshe. Carnival group organized by Negro members of a *candomblé*.

Aganju. One of the forms of the god Shangô.

age. Priest of the dead.

agôgô. Single or double iron bell struck with a metal rod, used as a musical instrument to summon the gods in Rio, Bahia, and Pernambuco.

Agongonu or *Agun-gono* or *Agonglo*. God of the *Casa das Minas* in São Luiz do Maranhão. This is the posthumously deified King Agonglo, who reigned in Dahomey in the late eighteenth and early nineteenth centuries. This god is also found in Amazonas under the name Agun-gono.

agregado. Tenant farmer who works a stipulated number of days (for which he is paid) for the owner of a sugar or coffee plantation.

Ague. Dahoman counterpart of Oxóssi, god of the hunt, son of Mawu and Lisa.

Aguê. Angola counterpart of Ossain, god of herbs or leaves.

Aido-wedo. Dahoman god.

ajibona (*agibonan, jibonan*). Priestess who directs the African cult and assists the high priest. Also known as the *mãe pequena.*

ajua. See *jurema.*

Ajuka. The bottom of the sea.

Akaba. King of Dahomey (1680–1708) posthumously deified and worshiped as a *vodun* in the *Casa das Minas.*

ala. White cloth.

alabé. Chief musician of the *candomblé.* The *alabé-huntor*, the drummer-singer, plays the biggest of the three drums.

Ali Babâ. Director of the house of the dead.

aligenun. Evil spirit, djin.

alikali. Priest responsible for judicial matters in the Malê "nation."

Aloge or *Alogbwe.* Dahoman god of the smallpox family.

alpendre. Portico; covered space at the entrance to a church.

alufa. Priest of Mohammedan Negroes in Brazil.

Aluvala. Angola counterpart of the Yoruba god Exú.

amasia. Common-law marriage; concubinage.

amasin. Infusion of herbs used in purificatory baths.

amure. Marriage in the Mussulman "nation" of Bahia or Rio.

Anamburucú. See *Nanamburucú.*

Angana-Nzambi. Supreme god of certain Bantu "nations."

Angoro. Angola counterpart of the Yoruba god of the rainbow.

Angoromea. Congo counterpart of the Yoruba god of the rainbow.

anuchan. Priest of the cult of the dead.

apetebi. Priestess who assists the *babalaô.*

ara-urun. Ghosts.

assivajui. Master of ceremonies in the Brazilian Mussulman sects.

ato. Prayer written by Brazilian Mussulmans on wooden tablets with ink made of burned rice.

Avrekete or *Afrékété.* Dahoman god, son of Agbê and his sister Naété.

Aziri. Dahoman goddess, counterpart of the Yoruba Oxun, also found in Haiti under the name Mistress Ezili (see Milo Marcelin, *Mythologie Vodou* [Port-au-Prince, 1949], 1: 77–85).

Azoani. Dahoman counterpart of Omolú, god of smallpox.

baba. Father; ancestor. This term designates both the dead and the leaders of the African sect.

babalaô. Priest of Ifá. Diviner in northeastern Brazil; cult leader in Rio.

babalorixá. Cult leader (male) in northeastern Brazil.

Babassuê. Afro-Indian sect in Amazonas.

bacharel (pl. *bachareis*). Graduate of a university or secondary school.

Badê (*Gbadê*). One of the Dahoman gods of lightning.

bairro. Neighborhood; region.

Balaiada. Civil war in the province of Maranhão (1838–1841) accompanied by much bloodshed. The uprising was named after its leader, Manuel dos Anjos Ferreira, nicknamed O Balaio because he was a maker and seller of baskets.

Balaio. Black wicker basket. Nickname of the leader of the *Balaiada* uprising.

balangandan. Ornamental frame hung with amulets, worn by the women of Bahia.

bandeira. Armed band of adventurers which in colonial days made expeditions into the back country to enslave the Indians, seek gold or precious stones, or wipe out the *quilombos* of runaway Negroes.

bandeirante. Member of a *bandeira.*

banguê. Sugarmill of the colonial era operated by animal traction or a water race. Also called the *engenho.*

banzo. Nostalgia; homesickness. The word is probably derived from the Quimbunda word for village, *mbanza.*

Bara or *Barabara.* One of the names of the god Exú (Exú of the Earth).

barracão. Pavilion where public ceremonies of an Afro-Brazilian cult are held.

batuque. (1) Erotic Negro dance. (2) Term used in Rio Grande do Sul to designate an African sect.

Beji. See *Ibeji.*

Bemtevi. A political party in Maranhão during the regency.

Bombonjira (Bombomgira). Congo god, counterpart of the Yoruba Exú.

Boroco. Corrupt form of *Nanamburucú.*

Bosuko. Dahoman god of the smallpox family.

brejo. Literally, "swamp." The region in northeastern Brazil where the slow rivers water and fertilize the land in their yearly floods.

budun (bogun, budu). Corruption of *vodun.*

bumba-meu-boi. Popular festival featuring a dramatic dance, the climax of which depicts the death and resurrection of an ox.

búzio. Cowrie shell; used as money in Africa and for foretelling the future.

caatinga. Indian name for an arid region of Brazil covered with scrub and prickly vegetation.

Cabanada. Revolt that broke out in Pernambuco and Alagoas in 1832 with the object of restoring Pedro I, who had abdicated the previous year. So named by its adversaries after the *cabanas* in which the proletarian insurgents lived.

caboclo. (1) A civilized Brazilian Indian. (2) Person of mixed Indian and white blood. (3) A peasant, especially one whose skin is copper-colored. (4) An Indian god worshiped in a *caboclo candomblé, macumba,* or *catimbó.*

caboclo candomblé. Syncretistic Afro-Amerindian cult.

cabra. This term is used by different writers in different senses. Sometimes it designates a black-mulatto mixed-blood, sometimes an Indian-African one. To quote Rodolpho Theophilo, a *cabra* is a "vigorous, violent, bloodthirsty mixed-blood quite different from the mulatto and lacking his manners and intelligence."

cabula. African religious sect of Bantu origin in Espírito Santo.

cachaça. Brandy made from sugar cane (often of inferior quality).

cachimbo. See *catimbó.*

cafioto. Member of the *cabula* sect. The term originally meant "child."

cafuné. The snapping sound made by the fingernails when killing fleas while grooming someone's hair.

cafuso. An Indian-Negro mixed-blood.

caiálo. One who is not a member of a *cabula*; an outsider.

Caipora. See *Curupira.*

Cajanja. One of the Angola counterparts of the Yoruba god of smallpox.

calundu. Old name for an African religious sect.

Calunga. (1) Bantu goddess of the sea and of death. (2) Doll carried in the carnival procession of the *maracatú.*

camaná. Cabula initiate.

camarinha. Sacred room where future daughters of the gods live during their training and initiation.

cambone. Assistant to the priests and mediums in the *cabula* and *macumba.*

camolélé. Headdress of the *cabula* priest.

camucite. Cabula temple.

candaru. Embers of incense or burning aromatic herbs.

candomblé. (1) The religion of the Negroes of Bahia, the great ceremonies honoring the *orixás,* and the sanctuary in which they are held. (2) In southern Brazil, Uruguay, and Argentina, a profane Negro dance.

cangaceiro. Member of a group of bandits living in the *sertão.*

canjere. African religious ceremonies in the Minas region. The term is also applied to profane Negro dances.

Canjira-Mungongon. A *macumba* spirit.

canto. Group of Negroes working for hire, generally as porters, directed by a "captain."

canzol. Macumba sanctuary.

capim. Kind of grass or hay.

capitão do mato. Bush captain who pursued and captured runaway slaves.

capoeira. African contest introduced into Brazil by the Angola blacks. In Rio the name is also applied to ruffians responsible for all kinds of nocturnal violence and assaults.

caqui. Witch doctor (Minas region).

Cariapemba. Bantu deity corresponding to the Christian devil.

carpideira. Hired mourner (female).

Casa das Minas. Dahoman sect in São Luiz do Maranhão.

casa do candomblé. House where African religion is practiced in Bahia.

casa grande. The big house of the plantation owner.

Cassumbenca. Angola counterpart of the Yoruba god of the sky, Oxalá.

catalo. Postulant in the *cabula* sect.

Catendê. Bantu god; time.

catérété. Rural dance of southern Brazil characterized by hand clapping and foot stamping. The dancers, who are usually men, face one another in two lines.

catimbó. Sect of Amerindian origin, very widespread in northern Brazil.

catimbozeiro(a). The director of the *catimbó* cult. Today the term implies a formidable witch doctor and master of black magic.

Caviungo. Angola counterpart of the Yoruba god of smallpox, Omolú.

chacara. House with a garden on the outskirts of a town.

Cháchá. Honorific associated with certain privileges.

charqueada. Process of drying salt meat in the sun.

chegança. Dramatic ballet. There is a "Moorish *chegança*" recalling the struggle of the Christians against the Moors, and a "sailors' *chegança*" recalling Portuguese expeditions.

coco. Folk dance of northeastern Brazil accompanied by singing. The soloist stands in the center and the dancers take up the refrain after each couplet.

combarca. Concubine.

come. Sanctuary (in the Dahoman sect of São Luiz do Maranhão).

compadre. Godfather; sponsor; friend.

compadrismo. "Godparenthood"; a social bond that has become very prevalent throughout Latin America. There are baptismal godparents, godparents for the festivities celebrating the Eve of Saint John, and godparents who sponsor a girl's initiation as a daughter of the gods.

congada or *congo.* Folk drama on African themes (tribal warfare, embassies, death and resurrection of a prince). Mario de Andrade has described these as dramatic ballets interspersed with songs and spoken dialogue.

cortico. Hovel.

cucumbi. Name used for certain forms of the *congada* in some regions of Brazil, notably in Bahia.

curandeirismo. The art of the *curandeiro* or *curador*, the healer who treats both people and animals, using herbal infusions and plasters as well as purely magical procedures.

curumiri. A young Tupí Indian between the ages of one and eight years.

Curupira. Indian god of Amazonas, protector of the forests. Curupira is represented as an agile little Indian with red hair whose feet point the wrong way. In Pernambuco he has only one leg, like the Saci, another god of the hunt. In southern Brazil he is known as Caapora or Caipora.

cururú. (1) Dance of Jesuit origin almost without choreography and dominated by singing. The singers compete against one another, improvising on given themes, religious or profane, and using given rhymes. (2) Argument, quarrel.

Da or *Danbira.* Dahoman god of life, fecundity, and movement; represented by snakes, the rainbow, smoke, and running water.

Dadaho. Dahoman deity of the royal family (*Casa das Minas*). According to Verger, Dadaho is Agassou, the *vodun* of the kings of Abomey.

dagan. The senior of the two daughters of the gods who perform the sacrifice to Exú.

damatá. Symbol of the god Oxóssi consisting of a miniature iron bow and arrow.

Dance of Saint Gonçalves. Dance of Portuguese origin "promised" to the saint in gratitude for a grace received. Originally performed in the church, it was later banned but survives in rural Brazil.

Dance of the Holy Cross. Dance performed around the Catholic cross early in May, chiefly in southern Brazil. The priest has no part in it; the people themselves organize the dance.

Dandalunda. Angola counterpart of Yemanjá, Yoruba goddess of the sea.

Davise. Family name of the posthumously deified kings of Dahomey.

desafio. Literary or musical genre in which contestants improvise verses in a sort of duel.

despachado. Dismissed; sent away.

despacho. Sacrifice to an *orixá.* By extension, the dismissal of a deity. The term is sometimes used in a popular sense to mean a magical offering.

diamba-liamba. Angola name for hemp.

dilogun or *dologun.* Consultation of the gods through the use of sixteen shells.

Doçu or *Dosu.* God of the *Casa das Minas* (King Dossu Agadja).

ebo. Sacrifice to the gods.

ebomin. Title conferred on Ketu or Jesha initiates after seven years.

eguns. (1) The souls of the dead, skeletons, ghosts, ancestors. (2) Secret society that summons the souls of the dead.

eho. In the Yoruba "nation," that which is taboo. The Bantu equivalent is *quizilla.*

ekedi. Servants of the *orixás* while they are possessing their daughters (E. Carneiro's definition).

Elegba or *Legba.* Dahoman counterpart of Exú.

elima. Magical power (Bantu).

embanda. Cabula or *macumba* priest.

enba. Magic powder.

encantado. Spirit worshiped by the syncretistic sects in northern and north-eastern Brazil.

encosta. Spirit that takes possession of a person and makes him ill and that must therefore be expelled.

engenho. Sugar mill; sugar plantation.

engira. The *cabula* sect.

entrada. An expedition into the interior of Brazil sponsored by the crown or the governor.

esteira. Straw mat.

esturaque. Sacred plant.

exú. Divine messenger and tutelary spirit.

Farrapos. Literally, "ragged ones." Pejorative name for the Brazilians in Rio Grande do Sul who revolted against the central power in 1835–1845.

favelas. Wooden shacks where the proletariat of Rio de Janeiro live in squalor.

fazenda. Large estate, ranch, or plantation.

fazendeiro. Owner of a *fazenda.*

feijão. Bean.

feiticeiro. Practitioner of black magic; witch doctor.

feitor. Overseer.

festeiro. Church member elected to direct one of the great Catholic festivals.

fila. Generic term for headdress in the Mussulman sects. Today, in the *candomblé,* the hood of Omolú.

Filha or *filho de santo.* Daughter or son of a god; an initiate of the Afro-Brazilian cult.

folia. An organized group with lifetime membership which roams the *sertão* soliciting resources for the great Catholic festivals.

ganga. (1) Bantu priest. (2) Bantu counterpart of Exú. (3) Bantu witchcraft.

ganza. Musical instrument consisting of a small closed tin cylinder that is shaken.

garapa. Refreshing beverage.

garimpeiro. Originally a prospector for gold or precious stones who "poached" in rivers to which he had no rights. Today any prospector.

gaucho. Cowboy in the extreme south of Brazil. The cowboy spends most of the day on horseback, watching his herd.

Gêgê. Name given to the Dahoman "nation" in Recife, Bahia, and Pôrto Alegre.

Gongonbira. Bantu counterpart of Oxóssi, Yoruba god of the hunt.

Guabirus. Name given to the members of the Conservative party against which the *Praieiro* rebelled in 1849.

guides. Celestial spirits, souls of the dead who guide their mediums.

Gum. Dahoman name for Ogun.

gume. Interior courtyard of the *Casa das Minas* planted with trees and sacred shrubs.

horta. Garden; pleasure garden; vegetable garden or orchard.

hunbono. High priestess of the Dahoman "nation."

hunto or *huntor.* Drummer.

Ibeji. The sacred twins of the Yoruba.

Ifá. God of divination.

igbale. Luturgical broom.

ile. House.

ile orixá. House of the gods.

ile saim or *sahim.* House of the dead. In Pernambuco the house of the dead is called the *"balé* room."

ilu. Small drum.

Ilu-aye. Africa.

iman. See *lemano.*

Incossi Mucumbe. Congo counterpart of Ogun.

ingome. Type of drum.

iniam. Red-and-white cloth with which one of the *batuque* drums is covered.

inkisse. Any of the gods of the Angola and Congo "nations."

irôkô. The sacred tree of the Yoruba.

iya. Mother.

iya bassé. The woman who cooks for the gods.

iya kêkêrê. The assistant and deputy of the *yalorixá* and the *babalorixá.*

iya têbêxê. Singer who starts each hymn and sings solos.

jaboti. Turtle, the leading character of Indian folk tales in Amazonas.

Jaci. Indian deity, the moon. This deity reappears as a *caboclo* in the syncretistic sects of northern and northeastern Brazil.

jongo. Dance in the round of blacks in São Paulo, Minas, Rio de Janeiro, and Espírito Santo.

jujuism (from the Hausa *djudju,* meaning "fetish"). Religion of certain Nigerian tribes.

Jurapari. Tupí god associated with the sun and identified with the devil by missionaries. Certain tribes in Amazonas still worship him, and he also appears in the syncretistic sects of the northeast.

jurema. (1) Tree of the mimosa family. (2) Beverage made of the fruit, bark, or root of that tree which produces hallucinatory states. (3) Kingdom of the *encantados* and name of a *caboclo.*

Kaiala. Congo counterpart of Yemanjá.

Kakamado. The leading *encantado* in the rural African sects of Maranhão.

Kambararanguanje. Counterpart of Shangô in the Congo "nation."

kardenko. *Pegi*, or altar, of the Dahoman gods of Maranhão.

Katende. Time (one of the forms of Irôkô).

Kevioso. Ewe god of thunder.

Kiassubangango or *Kibuco.* Angola god of thunder.

kissium. Prayer of the Brazilian Mussulmans.

Koisi. Koassina, brother of King Agadja of Abomey, posthumously deified and worshiped as a *vodun* in the *Casa das Minas*.

kpoli. Small bag, made of white cloth, containing sacred leaves and the dust in which the name of the god was traced when it was revealed by divination. This dust is the personal *odu* of the consultant.

kulona. One of the masked dances of the "little devils" performed during the Festival of the Three Kings in Cuba.

Labara. See Bara.

Lambarenganga. Angola counterpart of Oxalá.

ledamo. Priest of the Mussulman "nation" in Bahia or Rio.

Legba. See Elegba.

lemano. High priest of the Mussulman sects.

limpar o sangue. To purify the blood by mixing it with white blood.

liquaqua. Rhythmic hand clapping accompanying a hymn.

Lisa. Companion of the Fon deity Mawu, hence a sky god, counterpart of Oxalá, in the Dahoman sects of Maranhão. According to Manuel Querino, the Gêgê "nation" worshiped this god under the name of Ulissa.

Lôkô or *Lôcô.* Dahoman counterpart of Irôkô.

lorogun. Ceremony in which the *candomblé* is closed for Holy Week.

lundu. Dance of black Brazilians.

machachali. Chapel or oratory of black Mussulmans in Brazil.

maconha. Popular name for hemp smoked in cigarettes.

macumba. African sect in Rio. By extension, black magic.

macumbeiro. (1) Director of a *macumba*. (2) Witch doctor.

mãe d'agua. Female deity, of the Afro-Brazilian cult, who inhabits water.

mãe de santo. Popular name for the *yalorixá*.

mãe pequena. "Little mother"; deputy director of the *candomblé*. The *iya kêkêrê*.

mãe preta. "Black mammy."

magba. Priest of Shangô.

Malê. Possibly a contraction of *Malinke*; Mussulman "nation" of Brazil.

Malemba. See *Lemba*.

malungo. Name given by Africans to their fellow-slaves on the ships that transported them to America.

mandinga. Witchcraft.

mandingueiro. Witch doctor.

mandraca. White magic.

maracatú. Dance with Afro-Brazilian religious elements originally performed in front of the Catholic church but now purely a carnival dance.

marafo. Brandy.

Maronga. One of the *caboclos* of the syncretistic sects of northern and northeastern Brazil.

Matamba. Angola counterpart of Yansan.

matuto. Backwoodsman. Term used (often pejoratively) in the states of Minas, Rio, Bahia, Alagoas, Pernambuco, and even Rio Grande do Norte.

mesa. Table that serves as an altar.

mironga. Secret.

mocambo (mucambo). (1) Synonym for *quilombo.* (2) Miserable huts or shanties (Pernambuco region).

muamba. Witchcraft; black magic.

mucharabi. Balcony with grille, of Arabic origin.

mulungo. African music.

mungunzá (munguzá). Pudding made of cornmeal, coconut milk, butter, sugar, and spices.

Mussurumi. The Mussulman "nations" in Brazil.

Mutacalombo. Congo counterpart of Oxóssi.

Mutalombo. Angola counterpart of Oxóssi.

mutirão. Communal labor contributed at planting or harvest time or for other agricultural needs in return for food and a big celebration with dancing. The term has many synonyms: *muxirão, puchirão, bandeira, adjutorio.* *Mutirão* is not to be confused with the "exchange of days" (*trocar dias*), a system by which labor is contributed and later repaid.

Naété or *Naê* or *Naedona.* Probably Naété, Fon goddess of the sea (Dahomey).

Nanamburucú or *Nanan.* God known and worshiped in Nigeria, Dahomey, Togo, and the Gold Coast. In Togo, the supreme god. In certain parts of Nigeria, the mother of Omolú, though still characterized as the creator-goddess. In Brazil the name is often abbreviated to *Nanan.*

negro de ganho. Slave hired out by his owner or sent out to peddle merchandise in the streets, returning some of the proceeds to his master.

negro de recado. Messenger, usually a little boy.

nganga. High priest. The term is of Bantu origin.

ninbù. A *cabula* song or canticle.

Nunvurucemabuva. Congo counterpart of Yansan.

Obá. (1) Yoruba goddess of the river Obá, the third wife of Shangô. (2) King. By extension, the title given to the ministers of Shangô in a Bahia *candomblé.*

Obaluayé. See *Abaluaie.*

Obatalá. Yoruba sky god, the creator.

obî (orobo). African fruit, the *kola* nut, used in consulting the gods and for sacrifices.

Odé. Counterpart of Oxóssi in the Dahoman sects. Worshiped chiefly in the *xangôs* of Pernambuco.

odu. Generic name for the tokens of divination.

Odudua. Yoruba earth goddess, female persona of Obatalá.

ofa. Necklace.

ogan. Lay protector of the *candomblé*, selected by the *orixás*, subject to a minor initiation ritual.

ogan-ilu. Drummer.

ogboni. The elders. Secret secular council responsible for the earth cult and for certain political activities.

Ogillon. Yoruba god of certain metals and hence of blacksmiths.

Ogodo. One of the names of Shangô.

Ogun. Yoruba god of iron, blacksmiths, warriors, farmers, and all those who use iron.

Oiâ or *Oya.* One of the names of Yansan, goddess of the Niger, wife of Shangô.

Olisassá. Dahoman counterpart of Oxalá, whose name the Fon cannot pronounce because of the *sh* sound.

ologbo. Leader of the *ogboni.*

Olokun. Yoruba god of the sea.

Olorun. The supreme god of the Yoruba.

olosain. Priest dedicated to the cult of Ossain and charged with gathering sacred and medicinal plants.

Omolú or *Omolun.* God of smallpox and illnesses in general.

oos. Bead necklace.

opa-suma. Dance of the black Mussulmans of Brazil.

opele. Kind of rosary used for divination, made from the half-kernels of African or Brazilian nuts (*kpele*).

ori. (1) The head. (2) The organic soul located in the head. (3) The ceremony of "giving food to the head" (*obori*).

Orixálá. Obatalá.

orixás. Generic name for the Yoruba deities, the intermediaries between Olorun and mortals.

Oro. Yoruba secret society. Through the "voice of Oro," produced by a bull-roarer, the spirits of the dead speak.

Orun. Yoruba god of the sun.

Orunmila. Ifá, god of divination.

Ossain, Ossaim, Ossahim, Ossanhe. Yoruba god of grasses and leaves.

ota. Specially treated stones in which the power of the *orixás* is concentrated.

Otin. Deity of the Pôrto Alegre *batuques.*

Oxaguian. Oxalá as a young god.

Oxalá. God of the sky and of procreation. Brazilian name of Obatalá.

Oxalufan. Oxalá as an old god.

oxe. Double-headed axe, symbol of Shangô.

Oxo. Yoruba god of agriculture.

Oxóssi. Yoruba goddess of the hunt.

Oxun. Yoruba goddess of the Oxun River. Second wife of Shangô. Assumes different forms: Oxun Pandá, Oxun Doco, etc.

Oxun-marê (Ochu-marê). Deity of Dahoman origin accepted by the Yoruba.

padé (of Exú). Propitiatory offering to Exú that opens *candomblé* ceremonies.

pagé. Indian priest, witch doctor, or medicine man.

pagelança. Folk cult of Indian origin in northern Brazil.

pai (formerly spelled *pae*) *de santo.* Popular name for the *babalorixá.*

panam. One of the final rites of initiation in the *candomblé.*

Panda. Congo counterpart of Yemanjá, goddess of the sea.

pandeiro. Drum.

pango. See *diamba-liamba.*

Pedro Malazarte. Hero of Brazilian folk tales who overcomes his stronger opponents by guile.

pegi. Altar on which the stones consecrated to the gods are placed.

pegi-gan. Candomblé official in charge of the *pegi.*

Polibogi. One of the names of the Dahoman god of smallpox.

Pomba Gira. Wife of Exú or female persona of Exú.

pontos cantados. *Macumba* canticles sung to induce the spirits to descend.

pontos riscados. Drawings, symbolizing the spirits, made on the ground in colored chalk to induce the spirits to descend.

Praieiro. Group of members of the Liberal party of Pernambuco who revolted against the Conservative provincial authorities in 1849. Named after the street where the liberal newspaper had its offices.

quatan. Rhythmic hand clapping accompanying singing or dancing.

quêrêbatan. Dahoman name for the *Casa das Minas.*

quianbo. Bantu priest.

quibungo. Monster of Bantu origin having a large hole in its back through which it swallows children.

quilombo. Fugitive-slave settlement. The term is sometimes used to designate old forms of the *candomblé.*

quilombola, quilomboleiro. Fugitive Negro living in a *quilombo.*

Quincongo. Congo god of smallpox.

rancho. Group of men and women who celebrate Christmas with singing and dancing. Originally these groups symbolized shepherds on their way to Bethlehem to worship the infant Jesus.

reisado. Group of singers and dancers (particularly in Alagoas) who perform dramatic ballets on various themes, usually on Epiphany, the Festival of the Three Kings.

reza. Prayers recited at peasant gatherings directed by a *sacristão.*

Rocho Macumbe. Angola counterpart of Ogun.

Sabinada. Revolution led by the surgeon Francisco Sabino da Rocha Vieira in 1837 in Bahia with the object of establishing a republic in that province until such time as Pedro II attained his majority.

sacristão. Leader of the rural prayer meetings known as *rezas.*

Sagbata. Fon god of smallpox and the earth.

sala. Morning and evening prayer of the Malê Negroes in Brazil.

samba. Dance of Bantu origin characterized by the *umbigada.*

santé. See *santidade.*

santidade. (1) The mystic power that possesses a person in trance. (2) A seventeenth-century Indian religious movement.

Sapata. Sagbata.

sara. Religious ceremony of the Mussulman "nations" in Brazil.

seita. Literally, "sect." In Bahia, an Afro-Brazilian cult center.

semba. Women members of the priestly hierarchy of the *macumba.*

sentados. Initiates.

senzale. The slave quarters on a plantation.

sertanejo. Inhabitant of the *sertão.*

sertanista. Pioneer who makes expeditions into the *sertão* in search of its fabulous riches or to enslave the Indians; a *bandeirante.*

sertão. The backlands; the sparsely populated interior areas of Brazil.

Shangô. Yoruba thunder god.

shiré. The order in which the songs invoking the gods are sung.

sidagan. The most recently initiated of the girls who perform the cult of Exú to open *candomblé* ceremonies.

silhun (sirrun). Funeral ceremony in the Dahoman sects.

soba. Minor African king.

Sobô or *Sogbo.* Fon thunder god.

sobrado. A plantation owner's town house.

suma. Mussulman baptism.

tabua. Tablet.

tafia. Brandy made of sugar cane.

tambor de Mina. Dahoman sect in Maranhão; the ceremonies held there.

taquara. (1) Bamboo that grows wild in Brazil. (2) Musical instrument made from this bamboo.

tata. Tutelary spirit of the *cabula* sects; also found in *macumba.*

tayera. Group of women accompanying the procession of Our Lady of the Rosary (Bahia region).

teceba (teshuba). Kind of rosary used by the Malê in Brazil.

terreiro. Afro-Brazilian cult center.

tobossa. Child deity worshiped in the *Casa das Minas.* Manoel Querino gives Tobossi as the Dahoman name of Nanamburucú.

tokhueni. Young *voduns* who "open the way" for the other *voduns.*

tore. Indian dance.

trocar dias. To "exchange days"; the system of cooperative labor in which one man donates a day's labor to another who will later repay it.

Tupan. God of the Tupí Indians, hurler of thunderbolts.

Tupinamba. Ancient Tupí tribe of Brazil. A *caboclo* in the syncretistic sects of northern and northeastern Brazil.

turundu. Dramatic dance of Minas Gerais similar to the *congada.*

uganga. See *nganga.*

umbanda. (1) Priest. (2) White magic. (3) African form of spiritism.

umbigada. Movement characterizing dances such as the *samba, jongo, coco,* etc., in which the partners dance navel-to-navel, rubbing their abdomens together.

uricuri. Brazilian plant.

Uruanda. Supernatural homeland of certain spirits.

urucabaca. Brazilian plant.

urucongo. Musical bow.

vardenko. Pegi; altar in the Yoruba cult centers of Maranhão.

velorio. Funeral wake.

Verekete. See Avrekete.

vêvê. Drawings made on the ground in Haiti, each symbolizing a specific *vodun.*

vissungo. Negro songs (Minas).

vodun. Generic name for Dahoman deity.

vodunsi. In Bahia, girls who have undergone more than seven years of initiation in a Gêgê *terreiro*. In São Luiz do Maranhão, the girls consecrated to the *voduns*. Here the *vodunsi-ahe*, who have not undergone formal initiation, are distinguished from the *vodunsi-hunjai*, who have been "made."

wassa. Nagô priest of the second degree.

xangô. Afro-Brazilian cult center in Pernambuco and Alagoas; the ceremonies performed there.

xangô-reisado-baixo. Literally, "Shangô-invoked sotto voce"; African ceremonies celebrated without musical accompaniment during periods of police persecution.

Xapanan. Sagbata.

yaba. Cult member who attends the daughters of the gods during their trances (Recife).

yabanian. Yellow-and-green fabric used to cover one of the drums in the Pôrto Alegre sects.

yalorixá, ialorixá, iyalorixá. High priestess of a *candomblé*.

Yansan or *Yassam*. One of the names of Oiâ.

yawo. "Wife of the gods"; a girl who has completed her initiation rites.

Yemanjá, Iemanjá, Emanjá. Yoruba goddess of the sea.

Zamadonu. A *tobossu*, the abnormal son of King Akaba, worshiped as a *vodun* in the *Casa das Minas*.

Zambi or *Zumbi*. (1) The great Bantu god. (2) Title of the king of Palmares.

Zambiapongo or *Zambiopungo*. The great Congo god.

Zaze. Angola counterpart of Shangô.

Index

Abolition, 399; compartmentalization and, 168–69; mysticism and, 378–79; religion and, 163, 377–78; urbanization and, 166–67

Abreu, J. Froès, 183

Acculturation, 21, 155, 282, 382; black/white, 70–71; collective memory and, 383; compartmentalization and, 386–87; double, 387–88; immunity to, 73; magic and, 400; problems of studying, 384–85; psychic mechanism of, 72; of slaves in U.S., 48; social disorganization and, 301; social status and, 68–69; social structure and, 401; studies of, 13–16, 25; symbols and, 389–90; syncretism and, 96; as synthesis, 391; values and, 404; white/black, 69–70. *See also* Counteracculturation

Adão, Father, 77

Africa, 313; intercommunication between Brazil and, 165; memory of, 248; myths from, 241; transplantation of, to Brazil, 191–201; Umbanda spiritism and, 321; valorization and, 308

African civilizations, 21, 46; cultural conflict of, 66; *marronage* and, 96; *quilombos* and, 93; re-creation of, 157–61, 163; slavery and, 43–45; trance in, 376

African cults: in Brazil, 133–35, 145; campaign against, 164–65; differences among, 205–6; disintegration of, 293–94; economy of, 229–32; faith and, 223; functioning of, 220–39; influence of, 186–91; of Mozambique Bantu, 59–61; racial integration and, 169; rural workers and, 287, 288; of sun and earth, 200; survival of, 160, 164, 168; transformation of, by church, 54. *See also* Cults

African culture: *candomblé* and, 167; compartmentalization of, 168–69; conflicts of, 66; Indians and, 90

African customs: adaptation of, to Catholicism, 53–54; *congadas* as, 120–21;

re-creation of, in *quilombos,* 88–89; slaves' sexual mores and, 61

African gods, 189–90, 205, 206, 259, 275; Bantu religion and, 201–2; *batuque* and, 207–8, 213; black brotherhoods and, 62; *budus,* 185; *candomblé* and, 192, 194, 195, 196, 197, 198–201, 288, 289; *catimbó* and, 181–82; characteristics of, 379; Christianization of, 275–76; collective memory and, 246; dualist structure of Brazilian society and, 157; identified with Catholic saints, 21, 60, 89, 188, 198, 218, 260–72, 283, 299, 349, 388, 390, 404; Indian religion and, 186–87, 196–97; inheritance of, 200–201; metamorphosis of memories and, 250–58; migration of, 216; mystic trance and, 376–77; process of selection of, 66; slavery and, 155; spiritism and, 322–24, 325, 326–31; syncretism and, 162; Yoruba religious system and, 59, 61. *See also names of individual gods*

African religions: adaptation of, in Brazil, 58–77; African time frames and, 274–75; agriculture and, 393; ancestor worship in, 59–61; black Catholicism and, 126–28, 140–42; *cabula* and, 202–4; *candomblé* and, 191–201; Catholicism and, 53–54, 89, 94–95, 146, 162–63, 188, 214, 260–71, 350; Christianity and, 275–84; class conflict and, 66–67; collective memory and, 240–59; mulattoes and, 76–77; mysticism and, 379; myths of, 241–45; in *quilombos,* 89, 95–96; rituals of, and urban slaves, 51–52; Rodrigues on, 19–21; secrets in, 249–50; sexuality and, 398; size of black population and, 393; slave trade and, 17, 47–48; social disorganization and, 300–303; spiritism and, 325, 331, 334; survival of, in Brazil, 19, 49–50, 54, 57, 75, 183–91, 394; whites' attitude toward, 139–40; whites' influence on,